Canada in the World

Canada in the World

Settler Capitalism
and the Colonial Imagination

Tyler A. Shipley

FERNWOOD PUBLISHING
HALIFAX & WINNIPEG

Copyright © 2020 Tyler A. Shipley

All rights reserved. No part of this book may be reproduced or transmitted in any form by any means without permission in writing from the publisher, except by a reviewer, who may quote brief passages in a review.

Cover design: John van der Woude Designs
Printed and bound in Canada

Published by Fernwood Publishing
32 Oceanvista Lane, Black Point, Nova Scotia, B0J 1B0
and 748 Broadway Avenue, Winnipeg, Manitoba, R3G 0X3
www.fernwoodpublishing.ca

Fernwood Publishing Company Limited gratefully acknowledges the financial support of the Government of Canada, the Canada Council for the Arts, the Manitoba Department of Culture, Heritage and Tourism under the Manitoba Publishers Marketing Assistance Program and the Province of Manitoba, through the Book Publishing Tax Credit, for our publishing program. We are pleased to work in partnership with the Province of Nova Scotia to develop and promote our creative industries for the benefit of all Nova Scotians.

Library and Archives Canada Cataloguing in Publication

Title: Canada in the world : settler capitalism and
the colonial imagination / Tyler Shipley.
Names: Shipley, Tyler A., author.
Description: Includes bibliographical references and index.
Identifiers: Canadiana 20200156519 | ISBN 9781773631141 (softcover)
Subjects: LCSH: Canada—Relations. | LCSH: Canada—
Colonial influence. | LCSH: Canada—Colonization.
Classification: LCC FC242 .S55 2020 | DDC 327.71—dc23

Praise for *Canada in the World*

On its own, Shipley's Canada in the World *is an exceptional scholarly accomplishment that will be indispensable to studies of Canadian culture, history, and political economy. When read against the same backdrop,* Canada in the World *properly dislodges and displaces the ghosts of Harold Innis and George Grant that continue to haunt our popular understanding of the nation and obscure Canada's colonialism from public memory and visions of the future. Shipley's outstanding scholarship is matched by the accessibility of his writing; this book will reach across audiences of all varieties, as it deserves. It is a book that made me very excited. It will be a text for all my classes for the foreseeable future.*

Veldon Coburn, University of Ottawa

As a settler colonial society, Canada is fundamentally a racial project of accumulation. Tyler Shipley meticulously traces the racial capitalist line that runs through Canadian history, insisting that we understand that Canada moves in the world as a state that is dedicated first and foremost to the interests of white capital. Forging alliances with fascists and colonial powers everywhere, even at one point with Hitler, Canada works hard to undermine anyone who poses a threat to capital and to white power. The argument may sound exaggerated, especially to those who seek refuge in the idea that Canadians are the nicest people on earth and those who are anxious to see Canada as a better class of white nation, especially when compared to the United States. No doubt some will use the passion that infuses this book as a reason to dismiss its core claims. The book is a reminder to interrogate our emotional investments in niceness, juxtaposing our insistent race to innocence to Canadian arms sales, the body count that comes with Canadian mining activities, the support rendered to fascist regimes the world over, and most of all to the relentless internal colonialism that continues apace.

Sherene H. Razack, Distinguished Professor and Penny Kanner Endowed Chair, UCLA and author of *Dying from Improvement: Inquests and Inquiries into Indigenous Deaths in Custody*

This book will be a vital resource for those interested in a critical account of Canada's role in the world for many years to come. Shipley provides a vast and rigorous historical account of how Canadian actors have engaged with the world outside our borders, but importantly, he also grounds his study in an analysis of settler colonialism at home. The book fundamentally disrupts the notion that Canada is a benevolent, helpful, middle power, and sets the record straight on the colonial and imperial aspects of the Canadian state.

David P. Thomas, Mount Allison University, author of *Bombardier Abroad*

Canada in the World *is an unflinching and bold polemic that sweeps through centuries of history to support its central thesis: as an integral project of settler colonialism, 'Canada' entailed subjugation within and exploitation without, in a coherent and consistent quest to render the world safe for capitalism, colonialism and white supremacy. It should be both rigorously studied and strenuously debated by all who seek to understand the country's past, transform its present, and reimagine its future.*

Ian McKay, McMaster University, author of *Warrior Nation*

Contents

Preface and Acknowledgements ... xi

Introduction ... 1

Part I — Conquest and Colonialism ... 13

1. Colonial Encounters ... 14
New Worlds, East and West ... 15
Before Canada ... 23
Cartier's *Sauvages* ... 26
Puritan Pathologies ... 28
On the Eve of Canada ... 31

2. Conquest and Genocide ... 37
The Roots of Confederation ... 39
1867: The Birth of Canada ... 42
Clearing the Plains ... 45
Conquering the West ... 50
The Indian Act ... 53

3. From the Potlatch to the Residential Schools ... 63
The War of 1885 ... 65
Métis Resistance ... 67
Assimilation, Extermination, Cultural Genocide ... 71
The Residential School System ... 74
Policing the Colonized ... 78
Colonialism and Resistance ... 86

Part II — Canada in the Catastrophe Years ... 99

4. Great Wars and National Nativity ... 100
Canada at the *Fin de Siècle* ... 101
Canadian Imperialism ... 105
The South African War ... 109
Imperialism and the Great War ... 113
Canada's Great War ... 117
Vimyism ... 122

5. Flirting with Fascism ... 131
The 20th Century Begins ... 133
Between the Wars ... 138
Canadian Monopolists ... 141
The Spanish Civil War ... 146
The Mackenzie-Papineau Battalion ... 150
Hitler's Eyes ... 155
The Myth of Appeasement ... 161

6. The Mythologies of Canada's "Good War" ... 171
The Second World War ... 173
The Spectre of Jewish Bolshevism ... 178
None Is Too Many ... 183
Crimes and Contradictions ... 185
At War's End ... 189
Death from Above, Death from Below ... 191

Part III — Peacekeeping the Cold War ... 199

7. Peace and Scorched Earth ... 200
The Cold War ... 201
Israel, Suez and Canadian Mythology ... 204
The Dominion and the Rising Sun ... 211
The Scorched Earth of Korea ... 219
The Heroes of Dien Bien Phu ... 227
Saving Somoza: Falconbridge, Inco and Canada's Cold War ... 231
Consolidating the Cold War ... 236

8. Colonialism, a Part of Our Heritage ... 249
To Quarantine the Colonies ... 252
Heritage Minute: The Assassination of Patrice Lumumba ... 259
The Butcher of Zacapa ... 266
The Riff-Raff of the Latin American Left ... 270
Quiet Complicity in Vietnam ... 276
Moderate, Sensible, Progressive Leadership in Indonesia ... 282

9. Canada and the "End of History" ... 294
Twilight of the Global 1960s ... 296
A "Middle Power" in the Middle East ... 303
Red Menace: Canada and the Contra Wars ... 307
Canada, Cabora Bossa and Apartheid ... 314
The Complicated End of Apartheid ... 320
The Defeat of the Soviet Union ... 325
Soviet Nostalgia and the Making of Vladimir Putin ... 329

Part IV — The New Canadian Imperialism ... 343

10. The Dark Heart of Peacekeeping ... 344
War in the Gulf ... 346
The Peacekeeping Horizon ... 350
The Somalia Affair ... 353
"Ethnic Tension" and the Rwanda Genocides ... 359
Saint Roméo Dallaire ... 365
Paul Kagame, Celebrity Dictator ... 371
"Balkanizing" the Balkans ... 373
The War on Terror ... 381

11. Canada's War on Terror ... 394
Afghanistan: Canada's Longest War ... 395
"They Don't Deserve Our Help" ... 401
"What the Afghans Need Is Colonizing" ... 405
Canada in the War on Terror ... 408
The Shadows of Israeli Apartheid ... 414
A New Day for Democracy in Haiti ... 421
"Friends of Haiti" ... 426
Ottawa and Empire: Canada and the Honduran Dictatorship ... 432

12. Contemporary Canada and the Rise of Fascism ... 448
Armoured Neoliberalism ... 449
The Ukraine Crisis ... 452
Uncreating Hugo Chávez ... 458
The Friendly Far Right: Colombia and Brazil ... 467
Blood of Extraction ... 474
Poisoning the Well ... 479
Reorienting the Imperial Machine ... 482
The New Warriors, the Far-Right and the Heart of Canada ... 488

Conclusion — Decolonizing Canada ... 503

Index ... 511

Preface and Acknowledgements

To thank everyone who contributed to this book would be impossible, given the extent to which I have leaned on the conversations, research and analysis of friends, colleagues and students over the many years that I developed this project. You are all, in some form or fashion, in these pages.

Special thanks to Warren Bernauer, Kelly Anne Butler, Sean Carleton, Benedetta Piola Caselli, Jordy Cummings, Kole Kilibarda, Donald Kingsbury, Jerome Klassen, Robin Philpot, Greg Shupak and Chris Webb for their guidance and support in specific areas. Aliya Amarshi read significant sections of the text and workshopped with me several thematic points, adding layers that I would not have come to on my own and for which I am deeply grateful. Josh Moufawad-Paul read the entire first draft, over 700 pages of it, offering substantive editorial commentary that strengthened the work considerably. Finally, thank you to my first mentor in the study of history, Mark Gabbert, from whom I learned so much and whose influence is so deeply embedded in this book.

Thank you also to everyone at Fernwood who has supported this project, most notably Errol Sharpe, Brenda Conroy, Beverley Rach and Jenn Harris. The size and scope of the work posed some challenges, and I am lucky to have had the assistance and direction of experienced and committed editors and publishers to bring these words into the light.

The manuscript was completed as much of the world grappled with the covid-19 pandemic, the spark which appears to have ignited the next great capitalist crisis and which harkens the age of full-fledged climate catastrophe. The precise consequences of this moment are hard to predict, but it seems clear that it portends the further slide into capitalist dystopia and renewed rounds of class struggle and inter-imperial rivalry that could generate epoch-changing events.

To the extent that the calamities of 2020 are a logical consequence of the world Canada has worked so hard to build, they validate the critiques at the heart of this book. To the extent that this moment illustrates the absurdities and injustices of the systems that currently shape our lives and opens us to the necessity of building something better, I hope that this book will help to steer us away from the pitfalls of the past and towards a truly emancipatory future. I dedicate this book to my students, whose energy, enthusiasm and curiosity sustains my own commitment to that future.

Introduction

When the European settlers arrived, they needed land to live on. The First Nations peoples agreed to move to different areas to make room for the new settlements.
— Complete Canadian Curriculum (Grade 3), 2017[1]

IN 2017, THE COMPLETE CANADIAN Curriculum guide for third graders claimed that "the First Nations peoples moved to areas called reserves, where they could live undisturbed by the hustle and bustle of the settlers."[2] This was a radical and absurd misrepresentation of Canadian history, but it was reflective of a longstanding ideological project to convince Canadians that their country was a well-intentioned contributor to the greater good of the world. In that version of history, Canada has been a haven for refugees, it has been a voice of reason in times of international crisis, it has sought to preserve peace when others wanted war, it has made sacrifices when war was necessary to defeat injustice, and it has helped other nations build prosperous and functional societies like the one Canada built after Indigenous people, presumably, moved to the reserves where they could live "undisturbed by the hustle and bustle of the settlers."

This book offers a sober re-assessment of that story, providing a broad history of Canada's engagements in the world since Confederation. Unlike many such studies, I treat the relations between the French, British, and then Canadian settlers and the Indigenous Peoples they encountered as a foundational element of what Canada became, and I also demonstrate that the legacy and logic of Canadian colonialism runs through the entire history of Canada in the world. Canada's colonial project was driven by one fundamental material goal — the destruction of Indigenous political economic practices and their displacement by capitalism — and an equally important ideological foundation in the claim that Europeans were racially and culturally advanced and, thus, that their conquest of the Indigenous Peoples represented "progress." The interplay between this economic compulsion and its ideological framing has remained integral to the story of Canada.

The structure of this book is designed to highlight the central thesis that Canada's relationships in the world have consistently followed the patterns set during its colonial founding. Part I provides an overview of the colonial project that created Canada, with emphasis on the period around Confederation, a key point in the genocidal effort to eliminate what Canadian officials called the "Indian problem." The creation of Canada took place within the broader dynamics of the emergence of capitalism, the spread of European colonialism and the trans-Atlantic slave trade, which I discuss briefly.

As a new world order was constructed around those dynamics, the foundation for what would become Canada was being established in the minds and in the material conditions of its colonial architects. First, Canada was rooted in the desire to establish a private market in land and labour and create the conditions for capitalist wealth accumulation. Thus, like any settler capitalist state, Canada was designed to destroy the Indigenous inhabitants — by extermination, expulsion, assimilation or whatever other method — and replace their societies with one that would be dominated by a handful of wealthy capitalists and the laws and institutions that support a capitalist society.

Second, it was premised on the notion that white, European society was more advanced, intelligent, rational and just, and that white settlers were providentially destined to conquer the world. Though this notion took many forms, the various ideas that came to be known as white supremacy were deeply inculcated in the project to create Canada, justifying — in the minds of white settlers — the genocidal practices and policies that were facilitating the theft of land and destruction of Indigenous societies that settler capitalism required. White settlers were possessed by a colonial imagination, a fantasy of their superiority — and of the inferiority of those others they encountered — that permeated nearly every aspect of what became Canadian society. This colonial imagination was manifest in the most overtly genocidal expressions, like John A. Macdonald's assertions of the superiority of the Aryan races, but it was often also present in the attitudes of settlers, who believed themselves to be more progressive and enlightened, like Canadian missionaries or members of the suffragist movement in its early days.

Looking back at the period around Confederation and the conquest of the west, 21st-century Canadians are often tempted to assert that, while the racism of the early settlers was terrible, it was a product of the period in which they lived and it is unfair to judge them by the standards of the present. This is profoundly inadequate. It ignores the fact that those attitudes never went away, even if they were gradually refashioned and new language used to express them. Though Part I emphasizes the moments around Canada's creation, it carries the story forward to the 21st century to illustrate that colonialism never ended but, rather, remained a pervasive part of the Canadian story. This reality is tragically evident, for instance, in the appalling rate at which Indigenous women and children are murdered or disappeared in Canada, often with little, if any, investigation. Furthermore, as the rest of the book illustrates, Canadians' attitudes towards people outside of its borders remained steeped in the same attitudes; what was said of people in Afghanistan in the 21st century reflected what was said about Indigenous people in the 1880s.

Even in the 1880s, there was no global consensus that white supremacist values were correct. While most wealthy white people more or less accepted its basic premises, the overwhelming majority of the world was not white and did not consent to the theft of their land, the destruction of their societies and the denigration of their cultures by Europeans. Colonialism was always met with resistance. Even within European societies and settler colonies, there gradually emerged in the 19th century a current of anti-colonial politics. Though these individuals often failed to completely transcend the white supremacy of their society, they increasingly built connections with colonized people in struggles to overthrow the capitalist, colonial world order. The left, as this resistance came to be known, was always present in both the colonized and settler communities, and put the lie to any notion that "everyone" believed in the ideas of white supremacy.

Part I, then, lays the groundwork for the argument at the heart of this book, which is that those key components of Canada's founding — settler capitalism and the colonial imagination — remained central to Canada's engagements in the world henceforth. In Part II, I return to the period around Confederation and track the parallel dynamics of Canada's looking outward to the rest of the world, illustrating the ways in which the very same Canadians who were consolidating colonialism in Canada were projecting it elsewhere. Sam Steele, celebrated police officer who helped conquer the Indigenous Peoples and supervised the virtual slave labour of Chinese workers on the Canadian Pacific Railway (CPR), would later travel to South Africa to administer concentration camps holding mostly black South Africans on behalf of the British Empire. Cornelius Van Horne, capitalist tycoon who was the president of the CPR, was quickly off to Cuba where he brought his "clearer northern brain" to monopolize the island and extract profits.[3] By the 1930s, the Canadian military would be supporting a massacre of thousands of Indigenous farmers — "communist Indians," Prime Minister R.B. Bennett called them[4] — in El Salvador, in order to protect the profits of the Canadian company which monopolized electricity provision in the country.

This section of the book then locates Canada within the period of global tumult that developed in the early 20th century and exploded between 1914 and 1945 with two world wars and an economic catastrophe. The class dynamics of Canadian society — muted somewhat by the early stages of colonial conquest — became much clearer in this period as working-class Canadians, often immigrants, were sacrificed on behalf of the British Empire and the global supremacy of the Anglo-American powers. Central to this section is a re-assessment of Canada's place in a world gripped by left-wing revolution and fascist reaction; most notably, Part II critically examines Canada's relationship to the far-right movements that rose around the world in the 1920s and 1930s to illustrate that Canada often did more to foster their emergence than to stop them. Although Canada's participation in the Second World War was mythologized as selfless and heroic, the defeat of Nazi Germany would have been much easier had Canada not spent so long supporting Hitler, refusing to accept Jewish refugees and abandoning countries like Spain and Portugal to fascist domination.

Explaining Canada's behaviour in this period is difficult unless one remains clear about its founding principles. Canada's commitment was to a capitalist world, and thus it shared with the fascist powers a deep-rooted desire to crush the movements of the left that had risen up dramatically in the early 20th century in opposition to the poverty and immiseration of capitalism. In particular, Canada sought the destruction of the Soviet Union and, when Canada's own invasion failed to defeat the Russian Revolution, it hoped to wield fascism abroad as a hammer against communism. Furthermore, like the fascist powers, the Canadian ruling classes nurtured an abiding belief in hierarchy, in the idea that the world was divided into categories of people who, based on their race, gender, class or religion, were more or less fit to rule over others. Hitler, after all, admired Canada's genocidal policies towards Indigenous Peoples, just as Canadian Prime Minister William Lyon Mackenzie King admired "the constructive work" Hitler's Germany was doing in having "met the Communist menace at the time she did, and in the way she did," which was, of course, by mass murder.[5] King and Hitler also, notably, agreed "that in a large percentage of the [Jewish] race there are tendencies and trends which are dangerous indeed."[6] Ideologically, then, the Canadian government was not so distant from the fascists, even while many individual Canadians abhorred them.

The world looked very different after the Second World War, and Part III grapples with Canada's emergence as a so-called "middle power" during the Cold War. This was the era when peacekeeping became part of Canadian identity, when an image was built of a Canada that was a neutral and well-intentioned arbiter in international affairs. The reality was much different: as the people of Africa, Asia and Latin America fought for their freedom from Euro-American colonial or neocolonial authority, Canada consistently sided with the colonial powers and undermined those struggles for freedom. Canadian magazines declared that India was not a nation, Canadian officials urged Britain not to relinquish control of its colonial possessions to politically "immature" Africans, and Canadian weapons were donated to France to oppose the Vietnamese fight for independence. Across the globe, Canada insisted that colonized people were not capable of self-governance and mobilized racist stereotypes of Congolese cannibals, Papuan people living in trees and South Asian leaders wearing diapers.

These were all manifestations of the same colonial imagination that Canada had applied to its own conquered peoples, so it should come as no surprise that white supremacy mobilized at home would be similarly mobilized abroad. But Canada's undermining of the freedom struggles of colonized people was not simply ideological; by the Cold War period, Canadian capital had expanded into the world, from banking to mining to manufacturing, and the movements struggling against colonialism could not always be trusted to protect Canadian investments. As such, part of Canada's Cold War calculation was always to support those movements that were most amenable to maintaining a global capitalist system in a world where the existence of the Soviet Union made communism or socialism a viable option.

Canada thus became an important player in the Cold War, working closely with the United States to undermine those movements in the decolonizing world that posed a threat to the capitalist order and seeking to support those which would maintain neocolonial relations with the West. Canada opposed Indonesian freedom when it was oriented to the left, but supported it when it was ruled by a dictatorship that murdered millions of communists and welcomed foreign capital. Canada resisted the idea of Congolese independence when it was led by the charismatic left-leaning Patrice Lumumba, but quickly assisted an independent Congo taken over by right-wing forces which had assassinated Lumumba. Canada built close relations with the government of Chile and gave millions of dollars in foreign aid until Chileans elected the socialist Salvador Allende. Aid and relations were then suspended until a *coup d'etat* by the notorious butcher Augusto Pinochet — supported by Canada — turned Chile into a violent, capitalist laboratory.

It was all geared towards the larger goal of winning the Cold War, definitively conquering the socialist bloc that was centred around the Soviet Union, which, for all its flaws and problems, remained a key source of support for popular movements around the world. Canada had, from its inception, been driven by the permanent need to expand the frontiers of capitalism, and that project got a boost in the late 1980s, when the Soviet Union collapsed and Canada found itself part of an Anglo-American alliance that effectively ruled the world. Part IV of this book assesses what Canada did with this new power. It may have seemed, to some Canadians, that whatever violence was necessary to defeat the Soviet "Evil Empire" was worth it, even if it was unsavoury. For those who accepted that logic, the 1990s likely came as a shock, as Canada involved itself in global affairs that had disastrous consequences but did not have the Cold War as an excuse.

Part IV begins by addressing the 1990s, from the catastrophic dismantling of the economies of Russia and Eastern Europe, to the wanton violence of the Persian Gulf War, to the torture and murder of Somali youth, to the chaotic and confusing war in Yugoslavia and, perhaps most notably, the deeply tragic and misunderstood crisis in Rwanda. It was a terrible victory lap for the capitalist world and, especially, for Canada.

Introduction

In 2001, when decades of US interference in the Middle East produced a predictable retaliation in the form of the terrorist attacks against New York and Washington, a new era in world politics was declared under the banner of the War on Terror. Devastating and calamitous invasions of Afghanistan and Iraq quickly expanded to Libya, Syria, Mali and elsewhere, and the world veered ever closer to the dystopian fantasies that permeated western pop culture. The 21st century has offered endless war, climate catastrophe, capitalist crises and the rise of fascism, and Canada has consistently been found exacerbating all of these problems.

Canada has become one of the world's largest exporters of weapons. Canada is one of the world's worst polluters. Canada has routinely intervened in other countries' affairs — Haiti, Honduras, Colombia, Venezuela — to neutralize popular movements trying to reform or replace the capitalist structures causing the crisis. And Canada is cozying up to a new wave of fascists — in Brazil, Ukraine, Poland, Saudi Arabia, Israel and arguably the United States itself — who seem possessed by a pathological death drive that leaves children in concentration camps in Texas, an entire people imprisoned by an apartheid wall in Israel and the Amazon rainforest in flames. If the world is in crisis, Canada is a co-author, and through it all the logic has remained the same.

Behind the cascading crises of the 21st century is the endless desire for capitalist profits, of which Canada is in pursuit, especially in the environmentally destructive extractive industries. And in every struggle over Canadian access to some resource in some place, there have been people saying no, but being ignored or overruled. The same colonial imagination that led Canadians to assert their right to conquer Canada and write its laws drove Canadians to insert themselves into Honduras and re-write Honduran laws. The same certainty that Canada knew best was inherent in its transparent efforts to overthrow the Venezuelan government in favour of a pro-Western oligarch, even if the vast majority of Venezuelans had not and would not choose it. The same assumption of Canadian superiority led Canadian soldiers to claim that Afghans were "two thousand years behind" and needed the Canadian occupation to help develop the country and its industries.[7]

When people oppose Canadian intervention — as they often have — they are chastised as immature, irrational, hysterical and backwards. When Indigenous Guatemalans opposed a Canadian mine, the Canadian ambassador told them that they needed "to face the reality of a global society."⁸ If they were not insulted, they were attacked; after a Colombian opponent of a Canadian hydro dam travelled to Canada to denounce the project, he returned to Colombia to be murdered, without a word from the Canadian government or media. Back in Canada, when an Indigenous protestor interrupted Prime Minister Justin Trudeau at a fundraising dinner to raise the issue of people dying from poisoned water at Grassy Narrows First Nation, Trudeau sarcastically mocked the protestor while he was escorted out.

It is these continuities in Canada's engagements in the world that this book seeks to highlight. Canada's behaviour in more than 150 years of colonial relations with Indigenous Peoples is a terrible story in itself, but it is given another dimension when understood to be a consistent expression of what Canada is in the world. Canadian settlers' pervasive and ongoing practice of sexual violence against Indigenous women was reflected in the same behaviours by Canadian soldiers in Korea. The mixture of violence and manipulation that Canada used to seize land from Indigenous communities was replicated by Canadian capitalists in Honduras in the 21st century. Perhaps most telling of all, in nearly every setting the Canadian military found itself — Somalia, Yugoslavia, Afghanistan — soldiers consistently ended up calling that place "Indian Country."

This book offers a broad history of Canada in the world, but it is not exhaustive. Such a task would be impossible to write and overwhelming to read. Instead, I have made decisions about what to emphasize, what to note briefly and what to leave out. Those choices, naturally, betray my own interests in writing a book like this. Where many Canadian historians have spent much time dissecting the personalities at the highest level of Canadian politics, my focus tends to be on the broader dynamics of historical change. This is because I seek to understand *why* things happen, and I do not believe this question can be answered merely by examining the decisions of a few typically wealthy men who claim to speak on behalf on an entire nation. That those people in positions of power have an effect is undeniably true and, as such, the prime ministers are a big part of this story. But the flow of history runs much deeper than these individuals; this book suggests that Canada, regardless of its prime minister, has always been driven by a material compulsion towards the accumulation of capital and an ideological commitment to colonialism and white supremacy.

Indeed, many studies of Canadian foreign policy begin from an unsubstantiated assumption that Canadian policy is generally well-intentioned and seeks to strike a balance between the well-being of Canadians and the greater interests of the international community. Such an approach ignores the fact that Canada, like the rest of the world, is divided into different classes of people with different interests; what is good for some may be bad for others. I understand history as being shaped by conflict between and within that range of social classes and communities. The Canadian state, in this framework, acts as an institution that seeks to manage class conflict to the ultimate benefit of the Canadian capitalist class. Hence, the phases and episodes in Canada's foreign engagements are reflective of the evolving needs of the ruling classes. This book not only recounts various pieces of Canadian history but, in addition, contextualizes them within the framework of the Canadian colonial capitalist project.

Naturally, individual people in Canada often took on the goals and ideologies that emanated from the state, especially those whose interests most closely aligned with the ruling class, but many others found themselves on the opposite side for a variety of reasons. Gabriel Dumont, Mewa Singh, Alice Chown, Arthur Roy, Freda Coodin, Red Walsh, Norman Bethune, Edgar Harris, Kanao Inouye, James Endicott, Herbert Norman, Claire Culhane, Rocky Jones, Lee Maracle, Jean Claude Parrot; they all found themselves on the wrong side of Canada, at some point and for some reason, but their stories are just as significant as those of the prime ministers. They represent the cracks in the edifice of Canada; those who were excluded from it, who were broken by it or who extricated themselves from it and came to oppose it. In some of their lives — a soldier who refused to fight against the Bolsheviks, a nurse in Vietnam who exposed Canadian complicity in that conflict, or a nun who travelled to the Honduran border to block the passage of Canadian-supported paramilitaries — there were hints at something different that could have been, or that could yet be, in place of the Canada that is.

Still, this book is an examination of the Canada that is: how it has fit into the world, what role it has played, how it has shaped and been shaped by the dynamics around it. There is much covered here that is not typically included in foreign policy studies, ranging from the dynamics of class and race in Canada, the relationship between early waves of Canadian feminism and the Great War, and shifting attitudes towards immigration and who was included as "white" and/or "Canadian." There are also forays into global and regional politics that may, on occasion, seem not to be directly related to Canada. One of the weaknesses of many of the existing studies of Canada's engagements in the world is that the narrow focus on Canada means that the broader context in which Canada is engaging can be obscured. In fact, the Canadian government has often relied upon simplistic and de-contextualized narratives of its activities in order to cloak them in an air of harmless, good intentions. To truly understand the role Canada plays in various historical moments, it is imperative that we properly understand those moments.

For instance, the story that emerged from the crisis in Rwanda in 1994 was that a Canadian general tried to stop a genocide from taking place but was thwarted by United Nations bureaucrats who refused to give him the resources he needed to prevent Rwandan Hutus from engaging in a vicious and coordinated spree of ethnic violence against Tutsis. That narrative is inaccurate, but explaining its inaccuracies requires some deeper understanding of the history of Great Lakes Africa. Thus, Chapter 10 diverges for several pages into that history, out of which the reader should emerge with a much fuller understanding of how Canada's interference in Rwanda may have directly contributed to the tragedies that engulfed that country, even before 1994, and which ended with a pro-Western dictatorship that perfectly suited Canada's interests.

There are many such explorations of regional and global history into which I insert Canada's place, and in crafting these historical accounts I am deeply indebted to the work of other scholars. Outside of several years of fieldwork in Honduras, and the occasional personal anecdote, the knowledge that I marshal for this book is drawn from secondary sources, hundreds of them, each one containing many years of work and thinking by someone else. Although I have tried to use these sources faithfully, even when I am criticizing them, it needs be said that in a book as broad in scope as this, there are likely moments where the nuance and texture of my sources gets lost. I can only implore the interested reader to follow up on the sources that I have drawn from to get the deeper picture that, on occasion, I have had to sacrifice for relevance and brevity.

There is a fundamental question at the heart of this book: what is Canada? What is at the core of the thing — the state, the society, the culture — that was built on the place that is now called Canada and which was once under the jurisdiction of hundreds of Indigenous nations? No single answer will ever be fully satisfactory, but my intention is to cast some light on this problem by looking at how Canada has engaged in the world. What did Canada say? What did it do? Who did it support?

Who did it oppose? What was Canada's contribution to the events that shaped people's lives over the past century and a half, and what role has it played in building the world our children will inherit? The answers to these questions will not be comforting to anyone who is committed to the idea of a nice, kind Canada trying to help people. But given the state of the 21st century world, I make no apologies if this book is jarring. The problems that Canada has helped create are so great that some view them as an existential threat to humanity itself. Even less dire interpretations of the coming calamities suggest that we must, as a species, change course urgently. A necessary first step for people located in Canada is an honest and unflinching look in the mirror.

Notes
1. Quoted in Philip Lee-Shanok, "GTA book publisher accused of whitewashing Indigenous history," *CBC News*, October 3, 2017.
2. Quoted in Philip Lee-Shanok, "GTA book publisher accused…"
3. Quoted in Yves Engler, *The Black Book of Canadian Foreign Policy*, Fernwood, Halifax, 2009, p. 18.
4. R.B. Bennett, quoted in Peter McFarlane, *Northern Shadows: Canadians and Central America*, Toronto, Between the Lines, 1989, p. 47.
5. William Lyon Mackenzie King, *The Mackenzie King Diaries, 1893–1947*, June 29, 1937, Microfiche Collection, University of Toronto, University of Toronto Press, 1980.
6. William Lyon Mackenzie King, quoted in Gerald Tulchinsky, "Goldwin Smith: Victorian Canadian Antisemite," in Alan Davies, ed., *Antisemitism in Canada: History and Interpretation*, Waterloo, Wilfrid Laurier University Press, 1992, p. 84.
7. Ash Van Leeuwen, quoted in Christie Blatchford, *Fifteen Days: Stories of Bravery, Friendship, Life and Death from Inside the Canadian Military*, Toronto, Anchor, 2008, p. 63.
8. James Lambert, quoted in Todd Gordon and Jeffery R. Webber, *Blood of Extraction: Canadian Imperialism in Latin America*, Halifax, Fernwood, 2016, p. 95–96.

Part I

Conquest and Colonialism

Canada's First Foreign Policy

1

Colonial Encounters

I knew that whites were looking at me through their racial stereotypes and I too began to see myself as stupid, dirty breed, drunken and irresponsible. It made me feel stripped of all humanity and decency, and left me with nothing but my Indianness, which at that time I did not value. I hated talking to whites because it was such an agonizing experience... not only did my sense of inferiority become inflamed, but I came to hate myself for the image I could see in their eyes. Everywhere white supremacy surrounded me. Even in solitary silence I felt the word "savage" deep in my soul.

— Howard Adams, 1975[1]

ONE OF THE FOUNDATIONAL MYTHS of Canada is that when European settlers arrived they discovered a vast, empty territory. The idea of this empty wilderness still permeates Canadians' self-image, regularly reflected in government brochures and beer commercials. It may seem like a harmless homage to the natural environment and our collective appreciation for hiking and canoeing, but it is nevertheless an image built upon a pernicious lie: this place was never empty. Rather, there was a concerted effort to empty it.

Indeed, it has been argued that the Western Hemisphere may have been more densely populated than Europe itself when Columbus' ships landed in the Caribbean. In the five centuries that followed, Indigenous civilizations great and small were subject to a variety of coercive pressures that caused calamitous declines in many places; war, disease, famine and other gifts from across the Atlantic reduced the Indigenous population of the Americas by as much as 90 million people.[2]

It was in the cauldron of that catastrophe that Canada was born. Its birth was directly tied to the processes which emptied the Americas of many of its original inhabitants. This fact makes many contemporary Canadians uncomfortable, so much so that Canada has spent a large part of its history denying and downplaying the scale of the tragedy that was brought upon the Indigenous Peoples. But that refusal to grapple with history undermines our ability to make sense of our present. The patterns that emerge when we examine 150 years of Canadian foreign policy in light of Canada's colonial heritage are clear; there is consistency in both the primary goals and the ideological framework through which we understand and express them. What Canada was, Canada is. This cannot change unless and until we address this problem directly. As such, this book begins by examining the colonial process through which Canada was formed, from the dynamics that set the stage for Canada's Confederation in 1867 through over 150 years of Canada's foreign policy towards Indigenous nations.

The encounter between Europe and the Indigenous Peoples of what became Canada is an immensely complex historical event. My treatment of this process here is necessarily brief, emphasizing broader dynamics, often at the expense of important specific cases, counterpoints and exceptions. Priority is often placed on assessing the actions and attitudes of the European colonizers, which, unfortunately, reproduces the dominant scholarly dynamic wherein the politics of and within Indigenous nations is deemed to be of less historical importance. I do not share that belief, and I hope this book will go some way to undermining it. Nevertheless, since this study is designed to assess Canada, specifically, my emphasis is on a critical exploration of what those early colonizers did, and what they thought, in order to link those actions and thoughts to broader Canadian policies. It is my hope that the pages that follow will establish — among other things — the necessity of building a society that rejects the Eurocentric notion that true history is that which flowed from Europe.

New Worlds, East and West

Between the 15th and the 19th centuries, the world was dramatically changed. Civilizations old and new, on every continent, experienced dramatic ruptures during this time, whether in single moments of crisis or through gradual processes that irreparably changed their central operating procedures and ideological foundations. It could be argued that this was the period when "globalization" really happened, eventually reconfiguring the entire planet around a new centre of power in Europe, which, for the first time, could shape historical events all over the world. That Europe emerged as the centre of world power was, indeed, a novelty; not even at the height of the Roman Empire could it have been said that Europe was in any way more "advanced" than other empires and civilizations around the world.

Explaining precisely how that happened is no simple task. But three phenomena were undeniably at the heart of the matter, all of which developed in relationship to one another. These three events, in no particular order, were 1) the emergence of capitalism, 2) the creation of vast European colonial empires and 3) the rise of the trans-Atlantic slave trade. There is much debate over precisely how and why each of these began, but it is clear that they developed in parallel and very much reinforced one another.[3]

Capitalism is a social and economic system — a mode of production — distinguished by the prevalence of private property, particularly in land and in human labour. While there was much variation in the nature of pre-capitalist societies, capitalism was always a radical break from the lived experience of most people, who, until being brought under the power of capital, had direct access to land and whose labour was not structured by a wage relationship. In capitalism, most land and labour came to be owned by a small fraction of the population, who would use their ownership of these crucial new commodities to extract profits for themselves. The majority — who did not own capital and who could not afford to purchase the land, materials and labour necessary to start a successful capitalist enterprise — were left with few legal options besides taking on wage labour for someone else, under conditions invariably shaped by the social, political and economic context in which they found themselves. A white male automotive worker in Oshawa in the 1970s, for instance, might have been in a position to earn wages that allowed him to live a comfortable life. On the other hand, a Honduran migrant worker picking fruit on a rural Ontario farm in the early 2000s would face much less favourable labour conditions.

In both cases, these circumstances were largely beyond the individual labourer's control and were shaped by market forces that were difficult to discern. Yet, despite this appearance of an all-powerful, inscrutable, so-called "free market," that market was often manipulated by political actors mobilized to support the capitalist classes. As such, the market was inherently unbalanced, and its logic consistently — almost like magic — led to greater profits for capital and a growing gap between the rich and poor. Though this may sound polemical, it is actually a rather obvious and visible fact; for instance, in 2018 it was reported that the eight richest individuals in the world possessed more wealth than the poorest four billion, or half of the human species at the time. The richest person in the world, Jeff Bezos, had a net worth of over $105 billion, making him the wealthiest person in human history.[4]

There is much debate over when and how capitalism first emerged, but scholars generally accept that the earliest capitalist systems emanated from western Europe, coalescing most prominently in England. The dominant explanations for this came from Europeans themselves and, as such, often imagined European culture to be intrinsically superior. One popular idea was that capitalism was a product of the "Protestant ethic" — the claim being that they were simply motivated by their religion to work harder than other people. Of course, this was nonsense; people worked hard all over the world, and that did not usually transform an entire mode of production. In contrast to such Eurocentric explanations, the more satisfying theory is that capitalism emerged as a consequence of the relatively fragmented and disorganized nature of European feudalism, compared to the standards set in China, India and the Middle East.[5] Indeed, the feudal monarchies of western Europe — especially England — were less effectively managed than most of their contemporaries, which allowed greater space for class struggle to emerge. The feudal middle classes began to tilt the balance of power in their direction, ultimately prompting a series of capitalist (or pre-capitalist) revolutions in Holland, England and France.[6]

Emblematic of this gradual process of change was the process known as the Enclosures in England, wherein English merchants and lesser members of the aristocracy began claiming private ownership over tracts of land. This was, of course, illegal. In England, as in most feudal monarchies, the land was assumed to belong to God, with the monarch serving as its steward on God's behalf. To claim that you owned a parcel of land would have seemed as absurd then as it would today if I claimed to have purchased all of the air above the city of Toronto and proceeded to charge people a fee to breathe it in.

But these merchants — who would later be called capitalists — were able to exert coercive power over the peasants who lived on the land being "enclosed," and in the early stages of this process, their complaints at being kicked off the land went unheeded. For better or worse, the English monarchy was ineffectual by the standards of the time and was routinely mired in internal conflict over the throne. Decentralized and disorganized, it was unable to muster any effective response to the gradual privatization of land until it was too late. By the 17th century these new capitalists were wealthy, organized and armed, and they successfully asserted their right to determine the laws of the land in what they called the Glorious Revolution of 1688.[7]

This new capitalist class could generate profits by hiring former peasants to work on these privately owned farms, paying them a wage but claiming ownership over the fruits of their labour. While most peasants did not want to submit to the indignity of growing food for someone else on the land where they had once provided for themselves, the very fact that they had been kicked off the land made them dependent on this new form of wage labour in order to survive. It was the germ of the capitalist system which would eventually be applied to nearly every industry in the world, and it depended on separating the peasantry from the land. Bereft of direct access to land, people were forced into wage labour. Given the weakness of their circumstance — after all, they now depended on these jobs — the capitalists could exploit their labour, paying them far less in wages than what they earned by selling that which they produced.

Of course, this process was not as fluid and straightforward as the above narrative suggests; it developed in fits and starts and with significant pushback, not just from the aristocracy, whose power waned as a result of the rise of capitalism, but also from the peasants, whose lives, livelihoods, communities and traditions were being overturned.[8] And while I have documented the case of England, similar processes played out at a slower pace in other parts of Europe and Japan across this period. They were also evident in India, Egypt and other large tributary societies, but these did not emerge as the first capitalist states in large part because their political systems were far more tightly and effectively regulated to block such actions. What is more, to the extent that nascent capitalist systems were beginning to emerge in the 18th and 19th centuries outside of Europe, these were typically stunted by the arrival of European colonizers.[9]

Indeed, one of the great mistakes some scholars have made in assessing the origins of capitalism has been to imagine that the process took place in isolation from the dynamics of colonialism and slavery. It is no coincidence that over precisely the same period that capitalism emerged, these European powers began to expand their reach across the globe, in search of land and labour to exploit. These colonial empires looked different, depending on their goals. The 16th-century Spanish Empire, for instance, typically viewed its colonies primarily as a source of natural resources, especially precious metals, and focused its efforts on conquering and enslaving the people it met in order to extract that wealth. By contrast, several of the colonies of England would develop with the long-term goal of settlement and the displacement of Indigenous Peoples to facilitate the expansion of their capitalist economies. Though no two cases are identical, it is possible to distinguish between these two categories of colonialism: those designed primarily for economic exploitation (Spanish America, British India and the Dutch East Indies) and a more settler-oriented colonialism (British North America, French Algeria and Portuguese Brazil).[10]

In each of these variants and the other forms that colonial projects took, no consideration was given to the fact that Europeans had not been invited to conquer, enslave or displace anyone. But they reassured themselves that they were doing their god's work by bringing "civilization" to people they deemed less advanced. Indeed, European colonialism had as its direct antecedent the expulsion of the Jews and Muslims from Spain; Christopher Columbus's voyage was funded by a Spanish monarchy drunk on its victory in Iberia, seeking to launch one final crusade to destroy the Islamic Empire.[11] Though it was expressed differently in different times and places, colonialism was consistent in its claim that the colonizer was superior and should be thanked for the work it was doing, no matter how ugly it may have looked in practice.

And it was certainly ugly. The vicious Spanish genocide on the island of Hispaniola in the 16th century nearly eliminated the entire Taíno civilization.[12] The Dutch and English introduced the practice of cutting off the scalps of Indigenous people for bounty in southern New York and New Jersey in the 17th and 18th centuries.[13] The French used organized rape as a weapon against Algerians in the 19th century, promising to "annihilate all who will not crawl beneath our feet like dogs."[14] The Belgian king had as many as ten to fifteen million people killed in the Congo on the eve of the 20th century, and that century was marked by the extreme violence of the US military ranging from the slaughter of Filipino children at the start of the century to the torture of Iraqi prisoners at its end. An almost endless list of similarly horrific examples could be drawn from the history of colonialism.

Meanwhile, the direct, naked violence of colonialism reflected a deeper, more systemic violence, which made colonialism a world-changing phenomenon. Everywhere that European colonizers went, they extracted wealth. In fact, that was the entire purpose of colonialism. The amount of wealth transferred from the colonies to the European powers is incalculably high; scholars have estimated that Britain plundered some $45 trillion from India alone, a staggering figure that helps explain why Europe emerged as the centre of world capitalism.[15] In effect, colonialism gave Europe a massive head start when it came to capitalism; it was like beginning a game of Monopoly by stealing everyone's money and property while insisting that everyone else play by the rules.

Not only did colonial powers extract wealth, they increasingly sought to actively destroy the civilizations they encountered. As capitalism developed, and as the new capitalist class became increasingly aware of their own interests and of the very existence of a capitalist economic system, colonialism took a progressively more capitalist approach, especially in the colonies characterized by large-scale settlement. Rather than following a more mercantile pattern of conquest, whereby the new rulers would extract wealth and taxes and enforce a handful of self-serving laws, the more capitalist-oriented settler form of colonialism sought to recreate the conditions for capitalism in the colonized place.

To the colonial powers, this typically necessitated the complete dismantling of the systems they encountered. This is a particularly important point for the study of Canada; Indigenous Peoples could not be allowed to continue to practise their ways of life — their political, economic, social and cultural practices — because these practices were in direct contradiction to the capitalist model that the colonizers wanted to build. As such, colonialism often could not stop at simply ruling people from afar, the way earlier empires might have, but rather needed to break people from their very civilizations.

That breaking was similarly reflected in the third phenomenon involved in this transformation: the trans-Atlantic slave trade. Beginning in the 16th century and reaching its height in the late 18th century, the entire process involved the kidnapping of some 14 million people from various parts of Africa to be sold as slaves in the Americas, including the colonies that became Canada. Although various forms of slavery had existed as far back as the ancient human civilizations, arguably nothing compares to the scale and character of this particular chapter in human brutality. Several factors distinguished the trans-Atlantic slave trade from other forms of slavery. For one thing, there had never existed such a massive, commercially oriented slave trade. The infrastructure, both physical and institutional, built to carry out and extract profit from the sale of African slaves was of an unprecedented magnitude. Indeed, its parallel development to the rise of capitalism and the infusion of wealth stolen from the colonies is no coincidence; the establishment of the slave trade required a huge amount of expenditure, and those who engaged in it did so in order to reap the tremendous profits it could bestow.

Furthermore, the treatment and use of slaves in the Americas was also unique. As noted above, this was a total breaking of people from their communities and cultures. Even by the time they were placed on slave ships bound for the "new world," many of these future slaves were already unable to speak the same languages as their fellow captives, having been drawn in from many different places. Those who survived the voyage were then sold and sent off to various places across the Western Hemisphere, even further disarticulating them from people with whom they had any connection. By the time they arrived at their destination, they were often bereft of any connection to their homes, a fact not lost on slave owners, who took advantage of these enslaved people's utter dislocation to reinforce their power. Many Europeans explicitly conveyed their preference for African over Indigenous slaves, since the former were deemed easier to control.

All the while, the logic of colonialism — and its assumption that Europeans were more advanced — was applied in equal measure to the victims of the slave trade. While no instance of slavery was ever kind to the enslaved, the trans-Atlantic trade took this to a new level in its utter dehumanization of its victims. If they were not human, then it was easier to reconcile the horrific ways in which they were treated, and there is ample evidence that enslaved Africans were routinely described and administered to in this way. The ideological project to view Africans more as animals than people reflected the logic of colonialism, which routinely applied the same sorts of assessments to Indigenous people. Thus, the ideology of colonialism both reinforced, and was reinforced by, the slave trade.[16]

Finally, the slave economy itself was a crucial part of the re-shaping of the world. If colonialism represented a massive transfer of wealth, the slave trade was a tremendous infusion of forced labour. King Louis XIV, of France, himself acknowledged that "there [was] nothing which contribut[ed] more to the development of the colonies and the cultivation of their soil than the laborious toil of the Negroes."[17] Small wonder that the ruling classes of Europe and America were positively flummoxed at the spectacle of a successful slave revolt in Haiti at the turn of the 19th century, which was to herald the beginning of the end of this form of slavery.[18]

As many people have pointed out, much of the US economy, which would ultimately inherit the primary place in world capitalism, was built by slave labour. Slavery's importance to the US economy was so great that even on the eve of the Civil War, the cotton plantations of the south were intricately linked to the burgeoning global capitalist economy.[19] What is more, the colonial justifications for slavery were, in some respects, growing stronger in the 19th century rather than weaker. James Laxer notes that, although slavery was initially defended as a necessary evil, by the time abolition was being widely considered, the elite of the US south "promulgated the view that slavery was a positive good, benefitting both the slaves… and the white owners, who were suited to their paternal position as a natural consequence of their racial superiority."[20] Twenty-first-century movements that are demanding reparations from the United States for slavery estimate the total value of that unpaid labour to be around \$4.7 trillion, and it was undeniably a critical factor in establishing the economic motor of capitalism and in placing boundaries around who would be allowed to enjoy its privileges.[21] The fact that African-descended people remain disproportionately poor in nearly every country in the Western Hemisphere is a rather obvious illustration of the lasting legacy of slavery.

It is important to remember that these three dynamics were emerging in parallel and reinforced one another. The success of European colonial conquests in the Western Hemisphere were based, in part, on military technologies that had developed as a result of increased commercial activity and rivalry around the emergence of capitalism.[22] At the same time, the increased compulsion towards expanding the sphere of their colonial economic activities was spurring on further advances in military technology. Distinguishing which of these factors constituted the "chicken" and which constituted the "egg" is probably a fruitless endeavour; the point is that they emerged together to great consequence.

Thus, in very broad strokes, was the world remade in the period during which Canada was conceived. While the Canada we know was not created until Confederation in 1867, its predecessors — New France and British North America — were very much a product of the dynamics described above. As we turn our attention to the details of Canada's arrival and the relationships it created with the Indigenous nations it met, it is important to keep this context in mind. After all, Canadian policies were not generated in a vacuum but out of the very fires that forged the contemporary world.

Before Canada

Seen through the eyes of many Indigenous nations, Canada is a foreign imposition.[23] The very fact that Canada treats its relations with Indigenous Peoples as an "internal" matter speaks to its colonial commitments; Indigenous nations invariably view themselves as sovereign, making this a matter of Canadian foreign policy. This becomes much more apparent when one takes a longer view of these relations. Both the early European settlers and the Indigenous nations always viewed their interactions as international, and, as such, I proceed from the premise that these encounters were a matter of foreign policy. Since this book is about modern Canada, it focuses on events that took place around and subsequent to Confederation in 1867. But, in order to make sense of those events, this chapter sketches out the historical context that Canada inherited, highlighting the ways that European patterns from before Confederation would set the tone for Canada's independent foreign policy towards Indigenous nations afterwards.

There is a tendency in Canada to treat Indigenous Peoples as though they are one large, homogenous group. This has been true of official policy, which has routinely applied blanket policies to all "Indians," and it is equally true of individual settler conceptions, which, even when well-intentioned, have often incorrectly assumed all Indigenous people to be from the same cultural heritage.[24] In fact, few things bind all Indigenous people to one another beyond a shared modern history of dealing with European conquerors and settlers. Otherwise, the nations that have populated the Americas have been extremely varied: from massive, centralized tributary societies like the Aztec, to complex, horizontally organized democratic nations like the Haudenosaunee Confederacy, to more widely dispersed and locally autonomous kinship societies like the

Plains Cree. These civilizations did not live without internal and external conflicts and challenges; war, hardship, disease and division were part of the histories of Indigenous nations like any others.[25]

Within what is now Canada, there existed many dozens of distinct civilizations, which were not static but, rather, adapted to changing economic, environmental, social and political circumstances. The encounter with European settlers was to be the most difficult circumstance they faced, though many of the surviving nations still strive to maintain their independent existence despite the trauma and dislocation bestowed upon them by the experience of colonization. In sketching a broad narrative of Canadian foreign policy, I am inevitably compelled to make reference to Indigenous Peoples as if they were one side of a bilateral relationship with Canada. It would be more accurate to describe these relationships as multilateral, with Canada increasingly and consciously positioning itself as the central spoke.

But it is also true that none of the Indigenous nations the European settlers encountered shared those settlers' desire to build and maintain a capitalist economy. None entered into the relationship with the same preconceived notion of inherent superiority that the Europeans did. None were possessed by the same drive for endless accumulation of new territory and wealth. None made any attempt to aggressively convert European settlers to their religions. Many Indigenous people today actively identify with the shared experience of being Indigenous, while also asserting their specific nationality as Mi'kmaq, Innu, Haida, etc. Thus, while painting a picture of Indigenous nations as monolithic is patently incorrect, there remain profound and generalizable differences between Indigenous nations and the European settler societies that became Canada.

Those differences between settlers and Indigenous Peoples were, above all, a product of the changes that I described above: the remaking of the world around the logic of capitalism, colonialism and slavery. These three phenomena combined to create, in Europe, a group of civilizations that were endlessly driven towards violent expansion, both because their new economic realities compelled it and because their ideologies demanded it.[26] When settlers arrived in what would eventually be called Canada, they arrived to make money and save souls; the former justified by the latter, and the latter made possible by the former. These would ultimately become the twin pillars of Canadian foreign policy: settler capitalism and the colonial imagination.

Anthropological records suggest that people have been living in what is now Canada for at least 13,000 years.[27] Indigenous Peoples settled in North America as the glaciers gradually melted,[28] and yet it is common practice among Canadian scholars to skip the first 12,500 years of the history of this place, as if nothing of consequence happened until Europeans arrived. By contrast, we are expected to have a working knowledge of English and French history before contact. We are led to believe that the Magna Carta was a formative moment for what would become Canada but that the rise and fall of the city of Cahokia — near present-day St. Louis, it was the largest city in North America's history until 18th-century Philadelphia — had no bearing.

But it did. Cahokia's rise in the 11th century was a consequence of a long cycle of favourable climatic conditions across the Northern Hemisphere, which had led to significant expansion of Indigenous agriculture over a period of several hundred years.[29] These years of plenty were, however, interrupted by the volcanic activity of the middle of the 13th century, which plunged the entire Northern Hemisphere into a minor ice age. Europe and North America alike were beset by crop failures and civilizational collapse; the lasting memory of this catastrophe in Europe is the Black Death, while a useful symbol of the crisis in North America was the abandonment of the metropolis of Cahokia.

The climatic shift and resulting crises created cascading waves of migration across the continent, like the movement of the Mortlach people into what is now Manitoba and Saskatchewan. The conflicts and adaptations that arose from this wave of migration re-shaped the political, economic and social dynamics of many Indigenous societies on the eve of the permanent European arrival. In some cases, the changed circumstances had led to the construction of new political alliances, like the Haudenosaunee Confederacy. In other cases, it left civilizations relatively weakened and vulnerable to the coming assault from across the Atlantic. In still others, the migratory waves had compelled the creation of effective new economic strategies, such as the non-disruptive buffalo hunt on the plains, which had the effect of making those Indigenous societies physically healthier and more resistant to European conquest.[30] The rise and fall of Cahokia, then, had consequences that shaped what later became Canada.

The point here is to remind ourselves that when Europeans arrived in what they called the "new world" they were engaging with civilizations that had been developing for millennia. Indeed, the first European settlers knew full well that they were dealing with large, complex, foreign nations. As late as the 1660s, there were still fewer than 3000 French colonists in Canada, utterly dwarfed in number by millions of Indigenous people.[31] With that in mind, it is worthwhile to look briefly at the first arrivals of the French and English settlers, whose early relations with Indigenous nations set the tone for Canada's international relations.

Cartier's *Sauvages*

While Norse explorers had some contact with Beothuk and other Indigenous nations in Newfoundland and Labrador in the 10th and 11th centuries, and Portuguese and Spanish sailors did some navigating and fishing along the east coast, the first real antecedents of Canadian foreign policy were established by Jacques Cartier, the French captain who sailed up the St. Lawrence River in 1535. Though 21st-century Canadians are often possessed by the idea that this was an encounter between politically and economically advanced Europeans and quaint, simple Indigenous nations, the reality was quite different. As Ramsay Cook notes in an introduction to *The Voyages of Jacques Cartier* (1993), "French life was not much different [from that of the Haudenosaunee] for most people," since, in France, "town labourers earned low wages while the peasantry's meagre standard of life fluctuated with the harvest."[32] If anything, Cook probably underestimates the standard of living of the Haudenosaunee, who were experiencing a golden age of art, culture and urban design.[33]

Still, the French always considered themselves to be the advanced race, dealing with a group of primitives without culture or history. Cartier immediately described the Haudenosaunee as "savages" and asserted that "they could easily be moulded in the way one would wish."[34] Ironically, Cartier noted that the Haudenosaunee were "wonderful thieves" who "steal everything they can carry off,"[35] even while he and his crew were squatting on Haudenosaunee territory.[36] Emblematic of the early colonial experience, Cartier's relationship with the local chief Donnacona began in uneasy peace and ended with betrayal; Cartier had Donnacona kidnapped after a false invitation to parley in the French fort. Upon Cartier's initial arrival at Stadacona (near present-day Québec City) in 1534, he seized two teenage boys to use them as guides; these were likely Donnacona's sons or nephews. When Cartier returned with the boys the next year, he set up camp near Stadacona without permission and declared his intention to sail up the river to Hochelaga (near present-day Montréal). Donnacona did not grant this passage, but Cartier defied these instructions. Though he was well-received at Hochelaga, he returned to winter near Stadacona, growing increasingly distrustful of the Haudenosaunee.

For their part, the Haudenosaunee clearly had grievances with the behaviour of the Europeans, especially after Cartier made a spectacle of raising a thirty-foot wooden cross on their territory, but there is no evidence to support Cartier's fear that they were plotting an attack.[37] In fact, the French only survived the winter of 1535 thanks to medicine provided by one of the teenagers Cartier had earlier kidnapped.[38] Nevertheless, Cartier grew increasingly hostile, and he ultimately kidnapped Donnacona and nine other Haudenosaunee and brought them to France, where they died. Unsurprisingly, when he returned to the St. Lawrence in 1541 to establish a permanent settlement, the Haudenosaunee attacked his colony.[39]

Without Indigenous support, the French were unable to survive the winters and maintain their presence, and so they abandoned the St. Lawrence for nearly a century. It was an instructive opening to nearly 500 years of relations between European settlers and Indigenous people in Canada, which was the name Cartier applied to this place after misunderstanding the Haudenosaunee word for "village." Reflecting on the behaviour of the French captain, Bruce Trigger notes: "Cartier's behaviour towards native people clearly became more cynical and opportunistic as his objectives shifted from peaceful exploration to conquest and control of North America."[40] Colonial goals, then, were key to understanding European behaviour.

The French gradually did establish a presence in what they called Acadie, and later Québec, in the early 17th century, while the British landed settlers along the eastern seaboard of North America and made attempts to establish colonies in Newfoundland and Nova Scotia (Acadia). Not surprisingly, rivalry between the two empires grew, colonialism being inherently a zero-sum game. Early settlements in New France were relatively small and primarily functioned as outposts to conduct the growing fur trade, with Indigenous traders engaging in the trade from a position of some strength and without significant disruption of Indigenous societies, at least by comparison to what had taken place elsewhere and what was yet to come.[41] In fact, several French attempts to settle in Québec would have failed without significant help from local Anishinaabeg and Innu, who taught colonists how to survive, as the Haudenosaunee had done for Cartier's crews in the 1530s.[42]

British colonies, by contrast, were oriented towards larger-scale settlement and were inscribed with the logic of capitalism and the need to dispossess Indigenous Peoples of the land itself. The early history of the British in North America, thus, was much more riven with conflict; it also offers the greatest insight into the deep roots of what became Canada since New France was shortly defeated by a British invasion from the south.

Puritan Pathologies

While it was not the first engagement between the English and Indigenous Peoples in North America (conflicts had already emerged around the Virginia colony) the most emblematic early encounter for a study of Canada was that which culminated in the Pequot War in the 1630s. The war was launched by the English Puritans of the Massachusetts Bay colony, who would later compel the British Crown to invade New France and claim Canada for Britain.[43]

The Puritans' Protestant extremism outstripped even their contemporaries in England, instilling in them a pious drive to utterly master their own and others' natural urges. Dancing, singing, sensuousness and embodied joy of any sort was the enemy; thus, their enemies even included other English settlers who built genuine relationships with Indigenous people, who suffered no such repressive dogma. Massachusetts governor John Endicott's greatest nemesis was another English settler, Thomas Morton, who, rather than conquer and kill, wished to live and learn with the Pequot people. His comparably respectful embrace of Indigenous hospitality represented a very different approach to foreign relations than that of the Puritans.[44]

The Puritans, more even than their English contemporaries, considered the Indigenous people to be "savages," who would either be saved by accepting the strict rule of God or be drowned in a "marsh of blood," with evident preference for the latter.[45] This bloodlust was made clear in the opening of the Pequot War. When a ruthless and quick-tempered English trader, John Oldham, was found dead off Brock Island, his contemporary, John Gallop, quickly killed a dozen Pequots in vengeance, though he had neither evidence that they had killed Oldham nor any insight into whether Oldham had himself initiated a conflict.

Unsatisfied by their revenge, the Puritans launched a surprise attack on a Pequot fort on the Mystic River, ultimately choosing to burn it and the 400 Pequots inside. By now the workings of colonial ferocity had hooks in the Massachusetts Puritans, who hunted down the remaining Pequots at every opportunity. Pequot land was now being taken by the colony and more was coveted; the new governor, Israel Stoughton, arrived in 1637, having been promised a piece of Pequot territory upon which he could build a warehouse. When he arrived to find a group of nearly a hundred Pequot refugees, he had them seized and turned over to the above-mentioned John Gallop. Gallop tied them up and threw them into the sea, while his mates scoured the area to hunt and kill any remaining Pequots.[46]

According to one Puritan leader, their god was kind enough to punish the Pequots "and to give us their Land for an Inheritance."[47] Indeed, the ease with which Puritan colonial ideals combined with the economic imperative to dispossess Indigenous people of their land is what I wish to highlight here. Richard Drinnon's *Facing West* (1980) illustrates the extent to which these two dynamics reinforced one another across the colonial history of the United States and the expansion of its empire. This pattern is mirrored in the creation of Canada, which took particular shape after the arrival of the Loyalists, many of whom were descendants of the Puritans.[48]

The Puritans explicitly sought to destroy the Pequot and "to cut off the Remembrance of them from the Earth."[49] Drinnon notes that eliminating the Pequots served to satisfy the profoundly suppressed desires of the Puritans, who were forbidden from enjoying the sensuality — be it sex, singing or dancing — that Indigenous life represented to them.[50] Destruction of the Pequots was a spiritual war against the worst temptations of their own subconscious. To the settlers, explains Drinnon, "the bestial Indians already *were* the nature that the colonists would fall back into should they yield to such impulses."[51] This is a point worth remembering when we consider modern Canadian musings on the conflict in Rwanda, where Gen. Roméo Dallaire "shook hands with the devil," or the peacekeeping mission in Somalia, where Canadians claimed that the evil of that country had led its otherwise pure soldiers to commit heinous acts of violence.[52]

And yet, at the same time, Drinnon reminds us that "the Pequot War was about extending English rule and laws."[53] Far from being simply a psychological manifestation, the genocidal impulse of the Puritans had a concrete material purpose. Speaking of John Mason, one of the leaders of these massacres, Drinnon notes that while he "enjoyed the psychic income accruing to an instrumental saviour," he also enjoyed the acquisition of "tangible assets as well, including an island of five hundred acres... that he claimed by right of conquest."[54] Settlers wanted land; they had come specifically to take it. As Patrick Wolfe argues, "whatever settlers may say — and they generally have a lot to say — the primary motive [of settler colonialism] is not race (or religion, ethnicity, grade of civilization, etc.) but access to territory."[55]

These twin themes — ideological claims of superiority masking naked theft of territory — would run through the entire English settlement of North America, from Kentucky to Florida to British Columbia. The attitudes of the Puritans may seem extreme, but they set the tone that would be followed with only minor variation over the ensuing centuries of the conquest and genocide that built Canada and the United States. The British expanded their influence over Canada in successive waves: in the claiming of Rupert's Land in 1670 for the Hudson's Bay Company; in the awarding of Newfoundland to Britain in 1713; in the establishment of the colony of Halifax and the expulsion of the French Acadians in the 1750s; and especially in the ultimate defeat of New France in 1763, the assertion of British North America and the influx of Loyalists after 1776. Throughout this period, Indigenous people were drawn into the century of wars between Britain, France and later the United States, which took place on their land, and they often played decisive roles in the outcomes of battles.[56] While various Indigenous nations tried to navigate the conflicts in ways that would best protect themselves, the end result was destabilization of Indigenous communities, disruption of Indigenous territories and dissolution of internal and international bonds between Indigenous nations.[57]

Meanwhile, the American Revolution exposed the contradiction in settler colonialism between the interests of the settlers and those of the metropolitan elite. Despite its lofty rhetoric, the American Revolution was effectively a struggle between different factions of the British ruling class. That is, the American Revolution was not anti-colonial, because the American settlers had not been colonized by Britain. They *were* the colonizers, fed up with playing by the rules their early sponsors had placed on them.[58]

Notably, one of the major points of friction was that London sought to contain the settlers' westward expansion into what was then called "Indian Territory."⁵⁹ The ambitions of the settlers had grown, spurred by the economic desire for land and the now deeply ingrained hatred of Indigenous people.⁶⁰ In the late 18th century, a complex political and military showdown played out between the British, the American settlers and the Indigenous people in the territory south of the Great Lakes. Though the British sought to restrict American expansion, they were not "protecting" Indigenous territory in any meaningful way. In fact, the British were still actively asserting their own dominance over the region; these conflicts are perhaps best captured by the infamous suggestion of British Commander Jeffrey Amherst that they gift Odawa and Wyandot people blankets infected with smallpox to "extirpate this execrable race."⁶¹

Nevertheless, as American settlers brought active genocide from the eastern colonies, many Indigenous nations found it expedient to ally with the British to try to protect themselves, while some threw in their lot on the American side. Both the British and Americans typically made promises in exchange for Indigenous allegiance, and those promises were invariably broken. For instance, when the British decided to capitulate and grant independence to the Americans, they gave up all the territory south of the Great Lakes without consulting any of the Indigenous allies, whose agreements to fight in the war were premised on the protection of that land. The British attempted to smooth things over with the Haudenosaunee by offering them an insulting consolation gift of 1800 gallons of rum.⁶²

On the Eve of Canada

The new reality was a continent divided between two groups of British settlers: the more aggressively expansionist United States (which would soon dramatically reduce the territory of a third settler state in Mexico), and the comparably conservative British North America. The latter, Canada's direct predecessor, was no less interested in claiming Indigenous territory and converting it into private property to be sold to settlers, though it sometimes sought less direct avenues of conquest than the Americans. Indeed, when American settlers loyal to Britain moved north after 1776, many claimed territory ceded by the Anishinaabe through processes that were, as Margaret Conrad explains, manipulative and misleading:

> Indigenous peoples willingly gave up use of land that they held

in common — but not exclusively and not forever. As they would discover to their regret, land once used for hunting and fishing quickly gave way to agricultural communities and exclusive ownership. More regrettably, a growing body of evidence confirms that the settlers and those who negotiated on their behalf bargained in bad faith. Treaties were couched in terms so vague that they could be interpreted in various ways, and both authorities and settlers pushed their advantage when they felt they could get away with it.[63]

Just as Cartier had lied to Donnacona, 18th-century colonial authorities would use deception and trickery to get Indigenous land. And just as they had in Massachusetts, English settlers would not hesitate to take matters into their own hands, seizing territory for themselves and backing up their claims with violence. For instance, defying the 1763 Royal Proclamation, which compelled settlers to sign treaties before claiming Indigenous land, Loyalists in the late 18th century seized Mi'kmaw territory on the Miramichi River, knowing that British authorities would not support the Mi'kmaw claim.[64] After all, only a few decades earlier, the British had authorized settlers to "take or destroy the savages commonly called Micmacks [sic] wherever they are found," and offered bounties "to be paid upon producing such savage taken or his scalp."[65]

The Mi'kmaq were not the only targets of the new settlers; the wave of Loyalist migration in the late 18th century also displaced the Beothuk and the Maliseet in the Maritimes, the Mohawk, Nipissing and Algonquin in Québec, and the Ojibwa and Mississauga in Ontario. These processes took several forms. The Beothuk died out after being forcibly cut off from the coastal resources they depended upon; the Mi'kmaq were told they had lost the rights to their territory when Britain defeated New France; the Mohawk, Nipissing and Algonquin had much of their reserve lands and hunting/fishing territory claimed by Loyalists, who were given the right to settle on "Waste Lands of the Crown"; the Ojibwa and Mississauga were encouraged to sell their land for lump sums or in exchange for perpetual annuities, in negotiations marred by deception and manipulation.[66]

The roots of Canadian colonial actions and attitudes, traced through Cartier, the Puritans and British North America, prove to be more consistent than many contemporary Canadians would imagine. At the end of the 18th century, British North America did not yet have the resources or numbers to expand beyond the Great Lakes, but it consolidated its position in Upper and Lower Canada (Ontario and Québec) and the maritime colonies, dispossessed remaining Indigenous people of much of their land there and developed the core of a new capitalist economy, benefitting from the labour of African and Indigenous slaves until abolition in the 1830s.[67]

By the middle of the 19th century, however, US expansion had begun to alarm the leaders of British North America. These two factions in the British colonial empire had already squabbled over territory in the War of 1812, and now the Americans were pushing west, threatening to swallow up the bulk of North America. The colonial elite in London and Canada became increasingly obsessed with the idea of connecting the Canadian colonies to British Columbia and asserting their claim to all of the territory in between. No longer a project for the distant future, Canada's west had to be settled immediately; there was only the problem of dozens of Indigenous nations who lived there and would not simply cede their territory and disappear into the mist. Thus was the stage set for the Confederation of Canada and the massive expansion and consolidation of Canadian colonialism.

Notes

1. Howard Adams, *Prison of Grass: Canada from a Native Point of View*, Saskatoon, Fifth House Publishers, 1989, p. 16.
2. Nicolás Sánchez-Albornoz, *Population of Latin America*, Berkeley, University of California Press, 1974. Other useful sources include Sherburne F. Cook and Woodrow Borah's *Essays in Population History: Mexico and the Caribbean, Vol I* (1971) and Roxanne Dunbar-Ortiz's *Indians of the Americas* (1984).
3. Henry Heller, *The Birth of Capitalism: A Twenty-First Century Perspective*, London, Pluto Press, 2011, p. 162–175.
4. Oxfam, "An economy for the 99 percent," Oxfam Briefing Paper, January 15, 2017. Available at: https://www.oxfamamerica.org/explore/research-publications/an-economy-for-the99-percet/.
5. Samir Amin, *Class and Nation: Historically and in the Current Crisis*, New York, Monthly Review Press, 1980.
6. Samir Amin, *Eurocentrism*, 2nd ed., New York, Monthly Review Press, 2009, p. 221–238.
7. Gerald Horne, *The Apocalypse of Settler Capitalism*, New York, Monthly Review Press, 2017, p. 163–178.
8. Examples include the Diggers and the Levellers, each arising in opposition to the Enclosures and capitalism, even before their historical implications were clear.
9. Samir Amin, *Eurocentrism*, 2nd ed., p. 246–248.
10. Robert J.C. Young, *Postcolonialism: An Historical Introduction*, Oxford, Blackwell, 2004, p. 17.

11. Young, *Postcolonialism*, p. 21.
12. Tony Castanha, *The Myth of Indigenous Caribbean Extinction: Continuity and Reclamation in Borikén (Puerto Rico)*, New York, Palgrave MacMillan, 2011.
13. P. Farb, *Man's Rise to Civilization*, New York, Dutton, 1968, p. 124.
14. Olivier Le Cour Grandmaison, "Liberty, equality, and colony," *Le Monde Diplomatique*, June 2001. The 1843 quotation elaborates: "All populations who do not accept our conditions must be despoiled. Everything must be seized, devastated, without age or sex distinction: grass must not grow any more where the French army has set foot… This is how, my dear friend, we must make war against Arabs: kill all men over the age of fifteen, take all their women and children."
15. Jason Hickel, "How Britain stole $45 trillion from India," *Al-Jazeera*, December 19, 2018.
16. The phenomenology of the slave trade is explored in recent work by scholars like Saidiya Hartman, Fred Moten, and Jared Sexton.
17. Louis XIV, quoted in Eric Williams, "Capitalism and Slavery," in Tanya Das Gupta ed., *Race and Racialization: Essential Readings*, Toronto, Canadian Scholars' Press, 2007, p. 149.
18. C.L.R. James, *The Black Jacobins, Toussaint L'Ouverture and the San Domingo Revolution*, 2nd ed., New York, Vintage, 1989.
19. James Laxer, *Staking Claims to a Continent: John A. Macdonald, Abraham Lincoln, Jefferson Davis, and the making of North America*, Toronto, House of Anansi Press, 2016, p. 21.
20. James Laxer, *Staking Claims*, p. 21.
21. "Six White Congressmen Endorse Reparations for Slavery," *The Journal of Blacks in Higher Education*, Vol. 27, January 2000, p. 20–21. The number is almost certainly a very low estimation.
22. Bruce G. Trigger, *Natives and Newcomers: Canada's "Heroic Age" Reconsidered*, Montreal, McGill-Queen's University Press, 1975, p. 120–121.
23. Esyllt Jones and Adele Perry, ed, *People's Citizenship Guide: a response to conservative Canada*, Winnipeg, Arbeiter Ring, 2011, p. 12.
24. Lisa Monchalin offers a good overview of these terms and their relative strengths and weaknesses in *The Colonial Problem: An Indigenous Perspective on Crime and Injustice in Canada*, Toronto, University of Toronto Press, 2017, p. 1–8. See also Gregory Younging's *Elements of Indigenous Style* (2018).
25. Scott Rutherford, "Indigenous Peoples, Colonialism and Canada," in Karen Dubinsky, Sean Mills and Scott Rutherford, ed., *Canada and the Third World: Overlapping Histories*, Toronto, University of Toronto Press, 2016, p. 15.
26. Francis Jennings has built a convincing case that the ferocious nature of European settler violence significantly surpassed the capacities of most Indigenous nations for cruelty, even in war. Jennings highlights, for instance, the Pequots' shock in discovering that English Puritans treated women and children as military targets. Francis Jennings, *The Invasion of America: Indians, Colonialism, and the Cant of Conquest*, Chapel Hill, University of North Carolina Press, 1975.
27. Margaret Conrad, *A Concise History of Canada*, Cambridge, Cambridge University Press, 2012, p. 11.
28. Doug Cuthand, "Canada's History Goes Beyond 150 Years," in Kiera L. Ladner

and Myra J. Tait, *Surviving Canada: Indigenous Peoples Celebrate 150 Years of Betrayal*, Winnipeg, Arbeiter Ring, 2017, p. 157.
29. James Daschuk, *Clearing the Plains: Disease, Politics of Starvation, and the Loss of Aboriginal Life*, Regina, University of Regina Press, 2013, p. 3.
30. James Daschuk, *Clearing the Plains*, p. 6–8.
31. Bruce G. Trigger, *Natives and Newcomers*, p. 7.
32. Ramsay Cook, *The Voyages of Jacques Cartier*, Toronto, University of Toronto Press, 1993, p. xiv–xv.
33. Bruce G. Trigger, *Natives and Newcomers*, p. 91–108.
34. Jacques Cartier, quoted in Ramsay Cook, *Voyages of Jacques Cartier*, p. 70.
35. Jacques Cartier, quoted in Ramsay Cook, *Voyages of Jacques Cartier*, p. 26.
36. Ramsay Cook, *Voyages of Jacques Cartier*, p. xxv.
37. Jacques Cartier, quoted in Ramsay Cook, *Voyages of Jacques Cartier*, p. 21.
38. Ramsay Cook, *Voyages of Jacques Cartier*, p. xxxvii.
39. Margaret Conrad, *Concise History*, p. 31.
40. Bruce G. Trigger, *Natives and Newcomers*, p. 133.
41. Scott Rutherford, "Indigenous Peoples, Colonialism and Canada," p. 18.
42. Margaret Conrad, Alvin Finkel and Donald Fyson, *History of the Canadian Peoples, Volume I, 6th ed*, Toronto, Pearson, 2015, p. 42.
43. Margaret Conrad, *Concise History*, p. 72.
44. Richard Drinnon, *Facing West: The Metaphysics of Indian-Hating and Empire-Building*, Minneapolis, University of Minnesota Press, 1980, p. 3–35.
45. Quoted in Richard Drinnon, *Facing West*, p. 4.
46. Richard Drinnon, *Facing West*, p. 33–61.
47. John Mason, quoted in Richard Drinnon, *Facing West*, p. 46.
48. Margaret Conrad, *Concise History*, p. 92.
49. John Mason, quoted in Richard Drinnon, *Facing West*, p. 55.
50. To be clear, the fact that the Puritans deemed the Indigenous people they met to be licentious and hypersexual does not mean that they were, indeed, those things. That they were not as repressed as the Puritans is certainly accurate, but the same could likely be said of a great many societies at the time, including that of the rest of England itself. Richard Drinnon, *Facing West*, p. 30.
51. Richard Drinnon, *Facing West*, p. 56. Emphasis in original.
52. Sherene Razack, *Dark Threats and White Knights: The Somalia Affair, Peacekeeping, and the New Imperialism*, Toronto, University of Toronto Press, 2004.
53. Richard Drinnon, *Facing West*, p. 48.
54. Richard Drinnon, *Facing West*, p. 47.
55. Patrick Wolfe, "Settler Colonialism and the Elimination of the Native," *Journal of Genocide Studies*, vol. 8, no. 4, 2006, p. 387–409.
56. James Laxer, *Tecumseh and Brock: The War of 1812*, Toronto, House of Anansi, 2012.
57. Scott Rutherford, "Indigenous Peoples, Colonialism and Canada," p. 18.
58. James Laxer, *Staking Claims*, p. 14.
59. Gerald Horne, *The Counter-Revolution of 1776: Slave Resistance and the Origins of the United States of America*, New York, New York University Press, 2014.
60. Richard Drinnon, *Facing West*, 119–215.

61. Margaret Conrad, *Concise History*, p. 81.
62. Margaret Conrad, *Concise History*, p. 91.
63. Margaret Conrad, *Concise History*, p. 93–94.
64. Conrad, Finkel and Fyson, *History of the Canadian Peoples, 6th ed.*, p. 178.
65. Edward Cornwallis, quoted in Conrad, Finkel and Fyson, *History of the Canadian Peoples, 6th ed.*, p. 136.
66. Arthur J. Ray, *I Have Lived Here Since the World Began: An Illustrated History of Canada's Native People*, Montreal, McGill-Queen's University Press, 2011, p. 142–159.
67. Scott Rutherford, "Indigenous Peoples, Colonialism and Canada," p. 17. In Montreal, for instance, half of all homeowners held at least one Indigenous slave, while many more owned African slaves as well. Many African slaves escaped from Canada to US states where slavery had already been abolished, like Michigan and Vermont.

2

Conquest and Genocide

We do not propose to expend large sums of money to give them food from the first day of the year to the last. We must give them enough to keep them alive; but the Indians must, under the regulations that have been sanctioned by Parliament, go to the reservations and cultivate their land... If, by accident, an Indian should starve, it is not the fault of the Government.

— Sir Hector-Louis Langevin, MP, House of Commons, April 15, 1886[1]

THROUGHOUT 2017, CANADIANS WERE ENCOURAGED to participate in a year-long celebration of Canada's 150th birthday. Many people enjoyed the various festivities — from fireworks to concerts to totem pole carving — without giving much thought to what it meant, but the party did not go off without a hitch. For a state spending $200 million to build its brand, Canada's celebration was awkwardly timed; Indigenous political activism was growing, and awareness of Canada's heritage of colonial violence was more widespread following the release of the report of the Truth and Reconciliation Commission on Canada's use of residential schools against Indigenous children.[2]

The problem was that, for the party to make any sense, Canadians had to think about 1867, the year of Confederation. But under any scrutiny, the dynamics of that moment are heavily shaped by racism and colonialism. How could we talk about Confederation without mentioning the conquest of the Indigenous west and the passing of the Indian Act? These were foundational elements of Confederation, reflecting both the inheritance and the completion of colonial genocide. Some party.

The Canada 150 celebration did, however, hit upon one fundamental truth: the Canada we know is a product of the dynamics of 1867. The moment of Confederation was the maturation of the settler colonialism that preceded it, the logical conclusion of the French and British occupation of this land. It was, by extension, the formative moment for what is now Canada, the point from which all of modern Canadian history flows.

While some of the 2017 celebrants fully ignored the painful legacy of Confederation, re-imagining it as little more than a gallant and glorious exercise in nation-building, many others tried to use the moment as an opportunity to reflect on how far Canada has come. While this latter group was willing to concede that 1867 was a key turning point in the genocide of the Indigenous Peoples, they sought to reassure themselves that 21st-century Canada was different and better than that. Prime Minister Justin Trudeau reflected that position:

> As we mark Canada 150, we also recognize that for many, today is not an occasion for celebration. Indigenous Peoples in this country have faced oppression for centuries. As a society, we must acknowledge and apologize for past wrongs, and chart a path forward for the next 150 years — one in which we continue to build our nation-to-nation, Inuit-Crown, and government-to-government relationship with the First Nations, Inuit, and Métis Nation. Our efforts toward reconciliation reflect a deep Canadian tradition — the belief that better is always possible.[3]

It sounded good, but what Trudeau and so many others ignored was the fact that the Canadian tradition they were celebrating would not exist without the darkest legacies of 1867. Even the idea that we should be concerned only about the *legacy* of 1867, rather than its ongoing manifestations, was sharply criticized by scholars like Glen Sean Coulthard.[4] 1867 is not simply a painful memory; its entire logical framework remains written into the DNA of contemporary Canada. This is true not only of Canada's contemporary relations with Indigenous nations, which I take up in Chapter 3, but also in the rest of Canada's foreign policy.

Thus, it is imperative that we properly understand the dynamics around this formative moment in the making of Canada. Typically, discussion about Confederation focuses on internal Canadian politics and the relations between Canada, Britain and the United States, and I address those dynamics. However, the heart of the Confederation project was the conquest of the west. As such, my emphasis is on Canada's relations with the Indigenous nations of the Great Plains. In those formative relations,

Canada was again encountering foreign powers, not dealing with an internal matter, and Canada's relationship with those foreign Indigenous nations was governed by the needs of a settler capitalist state and the ideology of white supremacy that lurks at the heart of colonialism.

The Roots of Confederation

The Confederation of Canada had plenty of moving parts and motivations. There was frustration over political deadlock between Ontario and Québec and a desire to reorganize to facilitate functional governance. There was dissatisfaction with the slower industrial development of Canada as compared to the United States. There were concerns that British imperial favour, with respect to trade and finance, was on the decline, leaving the nascent Canadian capitalist class to its own devices. This had already prompted some of the Canadian business elite to make a push for annexation by the United States in 1849.[5]

Indeed, chief among the factors that spurred Confederation was the awareness that the United States was expanding and that, if Canada was going to continue to be a viable national project of settler capitalism, it was going to have to unite in the east and expand to the west. In addition to the annexationist push, there was concern about American authorities disrespecting territorial boundaries, both in their wars against the Indigenous Peoples in the west and in border-area battles in the US Civil War (1861–1865). There was also a growing sense, especially after a tense standoff over American boarding of the British mail vessel *Trent*, that British appetite to send troops to protect the Canadian territories was limited.[6]

From the standpoint of the Canadian elite, the Civil War had illustrated the fragility of the 19th-century continental arrangements (a fact already apparent in Canada given the settler rebellions in the 1830s).[7] Nevertheless, the victory and consolidation of the North had served notice that the American machine would not be easily stopped. Already, by the middle of the 19th century, American adventurers, traders and would-be conquerors had moved north into what was then claimed as territory of the Hudson's Bay Company (HBC), from contemporary Winnipeg to the Rocky Mountains. Given the aggressive expansion of the United States in the early 19th century — from the Louisiana Purchase to the Mexican-American War — it was not unreasonable to think that the Americans might try to consolidate their hold over the northern plains, cutting off the Canadian colonies from British Columbia and thus limiting the expansion of Canadian settler capitalism.

This competition between different factions of European colonizers, then, was at the centre of the push for Confederation. Nevertheless, viewing Confederation as being motivated by rivalry with the US somewhat obscures the deeper motivation behind this rivalry. The race to settle the west wasn't simply a matter of abstract nationalism; it was about settlement. The Industrial Revolution was well underway in Europe and the rapid transformation of the European peasantries into urban working classes — especially in Great Britain — was producing a dramatic new impetus for emigration across the Atlantic. With capitalism entering a period of rapid growth, it was becoming increasingly clear that territorial expansion was going to be a matter of paramount importance. New urban centres in Europe and North America would need to be fed, their factories would need raw materials, and their unemployed would need a migratory release valve lest they become restive and revolutionary (as they had, dramatically, in Europe in the 1840s). The Canadian elite saw the west as a profitable solution to those problems.

No one better illustrates this than Canada's most famous Confederator, John A. Macdonald. Macdonald's family had immigrated to Kingston when John was five years old, and he grew up in comfortable middle-class conditions with an ambition for law and politics. Macdonald's legal practice was increasingly oriented to the corporate sector, and by the 1840s he was dabbling in property ownership himself. By the time he first ran for office he recognized that in an emerging capitalist state, the role of politics was to support capital, a point first made by his countryman Adam Smith a hundred years earlier.[8] As James Laxer described him, Macdonald was "close to the business community and anxious to promote its success... [and] did not see a separation between the interests of business and the role of the state."[9]

Indeed, the wealthy middle classes of Ontario and Québec had agreed on little about the management of British North America (BNA) but recognized that they had a shared economic interest in colonial expansion. The government had sunk huge amounts of subsidy money into the Grand Trunk Railroad, but it was faltering under poor management and inadequate demand.[10] Expansion to the west — to carry settlers west and to bring agricultural products east — would be a boon to the railroad, and, like Macdonald, most politicians had these interests as a priority (though some criticized the fact that Confederation seemed to be a scheme drawn up by the Grand Trunk).[11] While they bickered over the details, each of the signees of the British North America Act, which made official the creation of the Dominion of Canada, saw their economic fate tied to the expansion of east-west trade and thus viewed the project of settling the west as urgent.

Alas, from the standpoint of the colonizers, there was one major impediment to settling the west: it was already settled. Indigenous nations living west of the Red River colony (modern Winnipeg) had by no means been conquered. While the presence of the HBC had re-shaped Indigenous societies around their commercial relations, especially the fur trade, it had not established permanent agricultural settlements in the west and, as such, Indigenous control over the territory remained intact. By extension, many of the core dynamics of Indigenous life and society remained Indigenous.

This is not to say that Indigenous culture had remained static, nor that it was unaffected by many generations of contact with Europeans. Certainly, life on the prairies had already gone through massive changes prior to the 19th century; the introduction of horses and gunpowder had changed the nature of the buffalo hunt, the spread of European pathogens like smallpox and later tuberculosis had ravaged many communities, and migrations and movements that flowed from struggles with the colonizers had generated conflict between and within Indigenous nations that had re-shaped the geopolitical landscape of the west.[12] Furthermore, the HBC ran the fur trade in a notoriously tyrannical and colonial manner. For instance, Indigenous trappers were paid significantly less for furs than white trappers and they were forbidden from trading furs among themselves or even retaining furs for their personal use; HBC clerks would break into Indigenous homes, seizing furs they found and punishing their bearers.[13]

Nevertheless, Indigenous people still lived, by and large, in their communities and within the dynamic cultural traditions of their ancestors. And they were doing so on land increasingly coveted by the European settlers. As competition between the settler projects of Canada and the United States grew, plans for Canadian Confederation developed rapidly, and in turn pressure on the Indigenous Peoples of the west increased.

1867: The Birth of Canada

In the debates that led to the BNA Act, George Brown gushed at the sweeping away of hostilities between "a people comprised of two different races, speaking different languages, with religious and social and municipal and educational institutions totally different."[14] He was referring not to the Indigenous Peoples but to the English and French settlers. Indeed, much of the discussion surrounding Confederation, in 1867 as in 2017, was about the union of Canada's French and English settlers into one state. Indigenous nations featured minimally in the discussions at the time and indeed are barely mentioned in the story of 1867 in most Canadian history textbooks.[15]

But the absence of discussion of Indigenous Peoples is, itself, arguably the central story of Confederation. The flowery speeches given by the so-called "Fathers of Confederation" about their magnanimous decision to set aside their differences to build this new Dominion reflect the remarkable air of self-satisfaction that hung over a gathering of settlers effectively announcing their intention to complete the conquest of this land. Canadian nationalist historians often celebrate the settling of the west and the construction of the intercontinental railroad by pointing to the very real threat of US annexation of that territory. This plays well for Canadian audiences that like the idea of standing up to the "Yankees," but it misses a very important point: neither Canada nor the United States had a legitimate claim to this land. The Confederators did not mention the Indigenous Peoples precisely because the land they coveted was Indigenous territory.

Indeed, when Canada's first prime minister, John A. Macdonald, set out to purchase the northwest from the HBC, he was asked whether there would be any consultation with the Indigenous people living there; he replied that they were "incapable of the management of their own affairs."[16] His minister of public works, William McDougall, added that this purchase would allow "the whole expanse from the Atlantic to the Pacific [to] be peopled with a race the same as ourselves."[17] In private correspondence, Macdonald assured a colleague that "in another year the present residents will be altogether swamped by the influx of strangers who will go in with the idea of becoming industrious and peaceable settlers."[18]

Macdonald's intentions and ideology are clear; without consulting the nations that lived on the prairies, whom he deemed ignorant and lazy, he would purchase their land and flood it with more desirable settlers. It is worth noting that John A. Macdonald was an avowed white supremacist, and while this was not uncommon among wealthy white people in the late 19th century, he was a noteworthy racist even among his peers. He was among the pre-Confederation Canadians whose wealth was at least partially down to the slave trade, having married into Jamaican slave plantation money through his second wife.[19] He did not hesitate to extoll the virtues of the "Aryan race," and he was fond of comparing other races to animals. If the Canadian elite were divided on whether Indigenous people should be assimilated or exterminated, Macdonald gives us a clue to his position when he says, "the Aryan races will not wholesomely amalgamate with the Africans or the Asiatics… the cross of those races, like the cross of the dog and the fox, is not successful; it cannot be, and never will be. [Canada must protect] the Aryan character of the future of British America."[20]

To Macdonald's surprise, the people living in the territory he had just purchased were not ready to embrace his flood of Aryan settlers. When surveyors were sent to the Red River colony to prepare the colony for a wave of immigration, the largely Métis population of the colony intercepted them and made clear that they were not welcome. The Métis had already dealt with incursions into their territory in the past; some fifty years earlier they had their land "purchased" by the Earl of Selkirk who was determined to settle it with Scottish immigrants. Selkirk's forces were defeated by the Métis at the Battle of Seven Oaks in 1816, an important assertion of the growing sense of Métis identity.[21]

In 1869, the Métis were no less determined to protect the territory on which they had lived for centuries. Though they possessed no paper claim to it, the Métis — descendants of mixed European and Indigenous families — had occupied the area around the Red River settlement since the early days of the fur trade. By the 1860s, they considered themselves an independent nation and declared as much to the Canadians who arrived to assert their authority after Confederation. The Métis had typically elected councils of captains each year for the buffalo hunt and had effectively run their affairs based on this structure. Facing the threat of occupation by Canada, they formed a national committee along the same lines, seized the former HBC Fort Garry and reached out to English settlers who already lived in the colony to allow them to participate in its governance.[22]

While the Métis, under the leadership of Louis Riel, consolidated their autonomous government, Canadian officials continued to work towards the racial purification of the west, declaring that one day it would be populated by "an energetic and civilized race, able to improve its vast capabilities and appreciate its marvelous beauties."[23] To that end, Canada's appointed governor, William McDougall, proposed that the solution was to put out a call for European settlers and provide them with arms.[24] But when McDougall attempted to foment an uprising in the colony to undermine the Métis Provisional Government it failed; led by white supremacist Orangemen, it was quickly defeated and actually strengthened Métis commitment to their independence.

John A. Macdonald urgently wanted to defeat the Métis but needed to stall for time until a wave of settlement could be organized. Macdonald was wary of another attempt to unseat the Provisional Government by force, because it had developed relationships with the US state of Minnesota and would consider making a deal with the US for its protection.[25] He thus dispatched Donald A. Smith, an HBC commissioner-turned-Canadian Pacific Railway investor, to try to bribe the Métis and, when that failed, to negotiate a deal. Smith appeared accommodating to many of the Métis demands, offering affirmative but noncommittal answers to the most important demands around autonomy and land tenure.[26] But Canada had no intention of keeping Smith's word; it promptly passed the Manitoba Act, creating the new province around the Red River settlement while sending a military force of 1200 soldiers to occupy it and ensure that Riel's Provisional Government was supplanted by the new apparatus of Manitoba.

In a fitting prelude to the next 150 years of Canadian foreign policy, Col. Garnet Wolseley's campaign to crush the autonomous Métis nation was called a "a mission of peace."[27] Though Riel and his associates were not fooled, they were not equipped to defeat a military force that was so clearly designed for conquest. Indeed, the body of work of Wolseley himself spoke to the colonizing nature of the campaign; he had previously served in India, crushing the 1857 Mutiny, and would later make war in Africa on behalf of the Empire's West African colonies.[28] The army he brought to Winnipeg consisted of 400 British soldiers and several hundred Ontario Orangemen, who subsequently inflicted a reign of terror on the Métis, fuelled, according to one historian, by "rage and alcohol."[29] Many of the Métis were subjected to violence, sexual violence and murder.

That Louis Riel is remembered in much official history as the "founder of Manitoba" is a rather cheeky bit of misdirection; the founding of Manitoba was designed to eliminate Métis power and presence in Red River. Canada not only reneged on its promise to protect Métis land tenure, it also sent a force of belligerent racists to violently evict them from their lands. Most of the Métis abandoned Winnipeg and travelled west to follow the buffalo hunt, many settling near Batoche on the South Saskatchewan River. They quickly found themselves facing the same crises that plagued many of the Indigenous Peoples in the northwest; the disappearance of the buffalo and the encroachment of European settlement. As Canada tightened the noose in the 1870s and 1880s, the Métis would make a last stand in the War of 1885, but by that point Canada was well on the way to conquering the west.[30]

Clearing the Plains

The violent destruction of the Provisional Government of the Métis was the opening salvo in the process of settling the west. Over the two decades after Confederation, Canada would use manipulation, starvation and violence to clear the Great Plains of its Indigenous inhabitants, so as to make space for a wave of European settlement that would follow the construction of the intercontinental railroad.

Indigenous dominion over the plains had already seen significant disruption prior to the 1860s. During the era of the fur trade, European diseases — especially smallpox — had ravaged the prairies and caused major dislocations. Nationalities themselves changed, as entire cultural groups like the Basquia Cree disappeared and their survivors integrated into other nations. Indigenous nations displaced by French and English settlement, like the Haudenosaunee and Odawa, moved west and occupied territory left by those suffering from the losses to disease.[31] All the while, the changing economic and political dynamics of the region — especially as they re-oriented around trade with Europeans — generated conflict between nations that had previously enjoyed warm relations. The A'aninin, for instance, refused to hunt beaver out of respect for longstanding traditions, but this made their territory valuable to other groups seeking to trade beaver pelts.[32] This, as well as the A'aninin's abundance in horses for equestrian hunting, made them targets for Cree raids.

Nevertheless, even the significant changes in the 18th century could not compare to the catastrophe that would hit in the 19th century, when the settlers' goals shifted from commerce to capitalism. Through the middle of the century, from the 1820s to the 1860s, the HBC was granted a monopoly over the fur trade and tried to exercise its power over the entire area then known as Rupert's Land. It was hampered in that regard by its commercial core; seeking maximum returns on minimal investments, the HBC tried to run a lean organization, relying on Indigenous suppliers to do most of the labour and counting on its ability to dictate advantageous terms of trade.

As a result, the HBC was unable to assert dominance over the territory, which remained largely controlled by Indigenous nations. In the first half of the 19th century, many Indigenous nations were still able to thrive in societies that had been altered, but not completely undermined, by European relations. According to James Daschuk, "studies of skeletons have shown that, in the mid-nineteenth century, peoples of the plains were perhaps the tallest and best-nourished population in the world," a result of the nutrient-rich diet centred around the buffalo hunt.[33] Only a few decades later, these same people would be starving on reserves.

By the 1860s and 1870s, the pressures of growing European settlement on the Red River were changing the game significantly. Arthur J. Ray argues:

> This new breed of settler dreamed of turning the prairies and parklands into wheat fields, but… their dream was incompatible with the traditional land-use practices of the Native groups, which required large open areas for buffalo hunting and extensive common grazing and hay fields behind their Red River lots.[34]

In addition to the influx of these new settlers, the increased presence of American traders and miners moving north from Montana, and declines in animal stocks from overhunting, were leading to conflict on the plains. Violent wars against Indigenous Peoples in the US was adding to this pressure, sending more refugees north, and the result was increasing food scarcity and epidemics of scarlet fever, smallpox and especially tuberculosis, stemming from malnutrition.[35] Hunger — caused by the steadily increasing pressures of three centuries of European colonization — was emerging as the greatest enemy of Indigenous life.[36]

This problem reached its catastrophic height in the period immediately following Confederation, and Canada took full advantage of the situation. Between 1871 and 1877 Canada signed seven key treaties with the

Indigenous Peoples of the west, sometimes called the numbered treaties, which Canada used to effectively claim dominion over the entire territory of what was once Rupert's Land.[37] To be clear, many Indigenous leaders initially wanted to sign these treaties; their societies were suddenly faced with rapid decline in the context of food scarcity, disease and the influx of European settlers after the crushing of the Métis at Red River.[38] It was believed by some that the treaty process could salvage a just peace between Indigenous and settler societies involving appropriate and equitable stewardship of the land and — notably — guarantees of food and medicine from Canada in exchange for settlers' right to use Indigenous lands.

Instead, the treaty process was used by Canada to press its advantage in a time of Indigenous crisis. It is hardly surprising, given the history of Indigenous-settler relations and the imperatives of the new Canadian state, that the treaties were often struck in bad faith. Many careful studies of the treaty process suggest that Canadian authorities regularly penned written versions of the treaties that either changed or broke the spirit of the oral agreements. Scott Rutherford explains:

> Significant disagreement remains regarding the terms agreed to in the numbered treaties, especially the word "cede."... Instead of interpreting "cede" to mean the sharing of non-reserve land for mutual hunting and gathering activities, the Canadian state interpreted it as the total surrender of land in exchange for parcels of land called reserves. Rather than being accidental misinterpretations, such changes always favoured the Canadian government. The written version of Treaty No. 1 signed by Saulteaux and Cree leaders in 1871 reportedly leaves out several clauses regarding the size of reserve lands, promises of hunting rights, and promises of assistance that would have benefitted local Indigenous communities.[39]

This is significant in several respects, not the least of which is the fact that Canada's first foreign treaties were based in deception. What is more, it illustrates something critically important for contemporary discussions around Indigenous Peoples in Canadian society: Canada gained much of its present territory based on agreements it never fulfilled. My own ancestors bought farmland in Southern Manitoba in the 1880s from a Canadian state that had broken the terms of Treaty No. 1 and seized it from Indigenous people without carrying out its own obligations;

this, alone, calls into question any legal right my family had to settle in Manitoba.

And this was not the only problem with the treaties. In addition to manipulating the terms of the treaties themselves, Canada went to great lengths to ensure that it was bargaining from a position of power. This is clear in contrasting Treaty No. 1 (1871) with the later Treaty No. 6 (1876). The former relied on a sneaky interpretation of the meaning of "cede," whereas the latter was negotiated during a time of Indigenous crisis and therefore made its terms cruelly clear: "All Indians… do hereby cede, release, surrender, and yield up to the government forever, all their rights, titles, and privileges whatsoever to the lands included."[40] These are not terms of an agreement; they are terms of surrender. Indeed, key treaty negotiations often took place in the shadow of Indigenous people's starvation and death from tuberculosis caused by malnutrition.

Broadly speaking, this crisis was a result of colonialism, with its most immediate and visible manifestation being the disappearance of the buffalo, around which the plains economy was built. Pressure on the herds was primarily a consequence of overhunting, as more and more Indigenous people were pushed into the west by encroaching European settlement. This problem was exacerbated by the introduction of settler cattle ranching, which took grazing territory away from the buffalo, and also by the campaign of systematic slaughter of buffalo in the US.[41] While there is little evidence that Canadian authorities or settlers did the same, it is likely that some of the buffalo in Canada migrated south to graze on lands vacated by the slaughtered herds there, and some historians have speculated that the Northwest Mounted Police (NWMP) may have deliberately driven some of the herds into the US to increase the pressure on Indigenous people in Canada.[42] After a winter without snow in 1878, fires ravaged the grasslands and the herds collapsed forever.

The end of the buffalo hunt was the end of life as Indigenous Peoples on the plains had known it. Treaties were increasingly signed in desperation and with emphasis on insisting that the Canadian government provide seeds and implements to convert to agriculture economies and guarantees of food aid during crises. The Canadian government routinely failed to live up to its commitments, especially in the later treaties, and as Indigenous communities starved and died of tuberculosis, Canada refused to provide aid unless and until people moved to reserves. Despite promises that Canada would help Indigenous people transition into agriculture, the reserves were located on sandy, rocky or hilly territory that was typically poor farmland. By the 1880s, Indigenous life on the plains was utterly collapsing, with entire communities dying of hunger even as settlers' cattle grazed on the land.

The crisis on the plains in the late 1870s and early 1880s is described in harrowing detail in James Daschuk's *Clearing the Plains* (2013). What is most striking in this account is the extent to which the Canadian authorities both created the conditions for the catastrophe and then consciously refused to resolve it, letting thousands of Indigenous people die. As noted at the top of this chapter, Canadian leaders expressly proposed to give only enough food "to keep them alive" and even then absolved themselves if any should starve.[43] When Indigenous people flooded into the settler fort of Battleford demanding rations, Canadian authorities refused and instead gave food to settler labourers as payment for building a stockade to protect the fort from Indigenous raids.[44]

One obvious illustration of the coordinated famine on the prairies was the fact that Indigenous people were dying from protein-deficiency alongside grazing cattle. Some of the ranchers, concerned about the prospect of having their cattle poached but perhaps also motivated by some humanitarian impulse, offered to sell their herds to the government to give to the starving Indigenous people, but Indian Commissioner Edger Dewdney declined.[45] Dewdney may have been loath to harm the cattle industry since he had a stake in the success of I.G. Baker and Co., the largest meat contractor in Canada at the time.

Canadian officials not only refused to adequately address the crisis; they actively took advantage of the situation. Many Indigenous nations were refused aid unless they signed treaties, which even some within the Canadian government described as "a policy of submission shaped by a policy of starvation."[46] By the early 1880s, as the Canadian government was building the intercontinental railroad and beginning the permanent European settlement of the west, it needed to clear the Indigenous Peoples out of the way, so it began refusing food aid to anyone not already relocated to the reserves.[47] When even that didn't work, Canada simply expelled them by force, as when 5000 people were forced out of the Cypress Hills in 1883.

Even when Canada provided a little bit of relief, it was minimal, reluctant and sometimes rotten.[48] John A. Macdonald, in his second stint as prime minister, promised Parliament that he would not spend undue resources keeping Indigenous people alive: "We are doing all we can, by refusing food until the Indians are on the verge of starvation, to reduce the expense."[49] In some cases, the state would extract forced labour out of Indigenous people in exchange for food. "They must work or starve," blustered the well-fed finance minister Sir Leonard Tilley.[50] His colleague, Lawrence Vankoughnet, reinforced that position with added colonial zest:

> Strict instructions have been given to the agents to require labour from able-bodied Indians for supplies given them. This principle was laid down for the sake of the moral effect that it would have on the Indians in showing them that they must give something in return for what they receive, and also for the purpose of preventing them from hereafter expecting gratuitous assistance from the government.[51]

Thus, Canadian officials waxed poetic about teaching Indigenous people about fair exchange, in the midst of Canada's ethnic cleansing of Indigenous people by a combination of violence, deception and deliberate starvation. Vankoughnet's concern that Indigenous people might expect "gratuitous assistance" reflected the fact that they did, in fact, demand that Canada abide by the terms it had signed in the treaties, which specifically included food aid, medicine and assistance in establishing new farmlands on the reserves they had been confined to. It was Canada that was, quite literally, failing to "give something in return" for what it received; the support it had promised in exchange for the land that it had claimed.

Conquering the West

In 1873, after the conquest of Red River and as the numbered treaties were being signed, Canada created the Northwest Mounted Police (NWMP), predecessor of the Royal Canadian Mounted Police, to establish Canada's presence west of Winnipeg. In 1996, David Cruise and Alison Griffiths published a popular history of that first expedition of the NWMP, a book hailed by much of the Canadian press, including the *Toronto Star*, which called it "charmingly un-PC."[52] In the preface to *The Great Adventure: How the Mounties Conquered the West* (1996), the authors described the adventure:

> [It was] a swashbuckling, glorious, near-tragic, humorous, and

often poignant adventure... with little training and less experience [the police] signed up to march into the wild frontier and pacify the Indians, stop the whiskey trade, police the Canadian border, and bring law to a lawless land.[53]

This is a remarkable way to introduce modern audiences to the prelude to genocide. This "great adventure" was the first attempt by Canada to assert its claim to the west and to lay the foundations for a process that would lead to the near destruction of several Indigenous nations. It was instrumental in building the relationships and training necessary for Canada to crush the final significant Indigenous uprising of that era, in 1885. And it established patterns in the relationship between colonial police and the Indigenous Peoples that remain disturbingly present today. As such, the story Cruise and Griffiths tell is, in fact, significant; the glee with which they tell it illustrates something about the Canada of the 1990s.

Much of the story is told through the voices of this first contingent of Canadian police, giving us a clear window into the average settler understanding of Indigenous Peoples in the 1870s. Jean D'Artigue, a Montreal schoolteacher before joining the police, reported that a friend told him: "The Indians will [scalp you] as soon as soon as look at you. Civilized hair is like an aphrodisiac to those poor brutes, they can't help themselves." D'Artigue was taken by the idea of joining the force that would conquer them, writing, "I fancied I saw myself... fighting the Indians and the whiskey-traders. I saw settlements destroyed by the red men, the ladies carried away to worse than slavery, husbands and fathers calling upon us to rescue their wives and daughters."[54]

Right from the start, then, these conquerors were tapping into the colonial imagination: the white man would ride into the savage lands and rescue pure white women from the barbarous natives. D'Artigue was not alone in this fantasy; Fred Bagley expected to be "potting hostile savages and hobnobbing with haughty Indian Princes and lovely unsophisticated Princesses."[55] Even within this small company, the wide range of colonial fantasies was present, many of them imbued with the patriarchal colonial desire to take native brides (which must be understood to imply not just notions of romance but also of sexual violence, which was always an assumed part of the inherited rights of the colonizing man). One unnamed trainee understood his trek as an escape from "civilization," and he planned to "marry an Indian woman and settle down in a region entirely savage."[56]

Notably, the Canadian authors of this narrative, writing in 1996, do not themselves shy away from the language and ideology so common among the settler police of the 1870s. Though Cruise and Griffiths praise some individual Indigenous and mixed-race characters in their narrative — notably Jerry Potts, an Indigenous collaborator who worked closely with the police — they nevertheless describe the Great Plains as being "where the hand of civilization poked tenuous fingers into the last Indian stronghold on the frontier."[57] The idea that Canadian police were bringing "civilization" to the west is never questioned in the tale they tell. Indeed, Cruise and Griffiths uncritically cite a US army officer calling Indigenous society "a life of savagery" where "there is no right and wrong."[58]

The diaries of the Canadian settlers' vanguard establish several important facts about the conquest of the west. First, the Indigenous Peoples were considered a hostile, foreign power. Joseph Carscadden's diary describes his party of "300 men in a foe's country," John McIllree suggests that the Blackfoot "did not fancy our coming into their country," and Fred Bagley notes that the police force explicitly considered the Cypress Hills to be "enemy territory."[59] If the force Canada sent to "pacify" the west considered themselves to be dealing with a foreign enemy, it seems entirely reasonable that we, in the 21st century, call this a formative case of foreign policy. Indeed, historian J.R. Miller emphasizes that Canada made a conscious effort to re-frame these international relations as domestic affairs as its goals shifted towards outright conquest.[60]

Second, it is abundantly clear that the Canadian force was negotiating in bad faith with the Indigenous nations it encountered. The leader of the expedition, Colonel French, is quoted in a powwow with Sioux leaders, saying, "we do not want the land of the Dakota nor anyone else's." This was patently false; as the authors happily conclude, within a few years the North West Mounted Police "had become a full-fledged presence in the young Dominion... the Blackfoot Treaty had been signed, [Sioux chief] Sitting Bull had been routed from his Canadian sanctuary, Indians from the Great Lakes to the Rockies had been shepherded onto reservations, the buffalo were just a memory, Louis Riel was dead, and the last spike in the Canadian Pacific Railway had been driven home."[61]

Finally, their words illustrate the deeply engrained colonial mentality that possessed these conquerors. The Indigenous people they meet are "barbarous," "dirty and ugly," "lazy," "grotesque," "effeminate," "a nasty begging lot" who "crawled like snakes," were "skilled at evasion," and who were, when compared to the tales of writers like James Fenimore Cooper, "a low-browed, dull-eyed and brutish disappointment."[62] What is perhaps most striking is the casual and colonial sexualization of Indigenous women; this is a point I return to in the following chapter, but it is worth noting, alongside remarks in police diaries about Indigenous women's "grotesque coquetry," the fact that police and Indian agents regularly engaged in sexual violence and even established "bride pricing" systems wherein they would withhold rations in order to secure their access to teenaged Indigenous women. The practice was defended in Canada's Parliament as reasonable free market exchange.[63]

A telling footnote here is the fact that these colonial troops actively compared Indigenous people to the Irish, one declaring to the raucous laughter of his mates that the Sioux "sound exactly like the Irish" and following it up with a mockery of the two accents mashed-up.[64] Ireland, of course, was one of Britain's earliest colonial projects and the Irish were engaged in a very serious struggle against British colonialism, which was spilling over into Canada, where Irish Fenian rebels plotted attacks against British North American colonies and were subject to mass arrests and even a public hanging of one alleged Fenian.[65]

That these Canadian police would make that connection speaks to the way that colonial ideology pervaded their mindset. Indeed, many of the individuals involved in this expedition would go on to play key roles in the Canada's early foreign adventures; many remained connected to the police and helped win the War of 1885, while others went on to apply the skills they learned in the west to help the Empire crush revolts in Australia, India and South Africa.

The Indian Act

There is no document more foundational to Canadian foreign policy than the Indian Act of 1876, the first full, codified framework through which Canada dealt with its formative foreign relations. While the roots of Canadian policy must be traced through the histories of French and English colonial policies, the Indian Act is a truly Canadian product: a profound statement of what Canada was and what it would be. The Indian Act consolidated and bolstered laws, agreements and a general policy thrust that had already been put in place by the newly confederated dominion and borrowed heavily from a law passed prior to Confederation — the Gradual Civilization Act of 1857.[66] Indeed, nothing about the conquest of the west and the decimation of Indigenous nations in this period was particularly new; rather, it followed patterns and practices already developed during the French and British colonial era. Consider what Mi'kmaw leaders said in 1848 as their people starved on reserves in Nova Scotia:

> Some of your people say we are lazy, still we work. If you say we must go and hunt, we tell you again that to hunt is one thing but to find meat is another. They say to catch fish, and we try. They say make baskets, but we cannot sell them. They say make farms, this is very good; but will you help us till we cut away the trees and raise the crop. We cannot work without food.[67]

The problems identified by the Mi'kmaq — dispossession of land, disruption of hunting and fishing, collapsed markets for Indigenous goods and inadequate support in the transition to agriculture — are all mirrored in the crises imposed on Indigenous Peoples in the west. When the policymakers decided to populate the west with European settlers loyal to the Crown and the new dominion, this project presupposed the dislocation or destruction of the Indigenous people who lived there. The Indian Act was thus passed with a careful eye to the dispossession of Indigenous territory and an acute awareness that Indigenous and Métis resistance to their dispossession was likely and could be significant. As such, the Act's primary goals were to facilitate the seizure of territory while undermining the prospects for resistance.

In the service of that project — and inflected with the assumption of civilizational and racial superiority — the Indian Act presumed to dictate nearly every aspect of Indigenous life, from its political structures and limitations, to the physical movement of Indigenous people, to the very terms by which Indigeneity would be defined. The extreme degree to which Canada would control the lives of Indigenous people under the Indian Act made it comparable to the later Apartheid systems in South Africa and Israel, and there is evidence to suggest that Adolf Hitler reflected with admiration on the Canadian system for Indigenous segregation and subjugation. Contemplating the possible international responses to a wholesale extermination of European Jews, Hitler noted in 1941, "we also eat wheat from Canada and do not think of the Indians."[68] In other words, an effective campaign of genocide would erase not just people but the very memory of them.

Entire books have been dedicated to parsing out the terms of the Indian Act, which was subject to many adaptations in the ensuing years, but its fundamental purpose was to ensure that Indigenous people either assimilate or disappear.[69] Whether the Canadian government truly intended for Indigenous people to adapt themselves to settler society is an open question; for instance, while Canada insisted to Indigenous communities that they adopt agricultural production, it routinely failed to provide the seeds, tools and other technical assistance it promised in the treaties it signed. In fact, one of the most successful 19th-century Indigenous transitions to agriculture was that of the Sisseton Dakota, who actually refused to make treaty with Canada.[70] Did Canada want Indigenous people to turn the reserves into successful agricultural colonies or did it want them to die out and make space for European settlement? The answer probably varied from one colonial official to the next.

In practice, Canadian policy tended to have the latter effect, leading either to the outright starvation of Indigenous people or the less dramatic but equally profound destruction of Indigenous culture. We must be careful with this word: culture. A careless observer might think of culture as simply its outward reflections: clothing, art, recipes, dance and music. These are obviously important aspects of any people's cultural identity, but it is easy for a contemporary Canadian to downplay the notion of "cultural genocide" if one thinks only of these things. It can also lead to the over-simplistic notion that this damage can be undone if contemporary Indigenous Peoples are given the space and resources to re-discover and re-connect with their traditional clothing and art forms.

But while these are certainly positive steps, they reflect a misunderstanding of what culture means. A nation's culture is what *produces* things like language and art; culture exists not just in the artistic expressions of a people but in the political economy, ecology and epistemology to which music, clothing and art give expression.[71] Culture is a social understanding of our place in the universe, our relations with one another, our relations with nature and animal life, how we constitute families, how we relate to our bodies and our sexuality, how we work, how we communicate, how we conceive of justice, how we make decisions, how we divide wealth, what makes us happy or sad, and so much more. The cultural genocide of Indigenous nations was the breaking of those structures, those systems of knowledge, understanding and meaning, which had developed and changed over centuries and which formed the basis for the music, art and dances that contemporary Canada promotes as gestures towards its own tolerance and inclusion.[72]

A similar point is powerfully argued by Glen Sean Coulthard in his analysis of the anti-colonial struggles of the Dene in the 1970s and 1980s. Coulthard argues that culture should be understood as "the interconnected social totality... encompassing the economic, political, spiritual, and social," drawing from the broadest definition of Marx's category of "mode of production." Many social scientists think of mode of production as a purely economic category capturing the process by which things are produced. Coulthard insists that this term encompasses both those productive forces (technology, resources, labour and the way these are organized) and also "the forms of thought, behaviour, and social relationships that both condition and are conditioned by these productive forces."[73]

This broader definition of culture is what Canada sought to destroy, and many of the concrete processes it used flowed through the Indian Act, which — although it was passed and amended in parallel to the signing of treaties — often contradicted the letter and spirit of them. For instance, the Indian Act completely re-oriented Indigenous political structures to revolve around the Canadian government. In fact, it claimed the complete political authority of Canada over Indigenous Peoples, a remarkable statement given that Canada was still engaged in the process of signing nation-to-nation treaties. Ultimately, the Indian Act would create from scratch a political structure, known as the band council, through which Indigenous Peoples could govern themselves. However, the system, which had no roots in actual Indigenous governance structures, was created to be institutionally dominated by the Department of Indian Affairs (DIA), which had a veto power over any decision made through the band council system.

In addition to controlling Indigenous governance, the Indian Act would soon be amended to create a pass system whereby the DIA would track and restrict Indigenous people's movement in and out of reserves. Passes to leave the reserve had to be justified to an Indian agent, who had full authority to ask whatever questions and place whatever restrictions they wanted. Even hardened colonial officials like Edgar Dewdney insisted that this would require a re-negotiation of treaties, since it violated them so wildly.[74] Meanwhile, the officials who managed this system — the NWMP and the DIA — exhibited the full range of colonial abuses of power, from refusing certain individuals' movement due to petty grievances, to sexual harassment and violence in exchange for the granting of passes.[75]

Even the very definition of Indigeneity was to be determined by Canada. Holding official "Indian status" came to be a point of difficulty and contention for Indigenous people. As a "status Indian" one could not vote or participate in Canadian civic life, thus being relegated to participation only in the ineffectual band council system. Indigenous people could renounce their "Indian status" but once this was done it could never be regained, thus extinguishing forever a person's connection to their Indigenous heritage under Canadian law. What is more, the Canadian government itself got to decide who began as a "status Indian" based on labyrinthine measurements of quantities of Indigenous lineage, and it further determined that "Indian status" would flow exclusively through male bloodlines. An Indigenous woman who married a non-Indigenous man thereby lost her "Indian status." As Barrington Walker points out, the Indian Act did not exclusively define Indigeneity on the basis of blood; at 21 years old, "status Indians" could apply for voluntary enfranchisement in Canadian civic life, whereafter a DIA agent would assess "the degree of civilization to which [the Indigenous person] has attained, and the character for integrity, morality, and sobriety which he or she bears."[76]

Meanwhile, the reserve system, set up under the auspices of the supremely powerful DIA, divided Indigenous nations into small bands, scattered across the country at great distances from one another and often far away from the territory they knew. This was a conscious strategy of conquest and was in direct violation of the treaties Canada had signed, which had clearly allowed Indigenous nations to choose their own reserve territories. In fact, when Cree leaders Mistahimaskwa, Minahikosis and Piepot demanded contiguous reserves in order to carve out a small, united Indigenous region, Canada's official representative refused; Edgar Dewdney instead threatened to withhold food aid and arrest leaders who continued pursuing the plan.[77] Keeping the reserves separated was a simple divide-and-conquer strategy, which dovetailed with similar tactics described by Howard Adams:

> Consistent with colonization principles, Indian Affairs agents made a practice of sowing dissension by exaggerating band and tribal differences so that native people were led to believe that neighbouring Indians and Métis were mean, cruel, and unfriendly. This systematic colonization makes colonized people suspicious of their neighbours, while the colonizers appear peaceful and civilized. The colonizer encourages the different colonial

groups to distrust each other and thus keeps them divided and isolated, weaker and easier to control.[78]

These were only a few of the colonial measures embedded in the Indian Act, some of which I take up further in the next chapter. It was nothing less than the blueprint for genocide; a road map for the complete destruction of the Indigenous Peoples, whose resistance to colonialism had made them ineffective slaves and unwilling subjects and who, therefore, had to be cleared out of the way of Canadian settler capitalism. Even as the terms of the Indian Act were being drawn up, Canada established a colonial police force to administer them, and used violence and starvation to kettle Indigenous people into reserves where the new laws could be enforced. By the early 1880s, there were only a few hundred Indigenous people in the west who remained outside of the reserves, while some 20,000 were now locked into what Howard Adams called the "prison of grass."

Notes
1. Hugh Shewell, *Enough to Keep Them Alive: Indian Welfare in Canada, 1873–1965*, Toronto, University of Toronto Press, 2004, p. 41.
2. Daniel Leblanc, "Protestors rally for Indigenous rights as country gears up for Canada 150," *The Globe and Mail*, June 30, 2017.
3. Justin Trudeau, "Statement by the Prime Minister on Canada Day," July 1, 2017. https://pm.gc.ca/eng/news/2017/07/01/statement-prime-minister-canada-day.
4. Glen Sean Coulthard, *Red Skin, White Masks: Rejecting the Colonial Politics of Recognition*, Minneapolis, University of Minnesota Press, 2014, p. 109.
5. James Laxer, *Staking Claims to a Continent: John A. Macdonald, Abraham Lincoln, Jefferson Davis, and the making of North America*, Toronto, House of Anansi Press, 2016, p. 82.
6. James Laxer, *Staking Claims*, p. 221, 186.
7. Margaret Conrad, *A Concise History of Canada*, Cambridge, Cambridge University Press, 2012, p. 122–127.
8. As Smith wrote, "civil government, so far as it is instituted for the security of private property, is in reality instituted for the defence of the rich against the poor, or of those who have some property against those who have none at all." Adam Smith, *Wealth of Nations*, Book V, Chapter 1, Part II.
9. James Laxer, *Staking Claims*, p. 93.
10. Margaret Conrad, Alvin Finkel and Donald Fyson, *History of the Canadian Peoples, Volume I, 6th ed*, Toronto, Pearson, 2015, p. 18.
11. James Laxer, *Staking Claims*, p. 230.
12. James Daschuk, *Clearing the Plains: Disease, Politics of Starvation, and the Loss of Aboriginal Life*, Regina, University of Regina Press, 2013, p. 11–79.
13. Howard Adams, *Prison of Grass: Canada from a Native Point of View*, Saskatoon, Fifth House Publishers, 1989, p. 48.
14. James Laxer, *Staking Claims*, p. 228–229.

15. Robert A. Wardhaugh and Alan MacEachern, ed., *Destinies: Canadian History Since Confederation, 8th Edition,* Toronto, Nelson Education, 2012, p. 14.
16. John A. Macdonald, quoted in James Laxer, *Staking Claims,* 268.
17. William McDougall, quoted in James Laxer, *Staking Claims,* 268.
18. John A. Macdonald, quoted in James Laxer, *Staking Claims,* 270.
19. Karen Dubinsky and Mark Epprecht, "Canadian Business and the Business of Development," in Karen Dubinsky, Sean Mills and Scott Rutherford, ed., *Canada and the Third World: Overlapping Histories,* Toronto, University of Toronto Press, 2016, p. 67.
20. Canada, House of Commons, *Official Report of the Debates of the House of Commons of the Dominion of Canada,* Ottawa, Maclean, Rogers and Co., 1885, 18, May 4, 1885, p. 1588.
21. J.R. Miller, *Skyscrapers Hide the Heavens: A History of Indian-White Relations in Canada,* 3rd edition, Toronto, University of Toronto Press, 2000, p. 164.
22. A detailed account of the internal politics of the 1869–70 resistance is beyond the scope of this book, but it is worth noting that while the primary conflict appeared to be between Canada and the Métis, there was a separate but related conflict playing out between the industrially oriented Canadian elite and the network of settlers (and to a much lesser extent Métis and Indigenous Peoples), whose wealth was rooted in the fur trade. Canada's annexation of the northwest signalled the end of the commercial fur trade and the establishment of capitalist agriculture in support of industrial development, and this was an important subtext to the conflict. Howard Adams deftly argues that former HBC factors like William McTavish stoked the resistance while trying to ensure that the Métis remained on the front lines of it, carefully trying to advance their own interests while playing both sides. See Howard Adams, *Prison of Grass,* p. 46–59.
23. H.Y. Hind, quoted in James Laxer, *Staking Claims,* p. 276.
24. James Laxer, *Staking Claims,* p. 280.
25. Howard Adams, *Prison of Grass,* p. 56.
26. James Laxer, *Staking Claims,* 283.
27. Howard Adams, *Prison of Grass,* p. 58.
28. "I found the negro an objectionable animal," wrote Wolseley. "His vanity, pretensions, his vulgar swagger, made one feel how much more useful he would be if we had never emancipated him…he was intended to be the white man's servant." Hardly surprising views for a man whose life was dedicated to crushing resistance across the Empire. Indoctrinated into the imperial ideology from his childhood as an English settler in conquered Ireland, Wolseley fought in India and Burma, was involved in the Crimean War, and was then sent to China to help undermine the sovereignty of the Qing Dynasty in an adventure that sparked a civil war in China costing the lives of some 50–100 million people. He was recalled to India to defeat the mutiny of 1857, after which he was drawn to the clarion call of the Confederate Army of the US South, where he acted as a military advisor, before coming to Canada to defeat the Red River Resistance. From there, he was sent to West Africa where he helped defeat the Asanti in modern-day Ghana, and where he extolled the above piece of racial wisdom. Oddly, Wolseley had moments of critical reflection: "in the course of my North American wanderings I have never encountered any Indian tribes

without experiencing a feeling of remorse not only for having robbed them of their hunting grounds, but still more for killing them off with the fatal poison of whiskey." Elsewhere he writes of a Mi'kmaw chief, "I knew that his degradation was the result of the white man's rule, and before the booted European had ever been seen in the forests of Canada, their Indian inhabitants led a healthy life of savagery." Clearly, the white supremacist bent of Wolseley's thought could not be broken, but it is noteworthy that he — a foot soldier of empire — could speak plainly about the nature of the conquest. Field Marshall Viscount Wolseley, *The Story of a Soldier's Life*, Toronto, The Book Supply Company, 1904, p. 288, 191, 114.
29. A.H. de Tremaudan, quoted in Howard Adams, *Prison of Grass*, p. 58.
30. Traditional Canadian historians often refer to this conflict as the "1885 Rebellion" or the "Riel Rebellion." Following Howard Adams and other scholars, I prefer the term "War of 1885" since it reminds us that there were two sides contesting the future control over this land and it refuses the idea that Canada was a legitimate state suffering some kind of criminal rebellion. I apply the same logic to my discussion of the Red River Resistance, also typically labelled a "rebellion." Occasionally, for specificity and stylistic purposes, I still use terms like "rebellion" and "uprising" to describe specific instances of military resistance.
31. James Daschuk, *Clearing the Plains: Disease, Politics of Starvation, and the Loss of Aboriginal Life*, Regina, University of Regina Press, 2013, p. 40.
32. Daschuk, p. 44. The protection of the beaver derived from a centuries-old reliance on beaver dams to maintain a reliable water supply in an otherwise dry region.
33. James Daschuk, *Clearing the Plains*, p. 100.
34. Arthur J. Ray, *I Have Lived Here Since the World Began: An Illustrated History of Canada's Native People*, Montreal, McGill-Queen's University Press, 2011, p. 177.
35. James Daschuk, *Clearing the Plains*, p. 59–77.
36. Hunger and disease were afflicting Indigenous people in the east as well, with similar responses from Canadian authorities. Hugh Shewell, *Enough*, p. 41–67.
37. Scott Rutherford, "Indigenous Peoples, Colonialism and Canada," in Karen Dubinsky, Sean Mills and Scott Rutherford, ed., *Canada and the Third World: Overlapping Histories*, Toronto, University of Toronto Press, 2016, 22.
38. James Daschuk, *Clearing the Plains*, 79.
39. Scott Rutherford, "Indigenous Peoples, Colonialism and Canada," p 23.
40. Quoted in Howard Adams, *Prison of Grass*, p. 66.
41. This was undertaken with the express intent of exterminating the Indigenous Peoples of the American Midwest. J. Weston Phippen, "Kill Every Buffalo You Can! Every Buffalo Dead is an Indian Gone!," *The Atlantic*, May 3, 2016.
42. Howard Adams, *Prison of Grass*, p. 60.
43. Hector Langevin, quoted in Hugh Shewell, *Enough*, p. 41.
44. James Daschuk, *Clearing the Plains*, 108.
45. James Daschuk, *Clearing the Plains*, 114–115.
46. Macolm D. Cameron, quoted in James Daschuk, *Clearing the Plains*, 114.
47. James Daschuk, *Clearing the Plains*, 122.
48. Pork distributed at Touchwood Hills in 1880 was described by the Indian agents as "totally unfit for use," but it was handed out nevertheless. James Daschuk,

Clearing the Plains, 118.
49. John A. Macdonald, quoted in James Daschuk, *Clearing the Plains*, 123.
50. Leonard Tilley, quoted in James Daschuk, *Clearing the Plains*, 122.
51. Lawrence Vankoughnet, quoted in James Daschuk, *Clearing the Plains*, 116.
52. "PC" here means "politically correct," a pejorative term that emerged from Allan Bloom's *The Closing of the American Mind* (1987) as a way of mocking and subverting attempts to curb the use of explicitly offensive terms directed at women, people of colour, people with disabilities or other marginalized groups.
53. David Cruise and Alison Griffiths, *The Great Adventure: How the Mounties Conquered the West*, Toronto, Penguin Books, 1997, p. x-xi.
54. Jean D'Artigue, quoted in Cruise and Griffiths, *The Great Adventure*, p. 6.
55. Fred Bagley, quoted in Cruise and Griffiths, *The Great Adventure*, p. 11.
56. Quoted in Cruise and Griffiths, *The Great Adventure*, p. 18.
57. Cruise and Griffiths, *The Great Adventure*, p. 51.
58. Cruise and Griffiths, *The Great Adventure*, p. 154.
59. Cruise and Griffiths, *The Great Adventure*, p. 330.
60. J.R. Miller, *Skyscrapers Hide the Heavens: A History of Indian-White Relations in Canada*, 3rd edition, Toronto, University of Toronto Press, 2000, p. 125.
61. Cruise and Griffiths, *The Great Adventure*, p. 438.
62. Cruise and Griffiths, *The Great Adventure*.
63. During parliamentary debates in the 1880s, some MPs alleged that huge numbers of DIA officials were contracting sexually-transmitted diseases and purchasing thirteen-year-old "brides" for as little as ten dollars. Conservative MP Hector Langevin defended the DIA agents, insisting that bride pricing was normal for Indigenous Peoples and these constituted fair market exchanges. See James Daschuk, *Clearing the Plains*, p. 153.
64. Cruise and Griffiths, *The Great Adventure*, p. 314.
65. James Laxer, *Staking Claims*, p. 250–253.
66. J.R. Miller, *Skyscrapers*, p. 139.
67. Quoted in Arthur J. Ray, *I Have Lived Here*, p. 148.
68. Adolf Hitler, October 17, 1941, quoted in Czeslawa Madajczyka, *Generalny Plan Wschodni*, Instytut Historii Polskiej Akademii Nauk, Warsaw 1990, p. 69–70. Translated from German.
69. Margaret Conrad, *Concise History*, p. 155.
70. James Daschuk, *Clearing the Plains*, p. 124–126.
71. Language, for instance, is both a carrier of culture and also a reflection of it. Tomson Highway describes the way meanings conveyed in Cree cannot be properly translated into English without provoking a very different reaction. Tomson Highway, "Why Cree Is the Sexiest of All Languages," in Drew Hayden Taylor, ed. *Me Sexy: An Exploration of Native Sex and Sexuality*, Toronto, Douglas and McIntyre, 2008, p. 37.
72. In Canada's hosting of the 2010 Olympic Games in Vancouver, much of Canada's presentation of itself was laden with Indigenous imagery and iconography — Canada's hollow multiculturalism was to celebrate the symbols of what it had tried to destroy, to embrace the totem pole after waging war on the cultures that produced it.
73. Glen Sean Coulthard, *Red Skin, White Masks*, p. 65.

74. James Daschuk, *Clearing the Plains*, p. 162.
75. Some scholars suggest that the pass system was only sporadically enforced, owing to its questionable legality (under the terms of the treaties) and a generally unwillingness of Indigenous people to follow it and police to enforce it. While it was instrumental in preventing Indigenous people from coming together for spiritual celebrations like the Sun Dance and the Thirst Dance, it became increasingly unnecessary as the rapid European settlement of the west meant that fewer and fewer opportunities existed for Indigenous people off the reserves. Hunting and fishing were either depleting or would soon be accessible only to whites, homestead lands were being taken up by settlers, and Indigenous people had little interest in trying to find wage labour in the new settlements. Thus, while the system persisted into the 20th century, its importance was more in what it said about Canadian goals than in its long-term effects. See J.R. Miller, *Skyscrapers*, 258.
76. Indian Act, quoted in Barrington Walker, "Immigration Policy, Colonization, and the Development of a White Canada," in Karen Dubinsky, Sean Mills and Scott Rutherford, ed., *Canada and the Third World: Overlapping Histories*, Toronto, University of Toronto Press, 2016, p. 40.
77. Arthur J. Ray, *I Have Lived Here*, p. 216–217.
78. Howard Adams, *Prison of Grass*, p. 69.

3

From the Potlatch to the Residential Schools

The human race is divided into several broad families, distinguished as a rule by the colour of their skins. Asia is the home of the yellow man, Africa of the black man, Europe of the white man, and America of the red man. Today, Canada is inhabited mainly by the white or European race.

— W. Stewart Wallace, opening paragraph in *A First Book of Canadian History*, authorized by the Minister of Education for the Public Schools of Ontario, 1943[1]

In 2014, the Canadian government officially opened the Canadian Museum for Human Rights, built at the site where the Red and Assiniboine Rivers meet, an historic gathering place for Indigenous people and now a cultural/tourist centre in Winnipeg. Architecturally unique, the museum figures prominently into the Winnipeg skyline and is featured in plenty of postcards, sometimes framed by fireworks from Canada Day celebrations, which take place just outside the museum.

It seems to stand as a reminder to Canadians that this is a nation that cares about human rights, justice and equality. Visitors to the museum may be shocked by the stories of terrible things that have happened elsewhere in the world, but can leave at peace knowing that they live in a place where people care and wish to make the world a better place. Even the very premise of the museum — dedicated to improving the lives of people around the world — reinforces the ubiquitous and self-satisfied notion that it is "very Canadian" to want to help people.

If only it were so simple. In fact, the Museum of Human Rights is a deeply contradictory endeavour, manifestly developed by competing interests that could not cohere logically. There was mention of police violence against working-class movements, and yet the museum prominently thanked its extremely wealthy sponsors, including Great West Life, RBC and the Asper Family, the very class whose interests those police were defending. It devoted a small section to the plights of contemporary migrant workers, many of whom face extremely exploitative conditions in Canadian agribusinesses, but highlighted quotes from individual workers expressing their gratitude to Canada for giving them "opportunity" and "ensuring their rights are protected."[2] The visitor's guide rightly acknowledges that the museum's water is sourced from the Shoal Lake 40 First Nation but makes no mention of the fact that, as a result of the diversion of water to Winnipeg, the reserve itself has not had clean running water for decades.[3]

As Adele Perry argues, the case of Shoal Lake perfectly illustrates that the Canada we know was entirely dependent on the genocide of Indigenous Peoples; Winnipeg has water because Shoal Lake 40 does not.[4] This, ultimately, is why the Museum of Human Rights failed to achieve what its most idealistic designers and curators would have wanted. To do so would profoundly undermine the interests of its backers: the Canadian government and the capitalist class. While valiant attempts are made to tackle complex problems — racism, state violence, genocide — they cannot provide a coherent explanation of these problems without adequately addressing their root causes. After all, the sponsors of the museum do not want to be named as its villains.

The museum struggles most with how to present Canada's relations with Indigenous Peoples, named by the Truth and Reconciliation Commission in 2016 as "cultural genocide." Much space in the museum is devoted to showing respect for Indigenous traditions and culture, but relatively little has been done to highlight the conscious and concrete ways that Canada worked to destroy that culture. Museum-goers might easily be left with the impression that, while Canada made mistakes in the past, it is now working hard to address and resolve those problems. But genocide does not happen because of a few mistakes. It is the product of a conscious and concerted set of policies designed to eliminate — to erase — a group of people. The quote at the top of this chapter, drawn from an official Canadian history textbook in the 1940s and presented as a simple matter of fact, illustrates that Canadians well understood the process: a place that had once been home to "the red man" was now "inhabited by the white race." Its original inhabitants had been erased.

In this chapter, I illustrate that Canadian foreign policy towards Indigenous Peoples over the past century and a half has largely been consistent with the patterns established during the period of Confederation and the passing of the Indian Act. Far from righting the wrongs of the past, Canada has redoubled them. Whatever its new museum might say, Canada unswervingly prioritized the interests of Canadian capital over its international obligations to Indigenous Peoples. The colonial imagination that shaped its early encounters remains ever-present across this period.

The War of 1885

As the previous chapter documented, the period from the 1860s to the 1880s marked the beginning of Canada and the beginning of the end of Indigenous life as people knew it. Especially in the west, where many Indigenous survivors of colonialism had sought refuge, this was the period of catastrophe that turned once-strong and healthy nations into fragmented, isolated bands barely surviving on destitute reserves. These open-air prisons, guarded by agents of the Department of Indian Affairs (DIA), were often characterized by hunger, disease and demoralization; they were the ghettos which housed a people defeated, and their conquerors were arrogant and abusive.

The starvation crisis that had exploded with the collapse of the buffalo herds was, by the early 1880s, threatening the very existence of the Indigenous Peoples, whose numbers were falling drastically. Treaty promises of seeds and implements to support reserve agriculture were woefully inadequate, failing both due to government inattention and as a consequence of its fundamental colonial purpose. Canadian policy had sought to disperse Indigenous people widely to disrupt their traditional connection to the land and to one another; as a result, a reserve at Assissippi was located over a hundred miles away from the nearest mill, such that even when they successfully threshed grain, converting it into useful food was a monumental task.[5]

Canada's miserly policy of providing limited — sometimes rotten — food aid, often in exchange for forced labour, also played a key role in the crisis. On rare occasions, individual Canadian settlers would support Indigenous claims that food was rotten or tampered, as when Doctor F.X. Girard reported that bad flour had contributed to the deaths of twenty people on a Kainai reserve. Girard was denounced by his superiors for promoting inefficiencies.[6]

Violence almost erupted after more than a hundred Cree in Chief Piepot's band died from eating rancid pork delivered by the Canadian government. They had travelled over 350 miles from their home in the Cypress Hills to the reserve near Regina on the explicit premise that they would receive rations and had pointedly complained about the rotten meat. Indian Affairs Commissioner Edgar Dewdney had replied, "the Indians should eat the bacon or die."[7] This turned out to be a false binary; they did both. Only a few months before, the local settler newspaper, the *Regina Leader*, had reassured the white settlers of Regina that "the Government is bound to feed the Indians, so as they are fed, the poor creatures are no more likely to give trouble than a kennel of dogs fed at regular intervals."[8] This quote not only highlights the dehumanizing way settlers were encouraged to view the "Indians," but also reinforces the fact that they were well aware of the starvation crisis facing Indigenous people.

Control over these limited rations was given to local DIA agents, who often used this structural power to cast themselves as mini-dictators. So-called Indian agents carried out a wide range of abuses, and although most Indigenous people were too weakened by hunger and disease to mount significant resistance, their anger simmered and occasionally boiled over into violence. Incidents and conflicts increased in the early 1880s, and in 1884 the first major uprising took place at the Sakimay Reserve. When Indian agents refused to hand over food to starving people, Chief Sakimay and a group of armed men broke into the storehouse and seized the food themselves. Though no one was killed in the standoff, tension was clearly brewing.

That growing tension finally spilled over in 1885, in a series of minor conflicts between Cree and settlers — most notably the killing of nine Europeans at Frog Lake — and the larger Métis resistance that has come to be inaccurately termed the Riel Rebellion. At Frog Lake, two DIA agents had run the reserve like their own personal fiefdom and developed a reputation for their nastiness. John Delaney was "roundly hated for his relationships with very young women of the reserve, and his casual humiliations of the hungry people,"[9] and Thomas Quinn, himself of mixed ancestry, would withhold rations to extract teenage brides, and once summoned everyone to the ration house for food, only to declare it an April Fool's joke to the unimpressed, starving Cree.[10]

Though the settler press would call it the Frog Lake Massacre and use it to whip up support for repression, the Cree warriors had legitimate grievances against Quinn, Delaney and the other DIA agents they killed. As historian J.R. Miller notes, three of the twelve Europeans at Frog Lake were spared and treated humanely, even despite their indirect complicity in the crimes of the others.[11] As similar uprisings took place at other Cree reserves, the common denominator was that the killings of settlers were not random. Revenge was taken against those who had been cruel or withheld food, like farm instructor James Payne and rancher Barney Tremont, while those who had cultivated more or less respectful relationships with Indigenous people were spared and even assisted by groups of warriors during the uprisings.[12]

Nevertheless, Canadian authorities hunted the rebellious Cree, killed dozens of them and established what were effectively show trials at Battleford that resulted in the largest number of simultaneous public hangings in Canadian history. The bodies were left in the noose for fifteen minutes, for psychological effect.[13] After 1885, Canada effectively embarked on counter-insurgency warfare; Indigenous people were divided into loyal and disloyal factions, the pass system was enforced, local political structures were further dismantled, and reserves were subdivided to disrupt collective farming — and by extension political — practices. Indeed, the blending of Canada's ideological and material goals in this period was perfectly articulated in 1890 by the DIA commissioner, who proudly reported that "the work of sub-dividing reserves has begun in earnest. The policy of destroying the tribal or communist system is assailed in every possible way and every effort made to implant a system of individual responsibility instead."[14]

Métis Resistance

Concurrent to, but not in conjunction with, the Cree rebellions was the major Métis resistance around Batoche. Although Canadian authorities treated the events of 1885 as though they were a connected uprising across the northwest, in reality many of the Indigenous nations were too weak or intimidated, or their leaders were paid off too well, to join the resistance. Still, the mid-1880s presented the prospect of a major challenge for the fledgling Canadian national project. Although the Canadian Pacific Railroad had reached the prairies, construction was faltering due to lack of funds, and European settlement had slowed as the effects of the 1873 global recession began to set in.[15] In the area of Batoche, where most Métis had relocated after the Red River Resistance, even many of the white settlers were unhappy with the governance of the northwest. To European settlers, the Métis troubled the simplistic colonial ideologies they had otherwise accepted; were these people "civilized" Europeans or "savage" Indians?

It was clear that the Canadian government viewed them as the latter, most likely because they largely rejected the Canadian national project, viewed themselves as autonomous and independent, and employed self-governance structures that bore greater resemblance to their Indigenous heritage than to anything the whites had established. In 1884, when discontent began to build around settler towns like Prince Albert, the Canadian authorities noted with much alarm that — as in 1869 — many of the European settlers were finding common cause with the Métis. From the ranks of disgruntled settlers emerged leaders like William Henry Jackson, who worked with English mixed-race leaders like Charles Adams and Métis leaders like Gabriel Dumont, in building a broader people's movement in the central prairies.[16]

Prime Minister John A. Macdonald was extremely concerned about the prospect of a union of white and Indigenous resistance. He immediately set to work besetting division, taking control of the newspaper in Prince Albert and using it to spread propaganda, highlighting and exaggerating the violence of the Cree and Métis uprisings. Howard Adams explains that Macdonald resolved to "make certain concessions to the white residents of the Northwest, while at the same time allowing the Métis and Indian situation to aggravate itself to the point of desperation and hostility."[17]

This tactic allowed Canada to send a major military force into the region, on the premise that it was dealing with a violent Indigenous insurgency, while also subtly reinforcing Ottawa's dominion over the northwest. Settler capitalism, after all, requires a working class; while early waves of European settlement were imbued with the grandeur of colonial superiority, the reality of this economic system was that, before long, the majority of the settlers themselves became an exploited class. Their subservience to the system that exploited them was often won though the promotion of the colonial imagination; as Gerald Horne argues in *The Apocalypse of Settler Colonialism* (2017), white settlers, often escaping hardship in capitalist Europe, revelled in the knowledge that they were the true masters of their new land. Seduced by the idea of their supremacy, they became the foot soldiers of settler capitalism, battling with Indigenous people over land they believed they deserved and which represented the key to their ascension out of the ranks of the impoverished and exploited.[18]

These promises were typically illusory. John A. Macdonald and I.G. Baker didn't want to share their wealth with glorified peasants, even if they had English names. The horizon of settler capitalism was a highly stratified society where the majority worked hard and earned little, in order to sustain the enormous profits of the few. But in the establishment of that system, it needed a settler vanguard convinced that they would be the winners and that the only thing preventing them from realising their dreams was the presence of Indigenous people. Thus, in periods of Indigenous resistance, the elite needed to keep the settlers on their side or face outright catastrophe.

The prospect of interracial solidarity and upheaval was an old colonial problem in the Americas: in the 1720s, Indigenous and African slaves led a revolt in Natchez; in the 1730s a similar plan was uncovered in New Orleans; in the 1740s, a plot to poison slaveholders in South Carolina involved several white settlers; in 1741 colonial authorities blanched at the prospect of a "wicked and dangerous conspiracy" of "white people and diverse Negro slaves" to burn down Manhattan.[19] The prospect of marginalized groups — including poor white workers or indentured servants — joining forces struck terror in the heart of the American elite, which enacted a range of policies and laws to prevent such alliances from forming,[20] while simultaneously embarking on a psycho-cultural project to deepen the white supremacist logic at the heart of the white working class.[21]

This problem similarly animated the decisions of the Canadian government in 1884–85, as it worked to manage the resistance in the northwest and keep the settlers on side. Thus, the government reached out to angry whites, who were forming organizations like the Northwest Farmers Union, and tried to build bridges with them, while turning them against the Métis and Indigenous resisters.[22] Despite the efforts of settlers like William Henry Jackson to maintain solidarity, whites were increasingly willing to accept the claim from Ottawa that the Cree and Métis were engaging in a kind of race war, bent on killing settlers and seizing their land. Macdonald organized a massive police and military force to occupy the northwest, ostensibly to protect the settlers from Indigenous violence.

After much provocation from within the Métis community, where the government had employed the spy Charles Nolin to stir up violence, and the amassing of Canadian armed forces in the region, the conflict began with a police attack against the Métis at Duck Lake. Though outnumbered at a ratio of nearly 7 to 1, the Métis fighters had greater skill and awareness of the terrain and won an easy victory. Poised to inflict heavy losses, Louis Riel convinced Gabriel Dumont to show mercy, and thus only ten of the white police were killed. Nevertheless, the police set fire to Fort Carlton that night, claiming that the Métis had done it as part of their savage attack against settler authorities. This piece of theatre was effective, and thousands of whites in Ontario enlisted to join the force to crush the "savage and lawless mob" of Métis who were threatening the west. The new army was brought to Saskatchewan on the unfinished Canadian Pacific Railway,[23] and ultimately the small Métis guerrilla force would be faced with nearly 8000 Dominion soldiers and would be besieged and overrun at their home in Batoche.

The assault on Batoche was merciless; bullets were sprayed into civilian homes killing people as old as 93 years. As reported by observers to the *Toronto Mail* and even in the House of Commons, Canadian soldiers ransacked and set fire to Métis homes, literally looting and pillaging the village of their enemy. What they could not steal, like ovens and beds and tables, they smashed.[24] Métis leaders were executed or imprisoned, and John A. Macdonald wrote to Edgar Dewdney to explain that "the executions of the Indians... ought to convince the Red Man that the White Man governs."[25] Louis Riel — an important but by no means indispensable leader — was put on trial to prominently illustrate both Canada's victory and its magnanimity in offering its enemies their day in court. Indeed, Riel's ongoing use and misuse in Canadian politics and mythology generates some ambivalence from contemporary Métis.[26]

What is less discussed in the public sphere is that the Métis Resistance had been compelled by the fact that they were starving, their very survival imperiled by the Canadian government's refusal to provide them with land titles and seeds and farming implements. Rather than provide the relief that would have kept the Métis alive, the government had, in fact, replied by accusing them of squatting on valuable land. John A. Macdonald went as far as to demand payment from the starving Métis for the land they were trying to farm. Even the settler newspapers and the NWMP had acknowledged in 1884 that the Métis, decimated by the collapse of the buffalo hunt, would not survive without imminent support.[27] The full colonial depravity of Canada's refusal to support the Métis farmers is manifest in the fact that, after the slaughter and destruction of Batoche, Macdonald offered land grants twice the size of those the Métis had asked for, to the very soldiers who had just ransacked Batoche.[28] Despite all this, contemporary military historians still justify the assault by claiming it was a response to "open rebellion against the legitimate authority of Canada."[29]

Assimilation, Extermination, Cultural Genocide

The rebellious year of 1885 ended with mass executions of starving Indigenous people at Battleford and the burning of the starving Métis settlement at Batoche. Or, as military historian David Bercuson triumphantly put it, "the west had been saved for Canada."[30] White settlement was now a reality from coast to coast, and the Indigenous Peoples would no longer be allowed to disrupt that process in any way. The reserves were effectively converted into prisons, and the fact that they were typically on poor agricultural land meant that the ill-equipped prisoners would continue to starve. Canada's Indian Affairs commissioner Hayter Reed called Indigenous people "the scum of the prairies,"[31] and Canada actively recruited European settlers to populate the territories adjacent to the reserves in order to ensure white domination of the prairies.[32]

Fewer and fewer Indigenous people were given passes to leave the reserves to hunt, and they were further discouraged from doing so when the state began seizing guns, horses and ammunition to prevent future rebellion. Measures were taken to more effectively seal off the border with the US, to prevent Sioux resistance from spreading northward, though this concern was significantly reduced after the horrific massacre of the Sioux by US forces at Wounded Knee in 1890. The crisis of hunger and tuberculosis continued in the ensuing decades, with death rates as high as 127 per 1000 in the Qu'Appelle Valley. Within a few decades, Canada would create a Department of Health that specifically excluded Indigenous people; their health care, tellingly, fell under the portfolio of mines and resources.[33]

Having crushed Indigenous military action, the Canadian government sought to crush Indigenous spirits; resistance requires hope, and so measures were taken to stamp out any sources of Indigenous hope. As such, Canada embarked on a more rigorous effort to undermine whatever was left of Indigenous culture, by making Indigenous cultural institutions illegal and by breaking Indigenous children from their local and family traditions. Though many spiritual celebrations had already been deeply disrupted by the reserves and the pass system itself, all Indigenous religious ceremonies would soon be banned by the Dominion, as Canada increasingly possessed the capacity to target the very fabric of Indigenous culture.

Notable among these restrictions was the outlawing of the Potlatch ceremony after 1884. Practised by many nations of the Pacific Coast, most notably the Kwakwaka'wakw, the Potlatch was a gift-giving ceremony that was at the heart of the political economy of many of the Indigenous Peoples of the west coast. These were societies that were affluent and complex when European traders began arriving in the 18th century, their material abundance reflected in the amount of time that people of higher castes could devote to art and expression. Many contemporary Canadians still marvel, for instance, at their magnificent totem poles.

The Pacific Coast peoples did not experience significant dislocation in the early years of European trade, but pressure emerged in the late 1850s, when the prospect of gold brought Europeans in droves to the Fraser River valley. Until that point, British governors of the colony had been fairer in their dealings than elsewhere in Canada, generally preventing settlers from seizing land that Indigenous people wanted. This changed in the 1860s as British settlement — and conflict over land — grew. Without any formal treaty process, settlers began forcibly relocating Indigenous people away from the places they wanted, as when the Songhee were dispossessed of the area around Victoria. Settlement and displacement exploded after the arrival of the intercontinental railroad.

The Potlatch ceremony, though it appeared spiritual on the surface, was also profoundly economic, serving as a mechanism for wealth-redistribution and providing for collective economic security. If one band was ill-prepared for a coming winter, they could get what they needed at the Potlatch. If another was well-stocked, they could earn social and political capital by giving generously. Occasionally, surplus would actually be destroyed at a Potlatch in order to illustrate strength and prestige; Europeans expressed incredulity at such practices, which they saw as "bankrupting themselves" and "squandering" opportunities to accumulate wealth.[34]

As J.R. Miller notes, the "ethos [of the Potlatch] was the antithesis of the individualism and competitive accumulation that underlay

Euro-Canadian society," and so it is no surprise that Canadian officials were appalled by the ceremony and worked to undermine it. Missionary William Duncan called it "the most formidable of all obstacles in the way of the Indians becoming Christian, or even civilized."[35] For his part, Prime Minister Macdonald motivated the ban to Parliament by expressing concern that "the Indians feel yet that they are the lords of the country in British Columbia."[36]

The banning of the ceremony gave authorities one more tool to use against Indigenous people, though it didn't initially stop the Potlatching. Ceremonies continued in defiance of the law, sometimes taking place in secret. But in the 1910s and especially the 1920s, as the settler population on the west coast grew to engulf the Indigenous Peoples, arrests and repression of the Potlatch increased. Notable among these efforts was an episode that struck with all the chords of colonialism: in 1922, a number of people convicted of Potlatching at Alert Bay and Cape Mudge were offered a deal wherein their prison sentences would be commuted if they handed over all of their ceremonial regalia to the government. The elaborate masks, whistles, rattles and other Potlatch artifacts were sent to museums in Ontario.[37]

In addition to banning the Potlatch, the Canadian government amended the Indian Act to cover other Indigenous ceremonies, outlawing "any Indian festival, dance, or other ceremony of which the giving away or paying or giving back money, goods, or articles of any sort forms a part, or is a feature."[38] Any form of wealth redistribution by Indigenous people was now forbidden. This legislation was used to undermine the Sun and Thirst Dances of the plains though, like the Potlatch, enforcement was inconsistent. In extreme cases, Indigenous Elders were sentenced to jail time for hosting a dance and giving a dinner. More typically, dances were permitted but only in curtailed and limited fashion. In 1914, Indigenous people were legally mandated to get government authorization simply for wearing "Indian costume."[39]

By the turn of the century, the threat of Indigenous resistance was no longer taken seriously. The War of 1885 had been a final stand and the repression that followed, combined with the rapid influx of European settlers, had made Indigenous revolution a less pressing fear. Many settlers, in fact, began taking an anthropological interest in the people they now viewed as an ancient, dying race. Even as the political and economic hearts of ceremonies like the Potlatch and Sun Dance were being carved out, their superficial flavour was being preserved by settlers in museums and exhibitions, most notably the Calgary Stampede.[40] And while Indigenous people "performed" buffalo hunts for white audiences, the Canadian government was creating a national park to preserve the buffalo herds that had collapsed, but not for Indigenous hunters; Wood Buffalo Park forbade Indigenous hunting even while it considered a proposal to sell individual hunting licences to wealthy white sport hunters.[41]

The Residential School System

Defeated and debased, Indigenous Peoples were footnotes in Canada's *fin de siècle* imagination. As Canada welcomed the industrial future, with railroads and factories and bourgeois culture, Indigenous people were imprisoned in reserves, their culture deemed a relic of anthropology to be mocked or mystified but by no means respected. But what would Canada do with its Indigenous prisoners? It was never entirely clear whether the Canadian elite wanted to convert Indigenous people into agricultural labourers, preserve them as an industrial reserve army of labour or simply let them die. Glen Sean Coulthard argues persuasively that as Canada built its industrial capitalist base, it needed Indigenous land far more than Indigenous labour:

> Increased European settlement combined with an imported, hyper-exploited non-European workforce meant that, in the post fur trade period, Canadian state-formation and colonial-capitalist development required first and foremost land, and only secondarily the surplus value afforded by cheap, Indigenous labour. This is not to suggest, however, that the long-term goal of indoctrinating the Indigenous population to the principles of private property, possessive individualism, and menial wage work did not constitute an important feature of Canadian Indian policy. It did.[42]

The proletarianization of Indigenous people was secondary to their ghettoization and the permanent destruction of their will to resist the new state. Although the Canadian state used several different measures to accomplish these aims, none was as pervasive and pernicious as the infamous residential school system. The residential schools were so heinous that few contemporary Canadians will now defend them, and the radical cruelty of the apparatus around and within the schools was such that this history has forced a significant crack in the edifice of modern Canadian triumphalism. Most Canadians today know about the schools and view them as a shameful part of Canada's history.

That assessment is true, but it is also narrow and limited. The schools were not a disgraceful aberration but, rather, a single component of a broad and coherent colonial ideology and practice. Residential schools were not unique to Canada; similar models with similar goals were applied in several settler colonial states, including Australia and the United States, which also established such schools in its own colonies, like the Philippines. Canada undeniably excelled in the dubious art of kidnapping Indigenous children and subjecting them to isolation, abuse and traumatic cleavage from the world as they knew it. Though it may not have been the most significant factor in the near-collapse of the Indigenous world, it was surely among its most cruel.

The school system was part of the treaty negotiations on the plains, and Canadian official Alexander Morris may never have said anything so accidentally honest in those discussions as when, negotiating Treaty 4, he told the assembled: "The Queen wishes her red children to learn the cunning of the white man and when they are ready for it she will send schoolmasters on every Reserve and pay them."[43] Negotiators on the Indigenous side often recognized that a Canadian education might prove valuable for their younger generations and did not oppose the idea in principle, since they quite reasonably assumed that the schools would be set up in their communities and would supplement, not replace, their own systems of education. Indeed, these terms were clear enough in the treaties.

However, as early as 1847 — two decades before Confederation — the colonial agenda of the schools was clear. Egerton Ryerson, whose name is now given to a prominent Toronto university, asserted that any education for Indigenous children "must consist not merely of the training of the mind, but of the weaning from the habits and feelings of their ancestors, and the acquirements of the language, arts and customs of civilized life."[44] The schools would ultimately be established to do just that; teaching was in English and corporal punishment was meted out liberally to students who spoke their own languages. Sexual violence and abuse were also prevalent and linked to high suicide rates, alcoholism and drug abuse in survivors of the schools.

By the early 1900s, as children were emerging from the nightmarish experience of the schools, Indigenous parents increasingly refused to send them. In 1920, the Indian Act was amended to make attendance at the schools compulsory, and the police and Indian Affairs would now be empowered to take children to the schools — and keep them there — by force. At its height, some 75% of Indigenous children aged 7–15 were in the schools. The education itself was minimally useful; the Eurocentric curriculum was jarring and the Bible readings and histories of English kings was irrelevant and disconnected from anything Indigenous children knew. Students were actively taught that their own cultures were backwards and shameful; their traditional clothing was burned, their hair was cut short, and they were called by European names. Given the students' youth, that they had been physically separated from their homes and that they constantly feared physical and sexual violence, it is no surprise that the schools were utterly traumatic and left people irreparably broken from their very sense of themselves. Many survivors emerged alienated from both their own communities and the white society that had broken them.[45]

The testimonies of survivors, many compiled during the Truth and Reconciliation Commission hearings, are truly harrowing. The stories are so upsetting that I am often reluctant to share them in the classroom, my students sometimes leaving in tears. The schools were unsanitary, with raw sewage seeping into children's rooms. Students were experimented on by Canadian government researchers. Humiliation was rampant; children who wet the bed would be forced to wear their soiled clothing all day or pull down their pants and be lashed in front of the other students. Students who spoke their Indigenous language had needles stuck through their tongues. Many students were beaten into unconsciousness or even to death, in which case they were routinely deposited in unmarked mass graves. Children were sold into pedophile rings to be abused by clergy, police and business and government officials. Girls who got pregnant after being raped had their infant babies murdered. One testimony from a school in Saskatchewan described a newborn baby being put into an oven and burned to death.[46] These horrifying stories represent only a tiny fraction of the trauma inflicted and the long-term harm done.[47] These are actions that can only be understood in a context where the perpetrators — and here I mean not just the individuals carrying out these actions but the vast network of people committed to facilitating and justifying those actions — had fully accepted the idea that their victims were less than human.

The last residential school was closed in 1996, though most were shuttered by the late 1970s. The long-term damage and dislocation done to Indigenous individuals and communities is difficult to measure, and would qualify, on its own, as evidence of Canada's attempt to destroy Indigenous civilization. What is more, Canadian officials at various points in the history of the system made its intentions quite plain in quotes that are by now familiar to many Canadians. "The Indians must disappear before the march of civilization," said Canadian writer Duncan George MacDonald.[48] Taking it further, Canadian poet and DIA official Duncan Campbell Scott famously declared, "I want to get rid of the Indian problem… our object is to continue until there is not a single Indian in Canada that has not been absorbed by the body politic, and there is no Indian question, and no Indian Department."[49] John A. Macdonald, for his part, explicitly stated that "the schools [were] designed to kill the Indian in the child." These are inescapably the words of people committing genocide.

Following the release of the Truth and Reconciliation Commission report, there was no shortage of apologies from the Canadian government and from the various churches that ran the schools and were most directly responsible for them. But these apologies could not undo the damage, nor did they include significant measures for the decolonization of Canada. Indeed, the tragedies of the residential school system are only one component of the systematic colonization imposed on Indigenous Peoples. Even as the residential schools were falling out of fashion, Indigenous children were again being kidnapped in what came to be known as the Sixties Scoop, a set of policies that emanated from the social-democratic Co-operative Commonwealth Federation (CCF).[50] In this case, children were taken not to boarding schools but into the Canadian child welfare system, where they were fostered out to predominantly non-Indigenous families and, again, suffered extreme culture shock, trauma, abuse and pointed shaming for their Indigenous heritage. This dynamic is no relic of the past; Lauri Gilcrest notes that another such wave — a Millennium Scoop — has taken place in the past two decades.[51] In fact, by the late 2010s, there were more Indigenous children in government care — at various stages of the child welfare system — than were in the residential school system at its peak.[52]

Policing the Colonized

Colonialism is inextricably linked to gendered and sexualized violence. It was prevalent in the residential school system and in the more contemporary child welfare and foster care systems, a fact that still seems to shock modern Canadians. But it should not be so surprising; sexual abuse of children in residential schools is only a small part of the story. European colonialism was endowed with an intensely patriarchal ideology that sought to control women's bodies and sexuality, channeling "good" women's sexuality into marriage and childrearing, while preserving "bad" women's sexuality for the sexual satisfaction of men. Silvia Federici argues that this was not merely coincidental to the rise of capitalism but essential to it; controlling women's bodies meant controlling the reproduction of the labour force, arguably the most important commodity in capitalism.[53] Patriarchal values also sat neatly alongside the rest of the colonizers' ideological baggage — hierarchy, discipline, exploitation — which were the hallmarks of settler capitalism.[54]

Notably, while Indigenous civilizations in North America prior to European contact possessed a range of attitudes around gender and sexuality, much evidence suggests that the kind of patriarchy and sexualized violence exhibited by the colonizers was extremely rare.[55] Many Indigenous societies had considerably more egalitarian politics; indeed, European conquerors were surprised by the degree of respect that even male warriors had for women. One English general remarked on the fact that Indigenous war parties did not use sexual violence against their enemies, a fact that seemed to surprise the Europeans, for whom such behaviour had become normal. These patterns only began to change after centuries of relations with Europeans and, especially, as Indigenous societies were increasingly defeated and forced to assimilate.[56]

The earliest illustrations of this dynamic can be traced back to the efforts by French Jesuit missionaries to convert Indigenous people in the 17th century. In a pattern that would be repeated time and again across what became Canada, the greatest resistance to Christian conversion and other forms of assimilation came from Indigenous women. One of the primary reasons for this was that Indigenous gender relations tended to be much more egalitarian than the strict patriarchal authority the Europeans sought to impose. Jesuits were perplexed that Indigenous women exercised control over many aspects of family and community life, that their labour was valued as much or more than that of men, that women shared amongst one another the responsibility of raising children (as opposed to their being raised in nuclear families), that women were empowered to overrule their husbands or even leave them without difficulty or shame, and that the norms around sexuality were very relaxed.[57]

The Jesuits were horrified by this power — economic, political, social, sexual — that women possessed. In the 1630s, missionary Paul Le Jaune wrote: "The women have great power here… a man may promise you something, and, if he does not keep his promise… he tells you his wife did not wish to do it. I told him that he was the master and that in France women do not rule their husbands."[58] Another Jesuit was shocked by the "debauches, indecent dances, and shameful acts of concubinage" he witnessed among Indigenous women, and yet another bemoaned the fact that Indigenous women refused to be controlled: "a Young Woman, say they, is Master of her own Body… and free to do what she pleases."[59] The missionaries sought to curb women's power by explicitly courting the men for conversion and then encouraging them to assert their will over their wives.

Women, as a result, tended to be the most resistant to the changes being pushed by the missionaries and the fur trade. Carol Devens notes that "women declined conversion and stressed the importance of older rituals and practices" which were central to the existing social relationships. When one Jesuit preached the eternal fires of his hell, he reported that the women replied with sarcasm, "That if their Threats be well grounded, the Mountains of the other World must consist of the Ashes of souls."[60] When the priests persisted in their efforts, some women brought the fires of hell upon them directly, as when a Father Andre found his cabin torched. But women's resistance ultimately weakened, as the pressures of the fur trade and the growing incidence of disease and territorial encroachment made their communities more and more vulnerable.

The gradual degradation of Indigenous society by European conquest was reflected in the diminishing position of Indigenous women. Thus, the patterns that were present in New France were in many ways replicated in the Canadian conquest of the west. Dakelh (or Carrier) society, for instance, traditionally stressed gender equality; clans were matrilineal, and age, rather than gender, tended to determine political authority. The gendered division of labour was flexible and gave no advantage to men. In fact, women tended to organize and supervise that division of labour, and it was female elders who held the important role of storing and accounting for surplus production. This all changed gradually but decisively with European contact in the 19th century; whites promoted men into the role of "chief" and dealt exclusively with them, while missionaries established garrisons of coercive authority — magistrates, watchmen, soldiers — to enforce patriarchal Christian law.[61] Shortly thereafter, the Indian Act formalized Canada's establishment of male colonial domination.

Métis women came under particular pressure to conform to European gender roles, given their mixed-race heritage and the fact that Métis society more closely resembled that of the French. As such, even while other Indigenous women on the plains had retained some of their social status, Métis women at Red River were increasingly controlled, subject to domestic violence and relegated to inferior status. Even still, their subjugation was by no means complete, and Métis women in the late 19th century recognized that their best chances lay in the struggle for Métis sovereignty and autonomy. Many were active participants in the armed resistance in 1870 and especially 1885. Marie-Anne Parenteau threatened that if the police attacked Batoche she would "skin them like meat," and many women manufactured homemade bullets using kitchenware and knives. Women had an impact on strategy, as when Marguerite Caron admonished Louis Riel for not sending troops to support Métis fighters at Fish Creek. "*Si vous ne voulez pas aller, dites-le moi,*" she said, "*moi je vais aller* (if you're not going to go, tell me, I will go)."[62] Riel acquiesced and backup was sent to Fish Creek with success.

Nevertheless, despite their courage, the Métis were ultimately overwhelmed by the massive force of 8000 soldiers dispatched to destroy them, and women had to flee the town to avoid the carnage that the British soldiers unleashed. Those who did not escape were subject to indiscriminate violence and sexual violence. When they returned, it was to burned homes, destroyed crops and dead husbands. It was the women of Batoche who bore the burden of rebuilding their society from the wreckage of Canadian patriarchal annihilation.[63]

Thus, not only did European conquerors actively work to undermine egalitarian gender relations in Indigenous communities, they also acted out of their own deeply rooted patriarchal values. The very idea of male domination over women presupposes that violence may be necessary to sustain it; no domination is ever uncontested. Sexual violence, thus, should not be understood simply as individual pathology but as a behaviour framed and made possible by the social milieu around which it takes place.[64] European patriarchy always required a willingness to enact violence against women and anyone who undermined the gendered hierarchy that made women and their sexuality a commodity. Mapping that patriarchy onto colonialism, yet another system of hierarchy and domination, invariably made colonized women the targets of sexual harassment, abuse and violence at the hands of colonizing men.[65] Indeed, given the colonial emphasis on dominating its subjects in body and mind, colonialism makes for fertile ground for sexual violence and can be found all across the history and geography of European conquest.

In addition to being a subconscious manifestation of the twin hierarchies of patriarchy and colonialism, sexualized violence serves multiple concrete objectives for the colonizer. It belittles its victims and their lives and cultures, undermining their sense of self and self-worth, while simultaneously seeking to demoralize the colonized, whose humiliation in defeat is amplified by the desecration of their bodies and those of the loved ones they could not protect. Not only does it inflict trauma and shame upon the colonized, it also reinforces the superiority of the colonizer, who revels in the power bestowed upon him by his racial gifts. In shaming colonized men and women, and reducing them to such brutal submission, the colonizing patriarch now sees before him the justification for his actions, viewing his victims as base, shameful, beneath dignity. To the colonizer, they are less than human and the very fact that they submit to sexual violence is taken as evidence that they are sexually licentious. The act of violence produces the justification for it.[66]

"Everywhere around the world," argues Jean Barman, "Indigenous women presented an enormous dilemma to colonizers, at the heart of which lay their sexuality."[67] In the early days of conquest, Indigenous women were targets for colonizers' sexual gratification, but, especially as the settlement process got underway, this overlapped with a need to mark the racial and civilizational boundaries between them and their inferiors. Virtuous, Victorian sexuality would be "tainted" by settler men indulging in sexual affairs with Indigenous women, who were increasingly framed as prostitutes even when the evidence suggested a much less formal relationship. The very fact that Indigenous women expressed sexual agency in various ways was deemed a threat — they were tempting moral white men into sin — which served to reinforce the objectification of Indigenous women.[68] Thus, white men told themselves that Indigenous women were beneath them and that their sexuality was sinful, thus establishing a context in which sexual violence could be framed as inevitable and blamed on its victims.

European settlers in Canada applied this colonial attitude to Indigenous women right from the start.[69] It repeats itself again and again, in context after context, across the entire history of contact. Consider Henri Julien, one of the contingent involved in the 1874 march of the NWMP to conquer the west. In this, the arrival of the police to the prairies, Julien describes Sioux women in his diary:

> The women, even the budding girls, have not a single feminine grace. The men must be hard up indeed who takes such for a wife. And still, like their sisters the world over, these women put on airs. They have a certain grotesque coquetry about them. They cast sheep's eyes at you, and squint to see if you are admiring them.[70]

The civilized European settler, here, asserts his dominance over the colonized woman; he declares her ugly, unfit to be a wife, possessing none of the feminine grace of a white woman. At the same time, he insists that she is trying to tempt him with her "grotesque coquetry," desperate for his white, male approval. Consider now this remembrance from Howard Adams, Métis scholar who grew up in Saskatchewan in the 1940s. Hitchhiking to his job on a nearby farm, Adams was picked up by Mounties on the highway:

> As we started up, the driver asked if I was from [the Métis community] St. Louis, and before I had a chance to answer, the other cop remarked, "there's a lot of smoked meat around that town." I had heard that expression many times before and I knew what it meant. The comment really burned me but I was too scared to argue. As far as I was concerned, the girls in St. Louis were very decent. The Mountie continued, "I hear those half-breed babes like to have their fun lying down." I tried to change the subject, but the police were interested in pursuing it to the end. The driver asked in a mocking manner, "is it true they like it better from a white man?" I was getting really angry, while at the same time trying to explain that Métis girls were just as nice as white girls. They drove on with comments about "redskin hotboxes who didn't wear any pants at all" and kept calling me "chief" in

a sneering manner. Although they seemed to have an obsessive interest in native girls, they were also implying that Métis girls were little more than sluts and too dirty for the Mounties. One asked, "is it true that they'll go to bed with anyone for a beer?"... That is how the famous redcoats of law and order respect the native people and their society.[71]

The similarities in the attitude of these police, some seventy years apart, is striking. And the continuity in attitude is all the more profound when one jumps forward another seventy years to find police encounters with Indigenous people in the 21st century that possess precisely the same logic. In 2012, when an Indigenous teenager went to the Kelowna police to report that she had been sexually assaulted, she was subjected to more than two hours of humiliating cross-examination from the male officers at the station. Among the comments made by the interviewing officer were the following:

> Were you at all turned on during this at all? Even a little bit? You understand that when a guy tries to have sex with a female and the female is completely unwilling it is very difficult.... Go over again with me how did you try to get him to stop. Did you scream "no," did you say "get off me," did you say "this was rape, I need you to stop?"... Is one of the reasons why you came up with this is because you thought you might be pregnant and you thought you might need the pill?[72]

Just as the police in the previous two cases had done, the RCMP officer in Kelowna ascribed to the Indigenous youth a kind of distorted promiscuity and assumed that it was not possible that the girl could have been coerced into sex, that she must have asked for it and/or enjoyed it.

These are just three cases from the Canadian west, chosen for the way they mark temporal bookends in Canadian history. There is overwhelming evidence that these colonial attitudes towards Indigenous women have been pervasive throughout. Tens of thousands of Indigenous women are victimized by violence every year in modern Canada; Indigenous women are killed at a rate six times higher than non-Indigenous women, and perhaps most tellingly, they are three times more likely to be killed by a stranger.[73] Lisa Monchalin has described the ways that in North American pop culture — just as in the Victorian era — Indigenous women are portrayed as both hypersexual "temptresses" and simultaneously as brutish, ugly "squaws," and that these twin dehumanizations create the perception that Indigenous women are "rapable" subjects.[74] The notion that colonized women are acceptable targets for sexual violence is consistent in the history of colonialism and, as I illustrate in this book, throughout Canadian history; Latin American, African and Asian women have all been victims of Canadian sexual violence.

Nothing illustrates this crisis better than the fact that thousands of Indigenous women have been murdered or disappeared since the 1980s, with more than half of that number occurring since the year 2000. The vast majority of these cases were subject to minimal investigation and received little attention in the Canadian media until activist pressure from Indigenous communities forced the issue into public discourse and led to the striking of the National Inquiry into Missing and Murdered Indigenous Women and Girls.[75] As the inquiry report illustrates, poverty and precarity in Indigenous communities — itself a product of generations of colonialism — made the already "rapable" subjects even more vulnerable to settler violence, and the presence of class-coded addictions among Indigenous people fed into colonial stereotypes and reduced public sympathy.[76] In the context of such precarity, many Indigenous women become sex workers, giving white society yet another excuse to implicitly blame them for whatever violence they receive. The report concludes that Canada's treatment of Indigenous women constitutes genocide.

Even before the Canadian government was willing to entertain the idea that this was a problem, Human Rights Watch produced its own report, in 2013, specifically highlighting the murder and rape of Indigenous women in Northern British Columbia, identifying not just that women were being killed but that local settler authorities were complicit in the violence and were creating a climate of fear and vulnerability for the women. Women would be arrested for public intoxication — an offence committed by thousands of university students on most Saturday nights across Canada — and placed in cells where they would be attacked while guards watched. Indigenous sex workers were assaulted routinely and with impunity, since those committing the assaults were often police, judges, lawyers and other officials. Indeed, the police in particular were involved in a litany of offences, often involving both physical and sexual violence. One homeless Indigenous woman reported being raped in 2012 by four police officers, who stole her underwear afterwards. This utterly cruel extra step was so common that community workers began carrying packages of underwear to distribute to homeless women.[77]

The most infamous single case of such violence was that of Robert Pickton, a suburban pig farmer who murdered at least 33 — but as many as 68 — women in the late 1990s and early 2000s. Pickton had been arrested for trying to murder a sex worker in 1997, but the case was not pursued. As more and more women, many of them Indigenous, disappeared from Vancouver's Downtown Eastside, family and community members tried in vain to generate a proper police investigation; they were repeatedly met with disdain and disinterest. The mother of one of the victims conducted her own investigation and actually directed the police specifically to Pickton's farm, where he was bringing his victims, to rape and butcher them and feed them to his pigs. The police did not investigate and, indeed, didn't even log the information they had received. Pickton was arrested a few years later on an unrelated firearm violation charge, which ultimately broke the case on the worst serial killer in modern Canadian history.[78]

The Pickton case illustrated the extent to which Canadian society considered poor, Indigenous women to be disposable. The disappearances garnered little attention or investigation, even after some within the police had flagged that it seemed like the work of a serial killer, and the case only became well-known when the sensationally horrific details were discovered. Of course, Indigenous men are also targets for police and settler violence. Sherene H. Razack addresses the problem in *Dying from Improvement* (2015), a study of deaths of Indigenous people in police custody and the public narratives around them, and from that study I highlight three cases.

Paul Alphonse was a 67-year-old Secwepemc residential school survivor who died in police custody of pneumonia and "blunt force trauma" after being stomped so hard that several ribs were broken and he was left with a massive purple boot print on his chest. A jury found that Alphonse was a victim of homicide, but RCMP Constable Bob Irwin, who arrested Alphonse and was involved in a physical altercation with him shortly before his death, was not convicted. Frank Paul, a Mi'kmaw residential school survivor, was taken into custody by the Vancouver Police Department for public drunkenness, but instead of being brought to the drunk tank or taken to a detox centre, he was dumped in an alleyway, where he died within hours of hypothermia and alcohol poisoning. Neil Stonechild, an Indigenous teenager, was arrested and beaten up by police in Saskatoon and taken to a location outside of the city, where he froze to death. His was one of dozens of deaths caused by these so-called "starlight tours," a common enough police practice that it had a nickname.[79]

This roll call of settler murder does not adequately capture the nuanced argument Razack provides in the book, which emphasizes not just the fact that these travesties of justice took place, but that they were the product of an entire apparatus of settler society that made them possible. In each of these cases, pressure from families forced the state to open official inquiries into the deaths, and in each case the conclusions were that Indigenous people were "hard to police," that conflict with officers was a result of a "cultural chasm" and misunderstanding and that Indigenous people are "a disappearing race" whose bodies and minds are not equipped to manage modern life. That is, despite ostensibly investigating instances of state-sanctioned murder, the state concluded that ultimately there was nothing that could be done to prevent it. "People die," as one prison guard said after a prisoner died in his cells.[80]

Police violence and sexual abuse of Indigenous people across Canada's entire history has been rampant and routine, facilitated by a broader state apparatus committed to rationalizing police actions and networks of settler media who could be trusted to shift most of the blame onto Indigenous people themselves. The criminal justice system into which Indigenous people were increasingly funnelled was, itself, used as a tool to control and incarcerate them. Indigenous people are vastly overrepresented in the criminal system, prompting settlers to see them as "inherently" criminal and dangerous, when in truth there are a litany of structural — political and economic — factors that cause this overrepresentation. These range from racial profiling by police to lack of resources for legal representation to the ingrained racism of settler judges and juries.[81] In many ways, these systems inherited the roles played by the DIA and the residential schools in earlier periods: they demarcate the lines between colonizer and colonized, a distinction often written directly onto the bodies of Indigenous people.

Colonialism and Resistance

A century after the Great Plains were cleared of Indigenous people, who were penned into disparate reserves and quarantined from settler society, the dynamics of Canadian colonialism had changed. In several respects, the reserve system had outlived its usefulness for the Canadian government. Canada no longer feared any return to Indigenous forms of living; it would be manifestly impossible in most parts of the country for that to happen, given the decimation of Indigenous societies and the extent to which settler society had taken root and controlled the land itself.[82]

As this chapter documents, the post-Confederation period was about consolidating Canadian dominion over the land, and then systematically dismantling the structures and institutions of Indigenous culture, forcing them into utter dependence on the colonial government. By the middle of the 20th century, as Hugh Shewell notes, "most reserve communities had become government-managed slums where meagre relief was given in exchange for labour."[83] After the Second World War, the structures of Indian Affairs domination became less direct, as they gradually blended and interacted with other elements of the government bureaucracy. But Indigenous self-governance remained restricted, and local leadership was often coerced and co-opted by Canadian officials, creating a layer of Indigenous bureaucrats who — whatever their intentions — often served to further the interests of the settler state. Meanwhile, forced dependency on social services and support made it difficult for Indigenous people to organize opposition. Métis scholar Howard Adams was sharp in his critique:

> The three national organizations — Assembly of First Nations, the Native Council of Canada, and the Métis National Council — [were] typical middle-class bureaucracies that [were] not at all representative of the native masses. In some native organizations, the influential decision-makers [were] white consultants and, in the case of the Indian Brotherhood organizations, even employees of the Indian Affairs Branch — the colonizer.... Our real struggle is in the streets and in the native ghettos, fighting with our people against colonialism, not seeking prestigious but powerless positions.[84]

With most Indigenous land occupied by settlers and Indigenous governance largely controlled by Ottawa, it was no longer necessary for the Canadian state to restrict Indigenous people to the reserves, and so movement was much less regulated. The consequence was a gradual drift away from the reserves, especially beginning in the 1980s, as Indigenous youth moved to cities to try to find work and to escape the misery of the reserves, which tended to be underserviced, underfunded and bereft of economic opportunities.[85] Living conditions on many reserves in the 21st century have been described as "third world," a term attempting to capture the poverty and deprivation of places like Attawapiskat, a northern reserve where some 1500 people were "living in tents, sheds, shacks, or condemned houses... with black mould and no running water, electricity, insulation, or proper heating."[86] Attawapiskat was by no means a unique case. Similar situations existed on other reserves, several of which declared states of emergency in the 2010s; these conditions added fuel to myriad social problems already afflicting communities scarred by colonialism and trauma.[87]

All the while, Canadian capital continued to covet Indigenous land, even the small parcels of it that remained after the major land grabs of 19th century. Despite Canada's hold over formal Indigenous leadership, conflicts emerged around Canadian megaprojects — essential components of its capitalist development — like the Mackenzie Valley Pipeline, mining projects around James Bay, and the construction of massive hydroelectric dams in northern Manitoba.[88] Canadian mining companies claimed Indigenous territory in the north, oil and gas companies claimed Cree and Dene territory in Alberta, and pipelines were regularly built through Indigenous territory, despite communities like the Lubicon Cree rejecting such proposals.[89]

Theft of Indigenous territory spurred active resistance, through legal and diplomatic channels, but also in the form of direct action. An attempt to seize Mohawk territory to extend a golf course at Oka was stopped by Indigenous blockades. Efforts to steal Six Nations territory in southern Ontario for a real estate development were interrupted by direct action and occupation of that space. Despite killing Dudley George of the Ojibwa Nation, the Ontario Provincial Police were not able to claim Ojibwa territory to maintain their Ipperwash Provincial Park.[90] These mobilizations were not spontaneous expressions of sudden anger. Rather, they were a consequence of growing Indigenous militancy in the face of colonialism — militancy which had emerged in parallel to the official, bureaucratic Indigenous leadership that Canada had promoted.[91]

As early as the 1960s, Indigenous people had built anti-colonial movements like Red Power and the American Indian Movement, in spite of official leadership, tying their struggle to that of oppressed people around the world.[92] For the first time in several decades, Indigenous resistance was growing. There were at least 300 major Indigenous political demonstrations in the 1960s and 1970s, galvanized especially after Pierre Trudeau's government issued the White Paper in 1969, a clumsy attempt to scrap the treaties and privatize the reserves.[93] The 1980s saw the culmination of a major challenge from the Dene Nation in Canada's Northwest Territories, and standoffs like Oka and Ipperwash marked the 1990s and 2000s. Such confrontations over land continued, while the 2010s also featured the movement called Idle No More, a broad series of actions and demonstrations against Canadian colonial injustices and a social media campaign highlighting violence against Indigenous women, wherein they pointedly asked "Am I Next?"[94]

Settlers, their newspapers and their government often responded to these and other similar standoffs with a mixture of fear and anger. Who were these terrifying warriors wearing masks, wielding rifles and threatening violence? Where did they come from? How dare they try to interfere with the development of our businesses and our economy? Aren't they grateful to live in the greatest country in the world? In some cases, ideologically committed settlers actually mobilized counter-demonstrations against the Indigenous blockades. During the standoff at Caledonia — where Six Nations protestors blocked the entrance to a housing subdivision being built on their land — I witnessed an extraordinary spectacle of enraged white settlers screaming at the Six Nations protestors, trying to initiate a physical confrontation. They had been whipped into a fervour by noted neo-Nazi organizer Gary McHale, and on several occasions they broke out into spontaneous singing of the Canadian national anthem, waving Canadian flags as they sang of their "home and native land."[95] Similar spectacles were made at settler counter-protests during a wave of rail and highway blockades in early 2020 following Canada's attempt to force a pipeline project through Wet'suwet'en territory against the wishes of the community.

Inadvertently perhaps, they had put the lie to the claim that Canada included Indigenous Peoples. They were reminding us that Indigenous Peoples were only included in Canada as a subjugated minority and that at the first sign of any assertion of Indigenous autonomy — or even demands that Canada respect the treaties it signed in the first place — would evoke forceful reminders that Canada is a colonizing force. Settlers often celebrated crackdowns against Indigenous protestors, and the unit of police who killed Dudley George in 1995 even made t-shirts and mugs that glorified the attack.[96] These conflicts threw the ongoing Canadian colonial project into sharp relief: Canada was breaking treaties and stealing land for capitalist development and, in the face of Indigenous resistance, Canadian settlers reasserted all of the nascent colonial values that otherwise remain hidden. Indigenous artist and scholar Leanne Simpson describes it well:

> Over the past several centuries we have been violently dispossessed of most of our land to make room for settlement and resource development. The very active system of settler colonialism maintains that dispossession and erases us from the consciousness of settler Canadians except in ways that are deemed acceptable and non-threatening to the state. We start out dissenting… through state-sanctioned mechanisms like environmental impact assessments. Our dissent is ignored. Some of us explore Canadian legal strategies, even though the courts are stacked against us. Slowly but surely we get backed into a corner where the only thing left to do is to put our bodies on the land. The response is always the same — intimidation, force, violence, media smear campaigns, criminalization, silence, talk, negotiation, "new relationships," promises, placated resistance, and then more broken promises. Then the story repeats itself.[97]

Canadians today like to imagine that this country has moved beyond the racism of the past, but this is largely a myth sustained by the self-delusion of settlers who cannot bear the consequences of admitting that Canadians came as conquerors. The evidence that Canada remains a segregated society founded upon conquest is everywhere around us, if we only choose to look. Just as they once claimed Indigenous Peoples to be "savages" who "would scalp you as quickly as look at you," modern settlers peddle myths that bear equally little resemblance to the truth: They don't pay taxes. They only get jobs because of affirmative action. All they do is whine about the past. These misleading platitudes are shared and affirmed at every level of Canadian settler society.[98]

Anyone who doubts the extent to which these and other colonial attitudes remain hard-wired into the Canadian psyche would do well to read the comments sections in online news articles about two significant court cases: the 2017 acquittal of Gerald Stanley for shooting Colten Boushie in the head and the 2018 acquittal of Raymond Joseph Cormier for the rape and murder of Tina Fontaine. In the former, a white settler murdered an Indigenous youth for trespassing on his property, and a Saskatchewan jury acquitted him on the dubious claim that the gun misfired at precisely the moment he aimed it at Boushie's head. In the latter, a white settler was exonerated despite the jury's hearing evidence that he had spoken openly about killing Fontaine, a 15-year-old Indigenous sex worker. The public comment sections on articles about these cases revealed such disturbing levels of settler racism that many news sites had to disable commenting entirely.

Part I of this book spotlights the foundation of Canadian foreign policy. In this survey of Canada's formative relations with Indigenous nations, I have emphasized the capitalist imperatives and colonial ideologies at the heart of Canada. The picture is not flattering, nor is it exceptional; the development of Canada fit the predictable patterns of a settler colony born out of European expansion in the 15th to 19th centuries. Though it gradually took on a uniquely Canadian character, many of the same basic patterns are found in studies of the United States or Australia, or in more modern cases that follow similar logics, from South African Apartheid to Israel's occupation of Palestine.

These themes are crystallized in a booklet published in 1914 by the Board of Trade of The Pas. The Pas, its name a French adaptation of the Cree word for "wooded narrows," is a town in central Manitoba, near the border with Saskatchewan, where my father was born in 1944. The site is not far from where much of the fighting in the War of 1885 took place, and the town grew in the wake of their defeat. The themes of the Canadian project — capitalism and colonialism — are clear in the promotional booklet, published the same year that the MacKay Indian Residential School[99] was built seven miles northwest of the town:

> In 1910 the Dominion Government, having previously removed the Indians to the north side of the river, laid out the townsite of The Pas and placed it upon the market. At that time the whole white population did not exceed six families. Almost immediately people began to move in and so rapid was the settlement that in 1912 it was evident that The Pas was bound to become an important town and that the time was ripe for organization. Accordingly, the proper steps were taken and in May 1912 the town was incorporated under the name of The Pas and Herman Finger, manager of the Finger Lumber Company and a pioneer of the district, was elected Mayor.[100]

The "removal" of the Indigenous people and the development of a white settlement dominated by a lumber company were not distinct ideas or projects; settler capitalism and the colonial imagination are, in fact, inextricably linked. Understanding culture as an entire economic, political and social mode of life, it becomes clear that the colonial ideologies that denigrate and attack Indigenous cultures are part and parcel of the concrete material practice of stealing and settling land for the purposes of capitalist exploitation. One makes little sense without the other.

This is articulated clearly in Glen Sean Coulthard's careful analysis of the Dene Nation's struggle to protect its territory from the Mackenzie Valley Pipeline and related capitalist projects. As negotiations proceeded between Canadian and Dene leaders in the 1970s, Canada sought to placate Dene leaders with offers of cultural recognition while effectively privatizing Dene territory, irrespective of the fundamental contradiction that entailed. Citing government negotiators, Coulthard explains: "Recognizing the cultural claims of First Nations would be permitted, but only insofar as these claims could be reconciled with [the] 'predominantly private enterprise mode of organization.'"[101] In short, settler capitalism is, itself, a culture — one that will tolerate other cultures only after they have been drained of their essential content and reduced to a collection of tokenistic reference points that cannot threaten the capitalist order. Though it may sound radical, this logic has formed the core of Canadian foreign policy for 150 years.

Notes
1. W. Stewart Wallace, *First Book of Canadian History*, Toronto: MacMillan, 1943, p. 1.
2. Thom Workman, *If You're In My Way, I'm Walking: The Assault on Working People Since 1970,* Halifax, Fernwood, 2009, p. 79–97.
3. Visitor's Guide, Canadian Museum for Human Rights, p. 1. This is not an exceptional case but rather one of more than fifty Indigenous communities which do not have access to clean drinking water. The Grand River reserve in Ontario, for instance, lives without access to clean tap water, its residents forced to drive 10 kilometres to the nearest white town to buy bottled water. All the while, Nestlé pumps millions of litres of water out of Six Nations territory from a well that clearly belongs to the Six Nations under the terms of the 1701 Nanfan Treaty and the 1784 Haldimand Tract. Alexandra Shimo, "While Nestlé extracts millions of litres from their land, residents have no drinking water," *The Guardian*, October 4, 2018.
4. Adele Perry, "Drinking Dispossession: Shoal Lake 40, Winnipeg, and the Making of Canada, in Kiera L. Ladner and Myra J. Tait, ed, *Surviving Canada:*

Indigenous Peoples Celebrate 150 Years of Betrayal, Winnipeg, Arbeiter Ring, 2017, p. 261–273.
5. James Daschuk, *Clearing the Plains: Disease, Politics of Starvation, and the Loss of Aboriginal Life*, Regina, University of Regina Press, 2013, p. 150.
6. James Daschuk, *Clearing the Plains*, p. 140.
7. Edgar Dewdney, quoted in James Daschuk, *Clearing the Plains*, 143.
8. *Regina Leader*, Aug 16, 1883, p. 2.
9. Maureen Lux, quoted in James Daschuk, *Clearing the Plains*, 153.
10. James Daschuk, *Clearing the Plains*, 152–153.
11. J.R. Miller, *Skyscrapers Hide the Heavens: A History of Indian-White Relations in Canada*, 3rd edition, Toronto, University of Toronto Press, 2000, p. 240.
12. James Daschuk, *Clearing the Plains*, 154–155.
13. James Daschuk, *Clearing the Plains*, 157.
14. Quoted in Glen Sean Coulthard, *Red Skin, White Masks: Rejecting the Colonial Politics of Recognition*, Minneapolis, University of Minnesota Press, 2014, p. 13.
15. Howard Adams, *Prison of Grass: Canada from a Native Point of View*, Saskatoon, Fifth House Publishers, 1989, p. 71.
16. Howard Adams, *Prison of Grass*, p. 73.
17. Howard Adams, *Prison of Grass*, p. 75.
18. Gerald Horne, *The Apocalypse of Settler Capitalism*, New York, Monthly Review Press, 2017.
19. Gerald Horne, *The Counter-Revolution of 1776: Slave Resistance and the Origins of the United States of America*, New York, New York University Press, 2014, p. 136.
20. For instance, treaties signed by US states with Indigenous nations often demanded that runaway slaves be returned to their "owners," and black Americans were often prohibited from travelling to Indigenous territory.
21. David R. Roediger, *The Wages of Whiteness: Race and the Making of the American Working Class*, London, Verso, 1999.
22. The concessions made to the whites were minimal, but enough to weaken their resolve for any kind of confrontation with the government. These included reduction in freight rates and marginally improved representation in the governance of the northwest. See Howard Adams, *Prison of Grass*, p. 89.
23. My great-grandfather claimed that his brother, Thomas Shipley, would be the conductor on the first CPR passenger train travelling west from Brandon, Manitoba. He went on to become a kind of venture capitalist in Alberta, operating three hotels along the CPR trail on territory that had only just been seized by Canada.
24. Quoted in Howard Adams, *Prison of Grass*, p. 94.
25. John A. Macdonald, quoted in Tristan Hopper, "Here is what John A. Macdonald did to Indigenous people," *National Post*, August 28, 2018.
26. Riel's role, especially in the War of 1885, tends to be much exaggerated (as in its common referent, the Riel Rebellion) and serves to personify the struggle onto one man, remembered by many Canadians as a religious zealot. Thus, the entire resistance can quickly be brushed aside as the product of a madman, rather than a legitimate struggle by a people against oppression. In the same breath, Riel is sometimes morphed into a romantic figure who helped forge

Canada itself; despite participating in two armed conflicts against the Canadian state, he is taken up by Canadian politicians as a pioneering leader who stood up for the people of the west, as if he would somehow find common cause with contemporary conservatives' "western alienation." See J.R. Miller, *Skyscrapers*, p. 251–253.
27. Howard Adams, *Prison of Grass*, p. 77.
28. Howard Adams, *Prison of Grass*, p. 95.
29. David J. Bercuson, *The Fighting Canadians*, Toronto, Harper Collins, 2008, p. 110.
30. David J. Bercuson, *The Fighting Canadians*, p. 116.
31. Hayter Reed, quoted in Arthur J. Ray, *I Have Lived Here Since the World Began: An Illustrated History of Canada's Native People*, Montreal, McGill-Queen's University Press, 2011, p. 232.
32. Ryan Eyford, *White Settler Reserve: New Iceland and the Colonization of the Canadian West*, Vancouver, UBC Press, 2016, p. 186.
33. James Daschuk, *Clearing the Plains*, p. 177.
34. Arthur J. Ray, *I Have Lived Here*, p. 223.
35. William Duncan, quoted in J.R. Miller, *Skyscrapers*, p. 193.
36. John A. Macdonald, quoted in Arthur J. Ray, *I Have Lived Here*, p. 225.
37. Arthur J. Ray, *I Have Lived Here*, p. 230.
38. Indian Act, quoted in Arthur J. Ray, *I Have Lived Here*, p. 227.
39. Lisa Monchalin, *The Colonial Problem: An Indigenous Perspective on Crime and Injustice in Canada*, Toronto, University of Toronto press, 2017, p. 117.
40. It is worth remembering Glen Sean Coulthard's broader definition of culture, referenced in Chapter 2. When settlers felt confident that they had destroyed the bases for Indigenous cultures as "modes of life" — fully integrated economic, political and social totalities — they became more willing to indulge and even enthuse over those cultures' superficial manifestations. A tragically ironic manifestation of this was the fact that Gabriel Dumont, Métis leader who had played a central role in the resistance in the North West, found himself employed by Buffalo Bill's Wild Wild West Show, essentially performing a stereotype of himself for the entertainment of settlers.
41. J.R. Miller, *Skyscrapers*, p. 278.
42. Glen Sean Coulthard, *Red Skin, White Masks*, p. 13.
43. Alexander Morris, quoted in Arthur J. Ray, *I Have Lived Here*, p. 236.
44. Egerton Ryerson, quoted in Arthur J. Ray, *I have Lived Here*, p. 238.
45. Celia Haig-Brown, *Resistance and Renewal: Surviving the Indian Residential School*, Vancouver, Arsenal Pulp Press, 2006.
46. Lisa Monchalin, *The Colonial Problem*, p. 124–130.
47. In fact, the prevalence of sexual abuse in the residential school system so disturbs contemporary observers that they will often overemphasize that aspect of the schools over equally — if differently — traumatic elements of the experience. Highlighting acts that so deviate from conventional morality, however, serves to normalize the less dramatic abuses inherent in the system. To a modern Canadian, this history thus becomes reducible to the actions of a few deviant priests and nuns, and the responsibility for the entire apparatus of colonial violence around those incidents of sexual abuse is obfuscated. Sean Carleton

makes this point in his review of Gord Downie's "The Secret Path," which told the story of Chanie Wenjack, a victim of the schools, but which "disconnect[ed] Wenjack's story and the history of the residential schools generally from the wider processes of colonialism and capitalism in Canada." Sean Carleton, "Confronting the Secret Path and the Legacy of Residential Schools," *Active History*, October 26, 2016. Available at: https://activehistory.ca/2016/10/confronting-the-secret-path-and-the-legacy-of-residential-schools/.

48. George Duncan Forbes MacDonald, *British Columbia and Vancouver's Island*, London, Longman, Green, Roberts, Longman and Green, 1884, p. 125.
49. Duncan Campbell Scott, quoted in J.R. Miller, *Skyscrapers*, p. 281–282.
50. Allyson Stevenson, quoted in "Colonial Legacy of the CCF: An Interview with Allyson Stevenson," *Red Anthropology*, March 17, 2016.
51. Lisa Monchalin, *The Colonial Problem*, p. 168–169.
52. Sarah de Leeuw and Margo Greenwood, "Apprehensions of Indigenous children linked to misperceptions around neglect," *The Georgia Straight*, June 5, 2019.
53. Silvia Federici, *Caliban and the Witch*, Brooklyn, Autonomedia, 2009.
54. Lorenne Clark and Debra Lewis, *Rape: The Price of Coercive Sexuality*, The Women's Press, Toronto, 1977, p. 111–132.
55. Andrea Smith, *Conquest: Sexual Violence and American Indian Genocide*, Duke University press, 2015, p. 18–23.
56. Lisa Monchalin, *The Colonial Problem*, p. 176–177.
57. Carol Devens, "Separate Confrontations," in Veronica Strong-Boag and Anita Clair Fellman, ed., *Rethinking Canada: The Promise of Women's History*, 3rd ed., Toronto, Oxford University Press, 1997, p. 11–26.
58. Carol Devens, "Separate Confrontations," p. 18.
59. Carol Devens, "Separate Confrontations," p. 19.
60. Carol Devens, "Separate Confrontations," p. 19.
61. Jo-Anne Fiske, "Carrier Women and the Politics of Mothering," in Veronica Strong-Boag and Anita Clair Fellman, ed., *Rethinking Canada: The Promise of Women's History,* 3rd ed, Toronto, Oxford University Press, 1997, p. 361–365.
62. Diane P. Payment, "'La vie en rose?': Métis Women at Batoche, 1870 to 1920," in Veronica Strong-Boag and Anita Clair Fellman, ed., *Rethinking Canada: The Promise of Women's History,* 3rd ed, Toronto, Oxford University Press, 1997, p. 207–208.
63. Diane P. Payment, "La vie en rose?," p. 209–211.
64. Clark and Lewis, *Rape*, p. 111–132.
65. Andrea Smith, *Conquest*, p. 7–34.
66. There is not space in this book to do justice to the complex and critically important problem of the relationship between colonialism and sexual violence. Nevertheless, a very good starting point for making sense of the way that sexual violence is intricately linked with colonialism is Andrea Smith's work on the subject in *Conquest* (2015).
67. Jean Barman, "Taming Aboriginal Sexuality: Gender, Power, and Race in British Columbia, 1850–1900," *BC Studies* 115–116, 1997–1998, p. 240.
68. Jean Barman, "Taming Aboriginal Sexuality," p. 237–266.
69. Of course, male violence against women was by no means unique to Indigenous women. White women, too, were the targets of patriarchal sexual entitlement

and rage, a fact that remains as true today as it was in the 19th century. As Karen Dubinsky concludes, "it is [the] pervasive, random, and ordinary quality of male sexual violence which has led contemporary feminists to posit a direct relationship between rape and the maintenance of patriarchal power." Karen Dubinsky, "Sex and Shame," in Veronica Strong-Boag and Anita Clair Fellman, ed., *Rethinking Canada: The Promise of Women's History*, 3rd ed, Toronto, Oxford University Press, 1997, p. 172.

70. Henri Julien, quoted in David Cruise and Alison Griffiths, *The Great Adventure: How the Mounties Conquered the West*, Toronto, Penguin Books, 1997, p. 318.
71. Howard Adams, *Prison of Grass*, p. 38–39.
72. Quoted in Holly Moore and Brittany Guyot, "'Were you turned on by this at all?' RCMP officer asks Indigenous youth during sexual assault report," *Aboriginal People's Television Network*, May 13, 2019. Available at: https://aptnnews.ca/2019/05/13/were-you-turned-on-by-this-at-all-even-a-little-bit-rcmp-officer-asks-indigenous-youth-during-sexual-assault-report/.
73. Lisa Monchalin, *The Colonial Problem*, p. 175–176.
74. Lisa Monchalin, *The Colonial Problem*, p. 178–183.
75. The final report of the National Inquiry into Missing and Murdered Indigenous Women and Girls can be found at: https://www.mmiwg-ffada.ca/final-report/.
76. I describe such addiction as "class-coded" as a reminder that addictions of various forms exist in all sections of Canadian society. Wealthy, middle- and upper-class people tend to have addictions that can either be easily hidden or aren't deemed social problems, though they may harm the individual or society at large (caffeine, painkillers, prescription medications, social media, exercise, eating, not eating, shopping, anger, guns or television). By contrast, the addictions that poor people typically succumb to tend to be more difficult to conceal and are deemed to be social problems(public alcoholism, nicotine, drug abuse or use of solvents). The latter are invariably treated as though they are more harmful to society. Indigenous people's abuse of alcohol, for instance, is often cited as a burden on the Canadian health care system, but no such discourse surrounds the growing incidence of high blood pressure and heart disease caused by excessive use of caffeine among white middle-class professionals. Yet, the addictions that afflict poor and Indigenous people are chastised as "choices" that burden society. Consequently, the presence of addiction among Indigenous people is often used to subtly blame them for their own victimization. A signpost example of this was the reporting of the murder of Indigenous teenager Tina Fontaine, which often featured headlines like "Tina Fontaine had drugs, alcohol in system when she was killed: toxicologist" from the *Globe and Mail* and "Alcohol, THC were in Tina Fontaine's blood when she died: toxicologist testifies" from the CBC.
77. In fact, the word for "police" in Indigenous Dakelh language translates directly into English as "those who take us away." Human Rights Watch, *Those Who Take Us Away: Abusive Policing and Failures of Protection of Indigenous Women and Girls in Northern British Columbia, Canada*, New York, Human Rights Watch, 2013.
78. Lisa Monchalin, *The Colonial Problem*, p. 190–195.
79. Sherene H. Razack, *Dying from Improvement: Inquests and Inquiries into*

Indigenous Deaths in Custody, Toronto, University of Toronto Press, 2015.
80. Sherene H. Razack, *Dying from Improvement*, p. 193.
81. These are only a handful of the wide array of factors that lurk behind Indigenous criminalization rates. See Lisa Monchalin, *The Colonial Problem*, p. 143–145.
82. There are some exceptions to this, in places where the Canadian state has not yet fully established such a firm grip and Indigenous ways of living have survived or been revived. These are mostly in the more northern regions, especially in the Northwest Territories and Nunavut, but they are increasingly sites of colonial pressure as Canadian capital discovers resource deposits it wants to access. Peter Kulchyski and Warren Bernauer, Modern Treaties, Extraction, and Imperialism in Canada's Indigenous North: Two Case Studies," *Studies in Political Economy*, Vol. 93, No. 1, 2014.
83. Hugh Shewell, *Enough to Keep Them Alive: Indian Welfare in Canada, 1873–1965*, Toronto, University of Toronto Press, 2004, p. 330.
84. Howard Adams, *Prison of Grass*, p. 157–158.
85. As of 2006, around 53% of Indigenous people within Canada lived in urban centres, with Winnipeg comprising the largest urban Indigenous population at nearly 70,000 people, around 10% of the total population of the city. While plenty of employers have welcomed the influx of potential cheap labour, large sections of the urban middle-class has fretted about the presence of such uncivilized people living in their midst. Alan B. Anderson, ed, *Home in the City: Urban Aboriginal Housing and Living Conditions*, Toronto, University of Toronto Press, 2013, p. 32–34.
86. Lisa Monchalin, *The Colonial Problem*, p. 151.
87. Lisa Monchalin, *The Colonial Problem*, p. 151–159.
88. Todd Gordon, *Imperialist Canada*, Winnipeg, Arbeiter Ring, 2010, p. 108–123.
89. The pipeline built through Lubicon Lake First Nation burst in 2013, causing massive environmental destruction.
90. Todd Gordon, *Imperialist Canada*, p. 106.
91. Indeed, part of the motivation for creating the official structures of Indigenous leadership was to prevent the more radical movements from gaining ground. Howard Adams, *Prison of Grass*, p. 154–162.
92. Scott Rutherford, "Indigenous Peoples, Colonialism and Canada," in Karen Dubinsky, Sean Mills and Scott Rutherford, ed., *Canada and the Third World: Overlapping Histories*, Toronto, University of Toronto Press, 2016, p. 29.
93. Arthur J. Ray, *I Have Lived Here*, p. 334–335.
94. Scott Rutherford, "Indigenous Peoples, Colonialism and Canada," p. 31.
95. Alan Taylor, "Brant's vision," *The Globe and Mail*, May 31, 2006.
96. Government of Ontario, *Report of the Ipperwash Inquiry* v.4, Toronto, Queen's Printer for Ontario, 2007, p. 28–30.
97. Leanne Simpson, "Another Story from Elsipogtog," *The Tyee*, October 21, 2013.
98. Lisa Monchalin, *The Colonial Problem*, p. 14–22.
99. The Pas Historical Society, in a 1983 chronicle of the town, noted that the school was destroyed by fire in 1933, which "occasioned great sorrow… for it seemed to spell the end of a great endeavour." The author adds that "we can estimate the value of the building destroyed but we can never appraise the influence of that institution upon its children." He was correct, though hardly in the manner he

intended. Rev. D.L. Greene, "MacKay Indian Residential School," in *The Pas: Gateway to Northern Manitoba*, The Pas, The Pas Historical Society, 1983, p. 81–82.
100. The Pas Board of Trade, quoted in *The Pas: Gateway to Northern Manitoba*, p. 24.
101. Glen Sean Coulthard, *Red Skin, White Masks*, p. 72.

Part II

Canada in the Catastrophe Years

4

Great Wars and National Nativity

Unlike whites, there is no diversity among blacks. They lead the same kind of life, eat the same food, and concentrate their thoughts on the same few subjects. The result is that, little by little, they now have the same identical brain. We whites, on the other hand, learn to know so many different countries, inhabited by such varied people and we encounter so many different things that our ideas become as diverse as our characters.

— William Stairs,
Canadian Military Captain in Africa, 1891[1]

AMONG THE MOST DUBIOUS INVENTIONS of the late 19th century was the concept of "racial science," the idea that different races of people could be categorized and generalizations made about their relative physical and mental capacities. That this so-called science has long since been debunked is no great comfort to the millions of people around the world who suffered as a result of its application, or of the many different forms that white supremacy adapted through the 20th century.

Part I of this book detailed the colonial project from which Canada was born, a project that mobilized the ideas of white supremacy, including the "racial science" referred to in the quote above, to claim that white people had the right to conquer and seize the land that became Canada. The ideology that claimed superiority over Indigenous Peoples worked in harmony with the material goals of the settlers, namely the capture of the land and its conversion into capitalist private property. But neither that project nor its ideology operated in a bubble; Canadian colonialism paralleled that of other European settler colonies, and, while Canadian white supremacy had Indigenous Peoples as its initial and primary focus, the logic was nevertheless applied to all non-white people.

As such, when Canada looked outward from the territories it conquered in North America it saw plenty of "darker races" in need of civilizing, a fact that would remain consistent across more than 150 years of Canadian history. This chapter examines the period leading up to the Great War of 1914–1918, emphasizing Canada's role in buttressing and sustaining the goals and ideology of the British Empire, even while the shifting class character of Canada meant that the Canadian elite had to contend not only with external threats to its capitalist profits but also a growing internal revolt.

Canada at the *Fin de Siècle*

Canada was officially confederated in 1867 and its continental territorial boundaries were determined by the aggressive clearing of the Indigenous Peoples of the northwest. In the ensuing decades, Canada consolidated its genocidal campaign to eradicate Indigenous society through the apartheid-style reserve system, the curtailing of Indigenous political structures, the kidnapping of Indigenous children for re-education in residential schools and the aggressive use of police to enforce these rules. Many of these practices were just gaining steam in the early 1900s as Europe was drifting towards its internal war. To some observers, there may seem to be a strange contradiction between Canada sending soldiers to "fight for freedom" in Flanders Fields even while it was intentionally starving Indigenous people in open-air prisons on the plains.

This is only a contradiction if we believe that the Great War was, indeed, a fight for freedom. If, on the other hand, we recognize that the global war of 1914–1918 was really a struggle between European empires, not so different in motivation from the wars between the French and the English in North America in the 18th century, then Canada's participation makes much more sense. Canada, after all, was itself born of colonialism. The entire Canadian project was premised on the idea that the English were a superior race and should therefore expand the reaches of their empire, conquer all who stand in the way and grow the capitalist world market as widely as possible to their own advantage. The Canadian elite were emotionally and economically invested in the British Empire, and the Great War threatened to undermine the very empire they had helped build.[2]

That empire had created the settler capitalist project that Canada embodied, and the society Canada was building was increasingly divided along the lines of race and class. While white settlers — especially early homesteaders — were encouraged to consider themselves superior to Indigenous Peoples and African slaves, that sense of superiority did not prevent the ruling class from exploiting their labour in order to extract profits. The Canadian elite would use settler racism to keep the white working class divided from Indigenous and other marginalized peoples, especially during moments like the War of 1885, when it appeared that they might make common cause against Ottawa. But the elite also considered the growing working classes expendable; they could be useful as a garrison against Indigenous resistance or as labourers on farms and in factories, but they would be sacrificed for the Empire if necessary. And sacrificed they were.

Indeed, it is easy to get caught up in Canadian settler mythologies about pioneers and homesteaders such that we forget that a growing portion of the Canadian population in 1900 were urban and industrial workers, exploited in factories, paper mills, chemical plants, construction sites, mines and the railway. Despite the aggressive settlement of the west for agricultural production, the urbanization of Canada proceeded so rapidly that by the early 1920s there would be more people living in the cities than the countryside.[3] As elsewhere, industrialization and urbanization brought the harsh realities of class and capitalism into sharp relief; inequality and poverty became more visible and were reflected in the development of slums and ghettos and the privileged "reformers" who wanted to clean them up. Pearl-clutching over the dangers and vices of urban life tended to demonize the poor, and this fault-line of social conflict took on increasingly racialized dimensions.[4]

The Canadian ruling and professional classes were almost exclusively British (outside of Québec) as was the core of the settler population, which dominated the growing clerical and bureaucratic ranks. Notably, however, the later waves of immigration that swelled the ranks of the working class were not; Italians, Bulgarians, Poles, Ukrainians, Irish, Jews, Germans and other people from Eastern Europe and the Balkans arrived in cities like Montreal, Toronto and Winnipeg and were subject to varying degrees of racism and exploitation. Indeed, Canadian industry increasingly recruited non-British workers precisely because they had less wherewithal to complain or organize against poor labour conditions.[5] By and large, these groups of immigrants — in addition to black people and those Indigenous people not confined to reserves — did the hardest and poorest-paid jobs, even as the mostly Anglo owners of the largest corporations and banks generated significant profits. As early as the 1880s there were serious stirrings of a Canadian labour movement, and by the turn of the century, the prospect of a full social revolt was not fanciful.[6]

On the Pacific coast, Asian immigrants worked as farmers, fishers, merchants and miners but were segregated and subject to serious restrictions ranging from lack of voting rights to minimal access to housing. The most infamous case of mass exploitation in Canadian history was that of the Chinese workers who built the Canadian Pacific Railway; their lived experience was closer to forced labour than wage work and they were directly supervised by the Northwest Mounted Police (NWMP). The railroad was completed in 1885; no Chinese workers were allowed to pose for the famous photograph, naturally, but many still intended to stay in Canada and bring their families, especially given the waves of social upheaval in China at the time.[7] Their plans were upset by a Canadian government that feared a diminution of the British character of British Columbia and therefore imposed a head tax — essentially an entry fee, which was progressively increased from $10 to $500 — on every new Chinese immigrant.

Similar restrictions were placed on Japanese immigrants after 1907, after racist mobs attacked Asian sections of Vancouver.[8] Said Vancouver's *Daily Province* in 1907: "We are all of the opinion that this province must be a white man's country... we do not wish to look forward to a day when our descendants will be dominated by Japanese, or Chinese, or any other colour but their own."[9] A few years later another magazine took it further, explaining that "the Jap sets his teeth when difficulties arise and the only way to keep him down is to kill him."[10] A popular bar song in Canada at the time was "White Canada Forever," which featured the lyrics, "we welcome as brothers all white men still but the shifty yellow race, whose word is vain, who oppress the weak, must find another place." The Canadian government had to tread more lightly in its exclusion of Indian immigrants, given their British Imperial connection, but nevertheless found ways of discouraging immigration of South Asians in general, most famously in Canada's refusal to allow the *Komagata Maru*, an Indian ship carrying nearly 400 would-be immigrants from across South Asia, to dock in Vancouver.

Furthermore, when Canada did allow South Asian immigration, it policed their communities heavily in order to root out Indian nationalists who sought freedom from Britain. This policy was personified in the reviled immigration officer W.C. Hopkinson, who developed a network of informants within Vancouver's Sikh community to report on the Ghadr Party of Punjabi nationalists abroad working to undermine British rule.[11] After one of Hopkinson's informants opened fire and killed two Sikhs at a funeral in the Vancouver Gurdwara, Mewa Singh — a member of the Ghadr Party who was in the temple during the murders — assassinated Hopkinson. Singh had dealt with Hopkinson once before, when he was arrested for trying to provide provisions and support to the passengers of the *Komagata Maru*. He accepted full responsibility for the killing, telling the court that if Christians saw their people shot down in a church, they would act similarly against the perpetrators. Singh's trial was held almost immediately and he was sentenced to death in 1915; hundreds of Sikhs attended his funeral procession and he became a martyr in the Punjabi community.[12]

What becomes clear in any examination of Canada's post-Confederation waves of immigration is that race and racism are central to the story. This should come as no surprise, given the inherited colonial attitudes towards Indigenous people, the legacy of slavery and the segregationist (Jim Crow) tradition in Canada.[13] In the mid-19th century, Ontario newspapers proclaimed that not only were black people naturally "savage" in their "native wilds" of Africa, but also "reverting rapidly to the savage state wherever relieved from slavery."[14] By the 20th century, black immigrants from the United States were being frustrated in their efforts to settle on the prairies, and black people living in Canadian cities were subject to much of the same institutional racism found in the US.

As Canada was establishing its industrial base, then, it was also constructing a "liberal racial order," a system combining overt and subtle forms of legal and social discrimination to maintain a racially ordered class society.[15] As capitalism generated its expected inequalities, these were grafted onto the racial hierarchies that Canada was actively creating. Even the early attempts to organize the working classes were largely led by Anglo-Canadians, who often viewed other immigrants with suspicion; employers took advantage of this racial hierarchy, generating division within the working class by hiring Italians and others as scabs when Anglo workers organized strikes.[16] This racial hierarchy would prove to be of great significance in the ensuing period. Canadian conceptions of race would frame interventions in a global context, as the colonial imagination would be stretched to its limit in generating support for the Great War, a conflict which ultimately entailed the sacrifice of huge numbers of working-class Canadians, many of them recent immigrants.

Canadian Imperialism

Even while it consolidated its continental position and built an industrial capitalist economy, Canada was looking outward. Though it gained a kind of independence in 1867, it remained tethered to the British Empire in several key respects, not the least of which was in terms of foreign policy. Of course, in granting Canada dominion over Indigenous Peoples, Britain had handed over what was arguably the most important foreign portfolio, but, even then, British support had been crucial to the crushing of Indigenous and Métis resistance in Canada's first two decades of independence. What is more, the Canadian ruling class was ambivalent about its relationship to the Empire; while some craved greater independence, many still felt deep connections to the old country and held aloft the ideals of the British Empire. The possibility of American annexation still loomed, and the Empire seemed to offer some security.

The end of the 19th century was to be a high-water mark for the British Empire, which stretched across the globe, dominating and exploiting people on every continent. As British enthusiasm for empire waxed, buoyed by imperial cheerleaders like Rudyard Kipling, much of the Canadian elite blustered and longed to play a role in the great sport. Canada's new Royal Military College in Kingston began producing cadets for the Empire, and, as it turned out, Canadians had an aptitude for imperialism, having no doubt inculcated its primary lessons in their founding foreign policy. In addition to filling posts in other settler colonies like Australia and New Zealand, Canadians were sent to fight for the British Empire in India, Central Asia and Africa. In 1884, John A. Macdonald enthusiastically recruited 400 Canadian volunteers to help the British Empire crush a rebellion in Sudan, part of a long war to secure British control of the Nile region.[17]

One of Canada's earliest imperial soldiers, William Stairs, took part in a related British military endeavour in Egypt, during which time he documented his heroism and considered the disaster that would befall Africa were it not conquered by the British:

> Have we the right to divide among ourselves this vast continent, to throw out the local chiefs and impose our own ideas? To that there can only be one answer: yes! What value would it have in the hands of blacks who, in their natural state, are crueller to each other than the worst Arabs or wickedest whites?[18]

To Stairs, the "miserable, yellow-bellied Egyptians" and "the uneducated and uncivilized blacks"[19] were the antithesis of the civilization he was bringing to Africa. His first journey to Egypt was followed by one to the Congo only a few years later, this time as part of an imperial force to defeat Msiri, an indigenous leader in the Katanga region whose declaration of independence was interfering with the profits of the Compagnie du Katanga, a consortium of British and Belgian capital. Stairs' battalion killed Msiri, and Stairs triumphantly reported that "the European is [now] not only feared but respected" and that it would now be possible to "explore the country and open up its resources."[20]

Stairs' second expedition in Africa was undertaken at the behest of King Leopold II of Belgium — widely considered one of the most rapacious colonizers and responsible for the murder of as many as ten million people — who secured his hold over the Congo in part thanks to this Canadian adventurer. Stairs' expeditions left a trail of death; there is no way of knowing how many people were killed, but Stairs remarked casually upon the death he doled out to the "miserable, contemptible bushmen, [the] lowest form of man, [upon whom] the only weapon you can devise is one which inflicts a protracted, agonizing though certain death."[21] In addition to the wanton murder of Africans whom he encountered and the burning of their villages, Stairs worked and starved to death many African members of his own expedition, who were routinely beaten and lashed, had chains attached to their ankles for weeks and were even executed for minor offences.[22] His diaries are replete with racism and savagery, reflecting an almost surreal colonial pathology, and Ian McKay and Jamie Swift note that he was very much a product of Canada:

> In the Halifax of Stairs' youth, Afro-Nova Scotians were routinely ridiculed in the press and often confined to segregated institutions. In the history books, aboriginal peoples figured as bloodthirsty savages, tamed by the beneficent Anglos who planted Halifax… Stairs arrived in Africa with an already well-developed vocabulary of race and a firm belief in [social evolution].[23]

William Stairs was cut from the very mould of Canada; the attitude and the violence he brought to the Congo was precisely what he had been trained for. For the glory of the British Empire and for the capital of King Leopold II, he was applying the tactics of the Canadian colonizers to Africa. In fact, Stairs explicitly pointed to the example set by the NWMP, who, in Stairs' glowing review, had "ruled over 60,000 Indians in the west." Stairs even borrowed a page from the colonization of the Mi'kmaq in his home province, when he "cut off the heads of two men and placed them on poles one at each exit from the bush into the plantation,"[24] a tactic used by the early English settlers in Nova Scotia. And he made no secret of the fact his work was undertaken for capital, boasting proudly of "the openings that will be offered to the expansion of English and other trade in supplying new markets for the goods of the world."[25]

Canadian missionaries also found their way to Africa, some arriving as early as the 1860s. Applying much the same logic as they had in British North America, men like Walter Currie — who set up in Angola — worked closely with colonial authorities to teach the "backwards" to respect their "betters." Currie worked to eradicate local practices like drumming and dancing and to establish a sense of European superiority.[26] He also discouraged resistance to Portuguese authority, describing local villages as "filth[y] and immoral" and in need of Christian "cleanliness, intelligence, prosperity and morality."[27]

Another prominent Canadian imperialist was Percy Girouard, who so impressed Winston Churchill that he was appointed governor of the Northern Nigeria colony in 1907. Girouard called himself an "independent king" and used slave labour to build a railway line to increase colonial commerce.[28] When these practices sparked rebellion, Girouard sent his forces to kill at least 200 people. His rule was so effective that he was sent to govern British East Africa (Kenya) in 1909, which he promised to turn into a "white man's country."[29] His rule was so vicious that even British authorities grew weary, especially after he unilaterally abrogated a treaty the British had signed with the Masai, forcibly relocating 10,000 people to make space for more white settlers. It was a page taken straight out of Canada's settlement of the west; Girouard was hailed by the *Montreal Gazette* as one of the "ten greatest living Canadians."[30]

Stairs and Girouard were by no means unique in pledging themselves to the gospel of capital. Another famous Canadian — though born in the US — was Sir William Cornelius Van Horne, a ruthless capitalist who manipulated politicians and broke unions *en route* to being one of modern Canada's first great monopolists. Van Horne was obsessed with the virtues of war and manhood, and he admired German Kaiser Wilhelm II. He was the president of the Canadian Pacific Railway and amassed an enormous corporate empire in Canada and the United States. His success was such that after the US conquered and claimed Cuba in 1898, Van Horne was brought in to build the railway; it was hoped that his being Canadian would placate Cuban anger over the sudden invasion of Americans. He was later brought into a project to build a railroad in Guatemala to facilitate the growing banana industry.[31] Van Horne ultimately played a crucial role in cementing the presence and profits of the United Fruit Company in Guatemala and the dictator Estrada Cabrera, with whom Van Horne worked closely. While Cabrera viciously crushed Guatemalan opposition to his regime, the Canadian railroad man formed a close friendship and praised Cabrera for giving him every single concession he asked for.[32] A terrible precedent was set that would shape Canadian relations in Latin America for a century.

As the 19th century drew to a close, Europe was entering another active round of imperialism, conquering all who stood in the way of "progress" and capitalism, carving up the spoils with no small degree of rivalry. Indeed, there was a limited supply of world to carve up, and profits were harder to come by after a deep recession emerged in 1873. The European empires now jealously guarded the markets they required as outlets for overaccumulated capital. While they took it for granted that they, the Europeans, were the superior race, they nevertheless recognized that the colonies were a key component of their wealth and power and that these colonies would not be shared equally among the Europeans. Such rivalry became apparent in the brief war between France and the newly consolidated German Empire in 1871; Germany's victory and capture of the Alsace-Lorraine region both announced Germany's arrival as a growing power and spurred French urgency in its colonial endeavours. These developments were not lost on the British, who possessed the largest empire but well understood that the balance of power was in flux.[33]

The South African War

Conscious of growing imperial rivalry, Britain continued to expand and consolidate its global reach, even where that put it at risk of conflict with other European powers. There would be no clearer example of this than the South African War (1899–1902), sometimes called the Boer War, in which the British asserted dominion over the two republics in southern Africa which had previously been colonized by the Dutch. In the early 19th century, these Dutch and some French settlers considered themselves largely independent Afrikaners (or Boers), having settled in the area around Cape Town. But the British Empire wanted the Cape as a naval base and later for settlement; after Britain seized the colony, many of the Boers moved inland, creating two new colonies in Transvaal and the Orange Free State, but several grievances separated the two groups of colonizers.[34]

The South African War was immensely complicated and many of its nuances are beyond the scope of this book. But a few points are worth noting. First, despite its being characterized as a struggle between the Britons and the Boers, indigenous Africans were always a numeric majority in the area now called South Africa and, in fact, black soldiers often outnumbered whites in the actual war.[35] They are typically written out of this history in the same way that Indigenous Peoples are written out of the stories of wars between the French, English and Americans in North America in the 18th century. Africans fought on both sides for a variety of reasons, and, indeed, one of the key points of contention was the earlier Boer request for assistance from Britain in its war against the Zulu; the Boers had accepted British authority in exchange for support, but quickly thereafter rebelled and reclaimed their independence. Although they agreed on the need to repress indigenous Africans, it seemed clear that Britain and the Boers were on a collision course.[36]

The discovery of gold in the Boer Transvaal — and the proximity of German colonies that might be tempted to add to their treasure chest — made for immediate and compelling concerns for the British. British capitalists like Cecil Rhodes were already cashing in on the mineral wealth in nearby Kimberley; diamonds had been discovered in the 1860s and the English capitalists were intent on controlling the gold and diamond trade.[37] Tensions between the British and Boer were further heightened by the fact that the Boer states had been in dialogue with the Germans as the drums of war were beating. The British recognized by the turn of the century that Germany was emerging as its chief imperial rival, a fact that would come to shape British policy in this period and, indeed, lay at the heart of the larger catastrophe that would erupt in 1914. This rivalry over mineral wealth first spilled into a war in 1880–1881, in which the Boers successfully blocked a British annexation of Transvaal. When more gold was discovered on the Witwatersrand, the British determined to take over the Boer colonies for good; in 1899, they launched a bloody war to contain the ambition of the Boer settlers, protect the interests of British capitalists and undermine the possibility of a German foothold in southern Africa.[38]

From the Canadian standpoint, the South African War would be an opportunity to illustrate both its commitment to the British Empire and also its status as an independent nation. By the end of the 19th century, the Canadian elite craved greater power and autonomy within the Empire and sought to win that independence by proving Canada's capacities in service to the Crown. Prime Minister Wilfrid Laurier was not initially convinced, fearing a negative reaction in Québec; still, after rancorous debate, the Canadian government agreed to the path set by a powerful pro-Empire faction, and Canada ultimately sent three contingents of troops to South Africa — more than 7000 soldiers — in tacit exchange for greater autonomy.[39] It worked: by the end of the war, the British had removed their last remaining soldiers from Canada and granted the Canadian militia its own commander, and shortly thereafter, Canada assumed full responsibility for its own defence. Laurier further extracted Canada's right to make its own foreign trade agreements, a power it put to extensive use in the ensuing century.

Anglo-Canadian pundits were quick to get behind the South African adventure, which was soon branded a romantic and noble cause to protect South Africa from the dictatorship of a murderous band of cruel Boers and to deliver the country into the welcoming embrace of civilization and the British Empire. Canadian imperialists rallied to the cause, including wealthy women in the newly formed Imperial Order Daughters of the Empire. On the other hand, the small but growing socialist movement in Canada expressed anti-war sentiment, and many in Québec opposed the war on the grounds that it had no benefits for Canada and served only the needs of the British Empire. Opposition to the war should not, however, be celebrated uncritically; many Canadians expressed sympathy for the Boers because they represented a similar settler identity to their own. Ironically, labour journals which opposed this war of imperialism simultaneously praised the Boer pioneers for having successfully "tamed a wild country."[40]

Overall, most Canadians were willing to accept the idea that the British Empire represented progress and civilization, and that the Boers, despite their white skin and Christian faith, were closer on the evolutionary scale to the indigenous Africans they had colonized. Dissenters were labelled "Canadian Boers," and the still-fresh memory of the War of 1885 was mobilized to associate the Boers with the Métis, as Canada promised to carry "the banner of civilization into the very heart of Africa."[41] Indeed, on the day that the war broke out, a newspaper in Victoria declared: "Civilization Advances."[42]

But the war did not go as planned. After what it seemed would be a quick victory, the struggle shifted into a guerilla war, and the noble British Empire became mired in a counterinsurgency that quickly got ugly. In particular, the British and Canadian forces made extensive use of concentration camps, which historian Carman Miller describes as "places of death, disease and malnutrition."[43] The parallels with Canada's reserve system were striking, and the camps were administered directly by British-Canadian author, and staunch imperialist, John Buchan.

Having employed scorched-earth policies — burning crops, looting homes, sexual violence and executing hundreds of prisoners — to terrorize the population, soldiers of the Empire penned over 150,000 people into Buchan's concentration camps.[44] Thousands of prisoners died in the camps, though he described them as "health resorts," and Buchan used his position to coerce Boer prisoners into selling their land to be given to British settlers. Buchan no doubt lined his own pockets in the transfers, but his primary goal was to alter the character of the South African countryside, making it more British and less Boer. Again, the parallels to Canada's policies in conquering the west are impossible to miss. Buchan would later be a narrator of Canada's noble adventure in the First World War and an open admirer of fascism in the 1930s.[45]

Importantly, black South Africans, treated as an afterthought by much of the British and Canadian historiography, suffered greatly during the imperial scuffle. Nearly one-third of those imprisoned in Buchan's camps were black, and as dismissive as Buchan was of the character of the "unimaginative" Boers, he was unreserved in his assertion of black inferiority; through one of his fictional characters he blustered, "get these strange, sullen, childish, dark-skinned people hammered into a peaceable and prosperous society, and you have laid the foundation of all the virtues."[46]

Thus, when the British created the Constabulary force to pacify the defeated Boers, Canadians played a key role, especially Sam Steele of the NWMP, who explicitly modelled the imperial force after the police who had conquered the Canadian west.[47] It was in the Constabulary where one observes the attempt to reconcile the conflicted ideology that Canada had brought into the war; once the Boers were defeated, Canadians were anxious to mend relations with them at the expense of the black population. Boers were recruited into the Constabulary, only to discover that it entirely shared their colonial attitude towards black South Africans. Steele himself called black South Africans lazy and claimed that they were "untruthful and [in]capable of gratitude," and the Constabulary treated Boer farmers with preference while cracking down on black people.[48] Steele's experience supervising the hyper-exploitation of Chinese workers in Canada came in handy in South Africa, when he was called upon to crack down on black South Africans who escaped the compounds where they were kept when not working the mines.[49] What is more, Canadians participated in the effort to "civilize" South Africa, sending teachers to support a British imperial project that bore much similarity to the residential school system in Canada.[50]

While the South African War is typically not included in the popular canon of Canadian military history, it is a significant bridge between Canada's foundational foreign policy towards Indigenous Peoples and that which it would project into the rest of the world in the 20th century. Recruitment for the war drew explicitly from the veterans of colonialism, seeking those who possessed the "qualities of pioneers in a new country."[51] Some of its key personnel — like John Buchan and John McCrae — rubbed shoulders with great ideologues of the empire, such as Rudyard Kipling and Robert Baden-Powell, and would go on to be imperial cheerleaders themselves.[52] Indeed, though Buchan later claimed that Canada was "born" at Vimy Ridge in 1917, many Canadians initially claimed that mantle for the South African War. One writer declared, "today, Canada is a nation," while another mused that "a new power had arisen in the West," and some even suggested that Canada would soon be the centre of the British Empire.[53]

Behind all the bluster, Canadian capital was profiting. The British War Office had purchased some $7.5 million in war materials from Canada and, during a period of recession, companies like Simcoe Canning and Ottawa Car were pleased to get lucrative contracts for their products. When the war ended, Canadian investment flowed into South Africa with the active support of the Canadian government, which sent trade missions to establish links for private investment.[54] By 1905, Canadian trade with South Africa had grown by at least 1000%, as described by Carman Miller:

> That Canadian businessmen saw trade with South Africa as an attractive possibility is clear from a glance at the Canadian Manufacturers' Association's monthly journal Industrial Canada, which began publication in 1900. Its lead articles in the first two issues were on "Trade with South Africa," and "South Africa for Canadian Manufacturers."... It also prodded Canadian businessmen to be more active and vigilant in the pursuit of South African trade, placed advertisements in Cape Town newspapers, and pressed the government to subsidize better transportation links.[55]

Throughout, the South African War dominated much public discussion in Canada and it is by no means forgotten by the contemporary Canadian military; Canadian Forces Leadership Institute research officer Craig Leslie Mantle noted in 2007 that "the British campaign in South Africa against an enemy that blended easily with the local population, used unconventional tactics and possessed minimal resources is akin to those situations now being faced in Afghanistan and Iraq."[56] In sum, the South African War illustrated and reinforced many of the dynamics that had driven Canadian colonial policy and was an early preview of Canada's foreign adventures in the 20th century.

Imperialism and the Great War

The South African War was but a prelude to that which would tear the world apart in 1914. To many historians, then and now, the First World War marked a cataclysmic break between the old and the new. From the quaint era when professional cavalry would line up across a field and charge at one another to the brutality of modern warfare with machine guns and bombers targeting civilians. From the civility of settling disputes through noble warlike traditions to the barbarity and brutality of total war.

These claims were both true and false. There can be little doubt that the Great War marked an absolute rupture, perhaps most notably in the extent of carnage that could be doled out by mechanized, industrial weaponry from tanks to flamethrowers to horrific poison gases. But it was also the case that the older, "nobler" warfare imagined by those horrified by 1914 was an exaggerated mythology. The violence that Europeans had brought to the rest of the planet, from the late 15th century until the early 20th, looked nothing like the Battle of Waterloo. Indeed, many scholars argue that the Great War was an instance of "chickens coming home to roost"; the seeds of violence sown around the world for centuries harvested in the heartland of Europe to the shock and horror of people who had no idea what their leaders had been exporting. Even this is probably a stretch: the Napoleonic Wars may have been fought between cavalry on fields, but the conduct of these armies *en route* to their civilized battlefields would not be fondly remembered by the peasants whose homes they marauded and to whose bodies they laid claim.[57]

Nevertheless, the Great War was different. It was global in a way that was probably unprecedented and would not be repeated until the 1940s; while Canadians typically remember the Western Front, there were several theatres of war and soldiers were drawn from colonial empires the world over. To put this in perspective, more Africans were sacrificed for Great Britain in the war than Canadians.[58] Furthermore, no war in living memory had ever required such a mass mobilization; this was a war that mustered up to 70 million soldiers and killed 17 million people. No comparable bloodletting had ever taken place, and it should come as no surprise that several of the governments that led the belligerent powers into the war were toppled by its end. Indeed, a mobilization on this scale required the machinery of modern propaganda to ensure that the masses would fight for the flag instead of against it.

This would prove more difficult than 21st century observers might suspect. While the outbreak of war elicited great patriotic excitement, its devolution into an intractable and miserable trench massacre within the first few months made its popularity much more tenuous. For the soldiers in the trenches — enduring lice, rats, bombardment, disease, damp, dismemberment and death — the gap between them and the upper-class gentlemen who gave orders from encampments far away from the front seemed greater every day. For many, these resentments added fuel to a pre-existing fire of class antagonism; the period leading up to the war had been one of serious social conflict as working classes across Europe and the industrial world got organized and formed militant unions. Leaders in every mobilized country had to consider the consequences of creating an armed and trained working class. As it happened, they were right to worry; soldiers often found common cause with opposing soldiers — as in the famous Christmas truces on the Western Front[59] — and the tail end of the war was marked by significant left-wing rebellion and revolution across Europe.

Chief among the many causes for anger was the pervasive sense that the war, and all of that death and destruction, had been for nothing. Even the onslaught of propaganda claiming that one side or another posed some massive threat to the future of civilization failed to convince most people that the war had achieved anything that would make a difference in their lives. Far from a fight for freedom or democracy or any such abstraction, the First World War was a battle for empire. While each of the belligerents had a host of specific gains they wanted to make through the conflict, the core of it lay in the rivalry between Great Britain and Germany. The latter was poised to emerge as the centre of world capitalism if only it could expand; the former was intent on doing whatever was necessary to prevent that from happening. Even conservative historian J.L. Granatstein has admitted that this was "a battle of rival imperialisms."[60]

Where the South African War appeared simple but was, in fact, very complex, it could be argued that the Great War appeared complex but was quite simple. Capitalism was a global system. By the late 19th century, one could speak about a world economy, linked such that developments in markets around the globe had consequences for one another. Those links were tight enough that when a recession set in, in 1873, its effects were felt everywhere. So serious was the crisis of 1873 — the first of its kind but by no means the last — that it arguably set into motion the massive wave of empire-building that took place in the ensuing decades.[61] The colonies would act as mini-monopolies, where only the colonial power would have access to the resources, labour and markets that the colonies possessed.

The events described earlier in this chapter constituted part of the "Scramble for Africa," one component of this rapid carving up of the globe by the Euro-American powers. Despite the whimsical way this process was self-described — in Central Asia it was called "The Great Game" — every one of these conquests was violent and destructive and imbued with the kind of colonial arrogance displayed by characters like William Stairs and Sam Steele. But that violence was rooted in capitalist necessity; Eric Hobsbawm notes that "the 'natural frontiers' of Standard Oil, the Deutsche Bank or the De Beers Diamond Company were at the end of the universe, or rather at the limits of their capacity to expand."[62] Capital needed to expand, and empire was the squire of capital.

Great Britain was still the dominant imperial power, of that there was no doubt. France had accumulated a wide range of colonial possessions but was less capable of maintaining its hold over them in the long term. Germany and Italy had only recently unified into single nation-states, and as such they were latecomers to imperial expansion; neither was able to gain significant colonial territories, Italy's efforts being even less fruitful than Germany's. Other belligerents like Japan, Russia, Austria-Hungary and Turkey had mostly confined their empires to territory in the immediate vicinity of the metropole. While Britain and Germany amassed weapons and vied for the dominant position in world capitalism, the United States waited in the wings, consolidating its continental position though aggressive expansion and declaring the entire western hemisphere its *de facto* empire. It also took direct possession of the Philippines, Hawai'i, Alaska, Puerto Rico and Cuba. Ironically, the struggle between Britain and Germany for primacy in global capitalism would play a role in ensuring that the United States would ultimately inherit that role.

Heady stuff, for fans of geopolitical intrigue, but what bearing did all of this have on the average Canadian? The ebbs and flows of history have all manner of indirect consequences, but any sober assessment of the First World War has to conclude that the ambitions for which it was fought — the contest for a paramount position in the game of capitalist empire-building — were a world away from anything of significance to working people in Canada. What is more, it is hard to argue that the outcome of the war — a glorious victory for Great Britain and its allies — significantly improved the conditions of life for most Canadians. Nor did it better the situation of the many people around the world living under Euro-American domination, whether in Asia, Africa or the Americas.

Canada's Great War

As it had in the South African War, Canada joined the British war effort, this time without hesitation. "Ready, Aye, Ready!" went the call, as the Canadian parliament enthusiastically made its pledge, having assured Britain months earlier that it would. Prime Minister Robert Borden proudly declared the "future destiny of civilization and humanity" and the very "cause of freedom" to be at stake.[63]

For the elite, there was much on the line: Canada's reputation within the Empire, the prospect of asserting greater voice in Imperial policymaking and of course protecting the system through which the Canadian elite enriched themselves. If the Canadian project was capitalist, the framework in which that capitalism was fostered was the British Empire. Canada even had its own territorial ambitions, hoping to gain control over economically valuable parts of Alaska, Greenland, the islands of St. Pierre and Miquelon and even parts of the Caribbean.[64]

In fact, so great was Canada's ambition that its war of 1914–1918 was extended into 1919, in spite of its already having sacrificed some 60,000 working-class lives. Though rarely noted in discussions of Canada's Great War, Canada sent more than 3000 soldiers to Russia in 1918–1919 to try to defeat the Bolshevik Revolution, with Canadian officials expressing "great hopes for a huge Russian market after the Revolution was defeated."[65] Prime Minister Borden noted the "great advantage to Canada" in "gaining a foothold," and, indeed, the Royal Bank of Canada was among those planning to open a branch in Vladivostok.[66] A trade mission, sent alongside the troops in 1918, included representatives of the Canadian government, the Canadian Pacific Railway and the Bank of Montreal.[67]

Notably, Borden was one of the chief proponents of the adventure; he agreed with Lord Balfour's claim that Russians were "low on the scale of civilization" and helped to persuade US President Wilson to get on board. The invasion was begun in 1918; even as the Great War was ended by the Armistice in November, Canadian soldiers were engaged in shelling against the Red Army on the Dvina River.[68] They had been told that they were there to open up a new front against Germany, but now that Germany had collapsed, the absurdity of the war against Russia was laid bare. Borden remained steadfast, buoyed by the aggressive militarism of Winston Churchill, but by 1919, there was little appetite in Canada or amongst the soldiers to continue the invasion.[69] In fact, more than 4000

Canadian troops mutinied in Victoria at the prospect of being sent to fight in Siberia after the Armistice had ended the war; "*on y va pas!*" shouted one Québécois soldier as his officer fired a pistol at his feet. Other soldiers, like Arthur Roy, specifically refused to fight against the Bolsheviks, expressing sympathy with their cause. The leaders of the mutiny were shackled and whipped, and marched to the docks at bayonet point.[70]

That the end of the Great War was marked by soldiers being forced to fight to expand Canadian capitalism is reflective of how the war started. From the beginning, the Great War had been good for business. Industrial plants which had operated at half their capacity before the war were soon expanding their operations to account for the greater needs demanded by the war, and government-led inflationary policies were buffeting demand for Canadian products. Not surprisingly, the corporatist war economy model of state-driven capitalist development led to all kinds of corruption and profiteering, including in the Shell Committee, set up to sell war munitions to the British government, which provided handsome profits for the Hon. Col. J. Wesley Allison and several of his friends.[71]

Profits for the rich, while working people's wages were compressed and strikes banned, would never sell a war as awful as this. Instead, the focus was on Empire, duty, family, community, freedom, civilization. Though none of these things — save perhaps Empire — were on display in the trenches, these were the ideas used to maintain support for the war. The racial ordering noted above was to play an important role; Anglo-Canadians had been weaned on the idea that they were of a superior race — better not only than Indigenous, African and Asian people but also the newer immigrants from Southern and Eastern Europe — and these conceptions were easily bent to the purpose of building consensus for the Great War. Suddenly, it was the Germans and Central Europeans who were to be considered degenerates, mocked as animals and attributed to a lower rung on the racial ladder. It wasn't exactly a leap from the racisms they had already been honing for decades.

And it must not be forgotten that — in spite of all the patter about freedom and superior races and "conviction of duty to Empire"[72] — the primary motive for volunteers to the Canadian Expeditionary Force was poverty. Recruitment for the war was most effective in places where unemployment was highest, and, ironically perhaps, the pool of volunteers dried up in 1916 when the war economy had created new jobs that were slightly better than being cannon fodder in a muddy trench.[73] A war being fought for capitalist empires was being shaped by the exigencies of the capitalist labour market.

Indeed, a rather ironic consequence of the war which had placed such high ideological value on patriarchy and manhood was that it soon needed women to work in the factories — as many as 50,000 did during the war — and gave strength to Nellie McClung's demands for women's suffrage.[74] Of course, McClung's cause was limited to white, privileged women and rung with many of the tones of traditional colonial values; she was a product of the settlement of the west during the genocide and grew into an avid imperialist, fervently supporting the Great War and even the racial theories of eugenics, which advocated sterilization of the "feeble minded."[75] The suffrage movement, ironically, was deeply patriarchal in orientation, insisting that the health of Anglo-Canadian society was rooted in the family, and suffragists largely supported recruitment efforts for the war, which were consciously designed to play upon notions of manhood and masculinity.

McClung captured much of the mood of the early feminist movement in Canada, which Barbara Roberts describes as being "subordinated to their imperialism and to their bourgeois interests,"[76] especially insofar as it grew out of fear of the degradation of Anglo family life due to new waves of immigration. To this group of early feminists, votes for middle-class women would strengthen the Anglo-Saxon character of the nation, doubling the number of votes afforded to their race and class. Their movement clearly reflected Canadian settler ideology; missionary doctors like Margaret O'Hara, Elizabeth Beatty and Jean Hoyles Haslam travelled to India and China explicitly seeking to save women from the injustices foist upon them by their "backwards" cultures.[77] They were also opposed to the labour movement and rejected unions and strikes; famed suffragist Emily Murphy claimed that strikes "punished the [employer] far too dearly."[78]

Nevertheless, as industrial capitalism had grown in Canada, an increasing number of women and children were drawn into the ranks of the working class, comprising up to one in every three workers in Toronto in the late 19th century.[79] Though always outnumbered and less powerful, there gradually emerged a section of the feminist movement that was rooted in the working class and socialist in its orientation. Flora MacDonald Denison, for instance, worked as a dressmaker and rejected the conservative, Christian nature of much of the suffrage movement;

instead, she explicitly identified as a "feminist" and criticized the class snobbery of the suffragists.[80] Helena Gutteridge considered voting rights less important than labour rights, the latter a far more effective protection against exploitation. Alice Chown prioritized the needs of working women and tried to mobilize the women's movement to support the New York strike of the International Ladies' Garment Workers' Union, albeit without success. She was ardently and eloquently against the Great War, writing: "Europe is a vast charnel house, yet still the Molochs of War cry out [for] more… and still the monster is insatiate."[81]

Many working-class Jewish women also threw their weight into the left and labour movements, where they felt their immediate needs were located, rather than fighting with the suffragists for wealthy Anglo women's property rights. Although they got little credit, these women played a crucial role in major mobilizations and often suffered mightily for it. Jewish women, as Roz Usiskin argues, "served in minor positions such as secretaries of their locals. Despite this, women were in the front line of every demonstration and in every strike organized by the union." Those who were leaders and known to be communists were especially targeted; employers colluded in refusing to hire Polya Wolodarsky and Pearl Wedrow, and Freda Coodin was arrested and died in prison.[82] These women and others like them rejected much of the imperialism that surrounded the suffragists and, through their identification with the labour movement, often pushed anti-war positions after 1914 and criticized sections of the suffrage movement that had supported the war and especially conscription.[83] These and other more radical feminist activists endured harassment and intimidation — from the right and even men of the left — for arguing that the war was a capitalist folly, that all women deserved the vote and that their votes should be used to bring about more radical social change.[84]

Indeed, if the Great War was about freedom or democracy, the men running the Canadian government didn't get the memo. In addition to the obvious fact that Indigenous Peoples were experiencing ongoing genocide, Canada significantly curtailed the freedoms of its own settler population during the war. Workers' already-limited rights were reduced as all strikes were criminalized and agitators heavily repressed. Under the War Measures Act, the press was profoundly censored, and many foreign language and left-wing newspapers were shut down entirely.[85] Several organizations that included immigrants from outside of Britain were banned, especially left and labour organizations, like the Industrial Workers of the World (IWW), and people whose ancestry could be traced to "enemy" nations — principally Germans and Ukrainians — were disenfranchised and often thrown into concentration camps modelled after those run by John Buchan in South Africa.

Meanwhile, the crisis around conscription was as significant as any during the war; a government that had promised repeatedly that it would never force anyone to die for the British Empire began doing just that in 1917. The war was increasingly unpopular by this point — especially in Québec — and seven out of every ten men conscripted applied for exemption.[86] Few were exempt, and class played a significant role in such decisions. In the major protests in Québec over conscription, four working-class Québécois were killed by Canadian soldiers; among them was Georges Demeule, a 14-year old machinist. The weapons of the Great War would be turned against their own often as the war wound down; troops were called to put down a mutiny of Canadian soldiers in Victoria in 1918 and another in Wales in 1919, and police would kill one worker in Winnipeg during the General Strike that same year.[87]

Individual Canadians' responses to the war defy any attempt to generalize. They were, of course, shaped by race, gender and especially class. Many working-class people saw the world increasingly from the vantage point of a worker and, thus, came to oppose the war for a variety of reasons. Soldiers refused orders and mocked their generals in letters; civilians protested against conscription and expressed incredulity at the catastrophic conflict; trade unions swelled as anger at the absurd war translated into anger at the bosses whose wealth had flowed throughout. "This is a capitalist's war," expressed one Winnipeg worker at a labour congress, "so why should we let ourselves be gulled to fight their battle?"[88] By the war's end, anti-war sentiment was overlapping with the rise of the left, and when the workers of most industries in Winnipeg began building momentum towards a general strike, they often did so under the banner of communism. "Long live the Russian Soviet Republic!" went the cry at a packed meeting in December 1918. "Long live [German communist] Karl Liebknecht! Long live the working class!"[89] Indeed, the ruling class was nervous, and even a century later, conservative pundits reflected that fear. On the occasion of the centenary of the Winnipeg General Strike, for instance, conservative journalist Jenny Motkaluk described it as a "dangerous" moment in which the workers spoke the language of class.

Motkaluk concluded that police violence against the strike was necessary given the revolutionary possibility of the moment:

> This was the situation in May when the general strike was launched — a world in turmoil, Marxist revolutionaries in bloody revolution, labour leaders across the world praising Bolshevism and using the language of class warfare, and a struggling working class, now full of thousands of men accustomed to violence. *It was a dangerous mix.*[90]

Dangerous, perhaps, to the ruling classes. Of course, Motkaluk was exaggerating the extent to which the strike was a revolutionary event, but the urgency with which she tried to delegitimize its more radical components reflected the class struggle that had exploded in the aftermath of the Great War and which was, clearly, manifesting again when she was writing in the 2010s.

But even while noting the extent to which working-class Canadians were shifting to the left, it is important to bear in mind the paradoxes of a settler capitalist society like Canada; many other working people were still sold on the idea of the British Empire. Convinced of their racial and civilizational superiority, they readily accepted the idea that the Germans — like the Boers, the Métis or the Cree — were beneath them and that fighting for the British Empire was a fight for civilization itself. They dismissed those who opposed the war as cowards, foreigners, and communists, these three categories increasingly linked in the reactionary narrative. The colonial imagination may have been transposed awkwardly onto the Great War, but it nevertheless rallied enough Canadians to its clarion call to prevent an upheaval anything like those that befell Russia and Germany at war's end. And so, at a cost of 60,000 lives, Canada helped preserve Britain's supremacy in global imperialism for a few more decades.

Vimyism

A century after the Great War ended, its most enduring memory in Canada was the great battle at Vimy Ridge in 1917. Many believed it to be the moment that turned the tide of the war and that which crystalized the arrival of a new world power — Canada — to the stage. Canadians had, they were told, proven the true courage and nobility of their nation on that mud-soaked hill. It became the official story in Canada that Vimy

Ridge was a defining moment for the country. Conservative pundit and former minor-league hockey player Don Cherry — famous for pounding his desk while saying outrageous things about hockey, women and foreigners — was among a cast of Canadians who vigorously promoted the mythology of Vimy Ridge:

> On the 9th coming up is Vimy Day. It's very important in Canada — and I know the lefties don't like that — but it was [sic] made us a nation... the French and English tried to take Vimy Ridge for three years — three years and 150,000 casualties — we took up under General Arthur Currie and four divisions of Canadians, 35,000 guys, and it was the first time we ever had a general... and he said "gimme the four divisions of Canadians" — the Canadians took it in three days — they actually took it in one day — it was unbelievable, with General Currie, it was, it was, it was great. And you know [indecipherable] everybody says it was the birth of a nation... we had 3500 killed, we took 4000 prisoners, the Germans had 20,000 casualties, anyhow... we're the best troops of all time, all right?[91]

There are several problems with this thrilling tale. For one, the Battle of Vimy Ridge itself was, in purely military terms, as inconsequential as most of the battles in the war of attrition that was the First World War. In fact, outside of Canada, most military historians do not even consider it a separate battle, just a minor skirmish within the larger Battle of Arras. In trench warfare, where the front lines rarely moved much at all, what might be deemed a "victory" by one side was often simply a strategic repositioning to the other. As such, what Canadians were taught to celebrate as the victorious Battle of Vimy Ridge was considered by German strategists as a draw that allowed them to consolidate positions to the east.[92] Ironically, even the Canadian general who led the mission, Arthur Currie, considered its significance highly exaggerated.[93] It was a lot less exhilarating than the version of events spun by Don Cherry but, alas, the truth often is.

Historians Ian McKay and Jamie Swift call it "Vimyism," a phenomenon in Canadian culture rooted in the myth of a ferocious Canadian division training for months to do what no other Allied force could do: seize Vimy Ridge from the Germans. The actual battle, as experienced by the soldiers who fought in it, carried none of the romance later attributed to it. Its selection as a moment of "birth" for Canada was arbitrary, reflecting only the interests of those who wished to forge Canadian nationalism around the fires of war. The idea that Vimy illustrated Canadians' unique capacity for warfare is ludicrous, given the context of the chaotic and mechanized form that this war took. And even if Canadians did possess an exceptional aptitude for mass killing, choosing to make that the centre of a national project says a lot about the architects of that project. To the extent that Canadians had skill at warfare, it was honed in the slaughter of Indigenous Peoples in the west and Africans in Sudan, Congo and South Africa.

Yet, the mythology is stronger today than ever before. Vimyism, to McKay and Swift, is a kind of "martial nationalism" which insists that "war is fundamental to human flourishing, specifically because it toughens men and develops their characters."[94] Borrowing straight from the pages of the Imperial culture of the time, it is a vision of war wherein it liberates true manhood from the shackles of everyday life, creating moments of beauty and transcendence in the murder of other people for the greater good of the Empire. Despite the feelings of actual veterans of the Great War, it came to be told as a story of chivalry and gallantry in which, as McKay and Swift put it, "the Great War was a truly *great* war for Canada."[95]

In their important recent work, *The Vimy Trap* (2016), McKay and Swift lay out not only the errors and exaggerations of the myth of the "birth of the nation" but also the extent to which many Canadians after the war — especially surviving soldiers and families — were disinterested and uncompelled by the narratives of heroism and gallantry. Vimyism was not an easy sell in the 1920s. Postwar Canada was marked by an uptick in left and labour activism, which often explicitly rejected Imperial grandeur and nationalism as distractions from the real struggles taking place in workplaces and communities. Survivors of the war published their diaries, letters and stories from and about the war, drawing a wider section of the public into the realities they had been sheltered from in the tightly controlled press. Charles Yale Harrison's *Generals Die in Bed* marked a particularly biting, cynical Canadian contribution to the growing anti-war literature written by veterans, joining author-veterans like Erich Maria Remarque and Timothy Findley. The book was histrionically scorned by the Canadian establishment, which was especially scandalized by Harrison's frank portrayal of the savagery of Canadians' treatment of German prisoners.[96]

Of course, the war still had its ideologues. Notable Imperial trumpeters included John Buchan, who had run concentration camps in South Africa and who authored a voluminous history of the Great War he watched from a distance; J.W. Dafoe, crusading conservative editor of the *Manitoba Free Press* who called the war "the most romantic page in our national history"; and John McCrae, a man whose diary had him "aching for war" and hoping his support for conscription had "stabbed a French Canadian."[97] McCrae's famous poem "In Flanders Fields" has become a staple at Remembrance Day services. These men were not unlikely imperialists; many had fought for the British Empire in South Africa and believed in the masculine virtues of fighting for King and Country. Many felt that Canada's valorous effort in the war would translate into greater autonomy and prestige for the country. And, as usual, the voices that most loudly proclaimed the virtues of soldiering did so from well back of the front lines.[98]

In truth, the aftermath of the war was a period of reckoning for those who had lived through it. The contrasting perspectives and somewhat ambiguous relationship Canadians had with the war reflected the contradictory character of a settler capitalist society like Canada. While the elite lionized the war effort and tried to build an edifice of Imperial glory around it, the working classes were less enthusiastic, more conscious of the war's horrors and the fundamental fact that it was they who were sacrificed in its fires and would be again were another war to break out. This view was held especially by more recent, non-British immigrants and, of course, by the Québécois. Consequently, the 1920s and 1930s saw the rise of a kind of war commemoration that was geared towards peace.[99]

This was true of the Vimy Memorial itself, whose sculptor, Walter Allward, designed a monument to loss, grief and torment, describing it in 1933 as a "sermon against the futility of war."[100] It was similarly reflected in a series of war photographs published by the *Toronto Star* and the *Winnipeg Free Press* in 1934. Though the latter struck a more pro-militarist tone, both photo series' conveyed the prevailing anti-war sentiment of their moment. The images — striking, sometimes gruesome, and often identifying the similarities between soldiers of "enemy" nations — were published with captions that frequently mocked the stupidity of the war and mourned its many losses. This was especially true of the *Toronto Star* series, for which most of the captions were written by Great War veteran Gregory Clark, a highly respected writer who captured much in few words. Under an image of "damaged Canadians," Clark wrote of the one German soldier in the photo:

> There seems to be little hate here. But of course these are just

common front line soldiers. Every mile you went back of the line, the hate grew stronger, until at last, when you got right back to civilization, there you found hate in its pure, unadulterated essence. These boys called him Jerry. Back home, they called him the Hun.[101]

Clearly, the popular memory of the Great War in its immediate aftermath was much more critical than its architects would have liked. Nevertheless, plenty of Canadian settlers still believed in the ideas that had been at the heart of the war, even if they were disillusioned by the war itself. Working-class consciousness was limited and undermined by the sense, held by many Anglo-Canadians, of their unique civilizational position. These were conquerors; they had conquered the land, the Indians, the Africans and now the Germans. This Canada was their birthright, their prize, and even the horror of the Great War could not undo an ideology set so deep. Thus, Canada emerged with an equivocal memory of the catastrophic war that so scarred a generation in Europe and which led directly to the collapse of several European governments, a re-drawing of the world map and the rise of far-left and far-right movements that would utterly do away with the 19th century world.

Notes

1. William Stairs, quoted in Roy Maclaren, ed, *African Exploits: The Diaries of William Stairs, 1887–1892*, Kingston, McGill-Queens University Press, 1998, p. 333.
2. Carl Berger, *The Sense of Power: Studies in the Ideas of Canadian Imperialism 1867-1914*, 2nd ed., Toronto, University of Toronto Press, 2013.
3. Robert Craig Brown and Ramsay Cook, *Canada 1896-1921: A Nation Transformed*, Toronto, The Canadian Publishers, 1976, p. 2.
4. Barrington Walker, "Immigration Policy, Colonization, and the Development of a White Canada," in Karen Dubinsky, Sean Mills and Scott Rutherford, ed., *Canada and the Third World: Overlapping Histories*, Toronto, University of Toronto Press, 2016, p. 37–59.
5. J.M. Bumsted, *A History of the Canadian Peoples*, 4th ed, Oxford, Oxford University Press, 2011, p. 263.
6. Margaret Conrad, *A Concise History of Canada*, Cambridge, Cambridge University Press, 2012, p. 175–178.
7. These included the so-called Opium Wars — British wars against the Qing Dynasty to maintain British control of the drug trade — and the Taiping Rebellion, a millenarian peasant revolt which was fuelled in part by the material and psychological consequences of British and other foreign powers' successful imperial interventions in China.

8. Margaret Conrad, *Concise History*, p. 172.
9. Quoted in Ken Adachi, *The Enemy That Never Was: A History of Japanese Canadians*, Toronto, The Canadian Publishers, 1976, p. 63.
10. Quoted in Ken Adachi, *The Enemy*, p. 133.
11. Hugh J.M. Johnson, "The Surveillance of Indian Nationalists in North America," *BC Studies*, 78, Summer 1988.
12. Hugh J.M. Johnson, *The Voyage of the Komagata Maru: The Sikh Challenge to Canada's Colour Bar*, Vancouver, UBC Press, 2014.
13. Barrington Walker, "Immigration Policy, Colonization, and the Development of a White Canada," p. 48–49.
14. Quoted in Barrington Walker, "Immigration Policy, Colonization, and the Development of a White Canada," p. 51.
15. Ian McKay, cited in Barrington Walker, "Immigration Policy, Colonization, and the Development of a White Canada," p. 49.
16. J.M. Bumsted, *A History of the Canadian Peoples*, p. 264.
17. R.T. Naylor, *Canada in the European Age, 1453–1919*, Vancouver, New Star Books, 1987, p. 491.
18. William Stairs, quoted in Roy Maclaren, ed, *African Exploits*, p. 317.
19. William Stairs, in Roy Maclaren, ed, *African Exploits*, p. 340.
20. Ian McKay and Jamie Swift, *Warrior Nation: Rebranding Canada in an Age of Anxiety*, Toronto, Between the Lines, 2012, p. 41.
21. William Stairs, quoted in McKay and Swift, *Warrior Nation*, p. 50.
22. McKay and Swift, *Warrior Nation*, p. 45.
23. McKay and Swift, *Warrior Nation*, p. 49.
24. McKay and Swift, *Warrior Nation*, p. 47.
25. William Stairs, quoted in McKay and Swift, *Warrior Nation*, p. 53.
26. Yves Engler, *Canada in Africa: 300 Years of Aid and Exploitation*, Halifax, Fernwood, 2015, p. 63.
27. Walter Currie, quoted in Engler, *Canada in Africa*, p. 64–65.
28. Nearly a century later, Canadian Lt.-Col. Carol Mathieu called himself the "King of Belet Huen," shortly before playing a lead role in the torture and murder of Somali children in 1993.
29. Percy Girouard, quoted in Engler, *Canada in Africa*, p. 69.
30. Quoted in Engler, *Canada in Africa*, p. 71.
31. Van Horne pompously claimed that the Guatemalans were amazed by his courage and daring in riding his donkey along the cliffs on the mountains outside Guatemala City. It is doubtful that they were so awe-inspired. Peter McFarlane, *Northern Shadows: Canadians and Central America*, Toronto, Between the Lines, 1989, p. 35.
32. Peter McFarlane, *Northern Shadows*, p. 25–39.
33. This is described in detail in Eric Hobsbawm's classic *The Age of Empire* (1989), as well as in his introduction to *The Age of Extremes* (1994).
34. Martin Bossenbroek, *The Boer War*, New York, Seven Stories, 2018.
35. Carman Miller, *Canada's Little War: Fighting for the British Empire in Southern Africa*, Toronto, James Lorimer and Co, 2003, p. 8.
36. Carman Miller, *Painting the Map Red: Canada and the South African War, 1899–1902*, Montreal, McGill-Queen's Press, 1993, p. 3–15.

37. Martin Meredith, *Diamonds, Gold, and War: The British, the Boers, and the Making of South Africa*, New York, Public Affairs, 2007.
38. Martin Meredith, *Diamonds, Gold, and War*, p. 143–152.
39. Carman Miller, *Painting the Map Red*, p. 30–48.
40. Carman Miller, *Canada's Little War*, p. 16.
41. McKay and Swift, *Warrior Nation*, p. 58.
42. Carman Miller, *Canada's Little War*, 18.
43. Carman Miller, quoted in McKay and Swift, *Warrior Nation*, p. 58.
44. McKay and Swift, *Warrior Nation*, p. 58–59.
45. Eric Hobsbawm, *The Age of Extremes: A History of the World, 1914–1991*, New York, Vintage Books, 1996, p. 123.
46. John Buchan, quoted in McKay and Swift, *Warrior Nation*, p. 61.
47. Carman Miller, *Painting the Map Red*, p. 387.
48. Carman Miller, *Painting the Map Red*, p. 389.
49. Carman Miller, *Painting the Map Red*, p. 389.
50. Carman Miller, *Canada's Little War*, p. 90.
51. W.S. Evans, *The Canadian Contingents and Canadian Imperialism*, Toronto, Publisher's Syndicate Ltd, 1901, p. 124.
52. Carman Miller, *Painting the Map Red*, p. 198. Buchan and McCrae are central to the Canadian nationalist narrative of the First World War. McCrae was the author of the poem "In Flanders Fields," still recited every November 11 across Canada, and it was Buchan who coined the phrase that Canada's battle of Vimy Ridge was the "birth of a nation." Kipling, of course, was the archetype of imperialist culture, and Robert Baden-Powell was the founder of the intensely militarist and imperial Boy Scouts movement.
53. Carman Miller, *Canada's Little War*, p. 94.
54. Carman Miller, *Canada's Little War*, p. 95.
55. Carman Miller, *Painting the Map Red*, p. 428.
56. Craig Leslie Mantle, *Learning the Hard Way*, Kingston, Canadian Defense Academy Press, 2007, p. 2.
57. David Bell, *The First Total War: Napoleon's Europe and the Birth of Warfare as We Know It*, Boston, Houghton Mifflin, 2007.
58. Hew Strachan has estimated that some 90,000 African porters were killed in service to Britain during the war, nearly half again the approximately 60,000 Canadians. This number doesn't even include Africans who were forced or volunteered to fight for the other powers. Ian McKay and Jamie Swift, *The Vimy Trap*, Toronto, Between the Lines, 2016, p. 36.
59. These were a remarkable statement of class solidarity under the most extreme conditions, though they were typically not couched in such lofty terms. To those who gathered in "no-man's land" for impromptu football matches and Christmas masses, the overwhelming emotion tended to be relief at the short break from the horror. Soldiers who participated in the truces were punished and dispersed to different places along the front, and generals would subsequently order heavy shelling around the holiday season in order to prevent any further fraternizing. Ian McKay and Jamie Swift, *The Vimy Trap*, p. 57–59.
60. J.L. Granatstein, *The Last Good War: An Illustrated History of Canada in the Second World War, 1939–1945*, Toronto, Douglas and McIntyre, 2005, p. viii.

61. Many historians and economists have explained the dynamic within capitalism whereby the system periodically and inescapably produces excess capacity to produce goods but diminishing ability to profit from them. This is sometimes called "overaccumulation," and when it happens on a mass scale it triggers a capitalist crisis; since profits are declining, capital reduces the workforce to offset its losses. But this only compounds the crisis by creating a larger pool of people unable or unwilling to purchase commodities. Businesses begin to go bankrupt, unable to realise profits, forcing even more workers out of their jobs, deepening the crisis even further. In some cases, this has spiralled into massive contractions of the capitalist market, as during the Great Depression. Whenever such crises hit, the guardians and managers of the capitalist economy have to find some kind of solution, which they have historically done with only limited success. In the case of the 1873 crisis, the scramble to acquire and cordon off new territories for exploitation was the primary strategy undertaken by the European powers and, while it did give a boost to profits in the short term, it also set the explosives that would burn Europe to the ground in 1914. For more detail on the nature of capitalist overaccumulation and crisis, please see David Harvey, *The New Imperialism*, Oxford, Oxford University Press, 2003.
62. Eric Hobsbawm, *Age of Extremes*, p. 29–30.
63. Norman Hillmer and J.L. Granatstein, *Empire to Umpire*, Toronto, Irwin Publishing, 1994, p. 54.
64. Hillmer and Granatstein, *Empire to Umpire*, p. 61.
65. Dana Wilgress, quoted in Hillmer and Granatstein, *Empire to Umpire*, p. 70.
66. McKay and Swift, *Warrior Nation*, p. 78.
67. Aloysius Balawyder, *Canadian-Soviet Relations between the World Wars*, Toronto, University of Toronto Press, 1972, p. 12–14.
68. Aloysius Balawyder, *Canadian-Soviet Relations*, p. 8.
69. Robert Bothwell, "Borden and the Bolsheviks," in David Davies, ed., *Canada and the Soviet Experiment*, Toronto, Canadian Scholars' Press, 1994, p. 25–35.
70. Benjamin Isitt, *From Victoria to Vladivostok: Canada's Siberian Expedition, 1917-1919*, Vancouver, UBC Press, 2010.
71. Brown and Cook, *Canada 1896-1921*, p. 234–239.
72. Robert Borden, quoted in Brown and Cook, *Canada 1896-1921*, p. 275.
73. Brown and Cook, *Canada 1896-1921*, p. 239.
74. Brown and Cook, *Canada 1896-1921*, p. 241.
75. J.M. Bumsted, *A History of the Canadian Peoples*, p. 292.
76. Barbara Roberts, "'A Work of Empire:' Canadian Reformers and British Female Immigration," in Linda Kealey, ed., *A Not Unreasonable Claim: Women and Reform in Canada, 1880s-1920s*, Toronto, Women's Educational Press, 1979, p. 187.
77. Veronica Strong-Boag, "Canada's Women Doctors: Feminism Constrained," in Linda Kealey, ed., *A Not Unreasonable Claim: Women and Reform in Canada, 1880s-1920s*, Toronto, Women's Educational Press, 1979, p. 120–123.
78. Emily Murphy, quoted in Carol Bacchi, "Divided Allegiances: The Response of Farm and Labour Women to Suffrage," in Linda Kealey, ed., *A Not Unreasonable Claim: Women and Reform in Canada, 1880s-1920s*, Toronto, Women's Educational Press, 1979, p. 96.

79. Linda Kealey, "Introduction," in Linda Kealey, ed., *A Not Unreasonable Claim: Women and Reform in Canada, 1880s-1920s*, Toronto, Women's Educational Press, 1979, p. 4.
80. Deborah Gorham, "Flora MacDonald Denison: Canadian Feminist," in Linda Kealey, ed., *A Not Unreasonable Claim: Women and Reform in Canada, 1880s-1920s*, Toronto, Women's Educational Press, 1979, p. 47–70.
81. Alice Chown, quoted in McKay and Swift, *The Vimy Trap*, p. 54. Though chastised by church leaders as naïve, Chown was far more sharp-eyed in her analysis than most of her contemporaries; in 1918 she criticized the peace treaty that was so clearly designed to blame and punish Germany alone, correctly predicting that it would lay the groundwork for the next war.
82. Roz Usiskin, "Winnipeg's Jewish Women of the Left: Traditional and Radical," in Daniel Stone, ed., *Jewish Radicalism in Winnipeg, 1905–1960*, Winnipeg, Jewish Heritage Centre, 2002, p. 119.
83. Carol Bacchi, in Linda Kealey, ed., *A Not Unreasonable Claim: Women and Reform in Canada, 1880s–1920s*, Toronto, Women's Educational Press, 1979, p. 106.
84. Daniel Francis, *Seeing Reds: The Red Scare of 1918–1919, Canada's First War on Terror*, Vancouver, Arsenal Pulp Press, 2010, p. 170–177.
85. J.M. Bumsted, *A History of the Canadian Peoples*, p. 312–313.
86. McKay and Swift, *Warrior Nation*, p. 78.
87. Daniel Francis, *Seeing Reds*, p. 92–93.
88. Bob Russell, quoted in Daniel Francis, *Seeing Reds*, p. 45.
89. Jenny Motkaluk, "Let's not romanticize the 1919 Winnipeg General Strike," *National Post*, June 26, 2019.
90. Jenny Motkaluk, "Let's not romanticize the 1919 Winnipeg General Strike," *National Post*, June 26, 2019. Emphasis added.
91. Don Cherry, quoted in CBC Television, *Hockey Night in Canada*, March 7, 2012.
92. Andrew Godefroy, "The German Army at Vimy Ridge," in Geoffrey Hayes, Andrew Iarocci and Mike Bechthold, eds., *Vimy Ridge: A Canadian Reassessment*, Waterloo, Wilfrid Laurier University Press, p. 233–234.
93. McKay and Swift, *The Vimy Trap*, p. 10.
94. McKay and Swift, *The Vimy Trap*, p. 10.
95. Emphasis in original. McKay and Swift, *The Vimy Trap*, p. 10.
96. McKay and Swift, *Warrior Nation*, p. 74–75.
97. John McCrae, quoted in McKay and Swift, *The Vimy Trap*, p. 39.
98. McKay and Swift, *Warrior Nation*, p. 73.
99. McKay and Swift, *The Vimy Trap*, 105–166.
100. Walter Allward, quoted in McKay and Swift, *The Vimy Trap*, p. 131.
101. Gregory Clark, quoted in McKay and Swift, *The Vimy Trap*, p. 87–88.

5

Flirting with Fascism

> *[We should] conceal as much as possible from the public, all the facts concerning our business in São Paolo ... there is a feeling among the Brazilians that we are making a good deal of money which naturally gives rise to various demands, the most dangerous of which is that we should introduce second-class cars for the accommodation of the poorer classes.*
>
> — F.S. Pearson, president of Canadian-owned Brazilian Traction Light & Power Company, 1903[1]

EVERY YEAR IN NOVEMBER, I show my students some of the paintings of Frederick Varley, a member of the famous Group of Seven and a Canadian veteran of the First World War. Varley's reflection of the Great War is poignant and terrifying. It is misery and darkness. It is bodies dismembered and piled in heaps, in trenches or on carts. Above all, it is a sense of disorientation and confusion. One of his most famous works from that period is titled *For What?* as he pointedly questions the very cause for which he and so many other working-class people suffered or died.

For what? Good question, Fred. A century later, the war was routinely and reflexively explained away as a fight for "freedom," but that was less an answer and more an evasion. Whose freedom was won in the First World War? Certainly not the people whose lands had been colonized by Britain, France and other European powers in the 19th-century scrambles to extend their empires, as in Afghanistan, Egypt or Cuba. Nor those whose colonization was masked by the arrival of settlers claiming "vast, empty lands," a fate befalling Indigenous Peoples in the Americas but also in other settler colonies like Australia and New Zealand. Nor did the war liberate the marginalized or imprisoned within the belligerent countries; Roma and Jewish people remained persecuted in Europe, black people segregated in North America, and women and working people disenfranchised and exploited nearly everywhere.

On the other hand, the Canadian owners of massive electricity, transport and telecommunications monopolies in Latin America — actively deceiving their foreign customers as the above quote suggests — remained free to extract profits while Canada assisted the dictatorships that carried out violence to protect them. In one particularly heinous incident, Canada assisted in the massacre of thousands of Indigenous people in El Salvador in 1932, to preserve the position of Montreal-based International Power.[2]

Despite Fred Varley's four long years in the trenches, capitalism and colonialism were still the order of the day. The grand League of Nations formed after the war to construct a better world had little interest in actually changing its architecture. Ho Chi Minh's petition for Vietnamese freedom from French colonial control was ignored. W.E.B. Dubois's proposal to transfer Germany's African colonies to the League's jurisdiction was rejected in favour of handing them over to other European powers. Delegates to the League refused to accept a clause on racial equality proposed by Japan. At every step, Canada sided with the other colonial powers; Prime Minister Borden was particularly adamant in refusing the Japanese proposal for fear that it might empower Asians living in Canada.[3] The League also dismissed the case brought by the Six Nations (Haudenosaunee) Confederacy after Canadian representatives called "absurd" their claim to be "an organized and self-governing people."[4] In fact, a Canadian official told the League that the people of the Six Nations could not even be considered "moral," pointing specifically to the high degree of status, political power and marital freedom enjoyed by women as examples of their immorality.[5]

If the League of Nations was the legacy of the Great War, Fred Varley's question remained salient; for what was the war fought? To be sure, the calamity and catastrophe fomented by the Great War *did* have the unintended consequence of empowering some of the marginalized people whose voices would not be heard in the League. In fact, a significant turning point in the war was a women's march for peace and bread in Petrograd, which was the tipping point into the long-brewing Russian Revolution, which forever changed the course of history. But these were not part of the plans of any of the leaders who took their countries to war. Quite the contrary, the Great War was fought for empire, arguably the precise opposite of freedom. For the glory of the British Empire,

Canada mobilized nearly one of every 16 Canadians and sent some 60,000 working-class people to their deaths.

And so, as the dust settled, there was a pervasive sense among working people that nothing of value had been accomplished. Exploited and colonized workers and peasants around the world found themselves asking Fred Varley's question, some before the war had even ended. Indeed, it was precisely the arrival of a new round of class struggle — between many of those who had fought in the trenches and those who had sent them there — that was to be the primary consequence of the Great War and would shape the drift back into global war in the 1930s and 1940s. As these decades unfolded, an emerging fascist ideology arose to add a violent new dimension to that class struggle, and the Canadian elite saw in the rise of fascism an ally in the pursuit of its interests, a fact which would shape Canadian policy in that period.

The 20th Century Begins

The Great War had, indeed, marked a rupture between two distinct eras. It would prove to be the last major civil war of its era in the capitalist world, in the sense that all of the protagonist governments shared a similar ideology.[6] They believed in capitalism, colonialism, white supremacy and empire. They were simply fighting over who would be allowed to occupy the dominant position in that world order. But the totality of that struggle, compelled by the needs of capital for expansion, led to a quagmire beyond what any could have imagined when it began. In Europe, unlike in Canada, the seeds of social revolution had been planted earlier and deeper, and the war initiated a harvest of epic proportions.

In 1917, the extremely unpopular Tsarist autocracy in Russia collapsed and, in the space of a few months, had been replaced by a revolutionary communist government.[7] The revolutionary process in Russia dated back as far as the crushed rebellion in 1905, and by the time the Bolsheviks ascended to power they were, by far, the most popular organization in Petrograd, in large part due to their radically democratic and decentralized system of local councils, or *soviets*.[8] The Bolsheviks expected a wave of revolution to follow their own, and this was not a foolish belief. Only months after the October Revolution, mutinies and uprisings began in Vienna, Budapest and Prague. Bulgarian peasants abandoned the war and returned home to declare an independent republic. German troops crushed the Bulgarians, but, later that year, the pressures of the war became too much for the Kaiser's own government in Germany, and a mutiny at Keil quickly spiraled into the creation of a revolutionary socialist republic. Though it was defeated by German soldiers retreating from the front, a second socialist revolution took place in Bavaria the next year, which took months to put down.[9] Revolution was particularly potent in the collapsed Hapsburg Empire, with a socialist republic declared in Hungary in 1919, also lasting for several months.[10] A wave of strikes, protests and workplace occupations sometimes called the Bienno Rosso announced the arrival of a radical left in Italy, paralleled by the same in Spain, both threatening to reach revolutionary levels.[11]

At the same time, the world beyond Europe that had been conquered so glibly by emperors and adventurers sensed that the winds were shifting. Radical movements for independence, often — though not always — imbued with left politics, began stirring in Europe's periphery. Mexicans already engaged in a nationalist revolution against a US-sponsored dictatorship grew increasingly left in orientation. Workers in the US colony of Cuba began forming *soviets*, the Russian word for workers' councils that was now synonymous with revolution, and Argentinian revolutionaries filled the streets of Córdoba. Socialist principles were imbued into Sarekat Islam, a mass movement in Dutch-controlled Indonesia. Berbers in Morocco took up arms against both the French and Spanish colonizers in North Africa. Most significant was the growth of revolutionary movements in China, which would be frustrated for another forty years but would become a crucial stage for the world communist movement.

These troubles did not spare the victorious British Empire. Its first colony, Ireland, was seething with revolutionary fervour that was significantly shaped by the socialist ideals of leaders like James Connolly, while its colonial possessions in Egypt and India were already demanding greater autonomy, both seeing enormous upheaval and struggle in the years following the war. These movements in the colonized world tended to bring together a blending of nationalist demands for independence — either from direct colonial rule or indirect Euro-American domination — with socialist demands for equitable division of wealth, peasants' access to land and various forms of autonomous rule.

Even in countries that did not see revolutionary activity, the organized left was no longer simply a nuisance to be periodically smacked down. In Europe, it had seen its ranks swelled by the horror and indignity of the war and the hypocrisy and hubris of its leaders. These, combined with the galvanized anti-colonial movements in the colonized world, now posed a legitimate revolutionary challenge to the very wealth that the Great War belligerents were squabbling over. If these waves of revolution continued to spread, the wealthy elite would, at best, lose their privileged positions and, at worst, lose their heads.

But Canada was not ripe for revolution. The revolutionary potential of the Canadian working classes was tempered by most settlers' roots in the essentially conservative Anglo-loyalist tradition; a significant portion of Canada's population effectively imagined itself as part of the ruling class, even when material circumstances suggested otherwise. More recent immigrants from elsewhere in Europe or Asia were on precarious footing in Canada, already viewed with varying degrees of suspicion and derision, targeted for exploitation and quick to be subject to exclusion, criminalization and aggressive assimilation.[12] With Indigenous people kept largely confined to reserves, the prospects for social revolution in Canada were dim.

Still, the shockwaves from the Great War were felt in Canada too, especially as the wartime boom ended and recession set in in the early 1920s. Labour strife grew beyond anything Canada had seen before, marked by moments of minor rebellion like the Winnipeg General Strike of 1919 and the coal miners' strikes in Cape Breton. Workers' demands were typically around low wages and poor working conditions, but broader anti-capitalist politics were not uncommon, especially after the Russian Revolution in 1917. Leaders of the strikes in Winnipeg and Nova Scotia proudly declared themselves Bolsheviks, the socialist "Red Flag" was sung on Spadina Avenue in Toronto, and a radical labour conference in Calgary passed motions in favour of proletarian dictatorship and the One Big Union.[13] The Communist Party of Canada (CP) was formed in 1921, and its numbers grew rapidly, especially among new waves of immigrants like Finns, Ukrainians and Jews.[14]

Canadian authorities were spooked and thus emerged the first Red Scare; strikers and protestors were characterized as foreigners, immigrants, Jews and communists — left politics explicitly linked to the trusted tropes of racism — and the public was encouraged to fear their rapacious desire for violence and terror.[15] That the familiar strains of racism were inculcated into the anti-communist propaganda is no surprise; Arthur Racey's cartoons for the *Montreal Star* depicted Bolsheviks as cavemen who jailed capitalists for being clean, psychiatrists like Charles Clarke claimed that Bolshevism was a racially inherited mental illness, and when a Jewish labour activist had his dry-cleaning shop smashed up, the press noted that "these foreigners will learn to lie low and keep their mouths shut."[16]

When coal miners in Princeton, BC, held a series of strikes in 1932–33, they were subject to violence and kidnapping at the hands of the Ku Klux Klan, egged on by the local newspaper, which reported a KKK burning cross as "at once the symbol of terrorism and stern, unrelenting justice."[17] The editor had organized a "Citizen's League" to undermine the strikers, whom he disparaged as foreigners — many were immigrants from the Balkans — being manipulated by communists. He worked closely with the company and was likely connected to the KKK himself. The Klan boasted tens of thousands of members — some 15,000 in Saskatchewan alone — and tended to be drawn from the higher strata of society, defying the myth that racism was a working-class phenomenon.[18]

In truth, genuine revolutionaries were few and far outnumbered by less radical, though angry, workers. But the Red Scare of the late 1910s — and another in the early 1930s — served as a convenient excuse to crack down on labour activism while simultaneously delegitimizing the anti-capitalist politics that were starting to grow among the Canadian working classes. Repression was swift and heavy, using violence and intimidation but also a network of spies, informants and infiltrators to undermine groups from within. Working people were attacked and unions were broken in what historian J.M. Bumsted calls "the most bitter labour violence that Canada had ever seen."[19] Farmers, too, became increasingly frustrated by falling crop prices and high operating costs.

But resistance remained sporadic and isolated, as the Communist Party was unable to unite the angry masses into a common struggle. In 1932, in the midst of the Great Depression, the Canadian left gained a second mass organization in the social democratic Co-operative Commonwealth Federation (CCF). Though progressive in several respects, the CCF nevertheless siphoned energy and membership away from the more radical Communist Party, which had, from its outset, been heavily repressed by the Canadian government.[20] Other left organizations, including the Industrial Workers of the World and smaller labour unions, tried to facilitate larger working-class mobilizations, but these rarely materialized despite (or perhaps due to) the increasingly dire conditions faced by many in the 1930s.

Canadian capitalism, from its outset, had not been interested in providing for the poor. In its dealings with starving Indigenous people, Canadian officials had specifically refused food aid on the premise that it would lead to a general expectation of relief. That they were breaking the treaties they had signed was, by that point, irrelevant to the conquerors of the west, whose statements reflected the sentiments widely held by the rulers of the British Empire. Queen Victoria's representatives in India had said the very same to starving people there who were dying as a direct result of British policy during precisely the same period. "We cannot contemplate without serious apprehension," said Her Majesty's Famine Commission of 1878–1880, "the doctrine that in time of famine the poor are entitled to demand relief."[21]

It should, thus, be no surprise that Canada had nothing to offer its poor and unemployed in the catastrophic depression of the 1930s. Masses of unemployed men were offered only the opportunity to be sent to degrading, exploitative work camps in exchange for just enough sustenance to survive; initially promised two dollars per day of work, they were soon being paid as little as twenty cents per day.[22] The camps were run with military discipline and were explicitly designed to remove "Red agitators" from cities. Ironically, they quickly became sites of uprisings that culminated in the 1935 Regina Riot, which began after police attempted to disperse a group of men from the camps seeking an audience with the prime minister in Ottawa.[23]

Indeed, the Great Depression would intensify the social conflict that raged at the heart of the 20th century: the struggle between the rich and the poor, between the capitalist world and its socialist critics, between the left and the right. This was true in Canada but it was even more acute in Europe and the colonized world. Capitalism, for which so many lives had been sacrificed in the Great War, had by the 1930s brought wealth and power only to a very small minority, while the masses struggled to survive. As left movements grew in numbers, capacities and ambition, they elicited the forces of reaction; a new, aggressive right wing, rooted in the old institutions of authority like the military and police, many of its disciples hardened by the brutality of either the colonial wars or the Great War itself. In contrast to the 19th-century liberal and aristocratic elite, who seemed distant and divorced from the people, the new right was populist in orientation. But that populism was hyper-nationalist and capitalist; it was an intensification of the former prevailing ideology with an exaggerated emphasis on authority, domination and order. It called itself "fascism," and it had arrived to "cleanse" the world of communism and all of the "inferior" races and peoples infected by it.[24]

Between the Wars

The so-called "interwar" years were by no means peaceful and are considered by some scholars more as an interregnum between two rounds of a single war, like halftime in a football match with both sides making several substitutions. Both wars had, at their core, rivalries between German and Anglo-American capital over the profits of a global, industrial, capitalist economic system. In both cases, German leaders felt that their capacity to expand was being constrained by their rivals and sought to colonize parts of Europe in precisely the ways that Britain, France and the United States had colonized Africa, Asia and Latin America.[25] In each case, Russia was to play a significant role despite being peripheral to the inter-imperialist rivalry at the centre of it all. With the benefit of hindsight, some might look back at this period as a monumental failure of leaders around the world to prevent one of the ugliest chapters of human history from repeating itself just a few decades later.

But history is shaped by the material needs and realities of classes of people, as much as it is guided by the ideologies they wrap around those needs. The Great Depression, which began in the late 1920s, illustrated the extent to which capitalism was in crisis. Profits were at a premium and the industrialists of the various Euro-American ruling classes knew that if they did not find them, someone else would. Although they shared a disdain for working and colonized people and a hatred of the communist movements they were building, factions of the rich themselves were on a collision course with one another, no matter what steps they took to try to prevent it.

With that in mind, the interwar years appear as a tragedy unfolding in slow motion, an almost-inevitable slip back into the abyss, with nearly every step taken by the various characters in this drama inadvertently setting the stage for the coming crisis. The utter failure at Versailles to organize a sensible framework for peace was a logical consequence of British and French desire to maintain their imperial apparatus and block German expansion. The foolish refusal to regulate capitalism to prevent the catastrophic Great Depression was exactly what one would expect of governments entirely beholden to capital, as was the opening up of new realms of finance to sustain profits, which was the spark that lit the crash of 1929. The unconscionable sacrifice of Spanish democracy to the forces of fascism was an entirely predictable decision for Western capitalist states more afraid of the organized left than the organized right.

Canada's role in the events that took place between the wars should neither be exaggerated nor minimized. Canada was never a major broker in any of these epoch-shaping decisions; it was a bit player, the supporting cast for the heavyweights in Great Britain and the United States. Nevertheless, two things must be noted: 1) to the extent that Canada could place its weight in one direction or another, it consistently fell in line with the other Western powers, especially Britain, which both reflects Canada's own motivations and also had the effect of augmenting the position that emanated from the Anglo-American powers; and 2) Canada spent the interwar period gradually asserting its independence and accruing greater influence at the international level such that it did have an effect in whichever direction it pulled.

Many traditional studies of Canadian foreign policy emphasize this gradual assertion of autonomy and influence in the first half of the 20th century. It is not incorrect that Canada increasingly attained the full independence that had been set into motion in 1867, but this was hardly a surprise and the process by which this took form is described in great detail by historians more interested in the meetings, motions and letters of wealthy white men than myself.[26] These histories recount Canada's presence and limited participation in the Versailles proceedings, Canada's unique signature on the Versailles Treaty itself, Canadian refusal to offer troops to a possible British intervention in Chanak during a conflict with Turkey, the happenings of the Imperial Conferences of 1923 and 1926, and Canada's opening of foreign missions in France and Japan in 1928 and 1929. After 1931, Canada was participating actively and with full independence in international affairs, including the contentious decisions in the League of Nations over how to respond to acts of aggression like the Italian invasion of Ethiopia. Though certainly constrained by its relationships to Great Britain and the United States, Canada was, for all intents and purposes, operating as an ever more independent state.

Unlike much of the historiography of this period, what interests me is not how career diplomat O.D. Skelton managed to wrangle each piece of independence but, rather, what Canada wanted to *do* with the independence it was asserting. Even as the horrors of the Great War were subsiding, Canadian soldiers were sent to Russia to crush the workers' revolution and Canadians joined the British in the aerial bombardment of Afghanistan in the Third Afghan War. Like William Stairs and Percy Girouard before him, Canadian Gordon Guggisberg was named governor of an African colony — the Gold Coast (Ghana) — in 1919. He used forced Ashanti labour to build public works like railroads and a shipping port, in the hopes of improving access to "immensely valuable resources" like cocoa, timber and gold. Of course, this was all in the service of foreign, including Canadian, capital, but Guggisberg was skilful at covering his actions in a veneer of goodwill; he encouraged some political participation by local chiefs, such that he is remembered as a reformer, though his real intention was to use those chiefs as a bulwark against wider anti-colonial sentiment.[27]

Canadian capital was, indeed, expanding out into the world as banks, railroad barons and industrial magnates struck out to extract profits from those places where they could, especially in Latin America but as far as the Philippines. Initially, a large section of the Canadian elite wanted to build their own colonial empire in the Americas and sought British consent to annex its Latin American colonies in the West Indies, British Guyana, British Honduras (Belize), Bermuda and the Falklands. In 1916 — right in the middle of the Great War — Prime Minister Borden was certain he was on the brink of victory. With Britain preoccupied by the war, the opportunity was ripe for Canada to take over its imperial role in the West. Borden specifically enthused about "the extension of our territory," "the tropical products available" and the "responsibilities of governing subject races," but he worried about "the difficulty of dealing with the coloured population," to which end the British colonial office recommended that Canada send a wave of white settlers to prepare the ground for Canada's annexation.[28] Settler capitalism and the colonial imagination would be the basis for the Canadian Empire.

It did not pan out as Borden had hoped: by the end of the war it was clear that the United States had no intention of allowing such a scheme, and by 1921 Borden himself had been ousted from office. That year, the plan for Pax Canadiana had its last gasp in a proposal that Canada should assume control over Armenia; advocates framed Canada as having all the necessary qualities of a colonial power and being well equipped for the tutelage and leadership — some directly referenced the "White

Man's Burden" — needed to nurse Armenians into modernity. While the Armenians were cast as childlike, the Turks were framed as the barbaric savages from whom Canada must save the Armenians.[29] The plan was seriously considered but ultimately rejected. But even while these plans for the Canadian Empire were being kicked around, Canadian capital had been expanding in the shadow of the American Empire.

Canadian Monopolists

With the United States doing the dirty work of maintaining the semi-colonial status of much of the Western Hemisphere, Canadian money rushed in to capitalize. This had begun as early as the turn of the century and, as Peter McFarlane notes, it was directly connected to the conquest of the Indigenous west:

> European settlers began to flood the Canadian West, turning the prairies into the granary of the Empire and generating huge profits for the Central Canadian elite that owned the Western land-companies, railways, and banks. Canada ... finally had a capital surplus of its own, and Canadian businessmen began to look to the Central American-Caribbean region for their own hinterlands to conquer.[30]

Canadian money flowed south in the wake of William Van Horne's railroad monopoly in Cuba, which had made him so powerful in the country that he co-wrote the Cuban railroad laws his company was expected to follow. Canadian banks financed most business in Cuba — where "Canadian capital and clearer northern brains" were turning it into a "modern hive of industry," according to the *Canadian Journal of Commerce*[31] — and were dominant in much of the Caribbean. Canadian utility companies were prominent in Trinidad, Jamaica and Guyana, and increasingly expanded into the largest Latin American countries, like Brazil and Mexico.

In fact, a Canadian company provided all the electricity in Mexico City, and Canadians owned most of the tram systems in the country, where Canadian kingpins were particularly impressed by the dictatorship of Porfirio Díaz. Officials from Bank of Montreal praised his efforts on behalf of foreign capital and called it a "corporate Mecca."[32] Mexicans were less enthusiastic, and in 1910, the Mexican Revolution broke out against the hated Díaz. But Canadian capital was already heavily invested in the country and, especially as their own interests were threatened by the revolution, they threw their weight behind the dictator, acting as advisors to Díaz. He fled the country in 1913 and stopped off in Montreal on his way to reassure the Canadian oligarchs that their investments would "be safeguarded to the utmost ability" by a new dictator, Victoriana Huerta.[33]

The international presence of Canadian capital grew significantly after the Great War. The dream of a Canadian empire based in British Honduras (Belize) had not yet died, and Canadian banks, mines and electric companies had emerged as some of the primary investors in Central America. They immediately found that their interests were best served by the US-imposed dictatorships; the Canadian-owned Bonanza mine in Nicaragua benefitted greatly from its relationship with the Adolfo Díaz dictatorship, the Royal Bank financed the Federico Tinoco dictatorship in Costa Rica, and Canadian insurance companies swooped in to dominate the Caribbean.

Meanwhile, Canada's largest overseas investment was also its largest corporation and Brazil's largest private employer: the Brazilian Traction Light & Power Company, later Brascan, often called the Light, and sometimes referred to as the *polvo canadense* (Canadian Octopus). It began in 1899, and by the 1920s it had monopoly power over much of Brazil's electrical, telephone and transportation services. The Light got its monopoly through bribery and patronage and maintained it by manipulation and secrecy. It paid off politicians and bank managers, spied on Brazilians and played them against one another, and kept a cone of silence around its finances. As the quote at the top of this chapter indicated, the company was actively concealing its business from a Brazilian public that was angered by its rapacious and exploitative practices.[34]

By the 1920s workers at the Light were growing angry at low wages and began trying to organize a strike, a fact long-known by the company, which had embedded secret agents among them. In the meantime, the well-connected *polvo* was leaning on politicians and judges to extend its monopoly of the telephone system until 1990. This extension was granted in 1923. In the tumultuous 1930s the company continued to squeeze its workers, customers and competitors, relying on the efforts of men like Antonio Gallotti, who was both a company executive and a member of the Brazilian fascist party.[35] By the end of the Second World War even the politicians the company had bribed would grow incensed by what they viewed as "extortion of the people to benefit foreign shareholders."[36]

Ultimately, the Brazilian government would seek to supplant the power of the *polvo*, and, therefore, the company would support a *coup d'etat* to overthrow the government. It was no coincidence that the company — highly connected in Ottawa — received support from the Canadian government, which chose not to criticize the coup.

But arguably the most notable case in the interwar period was that of Montreal-based International Power, whose owner was the son of a Nova Scotia banking family. I.W. Killam would die, in his eighties, one of the wealthiest men in Canada, in part because his company seized a virtual monopoly of electricity generation in El Salvador in the late 1920s. No sooner had International Power gained its monopoly than it jacked up its rates; the Araújo dictatorship imposed no regulations to stop it. But Salvadoran peasants and workers were angry and began targeting the company with boycotts, strikes and demonstrations. As El Salvador drifted closer and closer to revolution, led by folk hero Augustín Farabundo Martí, anger directed at International Power was at the heart of the popular discontent; its offices were among those targeted by the rebels to be bombed.

By 1932, El Salvador was in the throes of a genuine social revolution, as left-wing peasants and workers, denied congressional seats despite winning them in an election, confronted the violent and corrupt dictatorship now run by General Maximiliano Hernández Martínez.[37] Officials at International Power loaned the dictator money to pay his soldiers, who themselves were threatening to rebel, and pressured the Canadian government to intervene on its behalf; luckily Prime Minister Bennett was an old friend of the owner of International Power, and quickly dispatched two Canadian gunboats to deal with the "communist Indians" in El Salvador.[38]

The ships arrived at Acajutla in January 1932. Commander Victor Brodeur ordered his platoon to land on the pier and set out to meet with the Salvadoran dictator. On the way he noted, dispassionately, that the country was obviously extremely unequal, with peasants working ten-hour days for twelve cents. "It is hardly to be wondered that Communism made many converts," he noted in his diary, before meeting with Hernández Martínez to plan the crackdown.[39] Hernández Martínez was jovial and viewed the arrival of the Canadian ships as a turning point; Brodeur offered to have his troops join the dictator's soldiers, but it was decided that the Canadians would — for the moment — remain a menacing presence in the harbour as a warning to the communists that they should give up.

The plan worked; Brodeur described having had a "wonderful morale effect" on the dictator's troops, who launched a new offensive and massacred thousands of Salvadoran peasants, almost all of them unarmed civilians. Brodeur also noted in his diary that many of corpses he passed in his daily patrols were wearing white flags, which they had used to indicate their peaceful intentions.[40] By the time it was over, Hernández Martínez had killed as many as 40,000 mostly Indigenous people, many of whom were forced to dig their own grave before being shot and deposited in it. It is remembered in El Salvador as La Matanza — the massacre — and the name of martyred Farabundo Martí would be taken up by a new generation of revolutionaries after the Second World War. The slaughter in El Salvador, Canada's first major military action since the 1919 invasion of Russia, was over in a few days. The Royal Canadian Navy had assisted the Salvadoran dictatorship in maintaining power and butchering unsatisfied Indigenous peasants, much to the pleasure of the Canadian electric company whose exploitative practices had been a focal point of the peoples' anger. Brodeur was invited to a luncheon, which he described as "exceedingly good," to be followed by the viewing of five executions of Salvadoran communists.[41]

Brodeur, evidently struck with a moment of moral uncertainty, skipped out after dessert and missed the executions. But the next day, after a round of golf with the leaders of the Salvadoran military, he reflected on his experience, noting that while the Indigenous peasants had good reason to be frustrated, their poverty was really their own fault, because "it is one of the outstanding characteristics of the Central American Indian that he is incapable of saving money; he spends it at once in the nearest *cantina*."[42] Brodeur's opinion of Indigenous people — that they were all drunks — was fostered in the upper echelons of Canadian society; his father, Louis-Phillipe, was a minister in the Laurier government. But the only Indigenous people he met in El Salvador were the corpses on the beach. As for the Salvadoran dictatorship, it held onto power until 1944, when it was removed by the US after becoming embarrassingly effusive in its praise for Nazi Germany.[43]

The Canadian media enjoyed the affair immensely, playing up the fact that Canadian ships had "rescued" the country from a "red revolt." Said the *Globe*: "Reds make trouble. Foreign population in peril. No protection… The Dominion fleet is roaming the seas in search of adventure; and finding it."[44] In fact it was the Salvadoran population that was in peril as the Canadians would, as Peter McFarlane put it, "stand by and observe one of the worst massacres of civilians in the history of the Americas."[45] The description in the *Globe* rung to the anti-communist tune that was popular among the Canadian elite in that moment — the *Vancouver Sun* similarly headlined "El Salvador Aflame with Red Revolt: Canadian Destroyers from British Columbia to the Rescue."

But these manipulations did not reflect even the views of many of the Canadian soldiers on the mission, who saw in the class dynamics of El Salvador a more extreme version of their own experience. "The lower decks were with the masses in El Salvador," explained one of the Canadian sailors on the mission. "The class function ashore in the country was like the class function in the navy."[46] The prime minister downplayed the central role of the Canadian electric company, noting only that a few Canadians were employed by the company and that the mission was "safeguarding life and property."[47] It was, clearly, a half-truth.

As Canada was expanding its empire of capital, it was accumulating unsavoury friends. Three of its closest allies in Central America — Hernández Martínez in El Salvador, Jorge Ubico in Guatemala and Anastasio Somoza in Nicaragua — would be admirers and even accomplices to Adolf Hitler.[48] Canada was clearly not bothered by this fact, since it gave funding and military support to these regimes. Indeed, what is noteworthy about Canadian engagements in the tumultuous world between the wars is not so much what Canada did, but what it did *not* do. Canada made little attempt to impose any penalties on Italy for its aggressive action against Ethiopia, in which it used chemical weapons and killed tens of thousands. Canada did not intervene to protect the Spanish Republic when it was attacked by the fascist General Francisco Franco, nor did Canada step in when Hitler's Luftwaffe rained bombs on the Basque-Spanish city of Guernica in support of Franco's cause. Canada did not try to halt Japanese expansion in East Asia; in fact, it offered much support. Canada refused to increase its absorption of Jewish refugees fleeing the Holocaust but, rather, placed stricter restrictions on them. And, perhaps most important, Canada made little effort to discourage Hitler from re-arming and re-embarking on the expansionary path that would inevitably lead to another war.

Each of these cases will be revisited in greater detail, either in this chapter or beyond. But, taken together, the pattern is unmistakable: Canada did not use its increased autonomy and economic power to take a stand against the rise of fascism. It did the opposite. Canada, in lockstep with its closest allies, Britain, France and the United States, tolerated — and in some cases encouraged — the ascension of the forces of the far right, which plunged the world into a nightmare even greater than that of 1914–1918. The prevailing explanation for this pattern of policies is patently unconvincing. We are routinely told that it was "appeasement," a willingness to give Hitler and his allies what they wanted out of a desire to avoid war. Depending on who is weaving the narrative, this may be characterized as weakness, naïveté, respect for domestic anti-war sentiment or some combination of the three. Yet it is almost never suggested that Canada and its allies might have been *sympathetic* to fascism. Such a notion is considered absurd, almost heretical, given that — in the end — Canadian soldiers like my dad's eldest brother-in-law were sent to pay the ultimate sacrifice to defeat Nazi Germany and its allies. And yet, contradictory though it might seem, Canada did much to facilitate the rise of the very fascist states my uncle ultimately fought against in the Second World War.

The Spanish Civil War

The dating of wars can be an odd formality. Few conflicts happen spontaneously, and those with global reach typically have multiple beginnings and endings depending on one's location or perspective. Thus, while the Second World War is typically dated 1939–1945, there are many who might insist upon an earlier start date, perhaps reflecting the timelines of Japanese conquests in Asia. There is also a strong argument to be made that what is called the Spanish Civil War marked the opening stage of the conflict in Europe. For many, it was considered the moment of truth for the so-called Western democracies, in which they were faced with a clear-cut case in which a democratic government was being attacked by a fascist military general with support from other fascist states. If there had ever been a time to send a message that fascism would not be tolerated, this would have been it. As it happened, fascism was tolerated.

By the middle of the 1930s, Hitler had consolidated power, had murdered thousands of German leftists, had initiated a whole series of measures against other "undesirables," was rapidly building a modern military and was making no secret of his ambition to expand German territory. At the same time, an internationally recognized democratic government in Spain was under attack by the forces of fascist General Francisco Franco; Hitler offered direct material support, most infamously in the 1937 aerial bombardment of Guernica. Over a thousand people, most of them civilians, were killed in that city by Hitler's bombs. There could hardly be clearer evidence that Hitler wanted to see a fascist Europe, and he was slaughtering people in Spain to ensure as much. If the Second World War was motivated by moral revulsion at the evils of Nazi Germany, one cannot help wondering why that revulsion did not kick in as Guernica burned.

But Guernica did not move the governments of the West. In the grand calculations of Britons, French, Canadians and Americans, the fall of Spain to a brutal tyranny was a domestic affair in which they had little interest. To the 21st-century audience this may seem odd. Why let Hitler drop bombs on civilians in Spain to consolidate a fascist government there, while drawing the line only two years later when he moved his forces into neighbouring Poland? Much of Poland had, in truth, been located within German territory prior to the First World War, whereas Spain was very clearly outside any "natural" orbit of German territorial sway and thus arguably marked a more egregious degree of expansionism on the part of the Nazis. The inconsistency is striking: what made Spain an acceptable concession but Poland a violation necessitating the greatest war in the history of humankind?

Plenty of justifications have been floated over the years — Germany did not directly annex Spain, the Western powers wanted to avoid war and so on — but the only satisfactory answer is to be found in a clear understanding of the ideological challenge at the heart of the 20th century. The Spanish Republic was governed by a coalition of the left which had won the elections of 1936. Franco's fascist uprising had been in direct response to that success, and the governments of the West had no desire to see Spanish workers effectively dismantle capitalism and prove the viability of socialist or communist economic principles in one of the old kingdoms of Europe.[49] The West had invaded Russia in 1918 to try to crush that revolution. They had systematically repressed the left in their own countries. They were intervening to prop up anti-communist dictatorships in Latin America. The pattern was clear.

Indeed, many in the West had applauded the rise of Mussolini in Italy — who coined the term fascism — on the grounds that it was an anti-communist movement which shared many of the same principles as their own governments. In 1927 Winston Churchill himself had visited Mussolini to praise his achievements:

> If I had been an Italian, I am sure that I should have been wholeheartedly with you from start to finish in your triumphant struggle against the bestial appetites and passions of Leninism. But in England we have not yet had to face this danger in the same deadly form… But that we shall succeed in grappling with communism and choking the life out of it — of that I am absolutely sure.[50]

This may be disappointing to anyone who has grown up on the myth of Winston Churchill, but it is hardly out of character for the rabid anti-communist aristocrat. Churchill was an ideologue of imperialism and anti-communism, perfectly content to crack any skulls necessary for the maintenance of the power of the rich over the rest. He was a product of patrician upbringing, upper-class schooling, imperialist training, white supremacist certainty and patriarchal ideology, and he possessed the supreme confidence of being one of the most powerful men in the British Empire.[51] In 1920 Churchill had ordered the bombing of an "ungrateful volcano" of Iraqi civilians who refused or were incapable of paying taxes to the British Empire, which had just seized the territory from Turkey.[52] He proclaimed himself "strongly in favour of using poisoned gas against uncivilized tribes" and mocked the "savage and barbarous" Afghans, hoping they would someday "put up a show" by giving Britain an excuse to launch another war against them.[53] When it came to Spain, Churchill considered the democratic government to be a "communist front" and was pleased by the "anti-Red movement" Franco was leading. He could hardly criticize Hitler for aerial bombardment of civilians when he, himself, had so recently done the same.

Churchill ultimately turned against the fascist powers for strategic, not ideological, reasons, to which I return in Chapter 6. When Britain liberated Greece from the Nazis in 1944, Churchill discovered a country that had already liberated itself. Greek communist partisans who had forced Nazi troops to retreat initially welcomed the Allies, but when Churchill demanded that they immediately surrender power to the British, they understandably refused. Churchill had his forces open fire against them.[54] Bodies on the streets of Athens, killed by British bullets, was an indication of just how similar Churchill's politics were to the Nazis he was fighting. Britain — and later the United States — would fight a bloody war to maintain its control over Greece well into the 1950s, a remarkable form of liberation that shaped Greek politics in the 20th century.

Here, then, we must reconcile ourselves to a point that may be difficult to digest: fascism was never ideologically that far away from the positions of the so-called Western democracies. Even a cursory consideration of the activities of the Anglo-American states in the first half of the 20th century illustrates that Winston Churchill was exceptional only insofar as he was unashamed of his own barbarity. Whether in the genocidal wars against Indigenous Peoples in North America, the rapacious colonial practices in Africa and Asia or the violent repression of militant trade unionists at home, the hallmarks of fascism were never far from the surface; intense and racialized nationalism, fetishization of the symbols and carriers of patriarchal authority, and fervent opposition to the organized left were all prominent in the policies of Great Britain, the United States and Canada.

Those states could, however, count on a relatively compliant popular base. Without a full-scale rebellion to quell, there was no compulsion to establish the same militarized apparatus of internal repression that the German, Italian and Spanish ruling classes had required.[55] Thus, as Churchill indicated in his letter to Mussolini, a capitalist agenda could be carried through in those states without need of a fascist movement to crush left opposition, a situation that capital itself typically preferred.[56] As the same time, fascism abroad was a welcome alternative to left revolution; the latter could generate momentum that might change the circumstances at home, and the former typically did not interfere significantly with business as usual. Indeed, the continued presence of Western capital in the fascist countries was best exemplified by Coca-Cola, which created Fanta, a new brand designed for its operations in Nazi Germany.

In that context, it seems hardly mysterious at all that the West would let Hitler and Franco crush Spanish democracy. If Spain was to be contested between the forces of left and right, there was little doubt which side governments like that of Canada would be on. Even while the German and Italian governments offered direct support to Franco, the governments of the West signed a non-intervention agreement in 1936 which not only declared official neutrality but also saw the signatories actively undermine any efforts by private individuals to volunteer to support the Spanish Republic. Though Canada did not sign onto the agreement, it effectively shared that position and passed its own law in 1937 which made it a criminal offence to enlist in the conflict in Spain.[57] The Canadian government was aware that some five hundred Canadians had already independently travelled to Spain to fight against fascism, but this was not great cause for concern; it would, in the words of one politician, "rid us of these undesirable people, provided they do not return here."[58]

The Mackenzie-Papineau Battalion

Those who Maxime Raymond called "undesirable people" were the Mackenzie-Papineau Battalion (Mac-Paps), a group of more than 1600 Canadians who joined the International Brigades to help defend the democratic Spanish Republic from the fascist insurgency between 1936 and 1939.[59] They were a group of mostly poor and working-class men, often unemployed and disproportionately drawn from non-British immigrant families, of whom nearly half were killed. Many of them had survived the labour camps Canada established for homeless men, and some had participated in the On-to-Ottawa trek and were among those attacked in Regina in 1935. Their journey to Spain was often clandestine, organized via the Communist Party of Canada with support from the Soviet Union.[60] Those who escaped the country before Franco's forces could kill them returned to Canada to no remembrance, no pension and no permission to enlist in the war against the Axis (though some did under false names).[61] They are still little more than a footnote in the annals of Canadian history, completely unknown to most Canadians, though they were the first volunteers in the fight against fascism.

The significance of their erasure from Canadian history cannot be overstated. A ruling class so desperate to create warrior heroes that it had proclaimed Vimy Ridge, a meaningless bloodbath in a war between rival empires, the "birth of a nation," made certain that the stories of Jules Paivio, Konstantin Olynyk, Red Walsh, Ross Russell, Charlie Sands and William Krehm were buried. They are never mentioned on Remembrance Day. They rarely show up in histories of Canada and are even hard to find in Canadian military histories. They have been the subject of just one documentary[62] and only a handful of books, many of them written by veterans themselves.

Norman Bethune's was the only name that ever made it into Canadian popular consciousness. A well-known doctor, Bethune had advocated for universal health care since the 1920s and had praised the Soviet Union's efforts to provide medical care for all, which had significantly reduced the incidence of tuberculosis, the disease that had killed so many Indigenous people in Canada's conquest of the west. By the 1930s, Bethune was openly a member of the Communist Party, imploring his colleagues in the Montreal medical community to do the same: "Twenty-five years ago it was thought contemptible to be called a socialist, today it is ridiculous not to be one."[63] In 1935, police in Montreal attacked a demonstration for jobs and bread, and Bethune immediately grabbed his medical kit and began treating people injured by the police. He was soon providing free medical care to poor people in Montreal's slums and earned the nickname "Comrade Bethune."[64] He also earned the attention of the growing fascist movement in Canada and had his home ransacked and swastikas painted on the walls.

When the police shrugged off the vandalism of his home, indicating that he had brought the problem onto himself, Bethune became convinced that Québec, and perhaps all of Canada, could be on the brink of slipping into fascism. The struggle in Spain came to represent to him the front line of what was a global struggle against an ideology that would bring only more suffering for the masses. He determined to join the volunteers, setting up a mobile blood transfusion system for the Spanish Republican forces. It was a successful effort, though there was never enough that Bethune and the other surgeons and medics could do. Bethune's work made him a minor celebrity, both in Spain and internationally, and his reports back to Canada did much to generate sympathy for the Republican cause. In particular, his description of the German and Italian bombing of civilian refugees in the town of Almeria was harrowing,[65] and when he conducted a tour of North America to generate support for the cause, it had some success. Following his time in Spain, Bethune travelled to China to help the communist partisans resist Japanese fascist occupation; he died there in 1939 and was commemorated in an essay by Mao Zedong. His story is still taught in many Chinese schools.[66]

Few of the other Mac-Paps are known at all, even the more prominent among them. James "Red" Walsh had been a labour organizer his entire life. He was a steelworker in New York City and longshoreman in British Columbia. He had survived the work camps, the On-to-Ottawa trek and the Regina Riot, he was a member of the Communist Party, and he had a stamp on his passport restricting his movements as a result. He was a contemporary of Arthur "Slim" Evans, one of the leaders of the BC miners' strike, and Tim Buck, the leader of the Communist Party, and when he went to Spain he was not just a volunteer but a political commissar, tasked with keeping up morale. This was not easy toward the end of the war, with his guts torn apart by shrapnel, as he struggled to help people escape to France. Even then, the organizer instincts kicked in, and when French guards tried to force Red and other wounded soldiers to walk across the Pyrenees mountains, he demanded that a bus be provided to transport the injured.[67]

Jules Paivio was the son of Finnish immigrants in northern Ontario, one of some 160 Finns whose more egalitarian settler communities had fostered a disproportionate number of volunteers. Paivio nearly died crossing into Spain through the Pyrenees and was promptly captured by Italian soldiers who threw him in one of Franco's prisons, where he was beaten, thrown down stairs, forced to live in filth and at one point mocked by the wife of British Prime Minister Neville Chamberlain.[68] He was one of the few prisoners to survive and recalled an emotional journey in which Franco's troops marched him and others ragged and barefoot through the streets of Burgos and San Sebastien to be humiliated by the crowds. But in San Sebastien, there was no humiliation: the crowds gathered in tears to thank the volunteers, to exchange addresses and to ask after loved ones who had also been imprisoned. The fascists were furious and locked Paivio and the others into cells, from which they would not leave for several months.

The stories of these volunteers reflect the fault lines of class struggle that connected Canada to the world. Tom Cacic had arrived in Spain from the Soviet Union, having only narrowly avoided execution in Yugoslavia as a communist. He was born Tomo, in Croatia, but immigrated in his youth to Canada and became a leader of a miners' strike in Ontario, where he was arrested and later deported for his work in the Communist Party. After fighting in Spain he returned to the place where he was born and fought with Tito's partisans against Nazi rule.[69] Charlie Sands had fought the Nazis as part of the communist movement in Germany until it became impossible to continue, at which point he fled to Canada and helped organize the trek to Ottawa. In Spain, he was remembered as a giant of a man who died at a battle in Belchite.[70] William Krehm was an idealistic young Jewish journalist from Toronto who was drawn to left politics during the Depression. In Spain, he revelled in the dynamics of Republican Barcelona but became caught up in the internal conflicts between anarchists and communists in the city and nearly died on the famed Passeig de Gracia.[71] He survived the war and later produced an important study of tyranny in Latin America.

Another young Jew, Ross Russell, was increasingly alarmed at the growing anti-Semitism in Montreal, where Adrien Arcand's Nazi thugs were given the green light by police to smash up Jewish stores and even attack Jews directly, as noted in the following chapter. Russell understood that this experience was connected to the struggle in Spain and the fascist menace in Europe. He barely survived his wounds in Spain and developed a terrible fear that his wounded leg would have to be amputated. He kept his leg, but the sight he beheld on the train out of Spain nearly broke his heart. On the French side of the border, along the rail line for miles, were Soviet weapons that had been blocked by the French government from entering Spain — weapons that could have saved the lives of his comrades and maybe saved Spain from the fascism that, by 1939, had taken full control of the country.[72]

In sharp contrast to these anti-fascist Canadians was government official Andrew O'Kelly, responsible for processing the movement of the last Canadians out of Spain. O'Kelly drew out and delayed the retreat, conducting long interviews to assess whether these were actual Canadians or communist spies. He regularly reminded the volunteers that they were criminals and tried to trick them into proving that they were spies by asking them to name famous Canadians or describe their hometowns.[73] He also separated the volunteers into ethnic categories, putting extra pressure on the non-British. Anti-communism, linked to racism against Eastern Europeans and Jews, was strong in Canada; not long before, former Prime Minister R.B. Bennett had stood in the House of Commons with a list of Slavic and Jewish communists, calling them "the scum of Canada."[74] Bennett had once sought the support of Adrien Arcand and the Canadian fascists and had been the architect of the Canadian labour camps, having created them to control the organized left after banning the Communist Party in 1931.[75]

O'Kelly's interrogations and segregations were an insult to everything the Mackenzie-Papineau Battalion had been fighting for, a startling reminder that the Canadian state was diametrically opposed to what the Mac-Paps represented. Bill Beeching recalled that while he was being questioned by O'Kelly, a squadron of fascist bombers flew overhead; O'Kelly, excited, "ran to the window, exclaiming that he would like to see for himself what a bombing raid was really like."[76] For the anti-fascist volunteers, who had spent years trying to avoid those fascist bombs, O'Kelly's excitement would have been a sharp illustration of the ideological gulf between them, a reminder that the ruling class in Canada had more sympathy for fascist bombers than for anti-fascist workers.

The contradiction between the actions of the individual Canadians who fought in solidarity with the Spanish Republic and the position of the Canadian government which denied them support is stark indeed. The war waged by the fascists was brutal, using German and Italian weapons and supported by Italian warships and a Nazi air force that was testing its capacities for aerial bombardment over civilian cities. The Canadian volunteers had little or no experience in fighting such a war, but they went, nonetheless, compelled by a sense of moral obligation and class consciousness. As Bill Beeching describes, "if there was one consideration common to all volunteers, it was that they were conscious anti-fascists… they believed that if fascism could be stopped in Spain, a second world war could be prevented."[77] Ron Liversedge specifically points to the fact that the volunteers were "politically conscious, all understanding what fascism meant for the common people."[78]

The Canadian government prevaricated — unwilling to support the Spanish government or the Canadian volunteers — precisely because it, too, was aware of the class conflict inherent in the Spanish struggle, and it fell on the other side. The prime minister, William Lyon Mackenzie King, whose grandfather was one of the namesakes of the Mackenzie-Papineau Battalion, was unmistakably hostile to the Canadian volunteers. He wanted no part in the Spanish Republican cause, part of the world communist conspiracy in King's mind, and he put it to Parliament that "there was imminent danger of the conflict spreading into a war of isms, of class conflict and of conflict of national strategic interests."[79] Perhaps that was why he made no complaint to British Prime Minister Neville Chamberlain after his wife, Lady Austen Chamberlain, toured Spain in 1938 and paid a visit to one of Franco's prisons, where several Canadian volunteers were being held; after failing to coax any of the Canadian prisoners into admitting that they were mercenaries, she shared a laugh with a fascist officer about the prisoners' stupidity.[80]

King was right, however, that the war in Spain was about "isms." It had always been about class, about the conflict between rich and poor, capitalism and communism, between those trying to build a more just society and those trying to re-assert the old hierarchies.[81] This was the conflict in Spain, as it had been in Germany and Italy, and in this the ruling classes of the Anglo-American countries had more common cause with the fascists than the Spanish Republicans. The Canadian prime minister, as Mark Zuehlke notes, "fully sympathized with governments, like that of [Nazi] Germany, which resorted to stamping out Communism by legalized repression."[82] On the other hand, the tens of thousands of Canadians who had been drawn to socialism and communism saw their fate attached to that of the Spanish Republic. Many understood that the *raison d'etre* of fascism was to destroy communism — and communists — and that, therefore, the rise of fascism would mean death not just to the cause of greater equality and justice but also potentially of anyone who believed in that cause. The spectacle of the Canadian Prime Minister meeting and praising Adolf Hitler confirmed that belief.

Hitler's Eyes

Prime Minister King met Hitler in the summer of 1937 in what is a remarkably underemphasized chronicle in Canadian history. When it is discussed, typically in biographies of King himself, Canadian historians tend to frame it as an unfortunate and awkward element of King's eccentric but well-intentioned desire for peace. Conservative historians like J.L. Granatstein and Robert Bothwell emphasize his skilful deference to "public opinion," as though the prime minister was not in a position to re-orient public opinion had he come out vocally and aggressively denouncing Hitler in the 1930s.[83] King first met with British Prime Minister Neville Chamberlain in London, where the leaders agreed that it would be easy enough to talk with the "admirable" German leader to remind him to moderate his territorial ambitions to avoid unduly interfering with the integrity of the British Commonwealth. In fact, Chamberlain spoke candidly about territorial issues that were at the heart of German ambitions, noting that "there was no doubt [Germany] wanted to expand," and that he, Chamberlain, saw no problem with that, provided it was contained to areas not of interest to Britain.[84]

Indeed, everyone at the Commonwealth conference in London agreed that Germany was on an aggressive posture, but none saw great problem with this and all felt that Germany was perfectly justified. The idea of a dividing of spheres of influence between the British Empire and a Greater Germany was considered a perfectly reasonable proposition. In fact, King had met a year earlier with the Soviet foreign minister Maxim Litvinoff, who had accurately predicted Nazi strategy, telling King that

Hitler's primary ambition would be in Eastern Europe and Russia. King was privately quite pleased, noting in his diary that he felt Hitler perhaps had no plans to look west at all and that Anglo-German peace could be achieved by allowing Hitler to conquer Russia. "If Russia were out of the picture," he wrote in 1936, "difficulties would soon adjust themselves."[85]

Following the visit with Chamberlain, the Canadian prime minister met with the newly crowned King George and conversed amiably with him about a variety of topics, including Italy's failure to send a representative to George's coronation and the problem of the rise of communism, or the "Reds," as King recorded it.[86] The prime minister also found time to have a pleasant lunch with his old friend John Buchan, now the Baron of Tweedsmuir, who had run concentration camps in South Africa and acted as chief propagandist for Canada's Great War.

King also had a warm and sprawling conversation with the German ambassador, Ludwig von Ribbentrop, who convinced King that the unfair terms of the Versailles Treaty had led to a rise of communism in Germany.[87] King was naturally compelled and noted in his diary, "Hitler [is] in deadly earnest about the suppression of Communism, and that it had become necessary to stamp it out in Germany... in doing that, he thought he was a friend to all countries." King agreed and noted that Von Ribbentrop was "a man I could get along with quite easily."[88] From there, King travelled to Berlin, where he met with the British ambassador, Nevile Henderson. They heartily agreed that the Nazis were doing good work and should be encouraged to proceed, including annexing greater territory in Europe, so long as they understood that the Commonwealth would stand together if its own interests were threatened. King put it thus in his diary:

> [Henderson] said he hoped I would not take up the Eastern question with Hitler. I said I had no desire to do this because it was not part of the situation in which Canada had a special interest. We had no desire to interfere in European politics. I hoped to impress upon him Canada's attitude alike toward Germany and Britain in the matter of seeing fair-play all round; that he must not judge because of our statement we would make no commitment in regard to Europe that we would be indifferent to acts of aggression which might threaten the liberty, the freedom which we enjoyed as members of the British Empire.[89]

The highest levels in British and Canadian governance were thus happily encouraging Hitler's expansion to the east, so long as his objectives did not interfere with those of the Empire. Henderson complained that the British left didn't approve of his warm disposition to the Nazis, but King reassured him that "there [was] a lot England [could] learn from Germany in treatment of masses of people [and] that Nazism was not all wrong."[90] This was June 1937; the Germans had burned the city of Guernica just three months earlier and Pablo Picasso's famous mural *Guernica* was unveiled that very summer in Paris.[91] King's tour of Berlin took him past Jewish citizens branded with the Star of David, and stores and hotels with signs banning Jews from the premises. Hitler's set of anti-Semitic laws had, in fact, been in effect since 1935 and were of little concern to King, who harboured his own anti-Semitism and had noted in his diary that Canada should avoid "too great an intermixture of foreign strains of blood."[92] Years earlier, King had written that there was "something in a Jew's nature which is detestable," though by 1936 he was ready to admit that there were "good as well as bad Jews."[93]

King was enthralled by his sojourn in Germany and could hardly wait for his audience with the Führer. The day finally arrived on June 29, and he first met with Nazi General Hermann Göring, who thanked the Canadian prime minister for the buffalo that Canada had sent to the Berlin Zoo; the choice of animal was auspicious, given that only 60 years earlier the buffalo herds had collapsed on the prairies, a key moment in Canada's conquest of the Indigenous Peoples of the west. After a pleasant exchange in which the German and Canadian expressed their desire for peace — Göring noting Germany's need for expansion and King making no suggestion that he would oppose it — King invited Göring to visit Canada at his next opportunity.

At last, he met with Hitler himself. King was entranced. After blustering his usual opening in conversation with Germans — the fact that he was born in Berlin, Ontario[94] — King praised Hitler for "the constructive work of his regime" and said that he "hoped that work would continue. That nothing would be permitted to destroy that work. That it was bound to be followed in other countries to the great advantage of mankind." In one rather absurd exchange, Hitler told King that he had to cultivate the support of the people because he "was not like Stalin who could shoot his generals and other members of his government who disagreed with him," to which King was most compelled, noting, "I confess I felt he was using exactly the same argument I had used in the Canadian parliament last session."[95] In fact, Hitler had, in 1934, done precisely that: in what was called the Night of the Long Knives, he had as many as a thousand members of his own party assassinated. It was widely reported in the international press, especially after Hitler delivered a speech justifying his having "cauterise[d] down to the raw flesh the ulcers of this poisoning of the wells in our domestic life."[96]

King and Hitler were particularly close on the subject of communism. "He spoke about the dangers of Bolshevism and Communism," wrote King, "he said that if Germany had not met the Communist menace at the time she did, and in the way she did, the condition of Germany today would be the same as the conditions of Spain."[97] Indeed, one of the least understood facets of Nazi Germany was that arguably its central, defining feature was anti-communism. Pre-fascist organizations like the Freikorps were responsible for crushing the popular revolutions of the German left following the Great War; they murdered Rosa Luxemburg, Karl Liebknecht, Kurt Eisner and other leaders of both the German Socialist Republic of 1918–1919 and the Bavarian Socialist Republic of 1919. A London reporter privately described the "liberation" of Munich by the Freikorps: "All suspected of extreme [communist] views are shot without trial. Numerous notables suspected of even moderate socialist views disappear without trace." Freikorps patrolled the streets, ordered to "shoot [the communists] and report that they attacked you," piling up enough bodies of suspected leftists that it raised the concern of Munich's health officials.[98]

This was only the beginning of the violence that would be shown to the German left. During the contested days of the Weimar Republic, the Weimar police often did as much to eliminate the left as did the fascists, but, once they attained power, the Nazis were ruthless. After falsely accusing the communists of starting a fire at the Reichstag — the German parliament — Hitler outlawed leftist political parties and suspended most civil liberties, while empowering his deputies to unleash a wave of violence against the German left.[99] There is no satisfactory figure capturing the number of socialists and communists killed in Germany between 1918 and 1945, but suffice it to say that even in the last free elections before Hitler's dictatorship, the left received millions of votes, far more than the Nazis.[100] Many of those millions of voters were killed, exiled to the Soviet Union or found themselves wearing red triangles in Hitler's concentration camps. Of the 300,000 members of the German Communist Party (KPD) alone, for instance, some 40% were killed and more than half were sent to the camps, and these were mostly captured in the first year of Hitler's rule.[101] Martin Niemöller's famous poem, used in so many Holocaust memorials, was a powerful reflection of this reality:

> First they came for the Communists and I did not speak out —
> Because I was not a Communist
>
> Then they came for the Socialists and I did not speak out —
> Because I was not a Socialist
>
> Then they came for the trade unionists and I did not speak out —
> Because I was not a trade unionist
>
> Then they came for the Jews and I did not speak out —
> Because I was not a Jew
>
> Then they came for me and there was no one left to speak out for me.[102]

The depth of this statement has often been reduced in popular capitalist culture, as if any social groups could be slotted into the structure of the verses and the lesson would be the same: we should always oppose oppression of particular groups of people. True. But Niemöller was also trying to tell us something specific: the Nazis killed the communists first. Then, having dealt with the hard left, they moved onto the soft left and attacked the trade unions. Then they expanded their operations to more widely target all Jews, even those not connected to the left, and their list of targets grew from there. Thus, importantly, it was anti-communism that lurked at the heart of the Nazi project, as it did with all fascist projects.

Mackenzie King's own hatred of the left made him receptive to Hitler's position, and King specifically noted Hitler's disapproval of the fact that leftists from England had joined the International Brigades in Spain. It was surely no coincidence that King very quickly, upon his return to Canada, moved to make it a criminal offence to fight with the Spanish Republic. After Hitler gave King a parting gift — an autographed picture — King "wished him well in his efforts to help mankind."[103]

King's diary entries on his meeting with Hitler are shocking to a modern audience. Posterity might have been more forgiving to King had he expressed something like grudging respect or cautious optimism, but King was star-struck. Some parts of the diaries are worth quoting at length:

> I then thanked him again for having given me the privilege of so long an interview. He smiled very pleasantly and indeed had a sort of appealing and affectionate look in his eyes. My sizing up of the man as I sat and talked with him was that he is really one who truly loves his fellow-men, and his country, and would make any sacrifice for their good. That he feels himself to be a deliverer of his people from tyranny. To understand Hitler, one has to remember his limited opportunities in his early life, his imprisonment, etc. It is truly marvelous what he has attained unto himself through his self education… His face is much more prepossessing than his pictures would give the impression of. It is not that of a fiery, over-strained nature, but of a calm, passive man, deeply and thoughtfully in earnest. His skin was smooth; his face did not present lines of fatigue or weariness; his eyes impressed me most of all. There was a liquid quality about them which indicate keen perception and profound sympathy… He has a very nice, sweet [sic] and, one could see, how particularly humble folk would come to have a profound love for the man… As I talked with him, I could not but think of Joan of Arc. He is distinctly a mystic.[104]

Though overshadowed by his meetings with Göring and Hitler, King also found time for a quick chat with Foreign Minister Baron von Neurath, whom he deemed "exceedingly pleasant and able." Von Neurath took the opportunity to be frank with King about Germany's need to expand: "The taking away of all German colonies at the end of the War was the greatest mistake England made," he told King, since it forced Germany to find other means of growing its economy. Indeed, von Neurath specifically mentioned the need for agricultural lands, citing Germany's growing population and proposing grain imports from Canada. What is particularly noteworthy in King's account of the "exceedingly pleasant" von Neurath was his discussion of the communists and Jews:

> He admitted that they had taken some pretty rough steps in clearing up the situation [with the communists and Jews] but the truth was the country was going to pieces at the time Hitler took over.

> He said to me that I would have loathed living in Berlin with the Jews, and the way in which they had increased their numbers in the City, and were taking possession of its more important part. He said there was no pleasure in going to a theatre which was filled with them. Many of them were very coarse and vulgar and assertive. They were getting control of all the business, the finance, and had really taken advantage of the necessity of the people. It was necessary to get them out and have the German people really control their own City and affairs. He told me I would have been surprised at the extent to which life and morals had become demoralized; that Hitler had set his face against all that kind of thing, and had tried to inspire desire for a good life in the minds of young people.[105]

King made no further comment in his diary, apparently taking this commentary at face value, moving right along to the next part of their discussion, von Neurath's affection for England. Shortly thereafter, they took a photograph together and went to von Neurath's house, where King met the von Neurath family for a luncheon that was "one of the pleasantest I have ever enjoyed." Evidently, the anti-Semitic rant did not put the Canadian prime minister off his lunch in the slightest. "I left him," King writes, "feeling that I had met a man whose confidence I would continue to enjoy through the rest of my days." They were fast friends! King concluded that diary entry: "Looking back over the German visit, I can honestly say it was as enjoyable, informative, and inspiring as any visit I have ever had anywhere. Indeed, I doubt I have ever had four days where were more interesting or indeed comparable in significance."[106] His only fear was that "the Press, through its misrepresentations and persistent propaganda," would undermine the peace and harmony he could clearly see in the future of British-German relations.

The Myth of Appeasement

Historical assessments of the period leading up to the Second World War often propose a soft justification for Western governments' allowing Hitler and the other fascist governments to grow, based on the assumption that the West was afraid of the prospect of another war. The story suggests that they pursued a policy of "appeasement," seeking to placate

Hitler's growing list of demands in order to prevent a conflict that would be costly and deadly. This was, no doubt, part of the story; the war was, indeed, those things. Certainly if one looks only at the years immediately preceding the breakout of hostilities, there is some evidence for this; as late as the summer of 1939, Mackenzie King still believed he could broker a peace with Hitler, appealing directly to the Führer to not "let anything imperil or destroy what you have already accomplished."[107] It is clear that King knew that war was close at hand and was seeking to prevent it. Still, while this narrative ascribes a certain degree of cowardice and foolishness to Western leaders, it couches that weakness in the idea that they were trying to prevent war and bloodshed. Their intentions, then, are beyond reproach.

Thoughtful analysis of this period fails to confirm the above thesis as the primary motivation of Canada and the Western powers. In fact, it appears as a massive cop-out, an attempt to rationalize a series of decisions that were, rather, developed primarily in the calculations of imperial and class politics. King describes in his diaries the expansion of German territory as "Germany's legitimate development,"[108] recognizing in Hitler's plans an impulse that was perfectly natural to all capitalist empires. He returned from his visit in Berlin with the intention of making it even more difficult for Canadians to fight fascism in Spain, convinced — just like Chamberlain and Churchill — that fascism was a positive bulwark against communism and offered a valuable way forward for Europe. His appeal to Hitler in 1939 praised everything he had accomplished, an astonishing statement given the horrors that had already happened by that point. He admired Hitler's humility, his patriotism and his liquid eyes.

While no doubt some leaders might have felt trepidation about the political fallout of leading their countries into another war, it is evident that what was operative in their discussions about the rise of fascism in Europe was that it was preferable to allow the rise of the right than that of the left. The discussions between Chamberlain, Henderson and King do not reflect trepidation but admiration. King's diaries betray gushing approval, not fear, of Hitler, and in his conversations with Henderson it becomes clear that King is, in fact, positioned within the faction that is most amenable to Hitler.

If there was naïveté in the political brain trust of the Anglosphere it was in their belief that the fascists would be satisfied in occupying a secondary status in global capitalism. It should have been obvious, given the nature of capitalism and the experience of the First World War, that inter-imperial rivalry was a permanent aspect of the system. No rising pole of capital accumulation could simply stop expanding; German capital in the first half of the 20th century would eventually, inevitably need greater *lebensraum*. Indeed, as it turned out, German expansion would not be limited in the way the West had hoped, and suddenly these same leaders' supposed fear of war evaporated. They were perfectly willing to put millions of other peoples' lives on the line once they had acknowledged the full extent of German and Japanese ambition and the fact that it threatened the wealth and power of the Western bourgeoisie itself.

What stands out about Canada's engagements in the world in the 1930s is that, during an exceptional time in history, Canada remained fundamentally Canada. Canada was created to facilitate the growth of a new capitalist economy, and its leaders remained steadfast in their goal of protecting and preserving the class system capitalism generated. Their commitment to that project was so great that even as a new, extreme version of traditional capitalist ideology — fascism — emerged in force, Canada resisted any plan to intercept it as long as the alternative was the rise of the left. The Canadian ruling class was neither naïve nor afraid; they recognized in the years between the world wars that the inequality and irrationality of capitalism had generated a wave of class struggle that threatened to bring down the entire system. Faced with the prospect of a revolutionary left — still small in Canada but strong enough to have led successful revolutions in Europe — the Canadian ruling class threw in their lot with those who were not afraid to use violence and coercion to defeat the left. And so, from Berlin to Madrid to San Salvador to Tokyo, Canada consciously and determinedly lined up with the far right.

Notes
1. F.S. Pearson, quoted in Rosana Barboso, *Brazil and Canada: Economic, Political, and Migratory Ties, 1820s to 1970s*, New York, Lexington Books, 2017, p. 37.
2. Peter McFarlane, *Northern Shadows: Canadians and Central America*, Toronto, Between the Lines, 1989, p. 49–62.
3. Prime Minister Borden worked vigorously and often duplicitously to undermine the proposal, at one point even trying to coerce the Japanese delegation into changing the wording of the clause such that instead of asserting the rights of people of all races, it would emphasize the rights of all nations. Francine McKenzie, "Race, Empire, and World Order: Robert Borden and Racial Equality at the Paris Peace Conference of 1919," in Laura Madokoro, Francine McKenzie, and David Meren, ed., *Dominion of Race: Rethinking Canada's International*

4. Sir Joseph Pope, quoted in David Webster, "'Red Indians in Geneva, 'Papuan Headhunters' in New York: Race, Mental Maps, and Two Global Appeals in the 1920s and 1960s," in Laura Madokoro, Francine McKenzie, and David Meren, ed., *Dominion of Race: Rethinking Canada's International History*, Vancouver, UBC Press, 2017, p. 263–264.
5. David Webster, "'Red Indians in Geneva, 'Papuan Headhunters' in New York: Race, Mental Maps, and Two Global Appeals in the 1920s and 1960s," p. 266.
6. The Second World War should certainly be read as Act II of the total war waged between 1914 and 1945, and in that sense it, too, expressed an uncontainable rivalry between ambitious would-be capitalist centres. However, it was complicated by the fact that the Soviet Union, crucial to the war's origins and outcomes, was ideologically completely different.
7. That collapse ultimately meant the exile of many Tsarist nobles, including the Count Paul Nicholayevich Ignatieff, father of Canadian diplomat George Ignatieff, himself the father of the unsuccessful Liberal Party leader Michael Ignatieff, who authored an important justification for modern, Canadian-style imperialism, *Empire Lite*. The unfortunate Count and his wife, Princess Natalie Nicholayevna Mestchersky, were able to extract a sum of 30,000 pounds sterling from Soviet Russia thanks to a sympathetic broker at the Midland Bank. This would be roughly equivalent to $1 million USD today, and helped to very quickly propel the aristocrat's son George into the University of Toronto, Oxford, and ultimately the Canadian foreign service, where he helped shape Canada's anti-communist Cold War policies. He was, however, forced to suffer the taunts of Soviet Secretary Nikita Khrushchev, who repeatedly called him "Count." George Ignatieff, *The Making of a Peacemonger*, Toronto, University of Toronto Press, 1985.
8. Scholarship, especially in English, on the Russian Revolution was hampered by the dominance of Cold War ideologues like Robert Conquest and Richard Pipes. However, solid sources on the revolution include the most famous first-hand English-language account, John Reed's *Ten Days That Shook the World* (1919), and the definitive accounts by Alexander Rabinowitch, including *Prelude to Revolution* (1968) and *The Bolsheviks Come to Power* (1976). A noteworthy 21st century account is China Miéville's *October: The Story of the Russian Revolution* (2017).
9. The forces that crushed these revolutions, the German Freikorps, would become the core of the rising fascist movement. An indispensable study of this movement is Klaus Theweleit's *Male Fantasies* (1977).
10. Among its denizens was Bela Lugosi, exiled after the revolution was defeated, who went on to become the actor famous for his portrayal of Count Dracula.
11. Eric Hobsbawm, *The Age of Extremes: A History of the World, 1914–1991*, New York, Vintage Books, 1996, p. 54–84.
12. Margaret Conrad, *A Concise History of Canada*, Cambridge, Cambridge University Press, 2012, p. 216.
13. Daniel Francis, *Seeing Reds: The Red Scare of 1918–1919, Canada's First War on Terror*, Vancouver, Arsenal Pulp Press, 2010, p. 89–114.
14. Stephen Lyon Endicott, *Raising the Workers' Flag: The Workers' Unity League of Canada, 1930–1936*, Toronto, University of Toronto Press, 2012, p. 27.

15. The characterization of the left as a "foreign" force was of course both true and false at the same time. The various left and labour organizations drew members from a wide variety of settler backgrounds; this certainly included Anglo-Canadians, but it also did include many more recent immigrants from southern and eastern Europe. Finns and Ukrainians were well-represented in these organizations, many having lived through serious mobilizations against the Tsarist authorities in Russia. Jews, too, brought a radical spirit, especially in the early-20th century waves of immigration. In Winnipeg's North End, for instance, the Jewish working class was able to "build a sub-culture in which working-class institutions and socialist ideas were hegemonic." This fact was seized upon by anti-Semites and anti-communists alike, each of whom emphasized and exaggerated the links between Jews and the left. Leo Panitch, "Back to the Future: Contextualizing the Legacy," in Daniel Stone, ed., *Jewish Radicalism in Winnipeg, 1905–1960*, Winnipeg, Jewish Heritage Centre of Western Canada, 2003, p. 17.
16. Daniel Francis, *Seeing Reds*, p. 98.
17. Dave Taylor, quoted in Jon Bartlett and Rika Ruebsaat, *Soviet Princeton: Slim Evans and the 1932–33 Miners' Strike*, Vancouver, New Star Books, 2015, p. 50.
18. Margaret Conrad, Alvin Finkel, and Donald Fyson, *History of the Canadian Peoples, Volume 2: 1867 to the Present*, Pearson, Toronto, 2015, p. 202–203.
19. J.M. Bumsted, *A History of the Canadian Peoples*, 4$ ed, Oxford, Oxford University Press, 2011, p. 320.
20. Drawing people away from the Communist Party and into a less radical formation was both an unintended consequence and also an explicit project of many of the CCF's leaders. Some in the CCF were openly hostile towards the Communists and actively opposed their presence. The CP was not without its flaws — especially insofar as its loyalty to the Soviet Union led it to adopt political lines that reflected the needs of the USSR rather than the needs of working people more broadly — but it was, nevertheless, of no use to the working classes to have the CCF and CP operating at cross purposes. See David Lewis, *The Good Fight: Political Memoirs, 1909–1958*, Toronto, MacMillan, 1981, p. 140–164.
21. Quoted in Mike Davis, *Late Victorian Holocausts: El Niño Famines and the Making of the Third World*, London, Verso, 2002, p. 33.
22. Bartlett and Ruebsaat, *Soviet Princeton*, p. 33.
23. J.M. Bumsted, *A History of the Canadian Peoples*, p. 318–331.
24. Fascism is notoriously difficult to define, especially since it has often been laced with an anti-intellectualism that defied the idea of a coherent ideology. Coined by Benito Mussolini's movement in Italy — fascism was a reference to the *fasces*, the rods used by Roman centurions to beat back angry mobs — Eric Hobsbawm illustrates that the factor which best linked the various fascist movements was populist, anti-communist nationalism; its strength was in its ability to mobilize reactionary politics from below, but its weakness in building international coalitions was that each fascism was so rooted in the idea of its own national superiority. Eric Hobsbawm, *The Age of Extremes*, p. 116–117.
25. Eric Hobsbawm, *The Age of Extremes*, p. 21–53.
26. For an overview of these developments, see Norman Hillmer and J.L. Granatstein's *Empire to Umpire* (1994).

27. Yves Engler, *Canada in Africa: 300 Years of Aid and Exploitation*, Halifax, Fernwood, 2015, p. 72-73.
28. Robert Borden, quoted in Peter McFarlane, *Northern Shadows*, p. 20.
29. David Webster, "Foreign Policy, Diplomacy, and Decolonization," in Karen Dubinsky, Sean Mills and Scott Rutherford, ed., *Canada and the Third World: Overlapping Histories*, Toronto, University of Toronto Press, 2016, p. 162-163. To be sure, the Ottoman Empire had carried out a horrendous genocidal campaign against Armenians between 1915 and 1923, which left as many as a million people dead. Nevertheless, it is important to note that it was precisely European intervention in the conflict between the Ottoman Empire and the Armenians that exacerbated the crisis and, according some scholars, was a critical factor in the path to genocide. Deborah Mayersen, for instance, argues that "Europe's intermittent intervention in Armenian affairs was key to the development and progression of the entire conflict," as concerns for the Armenian plight only seemed to emerge when it was politically expedient to undermine Turkey, but were rarely given the support they would have needed to successfully oppose the Ottoman Empire. Deborah Mayersen, *On the Path to Genocide: Armenia and Rwanda Reexamined*, New York, Berghahn Books, 2014, p. 87.
30. Peter McFarlane, *Northern Shadows*, p. 17.
31. Canadian Journal of Commerce, quoted in Yves Engler, *Black Book*, p. 18.
32. Quoted in R.T. Naylor, *Canada in the European Age, 1453-1919*, Vancouver, New Star Books, 1987, p. 486.
33. Porfirio Díaz, quoted in R.T. Naylor, *Canada in the European Age*, p. 487.
34. F.S. Pearson, quoted in Rosana Barboso, "Brazilian and Canadian relations: A Historical Survey," in Rosana Barbosa, ed., *Brazil and Canada in the Americas*, Halifax, Saint Mary's University, 2007, p. 35.
35. Yves Engler, *Black Book*, p. 97.
36. Frederico Trota, quoted in Rosana Barboso, *Brazil and Canada*, p. 38.
37. Peter McFarlane, *Northern Shadows*, p. 46-62.
38. R.B. Bennett, quoted in Peter McFarlane, *Northern Shadows*, p. 47.
39. Victor Brodeur, quoted in Peter McFarlane, *Northern Shadows*, p. 57.
40. Peter McFarlane, *Northern Shadows*, p. 59.
41. Peter McFarlane, *Northern Shadows*, p. 60.
42. Victor Brodeur, quoted in Peter McFarlane, *Northern Shadows*, p. 60.
43. David B. Green, "The Incredible Salvadoran Plot That Saved Thousands of Jews During the Holocaust," *Haaretz*, January 28, 2019.
44. Quoted in Peter McFarlane, *Northern Shadows*, p. 61.
45. Peter McFarlane, *Northern Shadows*, p. 48.
46. William Manfield, quoted in Peter McFarlane, *Northern Shadows*, p. 62.
47. R.B. Bennett, quoted in Peter McFarlane, *Northern Shadows*, p. 61.
48. Peter McFarlane, *Northern Shadows*, p. 70.
49. In addition to the socialist and communist movements in Spain, there was — especially in Catalonia — a strong contingent of anarchists who shared many of the goals of the communist left but differed significantly in their visions of a post-capitalist alternative.
50. Winston Churchill, quoted in Richard Seymour, "The Real Winston Churchill," *Jacobin*, January 11, 2018.

51. Richard Seymour, "The Real Winston Churchill," *Jacobin*, January 11, 2018. As Home Secretary, for instance, Churchill opposed Irish independence, women's suffrage, and trade unions' right to strike.
52. Mike Davis, *In Praise of Barbarians: Essays Against Empire*, Chicago, Haymarket Books, 2007, p. 108.
53. Ian McKay and Jamie Swift, *Warrior Nation: Rebranding Canada in an Age of Anxiety*, Toronto, Between the Lines, 2012, p. 85. These are only a few examples of Churchill's catalogue of racism, repression and cruelty in the service of the British elite. He fetishized the Great War, calling it "thrilling" and "delicious," though he was never himself under fire and mostly led disastrous campaigns. Even in ostensibly noble causes, like the fight against fascist Japan, Churchill's thirst for blood was unsettling: "we shall wipe them out, every one of them, men, women, and children," he said. "There shall not be a Japanese left on the face of the earth." In the oft-forgotten final chapters of his life, the then-knighted Sir Winston led vicious wars against indigenous people in Kenya and Malaysia, introducing in the latter case the use of Agent Orange and other toxic chemicals that would become ubiquitous in the Vietnam War.
54. Ed Vulliamy and Helena Smith, "Athens 1944: Britain's Dirty Secret," *The Guardian*, November 30, 2014.
55. This is not to suggest that fascism didn't also have a popular base in those societies. Fascists, especially in Germany and Italy, were very effective at drawing large sections of the working class into their movements. This was done, in part, by presenting the re-assertion of hyper-conservative values as being an action taken against liberal-minded elites. In Germany, for instance, the fascists held the Weimar Republic in contempt as a group of aristocratic elites who were weak in the face of left agitation (even while that regime was cracking down significantly on the left, notably during the Bloody May marches that left 33 people dead from police bullets), unduly tolerant of avant-garde movements in the arts (Berlin emerged in the 1920s as a hotspot for the modernist movement with all of its cultural subversiveness) and submitting Germany to international humiliation (respecting the terms of the Versailles agreement, which had exacerbated an already bad economic situation for the masses). As such, the elites of Weimar — who were largely remnants from the Kaiser's old apparatus — were an easy target for the fascists, who drew popular support from disaffected sections of the working class who had not been won over by the left.
56. While big business had no qualms about doing business within the structures of fascism, the operating procedures were typically different; fascist Germany and Japan, for instance, could be described as state-capitalist systems, whereby some of the rights of capital were actually curtailed in order to facilitate a capitalism directed from above. For those who cultivated good relationships with the regime and whose industries would be of value to it — like the auto industry, weapons manufacturing or chemical companies — there were massive profits to be made. Eric Hobsbawm, *The Age of Extremes*, p. 127–129.
57. Victor Howard, *The Mackenzie-Papineau Battalion*, Ottawa, Carleton University Press, 1986, p. 14.
58. Maxime Raymond, quoted in Victor Howard, *The Mackenzie-Papineau Battalion*, p. 25.

59. Mark Zuehlke, *The Gallant Cause: Canadians in the Spanish Civil War 1936–1939*, Vancouver, Whitecap Books, 1996, p. x.
60. Ronald Liversedge, *Mac-Pap: Memoir of a Canadian in the Spanish Civil War*, Vancouver, New Star Books, 2013, p. 34.
61. William C. Beeching, *Canadian Volunteers: Spain 1936–1939*, Regina, Canadian Plains Research Centre, 1989, p. xxxvi.
62. This was *Los Canadienses* (1976), an interesting if flawed effort by the National Film Board to capture some of the veterans' stories before their generation passed.
63. Bethune, quoted in Mark Zuehlke, *The Gallant Cause*, p. 43.
64. My own mother recalls singing the lyrics "Norman Bethune, he's our comrade" at a friend's house in the 1960s in Winnipeg.
65. William C. Beeching, *Canadian Volunteers*, p. 166.
66. And yet, he has drifted into relative obscurity in Canada. The last significant revival of Bethune's legacy in Canada was the unsatisfying 1990 biopic, *Bethune: The Making of a Hero* reviewed critically in Larry Hannant, "I'm Not Your Man: Norman Bethune and Women," *The Ormsby Review*, February 28, 2018.
67. William C. Beeching, *Canadian Volunteers*, p. 196.
68. Mark Zuehlke, *The Gallant Cause*, p. 227.
69. Ronald Liversedge, *Mac-Pap*, p. 111.
70. Victor Howard, *The Mackenzie-Papineau Battalion*, p. x.
71. Mark Zuehlke, *The Gallant Cause*, p. 115.
72. Mark Zuehlke, *The Gallant Cause*, p. 253.
73. Ronald Liversedge, *Mac-Pap*, p. 146.
74. R.B. Bennett, quoted in Mark Zuehlke, *The Gallant Cause*, p. 182.
75. Conrad, *Concise History*, p. 208.
76. William C. Beeching, *Canadian Volunteers*, p. 190–191.
77. William C. Beeching, *Canadian Volunteers*, p. 7.
78. Ronald Liversedge, *Mac-Pap*, p. 32.
79. William Lyon Mackenzie King, quoted in William C. Beeching, *Canadian Volunteers*, p. 6.
80. Mark Zuehlke, *The Gallant Cause*, p. 227.
81. Anarchism, as noted elsewhere, also figured prominently in the ideological swirl of Republican Spain. The Spanish left evolved in complicated ways in the 1930s, especially given the increasing distrust of much of the international left towards Stalin. Thus, the history of the Spanish Civil War was shaped in part by the internal conflict between those communists who were aligned with the Soviet Union, and those who were not, which included the large Spanish anarchist movement. It is certainly part of the tragedy of Spain that the Spanish left struggled to find unity in a context where it had mobilized the support of the international left and was positioned to strike a blow to the fascist movement before the worst of its violence could be enacted. The events in Spain also shaped the international left, insofar as prominent writers like the British volunteer George Orwell reached a wide audience with their particular takes on the internal split; Orwell's sympathy for the anarchist position, for instance, galvanized a wider anti-communism internationally.
82. Mark Zuehlke, *The Gallant Cause*, p. 125.

83. J.L. Granatstein and Robert Bothwell, "'A Self-Evident National Duty:' Canadian Foreign Policy, 1935-1939," *Journal of Imperial and Commonwealth History*, Vol. 3, No. 2, January 1975.
84. William Lyon Mackenzie King, *The Mackenzie King Diaries, 1893-1947*, June 15, 1937, Microfiche Collection, University of Toronto, University of Toronto Press, 1980.
85. William Lyon Mackenzie King, quoted in Norman Hillmer, "Canada and the 'Godless Country,' 1930-1939," in David Davies, ed., *Canada and the Soviet Experiment*, Toronto, Canadian Scholars' Press, 1994, p. 67.
86. Mussolini sent a representative, someone from Abyssinia, and it was this — not the invasion of Ethiopia– that so bothered His Majesty. William Lyon Mackenzie King, *The Mackenzie King Diaries, 1893-1947*, May 5, 1937.
87. This was a bold stretch of the truth; the German left had been very active in the period leading up to 1918 and had led two revolutions in 1918 and 1919 that were brutally repressed by the Freikorps. Versailles only took effect in 1919, so blaming Versailles for the popularity of communism was a thin claim. Of course, the economic catastrophe that Versailles contributed to did exacerbate the problems Germans faced and this generated a period of high tension with both the left and the right vying for position during the troubled Weimar Republic.
88. William Lyon Mackenzie King, *The Mackenzie King Diaries, 1893-1947*, May 26, 1937.
89. William Lyon Mackenzie King, *The Mackenzie King Diaries, 1893-1947*, June 27, 1937.
90. William Lyon Mackenzie King, *The Mackenzie King Diaries, 1893-1947*, June 27, 1937.
91. Even while Spain was engulfed in war, Japan was attacking mainland China, Italy had invaded Ethiopia, and a greater war seemed imminent, the European bourgeoisie pretended everything was fine and all of the future protagonists of the Second World War were invited to Paris for the International Exposition in 1937.
92. William Lyon Mackenzie King, quoted in Mark Zuehlke, *The Gallant Cause*, p. 128. King famously purchased a huge amount of land around his country house at Kingsmere to prevent Jews — he called them "undesirables" — from living near him.
93. William Lyon Mackenzie King, quoted in Allan Levine, *King: William Lyon Mackenzie King, A Life Guided by Destiny*, Toronto, Douglas & McIntyre, 2011, p. 286-287. Needless to say, King's racism extended beyond just the Jews; his diaries, for instance, include repeated references to "darkies," his epithet of choice for black people.
94. The name was changed to Kitchener during the hostilities with Germany during the Great War, but King nevertheless thought that it would impress upon the Germans his natural affinity for their culture.
95. William Lyon Mackenzie King, *The Mackenzie King Diaries, 1893-1947*, June 29, 1937.
96. Adolf Hitler, quoted in Joachim Fest, *Hitler*, New York, Harcourt, 1974, p. 469.
97. William Lyon Mackenzie King, *The Mackenzie King Diaries, 1893-1947*, June 29, 1937.

98. Quoted in G.S. Graber, *The History of the SS*, New York, Charter, 1978, p. 13.
99. A year earlier, Hitler had wrangled a way to orchestrate the acquittal of five Storm Troopers who had violently murdered a Silesian communist in Potempa. There can be no doubt that the Nazi project involved the complete liquidation of the left as a political option and, indeed, this has always been the orientation of the far-right, from Mussolini's brown shirts in Italy to Pinochet's soldiers in Chile. Richard Grunberger, *A Social History of the Third Reich*, Markham, Penguin Books, 1974, p. 33.
100. Marcel Bois, "Hitler Wasn't Inevitable," *Jacobin*, November 25, 2015.
101. As many as 100,000 members of the KPD had been interned by the end of 1933. The fate of those exiled to the Soviet Union was not always much better; given the climate of fear and insecurity in the USSR in the late 1930s, the Stalinist purges affected German communists in particular, since Stalin feared both that they might be Nazi spies and saboteurs and that they brought a different interpretation of Marxism-Leninism that would threaten the hegemony of his own. Eric D. Weitz, *Creating German Communism, 1890–1990*, Princeton, Princeton University Press, 1997, p. 4–13, 280–283. For a critical study of the purges, see J. Arch Getty's *Origins of the Great Purges* (1987).
102. Martin Niemöller, "First They Came…," 1946.
103. William Lyon Mackenzie King, *The Mackenzie King Diaries, 1893–1947*, June 29, 1937.
104. William Lyon Mackenzie King, *The Mackenzie King Diaries, 1893–1947*, June 29, 1937.
105. William Lyon Mackenzie King, *The Mackenzie King Diaries, 1893–1947*, June 30, 1937.
106. William Lyon Mackenzie King, *The Mackenzie King Diaries, 1893–1947*, June 30, 1937.
107. William Lyon Mackenzie King, quoted in Allan Levine, *King*, p. 297.
108. William Lyon Mackenzie King, *The Mackenzie King Diaries, 1893–1947*, June 27, 1937.

6

The Mythologies of Canada's "Good War"

> *There is a lot England can learn from Germany in treatment of masses of people... Nazism is not all wrong... [Hitler] will rank someday with Joan of Arc among the deliverers of his people, and if he is only careful may yet be the deliverer of Europe.*
>
> — Canadian Prime Minister
> William Lyon Mackenzie King, 1937[1]

GO TO THE SECTION OF any Canadian library that deals with the Second World War and you are likely to be inundated by books bearing titles like *The Good War, The Good Fight, Moral Combat, The Greatest Generation* and other variations on this theme. Surely no conflict has ever generated such a vast literature proclaiming its inherent goodness, and with so minimal a pushback. For a war that ultimately claimed the lives of some 70 million people, World War Two enjoys a remarkably positive reputation.

Of course, it is easy to understand the reasons for that reputation. The war in Europe had an obvious, and genuinely terrible, protagonist in Adolf Hitler. The particularly grotesque nature of his Holocaust gave added surety to the notion that Nazi Germany represented the worst of humankind and had to be stopped at all costs. Few besides the most hardened Nazi apologist — admittedly a growing demographic in the 21st century — would dispute that Nazi Germany was a radically evil apparatus of genocide and repression, though careful scholars remind us that its brutality was not unprecedented in the colonial era.[2] Still, given the depravity of the Nazis and the ubiquity of public remembrances of the Holocaust, the Second World War is remembered as a simple war, which probably accounts for its popularity among 20th-century Canadians like my father. Indeed, his affinity for World War Two documentaries was such that I can remember, as a teenager, routinely waking up to the sounds of machine guns and aerial bombardment on television.

But while the moral bankruptcy of fascism is beyond doubt, it is not so simple to assume that the attitudes and actions of the Allied powers — and Canada in particular — place them on indisputable moral high ground. What account should be taken of Allied and Canadian war crimes committed against Germany during the war? What do we do about the fact that even while the West battled fascism in Germany it allowed the same ideology to persevere in Spain? If the war was fought to liberate the Jews of Europe, why were they consistently refused refuge in countries like Canada before, during and even after the war? How do we reconcile the postwar elevation of recently defeated fascists into positions of authority in occupied Germany and Japan?

Indeed, how do we grapple with the popularity of fascism within the Western countries prior to the war? Given the extent to which the Second World War became the focal point of Western triumphalism, its heroes canonized and its memory mobilized to justify every war undertaken since 1945, it is worth lingering on the fact that many of those heroes had admired fascism. Winston Churchill, subject of an endless stream of fawning books and films, praised fascism for having "rendered a service to the whole world," in providing a blueprint for "the ultimate means of protection against the cancerous growth of Bolshevism."[3] All of this raises the possibility that the defeat of Nazi Germany might have been the right action taken for the wrong reasons.

These and other questions are inevitably raised in documenting Canada's "good war." Indeed, they have been raised before in Canada, and the reaction spoke volumes. In 1992, the CBC aired a National Film Board/Galafilm documentary called *The Valour and the Horror*, which attempted to grapple with a few of the less flattering chapters of Canada's Second World War. The documentary only scratched the surface in questioning the dominant mythology; it was rooted in the testimonies of veterans and was heavily sympathetic to their experiences. Nevertheless, it posed some difficult questions about decisions made by the Allied and Canadian commanders, most notably around the indiscriminate firebombing of German civilian cities.

The reaction was swift and aggressive; conservative historians lambasted the documentary, publishing screeds against it which denounced its supposed errors.⁴ One veterans' group launched a libel lawsuit — which failed because the documentary had not lied — packing the courtroom with Legion activists calling the filmmakers "Nazi lovers."⁵ The Senate launched an inquiry into the production of the film, and the lone copy of the book which accompanied the film at the University of Toronto's Trinity College library was defaced with the claim that its mistakes were "breathtakingly irresponsible." What is breathtaking is the extent to which sections of the Canadian establishment were scandalized by a fairly bland retelling of some widely accepted truths about the Second World War, including that indiscriminate bombings of German cities by Canadian pilots were ordered by Air Marshal Sir Arthur "Bomber" Harris, who himself described the bombing as a "deliberate terror attack."⁶

This chapter engages with these complicated problems in an effort to document the political content of Canada's Second World War. Rather than offer detailed accounts of the battles or the tactical and strategic decisions, I assess the broader politics that surrounded the war, highlighting the ways that Canada's foundational logic shaped its responses to the events that clouded the late 1930s and early 1940s. That Nazi Germany was defeated was indisputably a positive outcome to which many Canadians made valuable contributions and tremendous sacrifices. That the Canadian government spent years facilitating the rise of the very fascism those Canadians died fighting can only be explained by remaining clear about those elements — settler capitalism and the colonial imagination — that form the core of what Canada is.

The Second World War

World War Two, as the previous chapter suggested, was rooted in the same conflict that had torn Europe apart three decades before: rivalry between capitalist empires and would-be empires vying for a position of supremacy within the world system. Though framed as a battle to protect the "free world," the reality was that the gap between the Western capitalist powers and the fascist states was not nearly as wide as the West liked to imagine. In Philip K. Dick's fictional *The Man in the High Castle* (1962), Dick imagined a world where the Axis powers had won the war, and what was so chilling in his vision was that, in many respects, the alternate world did not look so different from the real one. Dick's point, skillfully made, was that fascist capitalism only differed from liberal capitalism by degrees.

A world capitalist system dominated by the Germans and Japanese would have been different, but not unrecognizable.

Though it may sound radical, Dick's point was not so farfetched. After all, the Western democracies 1) worked closely with the belligerent fascist states until just before the war; 2) respected the supposed neutrality of fascist states, like Spain and Portugal, throughout and after the war; 3) continued to administer many of their colonies and dependencies in a manner similar to the fascist states throughout and after the war; 4) would later actively promote the rise of fascist-style dictatorships in former colonies when it suited their interests; and 5) worked closely with many former-fascist administrators after the war, even restoring them to power in many of the countries where they were defeated. None of these facts are secrets and, taken together, they suggest that the liberal capitalist governments of the United States, Great Britain and Canada, among others, did not have any serious discomfort with fascism as an ideology. This would seem to be in sharp contradiction with another prominent fact: the Western capitalist states fought a war — a total war that by most metrics would be called the largest in human history — to defeat the fascist Axis powers. Some explanation is in order.

Capitalism is always in expansion or contraction, and one of the primary tasks of the national capitalist state is to ensure continuous expansion for its *own* fraction of capital. This emerged in great clarity in the period between the 1870s and the First World War, as imperial rivalry had seen a dramatic rise in predatory economic competition, protectionist tariffs against foreign products, growing territorial conflict, especially in the rush to acquire colonies, and a concurrent urgency to produce weapons to conquer those territories and maintain control over them. This competition between national states — increasingly representing the interests of large monopolistic blocs of capital — ultimately led to the Great War, but its conclusion was unsatisfactory to nearly everyone involved.[7]

The Russian Empire had been overthrown and replaced by a communist state that believed world revolution was around the corner, but this world revolution failed — or was defeated — and the new Soviet Union had to repel an international invasion, leading it to conclude that its only path was to focus on building what it called "Socialism in One Country." The United States, after the failure to defeat the Soviet Union, also withdrew from Europe to focus on growing its own, largely uncontested, sphere of influence and economic power in the Americas and the Pacific.

Britain and France assumed the leadership of postwar Europe, taking the opportunity to dismember their rivals in Germany (by imposing brutal economic penalties), Central Europe (by carving it up into fragmented states dependent on the West as a bulwark against German and Soviet expansion) and Turkey (by dividing its territories haphazardly into British and French colonies). The victorious European powers attempted to hold on to control of their colonies in East Asia but came under increasing pressure from the expanding Japanese Empire, which had already seized Korea and Taiwan in accordance with the same capitalist dynamics that plagued Europe.

This untenable world order began to fall apart when capitalism fell into its deepest crisis yet, the Great Depression, beginning in 1929. As the previous chapter described, growing working-class militancy and the presence of a socialist state on the eastern frontier of Europe had led to an intensified round of class struggle that saw fascist movements rise to power in Italy, Germany, Japan and elsewhere in the 1920s and 1930s. These fascists, imbued with a fervently militarist nationalism, would not accept their countries' relegation to the lower ranks of capitalist power and began asserting their right to greater territory, meeting only limited resistance. Fascism, remember, was by no means a radical departure from the forms of governance of the West and was seen as a useful antidote to growing socialist and communist momentum, especially in a time when capitalism could deliver little more than poverty and immiseration for the masses.

At the same time, the Western powers sought to place limits on German and Japanese expansion. This was reflected in the conversations between Prime Ministers King and Chamberlain in 1937, whose project was to rein in the otherwise favourable Nazi government and convince it to limit its expansion to areas that would not interfere with British supremacy. They had largely accepted the idea of a Greater Germany led by the Nazis, provided it did not unduly upset the balance of power in the capitalist world. Of course, this was folly; capital does not accept limits, and in the crisis years of the 1930s, with the world organized into cordoned-off colonial territories, acquiring greater territory was crucial to a growing capitalist economy, and the idea that a rising power like Germany would impose limits on its own growth was fanciful.

Once it became evident that Germany and Japan had no intention of limiting their expansion, war between the otherwise sympathetic states became almost inevitable. Even then, Hitler thought at the start that he might be able to avoid a larger war with Britain and certainly the United States since they had shown little interest in blocking the Japanese invasion of Manchuria in 1931, Italian aggression in Ethiopia in 1935, German and Italian intervention in Spain in 1936, the Japanese assault on Nanjing in 1937, German annexations of Austria in 1938 and Czechoslovakia in 1939, or any other acts of internal and external aggression on the part of the fascist powers.[8] Nevertheless, Hitler miscalculated and was surprised when France and England chose to intervene in response to his expansion into Poland. In a series of cascading decisions, the great powers were pulled into a total war that would ultimately cost the lives of some 70 million people, a figure so great it is almost impossible to truly grasp.

The Second World War ultimately concluded the inter-imperial rivalry that had begun in the 1870s, settled by the decisive victory of the United States as the undisputed centre of world capitalism. It simultaneously heralded the arrival of the next great geopolitical rivalry, the Cold War, which differed in that it was not a contest between like-minded capitalist empires but a struggle between ideologically divergent world systems. During World War Two, the United States and Soviet Union found themselves allied against the fascist states, but for vastly different reasons; while the West sought to reassert its dominance over world capitalism, the USSR was fighting for its very existence. And while the totalizing nature of the struggle meant that such an alliance against a common enemy was necessary for both, it did not mean that cooperation was undertaken in good faith; for instance, when Hitler bent the full weight of his armies upon the destruction of the Soviet Union in the early 1940s, Stalin begged the Western powers to open up a second front against the Nazis to relieve the pressure, to no avail. In fact, the West's refusal to build an alliance for collective security in the face of Hitler's aggression in the 1930s was precisely what motivated Stalin to briefly sign a peace treaty with Nazi Germany in the hope of delaying the inevitable war.[9]

That the Soviets were left to face Hitler almost entirely on their own, and nevertheless won, was both the decisive turning point in the war itself and also a clear reflection of the Cold War that was emerging. It is telling that future Prime Minister Lester Pearson's view, in 1938, was that he would be "delighted to see the sub-human Nazis and the equally sub-human Bolsheviks batter themselves to pieces against each other, while the Anglo-Saxons held the ring."[10] This is not so far from what really happened.

By the time the Anglo-American powers landed in Normandy in 1944, Hitler was in retreat on the Eastern Front. In purely military terms, it is beyond doubt that the Soviet Union's victory was the most significant single element of the defeat of Nazi Germany. This is also reflected in the staggeringly disproportionate losses that the Soviet Union suffered during the war: some 26 million Soviet citizens died compared to around 50,000 Canadians and half a million Americans. Pearson's desire to see the Nazis and the Soviets annihilate one another — a view shared by most in the Atlantic alliance — was very nearly fulfilled.[11]

With all of this in mind, the notion that Western powers went to war against Hitler out of a grand moral crusade against evil is frightfully misguided. Of course, millions of people did fight against fascism precisely because of the horrific ideology it represented. Partisans rose up across occupied territories in Europe and Asia to resist fascism, many of them dominated by socialist and communist organizations which had, by necessity, much experience operating covertly. Soviet soldiers were rallied to struggle against a fascism that sought to destroy everything positive the country had built.[12] Even soldiers in the armies of the West often recognized that the struggle against fascism was more than simply great power rivalry; many saw in this war the potential end of an age of militarized capitalist authority and the dawn of a new era where working people would be empowered to build a better world. Though they were likely a minority, these individuals shared with those who had fought in Spain the notion that fascism was the culmination of everything wrong with the capitalist world and — as the epitaph of Canadian soldier Edgar Harris, killed in World War Two, read — they "died that fascism be destroyed and that workers might build a new world."[13]

And yet, the governments that sent Edgar Harris and millions of others into the war against the Axis did not share his ideological opposition to fascism and desire for a new world. Rather, they demonstrated in a variety of ways that they were motivated primarily by great power rivalry and capitalist compulsion, and this was as true of Canada as it was of its allies. As the previous chapter illustrated, the highest levels of Canadian government were comfortable working with the Nazis and even admired their work, which reflected a more extreme version of Canada's own class struggle. They had largely ignored the expansion of fascist regimes — sometimes actively assisted them, as in El Salvador — and had abandoned the Spanish Republic even when hundreds of individual Canadians wanted to show solidarity; indeed, Canada maintained close diplomatic relations with fascist Spain until the dictator's death in 1970, even dropping all visa requirements between the two countries in 1959. Canada also had warm relations with the Portuguese far-right dictator António de Oliveira Salazar, who claimed neutrality during the war.

Meanwhile, Canada maintained, following the Boer War, a "special relationship" with South Africa as it drifted towards its own quasi-fascist Apartheid system. In 1942, Prime Minister King rather tellingly noted that Canada's "greatest problems have South African parallels" and that he had taken lessons from how South Africa had "coped with the difficulties" it faced.[14] Canada's record of support for Japanese fascism was equally disheartening, as the next chapter explores in more depth. But perhaps none among these hypocrisies makes Canada's assertion of moral superiority ring as hollow as the fact that it was populated by a great many settlers who shared Hitler's values, including a group of Canadian leaders so deeply anti-Semitic that they refused to open Canada's doors to Jewish refugees fleeing the Holocaust.

The Spectre of Jewish Bolshevism

Persecution and racism against Jews in Europe had, by the 20th century, a long and inglorious tradition. While rooted in Europe's long domination by the Catholic and later Protestant churches, its more modern manifestations reflected the changing patterns of political economy. Earlier forms of anti-Semitism were rooted in religious rivalry — for instance, fear that Jews would poison the wells from which Christians drank in order to assert their theological superiority — and this threat could theoretically be resolved were a Jew to renounce their faith. But by the 19th century, a more modern anti-Semitic panic had taken on a racial character; one could no longer convert out of being a Jew, it was considered an immutable racial quality. This new anti-Semitism was increasingly linked to matters of wealth and politics; Jews were blamed by disgraced aristocrats for the French Revolution, held responsible for the rise of socialism and regularly blamed for the Bolshevik Revolution in Russia. At the same time, contradictory accusations were levelled at Jews: that they were stingy money-grubbers who represented the worst of the parasitic banking and commercial classes. This latter mythology grew out of the diasporic nature of European Jewry in the Middle Ages. Regularly persecuted and denied access to land, many Jews became urban-dwellers and adapted into trades that could be carved out of medieval urban life, like commerce and artisanry.[15]

Jews could thus be scapegoated for any number of political economic problems and, in the early 20th century, were held in contempt on contradictory grounds. Somehow, they represented both the communist menace *and* the scheming bourgeoisie.[16] That these two categories were class enemies — and that Jews were represented in both — were facts that hardly troubled those who wished to mobilize anti-Semitism for their aims, and the essence that could be distilled from these two competing visions was that the Jews wanted to "rule the world." Whether as an all-powerful banking cabal or as a revolutionary party, the Jews were framed as beholden to an ancient conspiracy to undermine the good, Christian people of Europe and America.

In this way, anti-Semitism could be morphed to appeal to both the elite and the working classes, making it a very useful rallying point for fascism. That being said, it is important to recall that fascism could exist without anti-Semitism in particular; indeed, the original fascist, Benito Mussolini, did not inculcate any specific aversion to Jews in his program until pressured to do so by Hitler. Fascism was an ideological response to socialism; it was a nationalist, authoritarian reaction that sought to re-assert traditional authority, to protect liberal capitalism — by illiberal means — when it could not protect itself. Indeed, despite a mountain of literature seeking to present fascism as antithetical to liberalism, fascism was a product of precisely the 19th century liberal order — industrial capitalism, class struggle and the construction of racial hierarchy around colonialism — that it appeared to be destroying. As Ishay Landa describes it, fascism was "an extreme attempt at solving the crisis of liberalism, breaking out of its aporia, and saving the bourgeoisie from itself."[17]

Thus, fascism as an ideology cannot be reduced to anti-Semitism, as some seek to do. At the same time, the Nazi adaptation of fascism made anti-Semitism its emotional cornerstone, an element of Hitler's project that resonated across much of Europe and North America,[18] and thus linked the two in such a powerful way that many subsequent fascist movements adopted the anti-Semitic element as an almost symbolic gesture where it had little resonance in the society in question.[19] In the early 20th century, the anti-Semitic character of Nazism was not nostalgic but central: Jews were recast by Hitler as "the carriers of Bolshevism," a disease that needed to be eradicated, and "Jewish Bolshevism" was framed as the primary enemy in "the struggle for the existence of the German people and a defence of European culture against the Asiatic and Muscovite flood."[20]

In this way, Jews were linked with the non-white peoples of the colonized world, who were, in turn, linked with the working classes and the revolutionary left. Euro-American elites were adapting and applying colonial language to their own working classes as early as in the crushing of the Paris Commune in 1871, in which the socialists were directly compared to "wild beasts, stinking animals, venomous creatures, all the refractory perversities that civilization has been unable to tame."[21] This language was common; consider the ravings of Winston Churchill, who called communists "enemies of the human race," "vampires sucking the blood of their victims" and "atrocious baboons in the midst of ruined towns and heaps of corpses," with Lenin a "monster atop a pyramid of skulls" surrounded by a "vile group of cosmopolitan fanatics." The language of Churchill's patrician vitriol was similar to that directed at Jews, whom he called "a force hidden behind every subversive movement of the nineteenth century."[22]

Indeed, Churchill fully incorporated his anti-Semitism into his aristocratic disgust at working-class movements, bemoaning the fact that Jews had built "a worldwide conspiracy for the overthrow of civilization" and were "the mainspring of every subversive movement during the 19th century" and had gone on to "become practically the undisputed masters of that enormous empire," in reference to the Bolsheviks having seized power in Moscow. He added that this Jewish leftist conspiracy was seeking a society based on "arrested development, envious malevolence, and impossible equality." In other words, they were stupid and jealous and they did not understand that hierarchy was natural. Churchill was reflecting the standard hallmarks of ruling-class ideology.[23]

This language met with no great scandal in Canada. Indeed, as noted in the previous chapter, prominent Canadians like Prime Minister William Lyon Mackenzie King were well-disposed to hating both the poor and the Jews and had plenty of experience and comfort with both. In fact, anti-Semitism reached its heights in Canada in the 1920s and 1930s, as Canadian fascist organizations and Swastika Clubs were formed across the country, especially in Ontario, Québec, and Manitoba, under leaders like Otto Becker, Adrien Arcand and William Whittaker. While Becker was recruiting for Swastika Clubs in Kitchener, Ontario politicians were openly declaring their racial hatreds, as when R.K. Serviss called a political opponent "a bloody Jew" and added that he had "no more respect for a Jew than Hitler."[24] Whittaker's Canadian Nationalist Party advocated openly for fascism and violence and was given permission by Winnipeg's mayor, Col. Ralph Webb, to use Winnipeg's military barracks for training.[25] Arcand, the leader of the *chemises bleues* (Blueshirts), fashioned himself the "Führer Canadien" and had the support of the provincial government in Québec as late as 1938.[26]

Through it all, the link between anti-Semitism and anti-communism was always present and was perhaps most clearly refracted through the personage of Brig. Gen. Dennis Draper, Toronto's police chief, who used his position to crack down on both the left and the foreigners, creating a "Red Squad" to break up meetings, outlaw organizations and ban Yiddish and other foreign-language newspapers for fear that they were being used to foment revolution.[27] In 1929 Draper's officers attacked a group of people at Queen's Park in Toronto listening to Communist Party speeches, charging into the crowd on horseback and assaulting people — including children — with batons while shouting "get back to Russia."[28] Not surprisingly, institutions like the police and military were often hotbeds of white supremacy. In Ottawa, it was another police officer, Jean Tissot, who tried to mobilize a boycott of Jewish stores to drive them out of the city.[29]

Even outside of these far-right organizations, anti-Semitism in Canadian society ran deep. The *Globe and Mail* reminded Canadians that most communists were Jews,[30] and the magazine *Saturday Night* editorialized, with reference to Jews, "when this country puts up its bars against further immigration from certain parts of Europe… we will know where to start."[31] The rise of Hitler in 1933 led to a spike in aggressively anti-Semitic incidents in Canadian cities. In Toronto, for example, "Gentiles Only" signs began popping up, Jews began to be refused service at hotels or blocked from renting in particular neighbourhoods, and that summer in the east side community of the Beaches, the Balmy Beach Swastika Club was formed to preserve the neighbourhood of its Anglo-Saxon character. The club drew inspiration from Nazi Germany and sought to rid the beachfront area of a wide array of immigrants, especially Jews, and youths wearing Swastika armbands attacked Jews at Kew Beach and threw garbage on the porches of their homes.[32]

Violence escalated through that summer culminating in the Christie Pits Riot: in the middle of a baseball game featuring a Jewish team, fascists in the audience unveiled a massive Swastika flag, threw up "Heil Hitler" salutes and began attacking the players. Dennis Draper's police had ignored reports that such an event was being planned and chose instead to send the bulk of their officers to break up a labour union meeting elsewhere. Back at Christie Pits, the working-class Jews and Italians who lived in the neighbourhood had rallied and went toe-to-toe with the Swastika gang through the night. In the end, the fascists were trounced, no thanks to the almost entirely absent police and Draper's claim that "Hebrew people [had] arrived and caused trouble."[33] Nevertheless, Toronto could no longer deny — as its newspapers had done for months — that anti-Semitism and fascism were growing in strength.[34] Indeed it bears remembering that the appearance of fascism and anti-Semitism in Canada was a new manifestation of existing class antagonism and colonial racism; its roots went deep and had always been primarily an upper-middle-class phenomenon.[35] As early as 1933 Canadian cities saw major working-class mobilizations *against* Hitler, many of which were attacked by Canadian police for their left-wing politics.

One of Canada's celebrated early intellectuals, Goldwin Smith, was viciously anti-Semitic, and this was explicitly linked to his white supremacy. In addition to, as Ramsay Cook describes, "faith in the superiority of the Anglo-Saxon civilization" and absolute disdain for Irish, Roman Catholics, French Canadians and women, Smith was also one of the most prominent anti-Semites of his era, asserting in 1878 that they were a "danger to western civilization" and should be thus removed from Europe.[36] As Gerald Tuchinsky argues, Smith's revulsion of Jews was pathological and, indeed, bordered on genocidal in his ominous predictions that their end would come.[37] Smith's rabid white supremacy is noteworthy not just because he was one of Canada's most famous intellectuals in the late 19th century but also because he was a mentor and family friend to future Canadian prime minister William Lyon Mackenzie King. It was Smith who wrote a letter of reference for King to go to Harvard. King, whose anti-Semitism was documented in the previous chapter, said this of Smith:

> I recall Goldwin Smith feeling so strongly about the Jews. He expressed it at one time as follows: that they were poison in the veins of a community… the evidence is very strong, not against all Jews… that in a large percentage of the race there are tendencies and trends which are dangerous indeed.[38]

King wrote these words in his diary in 1946, after the full depth of the horror of Hitler's Holocaust had been revealed. That Canada's celebrated prime minister, once an admirer of Hitler himself, should have still agreed with one of Canada's leading intellectuals' virulent anti-Semitism even after the murder of millions of Jews in Europe is a chilling testament to the depth of white supremacy in Canada.

None Is Too Many

It is beyond doubt that the project of calculated extermination known as the Holocaust (or Shoah) was encouraged by the Western powers when they refused to accept Jewish refugees in the late 1930s. Canada's place in this ugly piece of history is perhaps the most damning; Canada admitted among the fewest Jewish refugees of any Western country and its government was among the most ideologically committed to such a refusal. Between 1933 and 1945, some 200,000 Jews were admitted into the United States, 70,000 into Great Britain, 50,000 to Argentina, 27,000 to Brazil and 15,000 to Australia.[39] While these numbers represented only a tiny fraction of the need, they still dwarf the 5000 that Canada accepted. Most notably, Canada refused to allow more than 900 Jewish refugees to disembark from the MS *St Louis* at Halifax in 1939; more than 200 of the people turned back from Canada's shores would return to Europe to be killed by the Nazis.[40]

In addition to Prime Minister King himself, key figures in his administration were sympathetic to Hitler's hatred of Jews. Director of Immigration Charles Blair, an avowed anti-Semite, explicitly argued for a broad-based, international refusal to accept Jewish refugees, on the grounds that this would force Germany to solve its Jewish problem internally.[41] Needless to say, that is precisely what Germany did, to horrifying effect. Blair regularly issued screeds against the Jews, suggesting that they needed "humiliation" and should be told more regularly why "certain of their habits" were so reviled, and as director of immigration he routinely characterized Jews as cheats who tricked their way into countries and then brought stampedes of relatives.[42] He chastised them as unfit to do real work and even claimed that refusing Jews entry into Canada was doing them a favour since widespread anti-Semitism would only make them persecuted in Canada too.

Though this was a thin and disingenuous argument, it was not, strictly speaking, incorrect: Canadian society *was* intensely anti-Semitic. Leaders like King and Blair got their marching orders from a public that was encouraged to hold Jews — like other immigrants from southern and eastern Europe — in contempt.[43] But even as the full scope of the Holocaust was revealed, turning public opinion in a more sympathetic direction, the Canadian government maintained its intransigence. In 1943, as the Warsaw ghetto was being razed and with over a million Polish Jews already killed, the Anglo-American powers saw fit to reassure the public that they cared about the plight of the Jews. King even expressed feelings of guilt in his diaries, on occasion.[44] None among them, however, wished to actually accept refugees.

As the British, Americans and Canadians pressured one another to do something about Jews fleeing the Holocaust, the idea for a conference to discuss the matter became a political football. When the Americans suggested it be held in Ottawa, the Canadian government refused to even entertain the idea, lest it add to the pressure that Canada accept refugees. Since none of the governments in question wanted to host the conference, it was held in Bermuda, where, predictably, the conclusion was that nothing more could be done.[45] The complicity of the Allied powers in the Holocaust itself is striking. A British memo in 1943 articulated the greatest fear, which was that Hitler would *stop* killing Jews, "chang[ing] over from a policy of extermination to one of extrusion, aim[ing] as they did before the war at embarrassing other countries by flooding them with alien immigrants."[46]

The systematic refusal — before, during and after the Second World War — to accept Jewish refugees is exhaustively detailed in Irving Abella and Harold Troper's *None Is Too Many: Canada and the Jews of Europe, 1933–1948*, a title derived from a candid statement made by a Canadian official in 1945: with the war coming to an end, he was asked how many Jews Canada would accept and his answer was "none is too many." It sums up decades of immigration policies that cast an incredible pall over what many Canadians believe about their "good war." If the Second World War was about saving the Jews from Hitler, why did Canada not save the Jews from Hitler? Indeed, in a striking historical irony, the extreme violence of Hitler's genocide combined with the utter refusal of the West to accept Jewish immigration led to an absurd compromise: Canadian support for the hitherto marginal Zionist movement which sought to conquer and claim Palestine as a Jewish settler state. The irony, discussed in later chapters, was that the new state of Israel, born in part out of the catastrophe of Western anti-Semitism, would model much of its colonial violence in Palestine after the settler states of Canada and the United States.

Crimes and Contradictions

Canada did eventually break relations with the fascist regimes it so admired and sent soldiers to defeat the Axis. As discussed above, this decision was undertaken when it became clear to Britain and France that German expansion could not be contained and would, therefore, pose a direct threat to the supremacy of the Western powers. Canada joined them in declaring war in 1939, and Canadian forces suffered significant defeats early in the war, first in their failed defence of Hong Kong and again in the bungled attempt to land troops at Dieppe in France. Nevertheless, outside of limited naval operations, Canada's combat role in the war only became significant after the 1943 invasion of Sicily and the D-Day invasion in 1944; as noted elsewhere, the Allies had left the Soviet Union to contend with Nazi Germany almost entirely on its own.

Still, by 1944, the Canadian government was being asked to send more troops to Europe and again introduced conscription; though opposition was not as strong as in 1917, many of the conscripts refused and the King government had to play public opinion carefully.[47] To that end, King established several new agencies to conduct propaganda, most notably the Wartime Information Board, which carefully gauged public opinion to ensure that it could best tailor the government's message.[48] By 1945, more than a million Canadians had fought in the war — nearly a tenth of the population — and at least 40,000 had died. The sacrifice needed to defeat Nazi Germany was significant, and the lives lost were overwhelmingly drawn from the working classes. Many believed themselves to be part of a noble struggle and, in several respects, they were. The defeat of some of the fascist states of Europe was a victory for humanity, and the people who made that happen deserve credit for it, irrespective of the larger manipulations their government might have been involved in.

Still, the clouds that hang over Canada's involvement in the Second World War remain thick and troubling. Unsurprisingly, as Jeffrey Keshen documents, war profiteering was a persistent and significant fact during the 1940s as capital found ways to take advantage of the crisis. In addition to corruption in the military-industrial complex, capital naturally took full advantage of legal ways of ramping up exploitation — for instance, landlords gouged tenants for exorbitant rents in centres of war production — and the state took the opportunity of war to justify interceding on behalf of capital to force wage freezes and suspend the right to strike.[49] Capital was capital; no great moral crusade against fascism was going to interrupt the accumulation of profits. But what of that moral crusade? The amorality of capital may not be surprising, but the mythology of Canada's war always relies on the assumption that the troops were selfless heroes who acquitted themselves with honour as they risked the ultimate sacrifice for the greater good. While that may be true of some — I, personally, hope that definition holds true of my eldest uncle — it did not apply to all. While it might be a simple matter to assert that the Nazis were bad and needed to be defeated, the conduct of Canadian and other Allied soldiers during the war raises questions about measures taken that went beyond what was necessary and prudent to actually defeat the Nazis.

For instance, it should hardly need to be said that the rape of German women would not exact justice for the crimes of Nazism. But Canadian soldiers nevertheless raped German women. It is unclear how widespread such behaviour was; research into the matter has largely been unpursued. The best estimates suggest that Allied soldiers — including Canadians — committed tens of thousands of acts of sexual violence in the European Theatre of World War Two.[50] Very few of the cases, however, were pursued by military authorities. Thus, only 52 cases were brought against Canadian soldiers, from which only 19 were convicted.[51] In most of these cases, the targets were German women, but Canadian soldiers also attacked women in other countries, including the particularly heinous case of Lance-Corp. Robert J. Kerr, who was involved in a gang rape of a Flemish woman at her home in Belgium. In Saxony, Canadian solders sexually assaulted a Russian woman who had originally been kidnapped by Nazi soldiers in Russia and sent to work as a slave labourer on a German farm.[52] One soldier described another attack this way:

> One of the guys I joined up with… got himself into a hell of a jam here just the other day. He and another fellow hurded [sic] a couple of German Frauleins "up them stairs" ahead of a Sten Gun. While one held the Sten Gun the other gave them a painless meat injection, now they are both up on a charge of rape, which isn't so good.[53]

Rape, at gunpoint, by two Canadian soldiers, in the liberation of Germany. It clashes sharply with the image of the good war that we have been so long committed to. But it should not come as a surprise; this Canadian military was the same that had facilitated a massacre in El Salvador, that had committed horrific atrocities in sub-Saharan Africa and that had conquered the Indigenous Peoples. It was a colonial army that had used torture and sexual violence in the past and, while the war against the Nazis might have been a nobler cause, militaries are notoriously traditional. That Canadian pilots sang songs around the piano in English pubs that made ambiguous, lighthearted references to rape is a fact that bears noting.[54] These traditions would, indeed, be carried on after the Second World War; in Korea, the Congo, Yugoslavia and many stops in between. It is likely that this violence was less prominent in Germany than elsewhere; after all, Germans were considered racial and civilizational equals and although wartime propaganda worked to dehumanize "the Hun" as much as possible, it could not have had the same resonance as in cases when Canadians were conquering those they had long viewed as their "lessers."[55]

These were not the only atrocities Canadians committed in World War Two. The concept of "war crimes" can be tricky; in a total war, it is not easy to determine what boundaries to place on the scope and tactics of organized murder. Still, to the extent that certain constraints are traditionally expected to be upheld — around matters like the execution of prisoners, the use of torture or the massacre of unarmed civilians — it is clear that Canadians, like other Allied soldiers, regularly violated those conventions.[56] Certainly, some people would argue that anyone who chose to fight for the Nazis deserved the treatment they got; that treatment included summary execution, use as human shields and being forced to walk ahead of Canadian soldiers through minefields. Asked about the murder of German prisoners, Canadian General Jacques Dextraze simply noted, "this happens in war."[57] Though the answer seems callous, it is not easy to muster up much sympathy for the armed forces of a fascist state, especially one that was so deeply committed to campaigns of mass execution.

But civilians arguably pose a more complex problem. While many Germans supported the Nazis and their ideology, many others considered themselves victims of a terrifying dictatorship and did whatever they felt they could to undermine it, most famously in efforts to shelter Jewish friends and neighbours from the Holocaust. How, then, do we address individual Canadians who killed civilians? And how should we remember the intensive aerial bombing of German cities, most notably Dresden, Berlin and Hamburg? The latter city had 9000 tons of bombs dropped on it, reducing more than half of the city to ashes and killing some 40,000 people, most of them civilians.[58] Survivors' stories are horrific, describing temperatures so hot that skin peeled and windpipes would burn from breathing. People hiding in bunkers were asphyxiated. A child stuck in tar on the street, burned alive while its mother watched hopelessly. Canadians played a key role in the firebombing.

For the Canadian pilots flying those raids, emotions were mixed and often laced with fear. The missions were dangerous and the trauma often had them breaking down in tears following a mission. Many suffered mental breakdowns and refused to continue flying; one even jumped out of his plane to his death.[59] Most did not know what their bombs were targeting, at least at the start, but had been assured they were military targets. This was false: by 1942, it was the explicit Allied policy to bomb civilian cities to erode German morale. "We shall destroy Germany's will to fight," said Air Vice Marshall Harris. "We shall drop one and a quarter million tons of bombs, render 25 million Germans homeless, kill 900,000 and seriously injure one million."[60]

As the pilots clued into what was happening their reactions were mixed. One recounted the moment he was given a direct order to target a train station: "I thought, Oh my God! They're telling us to aim for these people as a primary target."[61] Another remembered, "to watch those houses [being bombed] and to realise they were your bombs. It was very disturbing."[62] Nevertheless, the majority continued to carry out the raids, convinced that the strategy of breaking the enemy's morale was just and wise. Assessing the justice of the bombing is complicated, but its wisdom has been long called into question. An estimated 460,000 Germans were killed in the bombing of their cities across the length of the war, most of them civilian, and many historians have argued that the Allied bombing actually strengthened German morale. For German soldiers who may have been unsure of the moral virtue of their position, watching hundreds of thousands of people burn in Dresden and Hamburg did much to clarify the reasons they should continue fighting. It is impossible to know whether the war would have ended sooner if German civilians had not been burned in their homes, but the fact that they were — and the other crimes documented above — is undeniably part of the story of Canada's "good war."

At War's End

There are those who would argue that Nazi Germany was an enemy whose evil was as great as any the world had ever seen; whatever was necessary to defeat fascism was acceptable, including the forms of violence noted above. The argument is worth entertaining. Given the real threat that Nazism represented to so many people, perhaps there should have been no scruples when it came to the methods of its defeat. This was arguably the approach taken by the Soviet Red Army, which dealt out severe punishment to the Germans it met on its march west to Berlin; the distinction between German and Nazi was not always investigated, and individual soldiers carried out acts of serious violence and sexual violence. At a more pragmatic and official level, the USSR oversaw a thorough program of de-Nazification in the countries it occupied after the war. In this case, more serious efforts were taken to root out of hiding those who had significantly collaborated with the Nazis, and many were tried and/or purged by the Soviets and the local governments that emerged after their liberation in the Soviet sphere of influence in Europe.[63] It is important to note that de-Nazification was widely supported by the many who had lived for varying lengths of time under Nazi occupation.

Curiously, despite its having employed extreme violence against German civilians during the war, the Western Allies undertook only minimal de-Nazification measures after 1945. If the evil of Nazism had justified those atrocities that Western soldiers had carried out against Germans, then it stands as one of the most remarkable facts about the Second World War that the Western faction of the Allied occupation allowed tens of thousands of Nazis — not just frontline soldiers but high-ranking officials — to return to civic life.[64] Collaborators in the banks and big businesses, as well as the police and military, were routinely allowed to return to their positions; even the man chosen by Washington to be West Germany's first chancellor, Konrad Adenauer, had been admired by Hitler and could reasonably be described as sympathetic to the Nazis in the 1930s.[65] More than a thousand Nazis — some of astonishingly high rank — were quietly brought to the United States to work for the CIA, their "minor war crimes" dismissed as temporary "moral lapses."[66] This policy — most famously known as "Operation Paperclip" — was not a secret conspiracy by a handful of officials but, rather, a widely considered and accepted element of Western policy. More than fifty Nazi scientists were recruited into Canada between 1945 and 1950, which required adjustments to Canadian immigration policies to make allowances for those who had only a "nominal" connection to the Nazi party.[67]

Many more were offered political roles in the West German state that emerged after 1945, some in prominent positions. Perhaps the most notable example was Nazi General Reinhard Gehlen. Gehlen had been the head of Nazi Germany's intelligence operations in Eastern Europe; he knew Hitler personally, called him a "misplaced genius" and last met with him in February 1945 in the Reich Chancellery. Gehlen bragged in his memoirs that he had "played a not unimportant role in the war."[68] He was placed in charge of West German intelligence in 1946 and retired with a CIA pension in 1968.[69] One of his deputies was Franz Six, a noteworthy enough SS officer that his name appears in histories of the organization. He had joined the Nazi party in 1930, worked as a propagandist in the 1930s and later led several Einsatzgruppen death squads, rising rapidly through the ranks of the SS. After serving a reduced sentence for crimes against humanity, he joined Gehlen's organization and lived out his days as a free — and powerful — man in West Germany.[70]

Some of these decisions were taken outside of the direct purview of the Canadian government. By the end of the war it was abundantly clear that the United States was assuming the leadership of the capitalist world, and Canada worked hard to collaborate effectively with both the US and Britain in building a postwar world order that would be favourable to their interests. Nevertheless, Canada's interests broadly coincided with its Atlantic partners. The British Commonwealth Relations Office sent a telegram to Ottawa explaining, in 1948, that, with respect to fascist leaders, it was not interested in "meting out retribution of every guilty individual" and sought instead "to dispose of the past as soon as possible."[71] This was not met with any indignation in Canada, which itself admitted at least 2000 former Nazis in the years following the war, in addition to those brought over in Operation Paperclip,[72] even after it had refused to admit those fleeing Nazi violence. Canada may not have ordered the burning of Dresden or the appointment of Reinhard Gehlen, but it did not object to those decisions or interfere with them in any way.

Canada, like the United States, was comfortable with the idea of anti-communist former Nazis keeping West Germany as a bulwark against communism in the emerging Cold War. To that end, Canada kept a force of over 6000 troops stationed in West Germany to buttress the threat being levied against the Soviet side.[73] Within four years of the war's end, West Germany was essentially being managed by the same people who had administered the country for the Nazis, though it was now protected by North American soldiers.[74] Similar patterns emerged in many of the postwar states administered by the West. It serves as a reminder that the Western Allies did not have a problem with fascist, or even Nazi, ideology; as soon as their capacity to build a rival empire was destroyed, the West was able to work with the former Nazis and collaborators just as smoothly as it had before the war.

Death from Above, Death from Below

The "good war" ended with the detonation of the first — and only — nuclear bombs ever deployed. The instant obliteration of as many as 250,000 civilians is an odd way for a "good" war to end. The horrific bomb over Nagasaki burned at more than 3000 degrees Celsius, incinerating people in an instant, and survivors had a 46% likelihood of developing leukemia. Descriptions of the aftermath are harrowing: "Their faces were blackish and swollen like pumpkins, there were corpses in which the heads had been split open."[75] World opinion was decidedly critical of the wanton carnage, and even the US public reflected discomfort with the scale of the barbarity. Defenders of the decision claimed that the bombs were necessary to end the war quickly, since the Japanese military would have fought to the end. This claim was false — the Japanese command was already formulating terms for surrender — and was largely based in an absurd racist stereotype about Japanese fanaticism.

Exhaustive scholarly study has illustrated that "ending the war to save American lives" was not the primary reason the atomic weapons were used.[76] Rather, as US Secretary of War Henry Stimson put it, "the bomb was a psychological weapon" used to illustrate the awful power of the United States and to ensure that Japan surrendered before the Soviet Union arrived on the scene.[77] US officials would evoke the memory often to intimidate the USSR, as when William Dyess warned, in 1980, that "the Soviets know that this terrible weapon has been dropped on human beings twice in history and it was an American president who dropped it both times."[78] In 1945 it was already evident that the real ideological struggle was between the left and the right — represented geopolitically by the US and the USSR — and the new president, Harry Truman, was not content sharing the postwar administration of the world with the Soviets. Everyone understood that Japan would be a key player in postwar East Asia, and Truman did not want to share its governance as he would have to in Germany; he explicitly acknowledged this in his memoirs, discussing his concern that imminent Soviet ground invasion would mean joint occupation of postwar Japan.[79]

In fact, the atomic weapons alone did not convince Japan to surrender. Rather, it was the imminent Soviet invasion that provoked the Emperor's announcement that Japan would capitulate. The Japanese elite, aware that the war was nearly over, had already made one aborted effort to surrender, a few weeks earlier. Now, with the Soviets at their doorstep, they faced the prospect of not only losing the war but witnessing the rebirth of Japanese communism, which they had worked so hard to crush. They knew that US administration would maintain the existing class character of Japan — albeit under direction from Washington — whereas the Soviets would present an ideological break. Thus, in the final moments of the Second World War, fearing the dismantling of the system of capitalism and patronage that maintained their privilege, Japanese fascist leadership was acquiescing to US occupation because it provided the best guarantee of their continued dominance of Japan.[80] As the next chapter documents, they were correct in that calculation.

Canadians might want to imagine that this whole sordid business had nothing to do with us. The bombs were not ours, their victims are not on our conscience, we would never bargain a quarter of a million lives for the sake of maintaining the capitalist character of occupied Japan. Unfortunately, this could not be further from the truth. About an hour after Japanese civilians were vapourized in Hiroshima, Canadian Munitions and Supply Minister C.D. Howe announced that "Canadian scientists and Canadian institutions ha[d] played an intimate part" in the bombing, which "guarantee[d] us a front-line position in the scientific advance that lies ahead."[81] Howe sat on the Combined Policy Committee, a joint US-UK-Canadian council through which the coordination of research, production and strategic use of the weapons was carried out. Howe supported the decision to drop the bomb and took great pride in Canada's important role, pointing specifically to the Eldorado Mining and Refining Company, which had been nationalized by the Canadian government in order to provide uranium for the bombs.

Indeed, the uranium was mined on Dene territory near Great Bear

Lake; the lake became completely contaminated, and it was the people of the Sahtugot'ine First Nation who carried the uranium out of the mine. Though the government knew the danger associated with this work, it did not tell the Indigenous workers; most of them died of cancer, as did many other people living near the mine.[82] It is a remarkable footnote to the "good war" that it should end with Canada killing Indigenous people, in order to build a weapon to kill Japanese people, in order to win a war that had already been won, in order to preserve the capitalist character of Japan.

Notes
1. William Lyon Mackenzie King, *The Mackenzie King Diaries, 1893–1947*, June 27, 1937, and June 29, 1937, Microfiche Collection, University of Toronto, University of Toronto Press, 1980.
2. Mahmood Mamdani, *Good Muslim, Bad Muslim: America, the Cold War, and the Roots of Terror*, New York, Random House, 2004, p. 7.
3. Winston Churchill, quoted in Ishay Landa, *The Apprentice's Sorcerer: Liberal Tradition and Fascism*, Boston, Brill, 2010, p. 321. Meanwhile, the supposedly weak-kneed Neville Chamberlain, cast by most narratives as the leader who blanched in the face of Hitler's aggression, was in fact also a great admirer, calling Nazi Germany and England "the two pillars of European peace and buttresses against communism."
4. David Bercuson and S.F. Wise, eds., *The Valour and the Horror Revisited*, Montreal, McGill-Queen's Press, 1994. Bercuson and Wise denounced the film — and cast mocking assertions against its authors — for suggesting that the bombing of German cities was unnecessary, saying, "The kinds of rigorous criticism and analysis demanded of our honours and graduate students in history are unknown to the public and, it seems, to many journalists." But despite pulling rank as professional historians, they failed to grapple with the fact that one of the most comprehensive studies of the bombing campaign — contained within a sympathetic three volume history of the Royal Canadian Air Force — largely came to the same conclusions as had the filmmakers. Brereton Greenhous, Stephen J. Harris, William C. Johnson, and William G.P. Rawling, *The Crucible of War 1939–1945: The Official History of the Royal Canadian Air Force*, vol. 3., Toronto, University of Toronto Press, 1994.
5. Ian McKay and Jamie Swift, *Warrior Nation: Rebranding Canada in an Age of Anxiety*, Toronto, Between the Lines, 2012, p. 189.
6. Arthur "Bomber" Harris, quoted in McKay and Swift, *Warrior Nation*, p. 189.
7. Henry Heller, *The Cold War and the New Imperialism: A Global History, 1945–2005*, New York, Monthly Review Press, 2006, p. 15–16.
8. Eric Hobsbawm, *The Age of Extremes: A History of the World, 1914–1991*, New York, Vintage Books, 1996, p. 37.
9. Isaac Deutscher, *Stalin: A Political Biography*, Oxford, Oxford University Press, 1967, p. 414–461.
10. Lester Pearson, quoted in John English, "Lester Pearson Encounters the Enigma," in David Davies, ed., *Canada and the Soviet Experiment*, Toronto, Canadian

Scholars' Press, 1994, p. 106.
11. John English, "Lester Pearson Encounters the Enigma," p. 107.
12. Not everything the Soviet Union built was positive. Though born of a revolutionary struggle of the working class — and imbued with an ideology that sought genuine emancipation for all working people — the new country faced extraordinary challenges in its early years. Not the least was the three-year counter-revolution and invasion of foreign forces, even after Russians had suffered three years in the Great War under the Tsar. In addition, with no world revolution in the early 1920s, the USSR had to find an internal solution to having carried off a working-class revolution in a country that was predominantly made up of rural agrarian peasants. It thus had to solve the problem of how to bolster agricultural production to support the industrialization of its cities in a context where much of the peasantry was suspicious of urban proposals for collective agriculture. By the mid-1920s it was clear that this was an existential problem insofar as the Western powers, and especially those turning to fascism, would take whatever measures to defeat the revolution. Thus, if it were to survive, it would need to rapidly build an industrial base and a modern military. What transpired in the process of solving this (and other) pressing problems ranged from remarkable success to unmitigated tragedy. Fair assessments of the Soviet experience are exceptionally difficult to find, given the ideological challenge that the Soviet Union posed and the resultant polarization of positions towards it. Neither the Cold War demonization of the USSR nor left apologia for it are acceptable responses for any serious historian. A useful overview of Soviet historiography can be found in Ronald Grigor Suny's *Red Flag Unfurled: History, Historians, and the Russian Revolution* (2017), while a solid overview of the history of the Soviet Union is provided in Moshe Lewis's *The Soviet Century* (2005). Classic and indispensable, albeit dated, is Charles Bettelheim's *Class Struggles in the USSR* (1976).
13. McKay and Swift, *Warrior Nation*, p. 89
14. William Lyon Mackenzie King, quoted in Brian Tennyson, *Canadian Relations with South Africa: A Diplomatic History*, Washington, University Press of America, 1982, p. xi.
15. The combining of these contradictory accusations found expression most notably in the spreading of the absurd propaganda known as the *Protocols of the Elders of Zion*, a set of clumsy forgeries purporting to be evidence of a Jewish conspiracy to rule the world. These emerged from Tsarist Russia, where the decrepit monarchy had tapped into the older form of anti-Semitism in order to stoke its more modern version, hoping to use Jews as a scapegoat for the miserable conditions of the Russian Empire. These culminated in the pogroms, the massacres of Jews and the sacking and looting of their communities, which sent waves of refugees west and, eventually, to North America. After the Tsarists were overthrown in 1917, the *Protocols* were used as evidence that Jews were behind the Bolshevik Revolution and were soon published and spread widely. This served ruling-class interests in Euro-America well; Jewish immigration was increasing and these mostly working-class immigrants were, indeed, drawn to left politics. Henry Ford was among the many high-placed North Americans who accepted the *Protocols* as truth and hammered the readers of his newspaper

with talk of the "Jewish menace." Thus, the spreading of the *Protocols* represents a key marker in the transition from the old anti-Semitism to its modern version. Abigail B. Bakan, "Race, Class, and Colonialism: Reconsidering the 'Jewish Question,'" in Abigail B. Bakan and Enakshi Dua, ed., *Theorizing Anti-Racism: Linkages in Marxism and Critical Race Theories*, Toronto, University of Toronto Press, 2014, p. 257.

16. Allan Levine, *King: William Lyon Mackenzie King, A Life Guided by Destiny*, Toronto, Douglas & McIntyre, 2011, p. 287.
17. Ishay Landa, *The Apprentice's Sorcerer: Liberal Tradition and Fascism*, Boston, Brill, 2010, p. 9.
18. In fact, Enzo Traverso has argued that anti-Semitism was actually far more prevalent in the early 20th century outside of Germany than within it. Enzo Traverso, *The Origins of Nazi Violence*, New York, The New Press, 2003, p. 13.
19. This tension is evident in the fascist movements re-emerging today, especially in North America, which often attempt to maintain the symbols, language and tradition of anti-Semitism that ran so deep in the history they admired, even despite the fact that Jews in North America have, over the past 70 years, attained a qualified "whiteness" insofar as they are mostly included in the various privileges generally available to whites. Jews, like Italians or Ukrainians, are no longer the typical targets for exclusionary racist panics; that role is being filled predominantly by people from other continents, especially Arabs and Muslims, and people from Latin America. In fact, many on the far-right admire the state of Israel, itself having adopted a quasi-fascist, settler colonial role, further complicating the anti-Semitic element of fascism. Even still, their propaganda makes it clear that hating Jews is still a significant — if arguably nostalgic — component of the ideology. The Tree of Life Synagogue in Pittsburgh was targeted by a fascist shooter in 2018 specifically because it was organizing support for the migrant caravan fleeing violence in Central America and seeking refuge in the United States. Thus, the synagogue represented the classic fascist formulation of the "Jewish Bolshevik," framing Jews as outsiders who infect society with left wing politics.
20. Adolf Hitler, quoted in Enzo Traverso, *The Origins of Nazi Violence*, p. 101.
21. Théophile Gautier, quoted in Enzo Traverso, *The Origins of Nazi Violence*, p. 111.
22. Winston Churchill, quoted in Enzo Traverso, *The Origins of Nazi Violence*, p. 103.
23. Winston Churchill, "Zionism vs Bolshevism," *Illustrated Sunday Herald*, February 8, 1920.
24. R.K. Serviss, quoted in Stephen Speisman, "Antisemitism in Ontario: The Twentieth Century," in Alan Davies, ed., *Antisemitism in Canada: History and Interpretation*, Waterloo, Wilfrid Laurier University Press, 1992, p. 123.
25. Malak Abas, "Racism is an integral part of Winnipeg's history," *The Manitoban*, September 6, 2017.
26. Jean-Francois Nadeau, *Adrien Arcand, Führer Canadien*, Québec, Lux, 2010.
27. Stephen Speisman, "Antisemitism in Ontario: The Twentieth Century," p. 124.
28. Kevin Plummer, "Historicist: Get Draper!," *Torontoist*, September 5, 2015. Available at: https://torontoist.com/2015/09/historicist-get-draper/

29. Raymond Ouimet, *L'affaire Tissot: Campagne antisémite en Outauais*, Écrits des Hautes-Terres, Montpellier, 2006.
30. Stephen Speisman, "Antisemitism in Ontario: The Twentieth Century," p. 124.
31. Quoted in Stephen A. Speisman, *The Jews of Toronto: A History to 1937*, Toronto, McLelland and Stewart, 1979, p. 330.
32. Stephen Speisman, "Antisemitism in Ontario: The Twentieth Century," p. 113–125.
33. Dennis Draper, quoted in Kevin Plummer, "Historicist: Get Draper!"
34. Stephen Speisman, "Antisemitism in Ontario: The Twentieth Century," p. 332–335.
35. Howard Palmer, "Politics, Religion and Antisemitism in Alberta, 1880–1950," in Alan Davies, ed., *Antisemitism in Canada: History and Interpretation*, Waterloo, Wilfrid Laurier University Press, 1992, p. 173.
36. Goldwin Smith, quoted in Gerald Tulchinsky, "Goldwin Smith: Victorian Canadian Antisemite," in Alan Davies, ed., *Antisemitism in Canada: History and Interpretation*, Waterloo, Wilfrid Laurier University Press, 1992, p. 68.
37. Gerald Tulchinsky, "Goldwin Smith: Victorian Canadian Antisemite," p. 68.
38. William Lyon Mackenzie King, quoted in Gerald Tulchinsky, "Goldwin Smith: Victorian Canadian Antisemite," p. 84.
39. Irving Abella and Harold Troper, *None Is Too Many: Canada and the Jews of Europe, 1933–1948*, Toronto, Lester & Orpen Dennys Publishers, 1983, p. vi.
40. Sarah Ghabrial and Elena Razlogova, "Justin Trudeau Conflating BDS With Anti-Semitism Is Dangerous," *Huffington Post*, November 15, 2018.
41. Abella and Troper, *None Is Too Many*, p. 28.
42. Abella and Troper, *None Is Too Many*, p. 8–9.
43. Abella and Troper, *None Is Too Many*, p. 18.
44. Allan Levine, *King*, p. 292.
45. Abella and Troper, *None Is Too Many*, p. 126–147.
46. Quoted in Abella and Troper, *None Is Too Many*, p. 129.
47. Achille Michaud and Pierre Turgeon, *Canada: A People's History, Volume Two*, Toronto, McClelland & Stewart Ltd., 2002, p. 208.
48. Jeffrey A. Keshen, *Saints, Sinners, and Soldiers: Canada's Second World War*, Vancouver, UBC Press, 2004, p. 17–18.
49. Jeffrey A. Keshen, *Saints, Sinners, and Soldiers*, p. 5.
50. Hugh Avi Gordon, "Cheers and Tears: Relations Between Canadian Soldiers and German Civilians, 1944–46," Dissertation submitted to University of Victoria, Department of History, 2010, p. 201.
51. Hugh Avi Gordon, "Cheers and Tears," p. 208–210.
52. Hugh Avi Gordon, "Cheers and Tear," p. 212–215.
53. Quoted in Hugh Avi Gordon, "Cheers and Tears," p. 224.
54. Merily Weisbord and Merilyn Simonds Mohr, *The Valour and the Horror: The Untold Story of Canadians in the Second World War*, Toronto, Harper Collins, 1991, p. 76. A selection of the lyrics shared: "there was a young plumber from Dee, who was plumbing his girl by the sea, said the girl, stop your plumbing, for I hear someone coming, said the plumber, still plumbing, it's me."
55. Weisbord and Mohr, *The Valour and the Horror*, p. 77.
56. Antony Beevor, *D-Day: The Battle for Normandy*, London, Viking Books, 2009.

57. Jacques Dextraze, quoted in Weisbord and Mohr, p. 148.
58. Weisbord and Mohr, *The Valour and the Horror*, p. 104.
59. Weisbord and Mohr, *The Valour and the Horror*, p. 93.
60. Air Vice Marshall Harris, quoted in Weisbord and Mohr, *The Valour and the Horror*, p. 96.
61. Jim Moffat, quoted in Weisbord and Mohr, *The Valour and the Horror*, p. 112.
62. Doug Harvey, quoted in Weisbord and Mohr, *The Valour and the Horror*, p. 115.
63. Timothy Vogt has argued that Soviet de-Nazification in East Germany, specifically, has been overstated by historians and was not as far-reaching as it had been portrayed by both anti-communist historians trying to frame Stalin as a totalitarian or the GDR itself trying to boost its anti-fascist credentials. There may be merit to his argument, though it remains the case that Soviet efforts to purge fascists, in all of its occupied territories, were infinitely more extensive than those in the West. Timothy Vogt, *Denazification in Soviet-Occupied Germany: Brandenberg, 1945–1948*, Cambridge, Harvard University Press, 2000. Eliminate
64. Tom Bower, *The Paperclip Conspiracy: The Battle for the Spoils and Secrets of Nazi Germany*, London, Michael Joseph, 1987.
65. Adenauer was a staunch anti-communist and, during his time as mayor of Koln, went out of his way to defend the Nazis on several occasions. In 1932, he argued that the Nazis should be invited to participate in the leadership of the country and, in fact, Adenauer had argued for an alliance between his own Zentrum party with the Nazis. While he maintained his opposition to the Nazi government during the war years, that opposition was weak enough that he never spent more than a short time in prison. Given the political climate of Nazi Germany, the fact that Adenauer was able to stay in the country, live in relative comfort and even claim a pension should speak to the fact that he was no avowed anti-fascist. See Peter Koch, *Konrad Adenauer: Eine politische biographie*, Hamburg, Rowohlt, 1985.
66. Quoted in Eric Lichtblau, "In Cold War, US Spy Agencies Used 1,000 Nazis," *The New York Times*, October 26, 2014.
67. Brian E. Crim, *Our Germans: Project Paperclip and the National Security State*, Baltimore, Johns Hopkins University Press, 2018, p. 81–82.
68. Reinhard Gehlen, *The Service: The Memoirs of Reinhard Gehlen*, New York, World Publishing, 1972, p. 24, 3.
69. Noam Chomsky, *Deterring Democracy*, New York, Verso, 1991, p. 341.
70. G.S. Graber, *The History of the SS*, New York, Charter, 1978, p. 112.
71. Commonwealth Relations Office, quoted in Andrew Nagorski, *The Nazi Hunters*, Simon and Schuster, New York, 2016, p. 89.
72. Harold Troper and Morton Weinfeld, "Jewish-Ukrainian Relations in Canada Since World War II and the Nazi War Criminal Issue," in Alan Davies, ed., *Antisemitism in Canada: History and Interpretation*, Waterloo, Wilfrid Laurier University Press, 1992, p. 283.
73. Roy Rempel, *Counterweights*, Kingston, McGill-Queen's University Press, 1996, p. 212.
74. Tom Bower, *The Paperclip Conspiracy*, p. 310–311.
75. Tatsuichiro Akizuki, quoted in Jonah Walters, "A Guide to the Hiroshima and Nagasaki Attacks," *Jacobin*, August 9, 2015.

76. Gar Alperovitz, *The Decision to Use the Atomic Bomb*, New York, Vintage Books, 1996.
77. John Price, *Orienting Canada: Race, Empire, and the Transpacific*, Vancouver, UBC Press, 2011, p. 98.
78. William Dyess, quoted in Jonah Walters, "A Guide to the Hiroshima and Nagasaki Attacks," *Jacobin*, August 9, 2015.
79. Jonah Walters, "A Guide to the Hiroshima and Nagasaki Attacks," *Jacobin*, August 9, 2015.
80. John Price, *Orienting Canada*, p. 105–106.
81. Quoted in John Price, *Orienting Canada*, p. 92–93.
82. John Price, *Orienting Canada*, p. 102.

Part III

Peacekeeping the Cold War

7

Peace and Scorched Earth

> *Japan's expansion... is as irresistible a force as that which carried our own ancestors from the Atlantic seaboard to the prairies and beyond; but we found nothing in the way, except Indians and buffaloes, whereas China is nearly as overpopulated as Japan itself.*
> — *Toronto Daily Star* editorial, 1937[1]

ONLY A FEW YEARS BEFORE Canadians plotted to drop the most devastating weapons ever devised onto cities full of Japanese civilians, Canada had been a strong supporter of Japanese fascist expansion. Canadians routinely denigrated Korean and Chinese victims of Japanese aggression, placing them lower on an imagined racial hierarchy than the Japanese, who, in the very act of colonizing their neighbours, were proving themselves worthy of Western respect. Diplomats stationed in Japan regularly claimed that Japan was the most "civilized" state in East Asia and used this as justification for its expansion. On the eve of one of Japan's most heinous campaigns of the Second World War, the Nanjing Massacre, the *Toronto Daily Star* favourably compared Japanese conquest of China to Canadian conquest of the Indigenous nations.[2]

Ironically, as the previous chapter noted, it was Indigenous people who were forced to mine the uranium that went into the bombs that devastated Japan in 1945. While the Canadian ruling class could respect Japan's fascist, colonial ideology, it could not ultimately condone the rise of a rival imperial power in the Pacific. Thus, as it had in Europe, Canada participated in the defeat of Imperial Japan, to ensure that the Euro-American world maintained global supremacy. Once that was accomplished, Canada happily assisted in the re-composition of the Japanese ruling class — with many of the same people who had run the fascist apparatus — in order to maintain Japan as a bulwark against communism. Indeed, it was a Canadian judge who oversaw the dismissal of charges against one of Japan's most notorious war criminals, Kishi Nobosuke, paving the way for his rise to become Japan's head of state.

These actions reflect Canada's transition into the all-encompassing global dynamic that was the Cold War. For many Canadians, the most lasting legacy of the era was the mythology of peacekeeping, which, during this period, became indelibly embedded in the Canadian psyche. This chapter assesses Canada's transition into the Cold War, highlighting Canada's ongoing relations with former fascists and collaborators, especially in Asia, with emphasis on Canada's terrible and often overlooked war in Korea. That war was labelled a "peacekeeping" mission, and indeed, the historical record reveals a far less flattering picture of the peacekeeping era than the Heritage Minutes and commemorative postage stamps suggest. Instead, Canadian peacekeeping and Cold War interventions typically fit into at least one of four patterns: 1) they served to slow or undermine the decolonization process in countries trying to break from European rule; 2) they provided a veneer of legitimacy to campaigns that were substantively episodes of Cold War aggression or capitalist self-interest; 3) they worked to maintain harmony among the Euro-American allies to better serve Canadian interests; and 4) they were imbued with colonial ideology and violence.

None of these categories were mutually exclusive, and often many of these dynamics were present at once. But, notably, all four are linked to the foundational logic of Canada's policy towards Indigenous nations: protecting and expanding the sphere of Canadian capitalism while disparaging its victims as less advanced and in need of colonial guidance and leadership. Taken together, they represented Canada's contribution to the victory of the colonial, capitalist states over their Cold War rivals, an outcome that stood as triumphant to some but tragic to many more.

The Cold War

Some three decades after it ended, the Cold War remains a widely misunderstood phenomenon. While the generations of Canadians who lived through its later phases often hold onto the simple narrative it offered at the time — that the evil communist Russians were trying to take over the world and we had to protect and preserve freedom and democracy — there is a more clearheaded view that has gained some traction over time, which is that both sides were blinkered by ideological commitments to destroying one another and created enormously harmful policies that nearly brought nuclear disaster upon the world. This certainly comes closer to the truth; detailed examination of the policies of both of the superpowers and their allies reveals plenty of cynical and unsavoury business undertaken in order to win what both often saw as a fight to the death. Yet, even this conclusion is overly facile and leaves us with little more than an unsatisfactory claim that the Cold War happened because its leaders acted irrationally. To truly understand the second half of Canada's 20th century, we need a more sophisticated account of the great power rivalry that shaped it.

From the outset it needs be said that neither side in the Cold War had a monopoly on moral righteousness, though both sides routinely laid claim to just that. The United States and its Western allies insisted that they were protecting democracy — people's inherent right to determine the rules and rulers that shaped their lives — and dubiously claimed that free market capitalism was a necessary condition for such democracy. The Soviet Union countered that the principles of equality and justice necessitated a shift away from capitalism — which produced precisely the opposite — and positioned itself as the guardian and guarantor of all people who wished to pursue this alternative.

Both of the superpowers periodically abandoned the ideals they professed in order to gain tactical advantage over one another, but the fact remains that this was a genuine ideological struggle, not simply a geostrategic rivalry. Unlike the First and Second World Wars, the animosity at the heart of the Cold War reflected a real class antagonism; the Soviet Union supported revolutionary movements around the world made up of peasants, workers and other marginalized classes in their respective societies.[3] These were inevitably movements that were upsetting the established class structures, typically highly unequal capitalist and colonial or semi-colonial systems. As such, US interventions around the world tended to be in support of traditional authorities and the capitalist classes that had grown alongside them. So, while it is true that both sides prioritized their own national interests, it is also true that their national interests were inherently bound up in the class character of the Cold War, the inherent antagonism between the traditional elite and the hitherto marginalized masses of the world. Peaceful co-existence was never really an option. For the capitalist world, every state that broke away and closed its doors to foreign investment and integration was cutting into somebody's profits, and the possibility that such a movement could spread was unthinkable. For the communist world, which had been under attack since before it even had international representation, every state where the old authorities regained control was a step closer to the end of the dream of world revolution.

Understanding the Cold War in these terms helps us to appreciate why it became such an all-encompassing struggle. More importantly, it explains why it came to mean so much to people *outside* of Washington and Moscow. Assessments of the "proxy wars" of that period often infer that the superpowers would descend upon some small country and raise armies to fight one another, with the unfortunate, disinterested locals caught in the middle. This is patently incorrect. In each of the various hotspots of the Cold War, from Korea to Angola to Nicaragua to Afghanistan, the conflicts were rooted in class struggles within those countries — albeit heavily shaped by the Cold War, which overshadowed everything else. Thus, to most people in Euro-America, Western Europe and the Commonwealth — and to a minority in the more privileged or formerly privileged classes elsewhere — the United States truly did represent the best hope at stemming the growing momentum towards socialism, which, to them, was tyranny.[4] At the same time, for a large majority of people in Asia, Africa and Latin America — and a smaller percentage in the West — it was the Soviet Union (and later China, Cuba and Vietnam) that represented both an inspiration to pursue a better course in their own countries and also a source of material and technical support in building their own successful revolutions.[5]

The case for Western-style capitalism was not helped by the fact that, when the Cold War began, much of the world remained under the direct colonial domination of the capitalist powers. Would Vietnam have become a central player in the world revolution if France had not introduced its people to capitalism via a ruthless, exploitative colonial occupation? It is impossible to say and, besides, capitalist expansion did not have any kindly, egalitarian variants. Ironically, Canada's role in the Cold War often hinged upon the idea that it might represent a kinder capitalism. The image that Canada built of itself during this period was of a more reasonable "middle power," offering an example of the good life that capitalism could bring, while remaining a well-intentioned arbiter in the hostile geopolitics of the Cold War. In truth, the audience that most took to this performance was Canadian settlers themselves; outside of Canada, few saw Canada as anything more than a bit player in the Euro-American alliance, and Indigenous people would not have lauded Canadian capitalism if anyone had cared to ask. In fact, the rise of anti-colonial struggles abroad reverberated within Canada as Indigenous people began, by the 1960s, to connect with the very movements that Canada was seeking to undermine elsewhere in the world.

Even amongst Euro-Canadians, the shine of the Cold War was maintained as much by coercion as consent. James Endicott's peace movement was among the many circles of Canadian society targeted by anti-communist purges. Endicott, who had come to a critical position on Cold War politics by living alongside the poor in China, was denounced as "public enemy number one" and subject to strip searches at the border, direct violence on the streets of Toronto and the firebombing of his house.[6] These attacks were reflective of both official and unofficial anti-communist hysteria, whipped up by prominent politicians like Lester Pearson, who had vetted Winston Churchill's "Iron Curtain" speech and once suggested the use of germ warfare against the Soviets. Pearson had been weaned on Empire; he read Kipling and Henty, he called Macedonians a "treacherous, deceitful lot" and Egyptians "very low specimens of humanity," and believed the British "well equipped to govern... the world." A few decades later, he effectively advocated preventative war against the USSR, sharing Churchill's view that the Anglo-Saxon race constituted a "special edition of humankind" responsible for confronting the world communist conspiracy.

From there it was hardly a leap in Pearson's mind to call the Canadian peace movement "an agent of foreign aggressive imperialism," and Pearson even compared his struggle against subversive communists, tellingly, to that waged by "our forefathers in the struggles with any savages lurking in the woods."[7] Cold War Canada, then, stayed true to its roots, working alongside the old colonial powers to maintain the capitalist world system, from which it benefitted handsomely, all the while crushing internal or indigenous threats.

Israel, Suez and Canadian Mythology

Much of Canada's reputation as a middle power and peacekeeper was built around the story of Lester Pearson and the Suez Crisis, making it an important place to start. Still, there is some irony in the mythmaking that accompanied Pearson's role in the Suez Crisis: despite the narrative around Suez that suggested Canada's skill was in bringing conflicting parties together to settle a dispute in which it had no stake, Canada actually failed at this objective in several instances before and after Suez. Canada was unable to negotiate a successful solution to the Kashmir crisis in the late 1940s.[8] Canadian intervention in Korea in the 1950s was an outright catastrophe, as documented below. Canada would go on to fail to broker a settlement in Cyprus in the 1970s or enact a lasting peace in Lebanon in the 1980s. Indeed, even the Suez Crisis itself was not ended to the satisfaction of Egypt, suggesting that Canada's skill as a neutral arbiter was vastly exaggerated.

What is more — and this was central to why Canada failed so miserably as a peacemaker — Canada *did* have a stake in the 1956 Suez Crisis and, relatedly, in the most significant event in the Middle East in the early Cold War: the creation of the settler state of Israel. In both cases, Canadians tend to believe that Canada's role was to act as a neutral moderator, helping manage the otherwise fiery and unstable situations and conflicts believed to be endemic to that region. Contrary to this narrative, both Arabs and Israelis agree that Canada stood firmly on the side of the creation of Israel, against the wishes of the Arab majority who lived in Palestine. As for Pearson's great peace project in Egypt, it ended with Egyptian President Nasser angrily expelling the Canadians for violating Egyptian sovereignty and consistently acting on behalf of Israel. Some review of these events is in order.

As noted in Chapter 6, Canada's policy towards Jewish refugees in Europe was one of callous indifference. Even while the full horror of the Holocaust was being revealed, Canada largely barred its gates to Jews fleeing Europe, working hard to deflect them elsewhere. One of those elsewheres was the British mandate of Palestine, taken after the First World War from the Ottoman Empire. Immigration to Palestine was favoured by Zionist Jews — those who wanted to conquer Palestine and create a Jewish state — but the influx of Jewish immigrants to Palestine was already causing conflict with the local Arab population, making British authorities wary of further immigration. Several times in the years leading up to the Second World War, Arab Palestinians rose up in revolt against British colonial authorities, and Jewish settlements were often a target; older animosities between the two groups were inflamed by both the growing Zionist character of the immigrants (and their creation of armed militias like Irgun and the Stern Gang) and the perception that Jewish immigration was being fostered by the hated British authorities.

Britain had, of course, stoked tensions when, in the course of the First World War, it effectively promised Palestine to both the Jews and Arabs; the Balfour Declaration had, in 1917, promised the Jews a national home in Palestine in exchange for their support in the Great War, but Britain had already promised Palestinian Arabs national independence should they revolt against the Ottoman Empire. Instead, at war's end, the Middle East was divided up between the French and English, with both the Arab and Jewish claims ignored, leading to major, though unsuccessful, Arab revolts in the 1920s against European rule.

The context after the Second World War was very different. There were hundreds of thousands of Jewish refugees in Europe who had survived the nightmare of the Holocaust and were now desperately seeking a new start outside of Europe. At the same time, as the Cold War was setting in, the West increasingly recognized that it could benefit from having an essentially European, pro-Western presence in the Middle East to balance other regional powers and help prevent the Soviets from gaining a foothold.[9] The solution seemed to present itself: resolve the Jewish refugee crisis without actually bringing in large numbers of Jews, and undermine rising Arab nationalism by supporting the creation of a sympathetic settler state.

Much discussion and debate ensued, with Canada taking a lead role in negotiating a United Nations plan for the partition of Palestine. No Arab representatives ever approved Lester Pearson's plan, but its approval in the UN provided the Zionist cause enough legitimacy to justify taking unilateral military action. Zionist paramilitaries already active in Palestine initiated a war in 1948 that culminated in what Palestinians call the Nakba (catastrophe), wherein thousands of Arab Palestinians were murdered, assaulted, sexually assaulted and otherwise subject to violence, and as many as 900,000 — more than 80% of the population — displaced in the creation of an Israeli state double the size of what Pearson's plan had proposed.[10]

Canada's key role in this process fostered much distrust in the Arab world that would reverberate during the Suez Crisis and beyond. To the Zionists, Pearson was a hero, the "Canadian Balfour," who was given awards and honours from Zionist organizations for his "commitment to Jewish freedom and Israel."[11] Ivan Rand, a Canadian supreme court judge, sat on a UN committee on Palestine and couched his work in classic colonial terms, framing the Jews as a force for progress and democracy, the Arabs as backwards and uncivilized.[12] Leon Mayrand, who worked with Rand, acknowledged that the Arabs would not be happy that Jews, who represented a small minority of the population, would be granted more than half of its territory, but Mayrand asserted that "[the Arabs] should not be taken too seriously" and that they would be cowed by Western willingness "to impose a settlement whatever the means necessary."[13] About a thousand Canadians, mostly but not exclusively Jews, went to Palestine in 1948 to fight with the Zionists; Ben Dunkelman, for instance, son of the founder of Tip-Top Tailors, was in charge of one of the most violent brigades, aggressively attacking and emptying Palestinian villages to make space for Jewish settlers. Israel would later build a recreational facility called Canada Park in recognition of these efforts; the park, which received $15 million from Canadians, was built on the site where Imwas, a Palestinian village, had been bulldozed.[14]

What is remarkable in all of this is how quickly the Canadian narrative around the Jews had changed; after all, less than a decade before, the prime minister had commiserated with Hitler about the Jewish "tainting" of German institutions. It was a striking example of the dialectic relationship between political economy and ideology; if the Canadian imagination already possessed the colonial framework for understanding the world, shifting political economic circumstances meant that the Jews would come to occupy a different place within that framework. A noteworthy comparison is Canada's relationship to the Boers, who were initially framed as savage and backwards but who, almost immediately after the war, were re-fashioned as the guardians of European progress in the face of the *more* "savage" Africans. Similar sorts of transitions occurred in the framing of other groups — Irish and Italians, for instance — who at certain points were denigrated in a manner similar to colonized people outside of Europe — albeit to a far lesser extent — but who were later integrated into the category of "white."[15]

Indeed, there is much to learned about colonialism and capitalism in the transition from the late 1930s, when the leaders of the Western world conspired to facilitate the extermination of European Jews, to the late 1940s, when those same leaders effectively gave permission for conditional Jewish entry into the club of white, colonial nations. Abigail Bakan theorizes this transition, noting a confluence of factors in the postwar era that contributed to this. First, within Jewish communities, the hitherto marginal ideology of Zionism that called for the creation of Israel along European colonial lines in Palestine suddenly possessed great currency, given the conscious failure of the Western world to prevent the Holocaust.[16] Second, that complicity in the Holocaust was rooted in Western states' desire to prevent significant Jewish immigration; the creation of Israel provided a kind of moral redemption for the West even while it solved their "Jewish Problem" by funnelling immigration elsewhere. Third, the emerging Cold War made it politically valuable to have a controllable ally in the Middle East, a geostrategic fact that would grow in importance as movements for pan-Arab nationalism coalesced in the 1950s.

Finally, and perhaps most important, postwar Zionism embodied the ideals of European colonialism, which were still deeply rooted (and, indeed, foundational in settler societies like the US and Canada); the "new Jew" was aggressive, masculine and willing to enslave and exploit a lesser race in order to build a capitalist enclave. In that sense, the ticket to modern whiteness was precisely the project to create, in Palestinians, a backwards, uncivilized people worthy of colonial occupation, debasement and ethnic cleansing.[17] The archetypal colonizer, Winston Churchill, expressed his support for the Zionist project precisely by framing it in terms of racial and colonial hierarchies:

> I do not agree that the dog in the manger has the final right to the manger, even though he may have lain there for a very long time. I do not admit that right. I do not admit, for instance, that a great wrong has been done to the Red Indians of America, or the black people of Australia. I do not admit that a wrong has been done to those people by the fact that a stronger race, a more worldly-wise race, to put it that way, has come in and taken their place.[18]

For Jews to be white, they had to take up the White Man's Burden; Israel was that project. Israel would be a settler capitalist state *par excellence*, modelling itself after the Anglo-American conquests of North America, the exclusionary settler regimes in South Africa and Australia, and even the Nazi apparatus that had sought the complete destruction of European Jewry.[19] Israel did all this during a period when the thrust of history seemed to point in the opposite direction, towards at least formal decolonization if not outright anti-colonial revolution. As such, Canada's steadfast support for the Zionist project between the end of the

Second World War and the 21st century was an important illustration of its position vis-à-vis colonialism.

This support also served as a centrepiece for much of Canadian policy in the Middle East, not least the Suez Crisis, which earned Lester Pearson a Nobel Prize. Heavily promoted by the Canadian government as a cornerstone of the Canada's place in the world, generations of Canadians have learned about the Suez Crisis, but few can actually explain it. The crisis actually began in Palestine when, in 1955, Israeli forces attacked an Egyptian military base. During the 1948 war, the Arab states bordering Palestine had invaded to try to defeat the Zionist uprising; they failed in part due to technical inferiority and in part because many of their leaders were motivated by their own desires to claim territory in Palestine.

Indeed, at the conclusion of that conflict, Jordan had claimed the West Bank of the Jordan River and Egypt occupied parts of Gaza. But Egyptian politics were in flux; having gradually asserted some independence from Great Britain in the 1930s, Egyptian nationalists were humiliated when Britain imposed its favoured Egyptian leader in 1942. That humiliation was amplified by the failure to defeat the Zionist uprising, and by the late 1940s Egyptians were in open revolt over British rule. When Britain finally rescinded control of the country, it was General Gamal Abdal Nasser who emerged as Egypt's leader. An Arab nationalist, Nasser cracked down on both the Egyptian communists and the Muslim Brotherhood, both of which had played a role in the fight for independence, and emphasized the idea of broad Arab resistance to colonialism in the region.

By 1956 tensions were high. There was conflict between Egyptian-controlled Gaza and Israel, the French were angry at Nasser for supporting the Algerian struggle for national liberation, and the British were frustrated by the loss of the strategically and economically valuable Suez Canal. Though the canal was now controlled by Egypt, its profits still flowed to the French and British investors in the Suez Canal Company. But in the summer of 1956, Nasser nationalized the company, with the intention of using its profits to pay for the construction of a major hydroelectric dam to power Egyptian industrialization. Israel, France and Britain quickly conspired to undermine Nasser; Israel launched an attack from the north, and Britain and France followed up by invading on the pretext of separating the belligerent forces, but with the transparent aim of reclaiming the Suez Canal.[20] International reaction to the invasion was critical, and most notable was US recrimination; the Americans wanted an open door in the Middle East and wanted relatively weak, independent states that could be played off one another to maintain US dominance. Direct colonial occupation of Egypt by Britain and France would block US access and galvanize Arab unity.

Until this point, Canada had taken little interest in the troubles. As Robert Teigrob illustrates, Canada often distinguished itself from the United States by its support for the maintenance of European colonial empires into the postwar era.[21] But in 1956, with its primary allies divided over how to manage the conflict around the Suez, Canadian leaders sensed that their own interests could be jeopardized. Canadian foreign policy was rooted in the Anglo-American alliance, especially as the Cold War and anti-colonial struggles were creating zones of serious class antagonism, as in Korea and Vietnam. Motivated by the necessity of maintaining a solid Western capitalist block, Canada set to work repairing relations between its allies in Egypt, of which Egypt itself was not one. Indeed, it needs be emphasized that Canada did not like the idea of Egypt controlling the Suez Canal, despite the obvious fact that it fell squarely within Egyptian territory.[22] Lester Pearson's intervention in the Suez Crisis was never about asserting Egyptian sovereignty.

Pearson played to both sides of the Atlantic alliance. To the Americans, he noted his "regret that force was used" and asserted his desire to "bring the fighting to an end." Still, he insisted that he did "not for one minute criticize the motives of the governments of the United Kingdom and France."[23] In order to help Britain and France back out of Egypt "with as little loss of face as possible," Pearson proposed replacing the occupying armies with a UN peacekeeping force, while gradually normalizing Egypt's relations with its neighbours. This would ultimately appease the US, which wanted the Europeans out, but would allow a graceful withdrawal such that the Cold War alliance could remain healthy.

Any doubt that this was at the heart of Canada's motivations is put to rest by Pearson, himself, who explained, "the situation was deteriorating and the communists were working feverishly and destructively to exploit it."[24] He was likely referring to a Soviet/Czech arms deal with Egypt signed in 1955, though he may also have been aware that the Western intervention was likely to push people towards the Soviet Union and the left more broadly.

In sum, Canada's support for the Zionist colonization of Palestine illustrated its commitment to Cold War politics in the Middle East, even while the struggle around the new settler state set off cascading conflicts in the region, including the Suez Crisis. While Pearson's proposal to create a UN peacekeeping force was hailed as an act of liberal internationalism, it was in truth a much more calculated, strategic episode of crisis-management within its own Cold War camp. Nothing could illustrate this more than the fact that Nasser himself would ultimately order the Canadian contingent of the UN force out of Egypt. Indeed, in 1956, Pearson reassured Nasser that the peacekeeping mission would involve "no infringement on sovereignty," but just the next year he reframed this to assert that, having consented to allow the UN force to land, Egypt now had "no right to control the force, no right to order it about, [or] to tell the force when it shall leave."[25] Nasser would conclude, on the eve of the Six Day War in 1967, that the Canadian peacekeepers had become "a force serving neo-imperialism."[26]

The Dominion and the Rising Sun

Just as Canada had been comfortable with the rise of fascism in Europe — and therefore played a role in both the Jewish Holocaust and the subsequent conquest of Palestine — its relations with fascist Japan began in friendship and warmth. Japan represented an authoritarian, capitalist, imperial state in Asia, which made it not so different from Canada and its allies. Canadian capital made significant profits in Japan, especially in the metals used to produce war materials, so Canada benefitted from Japanese expansion both directly, insofar as it was a boost to profits, and indirectly, in that Japan was expanding the sphere of capitalism. Inherent in Japan's imperial project was the defeat of popular movements oriented to the left, both within Japan and also in its growing empire.

Given that Japan seemed to be following the path already beaten by the Euro-American powers, it was easy enough to claim that Japan was on the road to becoming a "modern" civilization and thus in a position to "improve" its neighbours. After the Japanese assault on Manchuria left 20,000 people dead in 1931, Canadian diplomat Hugh Keenleyside explained that Japan "must be recognized as a stabilizing and regulating force." Six years later, after the vicious 1937 attack on the city of Nanjing, Randolph Bruce, Canada's envoy to Japan, claimed that this was "simply an attempt to put her neighbour country in better shape, as [Japan] had already done in Manchuria."[27]

Nevertheless, Japan's imperial ambition grew too great for the Euro-American powers to tolerate, and, just as they had with Nazi Germany, the West eventually found it necessary to block further expansion. By the 1940s, there was no feasible way for the Western powers to co-exist with Imperial Japan as they had previously hoped they would and, in 1941, after the surprise attacks against various targets including Pearl Harbor, total war engulfed the Pacific.[28] Suddenly, Japan's position as a lesser civilization was re-emphasized, and anti-Japanese racism stoked. Within Canada, people with Japanese ancestors — even those who had been in Canada for multiple generations — were thrown into internment camps and had their assets seized. Canada would go on to play a key role in creating and sanctioning the use of nuclear weapons on Hiroshima and Nagasaki, after which Prime Minister King noted, "it is fortunate that the use of the bomb should have been upon the Japanese rather than upon the white races of Europe."[29] Indeed, by 1945, anti-Japanese racism had reached a fever pitch, as one contributor to the *Vancouver Sun* called Japan "the most evil thing that has ever existed," and another asserted that atomic annihilation was "a swift and merciful way of clearing a heap of filth from the path of human progress."[30]

Canadians' shifting attitude towards Japan illustrates the complex relationship between the political economy of empire and its ideological framework. In the early 1900s, the Canadian government had placed serious restrictions on Japanese immigration amidst an anti-Asian furor among whites in BC. But by the Versailles peace talks in 1919, Canada was willing to support the idea of Japan as a regional power in East Asia, allowing it to claim Germany's former territories in Shandong (China) and the Pacific. At the same time, Canadian Prime Minister Robert Borden vigorously opposed a Japanese proposal to include racial equality into the terms of the League of Nations, fearful that it might undermine systemic hyper-exploitation of Asian labourers in Canada.[31]

Still, as Japan extended is imperial influence into China in the 1920s and 1930s, Canada viewed this as a positive step, and Canadian public opinion reflected a complicated racial hierarchy. When news of the horrific Japanese assault on Nanjing reached Canada, the *Vancouver Sun* both chastised Japan as a "medieval child" carrying out "feudal abuses that white nations abandoned… many years ago" while also maintaining that the Japanese were higher on the civilizational ladder than "the ill-equipped hordes of China." An editorial in Toronto claimed that

"Japan's expansion... is as irresistible a force as that which carried our own ancestors from the Atlantic seaboard to the prairies and beyond," explicitly locating Japan's behaviour as colonial and, therefore, righteous and inexorable.[32]

Indeed, in the late 1930s, Japanese expansion was barely interrupted at all; just as they did with Germany, the Euro-American powers accepted the rise of an anti-communist regional power so long as it did not interfere with their own supremacy. Despite repeated pleas from Chinese anti-fascist partisans, whose impressive resistance — especially among the communists based in Yan'an — was facing the full brunt of Japanese attention, Canada continued doing business with Japan even in metals that were being used to manufacture weapons, to the tune of $17 million into 1939.[33] Norman Bethune, the Canadian doctor who had joined the Mackenzie-Papineau Battalion to fight fascism in Spain, again found himself supporting an anti-fascist cause without Canadian support, as he and a few other Canadians like Jean Ewan travelled to Yan'an to join the Chinese communists in resistance to Japanese occupation.

Many Chinese-Canadians wanted to join that fight, but the Canadian government maintained strict regulations on their movement and few were able to get there.[34] Meanwhile, Chinese organizations in Canada desperately tried to raise public support for their cause but Japanese officials reassured the Canadian public that Japan was simply protecting China from "herself and Bolsheviks."[35] Japan thus regularly presented itself as a guardian against Chinese communism, which held great appeal in the West. As one Canadian missionary proudly proclaimed, Japan was "fighting hard and with unity outside her own country against communism."[36] Indeed, despite a growing degree of discontent within North America over support for Japan, in 1940 the United States was still providing jet fuel for Japanese aircraft and, as late as 1941, Canada maintained warm relations with Japan.[37]

But by the early 1940s, Germany and Japan had formed an alliance, and it was evident that Japan's friendship with the West could not last forever. Japan determined to seize the initiative in the Pacific war and launched a massive offensive in December 1941 which targeted Euro-American territories, thus bringing the West fully into that theatre of war. In a fitting illustration of the class dynamics that still underpinned everything, both Canadian diplomats in Tokyo and Japanese officials in Ottawa reported being treated with exceptional respect during the outbreak of hostilities;

Canadians played golf, watched movies and were even given a Christmas dinner.[38]

But while the elite went to war almost apologetically, no such niceties were permitted for the working classes. Canadian soldiers were sent to garrison the indefensible Hong Kong, where they would be easily overrun and were placed in prisoner of war camps. There, they were worked to illness and sometimes even death, after which the 680 survivors suffered serious long term physical and mental health effects.[39] Notable among the stories of the survivors was a massacre on Christmas Day by Japanese troops at St. Stephen's College, where injured Canadian soldiers were being interned. Some 63 wounded soldiers were killed and several of the women working as medical staff were raped. It is impossible to ignore the tragic irony that the Canadian ruling class had happily condoned Japanese atrocities against Koreans and Chinese, only for those same forms of violence to now be enacted upon working-class Canadians.

The irony went even further: one of the most notorious Japanese soldiers at the Sham Shui Po prison camp was Kanao Inouye, who had grown up in Kamloops, BC. Having lived in the intensely racist climate of BC in the early 20th century, Inouye had suffered racial abuse his entire life; when the war broke out, he seized an opportunity to exact revenge. One of the Canadian POWs described his first encounter with the man they called the "Kamloops Kid":

> So [Inouye] stops and says, "So you're the Canadians, eh." Just like that. Well, Jesus, we're really lookin' at this guy now. He says, "I want you to know I was born and raised in Kamloops, BC, and I hate your goddamn guts." And he says when he was a kid and growin' up there, they'd call him "little yellow bastard" and stuff like this. He never forgot that.[40]

Another witness had Inouye say to a Canadian, "now where is your so-called superiority, you dirty scum?"[41] Inouye was by all accounts sadistic and cruel. He beat several prisoners mercilessly and almost to death, and he deserves no sympathy for his role in the apparatus of Japanese fascism. But it is, nevertheless, noteworthy that anti-Japanese racism in Canada should blowback against Canadian prisoners in this way; whatever Kanao Inouye was, it was produced in British Columbia.

And that racism was no relic of the past: Inouye actually escaped from Canada to join the Japanese army just as Japanese-Canadians were being herded up and sent into internment camps. As the public mood tapped back into anti-Japanese racism that had prevailed a few decades earlier, one Canadian military official justified internment by claiming that "every little slant-eyed Jap will wave the flag of the Rising Sun if his countrymen invade the coast."[42] Ultimately, some 23,000 Japanese-Canadians had their possessions — property, fishing boats and equipment worth as much as $1.3 million — stolen and were sent to the camps in the interior of British Columbia. Many died in the harsh conditions, and others remained in the camps long after the war had ended.[43]

The war ended with the detonation of nuclear weapons and the mass killing of nearly a quarter of a million mostly civilian Japanese. Fearing a Soviet occupation and the reversal of their class privilege, the Japanese leadership surrendered and the United States assumed administration under General Douglas MacArthur. With Japan secured, the Western Allies now prioritized the defeat of the Chinese communists, who had emerged as the most successful and popular partisans against Japanese fascism. Civil war in China, between Chiang Kai-shek's nationalists and Mao Zedong's communists, broke out immediately after the war; the communists were poised to win easily.

Canada was characteristically bullish in the anti-communist crusade, sending 170 airplanes and $60 million to support Chiang Kai-shek's bombing of northern Chinese villages, while denying it was taking a side in the civil war. Some in King's government questioned the decision, but they kept quiet in the increasingly chilly atmosphere of the Red Scare.[44] Canada even sent a destroyer, the HMCS *Crescent*, to menace the coastline in 1949 as their side, the nationalists, awaited their downfall at Nanjing. Canadian missionaries in China were almost uniformly anti-communist, which tended to alienate even moderate Chinese Christians, and those few Canadians who preached a more thoughtful approach to Canadian-Chinese relations were ignored, recalled and muzzled.[45]

Most notable among these was James Endicott, mentioned above, who was among a small group of United Church missionaries who came to sympathize with the communist project in China. Disgusted with the corruption and violence of the nationalists and increasingly drawn to the emerging democratic practices of the communists, Endicott and his contemporaries tried to publicize a counter-narrative in Canada. When Endicott revealed that UN forces were using chemical weapons in Korea in the early 1950s, he was mocked on the front page of *Maclean's* magazine as "Fronting for the Reds." Endicott was telling the truth but he was shut out of the public discussion while *Maclean's* and other media published sensationalist accounts like Stewart Allen's "I Was a Prisoner of the Chinese Reds."[46]

Meanwhile, to the shock and dismay of the victims of Japanese violence in China, Korea and elsewhere, the Tokyo Tribunals, which were meant to bring justice to fascist Japan's leadership, were even less thorough than the prosecution of the German Nazis. Though 28 Japanese leaders, including Tojo Hideki, were prosecuted, the Emperor Hirohito himself was not brought before the tribunal and hundreds of high-ranking officials in the Japanese wartime apparatus were released without charges. One of these was Kishi Nobusuke, whose fascist credentials were truly horrific. Kishi had governed conquered Manchuria, where he designed and implemented forced labour camps that used millions of Chinese peasants as virtual slaves. In just one camp alone, at Fushun, some 25,000 Chinese workers died each year.[47]

Kishi viewed Chinese and Koreans as animals who could only respond to brute force and he routinely compared them to feces. Men were worked to death, women were sold into sexual servitude, and *yakuza* gangsters were employed to terrorize prisoners. Kishi, nicknamed "the monster" in China, enriched himself and his friends in the oligarchy and availed himself of a hedonistic lifestyle of sex, drugs and huge sums of money. In fact, he became skilled at money-laundering and worked closely with Ayukawa Yoshisuke, the founder of Nissan, who based his operations in enslaved Manchuria in the 1930s.[48] Kishi's conversion of Manchuria into a massive slave labour camp was so successful that he was promoted; he emerged in the early 1940s as one of Tojo Hideki's closest allies at the centre of Japan's preparations for war with the Allies, which included bringing some 700,000 Chinese and Korean slaves to work in Japan, most of whom died.

During Kishi's short time in prison, awaiting his war crimes trial, he remembered his days as the divine ruler and sexual kingpin of Manchuria in grotesque fashion, claiming that he "came so much, it was hard to clean it all up."[49] Despite his central role as an architect of Japanese atrocities, he was released in 1948 without ever facing a tribunal. The well-connected Kishi re-entered politics in a postwar Japanese state that was populated by many of the same faces that had ruled it during the war, and in 1957 he was elected prime minister due in part to the banning of several leftist political parties. In 1960, he became the first Japanese prime minister to visit Canada, and by all accounts he got on splendidly with John Diefenbaker,[50] though his government was toppled shortly thereafter by massive public demonstrations in Japan. Nevertheless, he was one of hundreds of war criminals who not only escaped punishment but became leaders of postwar Japan, and the Kishi dynasty was so strong that both his brother and grandson would later serve as Japanese prime ministers.

Canada played a key role in this perversion of justice. E.S. McDougall, the Canadian judge who participated in the Tokyo Tribunal, was part of the inner circle that controlled its outcome. There is overwhelming evidence suggesting that he was part of a cover-up of an episode in which the Japanese conducted biological warfare and experimentation on thousands of Chinese prisoners in Manchuria.[51] Moreover, no atrocities committed against people in Korea, Taiwan or Indochina were considered by the tribunal, and the judges were selected such that the Euro-American powers would control its decisions (eight of eleven were drawn from Euro-American or Commonwealth countries). In 1948, the first 28 indictments were handed down, but the tribunal decided to drop the cases that were still pending, including that of future Prime Minister Kishi.

Many Japanese and especially non-Japanese people in East Asia saw the tribunal as a travesty of justice. Notably, there was one Canadian who could be counted among them, though he used milder language. Herbert Norman was an historian who, due to his skill with the Japanese language, found himself working in the Canadian embassy in Tokyo. After the war, he served as the head of the Canadian mission there, and he sent careful but critical reports to Ottawa even as Canada's man on the tribunal fulfilled the miscarriage of justice. Norman argued that failing to prosecute the emperor would be viewed as an insult to people in China, Korea, and other nations occupied by Japan during the war. He insisted that responsibility for Japanese war crimes should be placed on the oligarchy — the network of business, government and military elite — who designed and benefitted from Japanese expansionism. Norman was particularly incensed by the decision to release the second wave of war criminals, noting that while "they are not as well-known... this group includes some of the most fanatical and unsavoury leaders of aggressive Japanese imperialism."[52]

But his cables were ignored. Japan was emerging as the centrepiece in US Cold War planning for East Asia and was to be used as a base of anti-communist operations. The US military had already used Japanese soldiers as a garrison against the communists in China, and needed to re-establish the old structures of authority within Japan to curb the explosion of left politics that had erupted there following the end of the war. Tenants associations, labour unions, women's groups and socialist and communist parties had begun to take an active role in postwar reconstruction and were holding fascist-sympathizing bosses, landlords and politicians accountable for the nightmares they had imposed. In local elections in 1947, the Socialist Party gained a plurality, and by 1949 the more radical Communist Party was able to gain 10% of the popular vote.[53]

Hence, in 1948, the US began to suppress Japanese progressives, using troops to break a strike at the Toho movie studios and decreeing the dissolution of government workers' rights to bargain or strike. In 1949 more than 20,000 communists were purged from Japanese public life by an increasingly draconian MacArthur administration. In this context, and with communists in China, Korea and Indochina surging in popularity, the Western allies considered Emperor Hirohito "one of our greatest supports in Japan," despite his arguably having been the most important figure in the Japanese fascist apparatus.[54] The old Japanese elite were pleased and even consented to an extended US occupation, since it meant a strengthening of their own position vis-à-vis rising Japanese working-class militancy.

Canada was actively participating in the project to reconstitute imperial Japan, under MacArthur, and would soon to take a lead role in the anti-communist crusade in Korea. Herbert Norman was a nuisance. His fair-minded and thoughtful analysis had no place in campaigns of Cold War class warfare, and he was placed under investigation as a communist spy and later kicked out of Japan. He committed suicide in Egypt in 1957 while under further scrutiny. Norman was no communist, but hounding him in this way helped delegitimize communist politics in the Canadian public while simultaneously unburdening the government of a conscientious liberal.[55] Some 40 years later, Canadian Cold Warriors still held him in disdain: said Robert Bothwell in 1998, Canada did not "derive much benefit, in analysis or insight, from the presence of the fabled Dr. Herbert Norman."[56]

The Scorched Earth of Korea

Canada's participation in the Korean War (1950–53) is surely one of the least studied and discussed major conflicts, an odd fact given that it remains one of Canada's largest military operations, involving some 27,000 soldiers and a cost of $7.25 million in aid to South Korea over three years of war.[57] It also established the tense standoff on the Korean peninsula, which persists into the 21st century and has periodically threatened to spark a major — maybe even nuclear — confrontation. And yet it remains largely absent from the Canadian popular imagination, perhaps crossing most Canadians' minds only once a year when it is listed among the conflicts being remembered on Remembrance Day. The memories that do exist tend to be hazy, clouded by the peculiar fact that, despite its name, the Korean War was technically a peacekeeping mission.

Control over the once-independent monarchy of Korea had been the source of conflict at the start of the 20th century, with Japan ultimately defeating its rivals in China and Russia in 1910. From then on, Korea was subject to a ruthless, exploitative Japanese colonialism, undertaken with enthusiastic Canadian support. Korea's industrial and agricultural base was rapidly developed, but this was all geared towards supporting the Japanese economy; for instance, while total rice production significantly increased during the Japanese occupation, consumption of rice by Koreans actually declined.[58] Koreans were conscripted into the Japanese military and labour camps, and the Korean language and even Korean names were banned, building widespread resentment towards Japan.

Given that much of the former Korean elite were happy to collaborate with the Japanese occupation, the simmering resentment was channeled into a growing political left. Strikes, disruptions, protests and even guerrilla struggles increased over time, reaching their height in the early 1940s, as Japan's imperial ambitions crested. These movements contained a mix of centre and left organizations, and they asserted both Korean independence and also a more equitable share of wealth and access to land for Korean peasants. The US State Department, when not conducting propaganda, actually had a clear read on the situation in 1945:

> There is great disappointment that immediate independence and sweeping out of the Japanese did not eventuate. [Those Koreans who] achieved high rank under the Japanese are considered pro-Japanese and are hated almost as much as their masters...

the most encouraging single factor in the political situation is the presence in Seoul of several hundred conservatives among the older and better educated Koreans. Although many of them have served the Japanese, that stigma ought eventually to disappear.[59]

Save the last sentence, this was a prescient analysis. Koreans wanted the fascists and their collaborators out, while the US wanted to put them in charge. Instead, the Korean partisans who had opposed Japanese occupation created, immediately following Japanese defeat, the Korean People's Republic (KPR). The KPR was popular, offered much autonomy for local governance and quickly gained control of more than half of the country.[60] The KPR had earned people's trust, given that its leaders had resisted Japanese occupation, and the KPR was setting to work on the matters of highest priority to average Koreans, including the rebuilding of homes and infrastructure, the acquisition and distribution of food and the seizing of land from wealthy landowners to be returned to Korean peasants. Koreans were also acutely aware of the possibility that Japanese occupation could quickly give way to Soviet or American occupation if they didn't assert themselves.[61]

They were right to be concerned. Despite the objections of the KPR, the Americans insisted in 1945 that Korea be divided along the 38th parallel into a Soviet and US zone. Though it had troops poised to occupy the entire peninsula, the USSR agreed to the joint-occupation, Stalin's commitment to peaceful co-existence with the West undermining the wishes of Koreans. Still, administering the transition in North Korea proved to be a fairly simple task for the Soviet Union, since most of Korea was, at that point, oriented towards the left. The Soviets may have sought to place limitations on Korean autonomy and electoral democracy, but in the immediate postwar moment, most of what the Soviets would have expected from a satellite state was already being undertaken by Koreans of their own free will. Importantly, the transformation that was taking place in North Korea was hugely beneficial to the country's poor — 75% of whom were small peasant farmers — who received land, both as small family plots and as part of larger collective farms and were given the equipment and support needed to cultivate food successfully.[62]

The US zone of occupation was very different. Since the Americans had not yet landed troops in Korea when Japan surrendered, they asked the Japanese commander in Korea to "maintain order and preserve the machinery of government" in the South until they arrived.[63] The Korean reaction was predictably negative; just days after the dropping of the atomic bombs in Hiroshima and Nagasaki, the United States was inviting the Japanese to maintain their occupation of South Korea. When the Americans finally arrived to assert their authority, they were appalled to find Koreans urgently and effectively applying a variety of socialist practices to rebuild the country, under the auspices of the KPR.

To halt the success of the KPR, the US repatriated Syngman Rhee, a conservative Korean politician who had deep ties with the United States. Rhee's father was descended from the Korean royal family, and he had adopted a life as a Christian missionary in Hawai'i, recently conquered by the US. Rhee worked his way up in American political circles, sojourned in Japan with future fascist collaborators, attended Harvard University with Woodrow Wilson and made largely irrelevant pronouncements of Korean independence from the United States.[64] Given his loyalty to the US, his Christian conservatism and his disconnection from the dynamics of real life in Korea, he was the perfect candidate for Washington. The CIA specifically noted that his goal was "personal control" of Korea, to which end "he has shown few scruples about the elements which he has been willing to utilize for his personal advancement, with the important exception that he has always refused to deal with Communists."[65] For the Western powers it was a match made in heaven.

In 1946, Rhee was established as provisional head of state in South Korea, while the US engineered an electoral process they could control. Rhee's election victory in 1948 was marred by widespread allegations of violence, and most of the candidates from the left and even the centre boycotted the elections, knowing they would be fraudulent.[66] But Canada, flexing its muscles at the new United Nations, helped form a UN commission to validate the sham election. Syngman Rhee's authoritarian rule over South Korea is still remembered as one of the darkest chapters in the country's history, and it kicked off nearly four decades of dictatorship in South Korea. Canada was among the first countries to officially recognize his government.[67]

Despite Canada's enthusiasm, Rhee was viewed by most Koreans as a puppet dictator. The strength of the KPR in South Korea was such that it could mobilize massive strikes and protests against his government, which could only be defeated by naked violence. Hundreds of KPR activists were imprisoned or killed, and by 1947–48 the KPR essentially found itself fighting a guerrilla war against Rhee and his US sponsors. Rhee filled most of his important administrative positions with members of the Korean ruling class who had collaborated with the Japanese occupation. For people who had survived fascist rule, the spectacle of seeing the same people ruling the country again was intolerable. By 1950, Rhee's government had effectively defeated the KPR by killing over 100,000 Koreans, with violence and imprisonment handed out to many more. His government had even alienated many centre-right Koreans, who found themselves imprisoned and/or tortured if they disagreed with him.[68]

This was the government that Canada would support in the Korean War — a government of fascist collaborators that stole elections, ruled by force, shut down opposition newspapers, undermined legitimate efforts at reconstruction and defied the will of average Koreans. Small wonder Canadians are rarely encouraged to remember the Korean War, whose veterans returned home with "Syngman Rhee Volunteer Medals."[69] Meanwhile, no such upheaval was taking place in the North. While the election of partisan war hero Kim Il Sung in 1948 was certainly a welcome choice to the Soviets, it was nevertheless the case that Kim was massively popular and the reforms taking place in the North, now called the Democratic People's Republic of Korea (DPRK), were widely supported. Canadian diplomats privately admitted as much.[70]

The war itself began in 1950, after months of increased tension provoked by Rhee's embarrassing electoral failure that year. Despite rigging the elections, Rhee still could only muster a minority government, and the increasing fragility of his dictatorship appeared to provide an opening to those who still sought unification along the lines of the original KPR. When members of the North Korean government travelled to the South to meet with opposition leaders about the situation, Rhee had them arrested. This set off a series of diplomatic shots leading most observers to conclude that full-scale war was imminent. Indeed, both Kim Il Sung and Syngman Rhee openly discussed using military options to re-unite the country along their preferred lines; Rhee was arguably more aggressive in his planning, trying desperately to convince the US to support a pre-emptive attack.[71] Minor cross-border skirmishes occurred with some regularity between 1948 and 1950. Indeed, the government of North Korea claimed that the South had invaded over 2500 times to cause violence and unrest, a claim corroborated by American officials in Korea.[72]

The North made the first successful incursion — though much evidence suggests that it was actually a counter-attack after the South captured the

Northern city of Haeju[73] — marching into South Korea on June 25, 1950. Rhee's forces collapsed quickly, and there was little doubt, given South Koreans' hatred of Syngman Rhee, that they would lose the war in short order. Knowing as much, the United States immediately declared this an act of communist aggression and mobilized its military for war. Canada joined a group of countries at the United Nations which claimed that North Korea had launched an "unprovoked" attack against South Korea and pushed the UN to take action against North Korea. Though this description of events was extremely misleading, it became the dominant narrative and was glibly repeated by Canadian historians for decades.[74] The war would effectively be led by the US, while they legally operated under the jurisdiction of the UN.

Of course, it was not North Korea, *per se*, that was framed as the source of the conflict but rather the Soviet Union, Red China and communism more generally. Throughout the period leading up to the war, Canadians were fed a steady diet of fearmongering about the looming third world war being launched by the Soviets. This could not have been further from the truth: Stalin was desperately committed to a defensive, de-escalating approach to the Cold War, avoiding conflict even when it meant watching communists be killed by the West.[75] He was distinctly uninterested in seeing conflict engulf the Korean peninsula; far from ordering the attack, he only reluctantly gave it his consent when Kim Il Sung promised it would be quick and decisive.[76] But to bring a war-weary Canadian public on board for another major conflict, it had to be framed as "Kremlin-controlled armies" and "communist aggression," with the *Vancouver Sun* even suggesting this was a more dire threat than Hitler. The fearmongering worked; by 1950, 69% of Canadians believed that a third world war would be upon them in less than five years and were convinced that Korea was an emergency that threatened their very survival.[77]

Even as it was securing domestic support for the war, Canada played a key role in establishing the disingenuous UN "peacekeeping" mission. Taking advantage of the absence of the Soviet Union (which was boycotting the UN in response to its recognition of Taiwan as the true representative of China), the UN established its first peacekeeping mission, to intervene on behalf of South Korea. Canadian Prime Minister Louis St-Laurent described it as a "police action designed to prevent war by discouraging aggression."[78] That police action would ultimately end the lives of several million Koreans, at least three million of them civilian, as well as more than 500 Canadians, and it reduced North Korea to rubble.

This is not just an aphorism. The UN peacekeeping mission in Korea employed what it described as a "scorched earth policy," which used megabombs and napalm gas to burn crops, pulverize buildings, flatten homes and instil terror among North Koreans. Cities were firebombed, dams were destroyed, and by the time the war was over, it was reported that there was not a single building in North Korea standing more than one story off the ground.[79] Bombing targets became so scarce that one pilot dropped several bombs on a single motorcycle rider.[80] In the words of US General MacArthur, Korea would be "obliterated" and left a "desert."[81] The devastation paralleled, and in some ways surpassed, scenes from the fallout of the Second World War.

The war was so horrific that some of its own soldiers refused to fight. Between 1950 and 1953, hundreds of soldiers with the UN force, including some Canadians, chose to abandon their side and abet the North Koreans. These were soldiers who had been taken prisoner, of whom, according to a report commissioned by the US military, some 30% collaborated with North Korea and 13% became active members of the communist front, as propagandists, spies, etc.[82] The embarrassing fact that Western soldiers were so disillusioned with their mission was significant enough that military leaders had to go on record acknowledging and explaining it. Rather than admit that their mission might lack a persuasive moral claim, they instead suggested that the Korean and Chinese communists were using brainwashing techniques to manipulate their prisoners.

The CIA had, in fact, been working on such measures, experimenting on North Korean prisoners as early as 1950.[83] But while the public was led to believe that the communists were employing "all-powerful, irresistible, unfathomable, and magical" tricks to lure away their soldiers,[84] even the US military acknowledged that there was no evidence of such magic and that, in fact, North Korea rarely used physical violence. Instead — according to US army reports — they would show Western soldiers maps of East Asia dotted with US military bases and suggest to them that maybe it was the US that was the aggressor. "This argument seemed plausible to the prisoners," said the US report. "They had no idea that these bases showed not the United States' wish for war, but its wish for peace."[85] Indeed, the distinction was elusive.

But even while some soldiers were horrified by the missions they were being asked to carry out, many others embraced an opportunity to embody the superiority they believed themselves to represent. Canadian soldiers routinely denigrated Korean and Chinese soldiers as a "yellow horde," tapping into the deep colonial legacy of Europeans in Asia, as well as the more recent memory of World War Two propaganda, which made ample use of racist slurs and stereotypes. Indeed, the epithet "g--k," so associated with the war in Vietnam, was widely used by Canadians in Korea. For its part, the Canadian media served up ridiculous racial stereotypes, like the claim by the *Calgary Herald* that Koreans' "chief aim in life is to have as many children as possible,"[86] and reassured its readers that this war was a challenge to civilization itself.

The colonial view of Koreans was such that many Canadians assumed the only way to pursue such a conflict was by the use of overwhelming force, believing Asians to be inherently malleable and swayed by powerful leaders. Canada had long viewed Koreans as "lesser" on the civilizational hierarchy. When Canada established diplomatic ties with Japan in 1929, *chargé d'affairs* Hugh Keenleyside argued that Korea ought to be a Japanese dominion.[87] Canadian missionaries, who had been active in Korea (and especially in the areas bordering Manchuria) since the early 20th century, often found themselves at the centre of conflicts between Korean communist partisans and the Japanese occupation. They overwhelmingly sided with the Japanese and preached anti-communism, which ultimately saw them lose favour among Koreans.[88]

Indeed, Canadian support for fascist Japan had betrayed the colonial superiority with which Canada viewed East Asia in general and Korea in particular. Now, in 1950, Koreans were the direct target of Canadian force, and expressions of colonial arrogance were the superficial marks of an attitude expressed more dangerously in soldiers' actions. Canadian soldiers committed violent attacks — sometimes murder and rape — against even the South Koreans they were ostensibly there to support. This pattern, rooted in Canadian settler violence against Indigenous people, would become a dubious hallmark of Canadian peacekeeping. Most of these crimes went almost entirely unpunished. Canadian soldier John Steeves murdered Shin Yong-Dok, a South Korean farmer, in a drunken rage in 1951. He was court martialled and sentenced to 15 years for manslaughter but was released after less than six months.[89] Earlier that same year, three Canadian soldiers descended — again after much drinking and partying — on a South Korean farmhouse, where they savagely beat a group of South Korean soldiers and raped two women. A Canadian journalist, Bill Boss, tried to file a report on the story, but it was squashed by the Canadian embassy in Tokyo and Boss was labelled a "subversive." The three soldiers were convicted but all three were released in 1952.[90]

These were not isolated cases. Historian John Price estimates that there were hundreds and maybe thousands of incidents like it. It is worth noting that these are not new revelations. Attempts to block these stories from North American newspapers did not always succeed, and they certainly could not be hidden from Koreans, whose contempt for the occupation grew as a result of this racist violence. No less than Pierre Berton, one of Canada's most famous writers, described the harrowing, everyday violence Canadian soldiers unleashed on Koreans.[91] This situation, and especially the widespread use of napalm attacks to kill civilians, caught the attention of Lester Pearson; the great peacekeeper's priority in Korea was not to stop the violence but to push for greater censorship of the press from speaking about it.[92] Pearson took his own advice in 1952, when he lied to Parliament, denying that Canada had participated in the development of biological weapons for use in the Korean War.[93] The initial accusation was made by James Endicott, whom *Maclean's* had denounced as "fronting for the Reds."

In fact, Endicott was speaking a truth Canadians did not want to hear, then as now. More recent attempts to bring the Korean War back into popular awareness often tried to rescue it as a noble cause, even when the facts made that a tough sell. Ted Barris, for instance, called it "the war that history forgot" and lamented the fact that Canadian classrooms did not echo with the recitations of the great battle at Kapyong.[94] But Canadian soldiers at Kapyong were ordered to open fire on civilian refugees; the Korean War was thus a difficult one for Canadian mythmakers to spin.[95]

In fact, Canada's role in the Korean War embodies the colonial dynamics at the heart of this study As in Canada's relations with Indigenous nations, the overarching strategic goals were the establishment and maintenance of capitalism. Like so many Cold War conflicts that followed it, the key question in the Korean War was whether Koreans would be permitted to establish a socialist economic system across the peninsula. This was clearly what the majority of Koreans on both sides of the 38th parallel wanted at that time. But to the US, Canada and other stewards of the global capitalist system, Korea was a domino they couldn't allow to fall, especially given the success of the Chinese Revolution just a year before. Indeed, by the 1950s, Canada was taking an active role in the Cold War, and Canadians were encouraged to demonize any group of people connected to communism.[96]

Meanwhile, throughout the course of Canada's engagements with Korea, it was clear that both the Canadian state and many of its representatives — be they missionaries, diplomats or soldiers — viewed Koreans through the same colonial lens they did Indigenous Peoples. Missionaries evangelized them, diplomats infantilized them, soldiers dehumanized them and the Canadian state considered itself fully justified in using every means at its disposal to dictate the terms of Korean governance. And despite helping to create a social, political and humanitarian apocalypse in Korea, few Canadians thought about the Korean War more than to add it to the list of Canada's generous contributions to global security and peace.

The Heroes of Dien Bien Phu

The Korean War is often overshadowed by the calamity which followed hard on its heels in Vietnam. Indeed, Vietnam would ultimately occupy a pivotal place in the broader history of the Cold War and the anti-colonial struggles that shaped the century. The French had dominated the region called Indochina (Vietnam, Cambodia and Laos) since 1858. The colony was consolidated in 1895 and run by a small French bureaucracy and local collaborators from the old elite. Rice, rubber and coal — produced by poorly paid peasants and workers — were France's primary sources of profit, but in 1925 a significant wave of protests against French domination began. By the time Indochina was seized by the Japanese as part of their major offensive in 1941, a powerful movement for independence had formed under the leadership of Ho Chi Minh and the Indochina Communist Party.

This resistance became the Viet Minh, guerilla partisans who harried the joint occupation of Japanese and French collaborationist authorities in Vichy. When Japan and Germany were defeated, the newly liberated French government planned to re-assume control of its colony, but the Viet Minh had other ideas, seizing first Hanoi and then the rest of the country with little opposition. It was a jubilant moment; Vietnam was declared independent, but it was short-lived. With the spirit of liberation still in the air, hostile British troops arrived the next month to help the French regain control over their former colony. Major battles in and around Saigon eventually pushed the Viet Minh out of the city. Canada made no objections.

In fact, Canada emerged as a strong supporter of the French re-conquest of Indochina. Within NATO, Canada endorsed a controversial resolution that claimed France's war was "in fullest harmony with the aims and ideals of the Atlantic community," which was true if one considers that those aims and ideals had long been colonial capitalism. Canada also made a material contribution: $61.3 million in weapons, ammunition and aircraft sold to France between 1950 and 1954.[97] Indeed, Canada's support for the French and then American effort to defeat Vietnamese independence was consistent right through the crisis in the Suez (1956) that made Canada so famous for peacekeeping. When the French forces were defeated by the Vietnamese at Dien Bien Phu — now symbolic of Europe's desperate failed bid to hang on to its decaying empires — Canadian Prime Minister St-Laurent had the temerity to honour French heroism. Canadians, he said, "while lamenting the tragic ending of the legendary conflict at Dien Bien Phu, salute with pride and honour the heroic defenders of the fortress."[98] The Canadian prime minister believed that the defeated French conquerors were the real heroes. Of course, across most of the world, the victory at Dien Bien Phu was a celebrated moment, paving the way for peace talks in Geneva that led to the creation of independent states of Cambodia, Laos and Vietnam, though the latter would be divided down the middle just as Korea had been.

At the 1954 Geneva Conference, which took place just after the ceasefire in Korea, it was agreed that France would withdraw and Vietnam would have its sovereignty, though the US would maintain a presence in the south, until elections in 1956, which would re-unite the country. These, Ho Chi Minh insisted, should be "universal, free, democratic and secret" and supervised by international observers.[99] Since there was little doubt that the Viet Minh would easily win national elections, the US determined that it would not allow the elections to take place. Instead, it supported a local pro-Western strongman, Ngo Dinh Diem, to rule South Vietnam as though it were an independent state.

This was in direct violation of the Geneva Accords, but, fortunately for the US, Canada had volunteered to sit on the International Control Commission (ICC) to oversee and enforce the Accords. Canada helped to keep the ICC unable and unwilling to force South Vietnam to participate in the elections, as exhaustively documented in Victor Levant's *Quiet*

Complicity (1986). Given that the promise of elections was one of the only reasons Ho Chi Minh had accepted the Accords in the first place, it was inevitable that war would be the consequence as the North would seek to unite the country in spite of Western interference.

Canada's partiality on the ICC was always obvious. Indeed, the only mystery is how Canada ever claimed otherwise. While supposedly sitting on a neutral commission, Canada provided hundreds of millions of dollars in aid to South Vietnam, which was not even supposed to exist after 1956, as per the agreement Canada was tasked with enforcing. The aid was part of what Prime Minister St-Laurent called a "crusade" against communist forces. Indeed, Nik Cavell, who administered Canada's Columbo Plan aid program in South Asia, reminded Parliament in 1957 that skilful application of foreign aid could help strengthen anti-communist forces to prevent the "white races" from being overwhelmed by what he evidently thought was "non-white" communism. This was, after all, the express purpose of Columbo Plan aid, a point of pride for Canadian Cold Warriors.[100]

In addition to aid, Canada used its position on the ICC to consistently side with South Vietnam even when it bordered on the absurd. In one instance, North Vietnamese officials sent a letter to the ICC to protest that political prisoners reported "released" from a South Vietnamese jail had, in fact, disappeared, likely having been killed. In a quintessentially Canadian response, the complaint itself — the murder of prisoners — was ignored while Canadian officials protested at the "very unpleasant" North Vietnamese letter and the "offensive language" it contained.[101]

In fact, the ICC received more than 800 complaints from North Vietnam, alleging more than 1300 cases of murder, detention, torture, arrest, mass concentration and massacre by the South Vietnamese government. Even the US privately admitted these were true; their puppet dictator Ngo Dinh Diem himself had promised to "mercilessly wipe out the Viet Cong as if we were in a state of war with them, no longer considering them as human beings."[102] Still, Canada consistently took South Vietnam's side in the ICC and ensured that no real consequences would be felt by the Diem regime or its American sponsors. Indeed, as Vietnam drifted into a full-scale war involving the United States, Canada would provide arms to the Americans and South Vietnamese, and Canadian officials would conduct espionage against North Vietnam, furnishing the CIA with information on troop movements, morale and North Vietnamese discussions with foreign powers.[103]

Clearly, a pattern emerges from Canada's engagements in Asia in this period. Canada regularly resisted movements towards independence for colonized peoples, especially if they were led by popular left movements, even after the Second World War had been fought ostensibly for freedom. In addition to supporting the US administration of postwar Japan, the nationalist domination of China, an imposed dictatorship in Korea and French reconquest of Indochina, Canada also voted against the withdrawal of Dutch colonial domination in Indonesia in 1948. Lester Pearson worried about Indonesian people, "who wish political freedom [but] cannot achieve it by peaceful change."[104] That Canada sold weapons to the Netherlands to help it crush the independence movement was surely a factor in the impossibility of peaceful change.

Meanwhile, Canada did not participate directly in the savage British guerrilla war to delay and manage its relinquishing of Malaya, but the Canadian ambassador who attended its celebration of independence in 1957 remarked on the importance of maintaining Malaya as a "strong bastion against Communism."[105] The British war had borne similarities to the emerging conflict in Vietnam and had been largely aimed at wiping out the widely popular Communist Party such that when the country gained its independence there would be no question of its allegiance.[106] As Canada told the United Nations in 1951, "though we have sympathy for those who seek self-government, we also have a strong interest in preventing the development of trouble-spots that would endanger western defence."[107] To that end, Canada made no complaint when the United States brought back fascist collaborators in the Philippines and repressed the popular communist Hukbalahap movement to ensure capitalist, pro-Western dominance there.[108]

Indeed, across every case, concern for the integrity of the capitalist world order was paramount and usually couched within the hyperbolic language of the Cold War. "If… the whole of Asia were to be allowed to fall under Communist domination," fretted Lester Pearson, "the free world would be tragically maimed and would be exposed to ever greater dangers."[109] Another Canadian diplomat took it further, insisting that "if the free world were to be kept in existence, it would have to be expanded and strengthened."[110] All one needs to do is substitute the word "capitalism" for "free world" — they were considered synonymous by the speakers — and you had a pretty clear articulation of Canada's Cold War aims. Capitalism, as it had from its inception, needed to expand to survive.

Threats to capitalism needed to be contained and eliminated. These goals, ideologically linked to the certainty of the Euro-American world's supremacy, were at the heart of Canadian policy in this period and were also being applied — with even more direct benefits for the Canadian capitalist class — in Latin America and the Caribbean.

Saving Somoza: Falconbridge, Inco and Canada's Cold War

It has long been a popular belief among Canadian liberals that if and when Canada has ever done anything unsavoury in the world, it was only because Uncle Sam demanded it. This mythology, reflected in studies like Linda McQuaig's *Holding the Bully's Coat* (2007), does not stand up to serious investigation, and Canada's aggressive posture in Latin America in the early Cold War era acts as a useful example. While it is undoubtedly true that Canada often worked with the United States and, especially after 1945, made many of its decisions based on US policies and positions, it is patently false to suggest that Canada acted as a supplicant to American interests. One especially illuminating case is the remarkable tale of the Canadian effort to prop up the dictatorship of Anastasio Somoza in Nicaragua against the wishes of the United States.

The Somoza family had been in power since 1933 and ruled the country with an iron fist, which was just what the doctor ordered for the Canadian mining magnates who owned its most profitable gold mines, especially La Luz, owned by Toronto-based Falconbridge. The extraordinarily profitable mines were intensely exploitative and created epidemic levels of arsenic poisoning, making La Luz a flashpoint for rebellion in Nicaragua. In fact, when revolution swept the country in 1947 it began at La Luz; the Canadian mine was a symbol of the Somoza dictatorship, which was receiving financing and weapons from Canadian mining companies.[111] Even officials in Washington had long acknowledged that the Canadian mining companies were "the backbone of the Somoza regime."[112] Falconbridge was quick to note that it was not motivated by affection for the dictator, who kept pictures of Hitler and Mussolini on his desk during the war; no, they supported him because he "used the army to prevent native workers from stealing too much gold."[113] More precisely, Somoza used his repressive apparatus to guarantee union-free mines and a mollified labour force.

None of this breaks from the standard pattern of Canadian behaviour abroad, but what makes the case unique is that, in 1947, the United States wanted Somoza out. The Central American dictators of the 1930s had outlived their utility in Washington; their public affection for the Nazis was now an embarrassment and their quasi-monarchic positions undermined US claims that they represented freedom and democracy in the Cold War. Given that people in many of these countries were on the brink of rebellion, the US plan was to get there first and replace the old dictators with governments that would effectively perform the same function but generate less opposition. They succeeded in Honduras and El Salvador, replacing longstanding dictators with loyal but more conciliatory leaders. In Guatemala, the people got there first and overthrew Jorge Ubico to create a democratic state under a popular reformer. In Nicaragua, it was clear that the Americans were finished with Somoza; they withdrew military aid and threatened to cut ties with the country if Somoza did not step down.[114]

So the old dictator turned to his last friends, the Canadians. W.G. Hubler of Falconbridge quickly became Somoza's closest ally, working tirelessly over the next year to secure Somoza's position. Hubler engaged the Canadian ambassador to the United States, Humphrey Hume Wrong, and they worked with Somoza and other mining executives to hatch a plan to save the regime. Somoza was rebranded as a vigilant anti-communist — this was true, but had never been made so explicit — and the Canadian executives harangued the US State Department to convince them that Somoza's position could be maintained by re-arranging the chairs a little, placing Somoza's uncle as president and a Falconbridge lawyer as vice-president of Nicaragua. The Americans were nonplussed that Falconbridge had "consented to act as a front for Somoza," but when Canadian money and airplanes helped Somoza crush the popular rebellion, they were satisfied that his position could stand.[115] Canadian capitalists had saved the career of one of the most hated dictators in the Western Hemisphere.

While the heavy lifting was done by the private sector, the Canadian government was involved in the process. After the Americans intercepted a shipment of four military aircraft being funnelled to Somoza from Hubler, the Canadian government ignored the US State Department's complaints. Private Canadians were running guns to a dictator in Nicaragua with the full knowledge of the Canadian government, but the FBI could not get

Ottawa to pick up the phone. Canada, clearly, was able to look out for its own affairs, having defied the will of the United States in supporting the Somoza dictatorship. And Canada knew exactly what it was supporting: internal reports from another Canadian ambassador had critically described Somoza's relations with Nazi spies, his "despotism" and his "personal ambitions."[116] By 1950, Somoza was officially back in the office of the president, and Canada sent a cable congratulating his "Excellency" and promising to "strengthen the happy relations which exist between the two countries."[117]

Around the same time, Canadians were actively supporting the overthrow of an elected government in Costa Rica by the fascist sympathizer José Figueres. Figueres' closest ally was Alexander Murray McNair, born in Costa Rica to wealthy Canadian parents, intelligence officer for the Allies in World War Two and hero of the right-wing rebellion that brought Figueres to power in 1948. Murray promised to help Figueres "lick these bastard communists" and maintained close contact with the Canadian government throughout the civil war.[118] Figueres' forces initially carried out terrorist attacks in Costa Rica, waiting for the people to join their movement. Few were interested in joining the fascist coup, so Figueres launched a full-fledged war, which ended with thousands of people dead and Figueres in power. There he would remain — either directly or in the shadows — until the 1970s. Alex Murray became a founding owner of the Costa Rican Electricity Institute, a virtual monopoly in the country's electricity provision.[119] The Murray family remained prominent in Costa Rica, with Alex's son Cecil founding a profitable aviation company in the 1950s under the friendly skies of the Figueres dictatorship.

With Figueres and Somoza in place by 1950, the only remaining popular democratic government in Central America was that of Jacobo Arbenz in Guatemala. The United States orchestrated a now-infamous overthrow of his government in 1954, at the behest of the United Fruit Company, to install the dictatorship of Carlos Castillo Armas. Canada supported the coup indirectly, refusing to respond when Arbenz asked Canada to support his legitimate, elected government in 1953. When Arbenz had been elected in 1950, Canadian official Alfred Savard had criticized him for failing to criminalize union leaders and absurdly described the soft-spoken, intellectual Arbenz as "unscrupulous, daring, and ruthless… a drug addict [who] is especially egotistical and sadistic when under the influence of drugs and alcohol."[120] These ludicrous claims have never been corroborated by any legitimate source, but they helped create the political will in Canada to support the coup.

Canadian labour leaders and members of the social democratic CCF, increasingly pulled into the orbit of anti-communism, joined the furor against Arbenz, and church leaders became convinced of the need to send missionaries to the region to quell poor Central Americans of the Red Menace. In Ottawa, External Affairs Minister Lester Pearson coyly admittedly to Parliament that he knew the coup was coming and instructed his department to refuse to speak about Guatemala until the situation was resolved. When it was resolved in 1954, Castillo Armas was installed as the new dictator, thousands of Guatemalans were killed and arrested, and the Canadian International Nickel Company (Inco) had itself a brand-new mining concession on Lake Izabal.[121]

The above patterns were repeated across Latin America. In 1942, for instance, Montreal-based Alcan asked the Canadian government to station "white soldiers" at its bauxite mines in Guyana, since the "local coloured guards" could not be trusted. Guyana was still effectively a British colony until 1966 and it guaranteed favourable conditions for the company, which housed its workers in underserviced slums and exploited them heavily, while company bosses lived in luxury nearby. Alcan executives both benefitted from, and believed in the idea of, colonial rule. When Guyanese people rose up in revolt in 1953, Alcan executives were among the whites who were deputized to maintain British authority.[122]

Thus, in the 1940s and 1950s, Canada continued to support governments which offered the best guarantees for stable capitalist investment, even when they had fascist sympathies, like Juan Perón in Argentina. At the same time, Canadian officials were able to recognize that in some cases centre-left governments might represent the best chances for Canadian profits. Canadian capital had struggled mightily during and after the Mexican Revolution, for instance, and took the lesson that working with right-wing dictators could backfire if the people were allowed to overthrow them.[123] As such, Canada sought out, on a case-by-case basis, the options that it believed could best represent its interests.

Indeed, the promotion and maintenance of violent dictators in Latin America was creating serious blowback, with the coup against Arbenz in Guatemala as a particularly galling intervention. Viewed by many as the culmination of nearly a century of interference, dating back to the invasion of the mercenary American William Walker, criticism of "Yankee imperialism" grew to a fever pitch and manifested most dramatically in the successful Cuban Revolution, which secured its victory on January 1, 1959. Contemporary Canadians have been weaned on stories about Canada's warm relations with Cuba, and an urban legend even circulated during the early days of the Justin Trudeau government that Justin was, in fact, the child of Fidel Castro and Margaret Trudeau, conceived during one of their sensationalized visits to Cuba in the 1970s.[124]

The story is false, as is the perception that Canada stood in any kind of solidarity with the Cuban Revolution.[125] Canada's decision to maintain relations with Cuba when the US was kicked out was rooted in the strategic consideration that it is sometimes best to keep your enemies close. Canadian officials were avowedly anti-communist: in 1959 the Canadian ambassador to Cuba expressed a desire "to halt this cancerous growth," describing Fidel himself as an "infection."[126] He was convinced that Fidel was incapable of leadership and was on the brink of death from consuming excessive barbiturates. Nevertheless, Canada determined that its position was stronger if it remained connected, an approach that looked clever after the US was embarrassed in its failed attempt to overthrow Fidel during the Bay of Pigs invasion. Thus, even while Prime Minister Diefenbaker railed against the "Soviet threat," he kept an open door to Cuba, using the continued presence of the Canadian embassy in Havana to conduct extensive spying on the Cuban government. All of the information gathered was shared with the CIA.[127]

Nevertheless, the Cuban Revolution survived, illustrating to people across Latin America, Africa and Asia that it was possible to go up against the colonizers and win. It was to be a turning point in the struggles for national and often socialist revolution across the three continents, which would erupt in the 1960s and 1970s, forcing the capitalist powers to confront their ongoing commitment to the colonial and semi-colonial relationships they had established in the 19th century. It appeared that the world revolution Lenin had hoped for in 1917 might finally materialize out of the continents most heavily exploited by global capitalism. From Cuba, the latest inspirational example, Ernesto "Che" Guevara promised that the oppressed people of the world would give the West "one, two, many Vietnams." For a time, it appeared that he was right. But Canada would play a key role in ensuring that this world revolution failed.

Consolidating the Cold War

Throughout the early Cold War period, there were critical voices in Canada, though they were largely drowned out. Much of the vibrancy of the Canadian left of the 1930s had been siphoned away by the combined effects of the defeat in Spain, the emergence of the social-democratic CCF, the patriotism elicited by the Second World War, the economic improvements generated by the war and the postwar expansion of the welfare state and the anti-communist hysteria that set in in the late 1940s. Nevertheless, publications like *Canadian Forum* offered trenchant critique, noting in 1944 that Euro-American colonialism bore much resemblance to the Nazi project it was set to defeat, and pointing out that the Asians and Africans fighting alongside the Allies would return home to few of the rights the Allied war effort trumpeted.

The peace movement, galvanized by James Endicott, was able to fill Maple Leaf Gardens with tens of thousands of people, and trade unions were as defiant as they had ever been. But the Canadian ruling class — led by Lester Pearson — was quick to let slip the dogs of anti-communism. Pearson purged many who had once been his personal friends, including Endicott and Herbert Norman,[128] and the National Film Board (NFB) and elements of the civil service were purged of a wide range of suspected subversives, many of them targeted for their sexuality.[129] The right was so convinced that queer sexualities were linked to communism that, intent on preventing homosexual communists from infiltrating the civil service, they would later use a ludicrous and demeaning "fruit machine" to detect the erotic responses of job applicants.[130] Lists of names of "suspected" communists were swapped between the RCMP and the CIA as Fortress North America conspired to fight the enemy within. Buoyed by the sensationalized but insignificant Gouzenko Affair, in which a Russian cipher clerk claimed to be exposing a wide-reaching espionage campaign directed against Canada, the machinery of Canadian repression was cranked up.[131]

As Ian McKay and Jamie Swift describe it, "Cold Warriors used anti-communism to fight health insurance, undermine trade unions, regulate wayward youths, and persecute homosexuals — all vital 'moral crusades.'"[132] This is documented in great detail in Reg Whitaker and Gary Marcuse's *Cold War Canada* (1994), wherein they describe the creation of an "insecurity state" designed to track and monitor people within Canada, particularly those either connected to the Communist Party or to left politics more broadly. The goal was to tar progressive values — from social equality to anti-racism to fair wages to peace — with "the brush of illegitimacy: disloyalty, subversion, connections to an external enemy," to ensure that the postwar arrangement was favourable to capital and to social conservatism.[133]

Even as Canada was tightening the noose on progressives at home, it sought to undermine the international left through psychological operations, the most prominent of which was the Canadian Broadcasting Corporation's International Service (CBC-IS), which beamed propaganda into Eastern Europe. By 1951, it was broadcasting in fourteen European languages, with tailored programming sent to different countries. In 1954, the service established primary objectives that included "to counteract communist propaganda about conditions in Western countries and about the warlike intentions of these countries" and "to encourage the Soviet people both to question what their government told them and eventually to oppose the aggressive policies of Soviet government."[134] Also revealing was the directive to "strive constantly to identify communism as an instrument of Soviet imperialism," which was, indeed, a significant Cold War tactic for the West, since it denied the possibility that any group of people could ever choose communism for their own reasons. Though this was obviously false, it was standard procedure to attribute any left movement anywhere as an export of Moscow. Small wonder that a book should appear in Moscow in 1951, by the leading Soviet scholar of Canada, entitled *Canada — Fiefdom of American Imperialism*.[135]

It is impossible to say how effective such measures were; convincing the rest of the world that the West did not have warlike intentions — in the shadow of the atomic bombs and the aggressive wars of the 1950s — was a tough sell. Notably, the CBC-IS revised some of its guidelines in 1956 to "show respect for foreign listeners' intelligence, common sense and national feeling," which suggests that early Canadian propaganda was taken as clumsy or insulting.[136] In the meantime, Canada was increasingly opening its doors to what it termed "refugees" fleeing from Soviet tyranny, despite having so recently refused Jews fleeing Hitler. It is likely true that most of the new wave of refugees had cause for fear from Soviet authorities; what was rarely discussed was the *reasons* they were fleeing from the Soviets. Many of this wave of refugees were far-right ethnic nationalists who had collaborated with the Nazis during the war.[137] Their hatred of the Soviets was born of an ingrained ideological opposition, and their fear was a consequence of the de-Nazification programs the Soviets put into place in many of the territories they occupied.

In 1950 Canada even opened up its doors to those who had directly served in the Nazi war machine. Even the avowedly anti-communist Canadian Jewish Congress was appalled at the decision, especially after Canada admitted former members of the so-called Galicia Division.[138] This was a Nazi SS unit — a death squad — involved in some of the worst atrocities in Ukraine. Many Ukrainians already in Canada themselves criticized these measures, perhaps anticipating part of Canada's motivation, which was to weaken the left-wing cohesion of immigrant groups like the Ukrainians. Indeed, as Canada increasingly positioned itself as a haven for people fleeing Soviet persecution, it consciously accumulated a core of right-wing émigrés which would eventually overwhelm the more left-oriented immigrant groups of the 1920s and 1930s. This new model of immigration policy emphasized integration of newcomers not just into the expanding working classes but also into the ideology of liberal capitalism; schools training immigrants to speak English, for instance, would inculcate the values of free enterprise into language training.[139]

The vast majority of Western historiography of the Cold War period, if it was at all critical of the policies and practices of the Cold War, failed to adequately sketch the link between colonialism and the seemingly geopolitical, *realpolitik* struggle against world communism. Many reflections on that era suggested that leading politicians, journalists and indeed common citizens of the West were caught up in a high-stakes chess match such that their visions were clouded by the exaggerated sense of danger that the USSR and its allies supposedly posed. While this was true to some extent, it missed something crucial: the Cold Warriors believed they were engaged in a struggle for civilization itself. In fact, Canadian Prime Minister Louis St-Laurent explicitly argued as much in 1950, telling an audience at the University of Toronto that the fight against Soviet communism was for the very "preservation of civilization."[140] The old colonial logic was not subsumed by the Cold War; they were blended together. Thus, to the extent that Cold War leaders exaggerated threats posed by the communists, it was often a sincere reflection of the panic they felt at the prospect of losing the very centre of their moral and spiritual compass: colonial capitalism.

The communist challenge was, by its very nature, anti-colonial. This is not to say that communist states never engaged in what could be described as colonial practices; certainly, some of the Soviet interventions in Eastern Europe illustrated that a communist state could devolve into a coercive apparatus that betrayed its own ideals and imposed its decaying model of communism onto other states, largely for its own preservation. But the fact remained that modern colonialism had been nurtured in symbiosis with capitalism; the two phenomena were inextricable, and the Cold War illustrated as much. When anti-colonial struggles were led by groups that were anti-capitalist and seeking to de-link from the world capitalist system and the neocolonial powers, they were seen as a threat.[141] When, on the other hand, decolonization was managed by forces that were largely sympathetic to capitalism and the West, it was often greeted with relative warmth and in some cases encouraged, because it ensured that the former colonizers would remain dominant. As the old model of direct colonial domination gave way to a newer variant wherein power was exercised indirectly, the core of modern colonialism was exposed: it was never only about exercising political authority; it was always about a much deeper domination.

This was explicitly understood by Canadian officials. In their discussions about the rising anti-colonial movements in Africa, discussed in greater detail in the next chapter, they directly addressed the fact that postcolonial states would be unlikely to feel warmth towards their former colonial authorities and that this would push them towards the communist world. External Affairs noted, with respect to the independence of Ghana, that it was the first "all-African negro independent nation to emerge from colonial status" and that this would "not be lost on the rest of Africa, nor on the anti-colonial nations or the Soviet Union."[142] The same sentiment was expressed with respect to Kenya, with Canadian diplomat Robert Ford — former *chargé d'affairs* in the Soviet Union — suggesting that Canada help "prevent these scraps of territory from falling to the Communists after the departure of the British."[143] As historian Kevin Spooner concludes, "race, colonialism, and the Cold War were clearly converging."[144]

As such, the Cold War was, indeed, a struggle to preserve the civilization that had been created by modern colonialism and capitalism. That this was the case was clearly illustrated in the years immediately following the Second World War, when a new international body for collective security and cooperation — the United Nations — was sidelined by the Atlantic powers in favour of a more exclusive, primarily military, alliance known as the North Atlantic Treaty Organization (NATO). Unlike the UN, this was effectively a union of colonial powers seeking to maintain their domination of the rest of the world; within NATO there would be no need to engage in debate or discussion with the communist countries or the decolonizing nations, which were increasingly emerging from liberation struggles against the very powers that formed NATO. Instead, this was a space where those voices could be ignored and the interests of the Western capitalist powers could be pursued unencumbered.

Perhaps the most interesting note in the construction of the NATO alliance is that its chief proponent was Canada.[145] In the uncertainty of the early Cold War period, Canada needed to establish the architecture through which it could guarantee its own position in the capitalist world, and key to that position was a successful alliance between Britain and the United States. Canadian officials recognized that bilateral relations with the US would inevitably be one-sided and could lock Canada into a kind of subservient relationship, whereas a North Atlantic alliance would allow Canada to carve out space in between the powers within which to pursue its own interests. Thus, as Tom Keating argues, the Canadian government was seeking "an international order that would meet [its] aspirations and interests,"[146] and this explains Canada's pursuit of the alliance, pursuit so aggressive that even the US secretary of defence expressed shock at Canada's fervent advocacy for it.[147] Far from being forced into NATO by its bullying neighbours, Canada had accomplished in the creation of NATO its goal of preserving security and independence for the Canadian state to pursue the interests of its capitalist classes.[148]

On the surface, NATO was framed as a defensive agreement to discourage Soviet aggression, but it was well understood by Canadian diplomats that Stalin had no interest in a war with the West. Hume Wrong at External Affairs wrote in 1946 that the "Soviet threat" was exaggerated, and Dana Wilgress reported from Moscow that it was the West that needed to be more prudent with respect to preserving peace.[149] Both Wrong and Wilgress were anti-communists, but pragmatically they each recognized that the Soviet Union was unlikely to launch a surprise attack against Western Europe or North America, which was the chief concern NATO was ostensibly designed to allay.

Rather, at its heart, the creation of NATO was about consolidating the alliance that would work to destroy the threat that had risen up to "civilization": the anti-colonial and anti-capitalist movements that were emerging throughout the world in the postwar period. The colonial imagination that was at the centre of Canada's founding logic was to be institutionalized in the NATO alliance it pushed. Canadian official Leon Mayrand explained that NATO would serve "a long run policy of increasing the strength of western civilization."[150] NATO was never a defensive alliance; it was always about cementing the ties between the Western capitalist powers such that they would be best positioned to put pressure on the Soviet Union, contain and control the emerging revolutionary movements, expand the frontiers of the capitalist world and, ultimately, win the Cold War and re-assert global supremacy. That Canada was a chief architect of such a project is entirely consistent with its material and ideological goals.

Notes

1. "Premature Fireworks in China," *Toronto Daily Star*, July 29, 1937.
2. "Premature Fireworks in China," *Toronto Daily Star*, July 29, 1937.
3. Nevertheless, the Soviet Union engaged in the Cold War from a profoundly defensive position. Especially in the immediate postwar period, Stalin's foreign policy was so desperately geared towards peace with the West that leftists around the world increasingly lost faith in the USSR as a beacon of hope and a centre for world revolution. The USSR sometimes abandoned colonized people to their fate, supported Western powers' claims to their colonial possessions and went out of its way to avoid the appearance that it was fomenting revolution beyond its borders, as when it backed Chiang Kai-shek in China instead of the communists who were on the brink of victory. The Soviet Union's loss of prestige among the international left was reflected in the Sino-Soviet split, the increasingly dictatorial authority exercised in Eastern Europe, and the growing momentum towards different revolutionary models, from Cuba to Chile to the American Indian Movement (AIM). Still, none of this changes the fact that the Soviet Union did continue to provide resources and support for left movements around the world and understood the preservation of its own existence as a communist state to be at least somewhat dependent on the success of the international left.
4. This includes, of course, the former elite in the Soviet Union itself and in those other places that experienced socialist or communist revolutions during the Cold War. Indeed, these were the classes that had the greatest cause to decry communist tyranny, insofar as it was their wealth that was being expropriated by the masses.
5. Contrary to Cold War propaganda, this was also true of Eastern Europe. In 1945, when the Soviet Union occupied the territory between Russia and Germany, communism was widely popular and many local communist and socialist parties had long been leading the resistance against the Nazis. Some even managed to throw off Nazi occupation before the Soviets arrived, as in Yugoslavia, thus providing an opportunity to affect local communist revolutions independent of Moscow. As the realities of Cold War *realpolitik* set in, and the USSR began to give local governments orders instead of suggestions, opposition to Soviet authority grew. Nevertheless, it remains a stubborn fact that the Soviets arrived

primarily as liberators, not conquerors. Henry Heller, *The Cold War and the New Imperialism: A Global History, 1945–2005*, New York, Monthly Review Press, 2006, p. 46–47.
6. Ian McKay and Jamie Swift, *Warrior Nation: Rebranding Canada in an Age of Anxiety*, Toronto, Between the Lines, 2012, p. 131.
7. Lester Pearson, quoted in McKay and Swift, *Warrior Nation*, p. 110, 130.
8. Salim Mansur, "Canada and India-Pakistan: At the Beginning," in Arthur G. Rubinoff, *Canada and South Asia: Political and Strategic Relations*, Toronto, University of Toronto, Centre for Asian Studies, 1992, p. 44–47.
9. Stalin, for geostrategic reasons that were both a miscalculation and also a betrayal of Soviet anti-colonial principles, briefly supported the creation of the Israeli state in the hopes that it would weaken British influence in the Middle East. This ran against what the USSR had agreed to in the Second Congress of the Third International, where the defence of Palestinian self-determination against the Zionist project was affirmed with even the representatives of the Jewish Bund agreeing that Zionism was imperialism. Within two years the policy was reversed again, with the USSR resuming its policy of opposing Zionism, but by that point Israeli settlers had a foothold and would not let go.
10. Even Israeli historians — some of them self-identified as Zionists — have had to acknowledge the historical reality of the violence of 1948. A wave of so-called New Historians in Israel, chief among them Ilan Pappe, made reckoning with the creation of Israel a central pivot of their work. Still, notwithstanding Pappe's excellent work, especially in *The Ethnic Cleansing of Palestine* (2006) and *A History of Modern Palestine* (2004), many of the New Historians, like Benny Morris, were rightly criticized for not going far enough in allowing the weight of their own evidence to reshape their ideological understanding of the Zionist project.
11. Quoted in Tareq Ismael, *Canada and the Middle East: The Foreign Policy of a Client State*, Calgary, Temeron Books, 1994, p. 10.
12. Yves Engler, *The Black Book of Canadian Foreign Policy*, Halifax, Fernwood, 2009, p. 54.
13. Quoted in Yves Engler, *Black Book*, p. 56.
14. Tareq Ismael, *Canada and the Middle East*, p. 10.
15. Among many valuable contributions to the study of the creation and fluidity of "whiteness" are David R. Roediger's *Working Towards Whiteness* (2005), Noel Ignatieff's *How the Irish Became White* (1995) and Steve Garner's *Whiteness: An Introduction* (2007).
16. Zionism, as an ideology, emerged in the late 19th century as a messianic and largely theological ideal, so named for a desire to return to the biblical Zion (Jerusalem) of 2500 years earlier before the flight to Babylon. It only gained real political meaning when it was applied by Theodor Herzl to mean a literal colonization project, modelled after the British imperialist Cecil Rhodes, who conquered much of Southern Africa. Zionism today still refers to those who support the creation and maintenance of a Jewish settler state in Palestine, though in the 21st century there has been a concerted effort by the Israeli ruling class and its allies to treat anti-Zionism as anti-Semitism. This is rejected by those, including many Jews, who denounce the Zionist project as modern

colonialism and insist that one can be anti-Zionist without advocating hatred towards Jews.
17. Abigail B. Bakan, "Race, Class, and Colonialism: Reconsidering the 'Jewish Question,'" in Abigail B. Bakan and Enakshi Dua, ed., *Theorizing Anti-Racism: Linkages in Marxism and Critical Race Theories*, Toronto, University of Toronto Press, 2014, p. 252-273.
18. Winston Churchill, quoted in Ishay Landa, *The Apprentice's Sorcerer: Liberal Tradition and Fascism*, Brill, Boston, 2010, p. 343.
19. Patrick Wolfe, *Traces of History: Elementary Structures of Race*, London, Verso, 2016, p. 203-270. Zionist ideology was, in fact, explicitly packaged for North American audiences, in terms of the old "frontier." "The [North] American will give the Jewish settler in Palestine the benefit of the doubt," said one Zionist supporter in the 1940s, "and regard the Arab as the aboriginal who must go down before the march of civilization." South Africa was always an obvious comparator, and in 2002, an Israeli officer even insisted that the army "analyze and internalize the lessons of... how the German [Nazi] army fought in the Warsaw ghetto." The irony is uncomfortable, but it also serves as a reminder that racial violence and conflict is always linked to political economic realities that shape both people's attitudes and also their ability to act on them. Quotes drawn from Norman Finkelstein, *Image and Reality of the Israel-Palestine Conflict*, New York, Verso, 2003, p. xv, xxiii.
20. Henry Heller, *The Cold War*, p. 90-93.
21. Robert Teigrob, *Warming Up to the Cold War: Canada and the United States' coalition of the willing, from Hiroshima to Korea*, Toronto, University of Toronto Press, 2009, p. 92-125.
22. Tareq Ismael, *Canada and the Middle East*, p. 17.
23. Lester Pearson, quoted in Tareq Ismael, *Canada and the Middle East*, p. 18.
24. Lester Pearson, quoted in Tareq Ismael, *Canada and the Middle East*, p. 18.
25. Lester Pearson, quoted in Tareq Ismael, *Canada and the Middle East*, p. 20. Emphasis added.
26. Gamal Abdal Nasser, quoted in Tareq Ismael, *Canada and the Middle East*, p. 21.
27. John D. Meehan, *The Dominion and the Rising Sun: Canada Encounters Japan, 1929-41*, Vancouver, UBC Press, 2004, p. 40, 152. The assault has been called "the Rape of Nanjing" in reference to the fact that sexual violence was widely committed by occupying Japanese soldiers, reminiscent of the French assault in Algeria in 1837 and the Canadian attack against the Métis at Batoche in 1885.
28. Of course, it is worth remembering that Pearl Harbor was in Hawai'i, a territory only recently conquered by the United States. US mythologies of being attacked "on American soil," perpetuated by films like *Pearl Harbor* (2001) and *Midway* (2019), ring rather hollow when one recalls that indigenous Kanaka Maoli people considered themselves to be living under US occupation. The Japanese administration framed its propaganda precisely around this fact, portraying itself as having liberated Hawai'i, among other territories, from colonial powers.
29. William Lyon Mackenzie King, quoted in John Price, *Orienting Canada: Race, Empire, and the Transpacific*, Vancouver, UBC Press, 2011, p. 94.
30. Fred Gregg, quoted in John Price, *Orienting Canada*, p. 96.

31. Francine McKenzie, "Race, Empire, and World Order: Robert Borden and Racial Equality at the Paris Peace Conference of 1919," in Laura Madokoro, Francine McKenzie, and David Meren, ed., *Dominion of Race: Rethinking Canada's International History*, Vancouver, UBC Press, 2017, p. 73–88.
32. Quoted in John Price, *Orienting Canada*, p. 39.
33. John D. Meehan, *The Dominion and the Rising Sun*, p. 181.
34. John Price, *Orienting Canada*, p. 56.
35. John D. Meehan, *The Dominion and the Rising Sun*, p. 175.
36. Urbain M Clouthier, quoted in Alvyn J. Austin, *Saving China: Canadian Missionaries in the Middle Kingdom, 1888–1959*, Toronto, University of Toronto Press, 1986, p. 257.
37. John Price, *Orienting Canada*, p. 72.
38. John D. Meehan, *The Dominion and the Rising Sun*, p. 194–195.
39. Merrily Weisbrod and Merilyn Simonds Mohr, *The Valour and the Horror: The Untold Story of Canadians in the Second World War*, Harper Collins, Toronto, 1991, p. 56.
40. Bob Clayton, quoted in Weisbrod and Mohr, *The Valour and the Horror*, p. 45.
41. Terry Woo, "Responsibility," *The Fighting 44s*, April 17, 2006. Available at: https://web.archive.org/web/20110724020345/http://www.thefighting44s.com/archives/2006/04/17/responsibility-slug/.
42. Sutherland Brown, quoted in John Price, *Orienting Canada*, p. 68.
43. John Price, *Orienting Canada*, p. 69.
44. McKay and Swift, *Warrior Nation*, p. 125.
45. Alvyn J. Austin, *Saving China*, p. 314–323.
46. Allen was, indeed, imprisoned for eight months, during which time he refused to confess to crimes he did, in fact, commit. His tax evasion was arguably not significant enough to justify the length of his imprisonment, but his rabid anti-communism during an ongoing civil war wherein the Canadian government was actively supporting the other side makes it hardly surprising that he should have been held a bit longer. Alvyn J. Austin, *Saving China*, p. 319–321.
47. Mark Driscoll, *Absolute Erotic, Absolute Grotesque*, London, Duke University Press, 2010, p. 289.
48. Mark Driscoll, *Absolute Erotic*, p. 263–293.
49. Mark Driscoll, *Absolute Erotic*, p. 267.
50. John Price, *Orienting Canada*, p. 149.
51. John Price, *Orienting Canada*, p. 163–166.
52. Herbert Norman, quoted in John Price, *Orienting Canada*, p. 159.
53. Henry Heller, *The Cold War*, p. 54–56.
54. Quoted in John Price, *Orienting Canada*, p. 166.
55. See Roger Bowen's *Innocence Is Not Enough* (1986) and James Barros' *No Sense of Evil* (1986) for two differing takes on the matter.
56. Robert Bothwell, "Eyes West: Canada and the Cold War in Asia," in Greg Donaghy, ed., *Canada and the Early Cold War, 1943–1957*, Ottawa, Government of Canada, Foreign Affairs and International Trade, 1988, p. 65.
57. Yves Engler, *Black Book*, 123.
58. T.E. Vadney, *The World Since 1945*, New York, Penguin, 1998, p. 135.
59. H. Merrell Benninghof, quoted in Bruce Cumings, *Korea's Place in The Sun: A*

Modern History, New York, W.W. Norton & Co., 1997, p. 192–193.
60. Bruce Cumings, *Korea's Place in The Sun*, p. 185–186.
61. Bruce Cumings, *Korea's Place in The Sun*, p. 190–191.
62. Bruce Cumings, *North Korea: Another Country*, New York, The New Press, 2004, p. 130–131.
63. Joyce and Gabriel Kolko, *The Limits of Power: The World and United States Foreign Policy, 1945–1954*, London, 1972, p. 280.
64. Young Ick Lew, *The Making of the First Korean President: Syngman Rhee's Quest for Independence, 1875–1948*, Honolulu, University of Hawai'i Press, 2014.
65. Quoted in Bruce Cumings, *Korea's Place in The Sun*, p. 214–215.
66. Henry Heller, *The Cold War*, p. 69.
67. John Price, *Orienting Canada*, p. 183.
68. Indispensable among English-language studies of Korean history in this period is the work of Bruce Cumings, most notably *Korea's Place in The Sun* (1997), *North Korea: Another Country* (2004) and *The Korean War: A History* (2010), in addition to *Korea: The Unknown War* (1987), co-authored with Jon Halliday.
69. Ted Barris, "The War That History Forgot," in R.W.L. Gusso and Young-Sik Yoo, ed., *Canada and Korea: Perspectives 2000*, University of Toronto Press, Toronto, 2002, p. 72.
70. Ralph Collins and Herbert Norman, quoted in John Price, *Orienting Canada*, p. 180.
71. Bruce Cumings, *The Korean War: A History*, New York, Modern Library, 2010.
72. William Blum, *Killing Hope: US Military and CIA Interventions Since World War II*, London, Zed Books, 2014, p. 46.
73. William Blum, *Killing Hope*, p. 46–47.
74. See for instance, David J. Bercuson, *The Fighting Canadians: Our Regimental History from New France to Afghanistan*, Toronto, Harper Collins, 2008, p. 262.
75. Soviet non-intervention in the Greek Civil War was but one example. McKay and Swift, *Warrior Nation*, p. 119.
76. Robert Teigrob, *Warming Up*, p. 174.
77. Robert Teigrob, *Warming Up*, p. 178–184.
78. Louis St. Laurent, Debates, House of Commons, 1950, IV, p. 253.
79. Reg Whitaker and Gary Marcuse, *Cold War Canada: The Making of a National Insecurity State, 1945–1957*, Toronto, University of Toronto Press, 1994, p. 391.
80. John Price, *Orienting Canada*, p. 270.
81. Douglas MacArthur, cited in John Price, *Orienting Canada*, p. 270.
82. Eugene Kinkead, *Why They Collaborated*, London, Longmans, 1960, p. 17.
83. John Marks, *The Search for the Manchurian Candidate: The CIA and Mind Control*, New York, W.W. Norton & Co., 1988, p. 25.
84. Robert J. Lifton, *Thought Reform and the Psychology of Totalism: A Study of "Brainwashing" in China*, London, W.W. Norton & Co, 1961, p. 4.
85. Eugene Kinkead, *Why They Collaborated*, p. 105–106.
86. Richard Needham, quoted in Robert Teigrob, *Warming Up*, p. 183.
87. John D. Meehan, *The Dominion and the Rising Sun*, p. 54.
88. A. Hamish Ion, "Across the Tumen and Beyond: Canadian Missionaries, Korean Christians, and the Japanese on the Manchurian Border, 1911–41," in R.W.L. Gusso and Young-Sik Yoo, ed., *Canada and Korea: Perspectives 2000*, University

of Toronto Press, Toronto, 2002, p. 45–70.
89. John Price, *Orienting Canada*, p. 264.
90. John Price, *Orienting Canada*, p. 264–265.
91. Pierre Berton, *My Times: Living with History, 1947–1995*, Toronto, Seal Edition, 1996, p. 78–103.
92. John Price, *Orienting Canada*, p. 271.
93. John Price, *Orienting Canada*, p. 278.
94. Even Barris' own account includes a Canadian soldier's remembrance of his regiment's participation in a civilian massacre at Taegu. Ted Barris, "The War That History Forgot," in R.W.L. Gusso and Young-Sik Yoo, ed., *Canada and Korea: Perspectives 2000*, University of Toronto Press, Toronto, 2002, p. 72.
95. Robert Bothwell, "Eyes West: Canada and the Cold War in Asia," p. 64.
96. One Canadian bishop told a reporter for *La Presse* that "an atomic bomb or two dropped on China would do nothing but good for humanity" and that "the Chinese themselves wanted it." Bishop Phillipe Côte, quoted in Alvyn J. Austin, *Saving China*, p. 313.
97. Victor Levant, *Quiet Complicity: Canadian Involvement in the Vietnam War*, Toronto, Between the Lines, 1986, p. 43.
98. Louis St. Laurent, quoted in Victor Levant, *Quiet Complicity*, p. 44.
99. Ho Chi Minh, quoted in Victor Levant, *Quiet Complicity*, p. 122.
100. Robert Bothwell, "Eyes West: Canada and the Cold War in Asia," p. 65.
101. Quoted in Victor Levant, *Quiet Complicity*, p. 138.
102. Ngo Dinh Diem, quoted in Victor Levant, *Quiet Complicity*, p. 137.
103. Victor Levant, *Quiet Complicity*, p. 107–172.
104. Lester Pearson, quoted in David Webster, "Foreign Policy, Diplomacy, and Decolonization," in Karen Dubinsky, Sean Mills and Scott Rutherford, ed., *Canada and the Third World: Overlapping Histories*, Toronto, University of Toronto Press, 2016, p. 169.
105. J.M. Macdonnell, quoted in David Webster, "Foreign Policy, Diplomacy, and Decolonization," p. 168.
106. Souchou Yao, *The Malayan Emergency: Essays on a Small, Distant War*, Copenhagen, NIAS Press, 2016.
107. Quoted in David Webster, "Foreign Policy, Diplomacy, and Decolonization," p. 175.
108. Gabriel Kolko, *Confronting the Third World: United States Foreign Policy, 1945–1980*, New York, Pantheon Books, 1988, p. 25–30.
109. Lester Pearson, quoted in David Webster, "Foreign Policy, Diplomacy, and Decolonization," p. 164.
110. Nik Cavell, quoted in David Webster, "Foreign Policy, Diplomacy, and Decolonization," p. 165.
111. Peter McFarlane, *Northern Shadows*, p. 67.
112. Quoted in Peter McFarlane, *Northern Shadows: Canadians and Central America*, Toronto, Between the Lines, 1989, p. 81.
113. Humphrey Hume Wrong, quoted in Peter McFarlane, *Northern Shadows*, p. 85.
114. Peter McFarlane, *Northern Shadows*, p. 82–85.
115. Humphrey Hume Wrong, quoted in Peter McFarlane, *Northern Shadows*, p. 89.
116. Fraser Elliott, quoted in Peter McFarlane, *Northern Shadows*, p. 84.

117. Quoted in Peter McFarlane, *Northern Shadows*, p. 90.
118. Peter McFarlane, *Northern Shadows*, p. 92–93.
119. Benedicte Bull, *Aid, Power, and Privatization: The Politics of telecommunications Reform in Central America*, Edward Elgar Publishing, Cheltenham, 2005, p. 89.
120. Alfred Savard, quoted in Peter McFarlane, *Northern Shadows*, p. 96.
121. Peter McFarlane, *Northern Shadows*, p. 94–100.
122. Yves Engler, *Black Book*, p. 75–76.
123. J.C.M. Ogelsby, *Gringos from the Far North: Essays in the History of Canadian-Latin American Relations, 1866–1968*, Toronto, MacMillan, 1976, p. 154–181.
124. Tristan Hopper, "No, internet, Fidel Castro isn't Trudeau's real father. The Canadian Prime Minister just really, really looks like him," *National Post*, February 14, 2017.
125. Mark Milke, "The Trudeau family's love of tyrants," *Maclean's*, February 28, 2018.
126. Quoted in James Rochlin, *Discovering the Americas*, p. 50–52.
127. Don Munton, "Canadian Intelligence and Diplomacy in Cuba," in Luis René Fernández Tabío, Cynthia Wright, and Lana Wylie, ed., *Other Diplomacies, Other Ties: Cuba and Canada in the Shadow of the US*, Toronto, University of Toronto Press, 2018, p. 64–84.
128. Whitaker and Marcuse, *Cold War Canada*, p. 402.
129. Robert Teigrob, *Warming Up*, p. 117–118.
130. Margaret Conrad, Alvin Finkel, and Donald Fyson, *History of the Canadian Peoples, Volume 2: 1867 to the Present*, Pearson, Toronto, 2015, p. 311–312.
131. Evidence of "espionage" was thin, and mostly constituted sharing of information that was either in the public domain or was deemed valuable for Canada's wartime ally, the Soviet Union, with which it *was* jointly fighting to defeat Nazi Germany. Nevertheless, it provided suitable ammunition to initiate anti-communist hysteria, leading to a sensationalized rendering of the events (especially in the ludicrously clumsy and racist film *The Iron Curtain*) and a range of violations of citizens' rights that were serious enough to lead to at least one suicide. Robert Teigrob, *Warming Up*, 54–91.
132. McKay and Swift, *Warrior Nation*, p. 120.
133. Reg Whitaker and Gary Marcuse, *Cold War Canada*, p. 24.
134. Quoted in Aloysius Balawyder, *In the Clutches of the Kremlin: Canadian-East European Relations (1945–1962)*, New York, Columbia University Press, 2000, p. 118.
135. Sergei Shcherbatykh, *Kanada — votchina amerikanskogo imperializma*, Moscow, Gospolitizdat, 1951.
136. Aloysius Balawyder, *In the Clutches*, p. 119.
137. This included Michael Chomiak, Nazi propagandist in Krakow, whose granddaughter Chrystia Freeland would eventually become Canada's Deputy Prime Minister in the late 2010s.
138. Franca Iacovetta, *Gatekeepers: Reshaping Immigrant Lives in Cold War Canada*, Toronto, Between the Lines, 2006, p. 116–117.
139. Franca Iacovetta, *Gatekeepers*, p. 48.
140. Louis St. Laurent, quoted in David Webster, "Foreign Policy, Diplomacy, and Decolonization," p. 164.

141. Kevin A. Spooner, "Awakening Africa: Race and Canadian Views on Decolonizing Africa," in Laura Madokoro, Francine McKenzie, and David Meren, ed., *Dominion of Race: Rethinking Canada's International History*, Vancouver, UBC Press, 2017, p. 211–215.
142. Quoted in Kevin A. Spooner, "Awakening Africa," p. 215.
143. Robert Ford, quoted in Kevin A. Spooner, "Awakening Africa," p. 214.
144. Kevin A. Spooner, "Awakening Africa," p. 215.
145. Paul Kellogg, "From the Avro Arrow to Afghanistan: The Political Economy of Canadian Militarism," in Jerome Klassen and Greg Albo, ed., *Empire's Ally: Canada and the War in Afghanistan*, Toronto, University of Toronto Press, 2013, p. 187–190.
146. Tom Keating, *Canada and World Order: The Multilateralist Tradition in Canadian Foreign Policy*, 2nd ed., Oxford, Oxford University Press, 2002, p. 70.
147. Quoted in Paul Kellogg, "From the Avro Arrow to Afghanistan," p. 189.
148. Paul Kellogg, "From the Avro Arrow to Afghanistan," p. 187–190.
149. Tom Keating, *Canada and World Order*, p. 78–81.
150. Leon Mayrand, quoted in Tom Keating, *Canada and World Order*, p. 76.

8

Colonialism, a Part of Our Heritage

Those countries which still have direct responsibilities for non-self-governing territories should not be made to feel at the United Nations or elsewhere that they are oppressors to be deprived arbitrarily of their rights or indeed their reputations.
— Lester B. Pearson, 1957[1]

ANYONE SEARCHING FOR A WINDOW into the soul of Canada would do well to watch the series of Heritage Minutes produced between 1991 and 2005 to provide a carefully curated public education on Canadian history. These dramatized vignettes depicted scenes from Canada's past that exemplified what their authors — multi-billionaire Charles Bronfman and news broadcaster Patrick Watson — considered to be the core values of Canada.[2] They were designed with several criteria, one of which was to "reflect and celebrate Canadian social and cultural values: tolerance, fairness, courage, tenacity, resourcefulness, inventiveness."[3] Much of their purpose was also about instilling Canadian pride; Bronfman claimed that his initial motivation to design the Heritage Minutes was disappointment with Canadians' lack of awareness of their own history.

Whether the 90-second Heritage Minutes designed by a billionaire capitalist helped Canadians learn their own history is debatable. Defenders of the series claim that while the Minutes reflected "dominant cultural traits in Canadian society," they nevertheless contributed to the spirit of multiculturalism.[4] In a sense, this is true: multiculturalism was always about safely incorporating marginalized communities into the portrayal of Canadian society while limiting the capacity of those communities to break down the actual, material barriers to their full participation in that society, a point to which I return in Chapter 9. Even the most critically minded Heritage Minutes presented historical problems while reassuring their audience that the problem had been solved by modern Canada. For instance, "Nitro" (1992), an episode which highlighted the dreadful treatment of Chinese railroad workers in the 1880s, was set up such that the narrator was an elderly Chinese man, surrounded by his grandchildren in a comfortable middle-class home, telling them his story of the exploitation he experienced. Canadian history would, it seemed, always have a happy ending.

Of the 86 vignettes produced, only a handful featured Indigenous people, and those portrayals were not uncontroversial. "Louis Riel" (1991), for instance, was somewhat sympathetic to his role as a Métis leader but ended with the dramatic spectacle of his hanging.[5] An episode featuring Indigenous people sharing the secrets of maple syrup with European settlers, "Syrup" (1997), rather dubiously implied harmonious relations between conquerors and conquered. Questionable special effects and superficial rendering of Indigenous mythology marred an effort to portray the creation of the Haudenosaunee Confederacy in "Peacemaker" (1992).[6] Meanwhile, a substantial number of the Minutes depicted military history — with particular emphasis on the World Wars — often in ways that emphasized the heroism and sacrifice of the soldiers for a noble cause. "Vimy Ridge" (2005), for instance, repeated the mythology discussed in Chapter 4, while "John McCrae" (1992) said nothing about the poet's vehement racism or lust for war.

Perhaps most incredible was the more recently produced "John A. Macdonald" (2014), in which Canada's first prime minister is portrayed as the proud and articulate father of Confederation, uniting the country around the project of building an intercontinental Canada connected by a railroad. He receives a slow clap from the gathering of the Canadian elite, and the music and narration frame the glorious moment of Canada's birth. That, in 2014, the authors of the Heritage Minutes could depict Macdonald with no reference to the racism and genocide that were his signal legacy — the genocide that was the central project of Confederation — was a truly breathtaking feat of ideology.

Indeed, when it came to Canada's place in the world, the Heritage Minutes were very clear that Canadians should be proud of their accomplishments. "Lucille Teasdale" (2000) portrayed the surgeon as a hero for devoting her life to caring for the poor in Uganda. "Despite twenty years of civil war," the narrator explained "they built a modern hospital." Teasdale and her husband Piero Corti did provide valuable, low-cost medical care in Uganda, though their presence there was a product of British conquest and came with much of the baggage of the "civilizing" missionary tradition. The vignette's mention of "modernity" tapped into that, as did the inexplicable inclusion of a scene where Teasdale is depicted saving a patient who had the point of a spear embedded in his gut. The civil wars in Uganda were not primarily fought with spears, but spears figured heavily in racist epithets and depictions of Africans. Meanwhile, "John Humphrey" (1997) exalted the diplomat for writing the United Nations Universal Declaration of Human Rights, as if Canada had not worked to undermine the United Nations within the first years of its existence and spent much of the 20th century ignoring violations of human rights committed by its allies, including in Uganda. A whimsical episode, "Joseph-Armand Bombardier" (1993), featured the young Bombardier playing with toy trains. Today, his company has grown so notorious that an entire book is dedicated to exposing the social harms it has created.[7] In 2019, for instance, it received a massive aerospace contract from the Ugandan quasi-dictatorship which Canada supported, despite that country's more pressing need for spending on public services.[8]

Canadians were praised in "Water Pump" (1995) for helping people in an unnamed African country learn how to access water sustainably by adapting a kind of Mennonite pump, in an episode that so perfectly depicts the colonial fantasy it even features thankful Africans laughing as the white Canadian explains how they did it. "You Canadians have such modern ideas," an African woman says, to which our hero replies, "it's really a very old idea." A remarkable vignette, "Pauline Vanier" (1995), depicts her and her husband's tireless efforts to help refugees get settled during World War Two, remarkable, of course, in light of Canada's record of refusing to accept Jewish refugees during the Holocaust. Canada's role in providing safety for escaped slaves was lauded in "Underground Railroad" (1991) without mention of Canadian slavery and segregation. They even found time to celebrate a colonial NWMP veteran in "Sam Steele" (1993), which featured the man who cleared the plains of Indigenous people, supervised Chinese labourers on the railroad and established the racialized South African police force after the Boer War.

Nevertheless, the Heritage Minutes are an extremely valuable cultural artifact; they represent what Canada wanted Canadians to believe about themselves and the world. They present a Canada that had figured it out, a world that needed Canada's help and Canadians who were up to the task.

Selfless, tolerant, generous, rational and imbued with self-effacing wit, Canadians were everything the world should aspire to. The imagination of a Canadian billionaire was thus hardwired in the collective psyche of many people who grew up in Canada. The vignettes reflected the fundamental values of settler capitalism and the colonial imagination that were so central to the Canadian project and, in that sense, they truly did reflect something of Canada, though not as they intended. This was particularly well-illustrated in a vignette about the Congo, discussed in detail below.

Those values are consistent in the Canadian story, though they underwent a kind of transformation during the Cold War era. While extolling the virtues of imperialism was common practice in the 1930s, by the 1950s the colonized world was in open rebellion and it was not such a simple matter for Canadians to speak openly about the backwardness and savagery of the colonized people of the world. Indeed, it became necessary during this period for Canada to fashion a new image for itself, the image reflected in the Heritage Minutes. All of the hallmarks of colonialism were still there, but as the 20th century progressed, the colonial imagination would increasingly be obscured from view, implied rather than expressed, buried within new languages of peacekeeping, democracy and development. Indeed, Canada increasingly told itself and the world that it was a paragon of peace and freedom, and questioned whether the people of Asia, Africa and Latin America were prepared to engage in the world in the same good faith. Until they were, said Canada, perhaps it was best that they remain under the tutelage of the benevolent colonial powers for just a little longer. As criticism of colonialism mounted, Canada was always there to soften it and to counsel consideration for the hardships of being a colonial power. After all, as Lester Pearson insisted in the quote at the top of this chapter: they were not oppressors, they were simply responsible for "non-self-governing territories."

To Quarantine the Colonies

Consistently in the decolonization process that marked the 1950s to the 1970s, Canada laboured to curb, soften and slow the processes of national liberation. In an absurd, but repeated, rhetorical turn, Canada would suggest that other nations should follow the Canadian lead in a gradual, evolutionary, nonconfrontational path to independence. The absurdity lies in the fact that Canada was never colonized; Indigenous

Peoples were colonized *by* Canada and those Indigenous nations had not won their national liberation. Canada was a settler colony whose leaders maintained sincere fealty to the British Crown even well into Canada's process of separation. And yet, Canadian officials pompously lectured people in South Asia on the need for gradual weaning from the Empire's teat, as though they benefitted from colonialism when, in fact, they had been brutally conquered, administered and on multiple occasions starved by the British Empire.[9]

But Canada forged ahead with that approach during the postwar waves of decolonization. Canada had pushed to ensure that India, Pakistan and Ceylon (Sri Lanka) be incorporated into the Commonwealth as dominions, rather than strike off as independent nations on their own. In the mid-1940s, Canadian media had excoriated the idea of Indian independence; one *Saturday Night* headline insisted, "India Is Not a Nation, and Cannot Become One."[10] This article was published, ironically, just months before a British-administered famine in Bengal killed as many as three million people. It was hardly an endorsement of British rule. Still, Canadian public opinion had been groomed with the idea of Empire, and a survey in 1946 found that only 18% of Canadians believed that India should be granted independence.[11] When the process went ahead, Canadians steadfastly defended the Empire and used the occasion of Indian freedom to heap praise on the benevolence of imperialism. James McCook claimed that Britain had "protected India from invasion" and had cured the "princes in jeweled turbans" of "many savage customs."[12] The *Globe and Mail* assured its readers that this was the fulfillment of Britain's plan, "the deliberate aim of [which] has been to equip the Indians for full self-government."[13]

More than a century of anti-colonial struggle, in which millions of lives were lost, were thus erased by Canadian journalists, who asserted that this outcome had been achieved by "wise and statesman-like moves all down through the years of British rule and guidance."[14] Indeed, Ottawa often expressed dismay at Britain's willingness to concede freedom; many officials believed Britain to be "overly timid" given that "the United Kingdom colonial record was so good."[15] Still others smugly warned of the dangers of allowing infantile Asians to rule themselves: a cartoon in the *Winnipeg Tribune* portrayed India and Pakistan as turbaned infants in diapers being handed off by a British nanny to the unprepared new leaders.[16] At the same time, one of the first Canadian high commissioners in India, Escott

Reid, tried to draw Canada into closer relations with India but came up against a Canadian state that was increasingly leaning towards Pakistan, as the latter was more open to the West in the emerging Cold War context. Nevertheless, while Reid tried to counsel a more open Canadian door to India, his affection for India was rooted in a colonial romanticization and fetishization. In one particularly uncomfortable passage in his notes from a Commonwealth conference in 1950, Reid wrote of the delegates:

> Ten were coloured and the coloured members on the whole were much more good-looking than the non-coloured members… most of the Ceylonese are dark chocolate with pitch-black hair and usually fine-featured. The Indians vary from Mr. Nehru's pale grey to Mr. Menon's dark black.[17]

Reid's exoticized descriptions of the South Asians at the meeting reflect the same colonial imagination that was found in Canadian settlers marvelling at the physical features of Indigenous people or slave-traders commenting on the bodies of African slaves. They also remained embedded in the Canadian imagination long after the Cold War; conservative historian Robert Bothwell claimed in 1998 that the "mysterious and benighted East" was dangerous in the 1940s because "for reasons best known to itself [it] dwelt in poverty."[18]

Meanwhile, Reid, despite his colonial exoticization, was arguably on the more progressive side of the debate within the Canadian establishment, insofar as he at least believed South Asian people deserved statehood. Official Canadian statements worried that the pace of decolonization might be too quick:

> We wonder whether the speed at which the United Kingdom proposes to proceed with political emancipation, particularly in West Africa, may not inspire nationalist agitation in territories where the French, Belgians, and Portuguese have attempted to impose a political "quarantine" until such time as there is a solid economic and social base for political participation by the native population.[19]

It is evident from this External Affairs memorandum that Canada sided with the latter option, the political "quarantine" of colonized people, even as they were demanding independence. The "particularly in West Africa" serves as a reminder that while Canada generally viewed non-European people as beneath them, it nevertheless maintained some sense of hierarchy between them. Africans, evidently, were deemed particularly unfit for democracy. This was reflected even in Canada's assessments of the Indian diaspora in East Africa, wherein Canadian officials developed a complex hierarchy not only of Indians and Africans but even within the Indian community of Hindus — troublesome because of their "mystical bond to Mother India" — and Muslims, who were better workers thanks to "the influence of the Aga Khan."[20]

While anti-colonial struggles had erupted in Asia immediately following the Second World War, aided by the disruption of European colonial rule by Japanese fascist occupation, most of the colonial states of Africa had not experienced the same interruption, and such coordinated struggles were slower to develop. Nevertheless, by the late 1950s, the foundations of European domination were cracking there too, as anti-colonial nationalist movements — often but not always socialist and communist in nature — were growing increasingly militant. Canada, as far back as the 1860s, had been a strong proponent of African colonization and an active participant in it, and the rewards of that commitment could be expressed in dollar signs. By 1960, Canadian businesses had over $68 million invested in the continent, and the nationalist movements seeking to assert the rights of indigenous Africans often viewed foreign capital as a direct part of the problem. Those movements more oriented to the left sought a full-scale reorientation of the economic system, where those dominated by less radical nationalism wanted to rebalance the existing arrangement in favour of the majority. In either case, Canadian capital — Rio Tinto in Rhodesia, Falconbridge in Uganda or Bata Shoes in Tanzania — would be set to lose the advantages it reaped from colonial violence.

And so, conveniently, it was determined that Africans just were not ready for statehood; Canada consistently voted against UN resolutions supporting decolonization and supplied weapons to European powers seeking to maintain their position in Africa. In 1957, Lester Pearson perhaps struck his most absurd stance, as noted above, when he defended the integrity of the European colonial powers, whom he comically described as "countries which still have direct responsibility for non-self-governing territories." A rather cumbersome way to say "colonizers." He went on to assert that they "should not be made to feel at the United Nations or elsewhere that they are oppressors to be deprived arbitrarily of their rights or indeed their reputations."²¹ We would not want any of the colonial powers to have hurt feelings, now would we?

Perhaps Pearson was feeling defensive about the fact that Canada had supplied to those colonizers some $1.5 billion in free ammunition, armaments, anti-aircraft guns, minesweepers, military transport vehicles, communications and electronic equipment, fighter jets and engines.²² This "aid" was delivered as part of the NATO arrangement, and it also included training programs wherein tens of thousands of pilots learned their trade in Canada before being sent to repress independence movements in Kenya, Algeria, Cameroon and the Congo.

Direct Canadian involvement against the various struggles for African freedom varied from case to case. In Kenya, the British fought a savage war to repress the indigenous Kikuyu during the Mau Mau rebellion.²³ Between 1952 and 1960, tens of thousands were killed, many more were tortured, rape was used as a tactic to terrorize the population, and at least 1.5 million people were herded into concentration camps.²⁴ And yet, the *Ottawa Citizen* saw fit to call the Mau Mau, not the British, "the most savage and bestial killers in the world."²⁵ More Brits were killed in auto accidents in Kenya than by the Mau Mau. In Canada's Parliament, the Mau Mau were described as encouraging "racial hatred" and their leader Jomo Kenyatta as "essentially an evil man" who encouraged the "the more primitive tribes in Africa to indulge in secret societies and witchcraft."²⁶ Another official casually noted that "the black races have not produced alone anything comparable to the great civilizations of any other races."²⁷

Canadian officials worried about the "rights and privileges" of the white settlers in Kenya, including my uncle, who worked as a private security guard for a Canadian bank. External Affairs' Robert Ford noted that "the British are really rushing ahead much too fast in the plans to give independence to a number of colonies which have very little in the way of civilization or training at self-government."²⁸ Nonetheless, the British were not giving up Kenya easily or quickly and, to that end, the Canadian government supplied F-86 Sabre fighter jets for the operations, and an RCMP officer, John Timmerman, ran the Criminal Investigation Division in Nairobi. His division was notoriously cruel; Timmerman was nicknamed the "Himmler of Kenya," and he carried out widespread — and truly horrific — torture of the "filthy pigs" who were "causing trouble."²⁹ In addition to doling out sexualized corporal punishment involving knives, snakes and scorpions, he oversaw the arrest of the "evil" Jomo Kenyatta, who would become prime minister of Kenya after the British were defeated.

During the same period, Canada supported the French position regarding its colonies in North Africa. Canada voted against independence for Morocco and Tunisia at the UN and delayed in recognizing their new governments, while giving its direct material support to the French war against Algeria's Front de Libération Nationale (FLN). The Canadian government offered $127 million in free ammunition, dynamite, guns and shells to the French colonizers over the duration of the war and even censured the Canadian media when it ran coverage that seemed to sympathize with the Algerian independence movement. This despite the fact that the French war to maintain control of Algeria was among its most brutal, involving widespread torture and sexual violence.

When the FLN successfully defeated France, Canada opened its doors to immigration from Algeria, but only to the displaced French settlers. In addition to creating a detailed set of criteria to maintain a racial hierarchy in its immigration from French North Africa, Canada established a new rule that such immigration would only be granted to those "enterprising individuals" who made the trip to Paris to file their paperwork. This, naturally, excluded the poor, who were mostly Arab. That this was explicit policy is made clear in a statement by Canadian immigration official G.M. Mitchell: "We only have to study the problem of Algerians in Europe with its high criminal rate, great health hazards, etc., to shudder at the idea of initiating such a movement to Canada."[30] The quarantine metaphor persisted.

Canada similarly supported French colonialism in West Africa, with the Canadian ambassador travelling through the colonies in 1956 and insisting that "a further period of tutelage" was needed before the Africans should achieve their freedom.[31] An even more grotesque version of that argument was applied when Papua New Guinea — located in the Pacific Islands but claiming a shared ancestry with the people of Africa — demanded its freedom from the Netherlands in the early 1960s, which Canada claimed was "out of the question [since Papuan] civilization was still in a very primitive stage." Indeed, the internal memorandum went on to complain about other nations trying "to tempt the Papuans down from the tree-tops," an undisguised reference to Papuans as monkeys.[32]

The struggle against colonialism was a fight for freedom, for prosperity and for dignity, and Canada lined up on the opposite side. For a period in the 1950s, Britain's Gold Coast colony came to be the unlikely centre of African revolution. The Gold Coast — soon to be called Ghana — had not been aggressively settled by whites; its role in the Empire was to provide raw materials ranging from agricultural products to valuable minerals and, of course, gold. In some respects, this made the struggle for freedom easier, since there was not a large, entrenched white minority seeking to hold firm. Indeed, Canadian officials were far less preoccupied with the decolonization of Ghana than that of Kenya.[33] Given the growing organization of non-violent resistance in the form of strikes and protests and Britain's preoccupation in trying to maintain other colonies, Ghana was able to win its independence in 1957, with Britain hoping to maintain informal economic power over the new country. But its new leader, Kwame Nkrumah, had rubbed shoulders with some of the greatest black intellectuals of his age, from W.E.B. DuBois to C.L.R. James, and he pursued a kind of left nationalist program that would inspire African independence movements across the continent, including that of Congolese freedom fighter Patrice Lumumba. Perhaps most notably, Nkrumah openly called for — and organized networks to operationalize — the decolonization of all of Africa and a united movement of Africans to liberate their continent.

It was hoped, in the West, that this would prove to be empty rhetoric, and there were some hints that it might be. Nkrumah surprised many by continuing to trade with South Africa despite growing criticism of Apartheid, and when lack of capital from falling cocoa prices created a potential economic crisis, he imposed austerity on Ghanaian peasants and workers.[34] Even as he counselled and helped organize efforts for pan-African revolution, his own record in Ghana was mixed. Sensing Nkrumah's delicate position, Canada helped the British Empire maintain its grip over post-independence Ghana, offering the new country military assistance. There was concern that Nkrumah's pan-African project could still bear fruit; Canadian high commissioner Evan Gill complained that a gathering of African leaders and intellectuals in Accra would lead to "discussions and resolutions that lean to extreme denunciations of colonial powers." To his dismay, "irresponsible sections of black African opinion" were discouraging "a moderate and responsible approach." In case Gill's message was not clear, he added that African leaders "showed themselves as unrealistic and irrational in their cry 'Africa for the Africans.'"[35]

Gill's approach was reflective of Canada's position, and while Canadian military assistance was framed as benevolence, its primary purpose was to keep Nkrumah in check; the military still maintained much of its British character and was built to be a crucial site of counter-revolution should Nkrumah seriously threaten colonial interests. Canada took to the project with gusto, and by 1966, Nkrumah had been ousted by the military Canada had trained, albeit with CIA assistance.[36] A year earlier, Canada's High Commissioner in Ghana had happily reported that the Ghanaian military was fully oriented towards the West. This was in large part thanks to the Canadian officers at the Ghanaian Defence College. Indeed, the military training program, bragged the High Commissioner, produced "all of the chief participants of the coup" which overthrew Nkrumah in 1966. On the day it happened, he cabled Ottawa to report that "a wonderful thing [had] happened *for the West* in Ghana and Canada [had] played a worthy part." Noting that "all here welcome this development,"[37] he failed to mention the massive strikes and demonstrations that erupted in response to the coup and the new regime's repression of those protests.[38]

Back in Ottawa, Prime Minister Pearson had little to say about it, and External Affairs simply explained that "we shall carry on with the present arrangement for Ghana."[39] One of the most popular leaders in Africa had just been overthrown in a military coup, and Canadian officers in Ghana had known about the coup preparations and said nothing. The leader of the coup, Joseph Ankrah, was welcomed in a state visit to Canada later that year, and Canada provided some $22 million in grants and aid over the next decade.[40] This was the true spirit of Canadian generosity; it only needed to be funnelled to those who would not interfere with the colonial structure of world power. Canada had another reason to celebrate Nkrumah's downfall: he had been one of Canada's harshest critics for the central role it played in the dismantling of Congolese democracy, Congo's descent into civil war and the assassination of the first Congolese president.

Heritage Minute: The Assassination of Patrice Lumumba

As noted above, Canadian ideology got a boost in the 1990s with the production of the Heritage Minutes, 90-second docudramas that depicted key moments in Canadian history which spoke to the essence of what it meant to be Canadian. Unintentionally, the Heritage Minutes often illustrated precisely the depth of Canada's colonial roots, betraying Canadian white supremacy even as their authors believed themselves to be illustrating Canada's tolerance, multiculturalism and commitment to peace.

Perhaps the most revealing such case was "Dextraze in the Congo" (2005), which featured plucky Canadian peacekeepers pulling off a dangerous mission to arrest a "crazed" African soldier, who was caught in the act of carrying out sadistic violence against his own people. The stereotyping was comically lazy, with the "raving" African militant slapping a nun in the face and threatening to butcher everyone until being surprised and humiliated by the clever, restrained — eminently "civilized" — UN peacekeeper who disarmed and arrested him. "We have the building surrounded," he calmly informed the "frenzied" African, "drop your weapon." Bested by his "intellectual master," the African kidnapper had no choice but to give up. An innocent, grateful African priest looked up at the white man and asked in wonderment, "who are you?" The peacekeeper was then revealed to be Canadian Brig. J.A. Dextraze and the setting was the Congo, 1963.[41]

The presentation of the vignette is masterful, and anyone unfamiliar with Congolese history and unbothered by colonial stereotypes could find themselves standing up and applauding at the end, so thoroughly is the Canadian moral victory hammered home. Despite being produced in the 21st century, the tone of the vignette is unintentionally harmonized with what many Canadian officials expressed fifty years earlier about the Congo. For instance, in 1957, the Canadian Ambassador to Belgium, Charles Hébert, praised Belgian efforts to civilize the Congo, a place "inhabited by very backwards peoples few of whom can have any conception of government," and urged caution with respect to granting Congolese independence since it would be "asking a great deal to expect a transition… from tribal warfare and cannibalism to 20th century standards of justice, political development, orderly and responsible government."[42] Among other things, this was a remarkable endorsement of the 20th century, which had already produced two world wars, the Great Depression and the Holocaust.

These views were by no means exceptional. Canadian trade commissioner A.B. Brodie insisted that the Belgians had made "healthier and more useful citizens" out of the Congolese, and another rejected the idea that Congolese schools should teach indigenous African history, reporting that "better subjects could be found, since savagery is still very near the surface in most of the natives." These attitudes were reflected in mainstream Canada, where newspapers and citizens would soon be calling the Congolese "savages" and "apes who cannot read." "Let them eat one another," wrote a John Madden from Newfoundland, while a Mrs. C. Critchett wrote to Prime Minister Diefenbaker calling the Congolese "smelly dirty n-----s."[43] These ideas were not only reflective of longstanding colonial attitudes, they were also being stoked by the Canadian media, as when the *Toronto Star* asserted that Congolese people were eating their enemies — in this case a missing Irish UN soldier — in "secret tribal rituals." This was false, but that did not stop the *Globe and Mail* from repeating the claims with the headline screaming "Cannibalism Making Comeback," stoking fear of "primitives [on the] loose."[44]

These angry citizens were responding to an incident in which Canadian peacekeepers in the Congo had been beaten up by local authorities. The circumstances surrounding this and other incidents of violence between Congolese and Canadian peacekeepers are murky. According to the Canadian military, the Canadians were entirely innocent, had behaved in an exemplary fashion and were targeted simply because they were white. In other versions of the story, the Canadians were boorish and rude and provoked the assaults by the disrespectful way they treated the locals they encountered.[45] What is certain is that Canadian peacekeepers were regularly entreated to resist the habit of calling the Congolese "Black Bastards, Jigaboos and Coloureds," and at least one of the incidents of violence took place in the Léopoldville (Kinshasa) red-light district, outside a nightclub frequented by locals. The nightclub was later placed out of bounds to the peacekeepers because they had fomented so many violent incidents there, though even after these restrictions were placed, a senior medical officer still observed that "our troops apparently have quite an active sexual life."[46]

If Canadian peacekeepers were behaving badly, disrespecting local people and culture and carrying out violence and perhaps sexual violence, this would be entirely consistent with the longstanding practices of Canada's colonial forces, from the Canadian prairies to the Korean peninsula. Even if Canadian peacekeepers were "innocently" partaking in local nightlife and "legitimately" availing themselves of sex, it is quite reasonable to ask whether this is appropriate comportment for soldiers arriving in a poor, racially segregated country in the midst of serious civil strife. UN peacekeeping missions have a long and sordid history of sexual violence and exploitation, and peacekeepers' relations with local sex workers — usually impoverished and often children — was long treated as a normal part of the job.⁴⁷ Of course, there was likely also truth in the claim that Congolese people were, in some cases, targeting the Canadians because they were white; white peacekeepers were not trusted by most Congolese people and were seen to be aggravating, rather than de-escalating, the ongoing conflict in the country. In fact, the Congolese prime minister had already asked them to leave.

Canada's engagement in the Congo began in earnest in 1960, after the Belgian government had determined to make a hasty exit from a country it could no longer control. Until then, Belgium had fought to maintain its grip using, among other Canadian gifts, 53 Canadian-designed CF-100 fighter jets, which one military historian called "the backbone of the Royal Belgian air force."⁴⁸ The most significant Congolese leader was Patrice Lumumba, a brewery worker from Kasai, who had once been a defender of colonialism but had grown increasingly critical in the 1950s during time spent in prison on embezzlement charges.⁴⁹ There he saw the idiocies and injustices of Belgian racial segregation laid bare, and upon his release in 1957 he grew more and more radical. In 1958 he attended the pan-Africanist conference in Nkrumah's Ghana and was moved; he returned to Léopoldville believing independence to be "a right that the Congolese people [had] lost."⁵⁰ As rebellion broke loose in 1959, Lumumba was at its heart, articulating both an anti-colonial line and, especially after meeting Sékou Touré in Guinea, also the language of class struggle. By 1960, Lumumba had won the loyalty of the working classes and the rural poor, and the Belgians had plans for Lumumba's assassination; they simply had not found a viable Congolese candidate to carry it out.⁵¹

That year, the Congo won its struggle for independence and Belgium tried desperately to maintain a foothold in the country, framing its departure as though it were a choice Belgium had made out of respect for Congolese autonomy. When the Belgian king announced Congo's independence, he claimed it was "the crowning glory of the work conceived by the genius of King Léopold II" and took credit for the construction of Congolese society and infrastructure, suggesting the Congolese needed to prove themselves "worthy of [Belgian] confidence."⁵² Lumumba's response was defiant:

> We have known harassing work, exacted in exchange for salaries which did not permit us to eat enough or drive away hunger… we have known ironies, insults, blows that we endured morning, noon, and night, because we are Negroes… we have seen

our lands seized in the name of allegedly legal laws which in fact recognized only that might is right. We have seen that the law was not the same for a white and for a black... we have seen that in the towns there were magnificent houses for the whites and crumbling shanties for the blacks... who will ever forget the massacres where so many of our brothers perished, the cells into which those who refused to submit to a regime of oppression and exploitation were thrown?[53]

Malcolm X, upon hearing the speech, called Lumumba "the greatest black man who ever walked the African continent."[54] It was a day of unprecedented pride and joy for many Congolese who experienced it; Lumumba had tapped the heart of anti-colonial spirit and spoken for the masses like none other had in recent memory. Nevertheless, Lumumba inherited a country in disarray; Belgium's authorities were furious and its media demanded revenge. Belgium had explicitly avoided training Congolese administrators and bureaucrats — in fact they had made all education difficult to access for non-Europeans — and when many Belgian civil servants abandoned the country upon the transfer of power, it left institutional chaos. Rival factions attempted to seize power in different parts of the large country, and anger at nearly a century of truly extreme colonial degradation spilled into sporadic attacks against Europeans who had remained.

Still, the Canadian press exaggerated the violence and filtered it through its own colonial understanding of the world, describing black "rampages" and evoking sympathy for "panic-stricken Europeans," with one *Toronto Star* headline invoking "New Congo Terror: Two Whites Slain."[55] Despite a few relatively minor incidents, in fact, the situation was mostly being contained by Lumumba until Moise Tshombe, a pro-Belgian local authority in the rich province of Katanga, declared independence from the rest of the country. Fearing that pro-Belgian factions would be encouraged to break the country apart, Lumumba called upon the United Nations to help protect the Congo from what he felt was an external threat from the Belgians, who did not want to part with the wealth they had so long extracted from their colony.

Canada was part of the UN force that was sent in response to the crisis, but Lumumba quickly concluded that the Western powers sided with the Belgians and would favour those factions within the country that were pro-West and pro-capital. It was in that context that he called for all white peacekeepers to leave the country while non-white UN peacekeepers would remain. It was a demand that acknowledged the harrowing history of colonialism in the Congo and sought to ease the tensions that threatened to break apart the young republic. Indeed, a cursory glance at the Canadian press put the lie to any notion that Canada represented some sort of benevolent, colourblind interlocutor; the major dailies ran regular commentary and cartoons that denigrated the Congolese, depicting them as primitive apes, often literally stepping straight out of the jungle wearing loincloths. The *Globe and Mail* had not long ago asked "who will run the country if and when the Belgians go?" That the Congolese might run the Congo was not even considered an option, and no wonder: columnist Donald R. Gordon explained that they had "never been able to even begin to approach European standards of knowledge, competence, or intellectual ability."[56]

In this context, Lumumba's request that white peacekeepers be removed seems quite reasonable. Canada and other European nations in the UN force ignored Lumumba's request, calling it "inverted racism," and violent incidents continued.[57] Even when no violence occurred, the Canadian peacekeepers felt they were not getting the appreciation they deserved. In one rather murky incident, a group of Congolese soldiers was accused of making a joke about eating a Canadian — by licking his lips over a boiling pot of water — which resulted in a *Toronto Star* headline, "Thought They Would Eat Me Alive."[58] For this incident, the chief of the Congolese military offered Canada a rather surprising apology; this overture began the relationship between Canada and Col. Joseph Mobutu, who would emerge after 1964 as the dictator Mobutu Sese Seko and would rule the country with an iron fist for three decades.

Mobutu was Lumumba's chief rival and emerged as the most pro-West option among the aspiring rebel Congolese leaders. Though the UN force was divided on how to orient itself with respect to the Congolese factions, it was clear that Canada ultimately sided with Mobutu; in fact, it was a Canadian who facilitated the capture and subsequent execution of Patrice Lumumba, cementing Mobutu's rise to power. Canadian Lt. Col. J.A. Berthiaume had not developed a good reputation, even among others in the UN force. It was evident that he was fostering friendly relations with certain factions in the conflict, particularly Mobutu, despite the neutrality the peacekeepers were supposed to maintain. This was known to the Canadian government, after Indian and Ghanaian members of the UN force called his behaviour into question, but Canadian authorities did not recall Berthiaume or reprimand him, choosing to "let the matter rest."[59]

The matter in question was, in fact, Berthiaume's collusion in Lumumba's arrest. Peacekeepers had strict and specific instructions not to intercede or track Lumumba's movements, but Berthiaume defied the order, telling his friend Mobutu where to find Lumumba and laying out a plan to drop paratroopers to arrest him. Lumumba was seized, and shortly thereafter killed, by Mobutu's forces. Despite protests at home — most notably a demonstration of African students in Montreal lamenting "the assassination of a great African nationalist leader"[60] — Canada continued to tacitly support Mobutu, rather feebly blaming the Congolese crisis on the Soviet Union. Lumumba was eulogized and remembered across the decolonizing world as a martyr of anti-colonial liberation, though Canada's role in his murder was overshadowed by that of Belgium and the United States.

While the Canadian government did not expressly order the capture and subsequent assassination of Lumumba, it is nevertheless deeply implicated in the surrounding events. When Lumumba had visited Ottawa in 1960, hoping to build support for his new country through bilateral aid agreements, he was rebuked. Deferring to the wishes of the Belgians, Prime Minister Diefenbaker's government had given minimal fanfare to Lumumba's arrival. Lumumba aptly viewed Canada's sympathy for the Belgian position as evidence that Canada "was just another imperialist country," though Canadian officials weakly dismissed Lumumba's comments as anger that he had not been provided with prostitutes.[61] During the conflict over the presence of white peacekeepers, Lumumba had again invoked the colonial imagination he saw in the Canadians:

> How can you imagine that, just like that, a hat painted blue is enough to eliminate the complexes of conservative officers from Sweden or Canada or Great Britain? Their vision of Africa… was one of lion hunts, slave markets, and colonial conquests, and they sympathized with the Belgians because they had the same past, the same history, the same taste for our riches.[62]

Patrice Lumumba saw through the Canadian veneer; just below the surface presentation of a magnanimous Canada in the service of popular democracy and peace lay the Canada which had called the Congolese "the lowest form of man" and helped the Belgian King Leopold conquer the Congo in the 1890s. That blue paint slapped onto an old colonial helmet could not quite take, and Lumumba could see right through it. Indeed, when the first contingent of Canadians arrived in Léopoldville in 1960, there was great anxiety about the possibility that they would have to bunk with Congolese soldiers. Fearful of how it might be perceived, the Canadians worked extremely hard to conceal the fact that they were requesting separate barracks; Col. Mendelsohn was tasked with the "delicate" matter of making "cautious" inquiries about Canadians living with "native troops" while avoiding the appearance that they were "refusing to quarter Canadian soldiers with coloured soldiers," though "it would not be a matter of a colour bar" but rather differences in "customs" and "diet."[63]

The backflips taken to demand segregated quarters without demanding segregated quarters were farcical and clearly didn't fool Lumumba or many others. In the end the Canadians ironically bunked at Athenee Royal, a former segregated school for white children. The ongoing crisis in the country, which had been arguably exacerbated by the UN force, soon precipitated a major famine in the Kasai province, where Lumumba was born. By early 1961, hundreds of people were dying every day, mostly from diseases caused by malnourishment. The UN asked Canada to provide 3250 tons of dried fish to support relief efforts, and even the Canadian media urged Diefenbaker to send the support. Inexplicably, Diefenbaker refused, offering the incredible excuse that "surplus foodstuffs should be distributed to unemployed persons in Canada."[64] And thus, for the second time in a century, Canada brought its racist, colonial attitudes to the Congo and helped deliver it into the hands of a ruthless dictatorship, leaving devastation in its wake. "A part of our heritage," as the CBC Heritage Minutes remind us.

The Butcher of Zacapa

Anti-colonial struggle in Latin America shared much with that of Africa and Asia — indeed such movements increasingly worked together — but differed insofar as their colonizers were not, technically, colonizers. Nevertheless, the nominally independent states of Latin America and the Caribbean understood well that if they ran afoul of the Americans, their illusion of independence would be shattered quickly. The US marines landed hundreds of times in Latin America in the century following the declaration of the Munroe Doctrine, which effectively claimed the entire hemisphere as a grand US colony. And as Canadian capital had expanded into the region, even the Canadian military had seen fit to flex its muscles on a few occasions. But revolution in one of the quintessential neocolonial states — Cuba, former playground of North American gangsters and capitalists — had dramatically changed the dynamics in Latin America and, indeed, across the world. In its immediate aftermath, new US President John F. Kennedy went ahead with a plan to help right-wing exiles re-invade the country, landing at the Bay of Pigs. They were defeated easily and Kennedy was humiliated.

Prime Minister Diefenbaker took a personal dislike to the young president, and over the next few years they disagreed often on Canada's role in the region. Kennedy wanted a supplicant Canada to do as it was told; Diefenbaker wanted an independent Canada to do what it wanted. Some Canadians might observe this with pride, but it is worth remembering that the independence Canada was asserting was not motivated by significant moral or ideological opposition to US policy. Diefenbaker's defence minister, Pierre Sévigny, for instance, frustrated the US by failing to support it at a conference for Kennedy's Alliance for Progress scheme, but Sévigny did take the opportunity to mock the "highly emotional" Latin Americans with Canadian journalist Charles Lynch, who, for his part, derided Che Guevara for using "every trick in his Moscow-sharpened repertoire," despite Che having very little connection to the Soviet Union whatsoever.[65] More importantly, Canada's record in the hemisphere reflected a consistent pattern that was in ideological lockstep with the United States; what Canada wanted was to ensure that it benefitted from US imperialism rather than taking the fall for it.

To that end, Canada did, ultimately, join the Alliance for Progress and took full advantage. The massive aid program was touted as a way to soften anti-American sentiment in the hemisphere by providing generous aid packages to assist in economic development. In practice, these often functioned as subsidies for North American capital looking to invest in the region, with the Canadian Commercial Corporation controlling the spigot for its contributions; so, while Canada initially gave $20 million to the program, most of the money was distributed as loans to Canadian investors like Swan Wooster, which won the contract for port facilities at Acajutla in El Salvador, where Canadian troops had landed in 1932.[66]

Dozens of other Canadian companies got contracts for construction and engineering projects across Latin America, many of them having already earned bad reputations, like International Power in El Salvador. Meanwhile, other Canadian firms benefitted from the favourable terms of the recently signed Central American Common Market. The agreement included protections for foreign capital, tariff-free access to every market in the region and loopholes that allowed Canadian companies like Bata, Molson and Seagram — the company inherited by the creator of the Heritage Minutes — to avoid taxes.[67] At the same time, it was disastrous for most people in Central America, since it undercut local industry, depressed wages and dispossessed great swaths of land that were previously tilled by local peasants for food production. It was, of course, easy to get such favourable terms from dictators, installed and protected by the North Americans, who cared little for the people they ruled.

In the late 1960s, the Pierre Trudeau government worked to improve upon what Diefenbaker had built, while offering rhetoric suggesting a new foreign policy course that would stray from the despised Yankees. Beneath the rhetoric was a desire to further expand the opportunities for capital; Trudeau's external affairs minister, Mitchell Sharp, had been an executive at Brascan, the *polvo canadense* that dominated Brazil in the 1920s, and his primary initiatives included the creation of three organizations to assist in that expansion. The Canadian International Development Agency (CIDA) would be a source of aid money, some of which did go to valuable causes, but most of which was tied to Canadian companies or attached to nefarious political ambitions.[68] The Export Development Corporation (EDC) funded aggressive Canadian investments in some of Latin America's most heinous dictatorships or, as the EDC chair called it, "doing business with the devil."[69] The third, the Canadian Association on Latin America, actually received its funding from CIDA and acted as a business council for investors, marshalling political influence to support Canadian investments in the hemisphere. These new organizations were designed to create the optimal conditions for Canadian capital to penetrate Latin America, which usually meant that they generated the resources and political will to undermine popular democracy in poor countries.

They had done just that in Guatemala in 1954, having supported the overthrow of the elected Guatemalan government, and Canadian capital had hoped to reap the benefits. Instead, it found its efforts frustrated in the early 1960s by ongoing political turmoil that had been set off by the 1954 coup. In particular, International Nickel (Inco) wanted to exploit the nickel deposits in Zacapa, near Lake Izabal. The problem for Inco was that this happened to be the place chosen by Guatemalan revolutionary Luis Turcios Lima as a base of operations for guerrilla activity against the dictatorship.

Needing access to the region in order to exploit it, Inco fostered close relationships with a new military government that took over in another coup in 1963. To the great delight of Inco, Col. Carlos Arana Osorio was sent into Zacapa — with the help of US green berets — to sweep out the guerrillas. It was a vicious campaign that left anywhere from 3000 to 6000 people dead.[70] French journalist Régis Debray, who had been in the jungle conducting interviews with Lima and his *campañeros*, reported that many of the victims were mutilated while others were forced to torture one another. The Canadian trade officer in Guatemala City was effusive: "Prospects for the remainder of 1963 and 1964 are brighter than they have been in the last four years. Progress should be marked, provided that the current political stability is maintained."[71] Col. Arana would, indeed, see to it that stability was maintained.

Arana, nicknamed the "Butcher of Zacapa," would win a fraudulent election in 1970, promising "to turn the country into a cemetery" to stop mounting criticism of the government. In 1969, as the Trudeau government began to shower Inco in loans for the Lake Izabal project, a group of Guatemalan researchers published a report condemning the mine and its brazen theft of wealth from the country; it was to pay no taxes to the government and had already been the cause of the horrific violence in Zacapa. The next year, two of the lead researchers were gunned down in Guatemala City, and a third barely survived an assassination attempt. Just a month later, Inco signed the final agreement with President Arana.[72]

The Trudeau government was closely associated with the Inco project throughout the 1970s while it was under construction, and the association reflected poorly on the prime minister. In 1973, while withholding loans from Salvador Allende's Chile, discussed below, Trudeau boasted of the $17.5 million his government had given to the Inco project, overseen by the "Butcher of Zacapa." In an attempt to improve his image, Trudeau offered a gift of 45,000 kilos of powdered milk after an earthquake in 1976. It turned out that the Canadian milk industry had a massive oversupply and most Indigenous people in Guatemala did not drink milk and could not digest it. The propaganda was not working, but Canada was defiant, continuing to exhort its close relationship with the regime even while the US government under Jimmy Carter was beginning to condemn

Guatemala's abhorrent human rights record. In 1978, when the mine finally opened, the Canadian ambassador was present, the Canadian flag was raised and the Guatemalan military — which had killed thousands of poor Guatemalans on behalf of the Inco mine — struck up "O Canada."[73]

The Riff-Raff of the Latin American Left

But Guatemala was only a prelude to the most notorious coup in Latin American history, the 1973 overthrow of Chilean President Salvador Allende and the installation of the CIA-supported dictatorship of Gen. Augusto Pinochet. Chileans had been increasingly dissatisfied with their circumstances: grinding poverty in the countryside led to the formation of militant peasant organizations, and urban workers built the Central Unitaria de Trabajadores de Chile, through which they organized waves of strikes against tumbling wages and rising costs in the postwar period. In 1958, these forces coalesced into a left-wing party that offered Dr. Salvador Allende as an openly Marxist candidate for president.

Though the left lost the election, they continued to agitate for change, and Ottawa and Washington grew increasingly nervous. To forestall that momentum, they backed Eduardo Frei, a corporatist candidate who offered a much more moderate alternative to the status quo. Frei received a huge amount of support from the US through the Alliance for Progress, and managed to win the 1964 elections, though Allende garnered 39% of the vote. Following Frei's victory, Canada offered $8.6 million in aid to help Frei consolidate and maintain favour, while foreign capital poured into the country. But this only exacerbated the problem, and, in 1970, Chileans elected Salvador Allende to the presidency.

Right-wing forces in Chile, in cahoots with US President Nixon, moved to eliminate Allende immediately. Chile's top general — who was committed to upholding the constitution and would have therefore opposed action against Allende — was assassinated in what proved to be a bungled attempt to provoke a coup. Chileans filled the streets in anger and the plot failed, but the US kept up the pressure, applying a trade embargo while the CIA plotted sabotage and paramilitary violence. When Allende moved to nationalize the major US copper mines, a move that was broadly popular across Chile, a representative of US Secretary of State Henry Kissinger promised: "We shall do all within our power to condemn Chile and the Chileans to utmost deprivation and poverty."[74]

Colonialism, a Part of Our Heritage

It was an effective strategy; despite a number of progressive measures that improved the lot of poor Chileans, the opposition and the CIA were able to sow chaos and discontent, which Allende could only barely manage. Finally, on September 11, 1973, the coup was carried out; Allende delivered one last radio address before committing suicide in the burning Presidential Palace, and Pinochet immediately established one of the most terrifying governments in Latin American history. Thousands of Allende supporters were killed, including some 7000 who were immediately shepherded into the National Stadium, where many were shot on the spot.[75] Hundreds of thousands of Chileans would ultimately be exiled as Pinochet established total dictatorship:

> Congress was closed. The [opposition] parties were banned... a strict night-time curfew was imposed and not lifted for several years. Left-wing newspapers and magazines vanished from the kiosks. The public administration was extensively purged. In the opening stages of the regime, virtually all important national institutions (including the soccer federation) were assigned to generals or admirals, colonels or captains. In the universities (also extensively purged) uniformed "delegate-Rectors" took over. The atmosphere of Chile was transformed overnight.[76]

Indeed, Pinochet's reign of terror was marked by calculated cruelty: his soldiers smashed the hands of beloved folk singer and guitarist Víctor Jara and strung up his body outside the national stadium; his secret police converted an old mansion into a torture-chamber and nicknamed it *el palacio de las sonrisas* (the palace of laughter); exiled Chileans were assassinated by hit squads from Buenos Aires to Washington, DC; and Pinochet silenced forever one of the great poets of the 20th century, *el vate*, Pablo Neruda.[77]

These terrible events in Santiago were a perfect opportunity for Pierre Trudeau to illustrate that his government was different. Alas, it was not. After having given millions of dollars to the Frei government, Canada immediately cut off aid to Chile when the socialist Allende was elected, despite those elections being free and fair. Trudeau refused an invitation from Allende to visit Chile. Western banks withdrew from Chile, and Canada suspended EDC support for exports to Chile. In 1972, Canada helped persuade the IMF to cut off all assistance. Effectively, Trudeau endorsed the US embargo in a remarkable series of dramatic actions that he simultaneously refused to bring against South African Apartheid on the grounds that such actions were "ineffective." In fact, in 1971, even while Canada was turning off the faucet for Chile, Trudeau's external affairs minister insisted that Canada's "capacity to influence" the white minorities in Southern Africa was limited and that more economic connection — not less — was the best way to exert pressure for change.[78]

In 1973, Canada welcomed the coup and the arrival of Pinochet. Even as Chileans were being summarily executed in the National Stadium, Canada's ambassador to Chile, Andrew Ross, gleefully cabled Ottawa to report the "panic atmosphere" that was being imposed upon "the riff-raff of the Latin American left" and suggested that the new government would assume "the thankless task of sobering Chile up." A few weeks later, he assured Trudeau that there was "no useful purpose to withholding recognition" of the Pinochet government, and so Canada granted official recognition to a military general who had seized power by force.[79] Meanwhile, loans of $95 million (from the IMF) and $22 million (from the Inter-American Development Bank) were rushed through at Canada's behest, and private Canadian capital was the first to get into Chile's blood-soaked streets. By 1978 Canada had extended at least $50 million in loans, and Canadian companies had nearly $1 billion invested in Pinochet's dictatorship, which would last until 1990.[80]

Many Canadians were unimpressed. Although Chile rarely made headlines, civil society coalitions in Canada that comprised the social-democratic left, various church organizations, academics and labour unions found Canada's support for the tragedy in Chile unconscionable. Though many of these sectors had played along with the Cold War in its early stages, the 1960s had marked a transition in Canadian society; such groups would join the traditional left in the late decades of the 20th century in pushing a more progressive line in Canadian foreign policy. Following the coup in Chile, they organized a massive and sustained campaign to shame the Trudeau government, which did not effect any change in Canadian policy towards Pinochet but did successfully advocate on behalf of Chilean refugees, of whom around 7000 were able to find exile in Canada.[81] Those refugees, in turn, became an important element of the solidarity efforts that would oppose the disastrous wars in Central America in the 1980s.

Indeed, even as Pierre Trudeau talked a big game about human rights, Canadian investments in countries with abysmal human rights records was largely uninterrupted and often bolstered. Brascan remained the largest investor in Brazil, where a CIA-orchestrated coup had overthrown the popular democratic government of João Goulart in 1964, ushering in two decades of right-wing military dictatorship. At the time, Lester Pearson essentially ignored the coup and the Canadian press celebrated it, with the *Globe and Mail* declaring "Rio Celebrates Army Victory in Brazil Coup."[82] The Canadian owners of Brascan certainly celebrated; the dictatorship would be generous to the company, of which one senior official was a self-proclaimed fascist. Trudeau's government not only ignored what it acknowledged were "widespread" allegations of torture of prisoners, it communicated to the Brazilian military that it would "avoid drawing attention to this problem because [it was] anxious to build a vigorous and healthy relationship with Brazil." Canada was the second largest foreign investor in the country, at over $1 billion, and wanted to "take full advantage" of the military crackdown on labour and human rights or, as one Canadian official described it, the "Brazilian Miracle."[83]

Fascism had also taken hold of Argentina in 1976. During the "Dirty War," declared by the right-wing military government in Buenos Aires, as many as 20,000 people were disappeared, and tens of thousands more imprisoned without charges; these were people of the left and labour movements or simply those with whom someone in power had a score to settle. In the midst of these disastrous and terrifying years, Canada actively courted the Argentinian government in order to sell it a nuclear reactor. Undeterred by the criticism he received, Trudeau attempted to sell Argentina's military government a second reactor in 1979 but was unsuccessful despite having avoided serious critique of the widely reported violence the regime was carrying out.[84]

Canada's support for this wave of authoritarian violence in Latin America, especially in Chile, had proved a great embarrassment for the Trudeau government, which wanted to distinguish itself as a good neighbour to the region. Thus, it was determined that Cuba could be a target for Canadian diplomatic attention; Trudeau himself harboured a hobbyist's interest in the revolution and felt this could be an opportunity to appear different from the United States. As such, Canada gradually increased its diplomatic and economic relations — though they still remained paltry — and Trudeau included Cuba on a regional visit in early 1976. Many Canadians were and remain seduced by the whirlwind tour that briefly brought the prime minister and his wife and son into close, informal relations with Fidel. In typical Trudeau fashion, he ended his visit with a rousing cry — *viva Cuba!* — which mildly offended domestic conservatives but elicited scandalous pleasure from much of his base. The gesture was largely empty and fit neatly into the Trudeau canon: beyond signalling some vague desire to irritate the Americans and his own political rivals, it heralded no significant change in Canada's relationship to Cuba, notwithstanding a minor and temporary boost in trade and foreign aid. That it drew the contempt of conservative historians like Jack Granatstein speaks more to the vacuity of the scholarly debate than to any real policy significance.[85]

Indeed, what was much more interesting in Trudeau's Cuba policy was its continuities with the past. As it had since the Diefenbaker era, Canada continued to use its embassy to spy on Cuba on behalf of the CIA. By the 1960s, Canada's diplomatic corps was adept at intelligence gathering, most notably in Cuba and in Indochina, both hotspots of US Cold War aggression. The embassy used its own personnel but also ran Cuban agents, whose information sharing would have constituted criminal activity if caught. This information, which Canada shared with the US, included Cuban defence preparations, boats and patrols, engagements with the Soviet Union and other strategic intelligence; this is all particularly noteworthy since the United States was, in fact, using it to plot the active overthrow of the Cuban government.[86] In addition to the Bay of Pigs invasion, the CIA hatched several plots to assassinate Fidel and other Cuban leaders.

Not only that, Canada was actively collaborating with an increasingly violent network of Cuban exiles carrying out terrorist attacks both in Cuba and beyond. Cuban exiles, in fact, carried out several significant attacks in Canada, including a bombing of the Cuban pavilion at Expo '67 in Montreal. Other attacks included a bazooka blast in Ottawa, bombings of ships in the Montreal harbour and a bombing of the Cuban consulate in Toronto.[87] Several people, including some Canadians, were killed in these attacks, and at least one of the bombings was alleged to have been abetted by the RCMP, which had ties to the Cuban exiles.[88] Meanwhile, the bombing in Ottawa was attributed to Orlando Bosch, whom even US authorities considered to be an unhinged and deadly individual. Bosch was the mastermind of the bombing of Cubana Airlines Flight 455, which killed 72 Cubans, including the national fencing team. Bosch would ultimately be given a full pardon by US President George H.W. Bush.

Bosch and the other Cuban exiles were being supported by the Canadian government despite their putting both Canadians and Cuban lives at risk. Most of the attacks carried out by these organizations were in Cuba, and ranged from the bombings of villages to the intentional spreading of biological weapons, as when Eduardo Arocena introduced Dengue 2 to Cuba, making 300,000 people sick. In total, some 600 attacks killed at least 3500 Cubans, but Canada had little to say on the matter. They were, after all, on the same side; the information they were providing to the United States was helping facilitate several of these campaigns. Most notably, the US worked with anti-Castro elements in Cuba on Operation Mongoose, which has been called "one of the worst examples of state-sponsored terrorism of the twentieth century."[89] Its missions included the capture and torture of teenagers, the bombing of ships in harbour and the sadistic psy-op known as Operation Peter Pan, wherein Cuban parents were falsely told that the government was planning to kidnap their children and were thus encouraged to send them, nearly 14,000 children, to "safety" in the United States.[90]

Canada's participation in US subterfuge and espionage in Cuba made it even more absurd when Canada reacted with righteous indignation to allegations that Cubans were spying on the US through consular officials in Montreal in 1977. When Canada took a tough line — offering a paternalistic scolding of Cuba for having its "hand in the cookie jar" — Cuba replied by threatening to expose and arrest Canada's own spy ring. Ironically, only the year before, as part of the brief overtures towards better relations, Fidel had released Canadian Ronald Lippert, who was serving a thirty-year sentence for smuggling munitions into Cuba on behalf of the CIA.[91]

The attack in Montreal was connected to the ongoing war in Southern Africa, where Cuba was assisting the Angolan anti-colonial struggle against the collaborators with Portuguese colonialism and the invasion launched by Apartheid South Africa, discussed in greater detail in the next chapter. Pierre Trudeau was taken aback at Cuba's expression of anti-colonial solidarity: "Canada disapproves *with horror* [at the] participation of Cuban troops in Africa."[92] That Canada should be so aghast at Cuba's putting troops into action in clear harmony with the will of the majority of Angolan and several UN resolutions — to repel an invasion by Apartheid South Africa — is the epitome of hypocrisy given Canada's record of support for, and participation in, foreign interventions. The scandal, it seemed, was not just that the forces of the international left would use similar tactics, but also that Cuba — viewed as a backwards upstart, racialized and stigmatized and assumed to be incapable and incompetent — should prove both able and willing to send troops across the ocean to support the struggle against colonialism.

Any superficial rapprochement fostered by the Trudeaus' spectacle in Cuba, then, was quickly brought down to earth by the hard reality that these two governments were on fundamentally opposite sides of the global class struggle that shaped modern international relations. In Ottawa, Cuba was suddenly framed as "an impediment to peace in Africa" and the collapse of this brief romance was signalled by the cancellation of an exhibition baseball game between the Montreal Expos and a team from Cuba.[93]

Quiet Complicity in Vietnam

Interest in the Vietnam War ebbed and flowed in the years following Vietnamese victory. A notable reckoning appeared to take place in the late 1980s, around the release of films like *Platoon* (1986), *Full Metal Jacket* (1987) and *Good Morning, Vietnam* (1987), and another wave of interest was piqued in the late 2010s after the publication of Ken Burns and Lynn Novick's documentary *The Vietnam War* (2017). Although many criticisms were correctly levelled at the Burns and Novick series — not the least of which was its glib acceptance of America's "good intentions" — it nevertheless served to remind a younger generation of just how horrific and seemingly senseless was the US war upon Vietnam. But for Canadian audiences this narrative provoked a certain sense of superiority; several Canadian newspapers reviewed the documentary with reminders that they, like most Canadians, had always opposed the terrible war.[94] How proud Canadians should be that our enlightened governments did not take us down this foolish path!

If only it were that simple. As the previous chapter highlighted, Canada had supported and helped to finance France's attempt to reconquer Indochina and lionized its last stand at Dien Bien Phu, even while much of the world celebrated Vietnam's liberation as a tremendous anti-colonial victory. Canada then joined the International Control Commission (ICC) to help enforce the terms of peace agreed upon in Geneva in 1954, but used its position to undermine and spy on North Vietnam even while it aided and armed the US puppet dictatorship in South Vietnam.

US involvement in Vietnam gradually increased in an effort to sustain a pro-Western foothold in a country that would otherwise have overwhelmingly supported Ho Chi Minh's communists; not only had they liberated the people from France, but they were carrying out policies that people wanted. Even Canadians who were on the ground in the lead-up to what were supposed to be democratic nationwide elections in 1956 acknowledged as much: "As it looks now," said Canadian journalist Blair Fraser in 1954, "it's quite likely the Communists will come to power here by peaceful constitutional means."[95] As a result, the elections were cancelled by the US and its South Vietnamese client state, with Canada's assistance.[96]

The genuine popularity of the Vietnamese communists was often lost on those who saw the Cold War as purely geopolitical rivalries. But as Gabriel Kolko illustrates in his important study of the conflict, the seizure of land from wealthy landowners to be given to small farming families was key to the support that North Vietnam and the Viet Cong guerrillas received throughout the war. Indeed, nothing was so crucial to their eventual victory against overwhelming US firepower than the fact that the vast majority of the people supported the communists. They were not brainwashed or intimidated; they simply saw in North Vietnam the prospect of a better life. The more the colonizers tried to take that away, the more committed the Vietnamese people became to winning.[97]

Lester Pearson described Vietnamese anti-colonial sentiment as "irrational."[98] But as time went on and the realities of the war filtered through, many Canadians came to share some of that irrationality; hundreds of thousands of Canadians became vocally opposed to the war, staging protests, sit-ins, petitions and public prayers and supporting the nearly 100,000 American draft-dodgers and deserters who came to Canada, two of whom would later be my own mentors in the study of world history. Students uncovered their universities' links to companies selling weapons for the war and Canada's complicity was increasingly exposed by committed activists and journalists, despite efforts to keep it quiet. Blunt admissions by soldiers — echoing presidential candidate Barry Goldwater — that they were to turn Vietnam "into a parking lot" drove home the fact that this was no noble struggle against Hitler's fascism, despite relentless efforts by the authorities to make precisely that connection.[99]

One Canadian aid worker sent to South Vietnam as part of Canada's support for the fledgling puppet regime there came back disgusted with what she had seen. Claire Culhane tended to victims of the US war at a hospital in Quang Ngai, only a few miles from the site of the horrific My Lai massacre perpetrated by American troops in 1968. Culhane witnessed not only the carnage beset upon Vietnamese bodies but the also the often-sociopathic mentality of North American soldiers trained to see Vietnamese peasants as little more than animals to be slaughtered for sport. From the hospital where she worked, she reported the inconceivable violence she indirectly witnessed:

> In the Emergency Ward one became dazed with shock following upon shock — lifting a baby out of a pool of its own blood, a young girl with her breasts sliced off and a broken bottle rammed up her vagina, a child with a hole in its back large enough to put one's fist into… none of these could be diagnosed as routine wounds. Soon I was able to link them with the previous night's "Search-and-Destroy and… Harassment and Interdiction Missions." These were unreported, daily, mini-massacres."[100]

Upon her return to Canada in 1968, Culhane conducted a ten-day hunger strike on Parliament Hill, galvanizing an escalation of the anti-war movement in Canada. A few years later she chained herself to a seat in the visitor's gallery of the House of Commons and hurled leaflets at politicians, shouting "why is Canada building hospitals and also supplying bombs in Vietnam?" Her book on the subject, *Why Is Canada in Vietnam?* (1972), was one of the first of its kind and offered a forceful condemnation of Canadian policy. Tellingly, on the title page of the University of Toronto's copy of the book, some defensive Canadian reader scrawled "angry bitter woman, axe to grind!"

But Culhane was part of a global mass movement; the Vietnam War had become the symbol of everything that was wrong with the West, the Cold War, colonialism and capitalism. It generated protests and strikes and gave urgency to the many struggles being waged against the capitalist world order. The Canadian state, patently aware of what side it was on, attempted to crack down on the budding rebellion. The RCMP worked with the FBI to investigate activists in Canada, to open their mail and tap their phones, to have them beaten, intimidated, smeared and "red-baited."[101] After a Mrs. E.L. McKegney sent a letter to US President Johnson criticizing the war, she found US Secret Service operatives interrogating her in her Sarnia, Ontario, home.[102]

As opposition to the war grew, so too did right-wing reaction; radio hosts, church leaders, university deans and other authority figures often exercised their institutional and social power to ostracize and discredit those who joined the growing protest. While Canada's doors were initially open to draft-dodgers, it became increasingly difficult for Americans to escape to Canada, especially those who were deserters. While dodgers were typically white, middle-class and college-educated, deserters were more likely to be non-white and working class, and, by 1969, Canada had made it impossible for deserters to cross the border.[103]

Canadian opposition to the war was small compared to most of the world, where a momentous wave of popular resistance took place in the late 1960s, of which the massive demonstrations against the Vietnam War in the United States and around the world were just one part. And even as the famous black boxer Mohammad Ali was being arrested for refusing to fight — "no Viet Cong ever called me n----r," he famously declared — television news was for the first and perhaps only time allowing a relatively immediate and unfiltered view of the war. North American audiences were shocked at the sight of their own soldiers being so rapidly cut down but also by the brutality of modern colonial warfare. It had been nearly a century since the conquest of the North American west; since that time, the savagery of colonialism had been increasingly hidden from the broader white public. Canadians had not travelled with William Stairs when he beheaded Congolese people, they had not seen John Buchan's South African concentration camps, they had not witnessed the massacre in El Salvador, and they had no idea that their soldiers had raped South Korean women. The stark reality of Vietnam was driven home when the CBC aired the Beryl Fox documentary *The Mills of the Gods: Vietnam* (1965), and Canadians watched an American pilot gleefully machine-gun fleeing civilians like it was a game at the county fair, exclaiming "look at it burn!" as napalm engulfed the forest.[104]

But public discontent could not change the fact that Canada was deeply connected to the war. More than 400 Canadian companies had contracts with the US military, which totalled over $2.4 billion, producing everything from engines to ammunition to grenades to batteries to boots and even whiskey and the famous green berets worn by US Special Forces.[105] This was widely known: in May 1967, the weekly magazine of the *Toronto Star* tracked Canadian explosives produced in Québec which were mixed into bombs and sent to Vietnam. "With luck," said the magazine, "the explosives… could be hailing down on a Vietnamese village six weeks later."[106] That same month, many Canadians recoiled at headlines like the one run by *Maclean's* in 1967: "We're Making Millions Out of Vietnam."[107] Pearson tried to convince the editors that he had no choice but to support the war because the Americans had insisted and would not take no for an answer. American pressure certainly played a role — Pearson was always conscious of maintaining harmony amongst the Atlantic allies — but Canada had built up a thick dossier of support for colonialism and its associated projects in order to offer the best possible prospects for business. Vietnam was no different.

In fact, one of its most insidious contributions to the war was, indeed, a Canadian initiative: espionage. Despite any posturing that suggested Canada was only doing Uncle Sam's bidding, it was the Canadian ambassador in Washington, Arnold Heeney, who suggested that Canada could spy on behalf of the Americans. This was in 1954, five days *before* Canada agreed to sit on the ICC, along with representatives from India and Poland. Prime Minister Pearson, the architect of the plan, was clear with Heeney that it must be kept secret. "Should it become generally known that we are passing any information on to the United States government," said Pearson, "it would have very serious repercussions."[108]

Indeed, in 1965 the media got wind of it, and the *Montreal Star* ran a major piece detailing the important military information Canadians were passing on and criticizing Canadian officials for "functioning as spies when they are supposed to be serving as international civil servants."[109] External Affairs Minister Paul Martin denied the allegations feebly, but it was evident that even Canada's humanitarian aid to South Vietnam was part of intelligence-gathering efforts. Claire Culhane denounced Canada's actions, noting that while more hospitals *were* being built, the actual medical care being provided was diminished because the hospitals' primary purpose was to run Vietnamese "sleeper agents" who would report to their CIA handlers through go-betweens at the hospitals.[110]

The most infamous espionage case was the "Seaborn mission" wherein Canadian ICC commissioner Blair Seaborn was empowered to deliver threats to the North Vietnamese leadership on behalf of the US, while gathering information on that country's preparedness to fight. Seaborn was instructed to make ominous threats of US expansion of the war and to "convey [an] attitude of real personal concern." North Vietnamese Prime Minister Pham Von Dong was unfazed. "It is impossible," he replied, "for you westerners to understand the force of the people's will to resist."[111]

When the Seaborn mission was publicly exposed in 1971, one journalist suggested that Canada had acted as a "chore-boy for Moloch," an apt metaphor for a Canadian regime that had lied and deceived about its role in Vietnam since the early 1950s. Seaborn himself was still spouting platitudes in 2002 when he reflected on his decision, suggesting his goal was to "help the United States and its adversary in Vietnam to gain a better understanding of one another's thinking and intentions, and... thereby reduce the prospect of a deepening and widening war."[112]

External Affairs Minister Mitchell Sharp even had the audacity to claim that "the underlying problem" with the ICC "was that the East European delegations regarded themselves not as impartial — as Canada did — but as representatives of the North Vietnamese and Vietcong."[113] Indeed, Canadian politicians repeatedly debased themselves with such disingenuous claptrap and denied they were conducting espionage and sabotage, even while they manipulated the ICC and lied about their role in producing chemical weapons for use in Vietnam. One such weapon was napalm, a chemical agent which burned the South Asian jungle, reducing it by as much as 50% in Vietnam.[114] Napalm was produced in Canada and provided to the US as part of the Defence Production Sharing Agreement; this was public knowledge in Canada as of at least 1975 when it was discussed in detail on CBC Radio's *As It Happens*.[115]

Canada also generously offered up large sections of the forests of New Brunswick so that the US air force could test its toxic defoliants, most notably Agent Orange, which killed more than 4 million Vietnamese people and ultimately led to the deaths of more than 2 million American veterans of the war.[116] Canadian ICC commissioner Gordon E. Cox defended the use of defoliants, explaining that they were no different from those "which I myself have used in my garden in Canada."[117] Privately, External Affairs noted that one of the compounds in the defoliants was arsenic, and "the admission of its use in public could be taken up by Hanoi propaganda, since it could presumably be harmful to humans if applied in sufficiently strong solutions."[118] One did not need to be a Hanoi propagandist to see something wrong with dropping toxic chemicals on people. At the time, Cox deflected attention with a smug and false suggestion that the complaints had not come from anyone in Vietnam but, rather, "the Cauliflower Growers' Associations of the Lower Danube Valley."

Finally, contrary to popular belief, some 30,000 Canadians had their boots on the ground in Vietnam. Some were there as part of joint

Canadian-US units. Some had volunteered to join the US army for the war. Some were in South Vietnam as aid workers, where the Canadian government was making a concerted effort to "wave the flag," as ambassador Ormund Dier put it, such that Canada could lend legitimacy to the idea that it was an international coalition joined in an effort to protect South Vietnam. The Canadians who went to Vietnam had predictably polarized reactions. While some, like Claire Culhane, were appalled by what they saw, most viewed the conflict through the colonial ideology they had inherited and articulated politics similar to their American counterparts. And, just as they had in Korea and the Congo, Canadians in Vietnam availed themselves of colonized women: Lewis MacKenzie, who served as a Canadian on the ICC force, reported that he had to remove Canadian flag decals from the mirrors of brothels in Saigon. Like colonial conquerors had done for hundreds of years — indeed, like Jacques Cartier had done on the St. Lawrence in 1534 — Canadian soldiers who had conquered new territory were planting the flag to stake their claim.[119]

Moderate, Sensible, Progressive Leadership in Indonesia

A consistent pattern in Canada's Cold War politics was a willingness to aid and abet actions that might have caused controversy were Canada to participate publicly. Vietnam is a signpost example, but the case of Indonesia and East Timor is also instructive; quietly but effectively, Canada rewarded the Indonesian dictatorship of Suharto for its massacre of communists and its genocide against the Timorese people in the 1960s and 1970s.[120]

Suharto came to power after overthrowing the quasi-democratic government of Soekarno, whose early rule had certainly been marked by anti-communist purges and assistance from Washington but had later positioned itself as part of the non-aligned movement and had hosted one of the most important anti-colonial summits of the era at Bandung in 1955. Canada, in the first place, had not supported Soekarno's call for an independent Indonesia and had assisted the Dutch in maintaining what they called the Dutch East Indies. But when Soekarno crushed a communist uprising in 1948, the Americans decided to support him, and the Dutch were ousted in favour of what appeared to be a pro-Western capitalist state that could comprise a regional power. Canada helped achieve this end by proposing the terms of Dutch withdrawal at the United Nations, framing itself now as a supporter of Indonesian independence.[121]

But the man that the US had picked to rule Indonesia, Soekarno, increasingly went rogue — diplomatically if not economically — and aroused mounting suspicion in the West. Canadian aid to the country was limited and, by the mid-1960s, Canadian diplomats were describing Soekarno as representing "a collapse of world order."[122] In 1963, Indonesia initiated a low-intensity conflict with Malaysia, which had recently been defeated by a massive British intervention to ensure that its decolonization would be controlled by the UK. As the regional conflict grew between the Malaysian client state and the rogue Indonesian nationalists, Soekarno was increasingly bellicose in his criticisms of the war in Vietnam and of imperialism more broadly. Canada sent its air force to support the Malaysian/British side.[123]

Having contributed to the weakening of Soekarno's position in Indonesia, Canada then watched as a general in his army — Suharto — carried out a horrific coup against Soekarno, which entailed the murder of as many as 2 million people, most of them of the Indonesian left. The violence was often graphic and designed to instil terror: people were decapitated, disembowelled, dragged by trucks.[124] Soekarno had allowed a degree of space for the left to emerge, in the late 1950s and early 1960s, and while he had kept a lid on revolutionary activity, there was a deep well of discontent that threatened to bubble over into genuine social revolution. The Communist Party of Indonesia (PKI) had, by 1965, nearly 25 million members and Suharto's massacre was carried out on behalf of the Indonesian and foreign elite who feared the fact that, as Max Lane explains:

> More than half of the voting population were actively mobilized behind demands that, if fulfilled, would completely undermine the privileged position of aspiring military businessmen and rural landowners. This [was a] movement for worker control of state enterprises, land reform, further nationalization of the economy and deeper cooperation among non-aligned countries.[125]

Indeed, what is often misunderstood in Western accounts of Suharto's violence is that its class component was conscious and calculated. The PKI was crushed; its grassroots leaders were killed and its members terrorized, factories or villages with reputations for militancy were annihilated, all media connected in any way with the left was shut down and its members killed, and the very act of political mobilization was made impossible. Suharto's project was counter-revolution, to such an extent that the very memory of left politics was to be erased; Max Lane calls it "ideologicide," in which the most terrifying accusation that could be made was that one was a member of the PKI and where even thinking left-wing thoughts was imbued with fear.[126] Despite its absence from the popular consciousness of Euro-America, Suharto's anti-communist assault must surely be counted as one of the most horrific state-sponsored massacres of the 20th century.

Throughout, the Canadian ambassador was kept well-informed of the violence, but nevertheless described Suharto, the leader of the massacres, as a "moderate, sensible, and progressive leader."[127] Indeed, Canada lined up behind Suharto, as External Affairs gushed, "it is patently in our interests that the new regime be allowed to consolidate its internal position," an oblique reference to the carnage.[128] Paul Martin followed up by opening the faucet on foreign aid, even as private capital flowed in; the largest Canadian investor was Inco, infamous for its operations with the "Butcher of Zacapa" in Guatemala, but Canada also pushed into the transportation and forestry industries.[129] More than fifty years later, Canadian academics were still carrying water for the vicious Suharto regime; Louis A. Delvoie, in a 2010 report, skated past the murder of millions of people by briefly noting that "Soekarno was overthrown in the midst of much bloodshed and his regime was eventually replaced by that of General Suharto" as if the bloodshed were a weather pattern or a downturn in oil prices, rather than a catastrophic wave of violence that traumatized a nation.[130] Unperturbed, Delvoie moved right along to praise Suharto for "deliberately cultivat[ing] relations with Western countries to which it looked for... investment" and enthused over "the constructive role which [Suharto] was prepared to play in regional affairs."[131]

Indeed, Canada barely batted an eye as Suharto established a violent dictatorship, annexed Papua New Guinea and promptly invaded East Timor. The western part of Papua New Guinea had been a Dutch colony and, after much diplomatic wrangling, Suharto used violence and repression to seize control and effectively curtail Papuan self-governance, establishing a police state that killed at least 100,000 people. Canadian officials had described Papuans as "primitives" who lived in trees,[132] and one Canadian in Indonesia suggested that they were "not sophisticated enough to have personal views on their political status."[133] They said this despite the fact that Papuan representatives were travelling the world

— including a stopover in Ottawa — to promote the cause of Papuan independence. The Canadian embassy in Jakarta made it clear that it viewed West Papua as being part of Suharto's "manifest destiny," and Canada voted in favour of Indonesia at the UN.[134]

In East Timor, the departure of Portugal after 1974 was celebrated, and the most popular force on the ground was FRETILIN, a communist organization that had been active in the struggle against Portugal and had built links of solidarity with the African anti-colonial struggles, especially FRELIMO in Mozambique. Suharto's intervention was premised on the false claim that FRETILIN had imposed itself on the terrified civilians who had asked Indonesia to intervene for their protection. The invasion and ensuing war were again gruesome, flowing directly from that which had been imposed internally on the Indonesian left, and left some 200,000 Timorese dead, often amidst horrifying atrocities. Eyewitness accounts described "women [being] shot one by one with the onlookers ordered to count," and "entire families being shot for refusing to hand over their personal possessions." Indonesian troops devised several ways of killing people, of which one of the most popular was to dump people into the sea from helicopters, a practice they called *mandi laut* (gone for a swim).[135]

Canada appeared to be disinterested in the situation in East Timor, protesting that it was geographically distant and could not be a Canadian priority. But Canada was not indifferent at all: by 1975 it had an estimated annual trade of $1 billion with Indonesia, which it wanted to protect.[136] As such, it publicly accepted Suharto's claim that East Timor was a bubbling cauldron of communist agitation and that, like Cuba or nearby Vietnam, it could become an outpost of foreign-inspired insurrection. Suharto was playing a tune he knew would resonate with the Western capitalist powers. Indeed, Suharto's government replicated much of the language of colonialism; one military official explained: "It is the new Indonesian civilization we are bringing, and it is not easy to civilize backward people."[137]

Like other aspiring regional colonial powers, Indonesia was adopting the language and practice of the colonialism from which it had so recently been liberated.[138] This no doubt further ingratiated Suharto to the Western powers; he certainly inspired the confidence of the Canadians. Canada regularly abstained on UN resolutions criticizing Indonesia's occupation of East Timor, and in 1980 it even began openly voting against them. In fact, Canadian officials found international outcry over the atrocities in East Timor to be an irritant, worrying only that negative press might mar

Suharto's planned visit to Ottawa. Said one sarcastic Canadian at the UN, "there may be attempts by the high priests of decolonization to take the Indonesians to task," but Canada should "not do anything to increase Indonesian difficulties."[139]

Canada had done everything it could to minimize those difficulties; as far back as 1970, Pierre Trudeau had committed to increasing Canadian investments in Indonesia, as well as conducting military exchanges and exercises with the same military committing the atrocities described above.[140] Trudeau visited Suharto in 1971, and Suharto was welcomed to Ottawa in 1975, only a few months before he launched the assault on East Timor; the two proclaimed "very close and friendly relations" and a desire to "deepen their cooperation on all fields." Canada also pledged $200 million in development aid to facilitate Canadian investment.[141] When Trudeau visited Suharto again in 1983, he received some minor criticism in the Canadian media, which may have motivated the Mulroney government to affect a stronger rhetorical stance — the word "outrage" was used — after Suharto's forces committed another massacre in Dili in 1991. Nevertheless, for all the bluster, Canada did not adjust its policy course and Suharto visited Ottawa just three months after the 1991 killings.[142]

Tracing back through the history recounted in this chapter — from Indonesia to Vietnam to Chile to the Congo — even the most committed Cold Warrior would have to reckon with the mountain of human tragedy enacted in the project to defeat the struggles against colonialism and capitalism. It is hardly surprising that, in all of those places, millions of people put their lives on the line precisely to try to create a world that was *not* the one produced by the colonial capitalist states. This was, after all, a world that was not designed for the masses but a system of class rule, wherein a complicated hierarchy of wealth and power elevated a small number of people into positions of enormous privilege, and they used whatever means necessary to maintain it. But people had fought back: a major wave of resistance had peaked in the late 1960s and early 1970s that rivalled the revolutionary character of the period following the First World War, and the ruling classes of the capitalist countries had barely managed to contain it. In the 1980s, they went back on the offensive to destroy the movements that had posed this challenge, and Canada was to play its role in the preservation of the world it had helped create.

Notes

1. Lester Pearson, quoted in Yves Engler, *Canada in Africa: 300 Years of Aid and Exploitation*, Halifax, Fernwood, 2015, p. 88–89.
2. Bronfman was the owner of Seagram's and became the 14th wealthiest person in Canada in 2019.
3. Historica Canada, "Heritage Minutes." Available at: https://historicacanada.ca/heritageminutes.
4. Michael Barbour and Mark Evans, "History by the Minute: A Representative National History or Common Sense of the Majority?," *Canadian Social Studies*, Vol. 41, No. 1, Fall 2008.
5. This could certainly be read as critical of Canada, but there was also an argument that portraying his graphic hanging was a kind of fetishization of the murder of a Métis man.
6. A newer generation of vignettes produced between 2016 and 2018 made efforts to increase the presence and improve the depiction of Indigenous people, and were certainly an improvement over the lazy stereotyping featured in "Jacques Cartier" (1991). By contrast, "Chanie Wenjack" (2016) portrayed a sanitized but nevertheless upsetting vision of the Residential School System and included Wenjack's sister, Pearl Achneepineskum, herself a survivor of the schools. Still, the script — penned by Joseph Boyden, a Canadian writer who falsely claimed Indigenous ancestry and made himself a leading voice for Indigenous people until he was exposed — made no mention of the possibility that the genocide perpetrated through the schools might be ongoing in other Canadian institutions in the 21st century. "New Heritage Minute explored dark history of Indian residential schools," *CBC News*, June 21, 2016.
7. David P. Thomas, *Bombardier Abroad: Patterns of Dispossession*, Fernwood, Halifax, 2018.
8. "Uganda Airlines revival on course as country receives two bombardier jets," *The East African*, April 23, 2019.
9. Mike Davis, *Late Victorian Holocausts: El Niño Famines and the Making of the Third World*, London, Verso, 2002.
10. Quoted in Robert Teigrob, *Warming Up to the Cold War: Canada and the United States' coalition of the willing, from Hiroshima to Korea*, Toronto, University of Toronto Press, 2009, p. 110.
11. Robert Teigrob, *Warming Up*, p. 110.
12. Quoted in Robert Teigrob, *Warming Up*, p. 111.
13. Robert Teigrob, *Warming Up*, p. 113.
14. Quoted in Robert Teigrob, *Warming Up*, p. 112.
15. Quoted in Kevin A. Spooner, "Awakening Africa: Race and Canadian Views on Decolonizing Africa," in Laura Madokoro, Francine McKenzie, and David Meren, ed., *Dominion of Race: Rethinking Canada's International History*, Vancouver, UBC Press, 2017, p. 222.
16. Robert Teigrob, *Warming Up*, p. 113.
17. Escott Reid, quoted in Ryan Touhey, "Romanticism and Race: Escott Reid, the Department of External Affairs, and the Sundering of Canada-India Relations, 1952-1957," in Laura Madokoro, Francine McKenzie, and David Meren, ed., *Dominion of Race: Rethinking Canada's International History*, Vancouver, UBC

Press, 2017, p. 186.
18. Robert Bothwell, "Eyes West: Canada and the Cold War in Asia," in Greg Donaghy, ed., *Canada and the Early Cold War, 1943-1957*, Ottawa, Government of Canada, Foreign Affairs and International Trade, 1988, p. 60.
19. Quoted in David Webster, "Foreign Policy, Diplomacy, and Decolonization," in Karen Dubinsky, Sean Mills and Scott Rutherford, ed., *Canada and the Third World: Overlapping Histories*, Toronto, University of Toronto Press, 2016, p. 167.
20. Terrence MacDermott, quoted in Kevin A. Spooner, "Awakening Africa," p. 220.
21. Lester Pearson, quoted in Yves Engler, *Canada in Africa*, p. 88-89.
22. Yves Engler, *Canada in Africa*, p. 91.
23. Mau Mau was the term for the anti-colonial movement, which was made up of mostly Kikuyu but also Meru and Embu people, among others in Kenya.
24. Caroline Elkins, *Imperial Reckoning: The Untold Story of Britain's Gulag in Kenya*, New York, Henry Holt, 2005, p. 233-270.
25. "Terror Shadows Kenya Beat," *Ottawa Citizen*, July 27, 1954.
26. Quoted in Kevin A. Spooner, "Awakening Africa," p. 212-213.
27. D'Arcy McGreer, quoted in Kevin A. Spooner, "Awakening Africa," p. 217.
28. Robert Ford, quoted in Kevin A. Spooner, "Awakening Africa," p. 214.
29. Quoted in Yves Engler, *Canada in Africa*, p. 93. Per Engler, a favoured method of interrogation was "to hold a man upside down with his head in a bucket of water and ram sand into his rectum. In a bid to spread fear, men were raped with knives, snakes and scorpions while women were gang-raped or had their breasts mutilated with pliers." These methods have no value in extracting useful information, the usual justification for torturing prisoners, since the scale of the brutality is such that victims will say anything to try to end the torture. They are, instead, acts of power and violence, meant to mark the body of the colonized with their lesser status. Sherene Razack, "Canada's Afghan Detainee Torture Scandal," in Jerome Klassen and Greg Albo, ed., *Empire's Ally: Canada and the War in Afghanistan*, Toronto, University of Toronto Press, 2013, p. 376-383.
30. G.M. Mitchell, quoted in David Meren, "Crisis of the Nation," in Laura Madokoro, Francine McKenzie, and David Meren, ed., *Dominion of Race: Rethinking Canada's International History*, Vancouver, UBC Press, 2017, p. 238.
31. Yves Engler, *Canada in Africa*, p. 97.
32. Quoted in David Webster, "Foreign Policy, Diplomacy, and Decolonization," p. 184.
33. Kevin A. Spooner, "Awakening Africa," p. 212-220.
34. Henry Heller, *The Cold War and the New Imperialism: A Global History, 1945-2005*, New York, Monthly Review Press, p. 100-101.
35. Evan Gill, quoted in Kevin A. Spooner, "Awakening Africa," p. 218.
36. Ahmad A. Rahman, *The Regime Change of Kwame Nkrumah*, New York, Palgrave Macmillan, 2007, p. 198-199.
37. Christopher R. Kilford, *The Other Cold War: Canada's Military Assistance to the Developing World, 1945-1975*, Ottawa, Canadian Defence Academy Press, 2010, p. 154-155. Emphasis added.
38. Ahmad A. Rahman, *The Regime Change*, p. 202.
39. Christopher R. Kilford, *The Other Cold War*, p. 154-155.
40. Yves Engler, *Canada in Africa*, p. 124.

41. Dextraze was a General during WWII who admitted to having overseeing the execution German prisoners.
42. Charles Hebert, quoted in Kevin A. Spooner, *Canada, the Congo Crisis, and UN Peacekeeping, 1960–64*, Vancouver, UBC Press, 2009, p. 18.
43. Letters to Prime Minister Diefenbaker, quoted in Kevin A. Spooner, *Canada, the Congo Crisis, and UN Peacekeeping*, p. 92.
44. Quoted in Colin McCullough, "No Axe to Grind in Africa," in Karen Dubinsky et al, ed., *New World Coming: The Sixties and the Shaping of Global Consciousness*, Toronto, Between the Lines, 2009, p. 229.
45. Kevin A. Spooner, *Canada, the Congo Crisis, and UN Peacekeeping*, p. 73–81.
46. Quoted in Kevin A. Spooner, *Canada, the Congo Crisis, and UN Peacekeeping*, p. 153.
47. Kelly Neudorfer's *Sexual Exploitation and Abuse in UN Peacekeeping* (2015) is one of the few comprehensive efforts to document this, engaging both with the regularity of these incidents and the UN's general lack of interest in pursuing them.
48. Sean Maloney, quoted in Yves Engler, *Canada in Africa*, p. 94.
49. Lumumba had been serving on a local black association for the so-called *évolués*, more "evolved" colonial subjects. Nevertheless, his efforts to promote the organization were difficult given the meagre pay he received, and he engaged in some "creative accounting" as one biographer put it. Leo Zeilig, *Lumumba: Africa's Lost Leader*, London, Haus Publishing, 2015, p. 52.
50. Patrice Lumumba, quoted in Leo Zeilig, *Lumumba*, p. 69.
51. Leo Zeilig, *Lumumba*, p. 94.
52. King Badouin, quoted in Leo Zeilig, *Lumumba*, p. 96.
53. Patrice Lumumba, quoted in Leo Zeilig, *Lumumba*, p. 97–98.
54. Malcolm X, quoted in Leo Zeilig, *Lumumba*, p. 100.
55. Quoted in Colin McCullough, "No Axe to Grind," p. 232.
56. Donald R. Gordon, quoted in Colin McCullough, "No Axe to Grind," p. 236.
57. Quoted in Kevin A. Spooner, *Canada, the Congo Crisis, and UN Peacekeeping*, p. 79.
58. It is entirely unclear whether such an incident even occurred and, if it did, whether it was in fact a joke about cannibalism. If it did happen as Charles Bernier had described it, it seems most likely that the Congolese were mocking the Canadians for believing such absurdities. Quoted in Colin McCullough, "No Axe to Grind," p. 234.
59. Quoted in Kevin A. Spooner, *Canada, the Congo Crisis, and UN Peacekeeping*, p. 110.
60. Quoted in Kevin A. Spooner, *Canada, the Congo Crisis, and UN Peacekeeping*, p. 136.
61. The sources for this claim, made by Diefenbaker himself, were Charles Lynch, a journalist with a record of fabrications, including spectacularly false claims around Lumumba's death, and George Ignatieff. The latter was certainly not a crude propagandist like Lynch, but his account of the situation in the Congo was, itself, thin. He claimed the Congo fell into anarchy with "reports of widespread rape and massacre" when the Belgians left, and mocked Lumumba's assertion that Belgium was fomenting the crisis, even as he admitted that Belgium backed

the Katanga rebellion. He also heaped praise on the Canadian mission, claiming it "did a wonderful job, under frightful conditions of physical discomfort and in the absence of any protection from local authorities." He did not mention that local authorities did not want the Canadians there. As for Diefenbaker's story about Lumumba, it was certainly possible, though it seemed odd that the teetotalling family man would make such a crass, uncharacteristic and public demand. Rather, it appeared more likely a convenient smear against a foreign leader who was exposing, with clarity and force, the colonial position that Canada was trying to conceal beneath the veneer of peacekeeping. See John G. Diefenbaker, *One Canada, The Memoirs of the Right Honourable John G. Diefenbaker: The Tumultuous Years 1962-1967*, Signet, Scarborough, 1975, p. 128. Charles Lynch, *You Can't Print THAT!*, Edmonton, Hurtig, 1983, p. 188-190. George Ignatieff, *The Making of a Peacemonger*, Toronto, University of Toronto Press, 1985, p. 191-192.

62. Patrice Lumumba, quoted in Madeleine G. Kalb, *The Congo Cables*, New York, Macmillan, 1982, p. 49-50.
63. Quoted in Kevin A. Spooner, *Canada, the Congo Crisis, and UN Peacekeeping*, p. 73.
64. Quoted in Kevin A. Spooner, *Canada, the Congo Crisis, and UN Peacekeeping*, p. 129.
65. Quoted in Peter McFarlane, *Northern Shadows*, p. 114, 113.
66. Peter McFarlane, *Northern Shadows*, p. 118.
67. Peter McFarlane, *Northern Shadows*, p. 118-120.
68. Nikolas Barry-Shaw and Dru Oja Jay, *Paved with Good Intentions: Canada's development NGOs from idealism to imperialism*, Fernwood, Halifax, 2012, p. 154-165.
69. Quoted in Peter McFarlane, *Northern Shadows*, p. 135.
70. Only a few hundred of the dead were actual guerrillas, though an argument could be made that the ethical ramifications of the massacre would be little changed even if they had all been part of the resistance. Indeed, the documentary *When the Mountains Tremble* (1983) illustrated that the guerrillas tended to be from poor, Indigenous communities, and they worked closely with civilians in those communities.
71. Quoted in Peter McFarlane, *Northern Shadows*, p. 126.
72. Peter McFarlane, *Northern Shadows*, p. 129-131.
73. Peter McFarlane, Northern Shadows, p. 149.
74. Quoted in Richard Pithouse, "Blood in the Streets of Santiago: Forty Years Since the Coup in Chile," *South African Civil Society Information Service*, September 9, 2013. Available at: https://sacsis.org.za/site/srticle/1779.
75. Hugh O'Shaughnessy, "Chilean coup: 40 years ago I watched Pinochet crush a democratic dream," *The Guardian*, September 7, 2013.
76. Simon Collier and William F. Sater, *A History of Chile, 1808-2002*, 2nd ed., Cambridge, Cambridge University Press, 2004, p. 359.
77. Collier and Sater, *A History of Chile*, p. 360-361.
78. Linda Freeman, *The Ambiguous Champion: Canada and South Africa in the Trudeau and Mulroney Years*, Toronto, University of Toronto Press, 1999, p. 62.
79. Andrew Ross, quoted in Peter McFarlane, *Northern Shadows*, p. 136.

80. Yves Engler, *The Black Book of Canadian Foreign Policy*, Halifax, Fernwood, 2009, p. 100.
81. Peter McFarlane, *Northern Shadows*, p. 145.
82. Quoted in Rosana Barboso, "Brazilian and Canadian relations: A Historical Survey," in Rosana Barbosa, ed., *Brazil and Canada in the Americas*, Halifax, Saint Mary's University, 2007, p. 44.
83. Quoted in Rosana Barbara, "Brazilian and Canadian relations," p. 46.
84. James Rochlin, *Discovering the Americas: The Evolution of Canadian Foreign Policy Towards Latin America*, Vancouver, UBC Press, 1994, p. 101–102.
85. J.L. Granatstein and Robert Bothwell, *Pirouette: Pierre Trudeau and Canadian Foreign Policy*, Toronto, University of Toronto Press, 1990.
86. Don Munton, "Canadian Intelligence and Diplomacy in Cuba," in Luis Rene Fernandez Tabio, Cynthia Wright, and Lana Wylie, ed., *Other Diplomacies, Other Ties: Cuba and Canada in the Shadow of the US*, Toronto, University of Toronto Press, 2018, p. 64–84.
87. Keith Bolender, "When Cuban-American Terrorism Came to Canada," in Luis Rene Fernandez Tabio, Cynthia Wright, and Lana Wylie, ed., *Other Diplomacies, Other Ties: Cuba and Canada in the Shadow of the US*, Toronto, University of Toronto Press, 2018, p. 115–135.
88. John Kirk and Peter McKenna, *Canada-Cuba Relations: The Other Good Neighbor Policy*, Gainesville, University of Florida Press, 1997, p. 115.
89. Lars Schoultz, *That Infernal Little Cuban Republic*, Chapel Hill, University of North Carolina Press, 2011.
90. Keith Bolender, "When Cuban-American Terrorism Came to Canada," p. 115–135.
91. Greg Donaghy and Mary Halloran, "Viva el pueblo Cubano: Pierre Trudeau's Distant Cuba, 1968–78," in Robert Wright and Lana Wylie, ed, *Our Place in the Sun: Canada and Cuba in the Castro Era*, Toronto, University of Toronto Press, 2009, p. 149.
92. Pierre Trudeau, quoted in Yves Engler, *Canada in Africa*, p. 100. Emphasis added.
93. Greg Donaghy and Mary Halloran, "Viva el pueblo Cubano," 157.
94. Terry Mosher, "50 years of Aislin: The Vietnam War produced no heroes," *Montreal Gazette*, September 18, 2017.
95. Blair Fraser, quoted in Victor Levant, *Quiet Complicity*, p. 121. Eisenhower, himself, acknowledged that around 80% of the country supported Ho Chi Minh.
96. Victor Levant, *Quiet Complicity: Canadian Involvement in the Vietnam War*, Toronto, Between the Lines, 1986, p. 121–140.
97. Gabriel Kolko, *Anatomy of a War: Vietnam, The United States, and the Modern Historical Experience*, New York, Pantheon Books, 1985.
98. Pearson, quoted in Ian McKay and Jamie Swift, *Warrior Nation: Rebranding Canada in an Age of Anxiety*, Toronto, Between the Lines, 2012, p. 155.
99. Walter L. Hixson, *American Foreign Relations: A New Diplomatic History*, New York, Routledge, 2016, p. 340.
100. Claire Culhane, *Why Is Canada in Vietnam? The Truth About Our Foreign Aid*, Toronto, NC Press, 1972, p. 36.
101. Red-baiting was a common tactic in the stifling of dissent and effectively

amounted to discrediting anyone who was critical by accusing them of being communists. The accused would then be forced to either deny that they were communists, thus switching the terms of discussion onto proving whether they were or were not a communist, or admit that they were a communist, thus delegitimizing anything they might have to say, since it would be assumed that they were simply propagandists shilling for some Soviet cause. This served to both reinforce the assumed inherent "evil" of communism while simultaneously distracting attention away from the specific critique the individual was raising.

102. Victor Levant, *Quiet Complicity*, p. 207.
103. Victor Levant, *Quiet Complicity*, p. 207–208.
104. He went on to explain to the camera, "Ok, good hits, good hits! Real fun, real fun. That was an outstanding target all right. We bombed first of all and you could see the people running everywhere… it's very seldom we see Victor Charlie [the North Vietnamese] run like that, when we do, we know we're going to really going to hose him down. I just love that."
105. McKay and Swift, *Warrior Nation*, p. 159. A complete list is provided in Victor Levant, *Quiet Complicity*, p. 55–56.
106. Quoted in Victor Levant, *Quiet Complicity*, p. 54.
107. Quoted in Victor Levant, *Quiet Complicity*, p. 54.
108. Lester Pearson, quoted in Victor Levant, *Quiet Complicity*, p. 193.
109. Quoted in Victor Levant, *Quiet Complicity*, p. 193–194.
110. Claire Culhane, *Why Is Canada in Vietnam?*, p. 114.
111. Pham Von Dong, quoted in Victor Levant, *Quiet Complicity*, p. 179.
112. J. Blair Seaborn, "Mission to Hanoi: The Canadian Channel," in Arthur E. Blanchette, ed., *Canadian Peacekeepers in Indochina, 1954–1973*, Kemptville, The Golden Dog Press, 2002, p. 87. Louise Pommet-Dyer's contribution to this book about the crisis in Indochina is a 27-page tale of whimsey in Phnom Penh, where she worked for three years with the International Commission for Supervision and Control. Her recollections are entirely about cocktail parties, parks and avenues, leisurely get-aways and office romance. The last line of her essay reads, "What I lived in the sixties was a dream and I don't want to wake up." Despite ostensibly working for a commission dealing with an horrific conflict, Pommet-Dyer was so sheltered from its realities that the war is barely mentioned amidst the details of her journey to find an air-conditioned room or the perfect wedding gift for her friend. Louise Pommet-Dyer, "Memories of Cambodia," in Arthur E. Blanchette, ed., *Canadian Peacekeepers in Indochina, 1954–1973*, Kemptville, The Golden Dog Press, 2002, p. 122–149.
113. Mitchell Sharp, "Foreword," Arthur E. Blanchette, ed., *Canadian Peacekeepers in Indochina, 1954–1973*, Kemptville, The Golden Dog Press, 2002, p. xi.
114. Mike Ives, "In War-Scarred Landscape, Vietnam Replants Its Forests," *Yale Environment 360*, November 4, 2010. Available at: https://e360.edu/features/in_war_scarred_landscape_vietnam_replants_its_forests.
115. The program, broadcast on January 27, 1975, is available in the CBC's digital archives: https://cbc.ca/archives/entry/supplying-the-war-machine.
116. Le Ke Son and Charles R. Bailey, *From Enemies to Partners: Vietnam, the US, and Agent Orange*, Chicago, G. Anton Publishing, 2017.
117. Gordon E. Cox, quoted in Victor Levant, *Quiet Complicity*, p. 177.

118. Quoted in Victor Levant, *Quiet Complicity*, p. 176.
119. McKay and Swift, *Warrior Nation*, p. 160.
120. Sharon Scharfe, *Complicity: Human Rights and Canadian Foreign Policy, The Case of East Timor*, Chicago, Black Rose Books, 1995.
121. Louie A. Delvoie, *Canada and Indonesia: Perturbed Engagement*, Centre for International Relations, Queen's University, March 2010, p. 2–3.
122. Terry MacDermot, quoted in David Webster, *Fire and the Full Moon: Canada and Indonesia in a Decolonizing World*, Vancouver, UBC Press, 2009, p. 191.
123. David Webster, *Fire and the Full Moon*, p. 142–150.
124. Max Lane, *Unfinished Nation: Indonesia Before and After Suharto*, Verso, London, 2008, p. 43.
125. Max Lane, *Unfinished Nation*, p. 43.
126. Max Lane, *Unfinished Nation*, p. 48–50.
127. R.M. Macdonnell, quoted in David Webster, *Fire and the Full Moon*, p. 153.
128. Quoted in David Webster, *Fire and the Full Moon*, p. 154.
129. David Webster, *Fire and the Full Moon*, p. 193.
130. Louie A. Delvoie, *Canada and Indonesia*, p. 4. For a sense of the trauma of that period, Joshua Oppenheimer's challenging documentary *The Act of Killing* (2012) is a powerful evocation of the emotion still attached to such a harrowing chapter in Indonesian history.
131. Louie A. Delvoie, *Canada and Indonesia*, p. 4–5.
132. John P. Sigvaldson, quoted in David Webster, "Foreign Policy, Diplomacy, and Decolonization," p. 184.
133. Quoted in David Webster, "'Red Indians' in Geneva, 'Papuan Headhunters' in New York: Race, Mental Maps, and Two Global Appeals in the 1920s and 1930s," in Laura Madokoro, Francine McKenzie, and David Meren, ed., *Dominion of Race: Rethinking Canada's International History*, Vancouver, UBC Press, 2017, p. 271.
134. David Webster, "'Red Indians' in Geneva," p. 271.
135. Sharon Scharfe, *Complicity*, p. 56.
136. Sharon Scharfe, *Complicity*, p. 103.
137. Colonel Kalangi, quoted in Sharon Scharfe, *Complicity*, p. 50.
138. Anti-colonial nationalism, once liberated from the original colonial power, can sometimes adopt the same attitudes and understandings of others. Conflicts between the Sinhalese nationalists and the Tamil minority in Sri Lanka, for instance, reflected many of the same colonial dynamics that had originally been imposed on both groups by the British. Indeed, what increasingly came to be termed "ethnic tensions" in post-independence countries in the 1990s was often a by-product of old colonial dynamics, displaced or replicated in relations between different groups in the postcolonial situation. Other examples include the rise of Idi Amin in Uganda and his expulsion of South Asians in 1972, or the conflict between Hutu nationalists and Tutsis that catalyzed the Rwanda genocides.
139. Quoted in David Webster, *Fire and the Full Moon*, p. 168.
140. Louie A. Delvoie, *Canada and Indonesia*, p. 5.
141. Louie A. Delvoie, *Canada and Indonesia*, p. 6.
142. Louie A. Delvoie, *Canada and Indonesia*, p. 10.

9

Canada and the "End of History"

I had always maintained that Canada, with a third of its income and employment coming from exports, should never adopt a policy of turning down customers for political reasons.

— Frank Petrie, President of Canadian Exporters Association, on sanctions against Apartheid South Africa, 1979[1]

WHEN THE COLD WAR ENDED in the late 1980s there was an explosion of triumphalist writing in the West that celebrated its victory. Most notably, American writer Francis Fukuyama declared that capitalist victory meant the "end of history." The fall of the Berlin Wall, following Ronald Reagan's famous demand that Gorbachev tear it down, was largely viewed uncritically as a victory for humanity. For many, of course, life in East Germany had been difficult and a united Germany was worth celebrating; but given everything that was at stake in the Cold War, the simple notion that America's victory was the world's victory was a little too facile. Wolfgang Becker's film *Good Bye, Lenin!* (2003) illustrated the ambivalence many East Germans felt upon being folded into the West, especially those who stood to lose not just the material securities that the socialist states provided but, indeed, the existential purpose that many derived from their commitment to building socialism.

That Canada played a role in the defeat of the Soviet Union — and of the communist challenge more broadly — is hardly news. As the previous chapters have illustrated, Canada was a significant contributor to the Cold War and was always, unequivocally, on the American side. But what also becomes clear, under careful examination, is that despite ideological discipline insisting that the Cold War was a moral crusade, the actual cases in which Canada intervened built up a dossier of foreign misadventures that reflected very poorly on Canada. Perhaps that is why, in 2009, the Canadian government sought to reaffirm the correctness of its moral stance in the Cold War by commissioning an expensive "Monument to the Victims of Communism," a project roundly mocked for its ideological clumsiness, and which got stalled in the planning phases.

Indeed, the cascading crises of the 21st century — from the War on Terror to the financial crash of 2008 to the rise of fascism — ultimately knocked much of the wind out of those triumphant sails of the late 1980s. In fact, the same author who coined the "end of history" phrase to describe the ascendance of liberal capitalism as the pinnacle of human achievement, circled back in 2018 to admit that maybe history had not ended after all.[2] This was no surprise, given that victory in the Cold War had been premised on so much violence against people simply trying to carve out a better life for themselves. From Korea to Chile, from Indonesia to Palestine, poor people had organized movements to try to improve the conditions of their lives and found themselves under attack by local reactionaries defending their dominant position. Behind these reactionaries was always the money and guns of the United States and its allies, including Canada.

At its core, the Cold War was a war against the poor. It was a war to ensure that popular rejection of capitalism and its inequalities would be stamped out — by soft coercion and bribery if possible but by violence and terror if necessary — and by the 1980s it was finally paying dividends. Having survived the global rebellion of the late 1960s, the capitalist powers went on a new offensive in the 1980s and successfully destroyed not only the Soviet Union but several other pockets of anti-capitalist resistance. The world was to be closed off to those who wished to create alternatives to the grinding poverty and inequality of capitalism, a sign hung over the gates of every nation reading "No Admittance Except on Business."

Canada played its role in this project, helping to close off the possibilities for internal rebellion even as it worked to undermine the remaining forces of resistance — in the Middle East, Central America and Southern Africa — and indeed, in the Soviet Union itself. Often lost in the fog of the Cold War was the extent to which — for all its flaws — the presence of the Soviet Union, and the communist bloc more generally, opened up space for anti-colonial and anti-capitalist struggle around the world. Causes which would later be celebrated in the West, like the defeat of South African Apartheid, were achieved in part thanks to resources from the Soviet Union and its allies, even while the West continued to do business with the Apartheid government.³ Indeed, as a representative of the Canadian capitalist class noted in the quote above, there was good business to be done in Apartheid South Africa; it saw no point in refusing that business "for political reasons." But what James Petrie called "political reasons" was people's lives; the struggle against Apartheid and, indeed, the global revolt against capitalism and colonialism, was about the simple idea that people's lives did not need to be a constant battle against poverty and injustice. That belief in a better world reached its peak in the global 1960s, and the Cold Warriors sought to crush it.

Twilight of the Global 1960s

The legacy of the 1960s was often mythologized in North American pop culture, re-imagined later as a romantic era of peace, love, drugs, sex and rock 'n' roll. The political content of the rebellions of the 1960s was often reduced to its most superficial elements, as though a white kid from Oshawa growing out his hair and smoking pot was equivalent to the heroic resistance of the Vietnamese National Liberation Front. The emphasis on Jimi Hendrix — as opposed to say the Red Army Faction in Germany — was illustrative of the discomfort that the period provoked for the ruling classes. The period sometimes called the "global 1960s" actually stretched well into the 1970s and provoked a genuine fear among the elite that total social upheaval was imminent and that the structures of capitalist class power and colonial rule were going to be toppled.⁴ Those ruling classes urgently needed to find ways of crushing and co-opting the increasingly radical movements of that era in order to maintain their position, but it was not going to be easy.

The gradual process of decolonization had meant that "world opinion" in the middle of the 20th century increasingly reflected non-European perspectives. What was perfectly standard behaviour for a European settler colony prior to the Second World War had become increasingly unacceptable by the 1960s to an international community that now had no choice but to include some voices from the hitherto marginalized world. Bodies like the United Nations may never have held significant political power, but they reflected a new climate in which colonial actors had to operate and wherein powerful voices from the decolonizing world could not be entirely ignored. Among many outstanding performances at the UN by powerful speakers like Kwame Nkrumah, Yasser Arafat and Thomas

Sankara, perhaps none stood out more than Ernesto "Che" Guevara's 1964 speech in which he celebrated that "the final hour of colonialism ha[d] struck" even as colonized people were still "massacred for the crime of demanding their freedom." Speaking after the murder of Congolese President Patrice Lumumba, Guevara put to the assembly: "How can we forget the betrayal of the hope that Patrice Lumumba placed in the United Nations?"[5] Perhaps most powerfully, Guevara turned Western Cold War rhetoric upon itself, exposing its most obvious contradictions:

> The United States intervenes in Latin America invoking the defence of free institutions. The time will come when this Assembly will acquire greater maturity and demand of the US government guarantees for the lives of the blacks and Latin Americans who live in that country… those [like the US government] who kill their own children and discriminate daily against them because of the colour of their skin; those who let murderers of blacks remain free, protecting them and further punishing the black population because they demand their legitimate rights as free men — how can those who do this consider themselves the guardians of freedom?[6]

Whatever victories it may have won through violence and subterfuge, the West was increasingly confronted by the fact that it was losing the battle for "hearts and minds." Having conquered and colonized the entire world, committed genocide and imposed slavery in order to establish capitalist enclaves and controllable markets and open up access to valuable resources — all the while denigrating and humiliating the people whose lands and labour they were building their empires upon — the Europeans and their offspring could little expect to find goodwill from the rest of the world. But this problem could no longer be addressed by simply killing and terrorizing their opponents; the presence of the communist bloc, which could both serve as an inspiration but also as a source of material support, had radically altered the colonial dynamic. The colonized now had a choice, and, as they fought for their freedom, the option of pursuing a non-capitalist path held great appeal to many. For the first time, the colonial powers needed to try to convince the rest of the world that it had more to offer than the Soviet Union, China, Cuba, Vietnam or any of the other models of communist and socialist states that were emerging.

All the while, they were dealing with the most significant internal pushback since the interwar period. As powerfully depicted in Chris Marker's landmark documentary, *A Grin Without a Cat* (1977), resistance in the imperial heartlands was in dialogue with — and inspired by — the revolutionary movements that had gripped the margins. The left in Italy was organized and formed militant Red Brigades. The left in France organized general strikes that shut the country down. The left in West Germany was carrying out limited acts of urban guerrilla war. Even at the heart of world capitalism, black Americans built both the civil rights movement and the more militant Black Power activism that was most famously manifest in the Black Panther Party, a communist organization that not only armed itself for protection against police violence but also provided breakfasts for children and sought to build better, stronger communities. That the Black Panthers were portrayed as dangerous criminals and targeted relentlessly by the US government — which went as far as to carry out bombings and assassinations in its own cities to crush radical Black Power movements — illustrated just how significant a threat they represented to the ruling class.[7]

All of this was part of the equation in Canada too, albeit to a lesser extent. One of the leading intellectuals of the Black Panther Party, Stokely Carmichael, came to Canada in 1968 and spoke in several cities, connecting with a leader of Halifax's militant black community, Burnley "Rocky" Jones.[8] The slogans of Black Power were resonant with people who had been marginalized for two centuries and had suffered greatly at the hands of the white elite. This was especially manifest in the physical destruction of their community, Africville, by years of depriving it of public services, by the destruction of parts of the neighbourhood for rail lines to serve white Haligonians, by the locating of garbage dumps, slaughter houses, tar factories and an infectious disease centre in the neighbourhood and then, in the late 1960s, in the literal razing of the community and forced relocation of its people to develop highways, port facilities and the A. Murray MacKay Bridge.[9] MacKay was a former CEO of the Maritime Telegraph and Telephone Company. The destruction of Africville dislocated the community in many ways and was combined with the establishment of controllable organizations for black people, like the Black United Front, which helped to co-opt and limit the radical potential of the Black Power movement.[10]

As noted in Chapter 3, this period also saw the rise of Red Power, militant Indigenous organizations linked to the American Indian

Movement (AIM) which sought to reinvigorate revolutionary politics and practice among colonized people in North America. Conscious of the links between colonialism in Canada and throughout the world, the Red Power movement was significant in re-shaping Indigenous consciousness in the 1960s, a shift that is powerfully portrayed in Lee Maracle's *Bobbi Lee: Indian Rebel* (1975).[11] The Native Alliance for Red Power declared in 1969 its demands for full autonomy in Indigenous communities, a separate police and justice system made by and for Indigenous people and compensation for the litany of ways that Canada had broken the terms of the treaties.[12]

The Red Power movement was, importantly, explicitly communist and anti-colonial in its orientation. One of its publications noted that Indigenous society was "totally at odds with the capitalist ethic" and that Red Power would "play a leading role in the fight for socialism in Canada," since it could provide an example to white Canadians by showing them "the image of their own future" and would "concretize what socialists mean when they talk of a society founded not on avarice but on human solidarity and brotherhood."[13] The Red Power movement upset the colonial imagination not just by declaring itself a decolonizing agent of history — rather than simply a victim or footnote — but also by placing itself at the vanguard of revolutionary change. Even within the subculture of the left, Red Power rejected the assumption that Indigenous people would learn revolutionary politics from white people but, rather, that white people had to learn from them.

Red Power, like many of the most resonant radical movements of the era, was inherently transnational. This was a strength; activists in the Red Power movement read Frantz Fanon, they struggled against Apartheid and against Pinochet, they travelled to Cuba with the Venceremos Brigades; they understood their struggle to be global in nature, given the globalizing nature of capitalism and colonialism.[14] This meant, however, that when the US government declared war on the movement it was bound to affect the dynamics north of the border. A violent and thorough campaign of repression against AIM — their members had what Bryan Palmer called a "virtual extermination order" placed upon them in the US — chilled the movement in Canada, where the government sought to divide Indigenous people by offering extremely modest reforms to dull the radical edge of the masses and create the perception that the Red Power activists were "fringe fanatics."[15]

The demobilizing effect was most horrifically illustrated in the murder of Anna Mae Aquash, a Mi'kmaq AIM activist born in Nova Scotia, who participated in many of the most important Indigenous actions of the era, including the Wounded Knee occupation of 1973 and a major blockade at Kenora, Ontario. Although there are still uncertainties around her death, what is certain is that it was politically motivated and that it was wrapped up in FBI efforts to destroy AIM.[16] The edge of Red Power was blunted enough to forestall the broad-based challenge to Canadian colonialism that it seemed to loom in the 1960s; while Indigenous activism persisted and would erupt in particular moments, like the Oka Crisis, the dream of a united movement to create "collaborative decolonization" that would overturn colonialism in Canada and the rest of the world failed to materialize.[17]

Still, the movement had indeed played a leadership role in the wave of rebellions; a new surge of women's rights activism swirled and took cues from women like Sandra Nicholas Lovelace, a Maliseet woman who took her grievance against Canada — that she lost her Indian status when she married a white man — to the United Nations. The feminist movement in Canada had, from its inception, been contested between those who sought to make gains for women within the prevailing colonial order and those who sought a more dramatic break from the patriarchal capitalist system. Though this continued to be the case, major mobilizations, like the Abortion Caravan, used direct action tactics to agitate against the Canadian state's control over women's bodies.[18] These struggles often interacted with the project for queer liberation, which had faced enormous challenges in the Cold War era but which emerged with more militancy and urgency following the Stonewall Riots against anti-queer police violence in New York City in 1969.

That very year, Canada moved to decriminalize homosexuality but life did not get easier for LGBTQ people in Canada. Throughout the 1960s and into the 1970s, the Canadian government maintained lists of "suspected" homosexuals, who were subject to surveillance and interrogation and could find themselves purged from public life. The Canadian establishment believed the very act of being queer to be an act of communist subversion, and while this was, obviously, ludicrous, it did speak to a certain truth; marginalized people are typically drawn to politics that seek to upset the existing hierarchies that keep them marginalized. As such, as Gary Kinsman notes, movements for queer liberation increasingly *were* tied to the left and recognized struggles for justice in the realm of class, race and gender to be connected to that of sexuality; the building of more radical left movements for queer liberation in the 1970s made the ongoing efforts of the RCMP to repress LGBTQ people more difficult.[19]

Indeed, the Canadian state would ultimately shift its course to allow a greater degree of institutional support for LGBTQ people, adopting a strategy that came to be known as "pinkwashing": mobilizing the language of tolerance and celebration of queer culture to mask a politics that still favoured ruling-class interests at the expense of all marginalized people. Same-sex marriage was legalized, an increasing number of celebrities came out, pop culture increasingly featured queer characters as more than just the target of jokes, and politicians would increasingly march in Pride Parades. For those LGBTQ people who enjoyed a certain degree of class comfort and security, Canada seemed to be doing well.

But the consequences of this co-opting remain present today. LGBTQ people still face higher rates of poverty, illness and addiction and are over-represented among the homeless in Canada — comprising some 25–40% of homeless youth — while being underrepresented in homeless shelters, which often pose greater challenges and dangers for them.[20] More than half of Ontario's trans people still live on less than $15,000 per year, and LGBTQ youth are 14 times more likely to commit suicide. At the same time, once-militant events like Pride have been increasingly taken over by corporate sponsors and rebranded as celebrations; while there is certainly value in the assertion that queer people have the right to occupy public space and celebrate, the draining of Pride's radical political content has served the interests of the Canadian state insofar as it has channelled a marginalized group away from direct confrontation with the state that still, fundamentally, marginalizes them.[21] The spectacle of having police march in the Pride Parade — the same police who often directly target queer people — is as clear an illustration as any of the co-optation of privileged sections of the movement.[22]

Another movement whose class character was complicated was the struggle for an independent Québec. Rebellion in Québec adopted anti-colonial language — even if the Québécois themselves were a sub-colonial power in the territory they had stolen from Indigenous Peoples — and was most dramatically manifest in 1970 when the Front de Libération du Québec (FLQ) kidnapped a British trade commissioner and a provincial minister. In response, the Pierre Trudeau government suspended all civil liberties and dramatically expanded the power of the police to detain and interrogate anyone suspected of being connected to the FLQ. This prompted much criticism as hundreds of Québécois were rounded up and intimidated, and the aggressive tactics by the Trudeau government likely contributed to the eventual killing of the provincial minister — Pierre Laporte — presumably by his kidnappers.

The FLQ espoused a kind of left politics, and some of its founding members remained committed to those principles; Charles Gagnon, for instance, went on to be one of the founders of the more explicitly communist organization En Lutte. The FLQ manifesto criticized the "Anglo-Saxon capitalists" who "made Québec into their private preserve of cheap labour and of unscrupulous exploitation."[23] Nevertheless, its lack of a solid base of support and its use of adventurist tactics meant that, as a legitimate progressive social movement, it fizzled quickly. It also failed to effectively locate Québec within the apparatus of the Canadian settler system, overemphasizing the extent to which it was a victim of colonialism rather than a perpetrator. Pierre Vallières' notable contribution to Québécois nationalism — *Les Nègres blancs d'Amérique* (1968) — suggested that Québécois people were a racialized minority. This framing could only work, as David Meren argued, "by deliberately ignoring the province's black and Indigenous populations and the subordinate position they occupied in a settler society."[24]

Still, the support that the movement mobilized was indicative of the fact that Québécois workers were angry. And, as elsewhere in Canada, the working classes were as militant as they had been since the turn of the century, and Trudeau's crackdown on the FLQ came alongside a concerted effort to undermine growing trade union activity. By the middle of the 1960s, strikes were happening at a rate of more than a thousand per year, with roughly half of those illegal or "wildcat" strikes.[25] Workers were emboldened — the 1965 postal workers' strike forced the government to make real concessions — and the Canadian government increasingly took coercive measures like the passing of legislation to make strikes illegal and the use of police to physically end the strikes. At the same time, the processes by which legal strikes could occur were made increasingly complex, requiring a wider layer of professionally trained lawyers and staff to help workers navigate them. The effect was to make workers more dependent on professionals whose incomes were not directly tied to the outcomes of particular workplace negotiations and who served to conservatize their movements by bogging them down in legal processes that dampened militancy.[26]

In sum, Canada had seen the rising tide of rebellion — emanating from the colonized people abroad and at home and then taking root in the Canadian working classes — and had weathered the storm. Through a carefully applied mix of coercion and co-optation, the Canadian state had managed to dull the edges of social rebellion and mitigate the effects of the revolutionary 1960s and 1970s. By the end of that decade, much of the radical, internationalist spirit and momentum of the era had been sapped. Malcolm X and Martin Luther King had been assassinated. Che Guevara was dead, his body grotesquely displayed by the Bolivian military for the world to see. Patrice Lumumba executed. Salvador Allende bombed into suicide. Counter-revolution was stemming the tide, and Canada had played its role in maintaining the global status quo.

As the 1980s beckoned, the West steeled itself for a final Cold War offensive, one that would break the Soviet Union and fracture what remained of the communist bloc, isolating those few holdouts and choking the life out of the movements still seeking to build a better world. Canada's contributions to this project were many but were particularly noteworthy in three crucial regional struggles — in the Middle East, Central America and Southern Africa — that were pivotal during this period. In each of these geopolitical theatres, the West actively sought to expand the scope of war and conflict far beyond what anyone living in those places wanted. Whether in arming both sides of the Iran-Iraq War, in raising and funding the armies of the paramilitary Contras or Mujahideen or in trying to control the outcomes of the anti-colonial and anti-Apartheid struggles in Africa, the Western powers — including Canada — pursued policies that were designed to provoke and perpetuate violence. The result was catastrophic, traumatic conflicts, the effects of which are still reverberating today. It also achieved one of the paramount aims of the capitalist powers: the collapse of the Soviet Union and the final defeat of the revolutionary spirit of the 1960s.

A "Middle Power" in the Middle East

In the early Cold War, Canada had worked hard to cultivate an image as a neutral party, a "middle power" that could be relied upon to broker fair agreements between politically opposed parties. But outside of Canada, this perception was not as pervasive as many Canadians believed. This was especially evident in the Middle East; while Canadians had been told that Pearson's intervention in the Suez Crisis was a signal achievement of the new middle power, its intentions had been far more transparent than it thought. As such, when a new crisis broke out in the Arab-Israeli conflict in 1967, Canada was not welcomed into peace negotiations. In fact, as the drums of war were beating, Egyptian President Nasser specifically demanded that the Canadian contingent of the United Nations Emergency Force be expelled from Egypt, noting that "there were attempts to turn UNEF into a force serving neo-imperialism."[27]

He was not wrong. In April of 1967, Israel sent aircraft to sweep over the Syrian capital of Damascus as part of escalating war manoeuvres, but Canada barely reacted. George Ignatieff — the son of a tsarist count and a committed Canadian Zionist — was president of the UN Security Council that month and did not even convene a meeting.[28] Within a few months, Israel had launched the Six-Day War, wherein it routed the Arab armies and seized the West Bank, Gaza, the Golan Heights and the Sinai Peninsula. Canada wanted to participate in peacekeeping efforts during the crisis, hoping to maintain its middle-power standing and ensure that the peace settlement would be favourable to Israel, but the Arab states rejected Canadian participation. An Egyptian newspaper described Canada as "a stooge of the Western powers who seek to colonize the Arab world with Israel's help."[29]

Indeed, even from the sidelines, Canadian statements reflected its position: while it called for ceasefire and negotiations, it insisted that the withdrawal of Israeli forces should be tied to the settlement of other issues in the conflict, including the recognition of Israel by the Arab states. In practice, this served to reward Israel's seizure of further Arab territory; Canada created a situation wherein Israel could bargain the return of the newly seized territories in exchange for legitimation of its 1948 invasion. Ultimately, Israel would not retreat from *any* of it; when Egypt and Syria attempted to retake parts of Palestine in 1973 they were defeated and Israel emerged as the dominant military power in the region.

This, of course, was directly related to the weapons it was receiving from the West. The Arab states aligned with Nasser's Egypt had recognized that the West was backing Israel and had turned to the Soviet Union for aid and arms. Israel had, therefore, redoubled its efforts to build a highly advanced military force with the help of its Euro-American sponsors. The 1973 war was, then, clearly a Cold War showdown; the West threw its weight behind the side that guaranteed the best outcome for world capitalism, and the Soviets backed that which might undermine US power in the region. The class character of these conflicts, however, was complex. While there can be no doubt that the Israeli state was a colonial project that reflected the will of a Zionist-Israeli capitalist class, it was not entirely accurate to call the Egyptian, Syrian and Jordanian states reflective of the Arab masses in Palestine or even in their own countries.[30]

Nasser's Egypt was hostile to the West and economically nationalist, operating a corporatist state similar to that of Mexico at that time, and he was succeeded in 1970 by Anwar Sadat who was even more anti-communist and loosened Nasser's controls on the market. Indeed, after 1973, Sadat would steer Egypt back to the Western camp. Syria had, in the 1950s, drawn closer to the Soviet Union in response to the clear statements of Western interests in the Middle East during the Suez Crisis. After an unsuccessful union with Nasser's Egypt, Syria was taken over by the socialist-oriented Ba'ath Party, but power in the party was quickly consolidated by its more conservative, nationalist factions. Minor gestures towards welfare-state policies were embedded within a largely dictatorial and oligarchic state, a pattern later replicated in Iraq. Jordan, for its part, was ruled by a conservative monarchy that had only survived a wave of popular resistance in 1958 with military assistance from the United States.[31]

Thus, while each of these Arab states was ostensibly fighting for the rights of Palestinian victims of Israeli colonialism, their own motives were more complex and involved no small degree of self-interest, especially in the later stages of the Cold War. Syria tried on several occasions to occupy Lebanon. Jordan and Syria clashed over Jordan's attacks against Palestinians in the West Bank in 1970. Egypt under Sadat oriented itself to the West and gradually abandoned its support for Palestine. Thus, while in some respects the Arab-Israeli conflict pitted anti-colonial forces against the new Zionist settler colony, it could just as accurately be described as an inter-imperial struggle for regional dominance; the Arab states asserted their right to rule the Middle East largely on the basis of ethnic and national chauvinism rather than any desire to upset existing class structures.

Still, however suspect their motives, the Arab states were confronting an Israeli settler state that had displaced millions of people and was establishing an increasingly fascistic, authoritarian rule over remaining indigenous Palestinians. Canada's refusal to acknowledge this obvious and fundamental fact put it at odds with most of the international community. And still Canadian diplomats expressed shock at Arab refusals to include them in any peace negotiations: "We were very friendly to Israel," said one official, "but that does not mean we [were] against the Arabs."[32] Whether this was naïvete or wilful misdirection, it was abundantly clear that, by the 1970s, Canada sided with Israel in a dispute that left little room for neutrality. The Canadian media and political classes supported Israel, and Canada regularly voted against Palestinian claims at the UN.

In 1974, Canada voted against a motion to give the Palestine Liberation Organization (PLO) a permanent observer status — to speak on issues affecting the Middle East — a resolution described by the *Globe and Mail* as "institutionalized terrorism." The next year, the Canadian Parliament unanimously condemned a UN resolution calling Zionism a form of racism and accused the African nations in particular of "ganging up" to pass the resolution.[33] It needs be noted that Zionism is, by definition, an ideology that cannot be disentangled from racism, given that its core tenet is support for a Jewish settler state built on what was Arab territory that explicitly excludes Arabs on the basis of their being Arab.[34] Canada's support for Israel would grow stronger after the Cold War, even as widening Palestinian resistance exposed the horrifying dimensions of Israel's ethno-state ambitions. This is explored further in Chapter 12.

Meanwhile, Canada was connected to the other major struggle in the Middle East at the time, the devastating war between Iraq and Iran (1980–88), most notably in Canada's sale of $25 million in weapons to Iraq in 1981,[35] immediately following Saddam Hussein's launch of the war against Iran, with US backing. The Americans had facilitated Saddam's rise through the ranks of the Ba'ath Party — which was geared towards public spending and a welfare-state model but stopped short of being genuinely socialist — and wanted to use Iraq as a bludgeon against the new Iranian government, which had toppled a US-backed dictatorship in 1979. With the removal of the repressive Iranian monarch in that revolution, the Americans lost an important local ally; Saddam's gambit was to quickly conquer Iran before the Islamic forces that led the Iranian Revolution could consolidate. Had things gone according to his plan, Iraq would have emerged as the chief US ally in the Middle East, larger and more politically palatable than the repressive Islamic monarchy of

Saudi Arabia, poised to be the chief benefactor of American support in the region.[36]

The revolution in Iran was certainly of concern to the West. The ousted Shah Reza Pahlevi had been a valuable Cold War ally — he had purchased $60 million in Canadian weapons in the 1970s[37] — and it was unlikely that the new Islamic government in Iran would look favourably on the Shah's former sponsors. Thus, the US granted its support to Saddam's war — as did Canada — and the West encouraged a conflict that was calamitous for people in both countries. Over a million people died in a devastating and often horrifically violent eight-year struggle, and the war even provided a rare note of shame for the American puppet masters when, in 1986, it emerged that the United States had been secretly selling weapons to Iran — via Israel — even while it officially supported and armed Iraq and had given false intelligence to Saddam Hussein that the Iranian military was weak and would fall easily.[38] The macabre aim behind this policy was to maximize the carnage of that war in the hopes of weakening both sides to better maintain US dominance over the region; Canada participated in this project by, itself, selling weapons to both Iraq and Iran simultaneously.[39]

The scale of the scandal was broadened when it was discovered that profits from the secret arms sales to Iran were being funnelled to the Contras, the paramilitaries who were committing terrorist raids in Nicaragua to undermine its democratically elected socialist government. As the Iran-Contra Scandal captivated American audiences, it was revealed that the weapons being sold to Iran were financed in part by Canadian bankers and that some of the weapons and aircraft being sold to the Contras were produced by Canadian companies, like Trans World Arms and Propair. The latter even sent mechanics to help service the Contras' airplanes at their illegal paramilitary base in El Salvador.[40] Canada was ever a "helpful fixer" for its right-wing friends.

Red Menace: Canada and the Contra Wars

I was a child of the 1980s and, as such, early video games were a major part of my coming to terms with the world. My attention, like many of my friends', was rapt by the first wave of Nintendo games that swept North America, and I still remember the secret code you could enter to cheat the system and gain an infinite number of attempts to win a game called *Contra* (1987). Playing *Contra* was an adrenaline rush, though it did not require significant puzzling or problem-solving; you simply ran through the jungle shooting people who were vaguely assumed to be "bad guys." Occasionally you were expected to blow up a bridge or destroy some kind of factory. It was not until many years later that I read the game's description to discover that the enemy was an alien race called the "Red Menace."[41] The name of the game should have been a clue, but I was just a kid and the word "Contra" meant nothing to me. Had I grown up in Central America, it would have.

The Contras were paramilitary fighters trained by the United States to commit acts of violence and terror against the socialist government of Nicaragua. They killed tens of thousands of Nicaraguans, blew up bridges, factories and other infrastructure, and fomented fear of ceaseless paramilitary violence if Nicaraguans did not choose a different form of government. As Greg Grandin explained in *The Last Colonial Massacre* (2004), the Contras "destroyed cooperatives, schools, health clinics, and other government projects and murdered civilians to demonstrate to a wavering rural population that the Sandinistas could not establish effective sovereignty."[42] Terror was not simply the method, it was the goal; the Contras were vicious and unpredictable, intentionally fomenting fear to destabilize the project to build socialism. This markedly cynical strategy was, ultimately, effective in its aims. After more than a decade of US-funded terrorism, Nicaraguans grew weary and gradually acquiesced to abandoning the socialist project.

Though the war was focused on Nicaragua, the Contras were based in Honduras and attacks were also launched in Guatemala and El Salvador. The entire peninsula was engulfed in what would become, arguably, the most horrific chapter in its history, culminating in genocide and trauma that still reverberates through the collective, social consciousness of Central America. Articulating that kind of trauma is no easy task, but it is regularly invoked in scholarship on Central America.[43] Grandin captured something of the horror that befell Guatemala in particular:

> The killings were brutal beyond imagination. Soldiers murdered children by beating them with rocks as their parents watched. They extracted organs and fetuses, amputated genitalia and limbs, committed mass and multiple rapes, and burned some victims alive. In the logic that equated Indigenous culture with subversion, army units destroyed ceremonial sites and turned sacred places such as churches and caves into torture chambers. By the

time the war ended in 1996, the state had killed two hundred thousand people.[44]

Canada refused to take a consistent position regarding the civil wars that raged in Central America in the 1980s. The core motivations of Canadian policy certainly had not changed, but a series of factors intervened to occasionally give the suggestion that Canada might take a strong, principled position on one of the greatest humanitarian disasters of the era. One of those factors was that, after the election of US President Ronald Reagan on the slogan "Let's Make America Great Again," the US policy of fomenting and participating in a vicious anti-democratic conflict was an easy target for criticism. At the same time, civil society organizations in Canada were applying significant and sustained pressure on the government to take a stand against US intervention and the dictatorships it was supporting. These calls were magnified by the fact that several Canadians working in Central America were targeted for assassination.[45] Still, even with all of these forces compelling a more progressive stance, Canada was timid, at best, and duplicitous, at worst, in its calls for a more humane North American relationship to Central America. In the end, its policy would be summed up by External Affairs Minister Mark McGuigan when he promised Washington Canada's "quiet acquiescence" for its campaign of destabilization and terror.[46]

The civil wars in Central America were centred around Nicaragua, where the guerrilla struggle by the Sandinista movement against the decrepit dictatorship of the Somoza family — which had ruled since the 1930s — was able to take over the country in 1979.[47] A well-organized, deep-rooted socialist movement, the Sandinistas had toppled a regime that had been sponsored and financed by the US and Canada for half a century.[48] Still, the obvious depravity of Somoza's regime had left even the Carter administration in Washington torn between support and repudiation; in the shadow of Vietnam, Carter was trying in vain to sustain America's claim to be the leader of the free world.

Meanwhile, revolutionary guerrilla movements had emerged in both El Salvador and Guatemala, partly inspired by the Sandinistas but largely rooted in local concerns; both countries were ruled by hardline, neocolonial military regimes which served the interests of foreign capital and the local elite. These governments survived on the support they received from Washington, and the consequences of several decades of such rule in all three countries was that peasant farmers were increasingly deprived of land, which was being sucked up by wealthy landowners producing beef, coffee, sugar, cotton and bananas for the North American market. Without access to agricultural land, *campesino* families were increasingly pushed into urban centres, where work was limited and heavily exploited.[49] Endemic poverty created a well of discontent that, by the late 1970s, could no longer be contained by sporadic acts of state repression.

The victory of the Sandinistas, who easily won the first legitimate democratic election in Nicaragua in a century, was almost certainly a portent of the future for El Salvador and Guatemala. The progressive measures the Sandinistas put in place included significant land reform, promotion of food production over cash crops and massive literacy and health care programs.[50] Sandinista President Daniel Ortega won another commanding majority in the 1984 elections, and the former guerrillas illustrated, in material terms, how much better life could be with even mild reforms. Indeed, it is important to emphasize that while there were plenty of socialists in the movement, and the Sandinistas did build relationships with Cuba and the Soviet Union, this was by no means a full-fledged communist revolution. Many in Nicaragua were frustrated by the slow and sometimes tentative pace of change, a point that bears emphasis primarily because of the way the US government characterized it after the election of Ronald Reagan in 1980.[51] Notably, the Sandinista revolution sought to construct a radically democratic system and, as Katherine Hoyt argued, the Sandinistas ran considerably more democratic institutions than the regimes before or after it.[52] This revolutionary project received the solidarity of Indigenous organizations in North America, especially AIM, many of whose members went to Nicaragua to fight alongside the Sandinistas.[53]

But Reagan arrived with a mandate to destroy world communism, and his election marked a key turning point in the Cold War. Characterizing the long-suffering masses of Central America as "communist hordes" and framing the conflict as a "textbook case of indirect armed aggression by a Communist power through Cuba," the Reagan administration signalled immediately its intent to destroy the revolutionary forces in the isthmus.[54] Money and weapons poured into the armies of the dictatorships in Guatemala and El Salvador, and the United States trained, equipped and effectively led a force of some 30,000 paramilitary Contra fighters to attack, terrorize and weaken the Sandinista government in Nicaragua. The results were a catastrophic descent into what many described as hell for people living in all four countries.[55]

Body counts, in a book like this, can blur together into an abstraction that barely registers as something real. As such, it is worth highlighting that while the number of lives lost during the wars was incredibly large — hundreds of thousands — what is just as important is the horrific nature of the violence and its pervasive and chilling effect on people's lives. In Nicaragua, the Contras consciously created fear: unable to win a full-scale war, they instead targeted not just government buildings and critical infrastructure but also schools and hospitals. In El Salvador, the head of the Catholic Church, Archbishop Oscar Romero, was murdered while saying mass. In Guatemala, the class conflict took on racial dimensions, given that the country's poor majority was largely Indigenous; what ensued was a full-fledged genocide of Guatemala's Maya population.[56]

Even by the standards of the 20th century, these were dark times, and the United States was unambiguously pulling the strings. As such, Canada was in a position to distinguish itself; Reagan had few friends in this crusade, and Canada was experiencing a period of heightened nationalism around its creation of a new constitution in 1982. In addition, perhaps more than ever before, Canadian civil society groups were plugged into foreign affairs and taking an active role in trying to shape Canadian policy. External Affairs officials complained that activists would tell them, "we had a team down there last week and this is the way it is."[57] Churches, trade unions, NGOs, academics and activists — including a growing Latin American community in Canada — not only pushed the government to act, they took action themselves.[58] When the Sandinistas defeated Somoza, the dictator escaped with or destroyed much of the country's currency reserves and medical supplies; in response, Canadian activists launched Operation Solidarity, raising half a million dollars and delivering 80,000 kilos of badly needed supplies. Prime Minister Joe Clark belatedly offered aircraft to transport the supplies, which far outnumbered any direct assistance the government itself provided.[59]

The wars in Central America spanned the governments of Joe Clark, Pierre Trudeau and Brian Mulroney, but Canada's inconsistent responses to the crisis cannot be reduced to party politics. Rather, they reflect Canadian leaders' attempts to maintain domestic and international legitimacy in a context where their primary ally — strategically and ideologically — had abandoned the niceties of diplomacy and multilateralism in an effort to decisively win the Cold War and establish a new era in American-led capitalism. Canadian leaders broadly shared these goals — Canada had approved a $66 million loan to Somoza shortly before the revolution — but balked at some of the measures Reagan was willing to take in achieving them, especially insofar as they galvanized popular opposition.

Thus, in practical terms, Canada offered financial aid to the dictatorships of Guatemala and El Salvador, then reduced it to almost nothing by 1984, then gradually bumped it up again. Ultimately hundreds of millions of dollars would be made available for the dictatorships, and Canada would endorse their sham elections in 1984 (El Salvador) and 1985 (Guatemala). Canada would sometimes signal support for the Sandinistas but would inevitably fail to act on it. In one moment, Canada would claim that the guerrillas were simply a Soviet front. In the next, it would join international organizations in insisting on peaceful settlement. In the face of a migratory crisis, Canada spun from callous indifference to, in 1982, a comparatively receptive refugee program that brought in thousands of people and then, in 1987, slammed the door shut again.[60] Nonetheless, even at its height, Canada's refugee plan rejected anyone who had been connected to the guerrillas — who were often those in greatest danger — and routinely refused entry to poor *campesinos,* who would not "fit in" to Canadian society.[61] Canada rarely expressed open support for the paramilitary Contras, and yet Canadian companies sold them mortars, missiles, rocket launchers and rifle bullets.[62]

Part of the explanation for Canada's willingness to moderate its typically straightforward colonial attitude to Latin America was that the level of social chaos generated by the wars made "business as usual" an impossible task. Canadian companies that had investments in Central America often found it impractical to maintain their operations; the notorious Inco mine in Guatemala, for instance, bailed out in 1980 as falling nickel prices and guerrilla activity around the mine made it a losing venture. In Nicaragua, the Noranda mine was immediately nationalized by the new government, which not only raised the red-and-black Sandinista flag, but also raised wages by 300% and set up a variety of health and safety regulations to protect the miners who had hitherto been mercilessly exploited. Inco made no effort to salvage its holdings, knowing that to do so would have exposed its brutal labour practices, which included long shifts in shafts that reached temperatures of 60 degrees Celsius.[63] Tellingly, Canadian capital mostly chose to wait out the wars on the understanding that the outcome, however long it took, would likely be a Central America ripe for profitable investment. Indeed, as Part IV of this book illustrates, that is precisely what happened.

In 1987, the leaders of the five Central American countries initiated peace talks which would ultimately end the conflict. It was not going to be easy. The United States was refusing any kind of negotiation that did not involve the Sandinistas' dismantling the socialist state they had built and effectively bringing the terrorist Contras into government. And while all of the Central American governments were weary of the war — even those which had willingly participated — there was still the problem of 12,000 paramilitary Contras whose real boss was Ronald Reagan. In 1987, Canadian External Affairs Minister Joe Clark travelled to Nicaragua, ostensibly to support the peace process, but found himself facing heavy criticism for Canada's refusal to criticize the Contras; the criticism came from Canadian aid workers who called it a "typical spineless Canadian approach."[64] Clark even suggested that Canada could help the peace process by allowing some of the Contra fighters to emigrate to Canada; he was quickly reminded that they were violent terrorists who had been carrying out atrocities for nearly a decade and that Canada should have been condemning them, not offering them sanctuary.[65] Indeed, there was some irony in Clark's offer, given that Canada was simultaneously making it harder for legitimate refugees to get from Central America to Canada.

It was precisely those ironies and inconsistencies that seemed to mark Canada's participation in the crisis. In 1986 Prime Minister Mulroney asserted, "we do not approve of any country supplying arms to any faction in the area," despite the fact that Canada was supplying arms to the Contras.[66] While the government followed the US lead in supporting the dictatorships of Central America, Canadian popular opinion was largely against those dictatorships and the Contra Wars in general. Bruce Cockburn's popular album *Stealing Fire* (1984) included several songs that explicitly criticized the war: on "Nicaragua," he sang, "you're the best of what we are, don't let them stop you now, Nicaragua," and on "If I Had a Rocket Launcher," he effectively endorsed revolutionary violence against the Guatemalan puppet dictatorship that was carrying out genocide. The Canadian public — influenced by strong activist networks and cultural figures like Cockburn — was on the right side of history, but could not get its government to stand on the same side.

Ultimately, Canada adopted an approach that rhetorically highlighted the importance of human rights but materially emphasized bringing the various Central American countries into the capitalist restructuring process that characterized the neoliberal period. That is, Canada pushed structural-adjustment policies (SAPS) upon Central American governments that would lead to privatization of public services, limiting of government regulations and openness to foreign capital.[67] In exchange for such policies, Canada would increasingly provide aid and support for the peace process, which only really got underway when the Sandinistas failed to win the 1990 elections in Nicaragua.

That electoral loss, hardly surprising given a decade of civil war and violence that it had not been able to withstand, was what the Americans needed to support the demobilization of the Contras. The US had got its wish: popular socialism had been defeated, drenched in a river of blood that had engulfed the entire isthmus and traumatized millions of people. By 1996, more than 70% of Nicaraguans had been plunged back into poverty,[68] and things were as bad or worse elsewhere. Though overshadowed by the wars in Central America, the Reagan and Bush administrations bookended the Contra Wars with invasions of smaller nearby countries — Grenada in 1983 and Panama in 1989 — to which Canada offered no rebuke. In the latter case, Brian Mulroney expressed his regret at the use of violence, which killed 4000 Panamanians, but ensured Canadians that "the US was justified."[69]

The Western states also maintained steady support for the Philippine dictatorship of Ferdinand Marcos — which killed tens of thousands — and Pierre Trudeau visited him in Manila in 1983. When the winds shifted against Marcos in 1986, the Western powers allowed the victory of a popular movement to overthrow him. Canada then offered aid to the new government, provided it agree to the International Monetary Fund's "policy recommendations."[70] The new government was perfectly willing to accept these terms; it had opposed Marcos but was largely rooted in the Filipino oligarchy and proceeded to carry out repression against genuinely revolutionary groups in the country, including many that had helped overthrow Marcos.

Canada, Cabora Bossa and Apartheid

Canada's entire Cold War history had been marked by discomfort with the waves of decolonization and the wider global rebellion of the 1960s. When civil rights leader Martin Luther King Jr. asked Prime Minister Diefenbaker to take a stronger stand against South African Apartheid in 1957, Diefenbaker dismissed the idea. Canada disapproved of racism everywhere, he insisted, so there should be no reason to single out one country; it was a rhetorical turn that Canada would repeat some fifty years later with respect to another conspicuously segregated settler colony in Israel.[71]

Canada's relations with South Africa had been very close since the Boer War, after which many Canadians stayed in South Africa to help build what would become the basis for Apartheid. Canadians helped establish concentration camps and a colonial administration that heavily favoured the Boer settler minority. As early as 1906 and as late as 1962, Canada and South Africa were exchanging ideas on the practices of settler colonialism; South African officials were given tours of the reserves and residential schools in which Canada was carrying out a slow genocide that the Boers sought to replicate.[72] A Canadian diplomat in Pretoria, reporting in 1944, denied that non-whites were poorly treated in South Africa, even while he himself described black South Africans as "a very low type," who were "perfectly dumb and appear to have little brain capacity," but who needed to be kept down lest they "create much more trouble in this country than the Negroes do in the United States."[73]

During the Second World War, Prime Minister King found himself infatuated with South African Prime Minister Jan Christian Smuts, who fought in the Boer War, signed the peace treaties after both world wars and was an ardent supporter and architect of racial segregation throughout his career. Smuts had lived a lifetime at the beating heart of a colonial project, and he and King supported a resolution in 1945 to "preserve their identity as white groups and the high standard of living they enjoyed."[74] But Smuts also anticipated the wave of communist and anti-colonial sentiment that would be unleashed by World War Two, which had by necessity awakened the age of mass politics; "with politics let loose among these peoples," he worried, "we might have a wave of disorder and wholesale communism."[75]

Smuts had articulated precisely the fear that lay at the heart of the Cold War West. Indeed, what is perhaps most striking in Canada's responses to Apartheid was the extent to which Canada tried to balance its desire to support the South African government with its awareness that doing so might further discredit Canada and lead to greater support for the communist bloc. One Canadian official worried in 1946 about the discussion of racial issues in South Africa at the UN, wherein the communist bloc might "have a field day in the capacity [of] champions and representatives of the oppressed peoples," leaving "the Soviet Union as the clear winner in this round of the important battle... for the loyalties of the coloured and colonial peoples."[76]

Thus, a guiding principle in Canadian policy towards Apartheid was to quietly support its ally unless and until it became politically impossible to do so. One such moment came in 1960, after the massacre of more than 200 people at Sharpeville. The outrage this event generated was such that Canada could no longer afford to appear to callously support South Africa (as it had in nearly every UN discussion or vote up to that point). Initially, Diefenbaker had stuck to the usual routine, but by 1961, several factors intervened to persuade him to take a hard line. Public opinion in Canada was largely against South Africa, especially after a Canadian journalist was arrested and deported for his coverage of Sharpeville. Moreover, Diefenbaker's more astute advisors recognized that, in the midst of the decolonization of Africa, it would be wise for Canada to present itself as an ally; this would, in the Diefenbaker administration's calculations, reduce the likelihood of communist forces gaining greater traction in Africa. As such, Canada supported the call for South Africa's expulsion from the Commonwealth.[77]

Though hailed as a crowning achievement of Canadian moral fortitude, it was anything but; Diefenbaker only briefly broke ranks with the other white powers in the Commonwealth and did so for strategic reasons, before immediately falling back into a pattern of quiet support for South Africa. In fact, it was the leaders of the other Commonwealth countries that had made it happen, particularly Jawaharlal Nehru and Julius Nyerere, who had effectively promised the other Commonwealth leaders that they would abandon it if South Africa remained. Fearing that an organization it found politically valuable would lose its significance, Canada grudgingly fell in line with the non-white leaders on this one occasion. This was emblematic of Canada's relationship to Apartheid, as later events would illustrate, and it reflected the dynamics of the 1960s; while Canada remained committed to its colonial and capitalist foundation, the realities of a powerful socialist bloc and a wave of anti-colonial movements and struggles was forcing Canada to make exceptions, to give ground and to cultivate an image as a trustworthy partner for the decolonizing world.

It was not. In those places where the decolonizing forces could not be stopped, Canada often acted to blunt the edge of their rejection of European colonialism in an effort to prevent them from shifting to the communist bloc, either in geostrategic relations with the Soviet Union or in terms of local economic policy or both. Canada worked to generate alliances and agreements with the former French colonies in Africa in an effort to build a Francophone alliance to stem the growing radicalism of pan-African leaders like Kwame Nkrumah and Julius Nyerere. Seeking to mitigate the loss of the British colony of Tanzania in 1961, Canada offered military aid and training after consulting with British officials who were fearful that the country would join the socialist camp. Canada exaggerated the threat posed by Nyerere, describing "a real danger [of] a communist country being given this golden opportunity to increase very substantially its influence in East Africa." Still, Canada set up the military agreement with Nyerere and used its close positioning to the Tanzanian government to spy on FRELIMO, the socialist independence movement fighting from Tanzania to liberate Mozambique.[78] Nyerere grew weary and suspicious of the Canadian presence and kicked them out in 1969; this was no doubt influenced by Canada's training of the Ghanaian military to overthrow Kwame Nkrumah only a few years prior.

It was Nyerere's government that eventually brought an end to the tyranny of another Canadian ally, Uganda's Idi Amin. Amin seized power in a British-orchestrated coup in 1971, overthrowing elected, left-leaning President Milton Obote, and Canadian officials praised "a move that promises to be an improvement" over the former government "favoured by the communists."[79] Amin's regime killed as many as 500,000 of his opponents and, in 1973, Canadian officials met with Amin just months after he was widely criticized for having expelled tens of thousands of South Asians from the country. Rather than use the opportunity to criticize the dictator, Ottawa was reassured that Bata Shoes had a new partnership with the government (the Obote government had nationalized its holdings) and Falconbridge was satisfied with the treatment of its Kilembe copper mines. By 1977, Canada had even established a new high commission in Amin's Uganda, but the dictator was erratic and began drifting into alliance with the Soviet Union, despite his utter lack of left-wing politics, thus losing favour in the West. He was overthrown in 1979 by Nyerere's Tanzanian military and democracy was briefly restored in Uganda.

Even after much of the colonized world had successfully achieved its independence — albeit often under neocolonial conditions — the fascist dictatorship in Portugal under António Salazar (and later Marcello Caetano) refused to relinquish its grip on Angola, Mozambique, Guinea-Bissau and other colonies in Africa. Salazar, like Franco in Spain, had been allowed to remain neutral during the Second World War despite the obviously fascistic nature of his rule. An admirer of Mussolini, Salazar was repressive in Portugal itself, and even more brutal in the colonies; in just one example from 1960, some 500 unarmed protestors were massacred by Portuguese authorities at Mueda.[80] The widespread violence of the colonial regime prompted ever more determined resistance, and, as momentum towards decolonization grew, Salazar and Caetano worked closely with the Apartheid state in South Africa to maintain the Portuguese position, such that between 1960 and 1973 well over 50,000 Africans — maybe as many as 100,000 — were killed in the colonies.

As early as 1966, the United Nations was condemning Portuguese colonialism and voting for economic sanctions; Canada consistently voted against these resolutions, in part because Canada was purchasing products like oil, kept cheap by Portugal's aggressively low labour standards. Instead of criticizing Portugal, Canada harped on the need for non-violence from the Africans, whose liberty was being prevented by violence. For its consistent support of Portuguese colonialism — and for its selling and even donating weapons to Portugal for use against Africans[81] — Canada was directly condemned in 1973 in the official publication of FRELIMO, the independence movement in Mozambique.[82]

Canada's most noteworthy involvement in the Portuguese colonial project was around the controversial Cabora Bassa Dam in Mozambique, a project designed to disrupt the advance of the FRELIMO rebels and deepen relations with Southern Rhodesia (Zimbabwe), a white settler state similar in nature to Apartheid South Africa.[83] Several Canadian companies won contracts associated with the dam, most notably Alcan, which provided aluminum rods for the massive project. This was undertaken in spite of a UN resolution condemning Cabora Bassa and after several other potential suppliers had refused to participate in what would constitute a breaking of economic sanctions against Rhodesia.[84]

Cabora Bassa was not just a hydroelectric dam; it was the centrepiece of a major colonial operation which was designed to create a new settler enclave for Portuguese workers and paramilitaries in Northern Mozambique. Among the plans for Cabora Bassa's development were military infrastructure such that it could be used as a base of counter-insurgency warfare against FRELIMO.[85] In 1968, Portugal had begun clearing the region of its indigenous inhabitants, to make space for the wave of Portuguese settlement; hundreds were killed, thousands fled to refugee camps across the Zambian border, and thousands more were placed in concentration camps. The parallels to Canada's clearing of the plains are striking, and it must be emphasized that the plan was undertaken with an eye to regional politics; South Africa and Southern Rhodesia were intimately involved in the project, economically, politically and militarily.[86] In Cabora Bassa, the white settlers of Southern Africa saw all of their interests aligned.

Indeed, in many respects, the period from the early 1970s to the early 1990s constituted a single, regional war in Southern Africa between two groupings of forces: one was predominantly left in orientation and — joined by Cuba and the Soviet Union — was fighting for indigenous African freedom. The other was made up of the mainstays of colonial reaction, which included the Portuguese and the governments of South Africa and Southern Rhodesia along with their Western colonial sponsors. Furthermore, while the conflict was often framed as being solely about freedom from colonial rule — or opposition to the specific racial dynamic of Apartheid in South Africa — the reality was that this was a struggle over the future class character of Southern Africa. At the centre of the resistance, from Mozambique to Namibia to Soweto, was a commitment to building a better, fairer, safer world. In short, the resistance was predominantly rooted in the principles of the left.[87]

The tipping point into all-out war was when the Portuguese dictatorship collapsed after its soldiers refused to keep fighting in Africa in 1974. With Portugal removed from the picture, it was the beginning of the end of traditional, direct colonial rule, but other forms of colonial and neocolonial domination remained. Those fighting for African independence were increasingly labelled "terrorists," especially by the Apartheid regime in South Africa, just one signal of the coming shift in the language applied to the enemies of Western capitalism and colonialism.[88] When Angola declared its independence, it was almost immediately invaded by South Africa (which would also invade Mozambique while trying to maintain its grip over an independence struggle in Namibia and resistance to the Apartheid system itself), but the Angolan revolutionaries found they had friends: thousands of troops arrived from Cuba to support the popular movement for freedom in Angola, to which Canada reacted "with horror."[89]

Given Canada's interest in maintaining a colonized Africa under the firm control of European power and capital, the presence of Cuban troops in Angola probably did generate horror for the Canadian establishment. The presence of Cuba's forces, indeed, made a significant difference in the regional civil war between the forces of liberation and reaction in Southern Africa.[90] The Apartheid state of South Africa had long shared a "special relationship" with Canada, but the systematized, legalized racial segregation of all aspects of South African life had become a dinosaur in the 1980s.

This is not to say that extreme colonial racism and marginalization, usually anchored in limited economic opportunity, was not a common element of the capitalist world; it most certainly was. But after the cascading swells of the Holocaust, the broadening communist challenge, global rebellion and decolonization, the civil rights movement and the Vietnam War, openly avowing to a formally racist system of government was not a good look for South Africa and its allies. Other settler colonies, like Canada and Australia, had long ago learned to frame their colonial projects as benign and marginalization as a thing of the past, even if this was not the case. Even Israel, which was rapidly developing a similar model, was careful about openly asserting its supposed racial superiority.

As such, South Africa became an increasingly difficult ally for the West, especially as the wars in Southern Africa were exposing the barbarity of Apartheid to a wider audience, generating a backlash in popular culture that could not but increase the pressure on Western governments to back down from decades of support for the racist regime. When Canadians reflect on these events, they are often encouraged to take pride in the strong stand that their governments took in opposition to Apartheid. Images of Brian Mulroney and Nelson Mandela in 1994 immortalized what appeared to be a heroic stand that the Canadian prime minister had taken. But, as Linda Freeman documents, the mythology that claims for Canada both a lead role in the fall of Apartheid and motives driven by moral obligation is little more than hagiography obscuring a much more self-interested legacy.[91]

The Complicated End of Apartheid

Prior to the Second World War, Canada barely gave a thought to South Africa's racial segregation. Over a roughly similar timeline to Canada, South Africa had been granted its independence from Britain and had maintained a white supremacist state which targeted not only the indigenous black population but also a large number of Indians. In the late 1940s, the issue became more difficult as the newly independent Indian state was insisting on better treatment of the Indian minority there. At the same time, in 1948, South Africa's far-right National Party, which had supported the Nazis, won the elections and created the formalized policy apparatus known as Apartheid, an Afrikaans word meaning "separate development."

The Diefenbaker government largely avoided criticizing Apartheid and even sold weapons to the regime, convinced that it was a valuable anti-communist ally. Pearson, for his part, helped ensure the survival of the white dictatorship in Rhodesia (Zimbabwe), which would be a key ally for South Africa in the critical decades of the 1970s and 1980s. The regime in Rhodesia had emerged in 1965 from the British colony called Southern Rhodesia, when the white settlers declared independence from Britain in order to avoid demands for more political representation for black people. The UN placed trade sanctions on Rhodesia, but they were widely violated by its primary trading partners in South Africa and the Portuguese colonies and even by businesses based in the West. Well into the 1970s, the Canadian company Falconbridge was still operating the Blanket Mine, which was described by a journalist writing for the *Montreal Gazette* as "a slave labour mine" and "a disgusting example of a Canadian company exploiting black workers."[92] Canada did nothing to stop Falconbridge, claiming no knowledge of ties between the company and the mine.[93]

The Pierre Trudeau government blustered its abhorrence at the racist systems in Rhodesia and South Africa but stubbornly refused to effect any meaningful interventions. In fact, even after South African police killed hundreds of students in Soweto in 1976, Trudeau insisted that Canada "[would] not interfere in trade or investment."[94] Indeed, many US companies invested in South Africa through Canadian subsidiaries because it was easier. Meanwhile, Trudeau sent RCMP officers to liaise and assist the Apartheid government's police, and he assisted the government in developing the capacity to produce nuclear weapons.[95] The Trudeau government saw South Africa as a key piece in the regional struggle against communism; arms dealers had no problem selling to South Africa and Western governments did little to stop them. By contrast, the liberation movements fighting against Apartheid and for freedom in Namibia, Rhodesia and the Portuguese colonies were denied access to any support because of their "violent methods." NATO maintained close links with the South African military and shared intelligence and strategy. South Africa purchased a "supergun" howitzer from Canadian Gerald Bull's Space Research Corporation, which it used in its invasion of Angola and Namibia.[96]

In effect, South Africa was a Cold War ally in a significant regional conflict, and the Apartheid system itself was little more than a PR nuisance which the West was willing to work around. Southern Africa was in the throes of serious class struggle; it was either Apartheid or a socialist revolution. This was placed in sharp relief by Cuba's decision to send thousands of troops to fight alongside Angolan socialists to defend the country's independence after the invasion by South Africa. Cuba's intervention prompted a sudden break in Canadian-Cuban relations, as Washington and Ottawa decried Cuba's actions as Soviet puppetry that would be a harm to peace. The former claim was known to be false — the Soviet Union had no knowledge of Cuba's plans and the move was motivated by nothing more than solidarity with Angolan resistance to the vile South African regime — and the latter claim was patently absurd, as Pretoria's troops were tearing through Angola towards Luanda at that very moment.[97]

Through the Trudeau governments and into the Mulroney era, there was a solid core of support in Canada for Apartheid: Canadian business mogul Conrad Black believed the white South Africans "should be commended for having the collective pride and motivation to defend themselves."[98] They did so with a $1 billion credit from the IMF in 1982; Canada's vote was decisive in getting the loan approved. Indeed, pro-Apartheid lobby groups and business associations like the Western Canadian Society of South Africa and the Canadian-South African Society were buttressed by right-wing journalists like Peter Worthington and even the husband of Canada's governor general, Jeanne Sauvé.[99] Activist networks opposed to Apartheid in Canada met stony silence from politicians and most media outlets, and business as usual was barely interrupted.

So how did Canada construct the mythology that it had been the saviour of black South Africa? The catalyst for this narrative was the Brian Mulroney government's adoption of serious economic sanctions in 1986, a somewhat stunning turn of events that reflected both Mulroney's awareness that the tides were shifting and also concern that if the West did not take charge of the transition from Apartheid the result would be communism. Indeed, a transformative moment in Mulroney's approach to South Africa was a speech by former Australian Prime Minister Malcolm Fraser warning that if the conflict were allowed to escalate "the government that emerged from all of this would be extremely radical, probably Marxist, and would nationalize all Western business interests."[100] It was the stuff of Mulroney's nightmares.

Suddenly, circumstances conspired to make a harder line on South Africa palatable and even expedient: black South Africans were in revolt, Rhodesia had fallen, the Namibian resistance was growing, and the days of Apartheid were clearly numbered.[101] As such, Mulroney was presented with an opening to take a moral stand that he would congratulate himself on for the rest of his career, even though in practical terms it fizzled out within a couple of years. Moreover, he was compelled to action by the growing wellspring of popular organizing in Canada — in the churches, NGOs, trade unions and communist parties — parallel and sometimes connected to that around the Central American crisis.[102] Still, for all of Mulroney's talk, Canadian sanctions were among the weakest — weaker even than those of the US — and trade during the seven years of sanctions still totalled $1.6 billion. When Mulroney met with Oliver Tambo of Nelson Mandela's African National Congress (ANC) party in 1987, he delivered a lesson on the ills of communism and terrorism, concerned as he was by the ANC's left politics and ties to the Soviet Union.[103]

That same year, South Africa's ambassador to Canada travelled the country trying to rekindle support for the Apartheid government, claiming that Apartheid itself was already being reformed and that continuing with hard sanctions would only weaken the forces trying to preserve capitalism and freedom from the communist ANC. In addition to the anti-communist angle, he played up racial ideas that he knew existed in Canada as in South Africa, emphasizing the "chaos" and violence of allowing blacks to govern, reinforcing the idea that non-whites are violent by nature and require white rule to contain their inherent aggression. He also generated minor public embarrassment for Canada by touring the Peguis First Nation Reserve, effectively illustrating the hypocrisy of Canada's moral stand on Apartheid. It was a canny manoeuvre that helped to blunt Mulroney's offensive, though most Indigenous people in Canada rejected the support of the equally vile Apartheid regime,[104] and indeed the more radical Indigenous groups that came out of the Red Power movement were deeply linked to the struggle against Apartheid.[105]

By the end of that year, Mulroney's opposition to Apartheid had been reduced to little more than rhetoric. Linda Freeman concludes that Mulroney's government "had its moments [but] it also had its weaknesses, compromises, and ambiguities."[106] Compromise might be valuable in some circumstances, but this was one of the most ruthless white supremacist governments on the planet. If ever there was a time for certainty and decisiveness, Apartheid South Africa fit the bill. Ultimately, the Apartheid regime was brought down, and Canada did, briefly, play a role in that. Credit for this needs to be given where it is due: persistent and principled critique of Canada's support for Apartheid by significant civil society mobilization within Canada which pressured politicians to act, which was itself spurred by the broader international groundswell of opposition to Apartheid.[107] That campaign would not have been possible without the long, painful battle waged by the masses of people in South Africa, Namibia, Zimbabwe and across all of Southern Africa over several decades, to say nothing of the intervention by Cuban forces. While Brian Mulroney briefly stepped onto the right side of history when it was political expedient to do so, the defeat of Apartheid was a victory won by the people.

And it was not the end: in the last years of Apartheid, the regime took advantage of the support it continued to receive from Western governments to lay the groundwork for a post-Apartheid South Africa that would remain capitalist and deeply — if informally — unequal.[108] This was a dynamic reflected across much of Southern Africa; already, by 1992, Canada was investing in mining in Namibia, cashing in on the weakness and dislocation of a country that had only just shaken off the yoke of South African invasion.[109] Meanwhile, Canada, after having labelled the ANC a "terrorist" organization for years, began to work with the party in 1984 in the hopes that it could "strengthen the hand of black moderates," as Joe Clark asserted. Canada would thus play a role in shaping the conditions for neoliberalism in the 1990s.[110]

Indeed, as Chris Webb notes, one complicated legacy of the anti-Apartheid struggle was that in order to earn the legitimacy needed to generate support from Western governments, the ANC had to distance itself somewhat from the anti-capitalist politics that had made it such a compelling force in the first place. John Saul, a long-time activist in solidarity with the struggle against Apartheid, pointedly asked whether the efforts to make the ANC "safe" for a government like Mulroney's had the effect of weakening its position vis-à-vis capital, such that post-Apartheid South Africa was vulnerable to the neoliberal onslaught that kept many black South Africans poor and marginalized.[111] As Saul wrote in 2011, the goal of the West was "to safeguard capital's long-run stake in a new South Africa" and to "water down the liberation impulse" within the ANC "at the expense of the hopes and aspirations of the vast mass of people." Canada, Saul concluded, had been a "junior but active partner" in this project.[112]

In fact, the sacrifices and difficulties presented by the struggle against white rule in Southern Africa — Portuguese, British and Boer — were such that many of the post-Apartheid states were unable to maintain the revolutionary left politics they initially asserted. Mozambique, once a centre of African socialist politics, was devastated by the wars and, in desperate need of capital for reconstruction and development, was sucked into the IMF–World Bank nexus.[113] Similar problems afflicted Tanzania, Angola, Zimbabwe, Namibia and other African states where socialism was, at some point in the late 20th century, a popular and viable option. Thus, while the defeat of Apartheid itself was undeniably positive, the post-Apartheid experience was not unfavourable to the ruling classes and fit into the emerging dynamics of the post–Cold War era. Explicit segregation and institutionalized racism had been eliminated, but capitalism — and the indirect segregation and racism that it brought — was maintained and even strengthened in the aftermath of Apartheid.

The Defeat of the Soviet Union

The Cold War ended, to the surprise of many, with a whimper. In spite of all those missiles and the many decades of claims that the Soviets would launch a surprise attack, such an attack never happened. Instead, a series of reforms began to take shape in the mid-1980s under Mikhail Gorbachev, which effectively unravelled the decaying state. Gorbachev did not originally intend to end the Soviet Union; in fact, he was attempting to apply calculated reforms to resolve problems of slowed growth and an entrenched bureaucracy. But his efforts to modernize the socialist economy were met with skepticism from many officials, who saw a potential threat to their own relatively comfortable positions. Gorbachev responded by trying to mobilize popular support for his reforms; the *glasnost* policies of wider political freedom, combined with minor market reforms known as *perestroika*, were designed to give Gorbachev the backing he needed to overcome those factions of the bureaucracy that were resisting change.[114]

This delicate plan backfired: ambitious members of the bureaucracy who could see the system overheating used the new space afforded to them by *glasnost* to press their advantage, and Gorbachev found himself on the defensive. Unable to manage the forces he had unleashed, Gorbachev spiralled between trying to push wider reform and trying to contain those reforms. In 1989, he could no longer resist pressure from the Eastern European republics for a break from Soviet leadership, and in 1991 the USSR itself fell apart. Boris Yeltsin, head of the new Russian Federation, usurped what was left of Soviet authority and initiated a process that would culminate in "shock therapy," a traumatic and chaotic dismantling of the apparatus of public institutions and Soviet infrastructure, to be replaced by market capitalism. "Shock therapy" — the brainchild of a group of Western economists, most notably Harvard University's Jeffery Sachs — utterly pulverized the material well-being of millions of people in the former-Soviet bloc and had significant consequences for the post-Soviet world. Up to 70% of Soviet state assets had been privatized by 1994, creating 40 new billionaires and leaving some 60 million people in poverty.[115] Gorbachev himself was featured in a 1997 Russian television ad for Pizza Hut, which explicitly tried to frame the transition to capitalism as a victory for freedom and ended with customers hailing Gorbachev with raised pizzas.

The internal pressures that had built up in the Soviet Union were compounded by similar pressures in Eastern Europe, which had led to increasing episodes of rebellion against Soviet authority. Most famously, these occurred in Hungary in 1956 and Czechoslovakia in 1968; the latter, dubbed the "Prague Spring," had taken place concurrent to the massive upheavals in the capitalist world. Its repression by Soviet tanks represented a crushing disappointment not just for Czech leftists, who wanted to pursue an independent socialist project, but for people of the international left, to whom it was now utterly clear that the USSR could not be relied upon as a genuine source of support for the kind of world revolution most wanted to see.[116] Though discontent was kept in check by Soviet coercion, it continued to simmer and exploded again in Poland in the 1980s; as the Soviet Union itself struggled to maintain a functional state apparatus in the late 1980s, it lost its capacity to manage the affairs of its satellite states. Beginning with the fall of the Berlin Wall in 1989, the republics of Eastern Europe each seceded from the Soviet Bloc and were quickly co-opted by the Western powers eager to feast upon the vast new economies opened up to capital.[117]

Indeed, the collapse of the USSR was as much caused by internal Soviet contradictions as it was by the aggressive posture of the United States and its allies in the 1980s. The Western ruling classes were on the offensive, crushing workers' rights in their own countries, slashing taxes for the rich and enshrining radically favourable terms for capital into free trade agreements with poor countries under their control. As they imposed austerity and more intense exploitation on the working classes within their own camp, they ratcheted up both the rhetoric and the practice of the Cold War, dragging the Soviets into a new and expensive arms race while continuing to fund and foment conflicts that would drain Soviet resources.[118] The most notable among these was in Afghanistan, but the conflicts in Central America and Southern Africa were also significant, as were the many theatres around the world where the USSR was funding resistance movements to oppressive right-wing governments with Western backing.[119] For the Soviet Union, the cost of maintaining its military rivalry with the US — and keeping up its commitment to support socialist revolutions abroad — was directly impeding its ability to improve the economy. Caught in the nexus of these contradictions, it appeared in retrospect that the fall of the Soviet Union was inevitable, though it came as a great shock to many in both camps at the time.

The fall of the Soviet Union was greeted by the ruling classes in Canada with much enthusiasm; an enemy they had sought to vanquish from its inception in 1917 had finally fallen. In the early 1980s, Joe Clark's government had effectively suspended relations with the USSR while demanding its "immediate withdrawal" from Afghanistan,[120] where the Soviets were fighting against the US-backed Islamists known as the Mujahideen, or holy warriors, which famously included Osama Bin Laden. Indeed, the US spent some $10 billion to maintain the Mujahideen militants and draw the Soviets into an unwinnable war, which would drain Soviet resources and morale. It was successful in that aim, and Canada helped to keep up that pressure, as Chapter 11 details. The cost, of course, was millions of Soviet and Afghan lives, the destruction of Afghan political institutions and physical infrastructure, the establishment of highly armed right-wing Islamic paramilitaries, who would fight over the scraps of Afghanistan for another decade while violently imposing sharp restrictions on Afghan society, and ultimately the creation of a safe haven for the plotters of the attacks of September 11, 2001, which would initiate the disastrous era of the War on Terror. The collateral damage of defeating the "Evil Empire" was incalculable.

After a brief and inconsequential period of détente by the Trudeau government, which left Soviet officials "absolutely baffled," the Mulroney government quickly reasserted Canada's tough line on the Soviet Union. In 1987, Mulroney claimed that Gorbachev's USSR had "violated virtually all of the principles guiding relations between states" in Afghanistan, a statement laden with irony given Canada's support for the US intervention there and, of course, Canada's own intervention little over a decade later.[121] But as the Soviet Union rapidly unravelled in 1989, Canada smelled blood and shifted its position to one of support for Gorbachev, now dubbed a "genuine reformer." As Gorbachev trod the road to capitalism, Canada opened its arms and its wallet, seeking opportunities for profitable investment in the market it had wanted to access in 1917. As the Canadian state locked in agreements for the protection of private capital, Canadian business pledged nearly $1 billion in investment. The opening of a joint Soviet-Canadian MacDonald's restaurant in Moscow's Pushkin Square in 1990 was as clear a sign as any that capitalism had arrived.[122]

Canada simultaneously offered massive "assistance programs" to the countries of Eastern Europe in order to establish the architecture necessary to facilitate an investment boom. The Canadian government was particularly assertive in quickly recognizing the independence of the former Soviet Republics, most notably Ukraine. Canada had cultivated a relationship with far-right Ukrainian nationalists — including former Nazi collaborators admitted to Canada after the war — and this immigrant community exercised some influence over Canadian policy in a dynamic not unlike the effect of the Miami Cubans in the United States. In 1991, Canada broke from its allies to be the first Western power to recognize Ukrainian independence and offer it new credits.[123] As Chapter 12 documents, Canada emerged as one of the chief supporters of the Ukrainian far-right in its ongoing rivalry with Russia.

The collapse of the Soviet Union heralded a triumphant reaction in the West, which claimed a moral, as well as political and economic victory, which seemed to retroactively justify every terrible deed that had been done in the past eight decades to that end. Capitalism, it was declared, was the "end of history," the highest point in human civilization. This system won, the argument went, because it was rational, it was right, it was civilized. Henceforth, everyone would get to share in the great prosperity that it showered upon its constituents, provided they worked hard and were deserving of those rewards. That this claim was largely a myth — that capitalism was, in fact, growing dramatically more unequal, that it had required horrific violence to sustain its Cold War position and that its alarming environmental consequences were beginning to appear — was hardly going to spoil the celebration.

Enmity between Canada and the Soviet Union had seen only brief intermissions in the 20th century, and, for the most part, Canada did whatever it could to contribute to the ultimate collapse of Soviet communism. Though constantly presented as a humanitarian concern, such nonsense hardly cut muster even at the time. Canada's goals were entirely rooted in the ideological rivalry that engulfed both sides and the very real sense that victory by one could only be achieved by defeat of the other. Nevertheless, the "Soviet threat" to Canada was consistently used in fearmongering anti-communist propaganda across an endless number of books, magazines, journals and pamphlets.[124] Ironically, one of the motifs of Canadian anti-communist propaganda was its denunciation of communist propaganda; in 1954, one Canadian official excoriated the Soviet Union for the psychological manipulation of circulating newspapers. "If somebody reads a paper for a considerable length of time," explained the official, "he will absorb at least something of the offered propaganda."[125] This, of course, is precisely how all politically oriented publications operate, not the least of which were those in Canada, which ranged from the prominent daily newspapers to the anti-communist "Alert" pamphlets circulated by right-wing citizens groups.[126]

Soviet Nostalgia and the Making of Vladimir Putin

Sifting through the back-and-forth accusations of overzealous ideologues for several decades is an overwhelming process that can leave one distanced from any sense of truth. Indeed, decades since the end of the Cold War, the fog has not really lifted; given the outcome, the story told by the West largely passed into accepted wisdom, despite its often being out of step with reality. Nevertheless, the real and unavoidable failures and shortcomings of the Soviet Union pose a challenge for anyone seeking an honest reckoning with this history. To draw up a sincere balance sheet that measures the positives and negatives brought to people's lives — within and beyond the borders of the USSR itself — is a difficult task, especially in the Anglo-American world that has been so saturated with anti-Soviet propaganda.[127] By contrast, researchers from elsewhere had no problem delineating both the successes and failures of the USSR. In *Re-Emerging Russia* (2017), Indian scholars Anuradha M. Chenoy and Rajan Kumar offer a thoughtful overview of the experience, noting not just the creation of an advanced industrial economy, universal literacy, defeat of Nazi Germany, secure jobs and housing for all and achievements in science and technology, but also that "it created an ideational structure which countered the hegemony of Western liberalism and capitalist economy with a socialist philosophy."[128]

The very existence of the Soviet Union provided an inspiration for a better world for the poor and marginalized, and the USSR often gave material support to those struggles. Still, while it dramatically improved the lives of millions of people around the world, it also failed to live up to many of its promises: it closed off the democratic channels that might have strengthened its cause, it developed what Chenoy and Kumar called a "dictatorship of the clique," and it adhered too long to policies which undermined its goals — with sometimes disastrous results, as in cases like the famine in Ukraine — ultimately establishing a structure that could not survive the reforms it needed by the 1980s.[129] Still, for all its faults, there is no pride to be taken in Canada's contribution to destroying this flawed attempt to build a better society; Canada by no means offered a better alternative for the masses.

Indeed, the post-Soviet experience in Russia and Eastern Europe was a nightmare, so much so that opinion polls showed a majority of people every year — save 2012 when it dropped to 49% — pining for a return to the days of the USSR and centrally planned economies, with the attendant security of guaranteed housing, education, transportation, wages, public services, pensions and so on.[130] In post-Soviet Russia, the collapse of the rouble wiped out peoples' savings and led farmers to horde food, exacerbating hunger in the cities. Pensions dried up, hospitals shut down, and property was snapped up by the rich, creating a new class of billionaires while poverty afflicted as much as 50% of the population in the late 1990s.[131]

Canadian capital played a role in the dismantling of Soviet infrastructure, licking its lips in the early 1990s about the prospect of "conquering

Europe" and accessing the post-Soviet market.¹³² A triumphant victory, indeed, as Western capital preyed upon the vulnerability of millions of people suddenly bereft of the economic security they had possessed for their entire lives, while denigrating them for "lack of work incentives" and "bad habits." Indeed, one Canadian business writer unintentionally exposed the core of Canada's attitude when he complained that, in post-Soviet economies, it was "difficult to get local managers to think in terms of profits and market measures of performance, rather than simply quantity of output or planned measures of performance."¹³³ Put differently, it was hard to shift people away from thinking about how to provide the best service, to instead focus on how to make the most profit. I find myself entirely unconvinced that the latter is a more rational way to think.

For working people, the defeat of the Soviet Union was disastrous. "The outcome of privatizations," as Chenoy and Kumar explain, "was catastrophic for the economy and the people — except for a few oligarchs who amassed wealth by stripping the state assets."¹³⁴ Among those oligarchs was Vladimir Putin, who would emerge in the early 2000s as a new capitalist dictator in Russia, who consolidated a kind of state capitalist economy, wherein key resources like oil and gas were renationalized but the core of the economy remained capitalist and exploitative. The emergence of Putin as an outspoken critic of the United States, and the assertion of Russia as part of a rival imperialist bloc, restored some sense of dignity to Russians, who felt shamed by Western chauvinism and triumphalism after the Cold War.¹³⁵

But Putin's rule did not improve the lives of most Russians; indeed, Putin is part of the legacy of the West's victory in the Cold War, since his rise to power was made possible by precisely the conditions the West imposed in the 1990s. By the 2010s, Putin's role in that rival bloc of capital would be a significant mitigating factor in the West's ability to impose its will in the War on Terror — most notably in Syria — and Canada would find itself provoking further conflict with Putin along the Russian-Ukrainian border. But Putin was ideologically on the right; in 2017, the Russian state ignored the 100th anniversary of the October Revolution and created a "National Unity Day" in its place.¹³⁶

Assessing how and why the USSR crumbled is a task beyond the scope of this book, but it is worth considering — given Canada's role in its defeat — whether the Soviet experiment might have yielded more impressive results if it had not been under attack from its very inception. It is impossible to say, since Soviet leaders were preoccupied with the fact that the West was trying to destroy it. The constant preoccupation with defence caused the USSR to divert resources away from valuable public services in order to project military power. Canada had participated in the project to create nuclear weapons, a feat the West accomplished and used — to horrific effect — in an effort to intimidate the Soviet Union. Acquiring its own nuclear deterrent was a reasonable measure for the Soviet Union to take, in that context, even though the arms race would place serious strain on its economic capacities. But it was not just bombs and missiles. Canada played a key role in the development of biological weapons — viruses that could be deployed to infect civilian populations — which were, in fact, used in the Korean War.[137] The constant escalation into more and different forms of weaponry was designed to threaten the Soviet Union and force it to respond in kind.[138]

What triumphalism is due, then, to the Western powers for their victory in the Cold War is reserved for the rich. For all its flaws, the Soviet Union was a project designed to improve the quality of life for people who had otherwise been crushed in the capitalist machine. It succeeded in that aim, albeit with significant drawbacks and flaws, and the lessons learned from the Soviet experiment were applied elsewhere in the world, as left movements adapted and matured in their understanding of how to build emancipatory political and economic systems. These later movements often rightly criticized the Soviet Union for its failures, as when Fidel Castro denounced the 1968 Soviet invasion of Czechoslovakia. But the Soviet Union was part of a political lineage that inspired liberation struggles around the world, which fought to overthrow both colonial occupiers and capitalist robber-barons and which made possible movements that dramatically improved the lives of millions of people. The fall of Apartheid depended on victory in Angola, which depended on intervention from Cuba, which survived thanks to support from the Soviet Union. Indeed, even when Soviet interest in supporting liberation movements was lacklustre, as it was in Southern Africa, its relatively minor material support still made a major impact.[139]

One does not need to ignore the flaws and failures that took place in the more than 70 years of Soviet history to acknowledge that it opened a window to the possibility of a better world. Among the spate of books written to commemorate the centenary of the 1917 revolutions, China Miéville called the October Revolution "far-reaching, contested, ultimately tragic, and ultimately inspiring,"[140] while Samir Amin asserted that humanity owed "an enormous debt" to the Soviet Union for defeating the Nazis, building a model of a plurinational state that raised the station of the most destitute and for supporting liberation movements in Asia and Africa which "forced the imperialist powers to retreat and to accept a polycentric globalization that was less unequal and more respectful of the sovereignty of nations and their cultures." Amin added, however, that its "mistakes and weaknesses" led to its defeat and the "brutal restoration of capitalism."[141] While Amin and Miéville differ significantly in their final assessment of the Russian Revolution, they share an awareness that careful scholarship of the Soviet Union must navigate a difficult contradiction between its monumental achievements and its devastating failures in seeking to understand an event that remains central to the story of the modern world.

Canada stood opposed to that possibility of a better world, from start to finish, from an invasion in 1918 designed "to cash in on the Russian market" to the efforts to "storm the fortress" as it collapsed in 1990.[142] What has come since the West's victory in the Cold War has been a consistent and unmistakable descent into global catastrophe. If the way of the West was better, the elimination of its chief competitor should have meant that the good life would finally arrive. Instead, a world dominated by the United States and its allies has produced a compounding cycle of human tragedy that has culminated in a global environmental crisis, wealth inequality on an unprecedented scale and a rise of fascism that heralds an even darker future on the horizon. It is this crisis, and Canada's role in generating it, that the final section of this book documents.

Notes

1. Frank Petrie, *As Far as Ever the Puffin Flew*, New York, Vantage, 1997, p. 309.
2. Louis Menand, "Francis Fukuyama Postpones the End of History," *The New Yorker*, August 27, 2018.
3. John S. Saul, *Recolonization and Resistance in Southern Africa in the 1990s*, Toronto, Between the Lines, 1993, p. 38–46.
4. Karen Dubinsky at al., ed., *New World Coming: The Sixties and the Shaping of Global Consciousness*, Toronto, Between the Lines, 2009, p. 1–6. Periodizations like this are always imperfect. Nevertheless it is reasonable to suggest that the late 1960s was a high point for what is sometimes called the New Left and from those movements emerged a range of more militant communist organizations that posed real challenges to capitalist states in the 1970s, from the Red Brigades in Italy to the Gauche Prolétarienne in France to the Naxal movement in India.
5. Ernesto "Che" Guevara, Speech at the United Nations, December 11, 1964.

6. Ernesto "Che" Guevara, Speech at the United Nations, December 11, 1964.
7. In 1969, the FBI orchestrated the killing of high-profile Black Panther Party leaders Fred Hampton and Mark Clark in Chicago, and launched raids against party headquarters in Los Angeles. In 1985, police in Philadelphia bombed a house in a residential neighbourhood, targeting members of another black radical organization called MOVE. In the 2010s, leaders of a wave of protests against police violence in Ferguson, Missouri were systemically assassinated, likely by police or affiliated right-wing organizations. The state, then, has been consistent in its willingness to use extreme violence to snuff out black radicalism.
8. James W. St G. Walker, "Black Confrontation in Sixties Halifax," in Lara Campbell, Dominique Clément, and Gregory S. Kealey, ed., *Debating Dissent: Canada and the Sixties*, Toronto, University of Toronto Press, 2012, p. 173–179.
9. Joseph Mensah, *Black Canadians: History, Experience, Social Conditions*, Fernwood, Halifax, 2010, p. 50–52.
10. James W. St G. Walker, "Black Confrontation in Sixties Halifax," p. 181–191.
11. Lee Maracle, *Bobbi Lee: Indian Rebel*, Toronto, Women's Press, 1990.
12. Quoted in Dick Fidler, *Red Power in Canada*, Toronto, Vanguard Publications, 1970, p. 8–9.
13. Dick Fidler, *Red Power in Canada*, p. 14–15.
14. Lee Maracle, "Red Power Legacies and Lives: An Interview by Scott Rutherford," in Karen Dubinsky at al., ed., *New World Coming: The Sixties and the Shaping of Global Consciousness*, Toronto, Between the Lines, 2009, p. 358–363.
15. Bryan D. Palmer, "'Indians of All Tribes': The Birth of Red Power," in Lara Campbell, Dominique Clément, and Gregory S. Kealey, ed., *Debating Dissent: Canada and the Sixties*, Toronto, University of Toronto Press, 2012, p. 207.
16. While it may have been an FBI assassination, it may also be possible that Aquash was killed by AIM itself, which believed Aquash to be an FBI informant. Either way, the FBI's campaign to infiltrate and destroy the movement was central to the dynamics which led to Aquash's death and which ultimately undermined militant Indigenous organizing of that era. Eric Konigsberg, "Who Killed Anna Mae?," *New York Times*, April 25, 2014. A chilling window into FBI efforts to undermine AIM can also be found in Roxanne Dunbar-Ortiz's memoir, *Outlaw Woman* (2014).
17. Lee Maracle, "Red Power Legacies and Lives: An Interview by Scott Rutherford," p. 358–361.
18. Margaret Conrad, Alvin Finkel, and Donald Fyson, *History of the Canadian Peoples, Volume 2: 1867 to the Present*, Pearson, Toronto, 2015, p. 311–314.
19. Gary Kinsman, "The Canadian National Security War on Queers and the Left," in Karen Dubinsky at al., ed., *New World Coming: The Sixties and the Shaping of Global Consciousness*, Toronto, Between the Lines, 2009, p. 77–83.
20. "LGBTQ2S Youth Homelessness in Canada," The 519. Available at: www.the519.org/education-training/lgbtq2s-youth-homelessness-in-canada/in-canada. See also BC Poverty Reduction Coalition, "Poverty Is a Queer and Trans Issue," available at: https://bcpovertyreduction.ca/wp-contentuploads/2014/08/2013_prc-lgbtqt-poverty-factsheet.pdf.
21. Stephan Dahl, "The Rise of Pride Marketing and the Curse of 'Pink Washing,'" *The Conversation*, August 26, 2014.

22. Christopher Joseph Lee, "No Pride in Police, No Police in Pride: Resisting the Pinkwashing of State Violence," *The Baffler,* June 28, 2019.
23. FLQ Manifesto, quoted in Conrad, Finkel, and Fyson, *History of the Canadian Peoples*, p. 269.
24. David Meren, "Crisis of the Nation: Race and Culture in the Canada-Québec-France Triangle of the 1960s," in Laura Madokoro, Francine McKenzie, and David Meren, ed., *Dominion of Race: Rethinking Canada's International History*, Vancouver, UBC Press, 2017, p. 241.
25. Peter S. McInnis, "'Hothead Troubles': Sixties-era Wildcat Strikes in Canada," in Lara Campbell, Dominique Clément, and Gregory S. Kealey, ed., *Debating Dissent: Canada and the Sixties*, Toronto, University of Toronto Press, 2012, p. 157.
26. Thom Workman, *If You're In My Way I'm Walking: The Assault on Working People Since 1970*, Halifax, Fernwood, 2009, p. 42–66.
27. Gamal Adbal Nasser, quoted in Tareq Ismael, *Canada and the Middle East: The Foreign Policy of a Client State*, Calgary, Temeron Books, 1994, p. 21.
28. Tareq Ismael, *Canada and the Middle East*, p. 20.
29. Quoted in Tareq Ismael, *Canada and the Middle East*, p. 22.
30. For a somewhat sympathetic take on the Ba'ath Party see Tareq Y. Ismael's *The Arab Left* (1976). For a more critical view, Maxime Rodinson's *Marxism and the Muslim World* (1979). The latter was republished in 2015 but both were written when Ba'ath still seemed to potentially offer a viable Arab reformist alternative. Ismael's reflections in *The Communist Movement in the Arab World* (2005) are considerably more critical.
31. Tareq Y. Ismael, *The Communist Movement in the Arab World*, London, Routledge, 2005, p. 17–40. Canada gave its endorsement of this and the simultaneous intervention in Lebanon, both designed to weaken pan-Arab unity and prevent a more popular and socialist uprising like that which had befallen Iraq.
32. Quoted in Tareq Ismael, *Canada and the Middle East*, p. 27.
33. Tareq Ismael, *Canada and the Middle East*, p. 40–49.
34. The complicated problem of the small number of Arab citizens of Israel is taken up in Shourideh C. Molavi, *Stateless Citizenship: The Palestinian-Arab Citizens of Israel*, Boston, Brill, 2013.
35. http://projects.sipri.se/armstrade/Trnd_Ind_IRQ_Imps_73-02.pdf.
36. Peter Gowan, *The Global Gamble: Washington's Faustian Bid for Global Dominance*, London, Verso, 1999, p. 174–177.
37. Ernie Regehr, *Arms Canada: The Deadly Business of Military Exports*, Toronto, James Lorimer & Co., 1987, p. xi.
38. Gabriel Kolko, *Another Century of War?*, New York, The New Press, 2002, p. 33.
39. Ernie Regehr, *Arms Canada*, p. xiii.
40. Peter McFarlane, *Northern Shadows*, p. 218–219.
41. When the game was initially designed and released in Japan, it made no effort to pretend that the Red Menace was an alien race. Indeed, the 1987 version of the game included an ending theme song titled "Sandinista," referring to the Nicaraguan government that the Contras were trained to terrorize.
42. Greg Grandin, *The Last Colonial Massacre: Latin America in the Cold War*,

Chicago, University of Chicago Press, 2004, p. 187.
43. Adrienne Pine's *Working Hard, Drinking Hard* (2008) captured some of the nuances of that collective trauma and how it played out in people's daily lives and their very sense of self and identity, even decades later, in the context of Honduras.
44. Greg Grandin, *The Last Colonial Massacre*, p. 3.
45. Peter McFarlane, *Northern Shadows*, 179.
46. Mark McGuigan, quoted in Peter McFarlane, *Northern Shadows*, p. 173.
47. Notably, that regime had been saved in the 1940s by Canada, when its American sponsors were ready to abandon it for its links to Nazism. See Chapter 7 for details.
48. Gioconda Belli, *The Country Under My Skin: A Memoir of Love and War*, New York, Knopf, 2002.
49. Henry Heller, *The Cold War and the New Imperialism: A Global History, 1945–2005*, New York, Monthly Review Press, 2006, p. 211.
50. Gary Prevost, "The Status of the Sandinista Revolutionary Project," in Gary Prevost and Harry E. Vanden, ed., *The Undermining of the Sandinista Revolution*, New York, St. Martin's Press, 1999, p. 9–14.
51. Liisa North and CAPA, *Between War and Peace in Central America*, Toronto, Between the Lines, 1990, p. 67–73.
52. Katherine Hoyt, *The Many Faces of Sandinista Democracy*, Athens, Ohio University Press, 1997, p. 186.
53. Roxanne Dunbar-Ortiz, *Blood on the Border: A Memoir of the Contra War*, Norman, University of Oklahoma Press, 2016.
54. Ronald Reagan and Alexander Haig, quoted in Peter McFarlane, *Northern Shadows*, p. 172.
55. John Simons, quoted in Peter McFarlane, *Northern Shadows*, p. 164.
56. Greg Grandin, *The Last Colonial Massacre: Latin America in the Cold War*, Chicago, University of Chicago Press, 2004.
57. David Bickford, quoted in Peter McFarlane, *Northern Shadows*, p. 166.
58. The legacy of these organizations is, to be sure, contested. As I detail in Chapter 12, these organizations often subtly served the interests of Canadian capital abroad. In the case of the wars in Central America, however, there was much solidarity work that was sincere in its motivations and, if nothing else, brought attention to the depravity of the war. In one remarkable incident in 1983, a group of eleven nuns travelled to the Honduran-Nicaraguan border to set a vigil and prevent Contra invaders from crossing the border. While the nuns were not ultimately permitted to land at the border, their effort did generate some attention in the Canadian media and proved an embarrassment to the Canadian government which was trying to keep a low profile in its support for the US war. Walter Stefaniuk, "11 leave for Honduras on pilgrimage for peace," *Toronto Star*, December 4, 1983.
59. McFarlane, 164–165.
60. Liisa North and CAPA, *Between War and Peace*, p. 131–164.
61. Of note, the opening of a more generous refugee policy was in response to significant public pressure, notably around particular incidents like the vicious murder and mutilation of Beatriz Barrios Marroquín in 1985 by Guatemalan

death squads while she was waiting for her immigration to Canada to be finalized. When refugee policies were tightened up in 1987, the government knew it would need to reverse public sentiment, so it emphasized the "problems" associated with an influx of Turkish, Portuguese, and especially Sikh immigrants; Canadians were whipped into a fervour over the coming 'invasion" of Sikhs, thus building consent for what the government ultimately wanted, which was to place greater restrictions on immigration in general.

62. The weapons were sold via several third-parties, a loophole that allowed the RCMP to look the other way. Peter McFarlane, *Northern Shadows*, p. 219.
63. Peter McFarlane, *Northern Shadows*, p. 161–162.
64. Wes Maultsaid, quoted in Peter McFarlane, *Northern Shadows*, p. 225.
65. Peter McFarlane, *Northern Shadows*, p. 226.
66. Brian Mulroney, quoted in Liisa North and CAPA, *Between War and Peace*, p. 49.
67. Elizabeth Spehar and Nancy Thede, "Canada and Central America's Democratization Process," in Jean Daudelin and Edgar J. Dosman, ed., *Beyond Mexico: Changing Americas, Vol. I*, Ottawa, Carleton University Press, 1995, p. 130–133.
68. Katherine Hoyt, *The Many Faces*, p. 189.
69. Brian Mulroney, quoted in Yves Engler, *Black Book*, p. 94.
70. Yves Engler, *Black Book*, p. 129.
71. Konrad Yakabuski, "On Israel, Trudeau is Harper's pupil," *Globe and Mail*, May 10, 2018.
72. Linda Freeman, *The Ambiguous Champion: Canada and South Africa in the Trudeau and Mulroney Years*, Toronto, University of Toronto Press, 1999, p. 16.
73. Charles Burchell, quoted in Brian Tennyson, *Canadian Relations with South Africa: A Diplomatic History*, Washington, University Press of America, 1982, p. 116.
74. Brian Tennyson, *Canadian Relations with South Africa*, p. 114–116.
75. Jan Christiaan Smuts, quoted in Noam Chomsky, *Deterring Democracy*, London, Verso, 1991, p. 334.
76. E.A. Coté, quoted in Brian Tennyson, *Canadian Relations with South Africa*, p. 116–117.
77. Linda Freeman, *The Ambiguous Champion*, p. 19–29
78. Quoted in Yves Engler, *Canada in Africa*, p. 114.
79. Quoted in Yves Engler, *Canada in Africa*, p. 341.
80. Ruy Guerra's *Mueda, Memoria e Massacre* (1979) documented people in Mueda recreating scenes from the massacre, a practice undertaken annually in commemoration.
81. John S. Saul, *The State and Revolution in Eastern Africa*, New York, Monthly Review Press, 1979, p. 123–126.
82. John S. Saul, *Canada and Mozambique*, Toronto, Development Education Centre, 1974, p. 75.
83. Southern Rhodesia was yet another colonial hangover that Canada continued to support: Canada repeatedly abstained or opposed UN resolutions demanding that the British settlers allow participation of the black majority in the country and cooperated with the regime even after it declared independence from Britain

in 1964 and maintained a system not dissimilar to Apartheid.
84. Yves Engler, *Canada in Africa*, p. 98.
85. "Cabora Bossa & the Struggle for Southern Africa," World Council of Churches, London, 1971, p. 1–6.
86. "Cabora Bossa & the Struggle for Southern Africa," p. 7–24.
87. John S. Saul, *Socialist Ideology and the Struggle for Southern Africa*, Trenton, Africa World Press, 1990, p. 33–63.
88. Consider this commentary on Cabora Bossa from a South African newspaper in 1969, in light of both its reflection of Canadian mythologies about "vast, empty lands" and also its preview of the war on terror: "What is today desolate and almost unpopulated country will provide a far better living for hundreds of thousands of people, and their presence and their prosperity will, there is every reason to believe, not only make it easier for the Portuguese to take their own people with them in resistance to terrorism, but also provide protection for others in South Africa. Cabora, in other words, makes a great deal of political as well as economic sense." *Johannesburg Star*, Sep. 6, 1969. Rhodesian media used the same language in talking about African liberation struggles. Cabora Bassa would be, according to the aptly titled Rhodesian periodical *Property and Finance*, "a solid barrier against any possible terrorist infiltration from further north" and would illustrate "what White initiative and skill is achieving in an otherwise 'Dark Continent.'" *Rhodesian Property and Finance*, August 1967.
89. Pierre Trudeau, quoted in Yves Engler, *Canada in Africa*, p. 100.
90. Christine Hatzky, *Cubans in Angola: South-South Cooperation and Transfer of Knowledge, 1976-1991*, Madison, University of Wisconsin Press, 2015.
91. To put this in perspective, at the height of the struggle against Apartheid, in 1985, the *Montreal Gazette* ran an editorial by Nick Auf Der Mar wherein he and two of his colleagues surmised that "Africa needs another Percy Girouard," referring to the Canadian who had acted as a vicious governor of Northern Nigeria in the 1890s. In the opinion of the *Gazette*, Africa had problems with transportation, and Girouard had been "the greatest Canadian builder Africa ha[d] ever seen." The journalists failed to note that his railroad projects were built by African slave labour. Nick Auf Der Mar, "Maybe Africa Needs Another Percy Girouard," *Montreal Gazette*, July 15, 1985.
92. Hugh Nangle, quoted in John Deverell and the Latin America Working Group, *Falconbridge: Portrait of a Canadian Mining Multinational*, Toronto, J. Lorimer & Co., 1975, p. 154.
93. The governor of the Hudson's Bay Company defended his company for operating in South African-occupied Namibia in 1976, claiming that it was "doing a service" by breaking the ban on trade there. George Richardson, quoted in John S. Saul, *The State and Revolution in Eastern Africa*, New York, Monthly Review Press, 1979, p. 128.
94. Pierre Trudeau, quoted in Linda Freeman, *The Ambiguous Champion: Canada and South Africa in the Trudeau and Mulroney Years*, Toronto, University of Toronto Press, 1999.
95. Linda Freeman, *The Ambiguous Champion*, p. 105.
96. Karen Dubinsky and Marc Epprecht, "Canadian Business and the Business of Development," in Karen Dubinsky, Sean Mills and Scott Rutherford, ed., *Canada*

and the Third World: Overlapping Histories, Toronto, University of Toronto Press, 2016, p. 63.

97. As was so often the case, and no doubt contributed to the vitriolic hatred he inspired in the West, Fidel's comments on the matter were incisive and struck at the very heart of colonialism. "The imperialists are irritated with us," he said in 1976. "Some of them wonder why we help the Angolans, what interests we have there. They are accustomed to thinking that whenever a country does something, it is in pursuit of oil, or copper, or diamonds, or some other natural resource. No! We are not after material interests, and, logically, the imperialists do not understand this, because they are exclusively guided by chauvinist, nationalist, and selfish criteria. We are fulfilling an elementary internationalist duty when we help the Angolan people. We are simply practicing a policy of principles." Fidel Castro, quoted in Robert Wright, *Three Nights in Havana*, Toronto, Harper Collins, 2007, p. 192.
98. Conrad Black, quoted in Linda Freeman, *The Ambiguous Champion*, p. 103.
99. John S. Saul, *Liberation Lite: The Roots of Recolonization in Southern Africa*, Trenton, Africa World Press, 2011, p. 35.
100. Malcolm Fraser, quoted in John S. Saul, *Liberation Lite*, p. 38.
101. Colin Leys and Susan Brown, *Histories of Namibia: Living through the liberation struggle*, London, The Merlin Press, 2005.
102. Chris Webb, "Hidden histories and political legacies of the Canadian anti-apartheid movement," *Canadian Dimension*, April 30, 2014.
103. Chris Webb, "Hidden histories…"
104. It was not the first time Canada had found itself nervous about criticizing South Africa for fear that attention would turn to itself; in the late 1940s, when India was demanding better treatment of Indians in South Africa, Prime Minister King was reluctant to speak up, knowing that the province of British Columbia still had explicitly racist laws concerning South Asians, who only gained the right to vote in 1947. Brian Tennyson, *Canadian Relations with South Africa*, p. 116–121.
105. Lee Maracle, "Red Power Legacies and Lives: An Interview by Scott Rutherford," in *New World Coming*, p. 361.
106. Linda Freeman, *The Ambiguous Champion*, p. 287.
107. John S, Saul, *Recolonization and Resistance in Southern Africa in the 1990s*, Toronto, Between the Lines, 1993, p. 181.
108. Martin J. Murray, *The Revolution Deferred: The Painful Birth of Post-Apartheid South Africa*, London, Verso, 2004.
109. Colin Leys and John S. Saul, *Namibia's Liberation Struggle: The Two-Edged Sword*, Athens, Ohio University Press, 1995, p. 196.
110. Joe Clark, quoted in Yves Engler, *Canada in Africa*, p. 110.
111. Chris Webb, "Hidden histories and political legacies of the Canadian anti-apartheid movement," *Canadian Dimension*, April 30, 2014.
112. John S. Saul, *Liberation Lite*, p. 6–7.
113. John S. Saul, *A Flawed Freedom: Rethinking Southern African Liberation*, Toronto, Between the Lines, 2014, p. 45–47.
114. Henry Heller, *The Cold War*, p. 252–255.
115. Anuradha M. Chenoy and Rajan Kumar, *Re-Emerging Russia: Structures,*

Institutions and Processes, Singapore, Palgrave MacMillan, 2017, p. 153–187.
116. Henry Heller, *The Cold War*, p. 184–188.
117. Henry Heller, *The Cold War*, p. 244–258.
118. Henry Heller, *The Cold War*, p. 231–244.
119. The governments to which Canada sold weapons in the 1970s and 1980s included the Saudi, Kuwaiti, Bahraini and Jordanian monarchies, and the military dictatorships in Brazil, Chile, Colombia, Honduras, El Salvador, Indonesia and the Philippines, in addition to both sides of the Iran-Iraq war. Ernie Regehr, *Arms Canada*, p. 218–230.
120. Joe Clark, quoted in Leigh Sarty, "A Rivalry Transformed: Canadian-Soviet Relations to the 1990s" in David Davies, ed., *Canada and the Soviet Experiment: Essays on Canadian Encounters with Russia and the Soviet Union, 1900–1991*, Toronto, Canadian Scholars Press, 1994, p. 152.
121. Joe Clark, quoted in Leigh Sarty, "A Rivalry Transformed: Canadian-Soviet Relations to the 1990s," p. 156.
122. Leigh Sarty, "A Rivalry Transformed: Canadian-Soviet Relations to the 1990s," p. 160.
123. Leigh Sarty, "A Rivalry Transformed: Canadian-Soviet Relations to the 1990s," p. 163–165.
124. William A.B. Campbell and Richard K. Melchin, *The Soviet Threat: How Real for Canada?*, Vancouver, Canadian Conservative Centre, 1986, p. 7.
125. Vladimir Kaye, quoted in Franca Iacovetta, *Gatekeepers: Reshaping Immigrant Lives in Cold War Canada*, Toronto, Between the Lines, 2006, p. 104.
126. Canadian newspapers like the *Globe and Mail* and *Toronto Star* reflected the mood of the ruling classes in Canada almost as faithfully as *Pravda* did the Soviet leadership; each had a party line and often stuck to it even when the evidence was against it, even while they also contained much legitimate news and analysis. Canadian state institutions like the National Film Board (NFB) made documentaries about Canadian overseas peacekeeping missions that were heavily vetted by the government and the military, just as *Pravda* expressed the ideology of the Soviet leadership. On the NFB, see Colin McCullough, *Creating Canada's Peacekeeping Past*, Vancouver, UBC Press, 2016, p. 84. On *Pravda*, see Leigh Sarty, "A Handshake Across the Pole: Canadian-Soviet Relations During the Era of Détente," in David Davies, ed., *Canada and the Soviet Experiment: Essays on Canadian Encounters with Russia and the Soviet Union, 1900–1991*, Toronto, Canadian Scholars' Press, 1994, p. 119.
127. One notable early exception to that rule was the work of Alexander Rabinowitch, who wrote some of the definitive studies of the Russian Revolution in a manner that was critical and sharp but was rooted in a deep engagement with source material, such that it disproved much of the mythology created by Cold Warriors like Robert Conquest. Rabinowitch's *The Bolsheviks Come to Power* (1976), for instance, completely undermined the myth that the October Revolution was an unpopular coup by the Bolsheviks, illustrating instead that the Bolsheviks' success was premised on the very fact that it was a radically democratic and decentralized party, and was thus the most popular organization, especially in Petrograd.
128. Chenoy and Kumar, *Re-Emerging Russia*, p. 1.

129. Chenoy and Kumar, *Re-Emerging Russia*, p. 2–3. The famine, and its complicated legacy, are addressed in greater detail in Chapter 12.
130. David Masci, "In Russia, nostalgia for Soviet Union and positive feelings for Stalin," Pew Research Centre, June 29, 2017. The Russian NGO Levada-Center tracked the opinion polls since the collapse of the Soviet Union in 1992, noting a spike to more than 70% wishing to return to the USSR in the early 2000s. Data available at: https://www.levada.ru/2018/12/19/nostalgiya-po-sssr-2/.
131. Chenoy and Kumar, *Re-Emerging Russia*, p. 153–187.
132. Gordon Pitts, *Storming the Fortress: How Canadian Business Can Conquer Europe in 1992*, Harper Collins, Toronto, 1990, p. 260.
133. Gordon Pitts, *Storming the Fortress*, p. 270.
134. Chenoy and Kumar, *Re-Emerging Russia*, p. 154.
135. Tomas Matza, *Shock Therapy: Psychology, Precarity, and Well-Being in Postsocialist Russia*, Durham, Duke University Press, 2018, p. 104–132.
136. Alex Steinberg, "Myths of the October Revolution: An Interview with Alexander Rabinowitch," Verso Books, February 13, 2018. Available at: https://www.versobooks.com/blogs/3615-myths-of-the-october-revolution-an-interview-with-alexander-rabinowitch.
137. Canadian researcher Guilford Reed helped to weaponize shellfish poison for use in CIA assassination operations. Donald Avery, *Pathogens for War: Biological Weapons, Canadian Life Sciences, and North American Biodefence*, Toronto, University of Toronto Press, 2013, p. 161.
138. Of course, once this cat-and-mouse game got underway, there is no question that the Soviets tried to get the drop on the West, developing weapons before their counterparts to get ahead. This dynamic is portrayed dramatically in the television series *The Americans* (2013–2018). Still, the compulsion to press on with the arms races was almost always initiated in the West, and only reluctantly reciprocated by a Kremlin that desperately needed to place its resources elsewhere.
139. "It is to Brezhnev, as much as anyone else outside South Africa itself, that credit for cracking the racist bloc should go," argued Fred Halliday in 1990. Even when its motives were more geopolitical than ideological, the resources offered by the Soviet Union were crucial to the success of many liberation struggles, and this was often ignored even by the international left, in its justifiable frustration and disappointment with the flawed, ossified USSR. Fred Halliday, "The Ends of the Cold War," *New Left Review*, No. 180, March-April 1990, p. 22–23.
140. China Miéville, *October: The Story of the Russian Revolution*, London, Verso, 2017, p. 1.
141. Samir Amin, *October 1917: A Century Later*, Montreal, Daraja Press, 2017, p. 5.
142. Gordon Pitts, *Storming the Fortress*, p. 250–272.

Part IV

The New Canadian Imperialism

10

The Dark Heart of Peacekeeping

We just said "Fuck this!!" and we gave them everything we got. You felt bad because you knew you killed people. I don't know the numbers.

— Cpl. David Margolin, describing Canadian soldiers ignoring the UN Rules of Engagement in the former Yugoslavia, 2002[1]

NO SINGLE IMAGE BETTER CAPTURED the construction of Canada's place in the world in the late 20th century than that of a middle-aged white man, dressed in military fatigues, wearing a blue peacekeeper's helmet, generously offering a teddy bear to a child in a poor, predominantly non-white country. This picture — of which many variations existed and could be pulled up with a quick internet search — contained so much of what mainstream Canada aspired and imagined itself to be. On the surface, it suggested a commitment to peace and international security, a willingness to invest in supporting the most vulnerable people even in the most difficult circumstances and an ideal of generosity and kindness.

Nevertheless, on careful inspection, it contained a variety of colonial reassurances: a white patriarch was rescuing and protecting non-white people, an image straight from the pages of Kipling's "White Man's Burden." The crisis in which the peacekeeper was intervening was invariably in a poor country many miles away, where, presumably, they had not quite figured out how to run a modern nation-state. And while the gun on our peacekeeper's hip reminded us that he was willing to use violence if necessary, the blue helmet promised us that our man was the "good guy," and we need not worry ourselves with the complicated details of the conflict he was now participating in.

As such, the broad appeal that this kind of image generated in Canada revealed much about the settler Canadian psyche. While some of the ideals of peacekeeping appeared progressive, the actual historical experience of Canadian peacekeeping typically represented a continuity with many of the dynamics described in the opening chapters on Canadian colonialism. Furthermore, the peacekeeping ideal was rooted in the idea that Canada needed to assist weaker, poorer, lesser peoples. Peacekeeping missions were not driven by an ideology of solidarity — peer-to-peer partnership — but rather with an overwhelming, pervasive air of paternalism. Thus, when Canadians arrived in Africa on peacekeeping missions, they came to "save" Africans, who could not save themselves. This stands in sharp contrast, for instance, to when Cubans travelled to Angola to stand beside Angolans in their national liberation struggle.[2]

The peacekeeping era was to crest in the 1990s, as the West sought to reconfigure and assert its place in the post–Cold War world. The disappearance of the Soviet Union and the communist governments of Eastern Europe loosely coincided with the shift of the Chinese Communist Party into a state-capitalist dictatorship that was communist in name only, and the defeat of left forces in Central America marked the end of the revolutionary energy of the 1960s. Thus, where the 1980s began with the world still divided into two ideologically opposed camps, the 1990s would see the consolidation of one world, policed by the United States and its allies on behalf of capitalism and its many attendant hierarchies. But justifying this new role posed a challenge: there was no longer the "Evil Empire" to use as an excuse for global militarism. This lack of an overarching force to struggle against meant that the 1990s saw a brief resurgence in the idea of peacekeeping. The Canadian ruling class understood itself to have helped win the Cold War and was excited to cash in on its spoils, but it also knew that it had a role to play in helping the United States police and maintain the now almost entirely capitalist world. Canada's most significant contribution to this project was its catastrophic failures in the realm of peacekeeping, wherein Canadian soldiers were revealed to be torturing teenagers in Somalia, abetting genocide in Rwanda and saying "fuck this" to the rules of engagement in Yugoslavia.

This chapter explores these cases, especially the widely misunderstood crisis in Rwanda. By the end of the 1990s, much of the shine of peacekeeping had worn off, and the terrorist attacks of September 2001 altered the global landscape such that Canada could refashion itself as a "warrior nation" as part of the US War on Terror. Canadians had found a new enemy — labelled "detestable murderers and scumbags" by one military general — and the early 21st century would be dominated by that new struggle.³ But the colonial imagination that Canadian soldiers took into the War on Terror was deeply rooted and manifested dramatically in those failed peacekeeping operations of the 1990s. It was also evident in the first major post–Cold War conflict, the 1991 assault on one of the few secular states in the Middle East. The patterns of the 21st century — unilateral military action, demonization of Arab and Muslim enemies, aggressive warfare to serve a capitalist agenda — were set by the West's decision to turn against an old ally in Iraq.

War in the Gulf

The 1991 Persian Gulf War was emblazoned into my head as a child. Live television coverage of the war was new and sensational; the grave and serious tones with which it was discussed signalled to me that something important was happening and captured my young imagination. Each day I would go to school and write, in my diary, an update on the previous day's events in the Gulf, drawing the "War in the Gulf" logo that CNN had created for its coverage. That I swallowed entirely the narrative of who was good and who was bad likely goes without saying — I was a 9-year-old white kid in Winnipeg — but it still stands as a testament to the power of propaganda that I built snow forts heavily stocked with snowballs in order to play out scenarios where the Iraqis would attack my now-impregnable front yard.

Though I knew nothing whatsoever about Iraq or its people, I knew that Saddam was the "bad guy," and that the Americans were the "good guys." This was regularly reinforced for me in popular culture, not least in the narratives of the World Wrestling Federation, where I watched the True American Hero, Hulk Hogan, smack down the vile and obnoxious Sgt. Slaughter, who was decked out in fatigues and sunglasses and waved an Iraqi flag.⁴ It was simple and easy for me: I was not Arab, I was not Muslim, I was not brown, no one in my family shared the name Hussein. Had these or any number of other factors been different, I might have had a very different reaction to the narrative that demonized Iraq; instead it became my first significant brush with the anti-Arab and anti-Muslim panic that would come to characterize the 21st century. It was not until several years later, upon the release of David O. Russell's satirical film

Three Kings (1999), that I found myself reflecting critically on a war I had believed to be — as one Canadian journalist put it — a simple "open and shut case."[5]

Canada was heavily involved in the Gulf War. Some 1700 Canadian soldiers fought in the war, and the Canadian military sent destroyers, supply vessels and CF-18 fighter jets.[6] Outside the United States, this made Canada's contribution one of the largest, to say nothing of the work Canada did to get UN support and approval for the war; External Affairs Minister Joe Clark bragged that Canada would be remembered for playing a "quite significant role in maintaining the consensus" in favour of the war.[7] The Mulroney government spent as much as $700 million on the Gulf War, a significant contribution to the restoration of an absolute monarch in Kuwait who had suspended parliament in 1986 and refused women the right to vote.

The Emir of Kuwait, Jaber Al-Ahmad Al-Sabah, was a close ally of the West, so when Saddam Hussein's Iraqi army invaded the small oil-producing kingdom, US President George H.W. Bush reacted quickly. American policy in the Middle East had long been to maintain a relative power balance between a range of different right-wing governments such that no one regional power could rival the United States. This had been the motivation for the US policy of equipping and funding both sides of the Iran-Iraq war of 1980–88, and the crisis provoked by the war contributed to Saddam Hussein's desperate move to invade Kuwait in order to shore up his position. Having long been a stooge of Washington, Saddam believed he would be allowed to seize Kuwait and then negotiate a withdrawal — and in the process resolve several economic disputes with the Emir — without incident.[8]

What was often ignored in discussions about Iraq and the decades of war in which it found itself was that, well into the 1980s, Iraq was one of most stable and economically prosperous countries in the Middle East. The Ba'ath Party, which governed Iraq in the latter half of the 20th century, claimed to be socialist — though in practice it was hostile to the left and limited itself to minor welfare state reforms — and had come to power during the popular overthrow of a British-installed monarchy. Saddam Hussein's position in the party grew as his personal ambition nudged him towards an alliance with the United States.[9] He consolidated his own power in Iraq with US resources, having assured the CIA that he would be a loyal Cold War ally; in 1979 he rose to the top of the Ba'ath Party and was famously photographed shaking hands with US Defense Secretary Donald Rumsfeld in 1983, who would later play a key role in Saddam's ouster. Still, Saddam had to placate the Iraqi masses — particularly its significant working classes — by maintaining some commitment to the social reform principles that led the revolution.

Before Saddam's rise — and even to some extent after — Iraq was a state that made legitimate efforts to redistribute wealth and to use the profits from oil sales to build up public infrastructure and social welfare. Peter Gowan, drawing from the work of Samir al-Khalil, notes that the Iraqi state had carried out land reform to improve the conditions of the rural poor and built a welfare state to support the urban working classes. "The regime dramatically modernized Iraqi society," explains Gowan, "led by its drive against illiteracy and for free education for all."[10] One component of this project was the inclusion and encouragement of women's participation in society, such that they made up a large percentage of the country's teachers, doctors, dentists and pharmacists. Notably, Iraq was also a secular state, surrounded by right-wing theocracies — Iran, Saudi Arabia and Israel — two of which relied heavily on US support.

The ruling party became more repressive after Saddam consolidated power, though it had already proven itself periodically intolerant of dissent: Iraq refused, for instance, to grant independence to ethnic minorities — like the Kurdish people — who had been lumped into the Iraqi state when it was created by Britain. Violence unleashed against these and other rebelling groups within Iraq was matched by the violence of the war with Iran, a brutal and intractable eight-year struggle that left as many as a million people dead. The US consistently avoided criticizing Iraq for this violence; the now-famous photograph of Donald Rumsfeld shaking hands with Saddam Hussein captured a moment in which the Iraqi dictator asked the US to water down any criticism of his use of chemical weapons, a request happily granted.[11]

No, Saddam's repressive streak was not what upset the leaders of the free world in 1991. His crime was to interfere with the delicate balance of power that kept the US and its allies in position to largely control the supply and sale of oil. The gulf monarchies were part of that balance; thus, in 1991, Saddam Hussein became enemy number one in the West and Canadians, like their southern neighbours, watched in real time on television as bombs rained down on the citizens of Baghdad. For all the talk of "smart bombs," the overwhelming number of sorties missed their targets and/or deliberately targeted non-military facilities like schools, hospitals and power plants; hundreds of thousands of Iraqis died.[12] A United Nations report described the bombing having had a "near apocalyptic impact," transforming a "highly urbanized and mechanized society" into a nation from the "preindustrial age."[13] The Iraqi army was pushed out of Kuwait with relative ease and the emir was reinstated. He promised to extend to women the right to vote — to reassure Western audiences that they had chosen the right side — but he did not fulfill that promise before dying in 2006.

The Canadian government and media carried water for the cynical war, with highly regarded journalists like Gwynne Dyer suggesting that Saddam's aggression was, as noted above, "an open and shut case," without the usual "wrong on both sides."[14] But despite the platitudes about human rights and democracy, the Kuwaiti monarchy ran a semi-feudal dictatorship wherein a small number of rich Kuwaiti citizens exploited the labour of migrant workers from Pakistan and Palestine. As for Saddam, he was allowed to remain in power in Iraq through the 1990s. What the US wanted was an Iraq under its control; thus, it refused to support popular movements seeking to oust Saddam in 1991, standing by while his forces crushed those rebellions in the aftermath of the Gulf War.

Instead, the US strategically bombed Iraq at various points in the 1990s, to keep Saddam in line and under their control. The actual effect of the bombing and subsequent economic sanctions was to create a humanitarian crisis in the country: US Secretary of State Madeline Albright was famously confronted in a television interview with the fact that half a million children had died in Iraq due to the campaign and claimed "it was worth it."[15] Canada supported the bombings, suggesting they were in compliance with UN resolutions and that Canada could not "sit on the sidelines." Canadian ships were sent to the Persian Gulf to ensure that the sanctions were maintained and badly needed goods were not delivered to starving Iraqis.[16] Still, Canada's role in the war was downplayed, as the Canadian military transitioned into a period that the right would later call the "decade of darkness," in which Canada seemed to reduce its military presence in the world. Budget cuts in the 1990s meant that fewer resources were given to the armed forces — though it felt far less a pinch than most other sectors of Canadian society — and with the disappearance of the "Soviet threat" it was unclear what role the Canadian military was supposed to play in the post–Cold War era.

This uncertainty was exacerbated by the temporary crisis that struck the Canadian military after it failed to successfully cover-up the scandal of torture and murder in Somalia in 1993 and, shortly thereafter, Canada's perceived inability to resolve the crisis that led to genocide in Rwanda in 1994. Failure to sell the image of a good, humanitarian UN intervention in the former Yugoslavia only added to the malaise. The culture of colonial patriarchy that had long pervaded the Canadian military appeared to be under threat, and, as one military historian reflected, "the decade of darkness after Somalia was not just about the shame and the budget cuts but also the frustration at being viewed as just blue-helmeted peacekeepers."[17] While peacekeeping had been effective cover for Canadian colonial adventures since the 1950s, large sections of the Canadian military establishment increasingly felt emasculated by those blue helmets, craving greater freedom to embrace aggressive war. They would, of course, get their wish after September 11, 2001.

The Peacekeeping Horizon

Peacekeeping, from its inception, was always laced with colonialism. While the missions themselves were typically motivated by interests that superseded any express moral obligations, their practitioners — just like the colonialists during the scramble for empire — imagined themselves to be the carriers of civilization. Thus, in missions like that in the Congo, Canadians were acting in the interest of capital while also believing themselves to be saving the Congo "from itself." In their efforts to facilitate Belgian interests, they were directly collaborating with the primary colonial power while taking for themselves a role in the neocolonial apparatus. Through it all, assumptions of superiority were plain; the logic of the peacekeeping mission was a perfect platform upon which to graft those colonial values.

It is instructive to reflect on how Canadians understood peacekeeping in its early phase. Colin McCullough's *Creating Canada's Peacekeeping Past* unpacks the generation of peacekeeping mythology through several National Film Board (NFB) documentaries. The NFB documentaries, which were heavily managed from above by External Affairs and the military, served to drain each mission of its real political content, while emphasizing the hard work and commitment of individual Canadian peacekeepers to help the world's "backward" people.

For instance, in *The Thin Blue Line* (1958), the Suez Canal mission was presented with no explanation of the nature of the conflict or the various interests at play, choosing instead to focus on Canadians working on hangar bays or delivering mail or relaxing in Lebanon. Egyptians were presented as "plying their ancient trade" next to "Canadian technicians," highlighting the assumed modernity of the white peacekeepers, even though it was likely that it was the Egyptians who were supervising the work. In one scene, a Canadian appeared to be dressed up mockingly like a Bedouin in the desert, while the narrator reassured the viewer that it was okay for the Canadian to "make light of local habits and hardships."[18] It was not clear that the Egyptians agreed, and Canadian peacekeepers were eventually ordered to leave.

A peacekeeping mission in Cyprus was presented with similar motifs in *You Are Welcome, Sirs, to Cyprus* (1964). As McCullough explained, the narration served to create a "depiction of the Canadians as strong, helpful white men and the Cypriots as either foolishly destructive or unable to govern themselves."[19] These hallmarks of colonialism ran through the film, which described the locals as "determined but confused, often violent yet sick of war"; their inability to manage their own emotions and serve their own interests was presented as the underlying reason for Canada's presence.[20] These themes linked back to colonialism in a different, but related, way in *A Life of Adventure* (1965), which functioned more as a recruitment tool and emphasized the fun and excitement that was on offer for Canadians serving in Gaza or Egypt. The narrator promised that taking on such important work offered "a life of adventure in the Canadian Forces," which could bring the recruit to "this exotic part of the world." The scene then shifted to the beach, where young men were surfing to the sounds of 1960s rock 'n' roll, and the camera hovered over a shot of women sunbathing in bikinis while the narrator slyly informed the viewer that "many a Canadian officer has reported that the scenery here is unexcelled."[21]

Given this kind of recruitment, the many incidents wherein Canadian peacekeepers committed acts of sexual violence or harassment against the people they were there to serve cannot be dismissed as simply the mistakes of disturbed individuals who misunderstood or marred otherwise pure operations. Quite the contrary, the values that made such acts possible were inculcated into the very recruitment and popular framing of peacekeeping from its outset, in documentaries shown in schools and on the

CBC, devised by the same politicians and military leaders who ordered and ran these operations. If a 1965 recruitment video could make a sly reference to sexual conquest then it could hardly be called a surprise that Canadian soldiers used their peacekeeping operations to act out these fantasies, especially given the way that sexual exploitation and violence had been so central to the colonial experience.[22]

Canadian understandings of peacekeeping had shifted somewhat by the 1980s. Less willing to accept the idyllic picture presented in the 1960s, peacekeeping was now being presented with a harder edge. Gwynne Dyer and Tina Viljoen's *Keeping the Elephants Away* (1986) criticized a peacekeeping milieu that lacked the teeth to deal with the threats it faced. This fundamentally right-wing critique of peacekeeping, far from identifying its colonial underpinnings, blamed its failures on the fact that the Canadians were not given the mandate and power they needed. Instead of recognizing that the conflicts in which peacekeepers engaged were, themselves, products of colonial and class struggles that Canada had a direct stake in — which was a large reason why they failed to achieve satisfactory peace — Dyer and Viljoen essentially argued that peacekeepers needed to be empowered to fight back against locals who did not really want peaceful settlements. This overly simplistic message rung with all the classic colonial notes: the natives were inherently violent and the civilized Canadians needed to use force to keep them in line.

Of course, the Canadians did use force. The mythology of innocent peacekeepers waving white flags amidst a hail of gunfire because UN bureaucrats would not let them engage the enemy was a right-wing fantasy from the outset, designed to undermine what few limits did exist to separate peacekeeping forces from traditional occupying armies. These debates became particularly fraught in the 1990s as peacekeeping missions in Somalia, Rwanda and the former Yugoslavia ended in catastrophe, each for different but related reasons. A series of NFB films by Garth Pritchard gave voice to that right-wing reaction, echoing and amplifying Dyer and Viljoen's position in the 1980s, in assessing the situation in the Balkans. *The Price of Duty* (1995) deified Canadian peacekeepers, presenting them almost as sacrificial figures who gave the best of themselves — and of Canada — to the largely ungrateful and oblivious people they were serving. Peacekeepers like Mark Isfeld — called "Izzy" in the film and given a martyr's treatment — were framed as being handcuffed by regulations that restricted their capacities in the field.

Reviews of the films harped on the same points, appreciating that it let the soldiers speak, instead of giving precedence to "political charlatans, lying diplomats, and howling victims."[23] Without the voices of the victims, the film obviously produced a narrow and misleading account. Indeed, Pritchard's goals were clear and by no means "neutral." He himself argued in 1995 that he avoided interviewing "retired colonels and professors being called on as the expert of the day to talk about something they know nothing about." Imagining his position to be in support of the "little guy," Pritchard was unable to understand that the Canadian peacekeeper was by no means the most vulnerable party in the situations in which they were placed. Indeed, Pritchard was explicitly reacting against the concerns that had been raised in the aftermath of Canadian peacekeepers' torture and murder of teenager Shidane Arone in 1993. Pritchard was incensed that while few knew about Izzy, "lots of Canadians know the name of the young Somali who was killed."[24]

Did they? Contrary to Garth Pritchard's complaints, Sherene Razack suggested in 2004 — only a decade later — that "few would now recognize the name of Shidane Arone and many would be outraged at the juxtaposition of the word peacekeeping with racial violence."[25] My own experience in the classroom has been that not one student, across many years of teaching courses in Canadian history, has ever been able to tell me who Shidane Arone was. His torture and murder were written out of the collective Canadian consciousness, in part because the so-called "Somalia Affair" was treated as an aberration, an exception to the rule of Canadian peacekeeping. This book illustrates that — quite the contrary — the behaviour of Canadian soldiers in Somalia in 1993 resonates with their behaviour from Germany to Korea to the Canadian prairies.

The Somalia Affair

The two incidents central to the 1993 Somalia Affair — the shooting of two Somalis on March 4 and the torture and murder of Shidane Arone on March 16 — were shocking to a Canadian public that believed its peacekeepers were good boys from "the clean snows of Petawawa."[26] In fact, many members of the Canadian Airborne Regiment stationed in Somalia knew about or participated in various levels of violence against Somalis during their time there, and superior officers condoned and encouraged the behaviour. Soldiers produced "trophy photos" with their tortured victims and "holiday videos" wherein they drank beer, laughed about cracking Somali heads and described their mission as "Operation Snatch Nig-Nog."²⁷ One soldier, a self-professed neo-Nazi, told the camera that they "hadn't killed enough n-----s yet," while another complained that Somalis "never work, they're lazy, they're slobs, and they stink." As these videos and stories accumulated, it also surfaced that the regiment practised violent and racist hazing rituals, including one where a black soldier was tied to a tree and covered in feces that spelled the words "I love the KKK."²⁸

Euro-American peacekeepers accumulated a laundry list of violent offences which they knew they would get away with, including destruction or theft of Somalis' personal property, collective deprivation of water, torture by electric shocks, beatings, cigarette burns, razor-wire cuts, rape, gang rape, murder, infanticide, swinging children above open flames and a case of sodomy and torture of a 13-year old inside the Italian Embassy.²⁹ Notably, no such reports exist with respect to Botswanan peacekeepers, suggesting that the colonial relationship was a key factor. Canadians called Somalia "Indian Country" and imagined that they were there to civilize a place of "pure evil," to bring order to chaos and to teach Somalis how to be modern. When Somalis did not greet them with the fanfare and gratitude they felt they deserved, they asserted their colonial superiority with violence.

As is common in such encounters, the colonial peacekeepers and public tended to ignore and erase local history in favour of a narrative wherein the natives were immutably and inevitably irrational, violent and backwards. Conflict in Somalia was treated as though it were the natural state of affairs for a savage African country wracked by "ethnic tension," which implied that war was a product of ancient, irresolvable tribal rivalries held by people who lacked the capacity to grow beyond these irrational racial hatreds. This was nonsense; Somalia had been devastated by conflict that was largely the result of Cold War rivalries and the infusion of American weapons to try to crush left-wing forces in Ethiopia.

After Europe had been forced to give up colonial authority in Somalia in 1960, it departed having ensured that the post-independence government would be a pro-Western quasi-dictatorship. Resentment simmered in both Somalia and Ethiopia as the rich exploited the poor under Western puppet governments, but, in 1974, left revolution stirred in Ethiopia.³⁰ This was unwelcome news in the West, which had sponsored the Ethiopian dictatorship of Haile Selassie.[31] To quell the momentum of the left in East Africa, the Americans funded and equipped a Somali invasion of Ethiopia. Left-wing forces in Ethiopia received some support from the USSR and Cuba, but ultimately American pockets were deeper. By the 1990s, the Ethiopian left was defeated, both countries were devastated, several smaller conflicts had emerged, and a food crisis affecting 4.5 million people exploded in the context of ongoing civil war.[32]

It was at that point that the West decided to make Somalia a test case in the new world order. Flush with Cold War victory, Somalia was an opportunity to illustrate that the American-dominated world was going to be governed by an enlightened empire, and Canada was to play a role. The story is thoroughly reviewed in Sherene Razack's *Dark Threats and White Knights* (2004), arguably one of the most important books on Canadian peacekeeping and its deep colonial roots. Razack illustrates that Canadians in Somalia were certain of their superiority — that the entire culture of the military was pervaded by this conviction — and that violence against their civilizational "lesser" was part of how they physically marked their superiority. These violent practices were, Razack argued, "intended to establish Northern nations as powerful and superior, nations in full control of the natives they had come to keep in line."[33]

While the official reporting of the case laboured to suggest that it was a "few bad apples" who had spoiled an otherwise noble mission, the very nature of the violence disproves this: it was widely known and condoned up the chain of command, it was actively documented in videos and diaries, and it was heavily sexualized and often targeted children. This latter point is noteworthy precisely because it falls so far outside of what would be considered acceptable behaviour in the home country. If only a handful of bad people were committing such egregiously terrible acts in Somalia, you would expect them to keep it secret; instead, these acts of barbarism were committed in very public ways, illustrating that they were widely accepted.

Any doubt that this was a colonial encounter is put to rest the language used by Canadians — not just the soldiers sent there but also the journalists who wrote about it and even the commissioners who reviewed the violence afterwards — which repeatedly invoked Somalia as an "ancient land" full of "savages who got ahead of themselves technologically" and which became a "victim of its own tribal warlords."[34] Canadians considered Somalis lazy and dirty, some refused to touch them without wearing gloves, and many characterized Somali men as either effeminate and homosexual or patriarchal and disrespectful to women, or both. Somalia was described as a frightening and evil place, where even children could be the enemy, despite the fact that Belet Huen — where the Canadians were stationed — was entirely peaceful throughout 1993. The militias had left the area before the Canadians got there, no Canadians were even wounded during the mission, and most of the people the peacekeepers encountered were starving refugees.[35]

Nevertheless, the Canadians acted as though they were under constant threat from these refugees, and in particular they became obsessed with the idea that items from their camp were being stolen. This theft was massively exaggerated, but the Canadians concluded that they needed to teach these ungrateful Somalis a lesson. Filtered through their colonial imagination, this meant that they would have to use violence, since that was considered the only language Somalis understood. This, in particular, framed the violent incidents that finally became a news story back home.

The shooting of two Somalis on March 4 was precipitated by an order from Lt.-Col. Carol Mathieu — the self-described "King of Belet Huen" — that any Somali seen fleeing from the Canadian camp should be shot "between the skirt and the flip-flops."[36] He then tasked one of his most aggressively racist and violent soldiers — Michel Rainville — with patrolling the camp to prevent theft. Rather than taking preventative measures like increasing lighting or reinforcing fencing, Rainville wanted to catch Somalis in the act of theft and punish them, so he set up visible displays of food and water inside the camp and had his patrol lie in wait, wearing night-vision goggles. The fact that he used food as bait raises an immediate and obvious point: people stealing food are not dangerous, they are hungry. Thus, it must have been common knowledge that the likely thieves were not, in fact, a threat. It speaks volumes about the mindset of the Canadian peacekeeping mission that Rainville would go to such lengths to entrap and punish a non-threatening "enemy" in order to "teach a lesson" to the very people Canada was ostensibly there to help.

The outcome was predictable: when two Somalis, Abdi Hamdare and Ahmad Aruush, saw the food and water they assumed it was a humanitarian aid camp and approached, only to be ambushed by a heavily armed platoon of Canadian soldiers. They were shot, in the backs, as they fled. Aruush was killed when a second flurry of gunfire was launched into his neck, which appeared suspiciously like an execution, since he had already been immobilized by shots to the chest. Rainville was congratulated by Lt.-Col. Mathieu and ordered to continue with the patrols.[37] Indeed, life continued with little interruption for the Canadian peacekeepers, despite the murder, and it was precisely that atmosphere of normalcy that bears noting; only twelve days later, another Somali would die in Canadian custody, with nearly everyone in the camp aware and seemingly unfazed.

On March 16, Shidane Arone, a 16-year-old Somali, who claimed he entered the Canadian camp to look for a missing child, was captured, tortured and murdered by Canadian peacekeepers. His last words before he died were "Canada, Canada, Canada."[38] The details of his torture, which was spread out over several hours, have been documented in great detail elsewhere and ranged from merciless beatings with phone books to cigarette burns on his penis. Testimony from the court-martial hearings suggest that many different soldiers, spanning a range of ranks, participated. Two soldiers — Clayton Matchee and Kyle Brown — were most directly involved and were characterized later as pathologically violent "bad apples."

But many other soldiers took photos, contributed weapons, shouted racial epithets at Arone, participated in beatings or at the very least looked the other way. As many as 80 people came and went from the area where the torture was taking place without intervening. Indeed, as Sherene Razack emphasizes, it was on the basis of "the very ordinariness and everyone's participation in it" that one of the soldiers involved was able to mount his own legal defence.[39] Another described hearing Arone howling in pain and compared it to the sound of an animal being slaughtered on a farm. Despite the sound, R.E. Campbell did not interrupt his video game to investigate, suggesting that the sound of torture was not uncommon.

The case was complicated by the fact that its primary participants — Matchee and Brown — were of Indigenous backgrounds. Some scholars argued that, in a white-supremacist environment like the Canadian military, Matchee and Brown were overcompensating in their attempts to "outwhite the white guys." Others noted that ascribing their actions to their racial background only replicated the kind of racial thinking that hung over the entire mission in Somalia in the first place and which made Shidane Arone an acceptable target for torture and murder. It was a worthwhile and complicated debate, but it took place mostly outside of the mainstream discussion in Canada; the Canadian military and broader public tended to simply settle on these two men as the chief villains from the Canadian side, men who had disgraced "their" country and brought shame upon the nation. This is an extremely important detail, since it allowed the Canadian public to shake off much of the shame — it wasn't really one of our boys, after all — and to remind itself that Canadians are still the good guys.

It is likely that Matchee's and Brown's experience of the Somalia mission — and the Canadian military in general — was different from that of their white counterparts. Several members of the unit were avowed neo-Nazis, and race clearly mediated relations in the regiment, given that a black soldier had been hazed with reference to the KKK. Matchee, in particular, appears to have been conscious of his racialized status, remarking on the night of the murder that now the black man would fear the Indian as he did the white man.[40] But it is worth emphasizing, as per Razack, that race had already overdetermined the relationship between soldiers serving in the Canadian military and the Somalis they encountered. To whatever extent Matchee's and Brown's Indigenous backgrounds adds a layer of tragedy to the story — since each would have inevitably been carriers of intergenerational trauma from the genocide that their families had suffered — it remains the case that they enacted colonial violence against Somalis. That violence was shaped and articulated through the dominant ideology that ran through the entire mission and indeed all Canadian encounters with colonial subjects: that Canada was civilized and its interlocutors were savages. As Razack concludes, peacekeeping was "a race war waged by those who constitute themselves as civilized, modern and democratic, against those who are constituted as savage, tribal and immoral."[41]

Through it all, the Canadians felt like *they* were the victims, and the Canadian public would ultimately accept that as the true story of the Somalia Affair. "It felt as if we were being mistreated," said one sad Canadian peacekeeper to the court, "we do so much and have it thrown back in our face."[42] The lawyer for Carol Mathieu — who along with Michel Rainville was court-martialled but found not guilty — explained that "extreme conditions existed over there: temperatures of 40, 50 degrees; the desert; the wind; the sand; complete anarchy; the absence of all forms of government."[43] Somalia itself did this to Canada. As in all colonial fantasies, the white nation went into the heart of darkness and discovered pure evil, and while most of its representatives maintained their dignity and civilization, a few succumbed to the evil around them and became it.

That those who "went native" were mostly Indigenous seemed to validate the entire narrative. Canada was punished for its good intentions, and Canadians remembered one of the ugliest episodes in its peacekeeping history as a tragedy that was done *to* it, rather than by it.

"Ethnic Tension" and the Rwanda Genocides

Many a student has approached me with a desire to write an essay about Canadian General Roméo Dallaire, the tragic figure at the heart of the Rwanda genocides, who, to so many Canadians, represented everything that is Canada: impartial, professional, compassionate, sacrificing himself for others. Dallaire's bestselling book, *Shake Hands with the Devil* (2003), told the tale of a naïve Canadian plunged into the heart of darkest Africa, where tribal and ethnic hatred was insurmountable and the bureaucratic shuffle of career diplomats at the United Nations failed to give Dallaire the resources and authorization he needed to prevent the wholesale slaughter of Africans by Africans. Given a few modern twists, at its core this is a story as popular today as when it was first written a century earlier to describe any number of imperial adventurers conquering and civilizing Africa.[44]

But, of course, this story ended badly. The white saviour Dallaire was unable to stop the carnage in Rwanda, and Western journalists flooded stores with trite books bearing sensationalist titles like *Season of Blood* and *Harvest of Skulls*, which sounded more like the names of heavy metal bands than serious engagements with a tragic episode in history. In his own lurid tale, Dallaire vividly describes his trauma as a result of witnessing the violence and he quickly became a celebrity in Canada; Dallaire, not any of the millions of people affected by the conflict in Rwanda, Burundi, Uganda or Zaire (Congo), became the real victim/hero in the eyes of Canadians.

The narrative that came to be accepted wisdom in the West was that "ancient, ethnic hatreds" had led to an horrific genocide committed by Rwandan Hutus against Tutsis, while neutral and ineffectual Western powers did nothing. To illustrate how distorted this narrative was requires some engagement with the history of the Great Lakes region of Africa, since it is precisely ignorance of that history that allows this distortion to go unchallenged. What follows is a brief overview designed to contextualize Canada's involvement in Rwanda, which I detail after providing this historical background. What develops is a picture of a crisis rooted more in the hierarchies of class and colonialism than in oversimplified narratives of "ethnic tension."

By most accounts, the Tutsi had migrated into the region already occupied by the Hutu (and the Twa) by at least the 14th century, and what emerged was a feudal society with shared religion and language, politically and economically dominated by Tutsi. In fact, many scholars have suggested that the terms Hutu and Tutsi corresponded less to ethnicity and more to social class; if you were a peasant you were Hutu, if you were a landlord or administrator you were Tutsi.[45] These distinctions were loose, at first, but became much more formalized under the modernizing Tutsi monarch Rwabugiri in the mid-19th century. When German and later Belgian colonizers took control of the countries, they mobilized this ethnic split to use the Tutsi as a collaborating local elite. Claiming that the Tutsi had an ancient European ancestry, the Belgians proclaimed them "Europeans with black skin." Racial identity became fixed and formal, ID cards were printed, and class was now more directly determined by whether one was Hutu or Tutsi. Using this structure, the Belgians enriched themselves while husbanding the precolonial class divide which would later explode as "ethnic violence."

Class and ethnicity had become linked; as Susan Thomson insists, it was "use and abuse of power by Tutsi chiefs that created Hutu consciousness," under the dominion of the Europeans.[46] Disruptions to mostly Hutu peasants' ability to maintain control over their land, their cattle and their labour aroused their ire and led to the 1959 revolution. Tutsi chiefs, since the mid-19th century, had exacted forced labour from mostly Hutu peasants, who had been largely shut out of opportunities for education and class mobility. But a small and subaltern Hutu elite had formed, gaining enough land and wealth to raise a serious challenge to Tutsi rule as the Belgians prepared to decolonize. When elections in 1952 and 1956 were stolen by Tutsi elite with Belgian support, Hutu nationalist movements began to launch a more violent challenge to Tutsi/Belgian authority. In 1959, the Belgians suddenly decided to cut their losses and side with the majority Hutu, facilitating the emergence of a Hutu-dominated Rwanda. In the now separated state of Burundi, the new government was led by Hutu seeking to build a pluralist multi-ethnic state, but the Tutsi elite refused to give up power, and, with the help of the CIA, they assassinated the first two leaders of independent Burundi and subsequently restored pro-West, neocolonial rule under Tutsi leadership.[47]

Back in Rwanda, many privileged Tutsis, abandoned by their Belgian benefactors, decided to leave the country as the prospect of a Hutu state became real. Some fled out of fear of Hutu violence, but most of this wave of émigrés were from the wealthy, collaborating classes and were also motivated by the desire to maintain their class power.[48] While some settled in Burundi and integrated into the Tutsi elite there, more travelled north to Uganda, from which they determined to regroup and launch attacks against the Hutu government in Rwanda in an effort to retake the country. Calling themselves *inyenzi*, or cockroaches, they carried out raids against primarily Hutu peasants in northern Rwanda, which generated a combination of panic and rage among these communities.[49] Hutus formed defensive militias in response, most famously the Interahamwe, which carried out reprisal attacks on *inyenzi* as well as Tutsi civilians still living in Rwanda.

In effect, then, colonialism and the postcolonial settlement had emboldened right-wing ethnic nationalists within both the Tutsi and Hutu. Many Tutsis who remained in Rwanda were politically moderate — some were socialists — or were themselves peasants who had more in common with Hutu peasants than with the Tutsi former elite. But the *inyenzi* raids provoked waves of violence among Hutu, especially after a 1963 attack menaced Kigali and raised the spectre of a Tutsi counter-revolution. Right-wing Hutus capitalized on that fear and fomented violence that left some ten thousand people killed, many of them Tutsi moderates who had no association with the *inyenzi* raiders. The situation was further inflamed in 1973 when the right-wing Tutsi government in Burundi carried out a massive ethnic cleansing of Hutus. The goal of the Michel Micombero government in Burundi, representing the Tutsi minority there, was to eliminate the ongoing resistance of Burundian Hutus. As such, at least 200,000 Hutus were killed and a similar number fled north into Rwanda. This wave of refugees brought not only increased pressure on Rwandan land for peasants but also collective trauma from the genocidal campaign they had survived.

A period of relative calm in Rwanda was established after a coup led by Juvénal Habyarimana in 1973. Habyarimana gestured towards reconciliation of Hutu and Tutsi and established quotas for civil service positions that were roughly based on population. These were complemented by economic reforms modelled after the centre-left government of Tanzania: for instance, lands previously held by wealthy Tutsi landlords and used for grazing were seized and redistributed to Hutu peasants, thus significantly increasing food production for a time. In the meantime, coffee production provided a relatively consistent source of capital, and Habyarimana improved public services and infrastructure, health and education. These reforms were limited and reliant on some coercion, but by several metrics Rwanda was doing better than any other state in the Great Lakes region. These were a legitimate attempt to pursue national development balanced between justice — after centuries of Tutsi domination — and reconciliation, designed to blunt the edge of Hutu resentment and affirm that Rwanda would remain a multi-ethnic state.[50]

But Habyarimana's government, if genuinely reformist, was not socialist. In a capitalist economy with significant semi-feudal dynamics, there remained an elite ruling class increasingly comprised of Hutu landowners, an urban bourgeoisie and the political mandarins connected to Habyarimana himself. Though primarily ethnic Hutus, they had gradually inherited the privilege once afforded to the Tutsi elite, and as the economy slumped in the late 1980s, Habyarimana was facing the prospect of class struggle emanating from the increasingly impoverished Hutu peasantry. The collapse of coffee prices in 1989 exacerbated an already serious problem, for which Habyarimana did not have a solution.[51] It was at that point that right-wing forces within both the Tutsi and Hutu communities found, in one another, a solution to their problems. The consequences would be catastrophic.

Leadership of the Tutsi right — which would emerge victorious after the genocides — came out of the émigré community in Uganda. Tutsi refugees there had failed to overthrow the Hutu government of Rwanda, but they saw an opportunity in the rise of Uganda's Yoweri Museveni in the 1970s. The Tutsi in Uganda had struggled with the vaguely left-leaning President Milton Obote, who viewed them with suspicion; he was likely channelling a combination of ethnic chauvinism and genuine concern over what was a quite militarized right-wing community.[52] By 1985, Museveni's forces had seized power in Uganda, and he was hailed in the West as a reformer, given his commitment to dismantling whatever architecture of state support Obote had built up, to be replaced by neoliberalism and austerity. Museveni was funded and supported by the West, and the Tutsi exiles now found themselves better positioned than ever before to launch a full-scale invasion to recapture Rwanda. With Museveni's help, they built the Rwandan Patriotic Front (RPF) under the leadership of Paul Kagame, who had a reputation for violent torture as Museveni's head of intelligence.[53] In 1990, they crossed the border into Rwanda and never looked back.

Rwandan President Habyarimana was presiding over an economic crisis, exacerbated by yet another wave of Hutu refugees fleeing Tutsi violence in Burundi in 1988. The 1990 RPF invasion added one more problem, but Habyarimana saw an opportunity to channel growing class frustration into anti-Tutsi anger. Fearmongering around the possibility of a Tutsi occupation and slaughter of Hutus was churned out from sources close to the government, particularly over right-wing radio, amplifying a sense of emergency among many Hutus. Habyarimana's motives might have been cynical, but the message was not farfetched. The RPF brought extreme violence as it invaded from the north, sending Hutu and even some Tutsi peasants fleeing south towards Kigali. As the RPF war continued, it became clear that they had, in fact, planted loyal agents inside Rwanda, giving added pitch to the fear that even regular, civilian Tutsis might be enemies of the Hutu.[54] The 1993 assassination of Burundi's first Hutu president by Tutsi military officials generated yet another massive upheaval in that country; as many as 100,000 Hutus and Tutsis were killed in the clashes that followed, and some 700,000 additional Hutu refugees fled Burundi, many to a Rwanda, already on edge from the RPF invasion and the economic collapse.

Poor Rwandans were caught between the competing right-wing projects of the Hutu and Tutsi elite, each stoking fear of one another, which itself generated violence, which in turn gave added pitch to that propaganda, in a cycle that escalated between 1990 and 1994. The 1990 RPF attack set off a cavalcade of panic; many Hutus feared they would lose what little they had or be subject to extreme violence at the hands of Tutsi extremists. As such, they were receptive to invocations of violence against Tutsis within Rwanda. Those Tutsis, as a result, increasingly lived in fear of their Hutu neighbours and grew to view the RPF as their only hope for survival. By 1993, President Habyarimana recognized that his army would likely lose against the RPF — which was better equipped and trained by the Anglophone powers, a point to which I will return — and determined his only course of action was to sue for peace and try to salvage a reasonable settlement wherein the Hutu elite and the Tutsi invaders could share power in Kigali. An agreement was signed in Tanzania, and there was hope that a crisis could be averted. But as Habyarimana's plane was about to land in the Rwandan capital city, it was shot down by a surface-to-air missile. The murder of the president was the tipping point into total chaos.

Debate still rages over who killed Habyarimana. Supporters of the RPF claim that it was Hutu extremists within Habyarimana's government who were seeking an excuse to carry out a pre-prepared genocide against all Tutsi in Rwanda. There is more evidence to suggest that it was, in fact, the RPF that killed Habyarimana, probably in an attempt to sabotage a peace process that would have prevented them from assuming total control of the country. Members of the RPF itself even testified that Paul Kagame claimed responsibility for the assassinations.[55] Whomever was behind the downing of that airplane, it is clear that right-wing elements on both sides encouraged the slide into outright catastrophe.

Habyarimana's murder triggered an horrendous outburst of violence by Hutu Interahamwe militias against primarily Tutsi civilians, but also against many Hutu "traitors" who were seen to be protecting or collaborating in some way with the Tutsi. This episode of violence lasted around 100 days and left as many as 500,000 people dead, and it makes up the core of what came to be known as the Rwanda Genocide. Meanwhile, the RPF carried out reprisal killings in the areas they occupied, in addition to the violence already associated with the war itself. They attacked refugee camps, executed Hutu prisoners and left people to die of dehydration and exposure in the sun.[56] In the end, the RPF easily routed the remnants of Habyarimana's government and occupied Kigali; they quickly established authoritarian Tutsi rule that harkened back to the precolonial era and, a quarter-century later, Paul Kagame still rules Rwanda.

While both the RPF and the Interahamwe were ideologically committed to ethnic supremacy, evidence does not support the claim that average Rwandans were universally accepting of the calls to genocide and war. Quite the contrary, interviews with survivors of the crisis suggest that many Hutu peasants-turned-killers were motivated by fear. It is instructive to read first-hand accounts, including this harrowing description by a Tutsi survivor who was a boy at the time:

> My older brother got killed at a roadblock not far from here. I was alone after that; I am the only survivor in my [immediate] family. The one that killed my brother was a famous Hutu... he and his wife used to visit us at least once a month... Since my family had been killed, I thought it would be smart to go home and hide there until the killing stopped. When I got there the Hutu that killed

my brother was there… I hid my face and hoped he would kill me quickly. But instead, he held onto me so tight, and he cried. He wept and wept and asked for my understanding. He said, "It is war. And we are killing all Tutsi. I am doing my duty. I killed many of my friends. You can't stay here. It's not safe because the [death] squads are on their way to loot and then burn this home." I couldn't believe my ears. This Hutu who killed my people was trying to protect me.[57]

Such stories offer a glimpse of the complexities of the situation. While the above by no means exonerates the perpetrator of the violence, it illustrates that any simple narrative of "ethnic hatred" utterly fails to explain this crisis; what comes up repeatedly in post-genocide testimonials is the sense, by those who carried out killings, that they had no choice. The Hutu militias were merciless with Hutu who refused to participate or protected Tutsis; many Hutu who murdered Tutsis did so out of fear that their own families would be murdered by the militia. Furthermore, hundreds of thousands of Rwandan Hutu were refugees from the horrific slaughters of Hutu by the Tutsi government in Burundi in 1973, 1988 and 1993, and carried the trauma of being survivors of genocide themselves, fearing that the Tutsi had arrived to finish the job.[58] The fact that the Tutsi RPF was, indeed, using indiscriminate violence against Hutu peasants only added to the fear that fuelled Hutu violence. The greatest part of the responsibility for this nightmare, then, must be placed on those parties that were in a position to encourage, facilitate and coerce more vulnerable people into carrying out the attacks. As such, the focus must come back to those far-right elements in both the Hutu and Tutsi leadership who were at the centre of it all. And that is where Canada comes in.

Saint Roméo Dallaire

Canada supported colonial rule and had urged the Belgians to hang on to their colonies in Africa; that colonial project ultimately empowered the right-wing, ethnic nationalist elements within both the Hutu and Tutsi communities. For instance, it was Belgian support that allowed the Tutsi elite to treat the Hutu majority with such contempt and cruelty. This, in turn, strengthened the position of Hutu nationalists and undermined voices from the Hutu left, like Joseph Gitera, who were less interested in the ethnic divide and sought, instead, to raise up the status of the poor masses, Hutu and Tutsi alike.[59] Later, France, as it inherited the role of regional neocolonial hegemon, built close relations with the right-wing Hutu nationalists who took over the Rwanda government, while the Anglo-American powers increasingly threw in their lot with the right-wing Tutsi exiles in Uganda. In the 1990s, the Americans, emboldened by the end of the Cold War and irritated by the presence of a centre-left government in Paris, provoked a minor wave of inter-imperial rivalry vis-à-vis France, which played out in various struggles for influence over postcolonial theatres, like Central Africa.[60] Canada categorically sided with the Anglosphere, but it chose to send primarily Francophone soldiers and diplomats, like Roméo Dallaire, to obscure that position.

It is ironic that so many Canadians think of Dallaire as a neutral man of peace, bedevilled by the African "darkness" and handcuffed by UN bureaucrats. In fact, Dallaire was active and partisan in his role in Rwanda, well beyond his legal mandate, and he unambiguously supported Paul Kagame and the RPF invaders. Dallaire did not actually deny this; he quickly became close friends with RPF supporters like Hélène Pinske and Landouald Ndasingwa,[61] and he described the future dictator Kagame as an "extraordinary man," claiming that his UN force and the RPF "had a good time together."[62] In many accounts, Dallaire and Kagame are uncritically presented as military allies, despite the fact that Dallaire was supposed to be preserving peace, not facilitating an invading army. Kagame told a *New Yorker* reporter that Dallaire provided him with military intelligence during the civil war and claimed that he, Kagame, persuaded Dallaire to "take a side."[63] In fact, Dallaire was so widely considered to be in league with the RPF that, according to several Rwandan refugees, Hutus at football matches who perceived a referee to be biased towards one team would boo and accuse that referee of being a "Dallaire."[64]

Dallaire's partisan interference caused friction among the UN force. Cameroonian Jacques-Roger Booh Booh was Dallaire's superior but found himself routinely undermined by Dallaire, who, against Booh Booh's orders, helped the RPF obtain weapons, training, intelligence and even food. Booh Booh insisted that the purpose of the force was to maintain peace and that this would require working with the Rwandan government to try to implement the peace agreement signed in 1993, but, as he put it in 2005, Dallaire became an "objective ally of one of the parties in the conflict."[65] Not only did Dallaire refuse to draw attention to RPF atrocities in northern Rwanda, he was even accused of complicity in an RPF massacre of Hutus in the national stadium in Kigali and was potentially implicated in the murder of two Rwandan presidents in 1993.[66]

In Dallaire's version of events, Booh Booh was incompetent; this is repackaged in even more dismissive language from Dallaire's Canadian fans: one called Booh Booh "blatantly unprepared for his job," unable "to grasp exactly what was going on in Rwanda" and "so ineffectual that Dallaire tried to take on more of the diplomat's role."[67] But Booh Booh believed that Dallaire's constant usurping of his authority had more to do with his unwillingness to take orders from an African.[68] It would certainly fit into Dallaire's colonial profile; he was a white man gone to save Africa, and when Bangladeshi peacekeepers arrived to supplement his force, he dismissed them as not "psychologically ready" for the task. He had been shocked when he arrived in Kigali to discover that there were educated Rwandans with political acumen; he had been expecting "an intellectual backwater."[69]

That Dallaire, a man who admitted he could not find Rwanda on a map before he had arrived there only a few months earlier, believed he knew better than Booh Booh, who had been involved in African politics for decades, is a remarkable bit of colonial hubris. Nevertheless, the post-genocide celebrity of Roméo Dallaire served to reassure Canadians of their "goodness" despite the horrible events in Rwanda and the shame that had just been exposed in Somalia. David Black explains that Dallaire came to represent "the best tradition of Canadian ethical or humane internationalism," and, as a result, "Canadians' own sense of themselves and their collective moral failure in Rwanda were at least partially mitigated, indeed transcended, by Dallaire's passionate advocacy."[70]

A key piece of the Roméo Dallaire mythology is the claim that he warned his UN superiors about the impending genocide but was ignored by tedious, ineffectual bureaucrats more concerned about protocols than saving lives. Through this tale, Canadians are collectively absolved of any role in the crisis, while, ironically, Africans like Kofi Annan and Jacques-Roger Booh Booh are blamed for it. In the words of Canadian journalist Carol Off, Dallaire was "struck dumb" by the UN's refusal to authorize major intervention by Dallaire's forces when an informant told him of a plan to distribute weapons for a planned genocide. With such overwhelming evidence of the looming catastrophe, the UN's failure to act was an "absurd" illustration of "everything that was wrong" with the

UN mission in Rwanda.[71] But Off drew most of her information here from Philip Gourevitch of the *New Yorker*, who claimed that Dallaire "had developed a remarkable intelligence source from within the highest echelons of the Interahamwe," who "explicitly described the plans to exterminate Tutsi."[72] The problem with this story was that its component pieces fell apart quickly under real scrutiny.

The claim was that Dallaire met an informant, pseudonym Jean-Pierre, who said that the Habyarimana government was stockpiling weapons and was paying him to make lists of Tutsis to kill. This was the basis of Dallaire's famous fax to the UN; Kofi Annan's office did not find the evidence compelling but still suggested Dallaire confront President Habyarimana with it and assess his reaction. In fact, Dallaire had not "developed" the informant at all; he never even met Jean-Pierre (whose real name was Abubakar Turutsinze).[73] Dallaire heard about Jean-Pierre from Faustin Twagiramungu, a politician in a rival party to President Habyarimana, who, himself, never met the famous Jean-Pierre. Twagiramungu passed along the Jean-Pierre rumour with a strong dose of skepticism about its validity. Even Dallaire, at the time, was unsure about Jean-Pierre, and the only UN representative who met him, Belgian Luc Marshal, later admitted he was "duped" by RPF propaganda. Jean-Pierre turned out to be a very questionable source, who could produce little solid evidence for his claims, which makes the UN decision to take restrained — rather than drastic — action, quite reasonable in retrospect.[74] It appears that Dallaire — assuming he knew better than the people around him — was inflaming the situation while people more familiar with the context were trying to restrain him.

The colonial dynamics around Dallaire's story are reflected in several other Canadian interventions in Rwanda. Canadian Louise Arbour took over as chief prosecutor of the International Criminal Tribunal for Rwanda (ICTR), after she was specially chosen by US Secretary of State Madeleine Albright. Oddly, she refused to even consider prosecuting members of the RPF and aggressively rejected the idea of investigating the assassination of President Habyarimana, even after the story broke in the *National Post* that the assassination was likely carried out by the RPF.[75] The ICTR was ultimately an entirely partisan affair — with prosecutors removed if they strayed from the line — and while it no doubt prosecuted some individuals who were culpable of serious crimes, its authority was seriously hampered by its selective application of justice.[76] The court became more a show trial than a serious investigation; access to information was largely controlled by the RPF government, and potential witnesses who might speak against the RPF line knew they would be punished for it. Defendants were not allowed to choose their own lawyers, and some were held for years in prison without ever being charged. Louise Arbour made a name for herself and earned a spot on the Canadian Supreme Court, but no meaningful justice or reconciliation was accomplished by the ICTR.

That didn't stop the Canadian media from making hay with the good works of Dallaire and Arbour. Colonialism finds its perfect articulation in *The Lion, the Fox and the Eagle* (2000) by Carol Off, wherein she celebrates the achievements of both Dallaire and Arbour in Rwanda. Replete with every hackneyed, orientalist turn of phrase one could imagine, Off provides her readers with the usual patter about the "darkness" in the heart of Africa, calling Rwanda "a place where there are no explanations for anything" and where a "wide-eyed" Dallaire faced "dark, random forces of hate and evil." Such claptrap was peppered throughout the book, as when she describes President Habyarimana as being "out of the classic African-dictator mould," who died in a "plane crash"; no mention of the missiles that made that plane crash. Habyarimana only exists in Off's story as a foil to her heroic Roméo, who was "trim, handsome" with "boundless energy," a "lion's courage" and "marooned in the middle of a country he was hardly able to find on a map a year earlier, with only his NATO training and a personal sense of right and wrong to guide him."[77]

Meanwhile, the "pretty" Louise Arbour was ready to tackle Africa's "culture of impunity." Ironically, Off applauds Arbour's willingness to break the law in order to achieve the results she wanted. "Due process, as understood in North America or Europe," Off explains, "would have made it impossible to arrest the prime suspects."[78] Off makes it clear that in lawless, backwards Africa, the white sheriff had to make her own rules to impose civilization. RPF leader Paul Kagame, for his part, played the role of the good colonial subject, whose troops were "polite and well disciplined." Though it was Off's name on the cover, credit for the book was arguably due to one Sian Cansfield, a ghost writer and researcher who worked on Off's book and Dallaire's *Shake Hands with the Devil*, which contains almost identical passages.[79] Mythmaking, it would seem, is all about repetition.

One other Canadian warrants mention. William Schabas did not receive as much limelight but he played an important role in precipitating the crisis. In March 1993, only about a year before the height of the massacre, he was part of a commission of mostly North American human rights organizations which released a report on Rwanda. Though it detailed the violence of Hutu militias, it did not cover the RPF invasion, which had initiated the crisis, and made almost no mention of RPF atrocities; as Schabas admitted, the investigators spent only two hours in territory occupied by the RPF, during which they were chaperoned by RPF soldiers and only met carefully selected witnesses. Six of the ten commissioners knew nothing about Rwanda before arriving in 1993, and none of them spoke Kinyarwanda. No responsible human rights organization would consider that a legitimate investigation. But the report was released to great fanfare, lauding its process as expansive and credible.[80]

If the goal was to generate a crisis for the Habyarimana government in Rwanda — a reasonable guess since some of the organizations were directly established by the RPF — it exceeded expectations. The flimsy, one-sided report became the gospel of the Western powers and provided justification for cutting aid and support for Rwanda, which played a key role in the descent into catastrophe in 1994. It was also used by the RPF to justify a deeper offensive into Rwandan territory, exacerbating the refugee crisis and Hutu panic at the prospect of RPF violence. Thus, it contributed directly to creating the conditions for the massacres of 1994.

Several of the authors of the report actually joined the RPF government after 1994, dropping any pretence of neutrality. Schabas, for his part, nicknamed himself "Humphrey Bogart, alias Bill" in reference to Bogart's adventurer in *The African Queen* (1951), a film steeped in colonial racism. After 1994 he worked with the RPF to obtain aid from Ottawa and travelled the world to act as a witness in criminal and extradition cases involving accused *génocidaires*.[81] Schabas helped the RPF government establish a new legal justice system, running a training program for new recruits. To be accepted into the program, potential Rwandan jurists had to successfully complete a questionnaire that Schabas designed, which included questions about Plato, Sartre and — unbelievably — the capital city of Canada.[82]

The support that these Canadians gave to the RPF reflected that of the Canadian government more generally. In 1990, with Rwanda's economy in convulsions due to the collapse of coffee prices, Canada slashed millions of dollars in aid money to Rwanda, trying to force Habyarimana to accept the neoliberal model of structural adjustments. This only encouraged greater resentment among Hutu peasants; if Habyarimana deflected the responsibility for the crisis onto the Tutsi, he was given plenty of ammunition by the poverty Mulroney's cuts were generating.[83] By 1993, Canada appeared fully committed to the regime change that was taking place and was further slashing its support for Habyarimana's government. Brian Mulroney chastised the Rwandan president for failing to enter peace talks with the invading forces of the RPF. By 1994, the Anglosphere had chosen Kagame and Museveni in Uganda, and these would become Canada's chief allies in Central Africa in the 21st century.

Paul Kagame, Celebrity Dictator

Peeling back the layers of this crisis utterly unravels the standard narrative of the Rwanda Genocide. In an important study of the overwhelming amount of disinformation — particularly that spun by the RPF government since 1994 — that surrounded the crisis, Johan Pottier insists that "Rwanda's bloodbath was not tribal," instead asserting that "it was a distinctly modern tragedy, a degenerated class conflict."[84] Furthermore, it was not an isolated incident that took place over a few months in 1994. The disaster of 1994 was a culmination of years of crisis, and it was followed by an ongoing humanitarian catastrophe in Rwanda, Burundi and Eastern Zaire (Congo), where as many as a million Rwandan refugees fled as the RPF consolidated power in Kigali and launched retribution killings.

Shortly thereafter, the Museveni and Kagame regimes plotted an assault into Zaire which not only targeted Hutu refugee camps but also sought to unseat Zaire's President Mobutu. Mobutu had seized the country some three decades earlier, when it was still called the Congo, with the direct assistance of Canadian peacekeepers, who facilitated his overthrow of the left-leaning Patrice Lumumba. Mobutu was a solid anti-communist ally to the West, but with the Cold War over, and with huge amounts of mineral wealth within Zaire's borders, the West was ready for new leadership there. Museveni and Kagame propped up Laurent Kabila to be their man in Kinshasa.

Kagame launched a major offensive against the refugee camps in Zaire; they were dismantled, thousands of refugees killed, and hundreds of thousands dispersed. Many streamed back into RPF-controlled Rwanda, while others fled further into Zaire. Meanwhile, Kabila's rebels had the direct support of Canada and the US. Canadian Commander Maurice

Baril risked heavy fire to meet with Laurent Kabila, who quickly secured his hold over Eastern Zaire. His soldiers' route mapped perfectly onto the locations of major mineral deposits; mining companies from the West had signed lucrative contracts with Kabila before he had even seized the territory. Vancouver-based First Quantum had contracts worth nearly $1 billion, Barrick Gold made a deal with Kabila for a concession on territory he had not yet "liberated," and the primary shareholder of Adastra Minerals actually provided a jet for Kabila while his forces pushed towards Kinshasa. Barrick's board included Brian Mulroney and George H.W. Bush, and First Quantum hired Joe Clark to liaise with the Kabila government on its behalf.[85]

Back in Rwanda, Paul Kagame built an authoritarian system which claimed to be eliminating ethnic distinctions — people were no longer officially classified as Hutu or Tutsi — but, in fact, it served to naturalize the domination of the Tutsi elite. Under Kagame's rule, all "former Hutu" were considered responsible for genocide and all "former Tutsi" were innocent victims, an ideology reinforced by compulsory re-education programs and the coercive arm of the state. Widely considered to be little more than show trials for enemies of the state, the ongoing efforts by the Kagame government to persecute the *génocidaires* have created a climate of fear, particularly for Hutu peasants, who are among the most economically and politically excluded groups in the world. In Susan Thomson's *Whispering Truth to Power* (2013), Rwandan peasants describe the psychologically twisted way in which the government forces people to accept its narrative; to question it brings charges of "genocide denial," for which hundreds of thousands of mostly "former Hutu" Rwandans have been imprisoned. Most have only one way of earning their freedom: forced labour. It is effectively a revival of precolonial serfdom.

In 2014 Kagame spoke at a rally, proclaiming that "whoever betrays the country will pay the price," an obvious reference to Patrick Karegeya, Rwanda's intelligence chief, who had quit Kagame's government and fled to South Africa, where he was found strangled in a hotel room.[86] In 2015, Kagame changed the constitution to allow himself to remain in office until 2034, provided he won the elections held in that time; but his electoral victory with an absurd 99% of the vote in 2017 was so obviously fraudulent that even the Western press raised its eyebrows.[87] And yet, Kagame is hailed across the Western world as a visionary leader, having cultivated a highly visible public image, including plenty of time spent in New York at the United Nations and arranging celebrity meetups like a 2018 visit with Ellen DeGeneres.

Kagame retains full Western support, in part because his Rwanda has been a devoted supporter of the American Empire, cultivating close ties with the Anglosphere by joining the Commonwealth and supporting the War on Terror while building a close relationship with the Apartheid government of Israel.[88] He visited Ottawa three times after 2004, received an honorary doctorate from the University of Sherbrooke in 2006, and continues to receive direct support from the Canadian government, including a donation of patrol vehicles for his police in 2010. In 2019, Canada sent representatives to attend Kagame's Genocide Memorial Day — which even the United States and Britain avoided, given the increasingly embarrassing state of Kagame's dictatorship — and the *Toronto Star* reported that Rwanda was "rebuilding with hope."[89]

"Balkanizing" the Balkans

While Rwanda's complicated story was refashioned as a simple tale of good and evil, the narrative around the crisis that simultaneously struck the former Yugoslavia never quite achieved the same simplicity, despite the best efforts of some of its propagandists. Indeed, for a series of wars that cost the lives of as many as 200,000 people and displaced up to 3 million, the crisis in the former Yugoslavia in the 1990s was a relatively underemphasized chapter in the story of the modern world. This was particularly odd in Canada, given its contribution not just to the physical devastation but also the authoring of the wars' narrative; as in Somalia and Rwanda, it was "ethnic hatred," we were told, uncorked by the dissolution of the decrepit socialist state and the cunning quasi-socialist dictators who stoked it, that set the Balkans ablaze in the 1990s.

It was, said Carol Off, "a blood feud that went back centuries," in which Canadians found themselves forced to choose which group of savage, serial killers they should support.[90] Only through the determination and sacrifice of Western intervention was the frenzied violence stopped and its architects brought to justice. Canada could proudly boast, among its accomplishments, that it had provided Louise "The Eagle" Arbour as the chief prosecutor for war crimes in the Balkans. As she had in Rwanda, Arbour "kept her eagle eye on the prize and helped to save the [war crimes] tribunals from an untimely demise."[91] The prize, of course, was the prosecution of Slobodan Milošević, named the chief architect of genocide.

This narrative bore only limited relation to the truth. While the faultlines of the conflict appeared to be "ethnic" in nature, the reality was that, as in Rwanda, ethnicity was often simply the matrix upon which larger geopolitical and class struggles were played out. As V.P. Gagnon Jr. powerfully illustrates in *The Myth of Ethnic War* (2004), the lurid tales of "primitive Yugoslavs nursing ancient ethnic hatreds, suddenly free to act out their fantasies of bloodlust" played well in Euro-American newspapers, affixing the old colonial stereotypes of uncivilized natives to the people of the Balkan Peninsula, but the evidence pointed to a far more nuanced and multi-dimensional set of causes for the conflict.[92]

In fact, those sections of the elite who were mobilizing racial violence often struggled to do so.[93] The leadership of both Serbia and Croatia had to heavily manipulate their electoral processes in order to stay in power, suggesting that they did not even enjoy significant popular support, which casts doubt on the notion that they effectively led campaigns of ethnic hate.[94] Indeed, it was striking that tension within urban centres like Zagreb, Belgrade and Sarajevo often fell along the lines of class or, at the very least, the urban/rural divide: refugees during the war who fled the countryside for haven in the cities were the target of scorn and animosity from the urbanites, who shared the same ethnic background but viewed these newcomers as outsiders.[95]

This is not to suggest that ethnically motivated violence did not take place; it most certainly did. But the assumption that it was motivated from the bottom-up — that is, that it dwelt within the hearts of the people who needed any excuse to let it out — was wildly false. When, for instance, Serbian forces attacked and expelled Croats and other non-Serbs living in the Krajina region, they did not have the unanimous support of even the local Serbian population. In fact, Serbian government violence was turned against Serbian moderates, who called for peaceful and equitable resolution of the conflict. Parallel dynamics took place within the Croatian forces, whose attempts to create a purely Croatian Bosnia-Hercegovina ran up against a local Croatian population that did not share such extreme desires; this was evident both in polling data from just before the war and in the very fact that the Croatian nationalists had to undertake a campaign of terror against Croatians who spoke out against the ethnic cleansing.[96]

The Western insistence on making the conflict about "ancient ethnic hatred" is best understood in its historical context. Yugoslavia had forged a unique path after the Second World War; having largely liberated themselves from the Nazis and their local fascist collaborators, the massive communist movement set about building an independent and multi-ethnic Yugoslavia under the leadership of Joseph Broz, more commonly called Tito. Tito's Yugoslavia radiated with hope for the future; Tito himself described it as a "big, beautiful contribution to the progressive movement,"[97] and in some respects it was one of the more successful socialist projects in Eastern Europe. It declared itself independent of both Washington and Moscow, it allowed greater political freedom and local governance than most of the other socialist states in Eastern Europe, and it effectively provided social and economic security such that most people in Yugoslavia enjoyed a fairly high standard of living. Most notably, it created a system of worker self-management that, while not without its flaws, gave workers unprecedented degrees of autonomy over their working conditions. Yugoslavia was not a utopia, and many have argued that its openness to Western market forces was precisely its undoing, but it nevertheless retained a certain prestige within the international left and still evokes a great deal of nostalgia among the people of post-Yugoslavia.[98]

Nevertheless, the waning years of the Cold War saw Yugoslavia's fortunes decline. After Tito's death in 1980 the balancing of federal and local power was not as easily found and the West could smell blood; preying upon the most opportunistic and self-serving leaders, Western banks and financial institutions increasingly drew Yugoslavia into debt and its attendant capitalist restructuring, such that by the 1990s austerity and poverty were increasing rapidly. As the Soviet Union collapsed and the United States swooped in to reap the harvest of its Cold War victory, the writing was clearly on the wall for Yugoslav socialism. Popular discontent rose although, importantly, it was not rooted in anti-communist rebellion, as Western ideological dogma insisted. While the far-right émigré communities were often virulently anti-communist — many such families had been fascists and collaborators and were anxious to exact their revenge on the socialists who had pushed them out[99] — those who actually lived in Yugoslavia had more modest demands, many seeking moderate reforms to the existing socialist system.[100] While there was no unanimous grievance behind the popular discontent of the early 1990s, it was not primarily motivated by anti-communism and it certainly was not rooted in any kind of "ethnic tension."

What came next is still a subject of some debate among critical scholars. What is undisputed is that in the tumult of the collapse of the USSR and the transformation of Eastern Europe, the Yugoslavian federation began to crumble, its dissolution stoked by nationalist far-right leaders in various countries. In Croatia, for instance, President Franjo Tudjman was a quasi-fascist Croatian nationalist who had organized support for his cause during his many years living in Canada; in fact, far-right nationalists were open about the fact that they were raising money for arms, telling the CBC that they needed weapons for "defence" and that they trusted the Croatian government to use the funds however was necessary.[101] By that point, Tudjman had already harnessed the most right-wing elements of Croatian society to generate violence that undermined the wishes of the majority of Croatians, who were mobilized towards more democratic, liberal or socialist aims.[102]

What is less certain is the role played by members of the former elite, who were trying to maintain power across the transition, most notably Serbian President Slobodan Milošević. According to some accounts, Milošević represented one of the best chances at preserving the socialist and federal character of Yugoslavia — and with it the protection of workers' self-management, guaranteed housing and social welfare and security.[103] In other analyses he is characterized as a corrupt and self-serving bureaucrat who knew that the old system was collapsing and sought to preside over its transformation such that he could emerge as a new oligarch.[104] The reality probably lies somewhere between these two positions; Milošević clearly built his base of support around the maintenance of a socialist Yugoslavia and likely did wish to maintain the integrity of the Yugoslavian federation, at least in the middle-term, though it is also beyond a doubt that he intended to maintain his own privileged position and ultimately was willing to use violence to achieve that end.

Whether Milošević was a quasi-socialist or a would-be capitalist oligarch, he was in either case blocking the interests of the Euro-American powers, which had just won the Cold War and were asserting their global domination. Their vision was of a neoliberal Balkan Peninsula with its public property and services privatized, its workers disciplined and capital flowing back to the West. Whatever else he was, Milošević was an impediment to that project; having enjoyed Western support at one point, he increasingly ran afoul of Washington, as when he nationalized the ICN pharmaceutical plant and turned it over to worker control, defying the privatizing dreams of Serbian-American capitalist Milan Panic. The ICN factory was bombed by NATO in 1999 and a narrative of Milošević-as-Hitler was used as justification for that Western intervention.[105]

As the instability created by the end of the Cold War generated increased tension in the Balkans in the late 1980s, the Western powers actually stoked that tension by actively supporting various factions in Yugoslavia in asserting national or sub-national autonomy; the newly reunited German government took a lead role in trying to pry small Balkan countries into alliance with the expanding European Community, while the United States and Canada applied economic pressure on each country to hold its own elections under US supervision. The struggle between those pushing for fragmentation and those trying to maintain Yugoslav unity was, thus, given added fuel by Western interference.[106] Indeed, careful studies of the conflict — even those that ultimately supported the intervention — noted the inconsistencies in Western support for certain groups over others. Most notably, perhaps, was the fact that the West offered significant support to the Kosovo Liberation Army (KLA) despite its having played a major role in the escalation of violence in Kosovo, while condemning the Serbian army for its crackdowns on the KLA.[107] Hypocrisies like this one permeated the conflict.

In that context, the period between 1991 and 2001 was one of perpetual conflict and violence in the Balkans. The US-led interventions, primarily carried out under the auspices of NATO and including a prominent Canadian presence, which conducted some 10% of the bombings in Serbia — were responsible for a tremendous amount of violence and destruction.[108] While typically billed as peacekeeping missions, the soldiers sent to the Balkans primarily behaved like an aggressive invasion force. The 1995 offensive in Bosnia was described by Ian McKay and Jamie Swift as having "encompassed mass bombings and ethnic cleansing [wherein] a blitzkrieg on a civilian population was officially presented as a form of peacekeeping."[109] Indeed, NATO bombing did not prevent humanitarian crisis, as was always claimed, but often created it. For instance, during the 1999 bombing of Kosovo, Foreign Affairs Minister Lloyd Axworthy claimed that NATO was "engaged in Kosovo to restore human security to the Kosovars."[110] And yet three weeks of NATO bombing killed more civilians in Kosovo than had died in the previous three months. Even Canada's former ambassador to Yugoslavia admitted that the medicine was worse than the disease.[111]

Indeed, the NATO bombing campaigns were utterly disastrous; more than a million Serbs were displaced by the war — whether across the new borders or within them — and not only did the bombing create millions of refugees of many ethnicities but it also destroyed the infrastructure needed to support them.[112] The degree of physical damage was hard to calculate, though it was valued at well over $1 billion, and the effects of this destruction were many. In addition to the loss of crucial systems of sanitation and electricity, many NATO bombs contained depleted uranium, the toxic effects of which would remain for years to come.[113] The bombed facilities included libraries, theatres, hospitals and senior care homes. Television and radio stations were also targeted, to help NATO achieve information dominance, and the Danube River, the source of drinking water for ten million people, was poisoned.[114] Peacekeepers sent to the Balkans engaged in sexual violence and rape in Bosnia and Kosovo — so much so that the UN was compelled to create a new code of sexual conduct — and they came to occupy an important role in the burgeoning market of sex trafficking.[115]

Michael Parenti lamented the destruction of Yugoslavia, which left it "a more privatized, deindustrialized, beggar-poor country of cheap labour and rich resources available at bargain prices, defenceless against capital penetration, so divided that it would never reunite."[116] The evidence for Parenti's claim was clear in examples like the publicly owned Zastava automotive factory, which had to shed 80% of its workforce after it was mostly destroyed by NATO bombs. Many in the former Yugoslavia believed that NATO was specifically targeting worker-owned factories, especially in the so-called "Red Belt," a region in southern Serbia that was solidly socialist in orientation and that was pounded with bombs despite not being industrially significant.[117]

For Canada, the wars in the Balkans were an opportunity to re-assert its place in the North Atlantic alliance. Proponents of Canada's active participation in Western military interventions argued that "Canada's credibility as a member of the international security community" was in question and that it "had to demonstrate that it was still a player" after its more limited participation in the Gulf War.[118] Nevertheless, most Canadian narratives of the war framed it in terms of "ethnic hatreds" and of "evil" men, like Milošević, committing genocide. Mainstream sources about Canada's role in the Balkans were almost exclusively studies of the minutiae of military strategy or the heroism of Canadian soldiers. As for the soldiers themselves, they seemed to have little understanding of the situation, one describing his witnessing of a crowd of refugees by explaining, "you know genocide was a big thing over there — it was rampant while we were there but we just didn't know it."[119] It did not cross the soldier's mind, evidently, that the refugees might have been fleeing NATO bombs or that the conflict might have been more complicated that a simple tale of Serbs committing genocides.

The outcome of the disastrous wars in the Balkans was ultimately satisfying to the Western powers that had fostered them. By the late 2010s, the fragmented republics of the Balkan Peninsula were firmly under the grip of neoliberal capitalism. Igor Štiks and Srećko Horvat describe the dismantling of Yugoslavia from the standpoint of its aftermath:

> Post-socialist citizens today feel largely excluded from decision-making processes: most elections have turned out to be little more than a reshuffling of the same political oligarchy with no serious differences in political programmes or rhetoric. Many lost their jobs (during the privatization campaigns) or saw their labour conditions worsen and their pensions evaporate; most of the previously guaranteed social benefits (such as free education and health care) gradually disappeared. In addition, citizens are heavily in debt, owing money to foreign banks that proliferated in the Balkans to the point of controlling its whole financial sector… when the dust [of the wars] finally settled, ordinary citizens found themselves not only with a devastated country, but also with empty pockets and without the old social safety net.[120]

The many books which celebrate the sacrifice and bravery of Canadian soldiers who fought in the Balkans, which document every troop movement, artillery formation and armoured vehicle, and which give us the soldiers' accounts of how much they missed their families and built comradery with fellow soldiers, consistently fail to account for the actual legacy of the wars.[121] In classic colonial fashion, the ends were assumed to be benevolent — these "backwards" people needed help so we helped them at great personal cost — even when the evidence clearly suggested otherwise. Meanwhile, the complicated history that led into the Balkan wars is simplified in order to frame Canada as unquestionably on the right side, especially in the vilification of Slobodan Milošević. That Milošević bears responsibility for violence that took place during this period is beyond doubt; that he was uniquely genocidal and villainous is a leap that has consistently failed to cut muster among critical scholars. Nevertheless, Canadian writer Carol Off describes him matter-of-factly as one of "history's villains…hungry for absolute power and control of Yugoslavia."[122]

That Off should so casually oversimplify this is hardly a surprise, given that the real subject of her study was Canadian judge Louise Arbour, responsible for prosecuting Milošević for crimes against humanity. The process of that trial, however, was widely criticized for being a politicized kangaroo court;[123] Arbour created anti-Milošević public media stunts in 1999 that helped build consent for the Kosovo bombing campaign, while making public appearances with high-ranking British and US officials as they announced escalations of the war against Milošević.[124] The Canadian judge was playing a critical role in building consensus around the NATO bombing that would prove so disastrous for millions of people, while reinforcing the Canadian role in bridging the Anglo-American imperial alliance. That it required some flexibility with the truth was nothing new for the Canadian establishment. As part of the ramping up towards war in Kosovo, CBC correspondent Nancy Durham interviewed an 18-year-old girl who claimed her six-year-old sister had been killed by Serbs. Though it had a powerful impact in Canada, the story turned out to be false, which was reported quietly after the war.[125]

Meanwhile, Canadian military academics published papers which repeated unprovable claims about the number of lives "saved" by the Canadian operations — evidently 350,000 in one operation in Sarajevo — and reassured themselves and their readers that "the villagers of Sector West…welcomed the arrival of the Canadians with baked sweets because they could finally live in peace." At the same time, they repeated the usual criticisms of the "weak" United Nations, noting that "it was unfortunate that the UN as a whole did not adhere to Canadian standards." Indeed, according to Major Dawn Hewitt, "the UN should never have hesitated to display force if it was necessary. No one in the Balkans respected the UN for soft-pedalling or backing down… every display of weakness was seized upon and exploited."[126]

This was in line with much of the discourse in Canada in the late 1990s, which viewed UN peacekeeping as weak and ineffectual and sought for Canada a more aggressive military role in the world. As the colonial logic went, the ruthless, uncivilized and cunning people of places like the Balkans would take advantage of northern kindness and would only respond to physical force. Thus, violence — more violence and displayed more quickly — was needed to keep the natives in line. Ironically, according to the soldiers themselves, they had little respect for the UN rules of engagement anyway: "Those rules went out the window when we got to Medak," explained one soldier, "we just said 'Fuck this!!' and we gave them everything we got. You felt bad because you knew you killed people. I don't know the numbers."[127] The numbers were significant. But the Canadians' frustrations with not being able to kill at will the people whose countries they had invaded would soon be assuaged. As the wars in the Balkans were winding down, the attacks of September 11, 2001, would give the colonial powers all the pretext they needed to set the UN aside and engage in the kind of aggressive wars they believed they had been unduly restrained from in Somalia, Rwanda and Yugoslavia.

The War on Terror

Writing at the end of the 1990s, just before the declaration of the War on Terror, Himani Bannerji summed up the moment clearly, describing "economic and political crisis," "the threat of fascism" and — perhaps most importantly — the retreat of the international left:

> Anti-imperialist politics [were] in disarray and national liberation movements [were] substituted by various right-wing nationalisms or capitalist state inspired multiculturalisms which [spoke] in the name of culture, tradition and identity.[128]

Bannerji was highlighting the extent to which the capitalist classes had defeated and co-opted the waves of resistance unleashed in the middle of the 20th century and, in the wake of their defeat, sought to instead placate the masses with politically vacuous, emptied versions of the ideas that had inspired real struggle; Bannerji's hypothesis would be reconfirmed some two decades later in Asad Haider's *Mistaken Identity* (2018), which reflected on precisely the problems that Bannerji had anticipated.[129] From its height in the 1960s, the global rebellion had been defeated by a concerted effort to break it; the nightmares of the post-Soviet experience exposed how much further there was to fall, and yet, the organized left was in disarray.[130]

Her observations were prescient, insofar as the War on Terror would illustrate both the confidence that the Western ruling classes possessed in their capacity to dominate the poor and marginalized, within and beyond their borders, and also the extent to which legitimately emancipatory movements had been sidelined by anti-American resistance which was, itself, often reactionary and regressive. This fact was borne out in, for instance, the prevalence of right-wing Islamic movements at the front of the challenge to US power in the Middle East. But this was also an insidious aspect of the internal failures of the North American left. As Bannerji concluded, the Canadian ruling class had seized upon the idea of a Canadian multicultural mosaic as a way of diffusing the real racial and cultural tensions that threatened to upset the settler capitalist project. The language of "diversity" would serve as a "diffusing or a muting device," undermining, for instance, Indigenous movements towards armed struggle over land claims and reducing them to "cultural demands."[131]

By the end of the 1990s, multiculturalism was a sacred Canadian value, so much so that immigrants perceived to have failed to "assimilate" would often be accused of rejecting Canadian multiculturalism. Meanwhile, this multiculturalism was part of the ideological apparatus that would be used to justify Canada's increasing presence in global affairs. The conflicts in Somalia, Rwanda and the Balkans were relentlessly framed as "ethnic violence" in a concerted effort to distinguish those places from Canada, a state which claimed to have transcended ethnicity and embraced modern multiculturalism. Indeed, even despite the pervasive sense of failure around Canada's interventions in those conflicts in the 1990s, the Canadian ruling class projected its purported expertise in building a harmonious, multicultural society as evidence for why — in the words of Irish pop singer Bono — "the world needed more Canada."[132] Bono was about to get his wish.

Multicultural Canada was to emerge as a central player in the War on Terror, the central defining dynamic of the early 21st century, through which the United States and its allies would justify a more aggressive and ambitious program to dominate the world through the projection of military power. To the extent that the Cold War had placed limits on the expansionary trajectory of the Western capitalist powers, its end had opened up vast new spaces to which the West felt entitled. The dismantling and devouring of the Soviet Bloc in the early 1990s provided a boost to profits and, combined with the entrenchment of neoliberalism, capital was flying high. But the boom years of the 1990s would inevitably sputter out, trapped within the contradictions of capitalism, wherein greater exploitation of the working class would ultimately make it impossible for those workers to purchase the products they were making. This problem, described originally by Karl Marx as "overaccumulation" of capital without space for profitable expansion, was signalled in the East Asian economic crisis of 1997–98, and the guardians of global capitalism — based in the Anglosphere — understood that they had to find a way to restore profitability.[133]

Their solution was twofold: domestically, they de-regulated the financial markets, allowing capital to turn Wall Street into a massive casino where it could buy and sell exotic and complex derivatives to generate short-term profits out of what David McNally describes as "paper claims to future wealth."[134] The future wealth that these paper claims represented — be they collateralized debt obligations, mortgage-backed securities, credit default swaps or any other related form of financial asset — was fundamentally rooted in working-class debt. In order to maintain consumer spending in a time when wages were being squeezed and costs were rising, working people had to take on greater amounts of debt. This debt allowed them to make purchases — particularly in housing — that their incomes would otherwise have prevented, which was good for the capitalists that needed to keep selling their products to earn a profit. But even with interest rates kept low so that consumers could borrow and spend, capital needed more; the buying and selling of that debt, in ever more complicated bundles and packages on Wall Street, would be a chief source of profits in the 2000s. That this fragile solution came unravelled in 2008 was a shock that everyone saw coming but no one bothered to fix, since the capitalist class correctly assumed that the US government would bail it out while passing on the punishment to the working class.[135]

The War on Terror would offer the second part of the solution. Just as capital had done during earlier crises — the scramble for empire following the crash of 1873, for instance — capital would cash in on the destruction and dispossession wrought by the War on Terror. David Harvey, building from Marx's theory of overaccumulation, would call this a process of "accumulation by dispossession."[136] Limited in its capacity to suck adequate profits out of the territory it already controlled, capital would enlist the US military and its trusted friends to create new spaces for profitable investment.

The centrepiece for this project would be the war in Iraq, a populous and resource-rich country which could provide a wide range of profitable investments, if not for the fact that Iraqis already owned or controlled most industries. This was a problem that could be solved by American bombs, which could physically destroy infrastructure while dislodging and disarticulating the structure of Iraqi society such that it would not have the capacity to protect local ownership — publicly or privately — of its resources and industries. For instance, Iraq had an extensive network of fibre optics that criss-crossed the country, but it was largely destroyed during the US bombing in 2003. In 2006, the puppet government of Iraq awarded a generous $20 million contract to the Canadian company, Nortel Networks, to build a new fibre optics network.[137] Thus, from the devastation inflicted by the War on Terror, came new opportunities for profits for capital.

Importantly, for all the talk in the 1990s of a global, transnational capitalist class, the spoils of the War on Terror were not distributed evenly. That there was an increasing degree of overlap and interconnection between blocs of capital in different parts of the world was certainly true, but the notion that this would end the old dynamics of interimperial rivalry was premature.[138] Capital — that nebulous, vampiric spirit that hangs above everything — is an abstraction that requires actual, existing capitalists to become concrete. Those capitalists are still human, no matter how inhuman they may behave, and humans still live in particular places and possess a range of social, cultural, emotional, psychological and even logistical loyalties to those places. Put differently, there are still US capitalists, competing for limited profits with Russian capitalists, Chinese capitalists and Brazilian capitalists. The War on Terror was designed not only to open up new spaces of profitable investment but also to ensure that they be cordoned off to be accessed only by those capitalists under the umbrella of the US Empire.[139]

Given this context, it is noteworthy that the War on Terror catalyzed a new closeness in the Anglo-American relationship, as British Prime Minister Tony Blair pledged himself completely at the altar of the war, seeking to ensure that British capital would cash in on the profit bonanza that was to come. Canada, naturally, also recognized that as a new rivalry emerged in world capitalism — with the United States increasingly challenged for hegemony by a bloc around China — it would need to earn its place in the Atlantic alliance.[140] Canada's emergence as a central agent in the War on Terror would be largely shaped by this dynamic, and the rewards for participating in US imperialism were sweet — for the

Canadian capitalists in a position to enjoy them — as Nortel Networks discovered in Iraq. The most significant stage upon which this would play out for Canada was in the destruction and occupation of Afghanistan.

Notes

1. Cpl. David Margolin, quoted in Sean M. Maloney and John Llambias, *Chances for Peace: Canadian Soldiers in the Balkans, 1992–1995*, Vanwell Publishing, St. Catherines, 2002, p. 220.
2. Christine Hatzky, *Cubans in Angola: South-South Cooperation and Transfer of Knowledge, 1976–1991,* Madison, University of Wisconsin Press, 2015.
3. Gen. Rick Hillier, quoted in Justin Podur and Sonali Kolhatkar, "'Detestable murderers and scumbags': Making sense of Canada's deployment in Afghanistan," *Briarpatch*, December 3, 2005.
4. The man who played Sgt. Slaughter, Robert Rudolph Remus, received countless death threats during his portrayal of the character and travelled with a security detail and bullet-proof vest.
5. Gwynne Dyer, quoted in Tom Keating, *Canada and World Order: The Multilateralist Tradition in Canadian Foreign Policy*, Oxford, Oxford University Press, 2002, p. 206.
6. Tom Keating, *Canada and World Order,* p. 207.
7. Joe Clark, quoted in Tom Keating, *Canada and World Order,* p. 208.
8. Henry Heller, *The Cold War and the New Imperialism: A Global History, 1945–2005*, New York, Monthly Review Press, p. 282. Setting aside the fact that Iraq, even under Saddam's rule, was far more progressive in most ways than Kuwait (in Iraq, for instance, women made up 46% of the country's dentists and 70% of its pharmacists, whereas in Kuwait, women were not even allowed to vote), some of Saddam's specific grievances with Kuwait were, in fact, quite reasonable. Iraq accused Kuwait of oil drilling that tapped into Iraqi reserves in the Rumaila field and was angry at the Gulf state for conspiring with Saudi Arabia in 1987 to flood the market with oil, thus lowering its price. This had harmed both Iranian and Iraqi producers, but Kuwait had extended loans to keep Iraq afloat. Now that the war was over and Iran had backed down, Kuwaiti creditors demanded Saddam repay the loans. For its part, the US gave several indications that it would support Saddam's war; the day before the Iraqi invasion, Assistant Secretary of State John Kelly specifically noted that the US was not obligated to intervene if Iraqi forces "charged across the border into Kuwait," and Saddam claimed the that US ambassador to Iraq, April Glaspie, told him the Americans had "no opinion on the Arab-Arab conflicts, like your border dispute with Kuwait." Quoted in William Blum, *Killing Hope: US Military and CIA Interventions Since World War II*, London, Zed Books, 2014, p. 322.
9. Gabriel Kolko, *Another Century of War?*, New York, The New Press, 2002, p. 33.
10. Peter Gowan, *The Global Gamble: Washington's Faustian Bin for Global Dominance*, London, Verso, 1999, p. 171–172.
11. "When Rumsfeld was chummy with Saddam…" *Al-Jazeera*, September 4, 2003. Available at: https://www.aljazeera.com/archive/2003/09/200849162656400767.html.

12. William Blum, *Killing Hope*, p. 335.
13. Quoted in William Blum, *Killing Hope*, p. 338.
14. Gwynne Dyer, quoted in Tom Keating, *Canada and World Order*, p. 206.
15. Madeleine Albright, quoted in Mark DeGeurin, "'Is the Price Worth It?' The Crippling Effects of UN Sanctions in Iraq," *Medium*, September 1, 2018.
16. Tom Keating, *Canada and World Order*, p. 209–210.
17. Stephen M. Saideman, *Adapting in the Dust: Lessons Learned from Canada's War in Afghanistan*, Toronto, University of Toronto Press, 2016, p. 91.
18. Colin McCullough, *Creating Canada's Peacekeeping Past*, Vancouver, UBC Press, 2016, p. 89, 91.
19. Colin McCullough, *Creating Canada's Peacekeeping Past*, p. 95.
20. Quoted in Colin McCullough, *Creating Canada's Peacekeeping Past*, p. 97.
21. Quoted in Colin McCullough, *Creating Canada's Peacekeeping Past*, p. 80.
22. Kelly Neudorfer, *Sexual Exploitation and Abuse in UN Peacekeeping: An Analysis of Risk and Prevention Factors*, London, Lexington Books, 2015.
23. Quoted in Colin McCullough, *Creating Canada's Peacekeeping Past*, p. 107.
24. Garth Pritchard, quoted in Colin McCullough, *Creating Canada's Peacekeeping Past*, p. 109.
25. Sherene H. Razack, *Dark Threats and White Knights: The Somalia Affair, Peacekeeping, and the New Imperialism*, University of Toronto Press, Toronto, 2004, p. 6.
26. Peter Debarats, *Somalia Cover-Up: A Commissioner's Journal*, McLelland and Stewart, Toronto, 1997, p. 63. Petawawa is the Southern Ontario location of one of Canada's largest military bases, and it was from there that most of the peacekeepers in Somalia were deployed. Its colonial roots are betrayed by its name; before it was a Canadian military base, it was an Algonquin settlement called *biidaawewe*.
27. Though arguably less loaded than the other word to which it slyly refers, the term "nig-nog" carried racial connotations since at least the 1950s, when it was often used by the English to refer to colonized people of colour.
28. Sherene H. Razack, *Dark Threats*, p. 4–5.
29. These cases are all well-documented by Inquiries undertaken by the governments of the other countries involved, and they stand in remarkable contrast to the behaviour of Botswanan peacekeepers, of whom there were no reports of violence or conflict with local civilians at all. Sherene H. Razack, *Dark Threats*, p. 52–54.
30. In 1969, a coup led by Said Barre ostensibly brought Somalia into the Soviet camp, but Barre's left credentials were always more sizzle than steak. His gambit was to try to play the Cold War adversaries against one another, so it was not long before he switched sides and accepted Western support, during his invasion of Ethiopia.
31. For instance, Canadian Robert Thompson commanded the Ethiopian air force. David Webster, "'Red Indians' in Geneva, 'Papuan Headhunters' in New York: Race, Mental Maps, and Two Global Appeals in the 1920s and 1930s," in Laura Madokoro, Francine McKenzie, and David Meren, ed., *Dominion of Race: Rethinking Canada's International History*, Vancouver, UBC Press, 2017, p. 273.
32. Ian McKay and Jamie Swift, *Warrior Nation: Rebranding Canada in an Age of*

Anxiety, Toronto, Between the Lines, 2012, p. 197.
33. Sherene H. Razack, *Dark Threats*, p. 55.
34. Peter Desbarats, *Somalia Cover-Up*, p. 2.
35. Sherene H. Razack, *Dark Threats*, p. 73.
36. Carol Mathieu, quoted in Sherene H. Razack, *Dark Threats*, p. 73. The casual and mocking feminization of Somalis in the order, itself, is a worthwhile reminder of the pervasive ideology in which Somalis were degraded and disdained by the Canadian military.
37. Sherene H. Razack, *Dark Threats*, p. 81.
38. Quoted in Jocelyn Coulon, *Soldiers of Diplomacy*, University of Toronto Press, Toronto, 1998, p. 94.
39. Sherene H. Razack, *Dark Threats*, p. 100.
40. Sherene H. Razack, *Dark Threats*, p. 98.
41. Sherene H. Razack, *Dark Threats*, p. 86.
42. GCM Private Brown, quoted in Sherene H. Razack, *Dark Threats*, p. 85.
43. Lt.-Col. D. Couture, quoted in Sherene H. Razack, *Dark Threats*, p. 84.
44. Few Westerners writing about Rwanda could resist the temptation to plumb Joseph Conrad's *Heart of Darkness* (1899) for metaphors and allusions, and that fact alone made it impossible for me to ignore the comparison, though I relegate it to a footnote. The lessons of Conrad's story were always ambiguous; it relied fundamentally on the colonial assumptions about European civilization and superiority, and it gave voice to a wide range of racist denigrations of Africans, while at the same time it offered notable discomfort with the enterprise of colonialism in practice. Nevertheless, in the hands of contemporary writers drawing parallels to Rwanda, it is often invoked simply to rehash stereotypes about the "savagery" of Africans and their inherently sinister continent, where white people experience a kind of crucible as they confront the darkest instincts of humanity and either rise above it or get pulled into its seductive shadow. A standout example of this framing can be found in Carol Off's *The Lion, the Fox, and the Eagle* (2000).
45. See, for instance, Susan Thomson's *Whispering Truth to Power* (2013) or Mahmoud Mamdani's *When Victims Become Killers* (2001) which articulate different versions of this position.
46. Susan Thomson, *Whispering Truth to Power: Everyday Resistance to Reconciliation in Postgenocide Rwanda*, Madison, University of Wisconsin Press, 2013, p. 65.
47. René Lemarchand, *Burundi: Ethnocide as Discourse and Practice*, Cambridge, Cambridge University Press, 1994. This was all taking place in the immediate context of the rise of Patrice Lumumba in the neighbouring Congo, among other left revolutionary struggles in Africa. US support for the Tutsi elite was not motivated by any particular concern for the ethnic rivalry but was a political economic calculation taken in the Cold War context.
48. Colin M. Waugh, *Paul Kagame and Rwanda*, London, McFarland & Company, 2004, p. 83.
49. The term *inyenzi* would later be held up as an example of Hutu racial hatred during the 1990s. To those who didn't know the context, the slandering of any group of people as cockroaches would appear to be an obvious precursor to genocide. While it was, no doubt, used as slander, the fact remains that it was

the Tutsi raiders in the early 1960s who gave themselves the nickname, because they travelled and launched attacks by night. Colin M. Waugh, *Paul Kagame and Rwanda*, p. 27.

50. Mahmood Mamdani, *When Victims Become Killers: Colonialism, Nativism, and the Genocide in Rwanda*, Princeton, Princeton University Press, 2002, p. 132–142.
51. This was a result of the end of the Cold War, which allowed Western governments to drop out of the International Coffee Agreement, no longer worried about pushing coffee producing countries into the arms of the Soviet Union.
52. Obote's rule was interrupted in the 1970s by the dictatorship of Idi Amin. Amin initially had the support of the Western powers and the Tutsi exiles, who both saw him as a traditional right-wing dictator willing to facilitate elite rule on behalf of foreign capital. He was overthrown in 1979 and Milton Obote won the next election and remained distrustful of the right-wing Tutsi exiles, who were easily convinced to fight with Museveni to overthrow Obote. Details on Canadian investments from Yves Engler, *Canada in Africa*, p. 83–85.
53. Judi Rever, *In Praise of Blood: The Crimes of the Rwandan Patriotic Front*, Toronto, Random House, 2018.
54. For instance, when RPF leader Paul Kagame left his training program in the United States to return to Rwanda to lead the invasion, he flew into Kigali and was met by RPF operatives inside the city, who quietly picked him up from the airport and transported him clandestinely to the Ugandan border, from where he assumed leadership of the RPF. Colin M. Waugh, *Paul Kagame and Rwanda*, p. 49.
55. Kyumba Nyamwasa, quoted in Judi Rever, *In Praise of Blood*, p. 193.
56. Judi Rever, *In Praise of Blood*, p. 81–106.
57. Quoted in Susan Thomson, *Whispering Truth*, p. 77.
58. René Lemarchand, *Burundi*, p. 76–130.
59. Susan Thomson, *Whispering Truth*, p. 67.
60. This rivalry lasted well into the early 2000s, and perhaps hit its peak in the absurd incident following France's refusal to support the 2003 war against Iraq; angered at French unwillingness to fall in line, Washington restaurants briefly changed their menus to replace "French fries" with "Freedom fries."
61. Carol Off, *The Lion, the Fox, and the Eagle: A Story of Generals and Justice in Rwanda and Yugoslavia*, Toronto, Vintage Canada, 2000, p. 31.
62. Roméo Dallaire, *Shake Hands with the Devil: The Failure of Humanity in Rwanda*, Toronto, Random House, 2003, p. 327, 156.
63. Philip Gourevitch, *We Wish to Inform You That Tomorrow We Will Be Killed with Our Families*, London, Picador, 1999, p. 160.
64. Journalist Robin Philpot was told this anecdote by different Rwandan exiles on separate occasions in Montreal and Belgium. Personal correspondence with Robin Philpot, September 1, 2018.
65. Jacques-Roger Booh Booh, quoted in Yves Engler, *Canada in Africa*, p. 203.
66. "Canadian General Romeo Dallaire Accused of Bias," *Hirondelle News Agency*, February 27, 2006. According to James Gasana — a member of the Rwandan government until 1993 — only a few months before President Habyarimana's plane was shot down, Dallaire agreed to an RPF request to close one of the

runways at the Kanombe Airport in Kigali. This meant that there was only one direction from which planes could land, which proved extremely useful in his assassination. Dallaire was also part of a meeting in the immediate aftermath of the assassination where he insisted that the new prime minister, Agathe Uwilingiyamana, make a radio address; she was assassinated *en route*, and Dallaire has refused to answer questions about the incident. It is unlikely that Roméo Dallaire was directly involved in, or aware of, the plots to have the two highest-ranking political authorities in Rwanda killed within two days. What is much more likely is that in his haste to work closely with the RPF, he was used by them to help destabilize the country to justify a full military take-over, as opposed to the negotiated agreement Habyarimana had agreed to. Either way, the great Canadian hero may have been directly implicated in the murder of two Rwandan leaders, which set off the worst of the horrors of 1994. James K. Gasana, *Rwanda: du parti-état à l'état-garrison*, L'Harmattan, 2002, p. 238.

67. Carol Off, *The Lion, the Fox, and the Eagle*, p. 37–38.
68. Jacques-Roger Booh Booh, *Le patron de Dallaire parle: Révélations sur les derives d'un general de l'ONU au Rwanda*, Paris, Duboiris, 2005, p. 15.
69. Carol Off, *The Lion, the Fox, and the Eagle*, p. 41.
70. David R. Black, *Canada and Africa in the New Millennium*, Waterloo, Wilfrid Laurier University Press, 2015, p. 69.
71. Carol Off, *The Lion, the Fox, and the Eagle*, p. 43.
72. Philip Gourevitch, *We Wish to Inform You*, p. 103, 105.
73. Robin Philpot, *Rwanda and the New Scramble for Africa: From Tragedy to Useful Imperial Fiction*, Montreal, Baraka Books, 2013, p. 91.
74. Jean-Pierre was a fairly low-level employee of the Habyarimana government who had been fired for peddling information. As reported in a sensationalist article in the *New Yorker* which became the basis for much of this narrative, Jean-Pierre claimed that "he was being paid about a thousand dollars a month... to compile lists of Tutsis," but Jean-Pierre was never able to provide any evidence of these lists. Philip Gourevitch, "The Genocide Fax," *New Yorker*, May 11, 1998, p. 42. The only verified evidence Jean-Pierre offered was a small cache of light weapons, but this, itself, was not exceptional in Kigali nor was it evidence of a genocidal conspiracy. The weakness of Jean-Pierre's intelligence casts doubt on the entire narrative of a carefully planned and systematically executed genocide by Hutu leadership, much of which hinged on the Dallaire fax. Faustin Twagiramungu testified that he did not find Jean-Pierre's story credible and found himself accused of genocide-denial and had to flee the country. Twagiramungu was not a Hutu extremist and had welcomed the RPF in 1994, serving as its first prime minister in the immediate aftermath of the worst violence in 1994. At no point did he deny that hundreds of thousands of Tutsi civilians had been killed in that terrible stretch in mid-1994; what he testified was that it was largely *spontaneous* violence that had been stoked by militants on both sides and was unleashed by charismatic right-wing Hutu leaders after the assassination of Habyarimana sabotaged the peace process. This is an entirely reasonable conclusion, backed up by a wide variety of accounts. Susan Thomson, *Whispering Truth*, p. 76–106. Twagiramungu offers detailed comment in an interview in Robin Philpot, *Rwanda and the New Scramble*, p. 89–99. Roméo Dallaire quoted in *Le Point*,

Radio-Canada, September 14, 1994.
75. Thierry Cruvellier, *Court of Remorse: Inside the International Criminal Tribunal for Rwanda*, Madison, University of Wisconsin Press, 2010, p. 157.
76. Even Carol Off's hagiography of Louise Arbour noted that Arbour was "coy when asked why the ICTR never indicted anyone in the RPF. The problem was always the same — how could you indict people who ran the country you were working in?" Carol Off, *The Lion, the Fox, and the Eagle*, p. 358.
77. Carol Off, *The Lion, the Fox, and the Eagle*, p. 29–46.
78. Carol Off, *The Lion, the Fox, and the Eagle*, p. 320.
79. Robin Philpot, *Rwanda and the New Scramble*, p. 146.
80. Robin Philpot, *Rwanda and the New Scramble*, p. 85
81. William A. Schabas, "Atrocities and the law," *Canadian Lawyer*, August/September 1993.
82. Carol Off, *The Lion, the Fox, and the Eagle*, p. 333.
83. Astri Suhrke and Howard Adelman, ed., *The Path of a Genocide: The Rwanda Crisis from Uganda to Zaire*, London, Transaction Publishers, 1999.
84. Johan Pottier, *Re-Imagining Rwanda: Conflict, Survival and Disinformation in the Late Twentieth Century*, Cambridge, Cambridge University Press, 2002, p. 9.
85. Two years after Kabila seized Kinshasa, he insisted that Rwandan and Ugandan forces withdraw. His former-champion Paul Kagame launched a massive assault into the country, which would have succeeded but for the intervention of Angola and Mozambique on behalf of Kabila. The war became a stalemate that cost as many as 5 million lives, with the RPF specifically accused by the UN of carrying out crimes that could constitute genocide.
86. In an interview published in 2015, Kagame acknowledged that he had ordered the killing. François Soudan, *Kagame: Conversations with the President of Rwanda*, New York, Enigma Books, 2015, p. 118.
87. Jason Burke, "Paul Kagame re-elected president with 99% of vote in Rwanda election," *The Guardian*, August 5, 2017.
88. Michael Bueckert, "Paul Kagame and Benjamin Netanyahu are enablers of each other's worst behaviours," *Africa Is a Country*, February 6, 2018.
89. Ignatius Ssuuna, "25 years after genocide, Rwanda has a new light, says leader," *Toronto Star*, April 7, 2019.
90. Maj. Gen. Lewis MacKenzie, quoted in Carol Off, *The Lion, the Fox and the Eagle*, p. 5. Perhaps the most prominent examples of this version of events is the popular *Balkan Ghosts* by Robert Kaplan (1994) and it finds echoes in the work of Canadian aristocrat-professor-politician Michael Ignatieff, especially his treatise on the virtues of empire, *Empire Lite* (2003).
91. Carol Off, *The Lion, the Fox and the Eagle*, p. 7.
92. V.P. Gagnon Jr., *The Myth of Ethnic War: Serbia and Croatia in the 1990s*, Ithaca, Cornell University Press, 2004, p. xiv.
93. Attempts by Serbian nationalists to draft young men into militias to defend the Serb people from purported Croatian brutality in 1991 were a dramatic failure; as much as 90% of the draftees in Belgrade refused to fight. If Serbs had truly been possessed of a frenzied ethnic rage, one would expect a higher level of enthusiasm for the opportunity to kill their blood enemies. V.P. Gagnon Jr., *The*

Myth of Ethnic War, p. 2.
94. V.P. Gagnon Jr., *The Myth of Ethnic War*, p. 178–179.
95. V.P. Gagnon Jr., *The Myth of Ethnic War*, p. 4.
96. V.P. Gagnon Jr., *The Myth of Ethnic War*, p. 4–5.
97. Joseph Broz Tito, quoted in Vladimir Unkovski-Korica, "Self-Management, Development and Debt: The Rise and Fall of the 'Yugoslav Experiment,'" in Srećko Horvat and Igor Štiks, *Welcome to the Desert of Post-Socialism: Radical Politics After Yugoslavia*, London, Verso, 2015, p. 23.
98. Mitja Velikonja, "Mapping Nostalgia for Tito: From Commemoration to Activism," in Srećko Horvat and Igor Štiks, *Welcome to the Desert of Post-Socialism: Radical Politics After Yugoslavia*, London, Verso, 2015, p. 173.
99. Though Carol Off's *The Ghosts of Medak Pocket* (2004) has many flaws, it does provide a useful window into the Canadian connection to the Yugoslav far-right, many of whose members lived and organized in Canada. In particular, thousands of members of the fascist Ustache settled in Canada after the Second World War, claiming to be "victims" of Tito's communist terror. Future Croatian far-right leader Franjo Tudjman gave a speech to some 20,000 Croats in Toronto in 1990 as part of efforts to build support and raise funds for Croatian militants. Carol Off, *The Ghosts of Medak Pocket: The Story of Canada's Secret War*, Random House, Toronto, 2004, p. 15–54.
100. These demands were heterogenous and defy simple generalization. Some wanted to move in the direction of Western-style liberalism as the flow of history seemed to be leading; others wanted to pursue a more effective market socialism, retaining the infrastructure of the current system while reducing corruption; many others wanted to rejuvenate the socialist project itself, which was stagnant and reeling from the Western capitalist interventions that had already been imposed in the 1980s.
101. Carol Off, *The Ghosts*, p. 51.
102. V.P. Gagnon Jr., *The Myth of Ethnic War*, p. 131–177.
103. Henry Heller, *The Cold War and the New Imperialism: A Global History, 1945–2005*, New York, Monthly Review Press, 2006, p. 309.
104. V.P. Gagnon Jr., *The Myth of Ethnic War*, p. 87–130.
105. Michael Parenti, *To Kill a Nation: The Attack on Yugoslavia*, London, Verso, 2000. p. 185.
106. Parenti, *To Kill a Nation*, p. 23–36.
107. Ray Murphy, *UN Peacekeeping in Lebanon, Somalia, and Kosovo*, Cambridge, Cambridge University Press, 2007, p. 71–73.
108. Yves Engler, *Black Book*, p. 220.
109. Ian McKay and Jamie Swift, "Military Intervention and Securing the Third World, 1945–2014," in Karen Dubinsky, Sean Mills and Scott Rutherford, ed., *Canada and the Third World: Overlapping Histories*, Toronto, University of Toronto Press, 2016, p. 205.
110. Lloyd Axworthy, quoted in Yves Engler, *Black Book*, p. 220.
111. James Bissett, quoted in Yves Engler, *Black Book*, p. 221.
112. Michael Parenti, *To Kill A Nation: The Attack on Yugoslavia*, Verso, London, 2000, p. 155–156.
113. Yves Engler, *Black Book*, p. 220.

114. Michael Parenti, *To Kill a Nation*, p. 173.
115. Peacekeepers from the United States even took children as sex slaves; it is unconfirmed whether Canadians participated, though it would hardly be surprising given their proximity during these missions. Kelly Neudorfer, *Sexual Exploitation and Abuse in UN Peacekeeping: An Analysis of Risk and Prevention Factors*, London, Lexington Books, 2015, p. 2, 22.
116. Michael Parenti, *To Kill a Nation*, p. 165–166
117. Michael Parenti, *To Kill a Nation*, p. 167–168.
118. Maloney and Llambias, *Chances for Peace*, p. 6–7.
119. Quoted in Matthew Bin, *On Guard for Thee: Canadian Peacekeeping Missions*, Bookland Press, Toronto, 2007, p. 137–138.
120. Igor Štiks and Srećko Horvat, "Introduction: Radical Politics in the Desert of the Transition," in Srećko Horvat and Igor Štiks, *Welcome to the Desert of Post-Socialism: Radical Politics After Yugoslavia*, London, Verso, 2015, p. 4–5.
121. Examples include Sean M. Maloney and John Llambias, *Chances for Peace* (2002), Matthew Bin, *On Guard for Thee* (2007) and Scott Taylor and Brian Nolan, *Tested Mettle* (1998).
122. Carol Off, *The Lion, the Fox, and the Eagle*, p. 340–341.
123. For a comprehensive account, see George Szamuely's *Bombs for Peace* (2013). The point was not that Milošević was innocent, but that the extent and the uniqueness of his guilt was exaggerated and politicized to serve NATO's aims, while others who bore similar responsibility for the violence in the Balkans — not least NATO members themselves — were absolved.
124. George Szamuely, *Bombs for Peace: NATO's Humanitarian War on Yugoslavia*, Amsterdam, Amsterdam University Press, 2003, p. 406–409.
125. John Allemang, "Patching Up the War's First Casualty," *Globe and Mail*, September 8, 1999.
126. Maj. Dawn M. Hewitt, *From Ottawa to Sarajevo: Canadian Peacekeepers in the Balkans*, Kingston, Centre for International Relations, Queen's University, 1998, p. 93–94.
127. Cpl. David Margolin, quoted in Maloney and Llambias, *Chances for Peace*, p. 220.
128. Himani Bannerji, *The Dark Side of the Nation: Essays on Multiculturalism, Nationalism and Gender*, Canadian Scholars' Press Inc, Toronto, 2000, p. 1.
129. Asad Haider, *Mistaken Identity: Race and Class in the Age of Trump*, London, Verso, 2018.
130. Naturally, such global generalizations must leave room for the particular pockets wherein such resistance persisted or was renewed. The Indigenous Zapatista movement in southern Mexico, for instance, achieved a remarkable degree of dual power in the 1990s and was a signal achievement of the anti-globalization movement. Nevertheless, it was swimming valiantly against the tide of history in that moment, which tended towards defeat and disorganization of working peoples' movements. James D. Cockcroft, *Mexico's Hope: An Encounter with Politics and History*, New York, Monthly Review Press, 1998, p. 295–384.
131. Himani Bannerji, *Dark Side*, p. 9.
132. "Bono endorses Martin, Canada in helping third world," *Globe and Mail*, November 16, 2003.

133. David Harvey, *The New Imperialism*, Oxford, Oxford University Press, 2003, p. 137–182.
134. David McNally, *Global Slump: The Economics and Politics of Crisis and Resistance*, Oakland, PM Press, 2011, p. 80.
135. David McNally, *Global Slump*.
136. David Harvey, *The New Imperialism*, p. 137–182.
137. Todd Gordon, *Imperialist Canada,* Winnipeg, Arbeiter Ring Publishing, 2010, p. 183.
138. The position that interimperial rivalry was a thing of the past was most notably put forward in the early 2000s by Michael Hardt and Antonio Negri in *Empire* (2000).
139. Adam Hanieh, "A 'Single War': The Political Economy of Intervention in the Middle East and Central Asia," in Jerome Klassen and Greg Albo, ed., *Empire's Ally: Canada and the War in Afghanistan*, Toronto, University of Toronto Press, 2013, p. 77–83.
140. Adam Hanieh, "A 'Single War,'" p. 82.

11

Canada's War on Terror

*My innocent children have been killed
by foreigners for no reason.*

— mother of two Afghan children killed by Canadian
soldiers at a checkpoint in Kandahar, 2008[1]

MARAKA, FOUR YEARS OLD, HAD a hole torn through her skull, while her two-year-old brother Tor Jan's chest was caved in. They were in a car with their father, Ruzi Mohammed, when it drove close to a Canadian convoy; soldiers opened fire on the car, leaving the children dead, their father injured and their mother grieving a loss that made no sense. Her children were not terrorists, they were not Taliban, they posed no threat to anyone. In a report on the case, CBC News described the children's grieving mother as "sobbing and shrieking that they were killed by foreigners for no reason."[2] The term "shrieking" was unmistakably derisive in this context; it conveyed that the Afghan woman was out of control, irrational, overreacting. It is inconceivable that a Canadian news agency would have described a grieving mother of a dead Canadian soldier — no matter how upset she might have been — as "shrieking." Read carefully, then, this was colonial denigration of a woman whose children had been killed by Canadian soldiers.

Meanwhile, the Canadian military and political classes circled the wagons for their soldiers. Defence Minister Peter MacKay explained that "a horrible decision had to be taken" because the vehicle was "behaving erratically."[3] The military issued a statement explaining that it regretted the incident, taking time to note that this was a difficult time for the Canadian soldiers who had killed the Afghan children: "This is a tough incident for the crews involved to deal with, as this is the last thing soldiers want to happen."[4] Grieve not for the dead Afghan children, the Canadian public was being told, but for their killers. The soldiers were quickly cleared of any wrongdoing in the matter and the children's father, Ruzi Mohammed, was supposed to be paid compensation for the family's loss and the fact that his own injuries cost him his job as a driller. It was not clear whether that compensation ever arrived, and when questioned about it, Canadian officials explained that "this being Afghanistan, these things can take time to make their way through the system."[5]

Should the soldiers who fired on that car have faced more severe punishment? There is no simple answer to that question. If the facts provided to the public were true and complete, then the defence they gave wasn't entirely unreasonable in its context; out of fear that the car might be carrying a bomb with the intention of crashing into a Canadian vehicle and exploding, the soldiers were ordered to open fire on the car to prevent that possibility. It all happened quickly, and, presumably, the soldiers made the best decision they could in the moment. This is plausible, at a certain level, though it also needs be noted that in Western counter-insurgency wars of this era, opening fire on people approaching convoys or roadblocks became such a common occurrence that some observers actually called it a "tactic" in the coverup of civilian deaths.[6]

Given a Canadian public disciplined to "support the troops," it was no surprise that they were absolved of any culpability. But it raised the larger and more difficult question that Canadians had been taught to ignore: should Canadian troops have been in Afghanistan at all? Had there been no occupation, no convoy, no insurgency, no counter-insurgency, would Maraka and Tor Jan Mohammed still be alive? What did it mean that Canada was so deeply enmeshed in the infinite, global War on Terror which produced human tragedy on a daily basis? Why were some lives deemed more expendable than others and why did the Canadian public so readily accept this? Was the "Afghan mission" itself beyond redemption?

Afghanistan: Canada's Longest War

"Death to Canada" was the chant repeated by hundreds of Afghan protestors at a highway blockade in September 2007. The blockade was protesting a violent raid, one of hundreds conducted by the invasion forces, that killed two civilian religious leaders outside Kandahar, where Canadian troops were primarily based.[7] Though the Canadian public was kept mostly in the dark about the worst details of the occupation of Afghanistan, the "death to Canada" chants cannot have helped buoy support for a war that had never generated much enthusiasm. Indeed, as Jean-Christophe Boucher and Kim Nossal describe it, "what support there was for the Canadian engagement in Afghanistan always remained tepid, with very few Canadians strongly in favour." Nevertheless, while there was often significant opposition to the war reflected in opinion polls, Boucher and Nossal rightly note that "the opposition always remained passive."[8]

Public apathy towards the war in Afghanistan was interesting, given that it was arguably Canada's most significant foreign policy file since the Second World War. Officially, the war lasted from 2001 to 2014, making it Canada's longest, though Canadian casualties were relatively few; 159 soldiers were killed and around 2000 injured. By contrast, over 100,000 Afghans were killed as a direct result of the conflict, a substantial portion of them civilians, and that number could be as high as 500,000 when considering indirect deaths caused by the war (destruction of crops and infrastructure, disruptions to hospitals and health care, poverty and malnutrition, etc.).[9] A decade into the war, 70% of Afghans were living in extreme poverty, and violence and instability were far worse than they had been before the invasion.[10] Canadians regularly reassured themselves that they were in Afghanistan to promote peace, to stabilize a "failed" state and to promote human rights, especially for women. That Afghan women's associations rejected this colonial logic was an uncomfortable disruption to the narrative and was, as such, typically ignored.[11] Still, despite a full-court press by the Canadian ruling class to sell the war in Afghanistan as a mission of peace and human rights, the nakedness — indeed the "Americanness" — of imperial aggression in Afghanistan prevented the Canadian public from ever fully embracing the war.

The "Afghan mission," as the Canadian elite typically called it, was launched in response to the attacks against symbolic centres of US power on September 11, 2001, the World Trade Centre and the Pentagon. The architect of the attacks was Osama Bin Laden, a wealthy Saudi militant who had once been on the CIA payroll but had turned on his one-time sponsors, resenting the overwhelming US presence in the Middle East, especially in Saudi Arabia. When US President George W. Bush declared the War on Terror, which would come to shape early 21st-century politics, Canada was quick to get on board, joining the invasion of Afghanistan almost immediately. No Afghans had participated in the 9/11 attacks, but US officials claimed that Bin Laden's organization, Al-Qaeda, had used a network of caves in that country as its base of operations. Accordingly, Afghanistan was to be subject to invasion and occupation with the ostensible aim of capturing Bin Laden, routing his organization and discouraging other countries from "harbouring terrorists."

Over many years of teaching Canada's war in Afghanistan, I have noticed a recurring and troubling pattern in my classes. When asked what they knew about Afghanistan from before 2001, few students have ever had an answer. The unspoken assumption held by many Canadians — including the soldiers who were sent there — was that Afghanistan effectively had no history. In the minds of Canadians, Afghanistan was a static society that had existed outside of time and modernity, frozen into a primordial state of "backwardness" that could only be interrupted by Western intervention. As one Canadian soldier put it, "we're in a country that's back two thousand years. It's like walking with people out of *National Geographic*."[12] These colonial assumptions were in harmony with those made hundreds of years earlier about Indigenous Peoples in the West or of Africans fighting for independence during the 1960s.

Afghanistan does, in fact, have a history, which actually sheds some light on the dynamics into which Canada plunged itself in 2001.[13] The country had been notoriously difficult for European powers to colonize, though both Britain and Russia attempted to do so in the 19th century. During the Cold War, Afghanistan was considered a relatively marginal player, initially non-aligned and ruled by a decentralized monarchy which downloaded local power to regional warlords, who controlled most of the land and whose power had carried over from the feudal era. Modernization efforts in the 1920s were thwarted by the British Empire, but by the 1950s, Afghans' appetite for change could no longer be suppressed.[14] As Prime Minister Muhammad Daud began building an industrial base and precipitating the emergence of more capitalist property relations, new class forces emerged in the country, including a growing communist presence, split between the People's Democratic Party of Afghanistan (PDPA) — which was linked closely with the Soviet Union — and the more organic, popular Shola Jawid. These groups sought to separate church and state, reduce the power of the large landowners and institute tribal and gender equality. Daud did not share these radical goals, but he recognized by the 1970s that if he was to seize power, he would need a mass mobilization, which only the communists could muster. They joined forces and, in 1973, the Republic of Afghanistan was born.

Its glory was short-lived; Daud immediately suspended parliament and the constitution and turned against the communists, having previously made that guarantee to his sponsors in the CIA and the regional warlords. His effort to liquidate the left was serious — hundreds of people were killed or arrested between 1973 and 1978 — but Daud underestimated the strength of the movement which had galvanized mass support like none other in recent Afghan history. In 1978, aware that Daud would never share power, the PDPA overthrew Daud and seized power against the wishes of the United States and the Afghan elite. The PDPA quickly made good on several of its promises, including eliminating the patriarchal bride-pricing system, enacting a national literacy program and, most importantly, seizing land from large landowners and redistributing it to Afghan peasants.[15]

Land reform was modest and the PDPA had serious limitations, but Afghanistan's turn to the left was still unacceptable to the United States. Life for most Afghans was getting better under the PDPA, and few believed that American intervention would improve matters. As such, the CIA had to look beyond Afghanistan to find people willing to die to reverse the reforms being enacted in that country. The solution came predominantly from the most right-wing sections of Islam, some within Afghanistan but many from abroad in Saudi Arabia and Pakistan, which resented the PDPA's marginalization of Islamic laws and its undermining of traditional hierarchies and structures of Afghan society.

These right-wing Islamic movements — which would later come to be known as "fundamentalist" — were resolutely anti-communist and incensed by the increasing presence of the Soviet Union in Afghanistan. Though the Soviets had not participated in the PDPA seizure of power, they did offer aid and technical support. Images of Soviet scientists teaching young men and women at the university in Kabul were, to many, a sign of progress; but that progress was unacceptable to the religious right, who immediately began carrying out terrorist attacks against the PDPA. Schools were burned, teachers were killed, and in 1979 an Islamist uprising at Herat ended with the murder, torture and dismembering of several PDPA and Soviet officials, their heads placed on spikes around the city.[16]

Thus was born the Mujahideen, a guerrilla force which would be funded, equipped and trained by the United States to undermine the PDPA government in Afghanistan and draw the Soviet Union into a conflict that would drain its resources and capacities. Among its leaders was Osama Bin

Laden, a wealthy young Saudi capitalist who helped finance and recruit fighters for the movement and who was featured in a fluffy 1993 article in the UK newspaper *The Independent* with the headline "Anti-Soviet warrior puts his army on the road to peace."[17] Peace is hardly what the Mujahideen brought to Afghanistan.

In what would prove to be a significant factor in the final unravelling of the Soviet Union, it sent troops to Afghanistan to protect the PDPA and spent nearly a decade mired in ceaseless struggle with the Mujahideen and local forces that joined it. While the PDPA had maintained some popularity, Afghans did not typically welcome the presence of Soviet troops, who often had little regard for local people or customs and were increasingly viewed as a kind of imperial imposition. The war was also unpopular in the Soviet Union — its own Vietnam — and the Americans poured over $10 billion into assisting the Mujahideen, to ensure that it would end in defeat for the Soviets and devastation for progressive forces in Afghanistan.[18]

When the dust settled, Afghanistan was in the hands of the Mujahideen, who could not decide who among them should exercise power. After a decade of war, the country would slide immediately back into civil war in the early 1990s, this time between different factions of the victorious Islamist forces. It was a group called the Taliban that ultimately emerged from the civil war in 1996 in control of Kabul and able to exert some influence over the rest of the country. Afghanistan was now ruled by forces and ideologies that had been marginalized since the 1950s. It was a major step backwards for the majority of Afghans, but it placed Afghanistan squarely in the US empire as it celebrated its Cold War victory. When the Taliban invited their old ally, Osama Bin Laden, to set up camp in Afghanistan, the US paid little attention. A few years later, planes were flying into the Twin Towers and Afghanistan was suddenly back on the radar in North America. The US-led coalition attacked Afghanistan and took control of the capital within a matter of months, establishing a puppet government under Hamid Karzai, but could only sustain that regime by maintaining a semi-permanent occupying force in the country.

Afghanistan before the invasion, then, had a complex history which involved many of the same kinds of class struggles that took place anywhere else in the world. Far from being frozen in time, Afghans had experienced the growth and consolidation of new class forces, revolution and counter-revolution, and perhaps more importantly, multiple foreign invasions. A people whom Canada tended to view as ancient and prehistoric had, in fact, lived through many of the quintessential struggles and crises of modernity. But little of this history was understood or respected by the Canadian soldiers that began pouring into the country in 2001. Instead, they brought high-calibre weapons and platitudes about "rescuing women" and "maintaining stability" in a country they believed to be a "failed state." Whatever failures were present in Afghanistan were, as Angela Joya concludes, a product of "the legacy of colonialism, the unequal structure of the world economy, the geopolitics of the Cold War, and the turn to neoliberalism since the 1980s."[19]

Yet Canadians continued to assume that Afghan problems were a result of Afghan backwardness and that only the more modern Canadian presence could get the country back on track. That the occupation did not make life better in Afghanistan did little to stop the flood of books published after 2001 valorizing the soldiers and their experiences. The authors of these books — typically journalists and sometimes academics — would often preface by disavowing themselves of any ethical judgement of the war itself. "I will leave the analysis to historians," wrote one, "whether Canada should have been in Afghanistan at all."[20] But the next 250 pages of his book effectively endorsed the war by treating the soldiers as heroes, detailing their inner life, their experience in Afghanistan, their bonds, their struggles and so on. There was nearly no mention of what it was like for Afghans.

Noteworthy in the avalanche of books that followed this pattern was *Fifteen Days* (2008) by right-wing columnist Christie Blatchford, which won a Governor-General's Literary Award. That the book was embraced by the Canadian establishment is telling: it led with a quote from Rudyard Kipling, opened with the bombastic claim that a Canadian unit in Kandahar was a "killing machine" and cartoonishly mocked and denigrated Afghans while lionizing Canadian soldiers, whose own descriptions of events made up much of the text. The book was, inadvertently, one of the single clearest articulations of Canada's colonial imagination in the 21st century.

"They Don't Deserve Our Help"

"Morally, you have to feel superior," explained one Canadian soldier to Christie Blatchford. And superior they certainly felt. Another Canadian is quoted at length yelling at a 25-year old wounded Afghan, claiming that the Afghan would not have shown the mercy he was showing: "That's bullshit. Because I'm better than you, because we're better than you, I will heal you up and patch you up and take you back."[21]

Indeed, throughout the book, Afghans are presented as one of three stereotypes, none of which have any agency or nuance, and all of which serve the Canadian colonial narrative. They are either: 1) bloodthirsty religious zealots who are barely human and disrespect women; 2) inept, cowardly and ungrateful allies who did not deserve Canada's help; or 3) simpering, grovelling victims who would spout platitudinous thanks for Canada's having saved them.

The first category was common ground for colonial occupations, and it was reflected even at the level of public discourse, as high-ranking military officials would speak to the media of Afghans who were "detestable murderers and scumbags," who wanted to "break our society" and were "insidious *by their very nature*."[22] General Rick Hillier was clearly suggesting that there was something intrinsic about Afghan evil; it was their nature, not their circumstances, or political-economic conditions, or a revulsion towards occupation and domination, that made them resist the Canadian presence.

Meanwhile, the second category — Canadian solders' perception of ingratitude from Afghans — is worth highlighting, given its hallowed position in the annals of colonialism. Rudyard Kipling himself mused about the "ungrateful" natives — "the blame of those ye better, the hate of those ye guard"[23] — and it figured prominently in the aftermath of the Somalia Affair, where Canadian peacekeepers' violence was justified by their feeling underappreciated by the Somalis they were there to "save." In Afghanistan, Canadians routinely chastised Afghans as ingrates, one admitting to "yelling and swearing" at a group of very old men for not helping the Canadians fix their country.[24] Indeed, the Canadians often had particular venom for their supposed allies in the Afghan National Police (ANP), created to protect the puppet government in Kabul. Canadian soldiers viewed the ANP as lazy and cowardly; the presence of Afghan troops was designed to obscure that this was a foreign occupation, but the colonial soldiers did not like it. Here, a soldier describes a mission in which the ANP were in the vanguard:

> Part of the plan was to get the ANP in front of us as we approached the school, because it's their fucking country, and every mission we're supposed to have an Afghan face on it, and I thought you know what it's about fucking time they started fucking coming good on this, let's get them up there. Fucking, you know what, I hate to say cannon fodder, but you know what, it's time for them to take a fucking lead. We'll push up behind and make sure they do it right.[25]

The soldier narrating would then get on the radio to his superior and complain that the Afghans were "hiding in the ditch" and was told "you're going to have to hold their hand." The framing of Afghans as cowardly children dovetails with the idea that they were ungrateful and undeserving of Canada's sacrifice on their behalf, as this soldier expressed:

> You're there to help people, to help the Afghan people make their country better. It's so frustrating to be in that position. You want to say "don't you people realise what you could have?" That's all we want. There were days… when I came back and said, "screw it, it's not worth it. This place is fucked. They don't deserve our help." [But other days] you drive around a corner and you see little kids and you say, "all right, we have to be here."[26]

In the last sentence, we see the third stereotype emerge: the thankful Afghan victim. Indeed, Canadians convinced themselves that "most of the people in Afghanistan want us to win, most of them want to help us,"[27] but it was a long way away from the truth. Opinion polls in Afghanistan throughout the war reflected a consistent opposition to the foreign presence, often as high as 80–90%.[28] It is the elephant in the room with all of these books; even while Canadian soldiers tell tales of barefoot Afghan children thanking them for allowing them to go to school,[29] the reality was that the occupation was always the subject of Afghan anger and resentment.

In keeping with much of the discourse around Canada's occupation of Afghanistan, Blatchford — through the people she interviews — raises the question of whether the war was a good idea only to subsume it under what she frames as the more important matter: supporting the troops. The sister of a Canadian soldier who died is quoted in the book, saying, "I didn't think we should go [to Afghanistan] but once we go, I support them."[30] This was a common theme in discussion around the war; Canadians were increasingly disciplined to "support the troops," whatever they thought of the specific mission in Afghanistan. Any meaningful dialogue about whether the war itself was good or bad was postponed indefinitely; Canadians' job was to simply line up behind the men and women who were putting themselves in harm's way on behalf of the rest of us. But what if the war in Afghanistan — like Somalia, Korea or the First World War — was never about protecting Canadians at all? What if the war in Afghanistan was about policing the world on behalf of capital and empire? The most important question about the war was precisely the one Canadians were being told to ignore.

That there was surprise at Afghans' lack of gratitude for Canada's benevolence was partly a product of the ignorance in which most Canadians were kept about Canada's vicious means and cynical ends in Afghanistan. The occupation, exhaustively documented in the edited volume *Empire's Ally* (2013), was a catastrophe for average Afghans. The establishment of the puppet Karzai government was a boon to capital from the Anglosphere, as US, British and Canadian companies secured lucrative contracts for construction, reconstruction, mining, telecommunications, energy and other industries. Among the Canadian companies that made major profits in Afghanistan after 2001 were Lockheed Martin Canada, Canaccord Financial and SRK Consulting, to say nothing of the massive engineering firm SNC-Lavalin, which seemed to be linked to nearly every Canadian adventure abroad and was briefly embarrassed in the late 2010s by a fraud and bribery scandal. Afghanistan's resource wealth was estimated at some $3 trillion, and the most notable Canadian investor in the country was Kilo Goldmines, awarded a contract for a massive iron mining deposit at Hajigak.[31]

And while the war brought windfall profits to a range of Canadian companies, its aims were broader than simply to bulge the pockets of Neil Bruce and other Canadian millionaires. The war in Afghanistan — like that in Iraq — was about establishing the architecture of the American Empire in the 21st century. US capital needed a world in which resistance to capital was defeated and demoralized, where local client states could be counted upon to maintain the legal and political conditions ideal for exploitation of labour and resources and where there was a multi-level security apparatus to protect the flow of profits from any possible threats. These threats could be anti-capitalist movements, but they could also take the form of general instability — which can upset the logistics of capital accumulation — or interference from rival blocs of capital. Afghanistan, located in a position of strategic importance for the transportation of fossil fuels, could have easily fallen under the sway of America's capitalist competitors — like Iran, Russia or China — and the war was one way of ensuring America's continued dominance in the region.[32]

Canada, as this book illustrates, was deeply invested in the idea of an American, capitalist empire. Canada's foreign policy across a century and a half had been aimed at protecting and promoting the British and US empires, with a keen understanding that Canada could carve out space for its own ruling classes' prosperity under that umbrella. Canada's significant contribution to the war in Afghanistan was to signal to Washington that Canada would "play ball," sacrificing resources, reputation and working-class lives to maintain the integrity and functionality of the US empire.[33] The payoff for Canada was that it would continue to receive preferential treatment within the empire; this included access to contracts, the sharing of information and a seat at the table where the big decisions would be made. Its participation in wars like Afghanistan was designed to be leveraged for those advantages. As Jerome Klassen explains:

> The goal of the conflict in Afghanistan [was] to impose occupation, assert western power, and globalize neoliberal economics. More specifically for Canada…the war [was] a deliberate and self-conscious strategy of the state and corporate elite to fashion a military infrastructure for managing the Third World in conjunction with US imperialism.[34]

Indeed, the war also served to transform the military itself, to shed the orientation towards peacekeeping and generate the enthusiasm, funding and firepower to be a full-fledged imperial army again.[35] By 2017, Canada was contributing just 62 of the over 90,000 UN peacekeepers around the world, ranked 72nd in the world by the numbers. This dramatic reduction in Canada's peacekeeping presence took place alongside an annual military budget that had ballooned from around $12 billion in the 1990s to well over $20 billion per year by the late 2010s.[36] The resources were there, but they were not being put into blue helmets. Canada was being transformed into a "warrior nation," its military restructured and empowered,[37] such that, as Greg Albo notes, even "the architecture of the Canadian state was redesigned significantly to give institutional prominence, permanency, and additional organizational breadth to the new security measures and foreign policy stance" that came with the War on Terror.[38]

"What the Afghans Need Is Colonizing"

In all of these imperial calculations, Afghans' needs were largely irrelevant in Canada's plans, which included using its military position in the country to exert considerable control over the Afghan government. Already beholden to the Western occupation to maintain his hold on power, the puppet president, Hamid Karzai, was actually structured into taking orders from Canadian military officials. Strategic Advisory Team-Afghanistan (SAT-A) was the deceptively dull title given to a cluster of Canadian military officers who were embedded within the apparatus of the Karzai government. SAT-A was in a position to craft Afghan legislation, and indeed it helped to establish the legal architecture of neoliberalism through which foreign capital was able to reap profits from the country.[39] Part of the reason SAT-A was in a position to exert such influence was that the occupation, when it redesigned the structures of Afghan governance, intentionally created a system wherein real power would rest in the hands of the president. As Daan Everts, a former head of NATO's mission in Afghanistan described it,

> It would have been better to have allowed more organized structures, more political actors like parties... the result [of not doing so] has been an extremely chaotic parliament. We deliberately did this. To reinforce presidential position, you weaken the parliament.[40]

Having consciously built a weak democratic system in which the puppet president held most of the power, Canada and its allies then ensured that their puppet did their bidding. The Karzai government welcomed foreign capital, sold off public assets, imposed austerity measures, maintained the power of the local elite and marshalled the limited resources of the Afghan state almost entirely to the violent counterinsurgency and the projection of military force to secure the conditions for foreign exploitation. Needless to say, this was an agenda that served foreign capital, not Afghan people. When Canada offered aid for reconstruction, it often did so only for Afghan communities that agreed to support the Karzai government, playing Afghans against one another and seeking to buy compliance with desperately needed reconstruction aid.[41]

Even when aid was given, much of it never even got to Afghanistan, being siphoned up by the Canadian NGOs and businesses that had been contracted to provide it.[42] Many of the projects — the construction of schools, for instance — that Canadians were told they were offering to Afghanistan were, in fact, unfinished, dysfunctional or non-existent.[43] In the meantime, in order to manage the growing popularity of the Taliban — popular because it was leading the counterinsurgency — Canada encouraged the Karzai government to make concessions to the religious right; with Canada's approval, Karzai re-established some of the most repressive and patriarchal laws that had originally been established by the Taliban, including "the legalization of child marriage, the starvation of spouses [for refusing sex], and the marrying of rapists to their victims."[44]

Despite Canada's being among the authors of this failing apparatus, Canadians were often encouraged, during the course of the war, to think of Afghanistan as a "basketcase" that could not build a functional state. If Canada could not solve Afghanistan's problems, the argument went, no one could. Certainly not Afghans themselves; the *National Post* declared in 2001, "what the Afghans need is colonizing."[45] In fact, there were plenty of Afghans who articulated what they actually needed, but Canada and its allies typically ignored them.

For instance, Afghan journalist Dad Noorani noted that Afghanistan needed a "third force," which lined up neither with the Islamist forces nor the foreign occupation. Noorani suggested that at the core of this third force could have been an alliance of left intellectuals, tribal elders who had remained outside of the power struggles and political movements that had resisted the temptation of using violence.[46] Other Afghans proposed more radical solutions; according to Hamayon Ragstar, the organization that still commanded the most respect among many poor Afghans was Shola Jawid, the communist party that had always had a solid base in the country and had earned the people's respect for having "not engaged in human rights violations [or] selling out the country."[47]

What is clear is that Afghans did not welcome the foreign occupation and were entirely capable of proposing workable alternatives to solve the crisis that had been churning since the arrival of the US-funded Mujahideen in the late 1970s. Canadians largely believed that no such

Afghans existed, and so the responsibility — the "burden" — for saving the country fell to Canadians. Thus, the assumption was always that Canada had good intentions, be they soldiers, generals, politicians, corporations, NGO workers, missionaries or folk singer Bruce Cockburn, who travelled to Afghanistan to entertain the troops.[48] Nevertheless, this book systematically illustrates that Canadians engaging in overseas wars have most often replicated the intentions of their colonial ancestors.

Indeed, it is a fitting testament to the way Canada viewed its mission in Afghanistan that soldiers again took to using the term "Indian Country" to describe where they were.[49] They had done the same, less than a decade earlier, during the operation in Somalia, which devolved into violence, torture and murder of starving Somalis. Not surprisingly, the same pattern emerged in Afghanistan. In the late 2000s, when the story began to leak out of Afghanistan that prisoners were being tortured the claim was that it was Afghan police who were torturing other Afghans and that Canada's only crime was in knowingly transferring prisoners to the Afghan National Police for torture. This version of events stayed comfortably within the narrative that Afghans were savage and violent, and — at worst — the Canadians were tainted and tempted by the dark, lawless "Indian Country" itself to look the other way at Afghans' violence.

Nevertheless, it became clear as early as 2007 that Canadians had, in fact, participated directly in torture.[50] By 2016, this was a matter of public record, reported even in the right-wing *National Post*, which picked up the story noting that Afghan prisoners — many of them poor farmers and workers with no ties to insurgent groups — were so terrified of the prison raids conducted by Canadian soldiers that they "defecated and urinated on the spot" when the Canadians arrived.[51]

Indeed, the torture was traumatic. The violence inflicted on Afghan prisoners included being "caged, beaten, killed, frozen, deprived of sleep, humiliated, hooded, stripped, kicked, electrocuted, executed, sexually assaulted, water boarded, threatened with rape and attacked with dogs."[52] In 2016, Prime Minister Justin Trudeau yet again refused a call to open a federal inquiry into torture in Afghanistan, and, as Sherene Razack notes, Canadians reassured themselves that whatever torture was inflicted on Afghans must have been necessary to extract information from "fanatical, misogynist Taliban prisoner[s]."[53] But this was false; intelligence agencies like the CIA and CSIS had long ago concluded that torture did not provide reliable information. It had no instrumental purpose whatsoever; rather, as Razack argues, it was about marking the space between colonizer and colonized, between the torturers' world — which mattered and had to be protected — and the irrelevant and dying world of the tortured.[54]

This was the precise rearticulation of the colonial imagination that Canada had been built upon. Canada represented the future; the colonized people were the past. Their only chance of survival was to adapt and assimilate — quickly, deferentially and with gratitude — to the colonizers' world. Just as a Canadian soldier had described Afghans as "two thousand years behind," a Canadian colonel explained that Canada had to "work with the Afghans and build their capacity, *starting from zero*." Col. Laurie Hawn, by then a Conservative MP, went on to explain that Canada should try to bring Afghanistan "to something like the standards we would expect in the West."[55] The Afghans were, in Rudyard Kipling's phrasing, Canada's "new-caught, sullen peoples, half-devil and half-child."[56] Like newborn infants, they had no history and the best they could hope for was to learn from the benevolent Canadian occupiers who were trying to mould them into modernity. The nightmare that the occupation had created in Afghanistan was, in this colonial understanding, framed as a gift its recipients did not — or could not — properly appreciate.

Canada in the War on Terror

While Afghanistan was the centrepiece of Canada's War on Terror, it was no means the only piece. In 2003, when the United States expanded the war to target Iraq, Canadian popular culture was gripped by debate. While a new militarism was taking hold of Canadian society, mobilizing the September 11 attacks and the "support the troops" mantra to justify Canada's wider involvement in the war, there was also reluctance among sections of Canadian society about going deeper into a war without end. Iraq had not played any role in the 9/11 attacks; in fact, Saddam Hussein was ideologically in direct opposition to Osama Bin Laden and the Al-Qaeda organization. Al-Qaeda's ideology was rooted in a right-wing version of Islam, whereas Iraq was a secular state, and, as the United States scrambled to assemble evidence of Saddam's construction of nuclear weapons, there was widespread skepticism that Iraq posed a legitimate or immediate threat to the Western world.[57]

As George W. Bush called for a "coalition of the willing" to topple the Iraqi government, the debate in Canada played out dramatically on

Hockey Night in Canada, as two of the country's chief ideologues hashed it out in the middle of a Habs game, after fans in Montreal booed during the US national anthem.⁵⁸ On the far-right was Don Cherry, insisting that Canada should stand beside its friends and go to war out of loyalty to the Americans. On the soft-right was Ron MacLean, insistent that Canada should only participate in the war if it gained United Nations approval. It was not a sophisticated deliberation, featuring only two versions of Canadian ruling-class ideology, but it was a reflection of the fact that Canada was in transition. MacLean's position harkened to the era when Canada cloaked the pursuit of its interests in multilateralism, peacekeeping and other gestures towards international consensus. Cherry, an anachronistic colonial racist, mobilized the language of "loyalty" and "brotherhood" with the US in advocating for war.⁵⁹

In 2003, Ron MacLean's version of Canada still prevailed; the Canadian government did not officially pledge itself to the war, citing the fact that the UN had not sanctioned it, and many Canadians congratulated themselves on taking a strong moral stand against an illegitimate war. Naturally, behind the scenes, the Canadian government worked closely with the US to facilitate the very war it claimed to be standing against. In addition to providing a surge of Canadian troops in Afghanistan to make up for redeployments of US soldiers to Iraq, the Canadian navy actively served alongside the Americans in the Persian Gulf, even taking command of the joint Canadian-US Taskforce 151.⁶⁰ Canadian soldiers participated in the ground war in Iraq; members of the vaunted Joint Task Force Two commando division fought alongside US and British special forces, and many later joined the private security companies — more commonly called mercenaries — that became notorious in Iraq. Canadian mercenary companies like Globe Risk, Global Impact, Gladius and GardaWorld all operated in the country, earning huge paydays while their employees protected Western businesses operating in occupied Iraq.⁶¹

Officially, Canada claimed that the "war" in Iraq happened in the initial weeks of the US invasion, and that everything after that was, instead, a period of "reconstruction." As such, by April 2003, Canada was offering police, prison experts, legal officers, combat engineers and transport planes to assist in that "reconstruction." Indeed, Canada headed the International Reconstruction Fund Facility for Iraq and played a central role in training both the Iraqi military and its police. The RCMP trained as many as 32,000 Iraqi police officers, working closely with its Interior

Ministry, which was notorious for death squads and torture.⁶² A Canadian firm, L-3 Wescam, provided guidance systems for missiles and drones while its parent company was sued for having provided "interrogation teams" to the Abu Ghraib detention centre, which became synonymous with torture and abuse of prisoners.⁶³

According to the US Ambassador in Ottawa, Canada was making a greater contribution to the war in Iraq than most of the countries officially listed in the "coalition of the willing."⁶⁴ For instance, while other countries withdrew their exchange officers in protest, Canada did not; its officers fought alongside the Americans and British, and one even received a Most Excellent Order of the British Empire from the Queen herself.⁶⁵ Another Canadian soldier was given deputy command of the US 18th Airborne division in Iraq, while the head of the Canadian Forces, Walter Natynczyk, was part of the planning of the war itself. The Canadian and US militaries had, by the early 2000s, been linked together to such an extent that a Canadian government refusal to participate in the war was somewhat meaningless; Canadians were bound to whatever the US military did.

This was not a sign of Canadian weakness, as some critics suggested, but rather a reflection of Canadian interests; the Canadian ruling class had long ago determined that the best chances for its success were rooted in Canada's becoming an indispensable part of the US military machine. The war in Iraq reflected the emergence of that project, described by Jerome Klassen:

> After 9/11, the Canadian corporate elite began to advocate a deep integration of the North American bloc and a global military force projection against terrorist groups, rogue states, and weapons of mass destruction. In this endeavour, it was supported by the defence lobby, which began to mobilize for a new foreign policy of cooperative specialization with US global primacy, selective engagement with multilateral institutions, and counterinsurgency warfare in failed or rogue states.⁶⁶

This was, explained Klassen, a "class-based effort at joining empire," a choice taken by the Canadian elite to pursue access to greater profits abroad by embedding itself within the US imperial machine. Whether in Afghanistan, Iraq, Libya or any other state targeted by the War on Terror, Canada would dutifully play its part in order to ensure that it had access to the rewards. In Iraq, those rewards were highlighted by major oil and gas concessions in Iraqi Kurdistan. Vast Exploration received one of the largest contracts; its CEO had developed a close friendship with Jay Garner, the US official who was placed in charge of Iraq. After his time running Iraq was over, Garner joined the company's board of directors.[67]

A lot of mutual back-scratching flowed between North American business and military over the ashes of Iraq, where even the *Washington Post* admitted to an estimate of some 600,000 people killed, mostly civilians, while there were credible estimates that placed the figure closer to a million.[68] A once relatively prosperous country now hosted as many as 10 million people living in poverty, who lacked consistent access to clean drinking water and electricity and who could not count on basic health care provision in their broken and polluted cities.[69] These facts put the lie to Canadian pro-war commentary like that of *National Post* columnist Mark Steyn, who claimed in 2002 that an American occupation would leave Iraq "at bare minimum, the least worst governed state in the Arab world, at best, pleasant, civilized and thriving."[70]

Given Canada's central role in Afghanistan and its significant, if hidden, contribution to the devastation of Iraq, it was clear that Canada was a big player in the War on Terror. By 2008, Canadian Forces general Rick Hillier was boastful about Canada's role: "We're not trying to be one of the big boys," he puffed, "we are one of the big boys."[71] As the War on Terror expanded to involve bombings, invasions, drone attacks and regime changes in several other countries, Canada was often involved. The Canadian military was one of the leaders of the campaign to oust Libyan President Muammar Gadhafi in 2011, sending more than 600 soldiers and a host of naval and air power to bomb the country and assist a rebel group in defeating Gadhafi.[72] The conflict barely made a blip in the Canadian popular consciousness; the few mentions it received in the Canadian media tended to be supportive, accepting without much question that Gadhafi was a bad guy and Canada was right to support the rebels, with little mention of the 20,000 civilians killed in the war. Once Gadhafi was ousted, Canada immediately offered $10 million in aid to the new government, which it believed would be a solid partner in the neoliberal reconstruction of Libya. "We saw a blatant wrong being perpetrated by a brutal regime," said Prime Minister Stephen Harper, "and Libyans now have an opportunity to create a more secure, just, and peaceful country."[73]

In fact, Libya descended into a chaotic civil war immediately following the 2011 attack and remains mired in political instability and violence.

The rebels Canada had backed were far-right Islamist militants who, once in power, had much in common with the far-right groups like the Islamic State of Iraq and Syria (ISIS), which had emerged in post-occupation Iraq. As many as 2 million people tried to escape from Libya, thousands dying in attempts to cross the Mediterranean Sea, and hundreds of thousands of others were swept up by criminal human-trafficking rings.[74] The net effect of Canada's bombing of Libya was to send the country into a spiral in which millions of people — always the most vulnerable — suffered terribly. By 2018, there was chatter in the West about another intervention in Libya to defeat the forces it had supported in 2011. And even as Libya reeled from the effects of Western intervention, the War on Terror began to target Syria.

The dismantling of the Ba'ath government in Iraq — even in its decrepit state under Saddam Hussein — opened the door to more radical right-wing Islamic forces which had had little room to operate under Saddam. By the 2010s, these forces had coalesced in organizations like ISIS which had aspirations beyond the borders of Iraq. Neighbouring Syria was ruled by a dictatorship not so different from that which had been defeated in Iraq; Bashar Al-Assad had also maintained his rule by offering a certain degree of economic stability, secularism and political pluralism for minority groups. Nevertheless, he repressed both right-wing Islamic fundamentalists like the Muslim Brotherhood and more left-leaning democratic activists who rose up during the Arab Spring with equal ferocity. As a full-fledged rebellion broke out against Assad's dictatorship, the secular and progressive character of the rebels in the Free Syria Army was compromised by its complicated and shifting alliances with Islamist organizations like ISIS.[75]

As Assad cracked down on the rebellion, the War on Terror expanded to Syria and thus the West found itself fighting "terrorism" by supporting "terrorists" trying to overthrow the Assad government. To be sure, there were plenty of Syrians who were not affiliated with ISIS or the Muslim Brotherhood and who still wanted Assad out; but the fact that these forces shared a common enemy in Assad made the war very difficult to parse.[76] Adding a NATO bombing campaign to the mix only made things worse. Assad, who still retained some support in Syria, was able to present himself as protecting the country from becoming another Iraq, while also soliciting support from rival regional powers like Russia and Iran. Assad's repression of the rebels became even more merciless, a fact that was brought home for me personally when one of his barrel bombs killed my friend, Toronto-based independent journalist Ali Mustafa.

With Assad now well-equipped and supported, nothing short of a full-scale invasion by the West would be likely to defeat him, and so the regime change was put on hold. Nevertheless, the Western powers carried out massive bombing campaigns against the country, within a strategy that sought to use Islamist organizations to weaken the Assad regime, while containing the growth of those Islamist groups like ISIS which posed a threat to US power in the region.[77] It was a delicate — and entirely cynical — balance that did not immediately yield the results the US wanted. More importantly, however, beneath these geopolitical manipulations, the war brought the full nightmare of the War on Terror upon the Syrian masses; a country of some 20 million people saw nearly half a million people killed, 2 million wounded and 10 million displaced. By 2015, 80% of the remaining people in Syria were living in poverty, its greatest cities were in ruins, and once-eradicated diseases like typhoid and measles were on the rise.[78]

Canada played its role, sending hundreds of military personnel to the region to conduct bombing raids between 2014 and 2016 and maintained a force near the Syrian/Iraqi border thereafter. Throughout the war, Canadian weapons flowed into the country; Canada had become, by 2015, the second largest arms dealer in the Middle East, and many of those arms were put to use in Syria.[79] The Canadian media was initially leery about the Syrian war, but quickly got on board, as the Canadian political classes led the jingoistic charge. Michael Ignatieff, former leader of the Liberal Party, stopped short of endorsing war but used the conflict as an opportunity to criticize Vladimir Putin, whom he claimed was Assad's "last remaining friend on Earth," and who, in backing Assad, was backing "a tyrant whose rule destabilized a region."[80] Ignatieff was right to call Assad a tyrant but blaming him, and not the War on Terror itself, for destabilizing the Middle East was obviously ludicrous. Meanwhile, Canadian senator Hugh Segal called for immediate intervention, comparing Assad to Hitler, and Louise Arbour — the judge who had presided over a travesty of justice in Rwanda and Yugoslavia — argued that Syria needed to be subject to "regime change."[81] Indeed, a few days after the *Globe and Mail* editorialized that "Syria must pay a price," former politicians Lloyd Axworthy and Allan Rock argued that intervention in Syria should be modelled after the mission in Kosovo in 1999.[82]

The war in Syria was complicated, and this brief overview cannot capture that complexity.[83] What is clear, however, is that the War on Terror did nothing to improve the lives of Syrians. There were no winners and, as Lakhdar Brahimi put it, "everybody had their agenda and the interests of the Syrian people came second, third, or not at all."[84] Western bombs served to escalate an already dangerous situation, provoking more violence from the Assad government without successfully defeating it. Even if Assad had been defeated, the forces that would have likely taken control of the country with Canada and its allies' support were, as in Libya, even more repressive and violent than Assad. Indeed, if any one piece of the War on Terror best illustrates its calamitous legacy, this is it.

Meanwhile, just as the war against Iraq had generated a deepening of the conflict in Syria, the dynamics unleashed by the intervention in Libya quickly led to a crisis in nearby Mali. In 2012, France and the United States took the lead on a regime change project in Mali, overthrowing its government not once but twice that year. Canada secretly joined the effort to "pacify" the country in 2013,[85] after the business section of the *National Post* fretted about how the crisis in the country was affecting Canadian gold mining operations, most notably those owned by Iamgold and Avion Gold.[86] The Canadian military presence gradually morphed into a UN peacekeeping mission which supported French and US efforts against a range of forces claimed to be "terrorists."[87] Canadian journalist Rosie DiManno channelled the colonial imagination, describing Mali as a "madhouse" and a "hellhole" and explaining to her readers that "there is always the potential for unforeseen consequences, in a strange land, and Mali is among the strangest lands of all."[88]

The Shadows of Israeli Apartheid

One state in the Middle East that was notably not targeted in the War on Terror was Israel, and Canada's support for that settler colony has remained a significant piece of its foreign policy into the 21st century. When Zionist forces conquered Palestine in 1948, Canada was looking for a way to deflect criticism for its record of refusing Jewish refugees during the Holocaust while also deflecting any commitment to accepting further Jewish refugees. The Zionist cause satisfied these needs and also provided a potential Cold War ally in the Middle East. As Israel consolidated its position, Canada was a consistent source of support, but this position was complicated by the explosion of Palestinian resistance in the late 1980s. Indeed, just as momentum for the end of Apartheid in South Africa reached its height, Palestinians launched the First Intifada, a rebellion which drew significant attention to the repressive, colonial state of Israel.

After Israel's defeat of the Arab armies in 1973, the Palestinians had been largely left to fend for themselves. Israeli occupation of the remaining Palestinian territories of Gaza and the West Bank became more intrusive and Israeli settlers began to heavily populate the ostensibly Arab territories. The presence of Israeli settlers — who typically settled on the best lands and used a disproportionate degree of crucial resources like water and electricity — was then used by the state to justify its increased presence. Palestinian resistance was initially limited by internal conflict, particularly the gap between the leadership of the umbrella organization, the Palestine Liberation Organization (PLO), and one of its more radical members, the Popular Front for the Liberation of Palestine. The latter had linked up with radical movements around the world and posed a serious challenge to the Zionist project but had, by the 1980s, been marginalized; Yasser Arafat's Fatah organization assumed leadership of the PLO, which increasingly claimed to be the sole representative of the Palestinian people.[89]

Arafat's PLO was willing to accept a variety of concessions in order to achieve separate Israeli and Palestinian states, but Israeli leadership had no intention of giving up Gaza and the West Bank and resented the PLO's "peace offensive."[90] As such, it launched an attack into Lebanon in 1982 ostensibly targeting PLO leadership, killing at least 20,000 Palestinian and Lebanese civilians, many of them refugees who had fled the Israeli occupation and were living in refugee camps at Sabra and Shatila.[91] Peace had been successfully avoided, and Israel could now focus on deepening its occupation of Palestine. But in 1987, mass rebellion broke out after an Israeli Defence Forces (IDF) truck killed four Palestinian civilians at a refugee camp in Jabalia. This First Intifada was primarily a series of peaceful demonstrations with violence typically limited to teenagers throwing stones at heavily fortified Israeli troops, but Israel nevertheless used overwhelming force against the uprising, and pressure mounted on the Canadian government to take a stand as it had just done in South Africa. Prime Minister Mulroney was not impressed, calling the comparison "false and odious" and ensuring CBC News that Israel had acted with "restraint."[92]

With the Intifada defeated, the now weakened and self-serving Fatah leadership signed the Oslo Accords, which effectively turned Gaza and the West Bank into areas of permanent occupation, with the PLO to serve as Israel's collaborating elite. Israeli settlements in Palestinian territory expanded — these settlers were subsidized and protected by the state and operated under Israeli law as opposed to that which Israel applied to Palestinians[93] — and the PLO was tasked with curbing the influence of armed factions of Palestinian resistance like Hamas. But the poverty and misery of the occupation only filled the ranks of those organizations that showed themselves to be willing to fight for Palestinian rights and dignity. As Israel erected barbed-wire fences and military checkpoints around Zionist settlements in the Palestinian territories, the already-small Palestinian territories became completely fragmented, and people trying to move products into or out of the territories had to go through multiple checkpoints, where they would be forced to unload all of their goods and then reload them. This had the effect of utterly choking already limited Palestinian economic opportunities; by the early 2000s, it was a human rights catastrophe with nearly half the population unemployed, many living on $2 per day.[94]

Hardly surprising, then, that the Second Intifada was soon launched, attempting to dislodge what was now widely being called Israeli Apartheid, a systematic, racialized occupation that had taken control of most of the former territory of Palestine and left Palestinians penned into impoverished, open-air prisons. While the Zionists and their supporters expended enormous resources to try to smear anyone who used the term "apartheid" — calling it anti-Semitic — this cynical manipulation failed to convince even much of the liberal mainstream in North America; no less than former US President Jimmy Carter insisted on calling it "a system of apartheid" in 2006.[95]

The cruelty of Israeli Apartheid was, by the 2010s, well-documented. With the aim of destroying Palestinian resistance utterly, Israel launched the deceptively named Operation Defensive Shield, described here by Norman Finkelstein:

> The targeting of Palestinian ambulances, the targeting of journalists, the killing of Palestinian children "for sport"... the rounding up, handcuffing, and blindfolding of Palestinian males between the ages of fifteen and fifty, and affixing of numbers on their wrists, the indiscriminate torture of Palestinian detainees, the

denial of food, water, electricity, medical treatment and burial to the Palestinian civilian population, indiscriminate air assaults on some Palestinian neighbourhoods, the systematic use of Palestinian civilians as human shields, [and] the bulldozing of Palestinian homes with the occupants huddled inside.[96]

These kinds of atrocities — and worse — became routine in the West Bank and Gaza. Mass and indiscriminate violence, such as the widely reported bombing of Palestinian children playing on a beach in 2014, was matched by wilful and systematic efforts to break Palestinian spirit through sabotage of institutions and humiliation of individuals. For instance, during an IDF assault on the Palestinian Ministry of Education, soldiers destroyed computer networks, televisions, overhead projectors and student transcripts and other documentation. In another case, the IDF attacked the Palestinian Ministry of Culture and destroyed children's paintings, while spreading their urine and feces throughout the building including inside the photocopy machine.[97]

Service in the IDF was compulsory for Israeli citizens and served to ensure that most civilians received a healthy dose of ideological training, finding themselves either participating, abetting or at the very least witnessing these kinds of actions. It was an effective means of limiting internal dissent, but by the 2010s Israeli society was, nevertheless, increasingly polarized. Sections of the Israeli middle class grew more uncomfortable with the horrific violence necessary to maintain Israeli society as it was; this discomfort was articulated by television talk show host Assaf Harel, who used his normally comedic program to denounce Israelis' "amazing ability to ignore what is happening mere kilometers away" and to acknowledge that "apartheid has been here for ages."[98] Nevertheless, the Israeli far-right was simultaneously gaining popularity, as evidenced by the rightward drift in Israeli electoral politics across the early 21st century. As in other settler societies, Israel could not escape its colonial roots; while some liberals wanted a "nicer" colonial occupation, many others were fully committed to apartheid.

Canada was unwavering in its political, economic and military support for the Israeli settler colony. CSIS and the Mossad — Canada's and Israeli's intelligence agencies — worked closely with one another and with the CIA, formalizing the arrangement in a 2008 "border management and security" agreement.[99] This meant, in practice, more sharing of technology with respect to counterinsurgency techniques vis-à-vis the Palestinians, border-control tactics to maintain the apartheid separation and biometric and other forms of identification to better control Palestinian movements.[100] Canadian police and military also operated closely with Israeli forces, with Canadian General Walter Natynczyk touring Israel in 2009, noting the similarities between Palestine and Afghanistan: "[We have] really come to understand and appreciate what the Israeli forces have had to counter... and the techniques, the way and the procedures that the Israeli military has adopted."[101]

The links between the Canadian and Israeli militaries were many. Israel was a significant source of profits for the Canadian military-industrial complex; over 140 different companies sold military equipment to Israel, from ammunition for large-calibre arms to the body armour worn by IDF soldiers while attacking Palestinian demonstrators. As far back as the 1990s, Nortel had earned a $70 million contract to build new communications technology for the Israeli Air Force, and by the 2000s Canadian and Israeli military producers were actually working together to produce drones and surveillance systems.[102] Meanwhile, the two militaries conducted training exercises together, and many Canadians actually joined the IDF itself. This was given a boost after Heather Reisman, owner of the Chapters/Indigo book empire in Canada, created scholarships for Canadians who returned from service in the IDF.[103] Reisman was not the only Canadian capitalist investing in Israel. Canadian firms like Green Park International and Green Mount International actually built parts of Israeli settlements in the Palestinian West Bank, and the Canadian Highways Infrastructure Corporation built the Trans-Israel Highway. Justin Podur described its significance:

> Israel's network of bypass roads is designed very deliberately to reach from the core areas of Israel itself into settlements in the West Bank without allowing traffic or communication between West Bank towns. These bypass roads are an integral component of [the process] by which Palestinians are isolated, surrounded, and disconnected from each other, made wholly dependent on the whims of the Israeli regime.[104]

Canadian capital was not only profiting but directly participating in the concrete process of constructing Israeli Apartheid. Alongside this material support for Israeli colonialism, Canada also stepped up its diplomatic support: in 2005, Canada began consistency voting against UN resolutions that condemned Israeli violence. The next year, when Israel launched a deadly assault against Lebanon that killed over 1000 people and displaced 25% of the Lebanese population, the Canadian government refused to criticize Israel, even after a Canadian peacekeeper stationed in Lebanon was killed by Israeli bombs. Moreover, an entire Lebanese-Canadian family, including four children, were killed in the assault, while some 20,000 joint-citizenship families were stranded and vulnerable to Israeli bombing.[105]

Israeli officials claimed the killing of a peacekeeper was an accident, but the UN had sent several notifications of the peacekeepers' locations, leading some observers to suggest that the UN was targeted intentionally to discourage it from criticizing Israeli violence.[106] But the Harper government called Israeli violence "measured" and Michael Ignatieff, Liberal Party leadership candidate at the time, reacted to the deaths of 28 Lebanese civilians by saying "this is the nature of the war that is going on… I'm not losing sleep about that."[107] Amazingly, as discussion developed in Canada around these comments, Ignatieff and Harper competed with one another over which of them could be more pro-Israel.[108] Not to be outdone, MPs from the social-democratic NDP, Judy Wasylycia-Leis and Pat Martin, went to Israel in 2004 and marvelled at the apartheid wall, the most dramatic physical manifestation of Israel's colonial system. "It was an incredible experience for me," said Wasylycia-Leis. "That fence shows a lot of restraint on Israel's part," added Martin. "If I were living there, I don't think I would be able to exhibit that much restraint."[109]

For the Jewish diaspora in Canada, Israel and its increasingly genocidal occupation of Palestine was divisive. Anti-Semitism in Canadian cities and during the 1930s and 1940s in Europe gave the Zionist project some appeal, and prominent figures on the Canadian left, like *Canadian Dimension* editor Cy Gonick, supported the creation of Israel and even defended it through the 1950s and 1960s.[110] Nevertheless, Gonick, like most others, increasingly shifted to a more critical position — he would later be a founder of the anti-Zionist Independent Jewish Voices — and, by the launch of the First Intifada, the Canadian left was more solidly behind the Palestinian struggle for freedom. At its mirror opposite were right-wing Jews in Canada who lined up ever more fully behind the Israeli state; by the 1990s and especially in the 2000s, demonstrations in Canadian cities supporting the Palestinian cause would be attacked by members of violent Zionist organizations like the Jewish Defence League.[111]

Always lurking behind the ideological clash over Israel was the spectre of anti-Semitism. From the standpoint of the Israeli state and its supporters, any criticism of Israel was grounds to smear the critic as an anti-Semite, and this strategy was taken up by the Canadian right more broadly. As sympathy for the Palestinian cause grew, Canadian politicians increasingly bemoaned what they called the growth of anti-Semitism on university campuses; both Prime Ministers Harper and Trudeau made this claim repeatedly, suggesting that campaigns to boycott Israeli Apartheid at universities intimidated Jewish students.[112] The Zionist organization B'nai Brith accused students of "inciting hatred" over a poster that featured an Israeli attack helicopter chasing a Palestinian child.[113] The featured helicopter, however, *was* part of the Israeli arsenal used to kill 1400 Palestinians in Gaza in 2008–09, over 400 of them children, and as many as 50 Canadian companies produced parts for the helicopters.[114]

The critique was valid and there were no grounds for labelling it anti-Semitic. But this tactic made it nearly impossible for any organization to engage in such criticism without it being deemed anti-Semitic; from student organizations to trade unions to magazine editorial boards and even to Jewish community groups, supporting Palestinian rights meant sustaining accusations of racism towards Jews.[115] Weaponizing the accusation of anti-Semitism was a cynical tactic used by supporters of Israeli colonialism; it invoked the real and ongoing legacy of violence against Jews to silence critics of Jewish-Israeli violence against Palestinians.[116] It was even more nefarious insofar as it generated an increasingly dismissive reaction from the many people and organizations falsely accused of anti-Semitism; nefarious because — in consistently misdirecting the accusation of anti-Semitism — it served to delegitimize *all* uses of the term.

In truth, anti-Semitism *did* persist, even within progressive movements in Canada; disentangling criticism of the right-wing settler colonial project called Israel from the people and religion that Israel claimed to represent was complicated, and many people and organizations struggled to find that line.[117] A critical position on Israeli capitalist exploitation, for instance, could easily start to sound like the old "Jewish bankers trying to rule the world" conspiracy that helped mobilize the Holocaust. As fascist movements have grown in strength and Nazi nostalgia has translated into a resurgence of genuine anti-Semitism, it has become increasingly important for the left to keep this distinction clear. Swastikas and anti-Semitic graffiti have increasingly appeared in Canadian cities. In 2018 a deadly attack was carried out against the Tree of Life synagogue in Pittsburgh, killing 11 people. In 2019, amid a series of anti-Semitic attacks in New Jersey and New York, the *New York Times* published an editorial reflecting old tropes about the unique "cunning" of the Jew.[118]

The increased presence of real anti-Semitism only made the misuse of the accusation by Zionists and their Canadian supporters that much more dangerous; as Holocaust survivor Suzanne Weiss argued in 2013, Canada had become:

> The world's number one apologist for the Israeli government and its oppression of the Palestinians [who] suffer mistreatment often reminiscent of what Hitler imposed on the Jews. The real threat to Israel's Jewish population comes from their own government's cruelty, its apartheid policies, its land grabs, its theft of resources, its long-term drive for ethnic cleansing… To be true to the memory of the victims of the Jewish Holocaust and all of Hitler's victims, we must defend the Palestinians.[119]

Indeed, Israel has become one of the most fascist-oriented states in the world and has ironically built bridges with fascist governments like that in Ukraine, which still celebrates the Nazi Holocaust. It is yet another in the rogue's gallery of Canada's closest friends, but it makes perfect sense in light of Canada's central goals and ideology. A settler capitalist state that colonized a people it considered beneath it on the civilizational ladder, Israel is a reflection of Canada itself. To condemn Israel's violent colonial apparatus would open the door to the very same criticism of Canada and would interrupt a culture of Canadian self-congratulation that is reaching new heights in the 21st century.

A New Day for Democracy in Haiti

Ideology works in subtle ways. It is often most powerful when it is transmitted not by an authority figure or institution but people who may not even be aware that they are reproducing that ideology. One summer evening in Toronto I found myself in a movie theatre, and, as I waited for the film to start, I sat through an advertisement for the MS Society of Canada. The ad was innocuous on the surface, as it tried to convince people to donate money for research on multiple sclerosis. One of my father's best friends battled with MS, and I have no qualms with the work of the MS

Society. But the premise of the ad was that Canadians were inherently helpful people and so we should apply that helpful nature to those who suffer from MS. The narrator casually explained that "as Canadians we have fought for others," just as it cut to an image of disaster-ravaged Haiti, where Canadians were making a heroic effort to help their neighbours in a time of need. A sign was visible on a rooftop that said "Thank you Canada."

The perception that Canada has been a generous benefactor to Haiti is so pervasive in Canada that conservative commentators have actually bemoaned it as a problem.[120] In mainstream circles, there is a deep-rooted belief that Canada has tried, against all odds, to help Haiti, a country suffering under the weight of natural disasters, political immaturity and local incompetence and corruption. Though Canada claimed no responsibility for these problems, its generous intervention to assist a "backwards" people in setting themselves on the right path reflected the best of Canadian idealism. Prime Minister Paul Martin explained in 2004 that Canada would "take a leadership role in providing the international support needed to produce a blueprint for Haitian society."[121]

Quite the contrary, Canadian policy towards the small Caribbean country helped ensure that it remain among the poorest and most exploited places in the Western Hemisphere, exploitation that was often at the hands of Canadian businesses and enforced by Canadian-trained police. That "blueprint for Haitian society" included the overthrow Haiti's popular and democratically elected president, Jean-Bertrand Aristide. The Western powers proclaimed it "a new day for democracy," but little good came to Haiti as a result of the undermining of its democratic process and the removal of a president who represented the wishes of the poor majority.[122] During a dramatic visit to Haiti in 2004, Prime Minister Martin spoke of a Haitian child: "This little girl is so cute… if she doesn't get an education what is going to happen to her?"[123] Martin's crocodile tears shrouded the fact that the chaos was an outcome of Canada's own policies, cooked up with the United States and France.

Haiti had long been a spectre haunting the colonial imagination. Before it was called Haiti it was a French slave colony known as Saint-Domingue. It was Christopher Columbus himself who marked his arrival at that island by writing that the Indigenous Taíno people he met were "fit to be ordered about and made to work," which Kirkpatrick Sale described as the "birth of American slavery."[124] The colony became a source of massive wealth for the French ruling class, and even as the principles of "liberty, equality and fraternity" were proclaimed by Robespierre in Paris in 1790, little changed for the slaves in Saint-Domingue. But the ideas of freedom expressed by the Jacobins were taken up across the Atlantic, and a slave revolt began in 1791 that would reach its ultimate, successful conclusion in 1804.

During that time, the Haitian revolutionaries, led by Toussaint L'Ouverture, would have to defeat not just the local slave-owning elite but also invasion forces from Spain and Britain — motivated by the desire to prevent any example of a successful rebellion — and a force of more than 35,000 French troops sent by Napoleon Bonaparte. That these "Black Jacobins" — so described by the historian C.L.R. James — were able to defeat the colonial powers and assert their freedom stands as one of the most remarkable stories in the history of the modern world.[125] Indeed, it shook the confidence of the rich in Europe and America — the latter particularly alarmed at Haiti's welcoming of marginalized African former slaves from the US — and there is a strong argument to be made that the victory of the Haitian Revolution heralded the end of the trans-Atlantic slave system itself.[126]

It did not, however, translate into the kind of freedom Haitians hoped it would. France accepted its defeat but only after demanding reparations; it considered the liberated slaves "stolen property" worth 150 million francs, a sum so great that it took Haiti more than a century to pay off the debt. To do so, Haiti was forced to borrow from British, American and other European banks, locking Haitians into a form of dependence, even as British and other merchants moved in to try to take advantage of Haiti's fragile position. Meanwhile, the Spanish and Americans fomented a rebellion on the eastern side of the island, which had previously been a Spanish colony, eventually carving out a separate Dominican Republic, from which the colonial powers tried ceaselessly to undermine Haitian independence. Throughout the first century of Haiti's existence, it was forced to play a dangerous game with the colonial powers, exploiting their own rivalries to maintain a delicate hold on its own sovereignty.[127]

It maintained this balance until the early 20th century, when the United States seized imperial control over Haiti, occupying the country between 1915 and 1934 to ensure that its constitution was favourable to US interests. In the pattern that was typical for American semi-colonies, a succession of military dictatorships ruled over a poor majority, to the benefit of foreign capital and a small local elite, which in Haiti was notable for its conspicuous whiteness. While the majority of the country were descendants of black slaves and spoke a range of Creole languages, the wealthy ruling class was dominated by a French-speaking elite whose ancestors had more likely owned slaves than been them.

In 1957 a US-trained doctor, François Duvalier, tapped into the black nationalism of poor Haitians and presented himself as an alternative to the traditional elite. His appropriation of the language of Négritude covered up the fact that he was an admirer of both the model of military dictatorship introduced by the United States during its occupation and also the economic status quo that had long kept black Haitians impoverished.[128] Duvalier established a dictatorship that would be inherited by his son and, between them, would last nearly 30 years. To keep the angry masses at bay, the Duvaliers established violent death squads called the Tontons Macoutes, who, alongside regular Haitian military and police, killed up to 30,000 people during the dictatorship.[129]

The Duvaliers lived in ostentatious luxury, but by the mid-1980s, popular anger could no longer be contained. Even the US backers of the Duvalier family recognized that it would not survive a wave of major social upheaval, and in 1986, Jean-Claude "Baby Doc" Duvalier was forced into exile. Initially, the US-trained military refused to cede power, but in the hopes of smoothing the transition into neoliberal democracy, it supported an electoral process in 1990. The outcome appalled them. In the waning years of the Duvalier dictatorship, an outspoken liberation theologist named Jean-Bertrand Aristide worked in one of the poorest parishes of Port-au-Prince and drew attention for his fiery speeches which denounced Duvalier, his US backers and the ruling elite that kept most Haitians poor. Speaking to the poor but addressing the colonial powers, he demanded reparations:

> We are asking that you acknowledge that you have stolen — that your countrymen have stolen — during the process of colonization. If you truly want to call yourselves developed countries, you need to acknowledge what you have done to us. But we are not asking for your pity, no, but for you to acknowledge that we have the right to recuperate a part of what has been stolen from us.[130]

Jean-Bertrand Aristide won the 1990 election easily, garnering 67% of the vote, well ahead of the candidate put forward by the United States. But before Aristide could make any serious effort to tackle the problems he inherited, his government was overthrown by the Haitian military at the behest of the CIA. What ensued was chaos; the majority, who backed Aristide, filled the streets and demanded justice and the restoration of democracy, while the military unleashed violence to try to quell the protests. Aristide barely escaped the country with his life, and up to 5000 people were killed in the street battles between 1991 and 1994. As many as 40,000 people tried to escape the violence by sailing to the United States, and the influx of refugees — combined with a remarkable international swell of support for Aristide — prompted the US government to bring back the president they had already overthrown.[131] Restored to power in 1994, Aristide was given strict orders from the World Bank: "The renovated state must focus on an economic strategy centred on the energy and initiative of civil society, especially the private sector, both foreign and national."[132] What the West wanted was an unambiguously capitalist Haiti, ideally ruled by someone who could convince the masses to quietly accept their lot.

Aristide presided over a new round of elections, peacefully transferred power to the winner and planned to campaign again in 2000. His party won handily in the 2000 elections and Aristide began a new term in office, on the promise that he would reform Haiti's economic system, bringing relief to the poor. On the spurious claim of election irregularities, the George W. Bush administration in Washington withheld aid and imposed sanctions on Aristide's government. In spite of that pressure, Aristide was able to take measures to alleviate poverty: he raised taxes on the rich and used the money to introduce literacy programs, to build new schools, hospitals and clinics, to create new public sector jobs, to subsidize the cost of essential goods and to raise the country's minimum wage.[133] Even these minor reforms were enough to make a substantial difference in the lives of the poorest Haitians, and Aristide's efforts were praised by the Food and Agricultural Organization, which awarded him a gold medal for providing food security.[134] Indeed, according to Peter Hallward, it was precisely Aristide's capacity to effect real change in Haiti that made him so dangerous to Western interests:

> Aristide was a threat because he proposed modest but practical steps toward popular political empowerment, because he proposed widely shared popular demands in terms that made immediate and compelling sense to most of the Haitian population, because he formulated these demands within the constraints of the existing constitutional structure, because he helped to

organize a relatively united and effective political party that quickly came to dominate that structure — and in particular because he did all this after eliminating the main mechanism that the elite had relied upon to squash all previous attempts at political change: the army.[135]

In addition to dramatically reducing the power and size of the armed forces, Aristide further set himself apart with his willingness to name colonialism, racism and capitalism as the source of the problems in the country. The French had banned all variations of the Haitian Vodu religion, but Aristide — the Catholic priest — gave them official recognition in the country.[136] Aristide also removed restrictions on the use of the Haitian Creole language and, indeed, to the masses he spoke Creole, not French, asserting the dignity, creativity and wisdom of Haiti's masses against colonial claims of superiority.[137] And he directly criticized capital and colonialism: "The exploiters justify and legalize the exploitation of the majority by a minority," he argued, and his new party, Lavalas, was built upon the Creole slogan, "*Yon sèl nou fèb; ansanm nou fò; ansanm, ansamn nou sé Lavalas*" (Alone we are weak; united we are strong; all together we are a cleansing torrent).[138]

This kind of language was never going to go over well in Ottawa. A state that was built on colonialism and had replicated its dynamics for over a century around the world was not predisposed to welcome such a critical position to the table of "civilized" nations. In the 1990s, Canada's direct involvement in Haiti was minimal and indirect. But by the early 2000s, Canada was anxious to take on a greater role in the maintenance of a capitalist workshop in Haiti, having increasingly invested itself both in the US imperial machine in general and in Haitian exploitation specifically.

"Friends of Haiti"

Most notable among Canadian investors in Haiti was Gildan Activewear, a sweatshop clothing manufacturer that had extensive operations in the two poorest countries in the Western Hemisphere, Haiti and Honduras. In addition to its own exploitative factories, Gildan also subcontracted in Haiti to a company owned by Andy Apaid, a member of the old elite and a violent opponent of Aristide. Apaid led a business council that opposed Aristide, had financially supported the first coup against him and forced his workers to attend anti-Aristide protests. He also had a lengthy record of wage theft and firing workers for complaining about it.[139] Not surprisingly, Canadian mining companies like KWG Resources, Ste-Genevieve Resources and Eurasian Minerals also had their eyes on Haiti and would gain major concessions after the 2004 coup.

Following the election of Aristide in 2000, Canada began stepping up its efforts to undermine the Haitian president. In addition to cutting off all aid, Secretary of State Denis Paradis hosted the "Ottawa Initiative on Haiti," wherein leaders from Canada, the US and France met in a beautiful house in Meech Lake, Québec, to discuss the future of Haiti. This 2003 gathering called itself the "Friends of Haiti" and, needless to say, no Haitians were present.[140] Paradis explained later that "the international community wouldn't wait for the five-year mandate of President Aristide to run its course through to 2005." Instead, said Paradis, "Aristide should go."[141] Haiti's "friends" claimed to be acting in the spirit of democracy promotion, claiming that a set of legislative elections in 2003 were illegitimate and proved that Aristide was establishing a dictatorship. That more than 60% of the Haitian population had participated in the elections, which were deemed free and fair by independent monitors, was a detail that did little to blunt Canada's edge. In fact, Aristide had, on several occasions after his re-election in 2000, offered to hold another round of elections to satisfy the complaints of the capitalist powers, knowing that his Lavalas Party would easily win.[142]

Canada's commitment to defying Haitian democracy was such that it sent officials to meet on several occasions with Haitian opposition groups. Many of these groups had links to the old Tonton Macoutes and other violent paramilitaries, but they received generous funding from Canada to support their project of overthrowing Aristide.[143] That funding was used to foment chaos and violence to undermine Aristide's project; basing themselves in the Dominican Republic, armed groups would attack government offices and police stations — and in one case the Presidential Palace itself — and kidnap and torture Aristide supporters. As this violence escalated, the fact that Aristide had dismantled much of the armed forces made it difficult for him to re-assert control. In fact, many of the insurgents attacking his government were former members of the military that had been reduced by Aristide.[144] As this opposition waged low-intensity civil war, occupying cities and killing those who resisted, the Canadian embassy reported it as "liberation."[145]

Canada's role in Haiti grew substantially around the event of Aristide's overthrow. Having taken a key place in the planning and preparation, Canada sent members of its Joint Task Force 2 to Haiti's capital city on February 29, 2004, to secure the airport for Aristide's removal. With the US doing the heavy lifting, Aristide was flown into exile for a second time. The architects of the coup established a council of "wise people" chosen by officials from Canada, the United States and France and that council appointed an interim government, choosing Gérard Latortue — a neoliberal economist who had lived in Florida for two decades — to be Haiti's new ruler.[146] Capital licked its lips as the World Bank noted that this regime provided "a window of opportunity for implementing economic governance reforms... that may be hard for a future government to undo."[147] The measures taken to intensify neoliberal capitalism in Haiti included: privatization of electricity, water, telecommunications and port facilities; reductions to minimum wage and to subsidies for poor farmers; a three-year tax holiday for big business; and the dismantling of many existing social programs, including the very successful literacy programs Aristide had fostered.[148]

Haiti was to be permanently remade by the very powers that had never forgiven it for revolting in the first place. The irony was palpable, and Haitians reacted with understandable anger. Protests rocked the country as people demanded the restoration of their legitimate government. It was in this moment that Canada stepped up to the plate to prove that it was one of the big boys in the delicate art of subverting democracy, stifling dissent and imposing predatory capitalism on a poor country.[149]

To strengthen Latortue's hold on power, Canada sent more than 500 troops to Haiti to smash the uprising of Aristide's supporters. The Haitian National Police (HNP) was reconstituted and filled with members of the paramilitary groups, who now turned their guns on the protestors demanding Aristide's return. As many as 1000 people were killed in the first weeks following the coup, and that number would more than triple within a few months. Not only did Canadian troops take part in the repression, but over 100 RCMP officers were sent to Haiti to train and provide "operational planning and implementation" for the HNP, particularly around crowd control and intelligence gathering. The HNP would receive $20 million in Canadian funding between 2004 and 2006, making Canada a direct partner and participant in the most horrific period of bloodshed Haiti had experienced since the days of military rule.[150]

After the toppling of its democracy, life in Haiti became a full-fledged nightmare. In addition to a steep decline into ever more extreme poverty — so much so that international journalists regularly reported people sifting through rotting garbage piles to find something to eat — violence and impunity surged following the coup. Locals reported that names of people targeted for assassination were being read over the radio, in an echo of the crisis in Rwanda:

> Every afternoon around 4 pm names are broadcast. Perhaps they are on a list of those whom the new government wants to arrest, or perhaps listeners call in with the name of so-and-so. All are linked with Aristide in some way. Some of those named soon disappear.[151]

While much of the violence was carried out by the Canadian-led HNP, the UN forces sent to support the new dictatorship also had blood on their hands; in just one incident in 2005, as many as 60 people were killed by UN troops in a Port-au-Prince slum. Anthony Fenton and Yves Engler detail it:

> Residents of Cité Soleil said UN forces shot out electric transformers in their neighbourhood. People were killed in their homes and on the street as they went to work. According to journalists and eyewitnesses, one man named Léon Cherry, age 46, was shot and killed on his way to work for a flower company. Another man, Mones Belizaire, was shot as he readied for work in a local sweatshop and died later from an infection. An unidentified street vendor was shot in the head and killed instantly. One man was shot in his ribs while brushing his teeth. Another was shot in the jaw as he left his house to make some money to pay his wife's medical costs and endured a slow death. Yet another man named Mira was shot and killed while urinating in his home. A mother, Sena Romelus, and her two young children were killed in their home, either by bullets or by an 83-CC grenade thrown by UN forces.[152]

This was not the end of Canada's imperial adventure in Haiti but, really, its beginning. "We're building a really nice hotel," explained Sgt. Maj. Kirby Burgess, describing the construction of a massive military base to house the mostly Canadian and US forces in Haiti.[153] After the coup, Canada began to establish a more permanent presence in the country, establishing deeper trade networks, a new embassy to be built by Canadian firm SNC-Lavalin and an extensive arrangement of aid programs mostly designed to maintain government dependence on Canada, rather than support communities. Canada spent $35 million trying to manufacture the outcome it wanted in the 2006 elections; the preferred Lavalas candidate was thrown in jail to prevent his even running a campaign, while the less-popular Lavalas candidate was allowed to run but faced a wide range of manipulations to try to prevent his victory.[154]

When a major earthquake hit the country in 2010, Canada seized the opportunity to play the hero, sending over 2000 troops to aid its neighbour in a time of need. But most Haitians saw, in the Canadian presence, an intensely militarized operation that focused more on rebuilding the infrastructure of economic exploitation than that of local communities. The earthquake was, by all accounts, disastrous, killing a quarter of a million people and displacing six times that number. Nonetheless, the level of devastation was, as Justin Podur notes, a consequence of "the quality of housing construction and the lack of enforcement of building codes, dense populations living in these unsafe buildings near the epicentre of the earthquake, and the lack of infrastructure for response."[155] In short, the dismantling of Haitian society, especially after 2004, is what made the earthquake of 2010 so deadly.

Furthermore, the actual earthquake aid and reconstruction was widely described as a "travesty."[156] The organization of relief efforts was chaotic, given that the Haitian state was effectively incapacitated and the work was contracted out to various foreign governments and NGOs. More importantly, most of the money that poured into Haiti was funnelled right back into the pockets of Canadian and US corporations and NGOs, and occasionally to wealthy Haitians. Problems as basic as the cleanup of rubble from the earthquake could have been solved by paying poor Haitians to do the work, thus performing a crucial task while pumping resources into a society that needed them. Instead, the work was given to big capital — companies like DRC, AshBritt, DAI, Chemonics — and big NGOs, which used a huge portion of the aid money they received to pay and support their own staff.[157] Even conservative estimates suggest that billions of dollars went to the salaries and amenities provided to NGO workers and the spectacle of luxury hotels springing up in a city literally reduced to rubble did little to assure Haitians that the international community had come to help.

Given all of this, how did Canadians emerge with the perception that — as per the MS Society — they had helped Haiti? In the most immediate sense, it was because a massive infrastructure of misinformation — in some cases full-fledged propaganda — had misled the Canadian public about what was happening there. Justin Podur elaborates:

> Many non-governmental institutions (NGOs), especially those that are well-funded, are an instrument of the foreign policy of powerful countries. These countries use their foreign agencies to fund NGOs in poor countries. These NGOs can do "development," "democracy promotion," "human rights promotion," or any number of very benevolent-sounding activities. The logic of their funding sources pushes their policies and public political statements in the direction of the foreign policy of their donors. These statements are then picked up by the press, by official spokespeople, and by progressives in the rich countries as being the voices of the grassroots of the poor countries.[158]

Thus, the directives of Canadian foreign policy were recast as though they came from the voices of poor Haitians. So that even while actual Haitians in Haiti were angry at the presence of militarized Canadian "aid" after the earthquake, Canadians were led to believe that Haitians were desperately clamouring for Canada's benevolence. This assumption was helped by the soothing public presence of Michaëlle Jean, Haitian-Canadian Governor-General, who reassured the public that Canada and Haiti had a strong and mutually beneficial relationship. But for this to work, the story needed to fit with what that public already thought it knew.

For Canadians, the dominant narrative remained rooted in the colonial imagination. Canadians believed that Haitians' struggles were a product of their own "backwardness," their lack of modern institutions, technology and political structures. Given that "backwardness," it could only be an act of generosity for Canada to have involved itself in that country at all, and any problems that may have come from Canada's presence could only have been a product of Haiti's own failings. Thus, even when Canada overthrew a democratic government, trained and supported a violent dictatorship and used the crisis as an opportunity to extract further wealth from a country already suffering, Canadians still believed they had gone there to help.

In 2016, with Haitian institutions in turmoil from so many years of northern interference, Canadian officials scolded the country for the problems that Canada had endeavoured to create, most notably, lack of functional democracy. "They need some tough love," said one official, after Haitians criticized Canada for donating money to Canadian NGOs rather than to the Haitian government directly. Canadian officials responded by claiming that they could not give money to the Haitian government because it was a "kleptocracy." Evan Dyer, reporting on the situation for the CBC, explained that "everyone had had it with Haiti," as if the country were a spoiled teenager. The article ironically drew an old quote from former president Jean-Bertrand Aristide on the problems with Haitian political parties, as if Canada had not twice had Aristide overthrown in order to empower the very "kleptocrats" it was now chastising for failing to hold proper elections. The imperial hubris was staggering, as Canada complained of the Haitian elite "playing political games on the donor's dime."[159]

Ottawa and Empire: Canada and the Honduran Dictatorship

Canada's intervention in Haiti was brash, but if there was an emblematic case of the new Canadian imperialism in the 21st century, it may actually have been Canada's more subtle support for a military coup in Honduras in 2009 and the dictatorship that followed. The coup interrupted a process of social reform that had only begun to gain momentum in the early 2000s but which had mobilized millions of people around a range of issues of serious consequence to their lives. These included the need for better jobs and higher wages, the recovery of *campesino* land from agribusiness and capitalist mega-projects, the protection of Indigenous and Garífuna land and resources, reversal of the privatization of public services, an end to impunity for police violence, confrontation of the patriarchal institutions and patterns that led to discrimination and violence against women and LGBTQ people, a reduction in the prevalence of criminal and street gangs and the insecurity that fostered, and ultimately the need to radically restructure society to facilitate a more equitable share of wealth and power.[160]

Honduras had been devastated by the US occupation in the 1980s during the Contra Wars and the imposition of neoliberalism in the 1990s, but by the 2000s people were ready to push back. What began as a series of scattered, local struggles coalesced into a national movement, which, in 2003, led a massive march on the capital city of Tegucigalpa; all of the major highways into the city were blocked and protestors converged on the Presidential Palace demanding reform. Two years later, Hondurans elected Manuel Zelaya as president, and immediately he was held accountable to the social movement that had supported his candidacy; he faced over a hundred protests in his first year in office and found it increasingly difficult to manage the country without accommodating that social movement.[161]

As such, Zelaya's time as president was marked by an inconsistent, but nevertheless notable, commitment to reform. The minimum wage was raised, *campesino* land claims were supported, and new concessions for environmentally destructive mining projects were halted while the government worked with affected communities to develop a new set of mining laws that would offer real protection to those communities. Furthermore, Zelaya explored the possibility of opening up the Honduran constitution — written under US occupation in the 1980s — to be redesigned by a cross-section of Hondurans from across various sectors of society. The efforts of the social movement were having a measurable impact on life in Honduras; across a variety of metrics, from health to income to crime, things were improving.[162]

Then, on the morning of June 28, 2009, the Honduran military kidnapped Manuel Zelaya in his pyjamas and took him to the US air force base at Palmerola, from where he was flown out of the country. Troops filled the streets, protestors were attacked, critical media stations were ransacked and a curfew was imposed on all citizens. A fake resignation letter was read in the Honduran Congress, and one of the *golpistas* (coup plotters), Roberto Micheletti, was declared president. The international response was quick, as one government after another denounced the *coup d'état*, demanding the immediate restoration of the legitimate president and insisting that the *golpistas* be punished. Some twelve hours later, Canada broke an awkwardly long silence and issued a statement which condemned the coup and "call[ed] upon all parties to show restraint."[163]

The statement played well for a Canadian audience, appearing to be a reasonable response that simply asked everyone to try to be calm and not act rashly in the midst of a crisis. But that perception relied on Canadians' ignorance of the real situation in Honduras. Canada was, in fact, engaged in wilful misdirection; the statement was suggesting that two equal parties were in a complicated conflict, when, in truth, one group had seized power by force and was attacking the other. The group that had seized power was the Honduran oligarchy, the small network of wealthy and powerful people who — along with the armed forces — had almost always run Honduras as their own private playground and extended a warm invitation to foreign capital to join in the exploitation of the country's land and people. Zelaya — and the movement that was pressuring him — threatened to interrupt their party. The coup was designed by the ruling class to put things back on track.

Canada was no disinterested party. By 2009 it had emerged as the second-largest foreign investor in Honduras, with over $600 million invested in particularly the mining, garment-manufacturing and tourist industries.[164] Montreal-based Gildan Activewear was the country's largest private-sector employer, with some 18,000 workers spread across dozens of sweatshops and industrial parks. As early as the 1990s, Canadian mining companies were poisoning Honduran soil and water, killing fish in rivers and toxifying entire communities; one region was described to me as being "condemned to death."[165] These companies formed an association — the Asociación Nacional de Mineros (ANAMINH) — designed to pressure the Honduran state to maintain lax regulation and low tariffs and taxes while providing a secure environment for their operations by cracking down on resistance and protest of their mines. Meanwhile, Canadian Randy Jorgensen — whose wealth was derived from his time as a shady pornography dealer — was actively stealing land from Honduran Garífuna communities on the Caribbean coast to build shopping centres, resort hotels and retirement villas.[166]

The social movement that had emerged in the 2000s was directly opposed to many of the practices that generated profits for these Canadian companies: the major mobilization in 2003 was specifically aimed at resisting Canadian mining companies; one of the organizations at the heart of the struggle was the Colectiva de Mujeres Hondureñas (CODEMUH), a women's organization that functioned as an advocacy collective for women who worked in Gildan's factories; another key component was the Organización Fraternal Negra Hondureña (OFRANEH), a Garífuna organization struggling against Canadian developers who were seizing their territory. The social movement was fighting for reform in Honduras that would have directly cut into Canadian profits. No surprise, then, that when the military took control of the country by force, there was little appetite in Canada to sing the praises of democracy and human rights.

Instead, the Canadian government took a lead role in supporting the coup and facilitating its normalization. Minister of State Peter Kent consistently used his statements to suggest that Zelaya had fomented the crisis and was the real villain, and he quickly shifted away from using the term "coup" at all, calling it simply a "political crisis." Hondurans rose up in defiance, and protests rocked the country, but even as hundreds of people were being tortured, disappeared and killed by the military crackdown, Canada repeatedly downplayed the violence and encouraged "all parties to show restraint" in the lead-up to elections scheduled for later that year. Honduras quickly descended into a country with the highest homicide rate in the world and was soon labelled the most dangerous place to be a journalist by Reporters Without Borders.[167]

The elections took place but were a predictable sham. Hundreds of social movement candidates dropped out, knowing that the military that was shooting them in the streets was not going to passively allow them to win an election. The presidential frontrunner, trade unionist Carlos H. Reyes, bowed out of the election after he received a blow to the head from a police baton. International elections-monitoring organizations like the Carter Centre refused to even send representatives, so obvious was the fact that these were not the conditions for legitimate elections. But when the sham was complete and the oligarchy declared their man, Pepe Lobo, the winner, Canada was among the first countries to offer its congratulations on "relatively free and fair elections."[168]

In the ensuing decade, Canada worked hard to minimize the visibility of the Honduran resistance and the repression against it and to, instead, present a picture of the country as being "back to normal." Peter Kent visited in 2010 and declared that he had had a "fruitful visit" with the new president. His choice of words was laden with irony; in the week prior to his visit, two Honduran activists were assassinated and the teenaged daughter of a critical journalist was found hanging from a tree outside her father's house. These were not exceptional cases but, rather, were representative of the macabre violence that had been unleashed in a country where the very highest level of legal and political authority used force and fear as its instruments of power. In the decade following the coup, tens of thousands of people would be subject to some form of state violence and several hundred would be killed. In 2016, the most prominent activist in the country, internationally recognized Indigenous land defender Berta Cáceres, was assassinated in response to her mobilizing opposition to the construction of the Agua Zarca hydroelectric dam project. Her murder sent a chill through the country; if they could kill Berta, no one was safe.

All the while, Canada doubled down on its relations with the new dictatorship. Prime Minister Stephen Harper was the first head of state to visit Honduras following the coup, and he had good reason to do so: Canada had signed a free-trade agreement with the new regime. Aware that a right-wing dictatorship would be the best guarantor of Canadian interests, Canada abruptly cut off multilateral trade talks with the CA4 (a coalition of Central American governments) to focus on signing a deal with Honduras only. Canada also sent a representative to help reform the Honduran police, and both the RCMP and the Canadian military ran training programs and joint exercises with the very Honduran armed forces that were carrying out the repression of activists and opponents of the regime.

At the same time, Canada helped to pressure international organizations to reinstate Honduras and recognize its government as legitimate, and Canada offered economic and military support to the dictatorship. In 2010, Canada sent a commissioner to sit on the Honduras Truth and Reconciliation Commission regarding the coup itself, but that commission was convened by the dictatorship as part of its efforts to whitewash its road to power. Canada played along, and the Canadian representative was Michael Kergin, a lawyer who had longstanding ties to the mining industry. Following the release of the report, Kergin characterized Zelaya as a "reckless" pawn of Venezuelan President Hugo Chávez, whose "partisans" protesting the new government were few and unrepresentative of wider Honduran society, which did not actually want the reforms Zelaya was enacting.

According to Kergin, average citizens preferred "the Honduran norm"; Kergin claimed that Hondurans wanted the neoliberal status quo despite the fact that millions of people had been actively protesting and voting against that status quo for over a decade. When he briefly addressed the military repression that had cemented the regime's control of the country, Kergin explained that Honduras had a "traditional culture of violence." Kergin was implying that, like all "backwards" people, Hondurans could not solve their problems with rational thought and that violence was necessary to keep the rabble in line, for their own good.[169] This was Michael Kergin's colonial encounter, and it sounded similar to so many others documented in this book.

Occasionally, Canada's close ties to such a heinous dictatorship did prove embarrassing. As massive protests marked the tenth anniversary of the coup in 2019, the regime sent out its troops to attack the crowds, but chose to equip those troops with vehicles donated by the Canadian government, which bore the maple leaf insignia and the word "Canada" on the side. The Canadian embassy was forced to disavow itself of the repression and ask that the vehicles only be used by the Ministry of Health.[170] That same year, the Canadian government had faced pressure from a coalition of citizens concerned about the imprisonment of Edwin Espinal, arrested during protests against the transparently fraudulent elections of 2017. Galvanized by Karen Spring, a Canadian solidarity activist who lived and worked in Honduras, this citizens coalition drew attention to the fact that Canada's closest partner in Central America was holding its political opponents in dangerous, maximum security prisons without due process. This was a particularly upsetting element of the story for me, as Karen and Edwin are dear friends of mine, who often opened their home to me during my visits to the country.[171]

The election Espinal was protesting had marked the consolidation of the dictatorship; Juan Orlando Hernández, who had come to power in another fraudulent election in 2013, had spent several years laying the groundwork for a long stay in office. In 2012, he stacked the Supreme Court with his supporters in what was called a "technical coup" and then, with the help of the Supreme Electoral Tribunal, he staged an absurd theft of an election wherein the numbers were clearly against him; following a 36-hour delay in announcing the official results, the government claimed that new ballots had been found which confirmed Juan Orlando as the winner.[172] Once in office, he created a new military-police unit, separate from the rest of the armed forces and loyal to him directly. In his *coup de grâce* in 2015, he changed the constitution of the country to allow himself to run for re-election. The irony was stark; when Manuel Zelaya was overthrown in 2009, the dominant narrative that the *golpistas* built, and which Canada repeated at every opportunity, was that Zelaya was planning to change the constitution to run for re-election and therefore had to be stopped.[173] It was a patently false accusation levelled at Zelaya, but when Juan Orlando took that very action, Canada's silence was deafening.

Canada's steadfast support for the dictatorship in Honduras did not occur in a vacuum, nor was it simply doing the bidding of a few big capitalist firms. It certainly was a big favour to companies like Gildan and

Goldcorp, the latter of which was part of a cluster of mining and extractive industry companies whose seizures of Indigenous land in Honduras bore remarkable similarity to the processes by which Canada gained access to Indigenous land within its own territory.[174] Nevertheless, Honduras was just one small piece of the neoliberal project to impose the most intense forms of capitalism into every corner of the globe, to be constantly expanding the scope of where and how capital can operate. Prying Honduras back from a project that had it drifting to the left was, in that sense, no different from a kind of Cold War domino-theory approach where any door that appears to be closing to capital is considered an existential threat. With that old colonial certainty that it knew best, Canada would go forth in the 21st century and save poor countries from themselves, taking whatever measures it could to keep them exposed and vulnerable to the vicissitudes of the free market. This often meant finding partners in those countries who, like the *golpistas* in Honduras, could be counted on to pursue the same project.

But by the 2010s it was clear that this was not going to be as easy as it may have been in the past. The War on Terror had created a cascading set of crises that had no simple solutions. Attempts to defeat the remaining leftist governments of Latin America provoked major civil unrest in places like Honduras, but they also threatened to incite larger-scale conflicts involving significant regional powers like Venezuela, Colombia and Brazil. Similar troubles would emerge in Eastern Europe, where aggressive Western posturing vis-à-vis Russia raised the spectre of a new round of inter-imperial rivalry.

These geopolitical problems would be magnified by the emergence of a new crisis of capitalism in the late 2000s, even as the global climate catastrophe began to take effect in earnest. Popular culture in the West became awash in dystopian images of the future, and with good reason; the world that had been built by the European colonial powers in the 17th and 18th centuries was generating crisis after crisis and offered little hope of any solution. Rosa Luxemburg had famously argued, in 1916, that the two choices facing humanity were socialism or barbarism. Though millions of people chose socialism, it was barbarism that won the day. This dilemma seemed as poignant as ever in the 21st century.[175]

Notes
1. Quoted in "'Horrible' choices of war," *Toronto Star*, July 29, 2008.
2. "Canadian troops kill 2 children after car nears convoy," CBC *News*, July 28, 2008.

3. Peter MacKay, quoted in "'Horrible' choices of war," *Toronto Star*, July 29, 2008.
4. Brig-Gen. Denis Thompson, quoted in "'Horrible' choices of war," *Toronto Star*, July 29, 2008.
5. Maj. Jay Janzen, quoted in The Canadian Press, "Father of children killed by Canadian soldiers threatened by Taliban," CBC News, September 15, 2008.
6. Justin Podur, *Haiti's New Dictatorship: The Coup, The Earthquake and the UN Occupation*, Pluto Press, London, 2012, p. 60.
7. "'Death to Canada,' some Afghan protestors chant," CBC News, September 26, 2007. The online version of the story was carefully edited after its original posting to clarify that only "some" Afghans were protesting Canada specifically.
8. Jean-Christophe Boucher and Kim Richard Nossal, *The Politics of War: Canada's Afghanistan Mission, 2001–2014*, Vancouver, UBC Press, 2017, p. 192.
9. Neta Crawford, "Update on the Human Costs of War for Afghanistan and Pakistan, 2001 to mid-2016," Watson Institute of International and Public Affairs, Costs of War Project, Brown University, August 2016. Available at: https://watson.brown.edu/costsofwar/files/cow/imce/papers/2016/War%20in%20Afghanistan%20and%20Pakistan%20UPDATE_FINAL_corrected%20date.pdf. The documentary *Living Beneath Drones* (2015) illustrates the extent to which individual Afghans had been deeply traumatized by the occupation, examining the mental health effects of aerial bombing and drone warfare.
10. Jerome Klassen, "Introduction: Empire, Afghanistan, and Canadian Foreign Policy," in Jerome Klassen and Greg Albo, ed., *Empire's Ally: Canada and the War in Afghanistan*, Toronto, University of Toronto Press, 2013, p. 4–9.
11. Andrea Smith, *Conquest: Sexual Violence and American Indian Genocide*, Durham, Duke University Press, 2015, p. 24–25.
12. Ash Van Leeuwen, quoted in Christie Blatchford, *Fifteen Days: Stories of Bravery, Friendship, Life and Death from Inside the Canadian Military*, Toronto, Anchor, 2008, p. 63.
13. See also Amin Saikal's *Modern Afghanistan: A History of Struggle and Survival* (2004), John Cooley's *Unholy Wars: Afghanistan, America, and International Terrorism*, (2002), Louis Dupree's *Afghanistan* (1980), or Jonathan L. Lee's *Afghanistan: A History from 1260 to the Present* (2018).
14. John Warnock, "Afghanistan and Empire," in Jerome Klassen and Greg Albo, ed., *Empire's Ally: Canada and the War in Afghanistan*, Toronto, University of Toronto Press, 2013, p. 46.
15. Oliver Roy, *Islam and Resistance in Afghanistan*, Cambridge, Cambridge University Press, 1985, p. 80–96.
16. John Warnock, "Afghanistan and Empire," p. 57.
17. Robert Fisk, "Anti-Soviet warrior puts his army on the road to peace," *The Independent*, Dec. 6, 1993.
18. John Warnock, "Afghanistan and Empire," p. 62.
19. Angela Joya, "Failed States and Canada's 3D Policy," in Jerome Klassen and Greg Albo, ed., *Empire's Ally: Canada and the War in Afghanistan*, Toronto, University of Toronto Press, 2013, p. 280.
20. T. Robert Fowler, *Combat Mission Kandahar: The Canadian Experience in Afghanistan*, Dundurn, Toronto, 2016, p. 11
21. Jon Hamilton, quoted in Christie Blatchford, *Fifteen Days*, p. 7.

22. Gen. Rick Hillier, quoted in CBC News, "Helping Afghanistan will protect Canada, says top soldier," CBC, July 15, 2005. Emphasis added.
23. Rudyard Kipling, "The White Man's Burden"
24. Kevin Schamuhn, quoted in Christie Blatchford, *Fifteen Days*, p. 127.
25. Jon Hamilton, quoted in Christie Blatchford, *Fifteen Days*, p. 23.
26. Nick Grimshaw, quoted in Christie Blatchford, *Fifteen Days*, p. 156–157.
27. Sean Ivanko, quoted in Christie Blatchford, *Fifteen Days*, p. 104.
28. For instance, in May 2011, 87% of respondents in Southern Afghanistan and 76% of respondents in Northern Afghanistan felt that NATO operations were "bad for the Afghan people." Jerome Klassen, "Introduction," p. 9.
29. Christie Blatchford, *Fifteen Days*, p. 62.
30. Victoria Goddard, quoted in Christie Blatchford, *Fifteen Days*, p. 181.
31. Zabihullah Hajanmal, "Ministry moves to start mining Hajigak," *Tolo News*, March 4, 2018. Available at: https://www.tolonews.com/business/ministry-moves-%C2%A0start-mining%C2%A0hajigak.
32. Adam Hanieh, "A 'Single War': The Political Economy of Intervention in the Middle East and Central Asia," in Jerome Klassen and Greg Albo, ed., *Empire's Ally: Canada and the War in Afghanistan*, Toronto, University of Toronto Press, 2013, p. 91–99.
33. Like most modern militaries, the Canadian Armed Forces tended to recruit from the Canadian working classes. Advertising often highlighted the economic and educational opportunities that a military career would provide — which would be of little interest to the already wealthy — and recruitment was often heaviest in rural areas and in the poorest provinces. The Atlantic provinces, for instance, produced more than 20% of military personnel despite representing close to 10% of the total population. The class composition of the military was thus skewed towards working-class youth, like a childhood friend of my family who was sent to Afghanistan. Jungwee Park, "A Profile of the Canadian Forces," *Perspectives*, Statistics Canada, July 2008.
34. Jerome Klassen, "Introduction," p. 14.
35. Ian McKay and Jamie Swift, *Warrior Nation: Rebranding Canada in an Age of Anxiety*, Toronto, Between the Lines, 2012, p. 235.
36. The Canadian right still was not satisfied; the *National Post* cried foul in 2019 when the Trudeau government did not spike the military budget from nearly $20 billion to the over $30 billion it had promised to hit by 2027. David Krayden, "Once again, the federal budget turns a blind eye to Canada's military needs," *National Post*, March 27, 2019.
37. Alexander Moens, "Afghanistan and the Revolution in Canadian Foreign Policy," *International Journal*, Vol. 63, No. 3, 2008, p. 569–586.
38. Greg Albo, "Fewer Illusions," in Jerome Klassen and Greg Albo, ed., *Empire's Ally: Canada and the War in Afghanistan*, Toronto, University of Toronto Press, 2013, p. 256.
39. Anthony Fenton and Jon Elmer, "Building an Expeditionary Force for Democracy Promotion, in Jerome Klassen and Greg Albo, ed., *Empire's Ally: Canada and the War in Afghanistan*, Toronto, University of Toronto Press, 2013, p. 319–328.
40. Daan Everts, quoted in Jerome Klassen, "Methods of Empire: State Building,

41. Todd Gordon, *Imperialist Canada*, Winnipeg, Arbeiter Ring, 2010, p. 358.
42. Justin Podur, "Incompatible Objectives: Counterinsurgency and Development in Afghanistan," in Jerome Klassen and Greg Albo, ed., *Empire's Ally: Canada and the War in Afghanistan*, Toronto, University of Toronto Press, 2013, p. 353.
43. A comprehensive report in the late 2000s indicated that of some $18 million in claims of foreign aid given to the Kandahar hospital by the Canadian International Development Agency (CIDA), there was only evidence of $5 million actually being spent on the hospital. A reported Maternal Waiting Home and other projects written up by CIDA did not exist. Todd Gordon, *Imperialist Canada*, p. 358-359.
44. These laws complemented those Karzai had already brought in with Canadian vetting, including a series of 2008 policies that disallowed women from wearing makeup in public, prevented young men from wearing female clothing, enforced the hijab at work and banned female dancing. Jerome Klassen, "Methods of Empire," in Jerome Klassen and Greg Albo, ed., *Empire's Ally: Canada and the War in Afghanistan*, Toronto, University of Toronto Press, 2013, p. 151.
45. Mark Steyn, "What the Afghans need is colonizing," *National Post*, October 9, 2001.
46. Thomas Ruttig, "Dad Noorani, critic of warlordism, passed away," *Afghanistan Analysts Network*. Available at: https://aan-afghanistan.com/index.asp?id=1930/.
47. Hamayon Ragstar, quoted in Kabir Joshi-Vijayan, "From Occupied Afghanistan: Part II, An Interview with Mike Skinner and Hamayon Ragstar," *The Dominion*, September 27, 2007.
48. Cockburn performed the song "If I Had a Rocket Launcher" to great applause from the Canadian troops, though it was originally written as a scathing criticism of the US war in Central America in the 1980s, which had many of the same motives and methods as that in Afghanistan. The Canadian Press, "Cockburn gets his rocket launcher," *Toronto Star*, September 11, 2009.
49. McKay and Swift, *Warrior Nation*, p. 234.
50. Paul Webster, "Canadian soldiers and doctors face torture allegations," *The Lancet*, Vol. 369, April 28, 2007.
51. David Pugliese, "Out-of-control Canadian military police terrorized Afghan prisoners in Kandahar, documents indicate," *National Post*, June 20, 2016.
52. Jerome Klassen, "Methods of Empire," p. 167.
53. Sherene H. Razack, "Canada's Afghan Detainee Torture Scandal," in Jerome Klassen and Greg Albo, ed., *Empire's Ally: Canada and the War in Afghanistan*, Toronto, University of Toronto Press, 2013, p. 370.
54. Sherene H. Razack, "Canada's Afghan Detainee Torture Scandal," p. 376-383.
55. Laurie Hawn, quoted in CBC Radio, *The Current*, December 11, 2009.
56. Rudyard Kipling, "The White Man's Burden."
57. US Secretary of State Colin Powell famously delivered a speech at the United Nations using visual evidence — photographs — purporting to prove that Saddam Hussein was building "weapons of mass destruction." After the invasion, the United States was forced to admit that it did not find any such weapons,

and Powell himself admitted that he was wrong, just a year later. David Corn, "Powell Admits False WMD Claim," *The Nation*, May 7, 2004.
58. "Coach's Corner on Iraq War riles viewers, CBC," *CBC News*, April 1, 2003.
59. Tyler A. Shipley, *Ottawa and Empire: Canada and the Military Coup in Honduras*, Toronto, Between the Lines, 2017, p. 63–65.
60. Patrick James, *Canada and Conflict*, Oxford, Oxford University Press, 2012, p. 89–91.
61. Yves Engler, *The Black Book of Canadian Foreign Policy*, Halifax, Fernwood, 2009, p. 46–47.
62. Colin Campbell, "A Dedicated Presence in Iraq," *Maclean's*, May 29, 2006.
63. Yves Engler, *Black Book*, p. 47.
64. Paul Cellucci, quoted in Richard Sanders, "Who says we're not at war?," *Globe and Mail*, March 31, 2003.
65. Janice Gross Stein and Eugene Lang, *The Unexpected War: Canada in Kandahar*, Toronto, Penguin, 2008.
66. Jerome Klassen, *Joining Empire: The Political Economy of the New Canadian Imperialism*, Toronto, University of Toronto Press, 2014, p. 251.
67. Anthony Fenton, "Drill, Garner, Drill," *Mother Jones*, November 24, 2008.
68. Philip Bump, "15 years after the Iraq War began, the death toll is still murky," *Washington Post*, March 20, 2018.
69. Maggie Wagner, "Poverty in Iraq after the war," *Borgen Magazine*, October 16, 2014. Available at: https://www.borgenmagazine.com/poverty-iraq-war/.
70. Mark Steyn, quoted in Tareq Y. Ismael and Jacqueline S. Ismael, "Canadian Mass Media and the Middle East," in George Melnyk, ed., *Canada and the New American Empire*, Calgary, University of Calgary Press, 2004, p. 33.
71. Gen. Rick Hillier, quoted in Jerome Klassen, *Joining Empire*, p. 220.
72. Patrick James, *Canada and Conflict*, p. 113–115
73. Stephen Harper, quoted in Patrick James, *Canada and Conflict*, p. 117.
74. Greg Shupak, "The Disaster in Libya," *Jacobin*, February 9, 2015.
75. Charles Glass, *Syria Burning: The Islamic State and the Death of the Arab Spring*, New York, OR Books, 2015, p. 1–53.
76. Christopher Phillips, *The Battle for Syria: International Rivalry in the New Middle East*, New Haven, Yale University Press, 2016, p. 189.
77. Christopher Phillips, *The Battle for Syria*, p. 105–147.
78. Christopher Phillips, *The Battle for Syria*, p. 1.
79. Diana Bashur, "What the West Owes Syrians: US and European Arms Sales to the Middle East 2011–2014, *Jadaliyya*, December 21, 2016. Available at: https://www.jadaliyya.com/Details/33857.
80. Michael Ignatieff, quoted in E. Donald Briggs, Walter C. Soderlund, and Tom Pierre Najem, *Syria, Press Framing, and the Responsibility to Protect*, Waterloo, Wilfrid Laurier Press, 2017, p. 100.
81. Louise Arbour, quoted in Briggs, Soderlund, and Najem, *Syria, Press Framing, and the Responsibility*, p. 101.
82. Briggs, Soderlund, and Najem, *Syria, Press Framing, and the Responsibility*, p. 161.
83. Useful studies of the conflict include Patrick Cockburn's *The Jihadis Return* (2014), Charles Glass' *Syria Burning* (2015), and Christopher Phillips' *The Battle*

for Syria (2016).
84. Lakhdar Brahimi, quoted in Christopher Phillips, *The Battle for Syria*, p. 232.
85. Derrick O'Keefe, "Canada joins military intervention in Mali — a reminder that we need more debate on foreign policy," *Rabble.ca*, January 15, 2013.
86. Peter Koven, "Mali coup could put gold miners at risk," *National Post*, March 22, 2012.
87. Roderick Ramsden, "Unrest in Mali: Canada's Role in Eradicating Terrorist Forces in West Africa," NATO Association of Canada, August 2, 2016. Available at: http://natoassociation.ca/unrest-in-mali-canadas-role-in-eradicating-terrorist-forces-in-west-africa/.
88. Rosie DiManno, "With Mali mission, Canadian troops are entering a madhouse," *Toronto Star*, March 22, 2018.
89. Ilan Pappe, *A History of Modern Palestine*, Cambridge, Cambridge University Press, 2006, p. 194–221.
90. Avner Yaniv, quoted in Norman Finkelstein, *Image and Reality of the Israel-Palestine Conflict*, New York, Verso, 2003, p. xix.
91. "Israel in Lebanon: Report of the International Commission to Enquire into Reported Violations of International Law by Israel during its Invasion of the Lebanon," *Journal of Palestine Studies*, Vol. 12, No. 3, Spring 1983, p. 117–133.
92. Brian Mulroney, quoted in Yves Engler, *Black Book*, p. 61.
93. As widely reported by B'Tselem, an Israeli human rights organization. Norman Finkelstein, *Image and Reality*, p. xx.
94. Norman Finkelstein, *Image and Reality*, p. xx.
95. Jimmy Carter, *Palestine: Peace not Apartheid*, New York, Simon & Schuster, 2006, p. 215.
96. Norman Finkelstein, *Image and Reality*, p. xxiii.
97. Norman Finkelstein, *Image and Reality*, p. xxv–xxvi.
98. Assaf Harel, quoted in Nick Visser, "Israeli TV Host Denounces Treatment of Palestinians: 'Apartheid Has Been Here for Ages,'" *Huffington Post*, March 1, 2017.
99. Yves Engler, *Canada and Israel: Building Apartheid*, Halifax, Fernwood, 2010, p. 51–56.
100. Todd Gordon, *Imperialist Canada*, p. 384.
101. Quoted in Yves Engler, *Canada and Israel*, p. 59.
102. Kole Kilibarda, "Canadian and Israeli Defence — Industrial and Homeland Security Ties: An Analysis" Queen's University Surveillance Project, November 2008.
103. Glenn Wheeler, "Indigo's Israel Problem: Activists throw book at CEO's scholarship fund for soldiers," *Now Toronto*, June 7, 2007.
104. Justin Podur, "Canada for anti-imperialists, Part II," *Z Magazine*, July 3, 2004.
105. Marie Joelle-Zahar, "Talking One Talk, Walking Another: Norm Entrepreneurship and Canada's Foreign Policy in the Middle East," in Paul Heinbecker and Bessma Momani, ed., *Canada and the Middle East: In Theory and Practice*, Waterloo, Wilfrid Laurier University Press, 2007, p. 55.
106. Marie Joelle-Zahar, "Talking One Talk, Walking Another," p. 55.
107. Michael Ignatieff, quoted in Marie Joelle-Zahar, "Talking One Talk, Walking Another," p. 55.

108. "Ignatieff defends 'war crimes' comment," CBC News, October 13, 2006.
109. Judy Wasylycia-Leis and Pat Martin, quoted in Yves Engler, *Canada and Israel*, p. 92.
110. Mordecai Briemberg, "A Journey from Israel to Palestine," in Cy Gonick, ed., *Canada Since 1960: A People's History*, Toronto, James Lorimer & Co., 2016, p. 344–356.
111. Dorit Naaman, "Coordinated Campaign Aimed to Stifle Academic Discussion about Israel Raises Critical Questions," Canadian Association of University Teachers Bulletin, October 2009.
112. "Trudeau blasts BDS movement as anti-Semitic," *Times of Israel*, January 17, 2019.
113. B'Nai Brith routinely collapsed and conflated the categories of anti-Semitism and legitimate critique of Israel, doing much damage in the process. In 2019, for instance, amidst a rash of genuinely anti-Semitic incidents that were tied into the rise of fascism more generally, B'Nai Brith reported on the increased prevalence of swastikas and messages like "kill all Jews" graffitied onto walls and transit cars. But in the same report, it linked these acts with the Boycott, Divestment, Sanctions (BDS) campaign, a legitimate international effort to penalize Israel for its brutal occupation of Palestinian land and people. Michelle Lalonde, "Anti-Semitic incidents in Québec increased by 50% in 2018, audit shows," *Montreal Gazette*, April 29, 2019.
114. Mordecai Briemberg, "A Journey from Israel to Palestine," p. 349.
115. Henry Heller, "Revolution and Imperialism: A North American Internationalism," in Cy Gonick, ed., *Canada Since 1960: A People's History*, Toronto, James Lorimer & Co., 2016, p. 337–340.
116. Mordecai Briemberg, "A Journey from Israel to Palestine," p. 349–352.
117. Eric Walberg's *The Canada-Israel Nexus* (2017), for instance, contains some useful data on Canadian state support for Israel, but it sacrifices its own credibility by veering headlong into anti-Semitic conspiracy theory, from criticizing Jews' "dual loyalties," to methodologically questionable quantifying of Jewish ownership of Canadian capital, and even going as far as to defend Holocaust deniers like Jim Keegstra. Walberg thus unwittingly plays right into the hands of Zionist propagandists who seek to equate criticism of Israel with anti-Semitism since, in fact, Walberg's criticism of Israel is actually anti-Semitic. Eric Walberg, *The Canada-Israel Nexus*, Atlanta, Clarity Press, 2017.
118. Bret Stephens, "The Secrets of Jewish Genius," *The New York Times*, December 27, 2019.
119. Suzanne Weiss, "Solidarity saved me from the Nazis; that's why I fight Israeli apartheid," *The Electronic Intifada*, November 26, 2013. Available at: https://electronicintifada.net/content/solidarity-saved-me-nazis-thats-why-i-fight-israeli-apartheid/12950.
120. Evan Dyer, "Canada showing Haiti some tough love," CBC News, November 22, 2016.
121. Paul Martin, quoted in Yves Engler and Anthony Fenton, *Canada in Haiti: Waging War on the Poor Majority*, Halifax, Fernwood, 2005, p. 11.
122. Quoted in Peter Hallward, *Damming the Flood: Haiti and the Politics of Containment*, Verso, London, 2011, p. xxxii.

123. Paul Martin, quoted in "Martin says violence preventing democracy from taking hold in Haiti," *CBC News*, November 14, 2004.
124. Kirkpatrick Sale, *The Conquest of Paradise: Christopher Columbus and the Columbian Legacy*, New York, Alfred A. Knopf, 1990, p. 97.
125. C.L.R. James, *The Black Jacobins, Toussaint L'Ouverture and the San Domingo Revolution*, 2nd ed, New York, Vintage, 1989.
126. Gerald Horne, *Confronting Black Jacobins: The United States, the Haitian Revolution, and the Origins of the Dominican Republic*, New York, Monthly Review Press, 2015.
127. Gerald Horne, *Confronting Black Jacobins*, p. 207–263.
128. The Négritude movement came out of Francophone Africa and combined pan-Africanist black pride with left, anti-colonial politics.
129. Michel-Rolph Trouillot, "Haiti's Nightmare and the Lessons of History," *NACLA Report on the Americas*, September 25, 2007.
130. Jean-Bertrand Aristide, quoted in Nicolas Rossier, dir., *Aristide and the Endless Revolution*, Baraka Productions, 2005.
131. That Aristide's overthrow became a *cause célèbre* is interesting; US involvement in the coup was kept relatively well-hidden, and American celebrities like Steven Spielberg and Robert de Niro demanded Aristide's restoration. When the US military brought him back, it was able to present itself as having saved Haiti from its own chaos. Peter Hallward, *Damming the Flood*, p. xxvi.
132. Quoted in Engler and Fenton, *Canada in Haiti*, p. 47.
133. Todd Gordon, *Imperialist Canada*, p. 328.
134. Quoted in Engler and Fenton, *Canada in Haiti*, p. 40.
135. Peter Hallward, *Damming the Flood*, p. xxx.
136. Carol J. Williams, "In Haiti, voodoo gets official recognition," *Chicago Tribune*, August 5, 2003.
137. Jean-Bertrand Aristide, *Dignity*, Charlottesville, University Press of Virginia, 1996.
138. Jean-Bertrand Aristide, quoted in Alex Dupuy, *The Prophet and Power: Jean-Bertrand Aristide, the International Community, and Haiti*, Lanham, Rowman and Littlefield, 2007, p. 79, 91.
139. Todd Gordon, *Imperialist Canada*, p. 252–253.
140. But US coup plotter extraordinaire Otto Reich did manage to make the guest list. Reich was one of the architects of the failed coup against Hugo Chávez in 2002. He worked on that plot with Elliot Abrams, who would later be made an advisor to President Trump on foreign affairs, where he again beat the drums for overthrows of both the Venezuelan and Iranian governments in 2019. Richard Sanders, "A Very Canadian Coup," Canadian Centre for Policy Alternatives, April 1, 2010.
141. Denis Paradis, quoted in Hallward, *Damming the Flood*, p. 91.
142. Todd Gordon, *Imperialist Canada*, p. 332.
143. Todd Gordon, *Imperialist Canada*, p. 329–331.
144. Aristide even asked the UN to send a small peacekeeping force to help him deal with the armed insurgency, but this request was ignored. Fenton and Engler, *Canada in Haiti*, p. 17.
145. Quoted in Jeb Sprague, *Paramilitarism and the Assault on Democracy in Haiti*,

New York, Monthly Review Press, 2012, p. 232
146. Fenton and Engler, *Canada in Haiti*, p. 19.
147. Quoted in Justin Podur, *Haiti's New Dictatorship*, p. 87.
148. Of the money saved by slashing programs, $30 million was paid out to former soldiers who had been de-commissioned by Aristide's government. Richard Sanders, "A Very Canadian Coup," Canadian Centre for Policy Alternatives, April 1, 2010.
149. Peter Hallward, *Damming the Flood*, p. 106.
150. Todd Gordon, *Imperialist Canada*, p. 334–338. One common tactic was that Canadian soldiers would enter poor neighbourhoods of Port-au-Prince, which were naturally filled with Aristide's supporters, and would break down barricades and other defensive positions built to protect communities from the HNP. Then, once "softened up" by foreign troops, the neighbourhoods would be attacked by the HNP.
151. Quoted in Justin Podur, *Haiti's New Dictatorship*, p. 61.
152. Fenton and Engler, *Canada in Haiti*, p. 75–76.
153. Sgt. Maj. Kirby Burgess, quoted in Justin Podur, *Haiti's New Dictatorship*, p. 60.
154. Todd Gordon, *Imperialist Canada*, p. 341.
155. Justin Podur, *Haiti's New Dictatorship*, p. 138.
156. Tim Schwartz, *Travesty in Haiti: A True Account of Christian Missions, Orphanages, Fraud, Food Aid and Drug Trafficking*, Charleston, BookSurge, 2008.
157. Tim Schwartz, quoted in Justin Podur, *Haiti's New Dictatorship*, p. 145–146.
158. Justin Podur, *Haiti's New Dictatorship*, p. 5.
159. Evan Dyer, "Canada showing Haiti some tough love," CBC *News*, November 22, 2016.
160. Street gangs were linked to larger narco-trafficking networks, which overlapped with police and military and the death squads, all of which engaged in politically motivated violence against activists in a variety of contexts, and which got their orders from both the business elite (legal and illegal) and the dictatorship. Joining gangs was one way out of grinding poverty and escaping via migration to the US was difficult and dangerous. Tyler Shipley, "'The Most Dangerous Country in the World': Violence and Capital in Post-Coup Honduras," in Simon Granovsky-Larsen and Dawn Paley, ed., *Organized Violence: Capitalist Warfare in Latin America*, Regina, University of Regina Press, 2019. Canada did little to intervene in what emerged in the late 2010s as a humanitarian crisis, wherein US border guards physically tore children away from their mothers, held refugees indefinitely in what amounted to concentration camps, and placed toddlers as young as three years old in front of judges to plead their deportation cases. Christina Jewett and Shefali Luthra, "Immigrant toddlers ordered to appear in court alone," *The Texas Tribune*, June 27, 2018.
161. Tyler Shipley, "Genealogy of a Social Movement: the Resistencia in Honduras," *Canadian Journal of Latin American and Caribbean Studies*, Vol. 41, No. 3, 2016.
162. John A. Booth, Christine J. Wade and Thomas W. Walker, *Understanding Central America: Global Forces, Rebellion, and Change*, 5th ed, Boulder, Westview Press, 2010, p. 174.
163. Department of Foreign Affairs and Trade, "Statement by Minister of State Kent

on the Situation in Honduras," No. 184, June 28, 2009.
164. Todd Gordon, "Canada Backs Profits, not Human Rights, in Honduras," *Toronto Star*, August 16, 2011.
165. Carlos Amador, Interview by Tyler Shipley, May 8, 2012.
166. Tyler Shipley, "Land Seizure, Dispossession, and Canadian Capital in Honduras," *Human Geography*, Vol. 8, No. 2, 2015.
167. Tyler Shipley, "Harper in Honduras: Left Solidarity and the Future of Coup Resistance," *The Bullet*, August 25, 2011.
168. It was never clear how Canada came to that conclusion; I was among the small number of Canadians actually in the country at the time, and all of my reports said the opposite. Tyler Shipley, "Honduras — where are the people?" *Toronto Media Co-op*, December 1, 2009.
169. Michael Kergin, "The Honduran Truth and Reconciliation Commission (2010–2011)," *Optimum Online*, Vol. 42, No. 3, September 2012, p. 42–45.
170. James K. Hill, "Declaración del Embajador de Canadá en Honduras," Government of Canada, June 27, 2019.
171. Erika Engel, "Simcoe County family fights for son living in inhumane Honduran prison," *Collingwood Today*, January 21, 2019.
172. Sarah Kinosian, "US recognizes re-election of Honduras president despite fraud allegations," *The Guardian*, December 22, 2017.
173. Zelaya's proposal to re-open the constitution was several steps — and probably years — away from implementation. The primaries for the November 2009 elections had already taken place, and Zelaya had already endorsed a candidate for those elections. Tyler Shipley, *Ottawa and Empire*, p. 47–49.
174. Tyler Shipley, "Land Seizure, Dispossession, and Canadian Capital in Honduras," *Human Geography*, Vol. 8, No. 2, 2015.
175. J. Moufawad-Paul, for instance, argued in *The Communist Necessity* (2014) that ending capitalism's ravaging of the planet and most of its people was not a utopian vision but, rather, a necessary condition for the continued existence of humanity.

12

Contemporary Canada and the Rise of Fascism

It is not in our past, nor within our power, to conquer or to dominate.

— Conservative Prime Minister Stephen Harper, 2007¹

[Canada] also [has] no history of colonialism.

— Conservative Prime Minister Stephen Harper, 2009²

[Canada has] a capacity to engage in the world in difficult places without some of the baggage that so many other Western countries have, either colonial pasts or perceptions of American imperialism, as a critique that's often out there.

— Liberal Prime Minister Justin Trudeau, 2016³

THE ELECTION OF A NEW government in Canada in 2015 provides a useful window into the exercise of Canadian power and politics. After nearly a decade of Conservative leadership under Stephen Harper, the election of a Liberal government led by Justin Trudeau heralded to many Canadians a new era. Trudeau's victory lap included several international forums at which he proudly declared "Canada is back," suggesting that the previous decade had been an interruption of the typical pattern of Canadian politics: support for peace, freedom, democracy, human rights and the environment. In fact, this was never what Canada had been about, and Trudeau's promises rung as falsely as his staged photo-ops, which were a recurring element of his first years in office.⁴

It is especially instructive to note the way that the Trudeau government doubled down not just on Canadian imperialism abroad but also colonialism at home. After years of struggle with Indigenous communities over the construction of the Trans Mountain Pipeline from Edmonton to Vancouver, the Trudeau government purchased the project from the Kinder Morgan company and pushed construction ahead. At the same time, the RCMP was preparing to use "lethal overwatch" and as much violence as necessary in evicting Wet'suwet'en protestors trying to block a Coastal Gaslink pipeline being built through their territory. Protestors called it "a continuation of what it must have been like 150 years ago,"[5] as the police sought, in their own words, to "sterilize the site."[6]

As Indigenous demonstrations repeatedly interrupted Trudeau's town hall discussions and photo-ops, he grew increasingly petulant and smug in his responses; when one of his speeches at a fundraiser was interrupted by a protestor demanding compensation for years of poisoned water at Grassy Narrows First Nation, Justin sarcastically thanked the protestor for his donation to the party while security escorted him out.[7] For a government that had promised "real change," it was the continuities in Trudeau's politics that were most striking.

Armoured Neoliberalism

In the late 2010s, the Trudeau government consolidated a form of Canadian imperialism that Jerome Klassen calls "armoured neoliberalism," which fused domestic and international policies of militarization and class struggle.[8] This imperial practice worked closely with the project of US empire in the hopes of carving out ever greater space for the expansion of Canadian capital abroad. In practice, Canada's role often included direct participation in imperial violence, from Afghanistan to Haiti to Honduras, but it also comprised more low-intensity intervention to preserve the crumbling US-led world order and a consistent position of support for right-wing allies of the Western powers. For instance, Trudeau's highly publicized visit from Mexican President Enrique Peña Nieto, complete with photos of the two leaders jogging in Ottawa, took place at the very moment the Mexican government was murdering striking teachers in the province of Oaxaca.[9]

Even more conspicuous was Trudeau's support for the quasi-fascist monarchy of Saudi Arabia. By the 2010s, the Saudi position as a regional power in the Middle East was being challenged by Iran, which had gained regional influence as a result of the hapless and chaotic occupation of Iraq.

Intent on toppling Saddam Hussein, the US occupation of Iraq had to ally itself with local Shia warlords who ultimately gained much sway over Iraqi politics and tended to orient towards Iran. The Saudi monarchy thus found its position threatened by an emboldened Iran, which commanded greater popular legitimacy in Middle East politics than the Saudis, who had consistently supported American intervention.

As a result, the Saudi monarchy was beset by regional rebellions and reacted with predictable violence in Bahrain, Syria and most notably in Yemen. Its crackdown on a Houthi uprising in Yemen was overwhelming; tens of thousands of civilians were killed and millions were left homeless and hungry as a result of the massive devastation, especially in cities like Sana'a. The destruction was so severe and the country so incapacitated that Yemen slid into an unprecedented humanitarian disaster, marked by a cholera epidemic that affected nearly a million people in 2017.[10]

And yet Justin Trudeau's shiny new government was a steadfast ally to the Saudi regime as it carried out this war. Canada provided not just diplomatic cover but also military equipment and training. One of the first actions of the Trudeau government in 2015 was to reaffirm the signing of a $15 billion deal to sell light armoured vehicles (LAV) to the Saudi military; this was the largest arms exporting contract in Canadian history, and it came with a promise of specialized training in how to operate the vehicles. These LAVs were put to use directly in Yemen, targeting civilians with their machine guns and high-calibre weapons. In addition to training the soldiers operating the LAVs, Canada also ran a series of training programs for Saudi pilots in Alberta and Saskatchewan.[11]

The Canadian government described Saudi Arabia as "a key military ally who backs efforts of the international community to fight the Islamic State in Iraq and Syria and the instability in Yemen," and claimed that Saudi Arabia "play[ed] an important role in promoting regional peace and stability."[12] A United Nations report in 2019, however, insisted that Saudi Arabia was carrying out war crimes and that its Western supporters were complicit.[13] International commentary began to take note of the contradiction between Canada's image and practice and Trudeau was thoroughly embarrassed in a 2019 appearance on the American television show *Patriot Act* when host Hasan Minhaj confronted Trudeau about its pursuit of the Trans Mountain Pipeline, its shady dealings with SNC-Lavalin and the Saudi weapons deal.

Indeed, Canada's role in the Middle East and its ongoing conflicts increased in the 2010s. By 2015, Canada was the second largest arms dealer to the region, most of which flowed to Saudi Arabia and its allies in the Gulf states.[14] With exports totaling over $3 billion annually, making it the 6th largest arms dealer in the world, Canada's weapons manufacturers sold their products at trade expos in Abu Dhabi, and Global Affairs Canada increased its dialogue with the monarchies of the Gulf Cooperation Council, which participated in the civil war in Syria.[15] Canada had played a role in the destruction of Syria, and, even as the Trudeau government tried to re-frame its involvement in the Syrian crisis by the heavily trumpeted admittance of 40,000 Syrian refugees, it continued to contravene international law in its ongoing bombing of Syrian targets.[16]

Though few Canadians knew anything about it, hundreds of Canadian combat troops were deployed in the Middle East — especially in Iraq and Syria but also in Bahrain, Kuwait and Qatar — and were engaging in direct battle.[17] Canada simultaneously joined what was called a UN peacekeeping mission in Mali in 2018; it had already assisted the French and US governments in carrying out a coup in that country in 2011, and then another in 2012, which had set off the crisis that was still spiralling nearly a decade later.[18] Meanwhile, Canada continued its longstanding policy of support for the apartheid system in Israel, which left it isolated in the international community, typically one of only a handful of countries that would vote against resolutions supporting Palestinian rights at the United Nations. And even as Canada ignored or defended the flagrant violations of Israel and Saudi Arabia, it spoke aggressively at the same forum about the abuses committed by Iran, Venezuela and other countries which were in the imperial crosshairs.

The consequence of being in those crosshairs was evident in places like Honduras and Haiti; the dictatorship of Honduras was shooting live rounds at protestors, and Haiti was so wracked by political turmoil that the Canadian government advised against travelling to the country.[19] Furthermore, in one of its most dangerous adventures, Canada was playing a significant role in stoking a crisis in Eastern Europe with the potential to spill into a serious international conflict.

The Ukraine Crisis

At the centre of an emerging crisis in Eastern Europe was Ukraine, ground zero for a contest between the Western capitalist powers and the defiant regional capitalist power in Russia. Russia under Vladimir Putin was a crony capitalist oligopoly which — to the extent that it could link into a bloc with China, Iran and other similarly placed powers — sought to form a rival imperialist camp to the United States.[20] If America's capacity to maintain its global empire was slipping, these rival capitalist centres were waiting to step in; the parallels to the inter-imperialist rivalry of 1914–18 were hard to ignore. News media in the United States through the early years of the Trump presidency screamed of the menace of Russia, massively exaggerating its capacity to interfere with US elections and information systems, while the expansion of NATO into Eastern Europe right up to the Russian border signalled that the West was serious about curbing the Russian ruling classes' ambition.

Ukraine emerged as the centre of that conflict when its own domestic politics shifted significantly in the 2010s. As Richard Sakwa illustrates in *Frontline Ukraine* (2016), the country was deeply divided between those cozying up to the West and those oriented towards Russia. This divide was old; Ukraine had long been pulled in both directions and Ukrainians had been forced to choose sides, most dramatically in the period of crisis that culminated in the Second World War. Those who sided with Nazi Germany held the upper hand in the early 1940s and carried out some of the worst atrocities, but these predominantly wealthy or middle-class Ukrainians were stripped of power and privilege — and sometimes their lives — when the Soviet army reversed the tide of the war. Under the Soviet Union, it was the pro-Russian Ukrainians who ruled the country, but with the end of the Cold War, Ukrainian politics shifted considerably. Many from the Soviet-era leadership were disgraced by their corruption and their quickness to become crony capitalists themselves, and the pro-West forces in the country grew in influence. Buoyed by material and political support from the West, these elements took ever greater control of the country in a series of events from the 2005 "Orange Revolution" to the 2014 Euromaidan protests.

Alarming, however, was the fact that this pro-West faction was heavily populated by organizations that were direct descendants of the Ukrainian Nazis who had collaborated with Hitler. By the late 2010s, the state had been effectively captured by the far right, and fascist militias patrolled

Ukrainian streets. In 2017 the Ukrainian government placed new statues in Lviv and other cities depicting Stepan Bandera, fascist leader in the 1930s and 1940s, responsible for the murder of hundreds of thousands of Jews, Poles and Russians.[21] As late as 1943, Bandera's followers in the Organization of Ukrainian Nationalists (OUN) were gouging out the eyes of families suspected of collaborating with the Soviet Union in its fight against the Nazis; now, the Ukrainian government was celebrating the OUN as the founders of the country.[22]

In addition to rebranding Ukrainian fascists as national heroes, the Ukrainian right pushed a nationalist narrative around a famine in the 1930s which it called the Holodomor. The famine in question was a disastrous consequence of Stalinist mismanagement and punitive purges of a wealthier class of peasants called *kulaks*, a class which included my mother's great-grandparents. This inadvertently led to a catastrophic collapse in production compounded by the diverting of food for export, to purchase machinery for industrial centres, which left between 2 and 3 million people to starve in parts of Ukraine, southern Russia and Kazakhstan. The famine was a devastating failure of Stalin's flawed collectivization policies and a tragic repercussion of the fear and instability instilled in his own bureaucracy in the 1930s. But Ukrainian nationalists increasingly insisted, against much of the historical evidence, that Stalin had orchestrated the famine intentionally in order to ethnically cleanse Ukrainians. The idea of a targeted ethnic attack by Russians against Ukrainians — despite the fact that Stalin was not Russian and many who died in the famine were not Ukrainian — was used to galvanize Ukrainian nationalist sentiment and enmity towards Russia.[23]

By the late 2010s, the Ukrainian far-right was openly declaring itself to be against "Yids, Russkies and other filth," invoking the classic Judeo-Bolshevik conspiracy theory, and the Ukrainian government passed laws banning the use of the Russian language, even in regions that were mostly Russian.[24] One of the far-right parties, Svoboda, distributed Nazi pamphlets translated into Ukrainian and increasingly took its violence to the streets. When Ukrainian-American actor Mila Kunis spoke about her persecution as a Jew in Ukraine, Svoboda called her a *zhydovka*, a racist epithet for a Jew.[25] All the while, the oligarchs who had seized control of most of the country's wealth during the post-Soviet nightmare often played both sides of the divide, seeking to maintain their power whichever direction Ukraine should go.

Petro Poroshenko, for instance, was born into a Russian family in Odessa but later built his capitalist empire in a Ukrainian region of the country. Poroshenko moved smoothly between business and government and as foreign minister in the 2000s he sought rapprochement between Ukraine and Russia. Nevertheless, as momentum grew for the pro-West faction in the 2010s, he quickly shifted to support that side and used his television network to promote their position.[26] In the meantime, oligarchs like Poroshenko — who served a term as president — ensured that Ukrainian politics were preoccupied with the debate about Russia, such that they could continue reaping the benefits of unfettered capitalist exploitation. Ukrainians grew increasingly poor, to the point where more than 30% of the population lived in poverty, and millions of Ukrainians had left the country to find work in Russia or the EU. Public services declined, wages stagnated, and governance slipped gradually into a more authoritarian state, ironically mirroring the dynamics in Russia.[27]

Vladimir Putin, for his part, sent troops to recapture the heavily Russian Crimea region while supporting a local Russian insurgency in Donbas. Putin's government claimed that its intervention was to protect ethnic Russians living in Ukraine from a government and paramilitaries that sought to marginalize and perhaps even eliminate them. In fact, Russians living in Ukraine had themselves risen up in defiance of the Ukrainian nationalists, most notably in the Donbas region in 2014. Russians filled the central square of Donetsk, motivated in large part by fear of the "Banderovtsy," the far-right followers of the Bandera movement, whom they had seen wearing Nazi regalia and attacking police in Maidan.[28] Putin was undoubtedly seizing an opportunity to expand his own territorial and political reach and to protect the Russian frontier from what it viewed as a puppet government of the West. Acknowledging that Putin's actions were taken out of self-interest, however, does not change the fact that his adversaries were fascists; the Ukrainian government had armed and enlisted paramilitaries Richard Sakwa describes as "proto-Freikorps."

What most people in Ukraine wanted was for the tensions to be reduced and some efforts towards reconciliation and compromise made between these factions within the country, such that it might be better insulated against the great power rivalry which was stoking the rise of the far right. Instead, however, Canada took a lead role in exacerbating the tensions, aggressively criticizing the Russian government and sending waves of economic and military support to the far-right, pro-West government in Ukraine. Nearly a thousand Canadian troops were stationed along Russia's border, from Latvia to the Black Sea to Ukraine itself. In 2014, when far-right forces launched the Euromaidan protests, which ultimately led to their seizure of power, Canada directly assisted them and provided haven in the Canadian embassy. In fact, Canada had been supporting these far-right forces for more than a decade already and had previously provided some $16 million in aid to support their "democratic reform."[29]

Canada's support for the far right in Ukraine contributed to a significant threat to peace and stability. Russian military capacity is substantial, and while it certainly could not win a full-fledged conventional war against the United States, its ability to project power into regional conflicts was demonstrated in its successful operation in Crimea in 2014 and its invention in Syria in 2015. Should a war be provoked along the Russian border, it is not clear what the outcome would be but it is certain that such a conflict would be devastating for the poor majority in the borderlands of all countries involved. Canada's stated position was to be a "visible and effective partner *of the United States* in Russia, Ukraine and zones of instability in Eastern Europe."[30] The priority, according to its own statement, was not peace in Eastern Europe. Rather, it was to strengthen its position within the US imperial apparatus, guarantee its own access to favourable trade opportunities in Ukraine and Eastern Europe and perhaps in a post-Putin Russia, and to satisfy the increasingly vocal Ukrainian diaspora in Canada, by now dominated by right-wing Ukrainians whose families came to Canada after the Second World War.

If Canada's commitment to this particular theatre of imperial politics seemed exaggerated in its importance, one clue to the significance it held in Ottawa could be found in the personage of Trudeau's minister of foreign affairs, and later deputy prime minister, Chrystia Freeland. Considered by many to be one of the real power players behind a spokesmodel prime minister, Freeland is the granddaughter of Ukrainian immigrants: her grandfather, Mykhailo Khomiak (anglicized as Michael Chomiak) was a prominent Ukrainian Nazi propagandist during the Second World War. He emigrated to Canada alongside at least 2000 members of a notorious Waffen-SS division of Ukrainian Nazis who were admitted to Canada in 1950.[31] When the story splashed in the Canadian press in 2017, Freeland initially denied the reports and claimed that it was Russian propaganda designed to discredit her. She later adjusted her story to suggest that if there was truth to the claims about her grandfather, she hadn't known it.

Freeland was lying, in both cases. Chomiak had, indeed, been the editor of *Krakivs'ki visti* (*News of Krakow*) reporting directly to Nazi authorities and even continuing to edit the paper after he fled with the Nazis to Vienna.[32] The newspaper had been seized from its original Jewish owners and given to Ukrainian collaborators, who were willing to publish articles welcoming the Nazi occupation and spreading anti-Jewish conspiracy theories. "With great joy," said the paper in the early 1940s, "the Ukrainian population welcomes the establishment of a just German order." It reported on a mass shooting of Jews that they had "got their comeuppance" and celebrated that there was "not a single [Jew] left in Kiev, while there were 350,000 under the Bolsheviks." Chomiak was personally set up in an apartment in Krakow that had been seized from Jews who had been sent to the camps.[33]

In 1943, the paper recruited volunteers for the Waffen-SS death squads, giving space to the highest-ranking Nazi in Ukraine to write: "The long-awaited moment has arrived when the Ukrainian people will again have the opportunity to come out with gun in hand to do battle against its most grievous foe — Bolshevism."[34] The Nazi who penned this callout was Volodomyr Kubijovych; in the 1970s, Chomiak reunited with his old Nazi friend to work on a project called *The Encyclopedia of Ukraine*, which touted a hardline, far-right and anti-Soviet position in its historical narrative. Chrystia Freeland worked on the project[35] and celebrated her grandparents' hard work "to return freedom and democracy to Ukraine," in a public statement in 2016 and in articles and books and stories which she consciously circulated publicly about her grandparents' life in Ukraine.[36] Freeland is credited with reading and editing the work of her uncle, John-Paul Himka, who was a professor at the University of Alberta and originally published the story of Chomiak's work as a Nazi propagandist in 1996.

Chrystia Freeland could not be expected to change the fact that her grandfather was a Nazi. But it is a troubling and persistent fact that her own political trajectory and ideology has followed a very similar pattern to that of her Nazi grandfather. Freeland's career, before she rose to become one of Canada's most powerful politicians, was in journalism and Ukrainian nationalist advocacy. She wrote avowedly anti-Russian articles, routinely derided the horrors of the Soviet Union and championed the cause of the far-right nationalists who took control of Ukraine in 2014. Her popular but unsophisticated *Sale of the Century* (2000) and various articles about Russia's 1990s routinely and bizarrely tapped into longstanding anti-Semitic language and themes, and at one point she specifically and inaccurately claimed that "in Russia, most of the oligarchs were Jewish."[37] She talked about her grandparents often, even evoked them in her first speech in the House of Commons, never saying a word about Chomiak's Nazism, but instead framing them as victims of the Soviet Union.

The editorial line of *Krakivs'ki visti* was actually quite similar; it celebrated the Ukrainian nation, fearmongered and caricatured the Soviets and Russians, and repeated anti-Semitic claims of a "Judeo-Bolshevik conspiracy."[38] There was no such conspiracy, but it was true that around 900,000 Jews who survived the Holocaust in Ukraine escaped to the Soviet Union that Freeland and her grandfather so reviled. Interestingly enough, Freeland seemed to represent a kind of Nazi-denial that her uncle John-Paul Himka had specifically articulated in his study of the Ukrainian diaspora:

> There persists a deafening silence about, as well as a reluctance to confront, even well-documented war crimes, such as the mass murder of Poles in Volhynia by the Ukrainian Insurgent Army (UPA) and the cooperation of the Ukrainian auxiliary police in the execution of the Jews.[39]

Indeed, Himka identified a common tactic among right-wing Ukrainians when confronted with evidence of the complicity of their organizations in the Holocaust, which was to deny the accusations and claim that they were Soviet propaganda. A remarkable parallel to Chrystia Freeland's 2017 denial of the well-documented fact that her grandfather worked for the Nazis and her choice to accuse Russia of spreading disinformation.

These details of Freeland's personal connection to Ukrainian Nazism could be more easily ignored had they not dovetailed so closely with the very real policies she was enacting with respect to Canada's foreign policy in Eastern Europe. Canada pledged more than $700 million to Ukraine beginning in 2014, including military and police training support. Indeed, Canada boasted of training of "more than 12,500 members of Ukraine's Security Forces"; troubling, given the extent to which those forces were populated by the Ukrainian far right.[40]

This was a Ukraine where the minister of internal affairs, Arsen Avakov, had direct ties to the fascist Azov Battalion, where fascists could safely hold a massive two-day rally — the Asagardsrei music festival — and where opponents of the government, like Kateryna Handziuk, were killed by fascists, who doused her in sulfuric acid.[41] Ironic, in light of Handziuk's vicious murder, that Canada's commitments to Ukraine were often framed in the language of feminism, which gave money to the country as part of its Feminist International Assistance Policy and emphasized the inclusion and empowerment of women and girls in the country.

Meanwhile, as part of its effort to re-assert Ukrainian control of the Donbas region, Canada declared in 2019 that it would not recognize Russian passports issued to people there. The announcement was made after a high-profile "Ukraine Reform Conference" in Toronto, in which Chrystia Freeland played a prominent role alongside new Ukrainian President Volodymyr Zelensky.[42] That same year, the Canadian ambassador was present as the Ukrainian government consecrated a monument to seventeen members of the fascist OUN, built on the site of a massacre of 1200 Jews in 1943, which was, as the head of the Ukrainian Jewish Committee put it, "erecting a monument to murderers on the graves of their victims."[43] Freeland was a willing participant in the construction of a Ukraine that would have made her grandfather proud.

Uncreating Hugo Chávez

Outside of its crusade in Ukraine, the foreign policy file wherein Trudeau and Freeland seemed likely to make a mark was in the project to defeat the Bolivarian Revolution in Venezuela. When Canada took a lead role in 2019 in supporting and officially recognizing Juan Guaidó as the self-proclaimed — though unelected — president of Venezuela, it was clear that Freeland wanted to preside over the endgame for the popular revolution in Venezuela. Guaidó's counter-revolution sputtered out by the middle of that year, despite the fact that Canada — alongside the members of a hastily constructed right-wing hemispheric alliance called the Lima Group — had granted official recognition to a comically illegitimate American-educated engineer. It was an indication of how little regard the Canadian state had, by the start of the 2020s, for the niceties of liberal consensus that a wealthy Venezuelan could simply tell everyone he was the country's real president and Canada was willing to go right along with it.

But Canada's aggressive posture towards Venezuela made sense in the context of the twin pillars of its foreign policy. Like Hondurans, like

Haitians, like Nicaraguans and Chileans, Venezuelans had embarked on a project that rebuked the global capitalism that had caused so much harm to so many and were seeking to build something unique and different. A gradual de-linking of Venezuela from the most predatory aspects of that system not only diminished the prospects for Canadian profits but it also set a powerful example that there were alternatives to capitalism. Furthermore, while Venezuela's story was often framed around the larger-than-life figure of President Hugo Chávez Frías, the much more disturbing reality — for the colonizers — was that the Bolivarian Revolution was rooted in the *barrios*, in the councils and communes that increasingly asserted local, democratic control over their neighbourhoods.[44]

When early Canadian settlers had encountered Indigenous nations without single, individual leaders to negotiate with, they were baffled and unnerved; one chief could be bribed, intimidated or bamboozled, but an entire community could not so easily be manipulated. Thus, when poor Venezuelans asserted that it was they who "created Chávez,"[45] and not the other way around, it provoked a kind of primordial panic among the leaders of the capitalist world. That the revolution survived the 2013 death of Chávez signalled that its roots did, indeed, go much deeper than the personage of Chávez himself, and, as such, it was the catalyst for a more aggressive Western push for intervention to end the revolution.

As George Ciccariello-Maher argues, the genesis of what became the Bolivarian Revolution was the crisis of the 1980s, which culminated in the Caracazo, a series of massive protests that rocked the capital city of Caracas, among others, in 1989. As the neoliberal wave swept Latin America in the 1980s, the country had been plunged into economic chaos, but its oligarchic leaders had simply prescribed deeper austerity. Prices for essential goods skyrocketed, subsidies on gas and public utilities were cut, wages plummeted, debt rose, unemployment soared, and anger simmered. When a new president, Carlos Andrés Pérez, failed to make good on his promise to stop the bleeding, leaving some 44% of Venezuelans living in poverty, Caracas erupted:

> Grainy news footage from the rebellion show[ed] the population looting unashamedly, some covering their faces but most not even bothering. After all, they were taking back things they deserved, but of which they had been deprived. Basic goods that had become too expensive or hard to find were soon discovered hoarded in warehouses and storerooms. These were now redistributed

directly by the people themselves, who carried everything from imported whiskey to entire sides of beef on their shoulders up into the *barrios* (shantytowns) surrounding the city.[46]

It was this expression of popular anger and redress that was to be the heart of the revolution which would ultimately be personified around Hugo Chávez, a former military officer who led an unsuccessful *coup d'état* in 1992 and won his first presidential election in 1998. Chávez, as well as anyone, understood that radical change in Venezuela could not be achieved under the decrepit system of representative democracy that had, for so long, stifled real popular dissent. Indeed, if the Caracazo had been an expression of that dissent, the massacre carried out by the Pérez government in its aftermath was the old system's answer. Hundreds — maybe thousands — of poor Venezuelans were slaughtered in a wave of indiscriminate violence unleashed upon the denizens of the *barrios*.[47]

The 1992 coup attempt made Chávez a hero, and his challenge to the oligarchy was more than rhetorical; after 1998 he initiated serious reform, striking a committee drawn from a wide range of Venezuelan society to rewrite the country's constitution. This was significant insofar as it shook up the existing political structures and left many of the old elite on the outside of the system they had ruled for so long.[48] It also created a significantly more progressive foundation for Venezuelan law, including, for instance, a clause that affirmed that women's domestic labour was equally valuable to other forms of labour and thus qualified those who did that work for social security.[49] Thereafter, Chávez tackled the endemic levels of poverty, repealing neoliberal austerity policies and replacing them with an array of social security measures.

Progress was slow, at first, but the challenge that the new government posed was serious enough that the United States and its allies tried to orchestrate a coup against Chávez in 2002, dramatically captured on video in *The Revolution Will Not Be Televised* (2003). The attempt failed, in large part because Chávez's base of support was wide enough to encompass not just the majority of the country's people but also large sections of its military.[50] Following his reinstatement, the private owners of Venezuela's oil industry tried to strangle the government by shutting down production. This, too, failed, as workers themselves seized control of the means of oil production. Once the state could marshal the wealth generated by the oil industry, it had the capital it needed to carry out a more systematic social reform, funding free health care, education, food and other essential goods and services for the poor. The gap between the rich and poor — once higher in Venezuela than anywhere else in Latin America — was reduced dramatically.[51]

Though Chávez was routinely disparaged in the North American media as a dictator, he actually commanded a massive swell of popular support. He won four legitimate presidential elections (1998, 2000, 2006, 2012), defeated a recall referendum (2004) and on several occasions held referenda on key pieces of his project, all of which were approved. During his time in office, his supporters almost always had a majority in the Venezuelan National Assembly, and, perhaps most notably, Chávez was remarkably tolerant of the vitriolic opposition of the oligarchy. Despite their use of the media to slander him, he permitted their continued ownership of most of its outlets. Despite repeated attempts to have him overthrown, there were almost no credible reports of any kind of violent retribution or even significant punishment doled out to those who plotted against him.

Meanwhile, what developed in Venezuela was a different kind of democracy, one rooted in community-level decision-making that empowered the poorest Venezuelans to help shape the conditions of their own lives. Even before the election of Hugo Chávez, the *barrios* had begun to self-organize, to create self-defence militias and to combat the biggest problems they faced, from gang violence to lack of running water. These were often far more successful at improving the conditions of life than anything the previous governments had ever done — the community of La Piedrita, for instance, pushed out the drug trade and the corrupt police that facilitated it — and when Chávez came to power they cooperated with him but did not submit to his authority.[52] Indeed, one of the most misunderstood elements of the Bolivarian Revolution was the very fact that Chávez and his successor, Nicolás Maduro, in fact presided over a massive network of somewhat self-governing communes. The building of this system was driven from below, but received a great deal of institutional support from above, and served to empower a wide range of hitherto marginalized groups in Venezuelan society, including women, LGBTQ and Indigenous people.[53]

None of this should suggest that Chávez had developed simple and harmonious relationships with the local councils and communes that rose up in Venezuela during the revolution. Conflict between a self-styled progressive *caudillo* like Chávez and the actual exercise of power by marginalized people was always going to be part of the story, as when social movement leaders complained in 1992 that Chávez had wanted the people to "applaud but not participate."[54] Nevertheless, Chávez also understood that if the revolution was to survive it would need the support of the masses, and that meant acquiescing to demands for local autonomy. In 2012, as Chávez was dying, he gave a speech in which he railed against his own ministers for having allowed corruption and inaction to stultify the transition to a genuine socialist democracy. "Popular power" he rallied, "does not come from Miraflores Palace."[55]

Both Chávez and the communes were trying to grapple with the tension between encouraging local democracy while maintaining some structures of centralized governance and order. When taken seriously, this is no easy problem to solve. In 2006, the Chávez government had established a structure through which local councils would exercise power and plug into national decision-making. After Chávez's death in 2013, the program grew under Nicolás Maduro, who made Reinaldo Iturriza — a long-time radical and activist for local democracy — a minister of the communes. Within a few years, there were some 50,000 communes registered across the country and they were expanding the scope of their authority.[56] Even as a collapse in oil prices sent the Venezuelan economy into a tailspin in 2014, Venezuela's version of democracy was, in many ways, more robust and direct than anywhere in the Western Hemisphere.

But that economic crisis, combined with the death of the immensely popular Chávez, proved to be a major opening for the Venezuelan right. Having been soundly defeated in the failed coup of 2002, and the litany of electoral losses that followed, the Venezuelan right was divided and in despair. The collapse in oil prices, however, opened the door for a reinvigorated assault on the Bolivarian Revolution. In the second half of the 2010s, they organized relentlessly — mostly by appealing to imperial power in North America — in an attempt to orchestrate the downfall of Maduro and the revolution. Both the Obama and Trump administrations were eager to see the Venezuelan example fail, and as Latin America was pulled gradually but certainly under the boot of the right, the target fell squarely on Caracas. The capitalist powers sought to foment a crisis in Venezuela, exacerbating the existing economic woes by imposing heavy sanctions and lavishing the opposition with resources, while building public consensus around the idea that Maduro was a dictator who was starving Venezuelans with his brutal policies.

As far back as the 2002 coup, Canada had been actively involved in supporting the groups trying to oust Chávez, and even brought leaders from those networks to Ottawa to deliver talks on the Venezuelan situation. In 2005, Ottawa resisted calls to meet with Chávez and instead hosted Maria Corina Machado, who had participated in the failed attempts to defeat him in the 2002 coup and 2004 recall. Her organization was one of at least three that were part of the 2002 coup attempt which received direct funding from the Canadian government.[57] Canada further stepped up its efforts to fund the Venezuelan right after 2007 when Chávez denounced and suspended American funding for such groups. The Canadian embassy in Caracas was pleased at the prospect of stepping up, noting that Canada now had an "opportunity to fill the gap created by [the suspension of US funding]."[58]

In the 2010s, the Canadian government seemed more and more seized by a frenetic desire to defeat Venezuela. In 2006, the Harper government, alone with the United States, refused to congratulate Hugo Chávez on his unambiguous victory in an election monitored by the Organization of American States (OAS). When, in 2010, the Chávez government shut down six radio stations for frequent violations of Venezuelan laws, Canada's Minister of State Peter Kent reacted sharply, calling it "evidence of shrinking democratic space in Venezuela."[59] Quite the contrary, Venezuela's privately owned media was rabidly anti-Chávez and had been allowed to spin ludicrous propaganda against him the entire time he had been in office; in fact, the 2002 coup attempt had been transparently carried out with the logistical support of several Venezuelan media outlets.[60] And still, Chávez had allowed them to remain on the air; in fact, they commanded 92–95% of Venezuelan television audiences.[61] Peter Kent's statement was made even more outrageous by the fact that it was issued on the very same day that he congratulated one of the plotters of the anti-democratic coup in Honduras on his victory in a sham election.[62]

Peter Kent's highly publicized and critical visit to Venezuela was noteworthy insofar as he refused to meet with any officials from the actual Venezuelan government. He did, however, have time to meet with the opposition that had been trying to oust Chávez for a decade; the Canadian government has never released the names of those opposition leaders, which suggests that they may have been involved in indefensible acts of violence or sabotage.[63] By this point, Chávez was no longer willing to spare Canada from the withering rhetoric he had long wielded against the

United States. Both Chávez and his representative at the OAS denounced Canada as a junior partner in imperialism and made specific reference to the fact that Canada had supported the coup in Honduras.[64]

Canada's support for the Honduran dictatorship was motivated in part by the needs of Canadian capital. Notably, Canadian capital had also been invested in Venezuela, particularly in mining for gold. Canadian mining projects have caused social conflict nearly everywhere they have gone, and Venezuela was no exception. As far back as 2001, the Venezuelan government found itself in conflict with Canadian companies, mostly surrounding the Las Cristinas mine, the country's largest gold deposit. Initially the mine was co-owned by the Venezuelan government and Placer Dome (later purchased by Barrick Gold), but a questionable sale of Placer Dome's rights to another Canadian company (Vanessa Ventures, later Infinito Gold) caused the Venezuelan government to block the purchase. Vanessa Ventures spent twelve years trying unsuccessfully to sue Venezuela under the Canada-Venezuela Foreign Investment Protection Agreement. The difficulty of extracting wealth from Venezuela was frustrating to the Canadian capitalist class, for whom Venezuela was its second-largest export market in South America and where it had up to $1 billion invested.[65]

While Vanessa Ventures tried to extract wealth by another route, Placer Dome's rights were transferred to yet another Canadian company, Crystallex. But a series of problems between Crystallex and the Venezuelan government — including a crash in the value of Crystallex — led to the nationalization of the gold mine. Crystallex eventually won a $1.2 billion payout in 2016, the same year that Rusoro Mining successfully won a $1 billion claim around another project.[66] Similar conflicts emerged involving Gold Reserve Inc. and Petro-Canada, leading Stephen Harper to assert in 2009 that Venezuela was "opposed to basically sound economic policies."[67] Venezuelan efforts to keep its mineral wealth within its borders also drew the ire of Canadian mining magnate Peter Munk, who penned a wild letter to the *Financial Times* which compared President Chávez to Hitler, Milošević and a range of other notorious historical figures. Munk's own company, Barrick Gold, included on its International Advisory Board Gustavo Cisneros, Venezuela's richest man and staunch opponent of Hugo Chávez.[68]

"Chávez failure," said the Canadian government in 2007, would be "a positive sign for Canadian interests in assisting in the development of good government, and in negotiating a free trade agreement, with the region."[69] That Canada should have viewed the failure of the Bolivarian Revolution as a positive sign is indicative of both its obsession with protecting the needs of capital and its colonial disregard for the autonomy and interests of those they believed to be beneath them. When Chávez died in 2013, the Canadian government and media could barely contain their glee; Stephen Harper celebrated the dawn of "a better, brighter future based on the principles of freedom, democracy, the rule of law and respect for human rights" for Venezuelans, and newspaper columnists fell upon themselves to pen screeds against Chávez as a dictator who tricked poor, "stupid" Venezuelans into supporting him while he cracked down on human rights and the media and also ruined the economy by giving handouts to the poor.[70]

This nonsense was immediately refuted by the Venezuelan government, which criticized Harper's statement and noted that Venezuela had a more robust democratic process than Canada; even Chávez's most narrow margin of victory — 56% of the popular vote — was larger than any mandate the Harper government had ever won. And unlike Harper's elections — two of which were called into question for irregularities — Chávez's fourteen electoral victories were beyond reproach, with even the Carter Centre calling Venezuela's elections "the best in the world."[71]

The Bolivarian Revolution reduced poverty by nearly 40%, reduced extreme poverty by nearly 60% and created a robust and direct form of democracy. It had built links with other progressive governments in the region, it had sold discounted oil to poor countries in the Caribbean, and it had helped inspire a new generation of resistance to imperialism. It was the classic "threat of a good example" that haunted governments like that in Ottawa, and from the moment of Chávez's death, Canada redoubled its efforts to defeat the revolution. After the first election of Chávez's former vice-president, one-time bus driver Nicolás Maduro, Canada claimed that his victory was tainted and called for an audit. The accusation was ludicrous; Venezuela's electoral process was widely recognized for its rigour. Canada and the United States were the only two countries in the world to make the accusation, and even then, the Venezuelan Electoral Council agreed to do an audit, which confirmed the initial result.[72] The North American powers were grasping at straws, but it was only the beginning of an intensified effort to galvanize opposition to Maduro and strangle the Venezuelan government until it would collapse.

Following the election of Maduro, the United States, Canada and the European Union placed economic sanctions on Venezuela designed to strangle its economy. The effects, combined with a crash in the price of oil, were catastrophic. One estimate suggests that between 2013 and 2019 the Venezuelan economy lost $114 billion, as a result of the sanctions and their secondary effects.[73] The UN also stated on several occasions that the sanctions constituted a form of collective punishment that was directly causing hunger and death, especially since they specifically obstructed the movement of food and medicine into the country. Nevertheless, Canada was steadfast in its effort to strangle the Venezuelan people into submission, a pattern that resembled Western policy towards Chile in the 1970s and Nicaragua in the 1980s. After sponsoring several waves of anti-Maduro protests in the hopes of fomenting a rebellion, Canada and its allies in the Lima Group latched onto the wealthy, American-educated Juan Guaidó in 2019, who proclaimed himself president.

Despite being supported by a wide range of subversive tactics from the West, Guaidó could not muster any effective rebellion against Maduro and rarely galvanized much popular sympathy. Guaidó's rallies were always dwarfed by those in support of the government, and the fact that Canada continued to refer to the powerless and unpopular Guaidó as Venezuela's president was increasingly embarrassing. Canada spent at least $55 million in its efforts to destabilize what it called the "illegitimate" Maduro government, but this claim fooled few, especially given that Canada's chief vehicle for this enterprise was the Lima Group.[74] That body, built in the aftermath of a coup in Brazil with the express purpose of regime change in Venezuela, was made up of the most far-right and dictatorial regimes in the hemisphere, including Brazil, Colombia and the regime Canada had sponsored in Honduras.

Thus, while it was true that Venezuelans were struggling, Canada's cynical misrepresentation of the causes of the crisis undermined any notion that it expressed genuine solidarity for poor Venezuelans. Ultimately, the economic crisis that had set in during the mid-2010s had much to do with the country's reliance on oil revenue, but its reliance on oil revenue was in part a function of the sanctions and restrictions placed upon it by United States and Canada. As in so many other cases, Canada helped generate a crisis in another country and then used the crisis as a justification for its intervention. Whether the model of socialist development advanced by the Bolivarian Revolution is sustainable and progressive is a complex question well beyond the scope of this work. What is certain is that Canada actively participated in efforts to subvert and dismantle a process built by and for the large majority of Venezuelans. Doing so is, inescapably, imperialism.

The Friendly Far Right: Colombia and Brazil

Canada's efforts to undermine the Bolivarian Revolution in Venezuela were often couched in the language of democracy, freedom and human rights, which — so went the claim — were problems in Venezuela that required Canadian attention. This book raises serious doubts about Canada's motivations when identifying such problems in the world and its justification in taking action in such cases. But it also illustrates that Canada has systematically used such rhetorical concerns as a smokescreen to conceal its real goals, which have typically been rooted in waging class struggle on behalf of the international and/or Canadian capitalist classes. That Venezuela fits this pattern is made especially evident by Canada's incongruent relationships to right-wing violence and dictatorship in Venezuela's largest neighbouring countries, Colombia and Brazil.

The Colombian comparison is particularly instructive. Though it receives less attention than many of its counterparts, the Colombian left managed to survive the great waves of counter-revolution in Latin America and continued to struggle for socialist revolution throughout the second half of the 20th century. Rooted in the rural peasantry, which was being forcibly dispossessed of land by the intensification of capitalism in the middle of the century, the Fuerzas Armadas Revolucionarias de Colombia (FARC) proved to be both an effective guerrilla force and also a shrewd political organization, maintaining a solid base of support throughout the struggle and establishing a wide network of local self-governance and self-defence units across rural Colombia.

Nevertheless, by the dawn of the 21st century, the FARC had lost some of its sway among the Colombian masses, and the Colombian ruling class was emboldened by foreign support and narcotrafficking dollars. The latter launched major offensives to defeat the FARC, especially in areas where foreign capital was seeking to open up investment. Often relying on the unchecked violence of paramilitary forces, the Colombian state was able to terrorize and demobilize much of FARC's base, and the rest of the Colombian peasant movement, with impunity. To be a human rights activist, a social movement defender, a trade unionist, indeed to be in any way supportive of social and collective rights was to be a target. Tens of thousands of mostly Indigenous and Afro-Colombians were killed in the late 1990s and early 2000s, and the majority of Colombians were plunged into poverty as neoliberal economic policies were imposed on the defeated communities.[75] At the same time, some 4 million people were displaced from their homes, at least half of that number from areas slated for mining development.[76]

The most decisive period in this right-wing onslaught was overseen by the government of Álvaro Uribe between 2002 and 2010, which spent some $80 billion on the military, though the violence continued well beyond his time in power.[77] There were few countries in Latin America that could boast such an appalling record with respect to violations of human rights, and yet, even as it was ramping up the pressure on the Chávez government in Venezuela, the Canadian government praised Colombia effusively. Prime Minister Harper declared that Colombia had chosen "to embrace political democracy and human rights and social development" and that Canada was "there to help."[78] Meanwhile, the Canadian Council for the Americas made the astounding decision to give its 2011 "statesman of the year" award to Uribe, who had overseen one of the most violent periods in Colombia's recent memory.

The unsurprising clue to solving this mystery was that Uribe had not only pried open Colombia's gates to Canadian investment, but his offensive against the rural insurgency had been undertaken with the express purpose of securing the conditions for profitable investments, especially in mining. Uribe had specifically promoted investment in Colombian mining by promising to create military battalions to protect company personnel during their exploration phases, assuring potential investors in Calgary and Toronto that community opposition to their operations would not be tolerated. Uribe changed Colombia's mining laws to reduce taxes from 15% to 4%, sped up the expropriation of land by limiting community consultations and weakened environmental protections to make good on his promise that Colombia would be "attractive to investors."[79] The new laws were, in fact, co-authored by Canada: CIDA funding between 1997 and 2002 directly contributed to the development of the new laws, from which Canadian companies were the direct beneficiaries. Officials connected to the Canadian company Corona Goldfields were specifically identified as authors of the laws.[80]

Despite these favourable laws, Canadian companies still faced opposition in their attempts to extract wealth from Colombia. For instance, in the Antioquia and Caldas regions, where Canadian firms were seeking to expand, local communities were refusing to leave. The problem was solved by aerial bombing from the Colombian military, which had, on occasion, been trained in Canada. This was nothing new; conflict around Canadian mining projects in Colombia was well documented as early as the 1990s. "The systematic massacres and displacements of Colombian citizens by a combined military-paramilitary assault," explained one report in 1997, "have the dual effect of creating a vast pool of cheaper labour and giving foreign companies access to valuable natural resources they may not otherwise have been able to obtain."[81] One prominent Colombian opponent of a Canadian hydro dam project, Kimy Pernía Domicó, travelled to Ottawa to testify in a parliamentary committee about the effects of the dam on his community. He warned the committee that his life was in danger for criticizing the dam; sure enough, only months after his second trip to Canada to talk about the dam, he disappeared, his body never found.[82] Even the *Toronto Star* had reported in 1999 that Canadian mining companies operating in the midst of military massacres could not possibly claim to have unbloodied hands.

Such blood had never been a problem for Canadian capital in the past, and it would not be in Colombia. By 2006 it had some $414 million invested in Colombia and by 2016 that figure had risen to $3.6 billion.[83] Put differently, Canada's investment in Colombia grew nearly eight times larger in the decade following the defeat of the social movements that had defended Colombia's rural poor and whose members continued to be murdered at an alarming rate. As elsewhere, violence was linked to capital development; hundreds of former FARC members and other social and environmental activists — and their families — were killed in the late 2010s around zones scheduled for business projects.

Even as Canada was supporting a project to overthrow the Venezuelan government for alleged human rights abuses in early 2019, it fell silent on the high-profile murder in Colombia of Dimar Torres, a former FARC guerrilla who had agreed to disarm as part of the peace process. Torres was tortured and executed after being grabbed on his way home from work in Convención, his brutalized body thrown into a shallow pit. He was one of more than 600 activists and former FARC members killed between 2016 and 2019 in what was called an "invisible genocide."[84] In July 2019, hundreds of people marched in Canadian cities to draw attention to the problem but to little avail; though the murder of Dimar Torres was a major news story in Colombia, Canada said not a word, and continued to support a process wherein the West was arming militants in Colombia and sending troops for a potential assault on Venezuela.[85]

All the while, the Canadian government promoted its role in Colombia as one in support of women's leadership, responsible mining and human rights. Thus, even while Canada ignored actual murders of activist men and women, it launched the "Women's Voice and Leadership" project, which claimed to include human rights defenders among its constituents.[86] The campaign launch focused, however, on economics. Indeed, alongside mining and other major infrastructure and telecommunications projects came Canadian bank capital, and notable among the list of Canadian banks and financial institutions operating in war-torn Colombia was Brookfield Asset Management.[87] Brookfield's progenitor company was Brascan, more colloquially known in Brazil as the *polvo canadense*, the Canadian octopus that was the country's largest company and had its tentacles in nearly every major industry, making it the source of public outrage in the 1920s and 1930s.

When the Brazilian government sought to limit the power of companies like Brascan in the 1960s, the Canadian media described Brazil as a "backward, illiterate, dirty country,"[88] and the Canadian government supported a counter-revolutionary *coup d'état*. In 1964 the Brazilian military took power by force and led the country through two decades of darkness and dictatorship. This period of dictatorship shaped Brazil's future significantly, insofar as Brazil's future leftist leaders — Luis Inácio Lula da Silva and Dilma Rousseff — were veterans of the struggle against that very dictatorship. Dilma, in particular, had fought in the guerrilla war and had been tortured by the military between 1972 and 1974, making her rise to the Brazilian presidency in 2011 a significant moment on several levels.[89]

But the arrival of the Worker's Party (PT) at the top of Brazilian politics in 2003 had been achieved, in part, by Lula's brokering a deal with one of the parties of the centre right; while it vaulted Lula into the presidency, it weakened his capacity to govern from the left. Indeed, in advance of the 2002 elections, the PT had specifically removed from its program the gradual transition to socialism that had long been part of its political line. As such, the early years of PT rule were not indicative of any major shift away from the Brazilian status quo; as Leslie Bethell pointedly asked, having made itself amenable to the oligarchy and the middle class, "was the PT still a party of the left?"[90] As it had in Colombia, Bell Canada International stepped into Brazil to fill the void left by the privatization waves of the neoliberal 1990s; the transition from state-provided telecommunications to private companies meant, predictably, a decline in good jobs and a reduction in the quality of service provision.[91] Neither Lula's nor Dilma's government was able to dramatically shift this dynamic.

Over time, however, and especially in Lula's second term in office, the reform project did grow more ambitious. Lula — born into poverty in Brazil's northeast and made famous by his charismatic leadership in the metalworkers' union in São Paolo — was always popular. But his popularity grew, especially among Brazil's poorest people, as the PT rolled out a more comprehensive poverty reduction plan in the mid-2000s. At the centre of this project was the Bolsa Família, a reformed social security measure which provided the equivalent of about $55 USD each month to the poorest Brazilian families, with priority given to single mothers. Though relatively modest — it represented less than 1% of Brazil's GDP — the Bolsa Família was life-changing for those who received it, which by 2010 was some 50 million people, nearly a quarter of the country's population.[92] For perspective, this meant that there were more people receiving the Bolsa Família in Brazil than the entire population of Canada. The PT was tackling extreme poverty in one of the most unequal countries in the world, without dramatically offending the ruling classes and, by the end of his second term, Lula's approval rating was as high as 75%. Nevertheless, the balancing act between rich and poor could not be maintained forever.

Dilma Rousseff won the presidency in 2010, but the petering out of the commodities boom — especially in agriculture, mining and oil — undermined her ability to maintain anti-poverty measures and public infrastructure without taking aim at the rich. Under Lula, the rich had stayed that way, largely avoiding taxation and enjoying a range of state subsidies, to say nothing of the endemic corruption that existed in the nexus of state and capital. As the economy began to unravel, Dilma took aim at the banks' decision to tighten access to credit, pushing her closer to a collision with the Brazilian right. Meanwhile, Dilma's inability to maintain public spending during the crisis generated anger amongst the poor; while the Bolsa Família pulled millions of people out of extreme poverty, it did not make them rich. The majority of Brazilians remained poor; public demonstrations accelerated and were then ignited by the final nail in the PT's coffin, the Lava-Jato (Car Wash) corruption scandal.[93]

What began as a stake-out of a car wash grew into a massive investigation into corruption at Petrobras, the state oil company, which ultimately implicated hundreds of high-level politicians and business executives. In its early stages, Lava-Jato had some support among the PT, even despite the fact that some of its own members were being caught in its web; Dilma herself even gave the operation a green light, in recognition of both the public distrust that would be generated by her squashing it and also the reality that corruption was playing a role in undermining her own ability to manage the state and run its public services. However, the investigators and judges who spearheaded Lava-Jato used it increasingly to hammer the PT; while several members of all political parties were caught up in it at the start, it increasingly targeted the PT and Lula and Dilma in particular.

In 2016, despite her having just won a second election, Dilma was impeached — she rightly called it a coup — by a congress that was stacked with her political enemies.[94] There was no evidence of corruption against her, only a minor implication of mismanagement. The biggest prize, however, for the forces behind Lava-Jato was Lula. Still the most popular politician in Brazil and sure to win the next round of elections, Lula was indicted in 2017 on a very thin corruption charge by a judicial system that was now completely controlled by the right. Barred from participation in the 2018 elections, the courts had effectively dismantled the party of the Brazilian left.[95]

Lurking behind much of the push to unseat the left was the fascist Jair Bolsonaro, who would win Brazil's 2018 elections. Having placed the more popular Lula in jail, Bolsonaro, open admirer of the military dictatorships, won the 2018 election and promised to rule with "the bible and the bullet." Four years earlier, he had responded to a speech by Congresswoman Maria do Rosário praising the work of the National Truth Commission, which had documented the violence and sexual violence of the military dictatorship, by yelling at her, "I would not rape you, you don't merit that."[96] This was the second time Bolsonaro had publicly made reference to raping do Rosário, and he was proud of it, sharing it widely through his social media accounts. In 2011 he had famously said that he would have preferred his son be hit by a car than be gay, and in a separate incident said that his son was "well raised" and would therefore never fall in love with a black woman.[97]

Canada did not express any concerns over Bolsonaro's hateful and fascist politics or the fact that he had effectively subverted democracy in Brazil. Though it had continued to do business in the country under PT leadership,⁹⁸ there was no doubt that Canada could achieve a better deal with a government that was not interested in supporting the poor. When Dilma was impeached in a technical coup in 2016, Canada made no objection and quietly reached out to the new government, led by the right-wing Michael Temer, to sign a new defensive cooperation agreement that forged closer links between the Canadian and Brazilian militaries.⁹⁹ That Canada would invite the head of the Brazilian military to bilateral talks immediately following what amounted to a coup spoke volumes about Canada's position and, perhaps, made it less surprising that Canada was so welcoming in 2018 to the fascist Jair Bolsonaro, a proudly racist, misogynist, homophobic former paratrooper who fetishized the armed forces, was highly placed in Brazil's criminal networks and had likely ordered the assassination of Rio de Janiero city councillor Marielle Franco.¹⁰⁰

Canada applauded Bolsonaro's electoral victory. CBC News was quick to declare that while "critics have lambasted the former paratrooper for his homophobic, racist and misogynist statements, his government could open new investment opportunities."¹⁰¹ The Canadian government quickly engaged with Bolsonaro in free trade talks, and Chrystia Freeland stood shoulder-to-shoulder with Bolsonaro as they plotted the overthrow of the Venezuelan government in early 2019. Given Canada's long record of working with fascists, this should not have come as a great surprise. Canadian investments in Brazil were significant; by 2018, Canada had over $11 billion invested in the country, much of it in the energy and extractive industries, and at the top of the list was the old octopus, Brookfield Asset Management.¹⁰²

While the PT had never been a major obstacle to their operations, it was clear that a Bolsonaro government would be very good for foreign investment. Bolsonaro almost immediately declared war on the Indigenous people of the Amazon, who had long fought to protect their land against capitalist expansion. Upon Bolsonaro's election, the CBC happily noted that he would "open new investment opportunities" as he had promised "to slash environmental regulations in the Amazon rainforest."¹⁰³ By the summer of 2019, the Amazon was in flames, after Bolsonaro had encouraged agribusiness and other capitalist developers to set the fires. In just his first eight months in office, Bolsonaro oversaw the destruction of 3500 square miles of forest, more than any year in recorded history, and cities like São Paolo were plunged into darkness from the smoke.

In addition to supporting fascist and proto-fascist governments in Colombia and Brazil, Canada also built strong relationships with fascist governments elsewhere. In the Philippines, where millions of people had organized into one of the largest communist insurgencies in the world, the government of Rodrigo Duterte declared itself fascist and promised to crush the communists with force. Framing them as "drug dealers," he dropped bombs containing white phosphorous on Filipino peasants and restricted their access to food, while arresting teachers and murdering activists.[104] Amnesty International called Duterte's campaign a "large scale murdering enterprise," but the limit of Justin Trudeau's outrage was to raise the question of human rights with Duterte during a meeting. Trudeau played it down, noting that there were "always human rights concerns to bring up with a wide range of leaders."[105]

Canada also fostered a close relationship with the fascist government of Narendra Modi in India, who attacked the communist Naxalite movement and advocated for Hindu supremacy amidst a growing nationalist paramilitary presence. Modi had facilitated a massacre of more than a thousand Muslims in 2002 and had stoked the rise of far-right violence. The Canadian press heaped praise on Modi for "making progress" with his neoliberal policies and deepening trade relations with Canada,[106] ignoring the massive human rights violations and the slide into fascism that is illustrated plainly in Anand Patwardhan's chilling documentary *Reason* (2018). In addition to those noted above, fascist and quasi-fascist governments were emerging in Poland, Hungary and Austria, among others, and Canada said little. As it had in the 1930s, Canada recognized that the shift to the right was good for business.

Blood of Extraction

By the 21st century, Canada's network of foreign investments and involvements has become so great that it is impossible to document it all in a book like this. Emblematic cases have, therefore, been chosen for closer examination. Nevertheless, it is worth noting that these episodes were not isolated incidents but, rather, reflective of the broader trend. By the 2010s, Canadian capital was investing more than $500 billion outside

Canada's borders, making it one of the world's highest sources of foreign direct investment, and had signed dozens of free trade agreements with countries around the world.[107]

These investments cover a wide range of industries, but tend to fall into three categories: 1) investment in natural resource extraction, which have to be undertaken in the place where the resources were located; 2) investment in low-wage industries, where capital can exploit cheaper labour abroad; and 3) investment in banking and finance, where privileged access to large amounts of capital make it possible for Canadian institutions to take advantage of clients and customers in poorer countries.[108] For all of these reasons, Canadian investment in the Global South accelerated rapidly in the 21st century. While each of these deserves some attention, the most prominent and notorious of Canada's foreign investments have tended to be in the mining sector. Todd Gordon and Jeffery R. Webber's *Blood of Extraction* (2016) documents the effects of Canada's mining industry in Latin America, illustrating both the violent and destructive practices of the companies and the systematic way in which the Canadian state works to support them. "As far as I can tell," said one Latin American government official, "the Canadian ambassador here is a representative for Canadian mining companies."[109]

Some 70% of the world's mining companies are based in Canada, which offers minimal taxation and regulation and a state apparatus bent to the industry's will. Net profits for individual companies are often in the billions and the average rate of profit for the industry is larger, by a massive degree, than in most other industries.[110] Meanwhile, these companies have some of the worst records in the world in terms of violations of human, environmental and labour rights.[111] It is significant that Canada is nurturing some of the world's most exploitative and profitable ventures, which are inevitably linked to both the theft and the poisoning of land in other countries. Canadian settler capitalism was, after all, rooted in the conquest of land.

Mining is also a noteworthy sector because it draws direct attention to Canada's particular place in the pantheon of exploitative capitalist powers. As Karen Dubinsky and Marc Epprecht note:

> It says something very disturbing when workers [in South Africa] voted Canada's Placer Dome as the second worst employer in the country in 2001… "The Killing Continues at a Canadian-owned Mine in Tanzania" is not the kind of headline that stirs Canadian

national pride. Toronto-listed Acres International... was the first international company to be found guilty of bribery of a state official [in Lesotho] and first to be debarred from World Bank contracts for corrupt practices.[112]

While the latter case was not directly tied to mining, it was part of the portfolio of Canadian extractive industry practices that have earned such a terrible reputation across Asia, Africa and Latin America.[113] The Marlin mine in Guatemala is a noteworthy case, especially given Canada's history of violent interference there.

Marlin was always controversial; it was built on Indigenous territory in the 1990s, not long after the end of the genocide. There was hardly any consultation with local communities, and the health effects of its cyanide-leaching process were disastrous. Moreover, as opposition to the mine grew, protestors were increasingly subject to violence. Blockades seeking to stop development of the mine were attacked by Guatemalan police, and several people were killed or injured for their opposition to the mine. Álvaro Sánchez, for instance, was shot dead in the street in March 2005 by a security guard who worked for Marlin (then owned by Glamis Gold, later Goldcorp). This was no isolated incident: in Las Nubes, where Skye Resources and later Hudbay Minerals were seeking to operate a nickel mine, violence against mostly Indigenous Maya Q'eqchi' opponents was rampant and horrific; several people were assassinated, live ammunition was routinely fired at protestors, a mini-bus carrying several community leaders was peppered with machine gun fire, there were incidents of gang rape, and one prominent activist — Adolfo Ich Chamán — was kidnapped and hacked to death by Hudbay security officers.[114]

Despite the extreme levels of violence being deployed against communities ravaged by Canadian mines, the Canadian embassy in Guatemala City did somersaults to defend the industry. In 2004, Ambassador James Lambert wrote an op-ed in Guatemala's primary national newspaper, *Prensa Libre*, claiming that "Canadian businesses [were] on the vanguard of high technology, environmental protection and social responsibility." Lambert's PR offensive was sustained over several weeks and also included a television appearance in which he lied about the standards Canadian mining companies had to meet in order to go ahead with their operations and — in a statement dripping with colonial arrogance — informed Guatemalans that "sooner or later, Indigenous communities in Guatemala [had] to face the reality of a global society."[115] In Lambert's view, then, "backwards" Indigenous people were once again trying to resist the sweep of modernity, as represented by violent and exploitative mining companies.

In Guatemala and elsewhere that Canadian mining was prominent, the very presence of the highly contested and heavily militarized mining operations served to increase the general level of violence and insecurity within the affected regions and countries. Conflicts around the mines and other mega-projects often generated a greater military and paramilitary presence, including armed security guards, thugs and death squads hired to intimidate activists; this is documented in detail in *Organized Violence* (2019), an edited volume which sketches out the dynamics of violence as they relate to major capitalist projects like mines and hydro dams in Latin America. While violence is often explained in the North American media as being "endemic" to Latin American countries and rooted in the drug trade, gang wars and general criminality of the population, the reality is that drugs, gangs and crime are more often a consequence of the violent practices of capitalism.[116]

Indeed, by the 21st century, much of the violence that took place around capital development had itself been privatized: while formal militaries and police still carried out violence, there was an increasing preference for the use of paramilitaries, private security, criminal gangs, *sicarios* and other "independent contractors" of violence. This often created a layer of deniability for the capitalist interests that remained at the centre of the story. Tahoe Resources, for instance, hired International Security and Defence Management, which then contracted Alberto Rotondo to be head of security at the Escobal silver mine in Guatemala; when Rotondo was found to have ordered his forces to open fire on protestors, Tahoe claimed innocence and cut ties with Rotondo.[117]

The overwhelmingly negative consequences of Canadian mining projects have generated massive mobilizations of people against those very projects around the world. A movement of people protesting the Barrick Gold mining project in Ancash, in Peru, led to a violent incident at a blockade in May 2006. Assassinations of opponents of the operations of the Ascendant Copper mine in Intag, Ecuador, led to a lawsuit against the company.[118] The body count connected to all Canadian mining companies has never been tallied, but it would easily range from hundreds of people to thousands, depending on how such a number were generated; even the notoriously pro-mining *Globe and Mail* admitted an extremely low estimate of 44 people killed between 2000 and 2015 around Canadian mining operations.¹¹⁹ Mariano Abarca, organizing against Blackfire Resources in southern Mexico: killed November 2009.¹²⁰ Mohamed Ould Machdhoufi, organizing against First Quantum Minerals in Mauritania: killed July 2012.¹²¹ Laura Leonor Vásquez Pineda, organizing against Tahoe Resources in Guatemala: killed January 2017.¹²²

While many of the examples I have drawn are from Latin America, similar dynamics are playing out across the rest of the Global South. Canada dominates the mining industry in Africa, with some 700 mines scattered across 35 countries, worth as much as $31 billion in profits in 2011.¹²³ Not surprisingly, those profits were built on the same violence and exploitation as elsewhere. The 2004 torture and massacre of over 100 Congolese protestors in Katanga, for instance, was facilitated by Canadian-owned Anvil Mining. Anvil transported the soldiers who carried out the massacre to its mine, which was being occupied by the protestors. After using Anvil's trucks to dump the bodies into a mass grave, the Congolese military commander thanked the company, noting that the operation was "made possible thanks to the logistics efforts provided by Anvil Mining."¹²⁴ The company did not deny its involvement but did not face any consequences.

At a Barrick Gold mine in Tanzania, dozens of local opponents of the mine were murdered between 2005 and 2015 by Barrick security, while at least 14 women were raped by the same security forces, and hundreds of other people were injured. What is more, in 2009 one of the mine's tailings ponds spilled, dumping sulphuric acid into the Tigithe River. "The Canadians are killing us," said Esther Mugusuhi, and indeed more than 40 people died due to the spill, in addition to thousands of animals.¹²⁵ Around the same time, Canadian-owned Golden Star leaked arsenic, mercury and lead into the water of two communities in Ghana. Citizens organized to defend themselves; at a demonstration of over 5000 people, the Ghanaian military opened fire on the protestors.¹²⁶

Perhaps the most noteworthy case in Africa was Canada's Iamgold and Semafo mines in Burkina Faso. To build its Essakane mine, Iamgold had to demolish 13 villages with promises of compensation that were largely unfulfilled. In 2011, Iamgold briefly closed the mine in order to fire all its workers, to illustrate that the company would not, as the CEO put it, "tolerate anything that has a negative impact on [its] stakeholders."¹²⁷ Iamgold was provided with an opportunity to train new workers, thanks to a CIDA-funded job-training project, co-sponsored by the Canadian charity organization Plan Canada. It was not Plan Canada's only intervention in Burkina Faso.

In fact, one of Plan Canada's directors, Benoit La Salle, decided to get into the mining industry himself. Having built connections with President Blaise Compaoré during his time "saving" children, he created Semafo when the president invited him to invest and gave him a massive tract of land to develop. Compaoré had come to power in 1987 after murdering one of Africa's most celebrated figures of liberation, Thomas Sankara, and was the kind of dictator Western governments dream of: he cracked down on rebellion, opened up the country to foreign investment and otherwise kept a low profile. His government was overthrown in 2014, but not before Canada could lock in an agreement on foreign investment that empowered its mining companies to sue any future government that undermined its operations.[128]

Poisoning the Well

Canadian companies and the governments that supported them often frame their opponents as too stupid or too criminal to understand that everyone will benefit from allowing the projects to move forward. This colonial framing is false; most of these projects are extremely destructive to the social and environmental fabric of the communities they affect and, indeed, to the environment that sustains all life on this planet. For instance, EnCana, a Canadian oil and gas company, sought to build a pipeline through the Ecuadorian Amazon that would threaten to destroy plant and animal species, would disrupt the Mindo Nambillo cloud forest, would compound the threat of earthquakes and would pose a serious risk of oil spills. A massive community mobilization eventually forced the company to withdraw from Ecuador in 2006. EnCana claimed that Ecuador had succumbed to the "Chávez disease."[129]

That disease spread to Chile, where Barrick Gold sought to expand the controversial Pascua Lama mine, which sits on the border between Chile and Argentina. Barrick was ultimately found guilty in Chile of breaking 33 environmental laws in its plans for the mine, which included moving three glaciers in order to get better access to deposits, as if these glaciers were not crucial elements of the Atacama Desert ecosystem. For the 70,000 people who live in the region, the glaciers were an important source of water, since rainfall is limited. Barrick also planned to use a cyanide-leaching process which typically leaves significant amounts of arsenic and other toxic chemicals in the water systems around its operations.[130]

Nevertheless, successful community mobilizations to block such destructive projects have been rare, and the list of toxic Canadian operations around the world is extensive. Placer Dome — later purchased by Barrick — dumped 200 million tons of toxic runoff into Calancan Bay in the Philippines, leading to the lead poisoning of Philippine children. The Chalillo dam in Belize, owned by Fortis Inc, poisoned water, flooded ancient Mayan temples and endangered several species, including the jaguar, scarlet macaw, red parrot and black howler monkey. La Mancha Resources cut down 300 hectares of forests in Côte d'Ivoire, as did SNC-Lavalin's Chamera dam projects in northern India, which destroyed forests, leading to soil erosion, landslides and desertification, all of which displaced hundreds of people whose lands were flooded.[131] Activists in Turkey scrawled "Canadian Go Home" on the side of a building owned by Alamos Gold in 2019, which cut down nearly 200,000 trees in Kirazli for a mining project that the community opposed, but which was given a green light by another Canadian ally, right-wing dictator Recep Erdoğan.[132]

These destructive operations find their mirror in similar capitalist mega-projects within the territory Canada now claims as its own. Canadian capital regularly clashes with Indigenous survivors of genocide trying to protect what is left of their access to the land. The Mackenzie Valley Pipeline project, the development of Manitoba Hydro projects on the Nelson River, the diamond mines of the Northwest Territories, the Alberta Tar Sands, the Trans Mountain Pipeline; there is a lengthy list of such ventures and, in nearly every case, capital found itself in conflict with the people who live on the land itself. Where capital has won, the damage has been great. A Murphy Oil Co Ltd pipeline burst, spilling millions of litres of oil on Lubicon Lake First Nation territory. An Imperial Metals tailing pond burst in Northern British Columbia, dumping 24 million cubic feet of sludge into the water system. A Prairie Mines & Royalty waste pit collapsed, pouring a billion litres of toxins into the Athabasca River.[133] Even the names of the companies evoked empire and royalty, as they poisoned the earth.

There is little room for compromise between the interests of settler capitalism and the needs of a dying planet. Despite rhetorical flourish to the contrary, Canada is one of the greatest contributors to environmental destruction and degradation in the world, including that which has driven up the planet's temperature to levels that threaten the very fabric of life on Earth. In 2018, the Canadian government was embarrassed by a major report that indicated that no country produced higher per capita rates of greenhouse gases than Canada, which emitted up to 100 million tonnes annually in the oil and gas industry alone.[134] After scientists at Environment Canada leaked a report that the country was warming up twice as fast as the global average, an independent audit criticized the government for not only failing to reduce carbon emissions but actually encouraging the crisis with subsidies for the fossil fuel and other industries which play a key role in climate change.[135] The effects are evident in record-breaking heatwaves and forest fires, and the melting of permafrost and glaciers in the north, all of which have serious consequences; just one heat wave in Québec in 2018 led to the deaths of some 70 people. But the consequences of climate change are hardly limited to localized weather events.

The climate crisis that has emerged in earnest in the 21st century is a global phenomenon that will — barring radical social, political, economic and technological change — exacerbate the human suffering produced by global capitalism to an unprecedented degree. Its consequences — including the desertification of arable land, the flooding of coastal cities, the further spread of new and old diseases, and the destruction of critical infrastructure, like highways, power plants, sanitation systems and hospitals — will invariably be borne most heavily by the poor. Hurricane Katrina, which struck the city of New Orleans in 2005, served as a microcosm of the advancing crisis; the rich were able to get in their cars and escape the city until the waters receded, to find their expensive houses on higher ground largely unaffected, while the poor were stranded on their rooftops waiting for help that rarely came.[136]

That the ruling classes would create a crisis that will most affect the poor is little surprise in a world where the richest eight people possess more wealth than half of the human species. The climate crisis, filtered through the logic of capitalism, will raise the price of protecting oneself from the ravages of an overheating planet. Reduced agricultural yields will make healthy food more expensive. More intense storms and floods will increase the cost of housing in more protected areas, leaving the poor to battle the rising water. In contexts where public services like electricity or water provision become limited, there is little doubt that the ruling classes will be served first; Canada has already established this pattern in its record of failing to provide clean drinking water to Indigenous communities.[137]

The very logic of the climate crisis — or illogic, insofar as destroying the optimal conditions for life on Earth is eminently irrational — is rooted in the project at the heart of Canada, which helps explain why Canada is such a significant contributor to it. As Linda Pannozzo noted in 2016, the Indigenous political economic systems that Canadian settlers worked so hard to destroy were designed for longevity.[138] One need not romanticize Indigenous economic practices to acknowledge that they were typically organized around the idea that humans existed in a relationship with nature; even if they did not always successfully protect it, there were political, cultural and religious safeguards in place to ensure that, generally speaking, their practices were sustainable.[139] This was rational; despite the ideology of colonialism that denigrated Indigenous knowledge and culture, it made sense to preserve the environment that the community depended upon.

Most precapitalist human civilizations recognized as fundamental their dependence on the land, a fact that is reflected in many religious and cultural traditions from that time, even in Europe.[140] But the rise of capitalism, combined with the establishment of colonialism and the trans-Atlantic slave trade, fostered a different understanding of humanity's relationship to the Earth. Now, certain humans claimed to be masters — masters of other humans but also of the environment itself — and the Earth was simply a provider of resources to feed the consumptive desires of the rich. Unfettered exploitation of land and labour was the heart of the capitalist, colonial project. Should it be any surprise that this project drove humanity into mass immiseration and the erosion of the planet's capacity to sustain human life? As Anishinabekwe scientist Robin Wall Kimmerer explains, "it is not just the land that has been broken, but our relationship to it."[141]

Reorienting the Imperial Machine

The Canadian ruling class is evidently untroubled by the crises, human and natural, it has provoked. As Canadian capital accumulated significantly in the 1980s and 1990s and was driven to look outward for new sources of profit, a central aspect of Canadian policy towards the postcolonial states of the Global South was to cultivate a favourable climate for Canadian investment and profit extraction in those countries. By the 2000s, Canadian governments no longer even tried to hide this fact; the 2013 Global Markets Action Plan, set out by the Harper government, made explicit that it would "ensure that all Government of Canada assets [be] harnessed to support the pursuit of commercial success by Canadian companies and investors in key foreign markets."[142]

Canada has increasingly restructured its own government to facilitate the goal of supporting capital and capitalism abroad, integrating trade and military policy and placing them in direct supervision of foreign aid and international development agencies, to ensure that all resources are, indeed, pointed to the same ends.[143] When Canada offers aid to poor countries, it may provide some ideological cover for its exploitative policies, but it is typically offered only on the condition that those states adopt measures that are favourable to foreign investment, which Canada dubs "Poverty Reduction Strategies."[144] Much of the foreign aid Canada gives is geared towards establishing the legal and political architecture for Canadian capital; as Canadian MP Julian Fantino explicitly put it, Canadian aid money should "make countries and people, trade and investment ready."[145]

Furthermore, Canadian aid money is often tied to projects that require giving contracts to Canadian companies. Millions of dollars listed as foreign aid are, in fact, funnelled right back to Canadian companies contracted to build infrastructure, like telecommunications, hydroelectric dams or highways. Often these projects are built with little consideration of the actual needs of the communities affected, and regularly they are built to support other Canadian investments; for instance, Canadian companies trying to build hydro megaprojects in Honduras were seeking to support the large network of Canadian-owned mining projects that needed to power their operations.[146]

Even Canada's NGO sector is increasingly part of the imperial project, as illustrated most egregiously following the 2004 coup in Haiti. As Nikolas Barry-Shaw and Dru Oja Jay explain:

> All of the major NGOs working in Haiti were either silent on the situation or openly hostile to Haitians seeking the return of the democratic government. None criticized the interim regime's bloody war on the slums or the support given to this endeavour by Canada. Many positively cheered the toppling of a democratically elected government.[147]

Indeed, this network of organizations ostensibly designed to do good in the world has been perverted by the powerful institutions of state and capital both to provide ideological cover for unsavoury political practices and also to help facilitate the actual operation of exploitative and imperial politics. While many individuals working in such organizations may believe they are making a positive difference, the parameters in which they work are increasingly circumscribed to prevent them from actually undermining the goals of Canadian foreign policy. NGOs that remain on a consistently critical footing are defunded, while those that survive have to play ball.

Indeed, the Canadian Forces explicitly spoke to this need in its 2007 Counter-Insurgency manual, highlighting the role of NGOs and explaining in patronizing terms that people in conquered societies may resist, given their "perception of oppression due to political, societal, and economic grievances," through which "the insurgent appears as the peoples' protector." Thus, the manual went on, an occupation required "lead administrators from various non-governmental organizations (NGOs) ... to counter the insurgency" and to provide "a valuable source of information to intelligence staff in creating a knowledge base of the environment." In case the military's purposes for NGOs were not already clear, the manual proceeded to state that "because of their ability to inform, demonstrate, and influence and even co-opt" their audiences, NGOs were crucial to winning the perception battle in 21st-century war.[148]

As ever, the dynamics of Canadian foreign interference reverberate back home. Canada's aggressive neoliberal impositions abroad are related to exploitative migrant worker programs in Canada. For instance, at precisely the same moment that Canada was facilitating the consolidation of a military dictatorship in Honduras that would crack down on dissent and impose ever greater levels of exploitation, dispossession and poverty, Canada was actively recruiting Hondurans into its Temporary Foreign Worker Program, to be exploited on Canadian farms.[149] And Canada's migrant worker programs are notoriously exploitative. A 2004 report on berry farms in British Columbia noted that workers were paid below minimum wages, weigh scales were fraudulent such that workers were paid for less than the work they actually did, vehicles provided to the workers for transport to and from work were unsafe, and housing failed to provide heat, water and sometimes even toilets. Workers were expected to live in homes with broken windows and appliances that did not work, while they slept in make-shift bunk beds in overcrowded basements and shared kitchen and bathroom facilities among as many as nine people.[150]

These terrible conditions often lead to sickness, injury and even death for the workers.[151] In 2012, eleven Peruvian workers were killed in Ontario when the van carrying them home from work was involved in a deadly crash. The vans had long been deemed unsafe, designed to carry cargo, not people; this is a telling illustration of how migrant workers are viewed in Canada.[152] Meanwhile, hundreds of thousands of people were desperately trying to escape the violence and hopelessness imposed upon Central America and chose to undertake the difficult and dangerous journey to the US border seeking refuge and work in North America. Thousands of these people died or were killed at some point in the journey, and the Trump administration established concentration camps at the border which constitute, by all reasonable standards of measurement, crimes against humanity. The horrendous spectacle included US soldiers grabbing children from the arms of their mothers, unarmed families being openly fired upon by immigration police, and children as young as two years old being stood up in front of judges to plead their immigration cases.[153]

Many Canadians are put off by the open bigotry of the Trump administration and the upsetting violence at the border. But Justin Trudeau's government acted in full cooperation with Trump's policies, ranging from a blanket ban on all Muslim travellers in 2018 to the full militarization of the border and the establishment of concentration camps, citing the Safe Third Country agreement as a hand-tying piece of legislation. Organizations like Amnesty International insist that Canada is violating human rights law in upholding the agreement.[154]

Much of Canada's national mythology is built around the idea of Canadian openness to immigrants, and the Trudeau government understood that it needed to make a gesture to its base, who deeply believed in that mythology. In 2015, Trudeau pledged to accept a limited number of refugees from Syria, where Canada had actively participated in the bombing that was partly responsible for the crisis. Ultimately, some 50,000 Syrians were allowed to settle in Canada, but while it made good headlines for Justin in the moment, the reality facing many of the refugees remains bleak. The average income for Syrian refugees in Canada is less than $20,000, well below the poverty line in Canada, and the path to Canadian citizenship is fraught with difficulty, preventing many from even applying.¹⁵⁵ Jobs are difficult to find, language training is often inaccessible, living conditions are expensive but often cramped and underserviced, and despite the persistent mythology of the "nice Canadian," many Syrians find their new neighbours intolerant and quick to conflict.¹⁵⁶ Canada had "generously" accepted refugees from places where it had helped create a crisis before; people fleeing Augusto Pinochet, Idi Amin, the Contras and the Tontons Macoute had all, to a limited extent, found refuge in Canada despite the fact that Canada supported their persecutors. But it was always limited: in 2017, for instance, less than 1% of the nearly 7000 Haitians that tried to find refuge in Canada were approved, and most never even had their cases considered.¹⁵⁷

In spite of Canada's tight immigration laws, the far-right in Canada has become increasingly agitated about a purported "invasion" of foreigners, with foreign values, who would "contaminate" Canada from the inside. Echoing similar panics in earlier eras, MP Kellie Leitch courted this section of Canadian society when she claimed that immigrants were not adhering to "Canadian values" and proposed that immigrants be forced to take a test to prove that they were ready to properly assimilate; polls suggested that as many as 67% of Canadians supported the idea of such a test.¹⁵⁸ Leitch had already been part of a Canadian government initiative to root out "barbaric cultural practices," an accusation directed primarily towards Muslims. This fearmongering translated into an attack in 2017 against a mosque in Québec, in which six people were killed by white supremacist Alexandre Bissonnette, who became a hero in far-right circles around the world.¹⁵⁹

But while this was the most deadly such attack, it is clear that this violence is bubbling just below the surface of Canadian society, given the increasingly common occurrence of racist tirades captured on video in parking lots, restaurants, buses and grocery stores, usually pivoting around the message "go back where you came from."¹⁶⁰ Indeed, even by the metrics used by the Canadian police, reported hate crimes rose consistently in the 2010s, spiking to over 2000 incidents in 2017.¹⁶¹ Needless to say, these reflect only a small portion of the total incidents, since the majority go unreported for a variety of reasons, not the least of which is that the police and military themselves are consistently shown to be racist in their own practices. In 2019, a high-ranking member of the Canadian Army Reserve, Patrik Mathews, was exposed to have been recruiting for a neo-Nazi organization that was preparing for a "race war." Earlier that year, reports surfaced that more than 50 members of the military were part of the US-based Atomwaffen neo-Nazi group.¹⁶²

The ground for this explosion of xenophobia had long been prepared by the Canadian establishment; in the late 2000s, the CBC offered up a television drama series that heralded the heroes who keep Canada safe from all the villains who would enter the country to do us harm in *The Border* (2008–2010). The show assured its viewers that the guards at Canada's border were the "good guys," while the "bad guys" were typically presented as Arab or Muslim, exacerbating the already difficult conditions faced by people of colour in Canada.¹⁶³

Indeed, there still exists a pervasive, normalized and often institutionalized racism that permeates Canadian immigration laws and practices, even in their regular application and enforcement. The authors of *Racialized Migrant Women in Canada* (2009) shed some light on matters that are often ignored in Canadian popular discussions: that the Canadian state contributes to the problem of violence against immigrant women, that immigrant women consistently earn less than their non-immigrant counterparts, that racist social structures and institutions lead directly to poorer health outcomes for women of colour and immigrants and that, put simply, the experience of dealing with daily, personal and impersonal racism is exhausting, traumatic and pervasive.¹⁶⁴ More than the structures and statistics, however, we need to understand the personal and immediate ways in which these white supremacist dynamics are felt by non-white people trying to navigate the system. Himani Bannerji recounts an experience during her Canadian immigration process that is at once harrowing and casual, sickening and normal, an accepted part of Canada's supposedly benevolent multiculturalism:

> I was facing an elderly, bald, white man, moustached and blue-eyed — who said he had been to India. I made some polite rejoinder and he asked me — "Do you speak Hindi?" I replied that I understood it very well and spoke it with mistakes. "Can you translate this sentence for me?" he asked, and proceeded to say in Hindi what in English amounts to "Do you want to fuck with me?" A wave of heat rose from my toes to my hair roots. I gripped the edge of my chair and stared at him — silently. His hand was on my passport, the pink slip of my "landing" document lay next to it. Steadying my voice I said "I don't know Hindi that well." "So you're a PhD student?" My interview continued. I sat

rigid and concluded it with a schizophrenic intensity. On Bloor Street in Toronto, sitting on the steps of a church — I vomited. I was a landed immigrant.[165]

That the experience of multicultural Canada could be so deeply traumatic might come as a shock to white Canadians who believe in their national mythology. In light of a sober assessment of Canada's history in the world, however, it is entirely predictable.

The New Warriors, the Far-Right and the Heart of Canada

In recent years, the Canadian right and far right have worked hard to cultivate a perception that Canada, like the United States, is enmeshed in a "culture war." On one side, so the story goes, are the liberal intellectuals, the academics, the politicians, the elite, embarked on a crusade to destroy civilization and the white men who built it.[166] On the other side of this mythical divide are the "true" Canadians, who work hard, pay their taxes, drink Tim Horton's coffee and respect the sacrifices of the military and police. In this narrative, the liberal elites are poisoning society by undermining the core values of Western civilization: strength, rationality, patriotism and order.

This story is an absurd creation of right-wing propaganda, but it serves the purpose of equating all left politics — even its most superficial forms — with weakness, insincerity and disloyalty to the nation. Any attempt to make Canadian society less patriarchal, less white supremacist, less unjust, is taken as an attack on the very idea of Canada itself. In a certain sense, of course, it is; Canada *is* premised upon such inequalities and to struggle against them is, indeed, running against the grain of Canadian history.[167]

But the conflation of the liberal elites with those fighting for justice and equality is marvellously silly. After all, it is the liberal elite who built the capitalist world order that is so deeply unequal and from which they maintain their elite status. The far right do not seem to understand the shell game those liberals have played so effectively for so long. When Ron MacLean and Don Cherry did their weekly liberal-conservative double act during the *Hockey Night in Canada* broadcast, the far right failed to comprehend that Ron and Don were on the same side, that Ron's entire purpose was to soften and sell Don's act. Covering a playoff series in

Washington, DC, in 2018, the pair brought a US military commander onto the set as a guest and gushed about the heroism and bravery of the troops, with Ron intervening to prompt Don into talking about how much he adored Donald Trump. Ron might not wear a Make America Great Again cap himself, but he nevertheless glowed with affection while Don recounted how excited he was to see Trump speak. The act served to suggest to Canadians that even a good liberal like Ron MacLean appreciated that some people like Donald Trump and that this was okay. Ron wanted viewers to be tolerant of such views, on the premise that this tolerance was what it meant to be Canadian.

And yet, while Ron preached tolerance of the far right, the views of the left were never given legitimacy on *Hockey Night in Canada*. Don was permitted to spout a range of bigoted platitudes on a semi-regular basis while Ron nodded along in various degrees of respectful disagreement, but there was no tolerance for questioning the war in Afghanistan, or asking why Canadian hockey fans still threw bananas at black players, or proposing that junior hockey players be allowed to form a union in order to earn a fair share of the profits they generate.[168] The reasonable, moderate liberal persona of Ron MacLean existed precisely to make Don Cherry's right-wing punditry an acceptable and normal part of Canadian life, which, in turn, pulled Canadian popular consciousness further to the right.

Liberal Canada has, in a sense, always been a clever mask worn by conservative Canada. But the far right has taken the bait; they believe Justin Trudeau when he cries crocodile tears about the injustices of colonialism, even as he seizes Indigenous territory to build pipelines. They believed Jean Chrétien when he said that Canada would not participate in the war in Iraq because it did not have UN approval, even as Canadian troops were on the ground in Iraq. They believed Michael Ignatieff when he said that Canada should use its power to do good in the world, even when his proposed method of doing so was, quite literally, imperialism.

Ignatieff, the grandson of a tsarist count and the son of a Pearsonian diplomat, fashioned himself a liberal intellectual. He taught at the University of Toronto in a school named after a gold mining tycoon, and he had a brief stint as the leader of the Liberal Party. His lack of charisma meant that his political career was a failure, but he nevertheless made one of the most important intellectual contributions to Canadian imperialism in *Empire Lite* (2003), his treatise on the value of humanitarian occupation.

Afghanistan, Ignatieff explained, was a place "where barbarians rule" and where self-government was "unattainable without some exercise of imperial power." Indeed, he expounded without evidence, "imperialism has become a precondition for democracy." "Humanitarians know," he concluded, "that there are some humanitarian problems for which there are only imperial solutions."[169]

The argument at the heart of Ignatieff's book is that while polite society do not like to speak of conquest anymore, it is only through conquest that "backwards" societies can evolve. Through "a distinctive new form of imperial tutelage called nation-building," the West can fix those people Ignatieff labels "barbarians" and, in so doing, save us all from their supposed "barbarism."[170] The War on Terror was, to Ignatieff, a struggle for the very future of civilization. It had to be won and the former terrorists had to be subjugated in order to make a better world. As long as the war was being fought for the right reasons — "the global eradication of terror," as he put it — then it was in the service of humanity.[171]

Ignatieff, probably unconsciously, tapped deep into the colonial imagination. He casually notes that the British Empire sought to rule people "with a view to preparing them for self-government." That this is empirically false and that the British had to be forced to leave by violence does not slow Ignatieff down in the slightest, as he goes on to explain, in the context of Canada, that "the British began preparing their white colonies for self-government in the 1840s," somehow forgetting that the Canadians were not the colonized people.[172] The Canadians were the colonizers; the British/Canadians never prepared the Indigenous Peoples for self-government — they conquered them and forcibly removed their right to self-government. With liberals like this, who needs conservatives? The far right mythology of "liberal elites" looks silliest when positioned next to the actual words and deeds of those same liberals. And for every supposedly liberal elite, there are also the conservative elites, like University of Calgary professor Tom Flanagan, who openly adopted the language of colonialism in a book praised by the *National Post* as "important and courageous," in which he claimed that "European civilization was several thousand years more advanced than the aboriginal cultures of North America," making conquest "inevitable" and "justifiable."[173] Handshakes across the aisle for Ignatieff and Flanagan.

Thus, despite its carving out an ever greater degree of public discourse in the 2010s, the nonsensical far-right fear of liberal elites does more to distract attention from the real sources of ideological clash and class struggle than they do to illuminate them. The Canadian ruling class — both its liberal and conservative factions — is committed to Canada playing a greater role in the War on Terror and its adjacent conflicts in places like Ukraine and Venezuela. Indeed, 21st-century Canadian culture has been swept by a wave of warrior culture that may be unprecedented and is certainly a sharp break from the *long durée* of the peacekeeping era. Throughout the Cold War, Canadians were steadily inculcated with the idea that their country was a force for peace. Now, that mythical, peaceful past is being mobilized to justify an aggressive, militaristic future.

Coinciding with the occupation of Afghanistan, the Canadian ruling class rolled out an overwhelming ideological push to weave militarism and warrior culture back into the fabric of Canadian life. The realm of professional sports was a significant platform for this cultural offensive, becoming a central pivot for a "support the troops" discipline that gripped Canada in the early 21st century. Commemorations of soldiers at sporting events has become standard practice, as has the expectation that fans should save their deepest respect and loudest applause for those soldiers. The Canadian military spent half a million dollars on military-themed pucks and jerseys for NHL teams to promote between 2007 and 2012, and my hometown franchise, the Winnipeg Jets, re-emerged in 2011 with its entire branding linked explicitly and legally to the Canadian Armed Forces.[174]

As Alyson McCready details in *Yellow Ribbons* (2013), the project to militarize Canadian national identity was both a "concerted cultural intervention by powerful forces" and a product of ordinary Canadians' engagements with that cultural intervention. Much of the "support the troops" push, then, came from above: yellow ribbons everywhere, even on public property; the renaming of public spaces to endorse militarism, like the "Highway of Heroes" in Southern Ontario; ubiquitous military advertising in the media and recruitment booths in colleges and universities; the presence of Canadian military installations at public festivals and popular spaces, including an Armoured Personnel Carrier at the Kingston Santa Claus Parade.[175] By the early 2010s, the Canadian government was budgeting millions of dollars every year on military advertising and propaganda.[176]

At the same time, the new militarism was being effectively interwoven into Canadian popular culture such that it would be reinforced from below.

A student in one of my classes once shared a story about failing to stand up for the Canadian national anthem at a Maple Leafs game; in addition to the racist and sexist abuse she received for it, she felt so frightened for her safety that she left. That ordinary Canadians should express that level of violence towards someone failing to display the appropriate degree of symbolic loyalty to the state is indicative of how effective the campaign to build a more aggressive patriotic militarism has been. It nevertheless also suggests that the ground for such a campaign was already fertile.

There is both continuity and rupture in Canada's new, aggressive military posture and culture. While the shift into more overt and self-conscious militarism in Canada is noteworthy, such foundations have always been in place in a nation built upon violent conquest. My paternal great-great-grandparents settled on land in Manitoba that had been stolen by force from Indigenous people only a few years before. Members of my great-grandparents' generation died in the service of British imperialism. My eldest uncle was revered by my father for his service in the Second World War. Another uncle worked as private security for a Canadian bank in Kenya during the Mau Mau rebellion. I watched the Persian Gulf War on live television. As a graduate student at York University, the York Centre for International and Security Studies invited the Canadian Armed Forces to our campus to try to recruit my colleagues and myself into service. As a faculty member at Humber College, I regularly see those same recruiters in the main entrance hall trying to draw in my students.

War and militarism have always been central to the Canadian story, because they have always been a necessary component of the world Canada seeks to build. When Canadian state and military rhetoric began shifting away from the language of peacekeeping in the early 2000s many liberal Canadians were shocked. In the mid-2000s, the head of the Canadian Armed Forces told a group of reporters that the job of the Canadian military was to "kill people"; his frank admission of the fundamental purpose of a military delighted some and scandalized others. Gen. Rick Hillier typified the new tone in the Canadian ruling class, rejecting the "soft" peacekeeper mentality and embracing the idea that Canadian soldiers are "warriors first and foremost… with a first responsibility to finish tough, often violent tasks when Canada needed them done."[177]

But the shift in tone has led many observers to exaggerate the extent of the shift in practice. In that sense, while this book owes a great deal of debt to the analysis provided by Ian McKay and Jamie Swift in *Warrior*

Nation (2012), I also diverge from their central argument that Canada has been torn between the competing tendencies of, on one hand, the bearers of warrior culture and, on the other, "people dangerously addicted to peaceful, complicated, often slow-acting remedies" for the problems of the world.[178] Against their suggestion that this latter group of Canadians "have a coherent and historically founded set of interests in the peaceful settlement of conflicts,"[179] I argue that the divide in Canada has not been between peacekeepers and new warriors, but between the rich and poor, the white and non-white, the settlers and the colonized, those who built Canada and those who have suffered it. Canada was a colonial imposition; despite claiming to represent progress, it has consistently impeded it. Despite claiming to represent civilization, it has generated violence and savagery. Despite claiming to be the future, it is a remnant of the past, of an era when European powers believed themselves to be entitled to conquer the world and claim its riches for themselves. For over a century and a half, that world order has been challenged, and Canada has struggled to preserve it. But Canada cannot outrun history forever.

Notes

1. Stephen Harper, quoted in Rosana Barbosa, "Conclusion," in Rosana Barbosa, ed., *Brazil and Canada in the Americas*, Gorsebrook Research Institute, Halifax, 2007, p. 109.
2. Stephen Harper, quoted in Derrick O'Keefe, "Harper in denial at G20: Canada has 'no history of colonialism,'" Rabble.ca, September 28, 2009.
3. Justin Trudeau, quoted in Christo Aivalis, "Justin Trudeau and Canada's Colonial Baggage: Past and Present," *Active History*, April 28, 2016.
4. These included appearances at pop cultural celebrations ranging from the final Tragically Hip concert to the annual Pride Parades in various cities to the Toronto Raptors' 2019 NBA Championship victory parade, but they also manifest as "spontaneous" episodes where Trudeau would assist a man in a wheelchair trying to descend a staircase, or "stumble upon" a wedding while jogging shirtless on the beach.
5. Molly Wickham, quoted in Angela Sterritt, "Wet'suwet'en arrests spark debate about Indigenous relations with RCMP," *CBC News*, January 18, 2019.
6. Quoted in Jaskiran Dhillon and Will Parrish, "Canada police prepared to shoot Indigenous activists, documents show," *The Guardian*, December 20, 2019.
7. Alex Bloomfield, "Trudeau apologizes for disrespecting Indigenous protestor at Liberal fundraiser," *City News*, March 28, 2019.
8. Jerome Klassen and Yves Engler, "What's Not to Like?: Justin Trudeau, the Global Disorder, and Liberal Illusions," in Norman Hillmer and Phillippe Legassé, *Justin Trudeau and Canadian Foreign Policy: Canada Among Nations 2017*, Palgrave MacMillan, Cham, Switzerland, 2018, p. 67.
9. John Ackerman, "Mexico is massacring its citizens and nobody seems to have

noticed," *Toronto Star*, June 27, 2016.
10. Kate Lyons, "Yemen's cholera outbreak now the worst in history as millionth case looms," *The Guardian*, October 12, 2017.
11. Klassen and Engler, "What's Not to Like?," p. 67–69.
12. Quoted in Klassen and Engler, "What's Not to Like?," p. 67–68.
13. Patrick Wintour, "UK, US and France may be complicit in Yemen war crimes — UN report," *The Guardian*, September 3, 2019.
14. Klassen and Engler, "What's Not to Like?," p. 68.
15. Steven Chase, "Canada now the second biggest arms exporter to Middle East, data show," *Globe and Mail*, June 14, 2016.
16. Klassen and Engler, "What's Not to Like?," p. 68.
17. Klassen and Engler, "What's Not to Like?," p. 68.
18. Roger Annis, "France launches bombing of northern Mali, with Canadian support," *Rabble.ca*, January 18, 2013.
19. Sidhartha Banerjee, "Canadians make harrowing trek to Haiti airport as Ottawa advises against travel," *The National Observer*, February 17, 2019.
20. Richard Sakwa, *Frontline Ukraine: Crisis in the Borderlands*, London, I.B. Taurus, 2006, p. 7.
21. Grzegorz Rossoliński-Liebe, *Stepan Bandera: The Life and Afterlife of a Ukrainian Nationalist*, Ibidem-Verlag, Stuttgart, 2014.
22. Richard Sakwa, *Frontline Ukraine*, p. 16–17.
23. The Holodomor debates are divisive and often difficult to navigate. There is no doubt that millions of people died in the famines of 1932–33, and that they were a direct consequence of Stalinist policies. The push to collectivize agriculture was central to Stalin's plan for rapid industrialization, deemed essential given the existential military threat that the Soviet Union faced. This motivated his aggressive campaign against the *kulaks*, wealthier peasants who had larger tracts of land and were resistant to the collectivization process, since it entailed their sharing their land with the many other, poorer peasant families. Stalin's deputies were ruthless in purging the *kulaks*, many of whom were exiled to Siberia. In 1932, during the chaotic process of collectivization, a severe drought hit the southwestern Soviet Union. Much of the harvest failed, a problem compounded by the fact that many people in the Stalinist bureaucracy refused — out of fear of reprisal — to admit the scale of the crop failures. Authorities thus proceeded with the export of food for the purchase of machinery to fuel industrialization. To the extent that Soviet officials knew that people were dying, they chose not to prioritize relief, to their shame. However, to frame the famine as an intentional, ethnically motivated genocide is to wilfully misread the historical record. The Holodomor narrative is designed to flatten out the actual historical record in favour of a story that feeds the myths and motivations of far-right Ukrainian nationalism. Nevertheless, the Canadian government created the Holodomor Memorial Day in 2008, around the same time it was planning a monument to the victims of communism. In his 2018 Holodomor Memorial Day address, Justin Trudeau accused the Soviet Union of having "used starvation as a weapon," an ironic accusation given that it more appropriately fits what took place in Canada in the 1870s and 1880s. Justin Trudeau, "Statement by the Prime Minister on Holodomor Memorial Day," November 24, 2018. Sources on the Holodomor

problem include Richard Sakwa's *Frontline Ukraine* (2016) and Matthew Kupfer and Thomas de Waal, "Crying genocide: Use and abuse of political rhetoric in Russia and Ukraine," Carnegie Endowment, July 28, 2014. English historiography of this problem is often rooted in the work of Cold Warrior historians like Robert Conquest and Richard Pipes, whose scholarship evokes much skepticism and has often been outright discredited by careful scholars like J. Arch Getty and James Harris. David Marples explicitly notes, in *Heroes and Villains* (2007), that asserting the existence of a Holodomor is a key piece of the Ukrainian nationalist project, and Douglas Tottle's *Fraud, Famine and Fascism* (1987) links the perpetuation of the genocide narrative to the Ukrainian far right, many of whom had relocated to Canada after the war. Also useful is George O. Liber's *Soviet Nationality Policy, Urban Growth, and Identity Change in the Ukrainian SSR 1923-1934* (1992).

24. Richard Sakwa, *Frontline Ukraine*, p. 20–23.
25. Oleksander Feldman, "First They Came for Mila Kunis," Gatestone Institute, February 4, 2013.
26. Richard Sakwa, *Frontline Ukraine*, p. 64–65.
27. Richard Sakwa, *Frontline Ukraine*, p. 72–75.
28. Richard Sakwa, *Frontline Ukraine*, p. 148–149.
29. Klassen and Engler, "What's Not to Like?," p. 70.
30. Department of Foreign Affairs and International Trade, 2006, quoted in Klassen and Engler, "What's Not to Like?," p. 70. Emphasis added.
31. Harold Troper and Morton Weinfeld, "Jewish-Ukrainian Relations in Canada Since World War II and the Nazi War Criminal Issue," in Alan Davies, ed., *Antisemitism in Canada: History and Interpretation*, Waterloo, Wilfrid Laurier University Press, 1992, p. 283.
32. David Pugliese, "Chrystia Freeland's granddad was indeed a Nazi collaborator — so much for Russian disinformation," *Ottawa Citizen*, March 8, 2017.
33. Mikhail Klikushin, "Why is this Canadian Foreign Minister 'Proud' of her Family's Nazi Past?," *The Observer*, March 22, 2017. Available at: https://observer.com/2017/03/chrystia-freeland-foreign-minister-canada-nazi-grandfather/.
34. Volodomyr Kubijovych, "Appeal to Ukrainian Citizens and Youth," *Krakivs'ki visti*, May 16, 1943, cited in Tadeusz Piotrowski, *Poland's Holocaust: Ethnic Strife, Collaboration with Occupying Forces and Genocide in the Second Republic, 1918-1947*, McFarland and Co, London, 1998, p. 226.
35. Canadian Institute of Ukrainian Studies newsletter, November 1986, p. 14. Available at: https://archive.org/stream/ciusnewsletter102cana/ciusnewsletter102cana_djvu.txt.
36. Robert Fife, "Freeland knew her grandfather was editor of Nazi newspaper," *Globe and Mail*, March 7, 2017.
37. "The Rise of the Global Super-Rich," interview with Chrystia Freeland, *Harvard Business Review*, December 13, 2012. In her book and articles and interviews, she repeatedly invoked the false assertion that there was a small cabal of mostly Jewish bankers who controlled more than half of the wealth in Russia. To those familiar with the tropes and motifs of anti-Semitic conspiracy theories, the tone was very clear. It is unclear whether Freeland was intentionally signalling anti-Semitism or subconsciously reproducing the ideology which surely

permeated the worldview of her grandfather and journalistic mentor. But it remains significant that her work sat so comfortably next to the propaganda her grandfather had written for the Nazis decades earlier.

38. Richard Sanders, "Historical Amnesia and the Blinding Effects of Propaganda," *Press for Conversation*, Coalition to Oppose the Arms Trade, March 22, 2017. Available at: https://coat.ncf.ca/research/Chomiak-Freeland/C-F_3.htm.
39. John-Paul Hinka, "War Criminality: A Blank Spot in the Collective Memory of the Ukrainian Diaspora," *Spaces of Identity, Special Issue: War Crimes*, Vol 5, No. 1, 2005.
40. Government of Canada, "Canada's Engagement in Ukraine." Available at: https://www.international.gc.ca/world-monde/country-pays/ukraine/relations/aspx?lang=eng.
41. Michael Colborne, "Why Does No One Care That Neo-Nazis Are Gaining Power in Ukraine?," *The Bullet*, January 18, 2019.
42. Volodymyr Ishchenko, "Ukraine: An Election for the Oligarchs," *The Bullet*, March 20, 2019.
43. Eduard Dolinski, quoted in Levon Sevunts, "Canada accused of promoting Holocaust revisionism with memorial in Ukraine," RCI *News*, September 3, 2019.
44. George Ciccariello-Maher, *We Created Chávez: A People's History of the Venezuelan Revolution*, London, Duke University Press, 2013, p. 7.
45. George Ciccariello-Maher, *We Created Chávez*, p. 21.
46. George Ciccariello-Maher, *Building the Commune: Radical Democracy in Venezuela*, New York, Verso, 2016, p. 1–2.
47. George Ciccariello-Maher, *Building the Commune*, p. 5.
48. Gregory Wilpert, *Changing Venezuela By Taking Power: The History and Policies of the Chávez Government*, New York, Verso, 2007, p. 5.
49. Michael McCaughan, *The Battle of Venezuela*, New York, Seven Stories Press, 2005, p. 94.
50. The Venezuelan military took a decisively different turn in the 1970s from many of its regional counterparts when it advanced a plan to send its soldiers to universities to study everything from social sciences to medicine. Unlike the Chilean military, which supported Pinochet, or that which ruled Argentina in the same period, which were pervaded by a kind of angry anti-intellectualism, the Venezuelan military was increasingly filled with educated people who embraced a range of social and political values. This partly explains how someone like Chávez himself came out of the ranks of military and why the revolution was able to count on its support for decades. Michael McCaughan, *The Battle of Venezuela*, p. 61–62.
51. Mark Weisbrot, *Failed: What the 'Experts' Got Wrong about the Global Economy*, Oxford, Oxford University Press, 2015, p. 218–220.
52. George Ciccariello-Maher, *We Created Chávez*, p. 3.
53. Luis Fernando Angosto-Ferrández, *Venezuela Reframed: Bolivarianism, Indigenous Peoples, and Socialisms of the Twenty-First Century*, London, Zed Books, 2015.
54. Douglas Bravo, quoted in Michael McCaughan, *The Battle of Venezuela*, p. 67.
55. Hugo Chávez, quoted in George Ciccariello-Maher, *Building the Commune*, p. 16–17.

56. George Ciccariello-Maher, *Building the Commune*, p. 25–27.
57. Yves Engler, *The Black Book of Canadian Foreign Policy*, Halifax, Fernwood, 2009, p. 108–109.
58. Quoted in Todd Gordon, *Imperialist Canada*, Winnipeg, Arbeiter Ring, 2010, p. 375.
59. Peter Kent, quoted in Tyler A. Shipley, *Ottawa and Empire: Canada and the Military Coup in Honduras*, Toronto, Between the Lines, 2017, p. 69.
60. Michael McCaughan, *The Battle of Venezuela*, p. 95.
61. Mark Weisbrot, "Why the U.S. Demonises Venezuela's Democracy," *The Guardian*, October 3, 2012.
62. Tyler A. Shipley, *Ottawa and Empire*, p. 67–70
63. Todd Gordon and Jeffery R. Webber, *Blood of Extraction: Canadian Imperialism in Latin America*, Halifax, Fernwood, 2016, p. 253–254.
64. Lesley M. Burn, "Between Rhetoric and Reality: Canada-Venezuela Relations," in Peter McKenna, ed. *Canada Looks South: In Search of an Americas Policy*, Toronto, University of Toronto Press, 2012, p. 295.
65. Gordon and Webber, *Blood of Extraction*, p. 244–245.
66. Yves Engler, quoted in Arnold August, "Why the Canadian government is bullying Venezuela," *Counterpunch*, July 19, 2019.
67. Stephen Harper, quoted in Gordon and Webber, *Blood of Extraction*, p. 249.
68. Yves Engler, *Black Book*, p. 110–111.
69. Privy Council Office Intelligence Assessment Secretariat, quoted in Gordon and Webber, *Blood of Extraction*, p. 247.
70. M. Blanchfield, "Venezuela Slams Harper for 'Blunt, Insensitive, Impertinent' Remarks on Hugo Chávez's Death," *National Post*, March 7, 2013.
71. Quoted in Mark Weisbrot, "Why the U.S. Demonises Venezuela's Democracy," *The Guardian*, October 3, 2012.
72. "Venezuelan Audit Can't Find Any Different Result in Presidential Election, Statistical Analysis Shows," Centre for Economic Policy Research, April 26, 2013.
73. Ruby Dagher, Peggy Mason, and Roy Culpeper, "Canada's misguided Venezuela policy and the inhumanity of sanctions," *The Conversation*, July 24, 2019.
74. Government of Canada, "Canada and the Venezuela Crisis." Available at: https://www.international.gc.ca/world-monde/issues_development-enjeux_developpement/response_conflict-reponse_conflits/crisis-crises/venezuela.aspx?lang=eng.
75. Jasmin Hristov, *Paramilitarism and Neoliberalism: Violent Systems of Capital Accumulation in Colombia and Beyond*, London, Pluto Press, 2014.
76. Forrest Hylton, *Evil Hour in Colombia*, London, Verso, 2006, p. 4.
77. Gordon and Webber, *Blood of Extraction*, p. 154.
78. Stephen Harper, quoted in R. Foot, "PM Defends Entering Free Trade Talks with Colombia," *National Post*, July 17, 2007.
79. Álvaro Uribe, quoted in Gordon and Webber, *Blood of Extraction*, p. 162.
80. Gordon and Webber, *Blood of Extraction*, p. 180.
81. Quoted in Gordon and Webber, *Blood of Extraction*, p. 161.
82. Todd Gordon, *Imperialist Canada*, p. 238.
83. Government of Canada, "Trade Commissioner Service — Colombia," October

3, 2018. Available at: https://www.tradecommissioner.gc.ca/colombia-colombie/index.aspx?lang=eng.
84. "Army admits extrajudicial execution of FARC member last week," Justice for Colombia, April 30, 2019. Available at: https://justiceforcolombia.org/news/army-admits-extrajudicial-execution-of-farc-member-last-week/.
85. Eli Rosenberg and Dan Lamothe, "'5000 troops,': Photo of John Bolton's notes raises questions about U.S. military role in Venezuela crisis," *The Washington Post*, January 28, 2019.
86. Embassy of Canada to Colombia, "Canada launch of the Women's Voice and Leadership project during "Mesa por la vida" event in Cali, Colombia," July 4, 2019. Available at: https://www.canadainternational.gc.ca/colombia-colombie/highlights-faits/2019/2019-07-mesa_por_la_vida.aspx?lang=eng.
87. Bell Canada International took particular advantage of the neoliberal privatization wave. Todd Gordon, *Imperialist Canada*, p. 247–248.
88. Quoted in Rosana Barbosa, "Brazilian and Canadian relations: An Historical Survey," in Rosana Barbosa, ed., *Brazil and Canada in the Americas*, Gorsebrook Research Institute, Halifax, 2007, p. 43.
89. Dilma was Brazil's first non-male president and had survived cancer while maintaining her position as President Lula's chief of staff before winning the presidency herself in 2011.
90. Leslie Bethell, *Brazil: Essays on History and Politics*, London, Institute of Latin American Studies, 2018, p. 213–215.
91. Todd Gordon, *Imperialist Canada*, p. 248.
92. Leslie Bethell, *Brazil*, p. 217–219.
93. Leslie Bethell, *Brazil*, p. 218–220.
94. Leslie Bethell, *Brazil*, p. 172.
95. Leslie Bethell, *Brazil*, p. 221.
96. Jair Bolsonaro, quoted in Glenn Greenwald and Andre Fishman, "The most misogynistic, hateful elected official in the democratic world: Brazil's Jair Bolsonaro," *The Intercept*, December 11, 2014.
97. Glenn Greenwald and Andre Fishman, "The most misogynistic, hateful elected official in the democratic world: Brazil's Jair Bolsonaro," *The Intercept*, December 11, 2014.
98. Canadian relations with Brazil in this period were often frosty; credible sources reported an absurd incident wherein Stephen Harper locked himself in a bathroom, during an official state visit in 2011, and refused to return to lunch until it was agreed that toasts would take place before, rather than after, lunch. Rosana Barbosa, *Brazil and Canada: Economic, Political, and Migratory Ties, 1820s to 1970s*, London, Lexington Books, 2017, p. 135.
99. Tyler A. Shipley, *Ottawa and Empire*, p. 162.
100. Glenn Greenwald and Victor Pougy, "As Brazil's Bolsonaro prepares to meet Donald Trump, his family's close ties to notorious paramilitary gangs draw scrutiny and outrage," *The Intercept*, March 18, 2019.
101. Chris Arsenault, "What a far-right Bolsonaro presidency in Brazil means for Canadian business," CBC News, October 26, 2018.
102. Chris Arsenault, "What a far-right Bolsonaro presidency…"
103. Chris Arsenault, "What a far-right Bolsonaro presidency…"

104. Amy Padilla, "Duterte's tyranny in the Philippines is an obstacle to people's development," *MR Online*, October 8, 2018.
105. Justin Trudeau, quoted in Andy Blatchford, "Philippines' Duterte helps secure Trudeau invitation to security event," *Toronto Star*, November 13, 2017.
106. Joe Chidley, "India's deepening economic ties with Canada show Modi evolution is making progress, even if it isn't perfect," *National Post*, July 4, 2019.
107. Todd Gordon, "Canada in the Third World," in Jerome Klassen and Greg Albo, ed., *Empire's Ally: Canada and the War in Afghanistan*, Toronto, University of Toronto Press, 2013, p. 215.
108. Canadian banks and financial firms took advantage of the global economic crisis of 2008, for instance, to buy out floundering foreign firms and increase their dominance in those markets. Gordon and Webber, *Blood of Extraction*, p. 16.
109. Quoted in Gordon and Webber, *Blood of Extraction*, p. 23.
110. Gordon and Webber, *Blood of Extraction*, p. 17.
111. L. Whittington, "Canadian mining firms the worse abusers: report," *Toronto Star*, October 19, 2010.
112. Karen Dubinsky and Mark Epprecht, "Canadian Business and the Business of Development," in Karen Dubinsky, Sean Mills and Scott Rutherford, ed., *Canada and the Third World: Overlapping Histories*, Toronto, University of Toronto Press, 2016, p. 71.
113. Gordon and Webber, *Blood of Extraction*, p. 119–145.
114. Simon Granovsky-Larsen and Dawn Paley, "Organized Violence and the Expansion of Capital," in Dawn Paley and Simon Granovsky-Larsen, ed. *Organized Violence: Capitalist Warfare in Latin America*, Regina, University of Regina Press, 2019, p. 1–2.
115. James Lambert, quoted in Gordon and Webber, *Blood of Extraction*, p. 95–96.
116. Granovsky-Larsen and Paley, "Organized Violence," p. 3–14.
117. Luis Solano, "Under Siege: Peaceful Resistance to Tahoe Resources and Militarization in Guatemala," in Dawn Paley and Simon Granovsky-Larsen, ed. *Organized Violence: Capitalist Warfare in Latin America*, Regina, University of Regina Press, 2019, p. 67–77.
118. Gloria Chicaiza, quoted in Gordon and Webber, *Blood of Extraction*, p. 222.
119. Duncan Hood, "People are dying because of Canadian mines. It's time for the killing to stop," *Globe and Mail*, February 19, 2019.
120. Gordon and Webber, *Blood of Extraction*, p. 280.
121. Afef Abrougui, "Mauritania: Outrage Over the Murder of a Worker," *Global Voices*, July 23, 2012. Available at: https://globalvoices.org/2012/07/23/mauritania-outrage-over-the-murder-of-a-worker/.
122. Nana Darkoa Sekyiamah, Lejla Medanhodzic and Liz Ford, "Remembering women killed fighting for human rights in 2017," *The Guardian*, November 29, 2017.
123. Yves Engler, *Canada in Africa: 300 Years of Aid and Exploitation*, Halifax, Fernwood, 2015, p. 139.
124. Quoted in Yves Engler, *Canada in Africa*, p. 155.
125. Esther Mugusuhi, quoted in Yves Engler, *Canada in Africa*, p. 172.
126. Yves Engler, *Canada in Africa*, p. 158.
127. Steve Letwin, quoted in Yves Engler, *Canada in Africa*, p. 152.

128. Yves Engler, *Canada in Africa*, p. 155.
129. Gwyn Morgan, quoted in Todd Gordon, *Imperialist Canada*, p. 232.
130. Todd Gordon, *Imperialist Canada*, p. 210–212.
131. Todd Gordon, *Imperialist Canada*, p. 214, 239, 242–243.
132. Reuters, "Thousands protest at Turkish gold mine owned by Canadian company," CBC News, August 6, 2019.
133. Gordon Kent, "Billion liters of coal-mine muck leaks into Athabasca River," *Edmonton Journal*, November 4, 2013.
134. Mia Rabson, "Canada produces more greenhouse gas emissions than any other G20 country, new report says," *Toronto Star*, November 14, 2018.
135. "Canada's failure to fight climate change 'disturbing,' environment watchdog says," CBC News, April 2, 2019.
136. Mike Davis, *In Praise of Barbarians: Essays Against Empire*, Chicago, Haymarket Books, 2007, p. 197–263.
137. Michael Mascarenhas, *Where the Waters Divide: Neoliberalism, White Privilege, and Environmental Racism in Canada*, Lanham, Lexington Books, 2012.
138. Linda Pannozzo, *The Environment*, Halifax, Fernwood, 2016, p. 1–19.
139. Daniel Paul, *We Were Not the Savages: A Mi'kmaq Perspective on the Collision between European and Native American Civilizations*, Halifax, Fernwood, 2006.
140. Chris Harman, *A People's History of the World*, London, Bookmarks, 1999, p. 87–100. See also Silvia Federici's *Caliban and the Witch* (2004).
141. Robin Wall Kimmerer, quoted in Linda Pannozzo, *The Environment*, p. 1.
142. Government of Canada, "Global Markets Action Plan: The Blueprint for Creating Jobs and Opportunities for Canadians through Foreign Trade," p. 6. Available at: https://international.gc.ca/global-markets-marches-mondiaux/assets/pdfs/plan-eng.pdf.
143. Greg Albo, "Fewer Illusions," in Jerome Klassen and Greg Albo, ed., *Empire's Ally: Canada and the War in Afghanistan*, Toronto, University of Toronto Press, 2013, p. 254–260.
144. Todd Gordon, "Canada in the Third World," p. 222.
145. Julian Fantino, quoted in Gordon and Webber, *Blood of Extraction*, p. 24.
146. Tyler Shipley, "Land Seizure, Dispossession, and Canadian Capital in Honduras," *Human Geography*, Vol. 8, No. 2, 2015.
147. Nikolas Barry-Shaw and Dru Oja Jay, *Paved with Good Intentions: Canada's development NGOs from idealism to imperialism,* Fernwood, Halifax, 2012, p. 210.
148. Canadian Forces Counter-Insurgency Operations Manual, quoted in Nikolas Barry-Shaw and Dru Oja Jay, *Paved with Good Intentions*, p. 210–211.
149. Karl Flecker, "Canada's Temporary Foreign Worker Program (TFWP) — Model Program or Mistake?" Canadian Labour Congress, April 2011.
150. Thom Workman, *If You're in My Way I'm Walking: The Assault on Working People since 1970*, Halifax, Fernwood, 2009, p. 79–80. These practices have not improved; in 2019, the owners of the Vancouver Canucks hockey team were the subject of a string of revelations about their own treatment of migrant workers on their farms, ranging from inadequate housing and facilities, to theft of wages, to the accusation that one of the owners refused to give the workers water until they completed their work. Aaron McArthur, "Migrant workers allege poor

working conditions at Aquilini-owned blueberry farm," *Global News*, May 28, 2019.
151. Thom Workman, *If You're in My Way*, p. 81–82.
152. Tyler Shipley, "Peruvian lives on Canada's conscience," *Rabble.ca*, February 10, 2012.
153. Vivian Yee and Miriam Jordan, "Migrant Children in Search of Justice: A 2-Year Old's Day in Immigration Court," *The New York Times*, October 8, 2018.
154. Brennan Macdonald and Vassy Kapelos, "Ottawa stands by U.S. as safe third country, despite new border policy," *CBC News*, July 18, 2019.
155. Michael Tutton, "Three years on, many Syrian refugees in Toronto find the path to Canadian citizenship is still stressful," *Globe and Mail*, December 23, 2018.
156. Dakshana Bascaramurty, "Syrian refugees still struggling to settle in Toronto and face uncertain future," *Globe and Mail*, April 21, 2017.
157. Kathleen Harris, "Nearly half of illegal border-crossers into Canada are from Haiti," *CBC News*, November 22, 2017.
158. Bruce Campion-Smith, "Canadians favour screening would-be immigrants for 'anti-Canadian' values, poll suggests," *Toronto Star*, September 10, 2016.
159. Andy Riga, "New Zealand mosque shooter references Québec killer Alexandre Bissonnette," *Montreal Gazette*, March 15, 2019.
160. A short list of recent incidents: a white man taunted an Arab woman with her child on the street in Montreal, calling her a "s--t" (2019); a white woman called a brown woman a "9/11 bloodsucker" and told her to go back where she came from in an Air Canada lineup (2019); a black woman in Ottawa had "n-----" graffitied on her garage door (2019); a group of Afghan-Canadians were told by a white woman at a Denny's Restaurant in Alberta to "speak English" or "go back where you came from," while the white woman asserted that she was a "real Canadian woman" not "one of your Syrian b----s" (2018); a white man tried to block a brown man from leaving a grocery store in London and threated to perform a "citizen's arrest" and have the man "deported" (2018); two brown men were beaten nearly to death in the street by a white man in Toronto (2018); a white man in Winnipeg told a brown woman in hijab to "go back to her country and take her head towel off" when she asked him for directions (2017); an illegally parked white man screamed racial abuse at a brown man in a parking lot in Vancouver (2016); and a bus mechanic in Halifax spent years harassing his co-workers with racial abuse that included writing "all minorities not welcome, show you care, burn a cross" on a bathroom wall alongside positive references to Adolf Hitler.
161. Statistics Canada, "Police-reported hate crime, number of incidents and rate per 100,000 population, Census Metropolitan Areas," August 3, 2019. Available at: https://www150.statcan.gc.ca/t1/tbl1/en/tv.action?pid=3510019101.
162. Mack Lamoureux and Ben Makuch, "Canadian Military Confirms Neo-Nazi Group Atomwaffen Was Within Its Ranks," *Vice*, May 28, 2019.
163. Jenna Hennebry and Bessma Momani, ed., *Targeted Transnational: The State, the Media, and Arab Canadians*, Vancouver, UBC Press, 2013.
164. Vijay Agnew, ed., *Racialized Migrant Women in Canada*, Toronto, University of Toronto Press, 2009.
165. Himani Bannerji, *The Dark Side of the Nation: Essays on Multiculturalism,*

Nationalism and Gender, Canadian Scholars' Press, Toronto, 2000, p. 89.
166. Don Cherry called them "bike-riding, left wing pinkos" and this mythical category of Canadians was claimed to be wealthy and powerful, sanctimonious and self-serving. They are portrayed as drinking expensive frappuccinos and embracing a wide range of causes that make them feel morally superior to everyone around them. Purported to be insincere in their motivations, these "social justice warriors" are said to be mobilizing "fake outrage" around false charges of racism, sexism, homophobia, and any other category that can draw attention to themselves as leaders of a struggle against the "demonized" white, straight, middle-class man.
167. Greater equality would, however, be beneficial to most Canadians, since Canada's richest 100 people possess more wealth than its poorest 6 million. Taylor Scollon, "Richest 100 Canadians have more wealth than bottom 6 million families combined," *North 99*, December 20, 2019. See also Stephen McBride and Heather Whiteside's *Private Affluence, Public Austerity* (2011) and Geoffrey McCormack and Thom Workman's *The Servant State* (2015).
168. Tyler Shipley, "Hockey Invented Canada: Questioning the Myths of Manufactured Nationalism," in Victorian Kannen and Neil Shyminsky, *The Spaces and Places of Canadian Culture*, Toronto, Canadian Scholars' Press, 2019
169. Michael Ignatieff, *Empire Lite: Nation-Building in Bosnia, Kosovo and Afghanistan*, Penguin, Toronto, 2003, p. 3, 24, 19.
170. Michael Ignatieff, *Empire Lite*, p. 2.
171. Michael Ignatieff, *Empire Lite*, p. 6.
172. Michael Ignatieff, *Empire Lite*, p. 114.
173. Tom Flanagan, *First Nations? Second Thoughts*, Montreal, McGill-Queen's University Press, 2008, p. 6.
174. Tyler Shipley, *Ottawa and Empire*, p. 167–169.
175. Alyson McCready, *Yellow Ribbons: The Militarization of Canadian National Identity*, Fernwood, Halifax, 2013.
176. Tyler Shipley, *Ottawa and Empire*, p. 167.
177. Gen. Rick Hillier, *A Soldier First: Bullets, Bureaucracy and the Politics of War*, Toronto, Harper Collins, 2009, p. 493.
178. Ian McKay and Jamie Swift, *Warrior Nation: Rebranding Canada in an Age of Anxiety*, Toronto, Between the Lines, 2012, p. 292.
179. McKay and Swift, *Warrior Nation*, p. 293.

Conclusion

Decolonizing Canada

Then and now an imperial people has awakened to the menace of the barbarians. Just beyond the zone of stable democratic states, which took the World Trade Centre and the Pentagon as its headquarters, there are border zones like Afghanistan where barbarians rule… Nobody likes empires, but there are some problems for which there are only imperial solutions.

— Michael Ignatieff, 2003[1]

FOR GENERATIONS, CANADIANS HAVE BEEN weaned on the idea that Canada is not like other nations: Canada is nicer, better, more inclusive, more multicultural, more tolerant. This book illustrates that this is painfully false and that great harm has been done to people in every corner of the world in the name of Canada and Canadian interests, and sometimes even in the name of the very values listed above. Indeed, the idea that Canada is better and more inclusive than Afghanistan led Canadian soldiers to carry out extreme violence against Afghans on the premise of improving Afghanistan. It was the very same logic that had driven Canada's colonial conquest of northern North America, taken from people who were deemed less civilized than the European settlers. The pattern established in that conquest has been repeated without interruption ever sense.

Lurking behind much of this history is a simple, but troubling, question: could Canada be different? For every decision that Canada took that made the world worse, was there another choice? Could Canada have refused to take part in the invasion of Afghanistan? Or insisted that its businesses stop selling weapons to Apartheid South Africa? Or allowed Chileans to pursue their democratic path to socialism without interference? Or properly punished soldiers who committed sexual violence in

Korea? Or accepted more Jewish refugees in the 1930s? Or stayed out of the First World War? Or respected the Indigenous Peoples' right to live where and how they wanted? Could European settlers have chosen to integrate peaceably into the Indigenous cultures they encountered?

Each question dives deeper into Canada's colonial legacy and becomes more difficult to answer. Of course, it is absolutely true that individuals make choices and, therefore, could have made different choices. John A. Macdonald did not have to starve Indigenous people on reserves: he chose to. His cabinet members chose to develop the specifics of those policies, his Indian agents and mounted police carried them out, and Canadian settlers like my own ancestors happily took advantage. They are all responsible for their choices. Any of these people, at any level, could have rejected these policies and attitudes; some, like William Henry Jackson, made real gestures in that direction.

In fact, in nearly every episode that this book documents, many individuals proved that different choices were possible. From the strikers in Winnipeg in 1919 to the Communist Party in the 1930s, from Flora MacDonald Denison to Kanahus Manuel, from Norman Bethune in China to Herbert Norman in Japan, from the anti-war movement in the 1960s to the activists who opposed Canada's role in Central America in the 1980s, from Jews speaking out against Canada's support for Israeli Apartheid to the campaigns for justice for migrant workers, Canadian policies and behaviours have never been carried out without resistance. But those individuals who chose differently have almost always been drowned out, overwhelmed, undermined, co-opted and marginalized, if not directly repressed, attacked, jailed or killed.

Indeed, there has always been a dominant ideological thread in Canada that is rooted in the structure and logic of almost every Canadian institution. That a state built on conquest and white supremacy should find itself carrying on the same traditions across a century and a half should not be surprising. There has been no radical break in Canada; the state that colonized this land is the same state that rules it today. It represents the same class interests and reflects the same assumptions and understandings of the world. The idea that this state — and the class it represents — could have made different choices appears to me utterly absurd, because this would mean acting against its own class interests.

Colonialism has been *good* for the Canadian ruling classes even while it has been a morally indefensible catastrophe for the Indigenous people it targeted. The same can be said of most of the choices this book documents; notwithstanding the inherently self-destructive dynamics of capitalism and colonialism in the long term, the short-term consequences of Canadian actions have typically advanced the interests of the Canadian elite in a variety of ways. On some occasions these actions have also brought benefits to privileged sections of the working class, though this has usually been limited and temporary.

To cite one seemingly small and isolated example: Canada's decision to sell weapons to Iraq and Iran in the early 1980s was not only good for arms dealers in the short haul but also helped make the Iran–Iraq War more deadly overall. The war weakened both sides, provoked divisions in the Middle East and better prepared the ground for US intervention in the 1990s and 2000s to ultimately take control of Iraq in a way that had huge benefits for Canadian capital. Not only did Canadian companies win contracts in Iraq, but US domination of the Middle East helps maintain the US-centred global capitalist empire, which Canadian capital needs, in general, in order to operate most effectively. Canada is deeply invested in the US imperial capitalist project, and one simple action — selling weapons to Iraq in 1981 — helped advance that project, even while it fuelled a nightmarish experience for people in Iraq and Iran.

This is not to say that Canada never took actions that undermined the goals of the ruling class. The state is not a monolithic, impenetrable structure that operates with perfect, calculated rationality. It is a complex mess of competing interests, mediated and managed by the ruling class to try to achieve its goals while minimizing resistance or interference. This fact sometimes meant that it acquiesced to demands that came from other sections of Canadian society — allowing refugees to come to Canada from Chile in the 1970s, for instance — to try to maintain broader public consent for the state. There were also cases where the state miscalculated and harmed its own interests; the attempt to effect a regime change in Syria in the 2010s clearly failed, and, in fact, the entire War on Terror had a mixed report card from the standpoint of how effectively it has advanced ruling-class interests in the West.

But what is indisputable is that it has always been the ruling class interests of the West that were foremost in the minds of policymakers in Canada and, indeed, which became embedded within the very DNA of what Canada is. Consider the sheer number of different choices Canada would have to make to genuinely reflect a different kind of position in the world and how massively different those decisions would have to be. Could Canada have refused to participate in the occupation of Afghanistan? Yes but, given what we know about Canada, what would it have done instead? Canada might have participated in a minor, supporting role as it did in Iraq. Or it might have funded, equipped and trained those elements it wanted to support from the sidelines, as it has in the conflict between Ukraine and Russia. Or it might have given diplomatic cover to its allies who fought directly to satisfy their objectives there, as it did in Southern Africa in the 1980s. But there is no conceivable version of Canada that would have abstained entirely from the War on Terror, rejected its premises, condemned its perpetrators or refused to profit from it.

There are, then, any number of other *tactics* Canada might have used to achieve its goals in Afghanistan without directly invading, but its *goals* would have remained the same. To imagine a Canada with different goals is to imagine something that is not Canada. Given the fundamental goals and ideology of the Canadian state — settler capitalism and the colonial imagination — debates about specific policy decisions are, in some ways, an absurd exercise. Even if we want to believe that Canada could make different decisions, to concretely picture Canada making radically different decisions is nearly impossible. In Afghanistan, as in Spain, Vietnam or Angola, what the people needed was solidarity in their struggle against injustice. Only something distinctly unlike Canada — only a state that represented an entirely different set of class interests — could possibly have intervened in Afghanistan or elsewhere in a manner that would manifest real solidarity.

Perhaps that is the point. Perhaps for the people who live in this place to be a progressive force in in the world — to line up on the side that is anti-colonial and anti-capitalist — and to genuinely fight for justice and equality for all people, we must build something that is not Canada. Nations are not immutable or permanent; they are built, they are dismantled, new nations are built. The question is: what sort of nation do we want, and can we achieve that with the institutions and legacies and structures of Canada? If the thing called Canada has always served the interests of a colonial capitalist elite, then it might be time to consider abandoning the idea — popular among left nationalists — that we can make Canada better. Instead of trying to reform something that has resisted such efforts for more than 150 years, why not replace it with something else?

There are still many on the Canadian left who believe that if we could redefine what Canada means — to make it inclusive rather than exclusive, or to represent the values of equality and justice — then we could build a Canada to be proud of. Of course, nations are contested ideas, and there are cases where values like solidarity and anti-colonialism became components of nationalist projects. Cuba falls into this category, but, importantly, Cuba was never a colonial power, it was always the colony. Canadian nationalism, by contrast, has from the very beginning been firmly embedded within the logic of colonialism and capitalism. In fact, Canadian patriotism has often been asserted in precisely the moments when Canadian colonialism was in action. White settlers sang the national anthem while protesting against Indigenous land defenders at Caledonia in the 2000s. That same anthem that was performed at the opening of a Canadian mine on a site of a massacre of Indigenous people in Guatemala in the 1970s. Calixa Lavallée was the composer of that anthem, "O Canada" (1880), and he also wrote the score for an operetta called "The Indian Question: Settled at Last."[2]

Even the Canadian national anthem cannot be disentangled from colonialism. In my synthesis of Canada's story across the preceding pages, I see only very exceptional cases where genuinely progressive politics were carried out by forces associated with Canadian nationalism and, even then, I would argue that they were limited — not strengthened — by their attachment to Canada. The greatest acts of solidarity and justice that Canadians have carried out have, by contrast, been undertaken with very little association with the idea of Canada. The soldiers who mutinied in Victoria rather than be sent to kill Bolsheviks in 1918; the Mackenzie-Papineau volunteers in Spain; the mostly Latin American activists who forced the Canadian state to accept refugees from Central America in the 1980s: they were all compelled by notions of justice, solidarity, class struggle and anti-colonialism but rarely were they compelled by Canadian nationalism. Above all, the efforts by Indigenous people to resist colonization and assert their right to live within independent nations have, by definition, existed in direct confrontation with the Canadian state. Canada, as we know it, is premised upon controlling this land. It cannot give it back and still be Canada.

As such, the famous image of Mohawk warriors standing face-to-face with Canadian soldiers during the Oka Crisis suggests a fundamental choice between two utterly different societies which cannot be reconciled in their current composition. Canadian left nationalists might wish to believe that the solution is to build a better Canada that would seek genuine reconciliation instead of pursuing ongoing colonialism. My response is to ask why we need to create a better Canada, where there is already A'nó:wara Tsi Kawè:note (Turtle Island).[3] Why must reconciliation take place within the context of the colonial imposition? To the extent that most Canadians — even those who are more thoughtful and progressive — would be terrified by the idea of dismantling Canada and living instead in A'nó:wara Tsi Kawè:note, then I submit that the thing called Canada remains fundamentally colonial.[4]

I therefore reject the idea that Canada can be made better. The central thesis of this book is that the core material and ideological premises of Canada — settler capitalism and the colonial imagination — are inseparable from what Canada is and does. The individuals who are currently called Canadians, however, are a different matter entirely. There is no reason that we — I am in this category — could not participate in the creation of something new and different, alongside and in solidarity with those people who have always been excluded from Canada. This book is not equipped to offer a program for how to build that alternative, but it clearly gestures towards certain necessary conditions for such a solution. The first and most obvious is to abandon the mythologies of Canada and, indeed, our very attachment to the idea of this nation and its national symbols. More specifically, we need to determine the values or symbols that we *are* committed to and detach them from any connection to Canada.

Second, whatever is built to replace Canada must have a completely different foundation and must reject both the logic of white supremacy and the class structure of capitalism. That these two dynamics are driving the world into a dystopia from which it may never emerge is increasingly obvious, as the emotional mood of this moment is permeated with depression, cynicism and a sense of the impossibility of change. This is beautifully, if tragically, captured in Mark Fisher's *Capitalist Realism* (2009) and even the American Psychological Association acknowledged, in a 2017 report, that the climate crisis alone is having a profound impact on people's mental health; a deeply pessimistic sense of the future has increasingly taken root.[5] The choice between socialism or barbarism, as it was framed by Rosa Luxemburg in 1916, is more salient today than ever before. The solution to our problems cannot be more of the colonial capitalism that has led us to where we currently stand. Instead, we need to build something that draws from the long tradition of resistance to that world order — from Indigenous anti-colonial movements and from the many anti-capitalist struggles that have risen up across its history — to extricate ourselves and each other from the doom machine that was built by imperial Europe and imposed around the world.

Greater awareness of that reality and willingness to confront the system head-on, however, will evoke the full wrath of the classes that seek to maintain their power. The widespread re-emergence of fascism is a manifestation of precisely that reaction, and, as we work to save ourselves from the crises we face, fascism will inevitably be one of the obstacles in our path. Thus, we need to adapt new and sustainable ways of organizing for change. Here I shrink from the responsibility of waving any particular flag; the international left has been — in broad terms — on the defensive for several decades and beset by theoretical and political splits of a wide variety. This book is not the place for me to name allegiance to any particular tradition, except to note that there is urgency in building a socialist or communist project that can succeed.

Having spent most of my life embedded in the left milieu of movementism — left politics dispersed into decentralized movements which react to particular problems but resist building the structures for a long-term confrontation with the ruling class — I have seen and sometimes lived its failures. As my friend and colleague J. Moufawad-Paul argues in *The Communist Necessity* (2014), "from its very emergence, capitalism has waged war upon humanity and the earth… the window in which we can make revolution is closing as the world approaches the armageddon promised by the logic of capital."[6] Moufawad-Paul concludes that building a communist alternative is a necessity if we are to prevent an utterly catastrophic collapse of humanity.

The choice between capitalist dystopia and the inevitably dangerous and destabilizing task of building left revolution is a terrifying reality. Given the history this book recounts, I fully admit that it would be much easier to cling to the hope that we can elect better leaders who will reform the system to make it gradually better. However, the evidence for this possibility is extremely thin. As such, I remain convinced that our only hope for a better world lies in fully subverting the old, and it is my strong belief that this cannot be achieved through or within the political and cultural institution known as Canada.

The contributions that Canada has made to this world have, on the balance, made most people's lives worse. Canada has furthered the causes of inequality and injustice, Canada has consistently supported the violent forces of the right and far right internationally, and Canada has relentlessly ravaged the environment we all depend upon. What Canada teaches us is that colonial powers can be polite, they can appear measured, they can mobilize the language of peace, and they can seem to offer help. They can do all these things and still be colonial powers. Several Canadian prime ministers have tried to reassure us that Canada has no colonial history. Not only does Canada have a colonial history, it has a colonial present. Perhaps there is still time to prevent Canada from having a colonial future.

Notes
1. Michael Ignatieff, *Empire Lite: Nation Building in Bosnia, Kosovo, and Afghanistan*, Penguin Books, New York, 2003, p. 3, 11.
2. The politics of the piece are not immediately apparent; some have suggested that it is a satire that is actually critical of colonialism while others emphasize the repetition of a wide variety of colonial stereotypes. Whatever Lavallée and his co-authors were trying to say, the point is that Canada's national anthem has always been wrapped up in the so-called "Indian Question," and separating the song from its colonial heritage is an impossible task. Rob Simms, "O Canada composer wrote music for unsettling operetta on 'The Indian Question,'" CBC *News*, June 28, 2017.
3. A'nó:wara Tsi Kawè:note (Turtle Island) is the name given to North America in the Kanien'kéha language, spoken by the Kanien'kehá:ka (Mohawk) people. Of course, not all Indigenous people use this term and thus it cannot claim universality either; a postcolonial Canada would have to build new relationships between Indigenous nations and former settlers but it would also involve a reformation of the relations between Indigenous nations.
4. Some of the difficult problems of how to approach the decolonization of the territory called Canada are raised in Eva Mackey's *Unsettled Expectations* (2016).
5. Susan Clayton, Kirra Krygsman, and Meighan Speiser, Mental Health and our Changing Climate: Impacts, Implications, and Guidance, Washington, American Psychological Association and ecoAmerica, 2017. Available at: https://www.apa.org/news/press/releases/2017/03/mental-health-climate.pdf.
6. J. Moufawad-Paul, *The Communist Necessity*, Montreal, Kesplebedeb, 2014, p. 155–157.

Index

9/11, 7, 327–28, 350, 381, 396, 408–10, 501n160
A'aninin people, 45
abolitionism, 22, 33
Acadia (Nova Scotia), 27, 30
Adenauer, Konrad, 189, 197n65
Adams, Howard, 14, 57–58, 59n22, 68, 82–83, 87
Afghanistan, 418, 439n7
    Canadian attitudes toward, 3, 8, 148, 396–97, 400–3, 406–9, 490
    civilian torture in, 398, 406–7, 449, 503
    geostrategic/capitalist importance of, 403–8
    history of, 397–400
    invasion of, 7, 113, 131, 396–97, 491
    occupation of, 327–28, 385, 403–9, 439n9, 506
    stereotypes of, 401–2
    war in, 140, 203, 394–96, 404–10, 489
    see also Al-Qaeda; Bin Laden, Osama; Mujahideen
Afghan National Police (ANP), 401–2, 407
Africa,
    anti-colonial struggle, 5, 134, 203, 235–39, 387n47
    "darkness" in, 358, 366, 369, 387n44
    decolonization, 255–66, 285, 296–97, 316–20, 355, 360, 397
    geostrategic occupation of, 132, 203, 245, 371
    mining in, 476–79
    neocolonialism, 5, 104–6, 126, 138–40, 257
    "Scramble for," 115–16, 350
    trans-Atlantic slave trade, 16, 20–22, 43, 100, 254, 423, 482
    see also Apartheid; South Africa; Rwanda
African National Congress (ANC), 323–25
Africans, 33, 423
    attitudes toward, 5, 43, 111–12, 118, 207, 251–60, 338n88, 354
    Canadian violence against, 59, 63, 84, 105–7, 124, 149
    erasure of, 109, 111–14, 128n58
    slave revolts, 22, 69, 423, 428
    South African War, 44, 109–15
    see also black people
Africville, 298
Afro-Nova Scotians, 106
agribusiness, Canadian, 432, 473–74
    exploitation in, 64
agriculture, 160, 194n12, 219, 258, 471, 494n23
    campesino access to, 310
    food security, 48–49, 425–26, 481
    Indigenous conversion to, 25, 32, 54–55, 65, 71, 74
    settler, 40–41, 59n22, 102
Albo, Greg, 403, 405
Albright Madeline, 349, 368
Algeria,
    colonialism in, 19
    liberation struggle, 209, 256–57
Algonquin people, 32, 386n26
Allende, Salvador, 6, 269–71, 303
Allied powers, 215
    Canada in, 123, 186–88, 236, 201–2
    Nazis and, 148, 185, 191

Normandy, 177
war crimes, 172, 184, 187, 189–90
Alphonse, Paul, 85
Al-Qaeda, 396, 408
American Indian Movement (AIM), 88–89, 241n3, 298–99
American Revolution, 30–31
Amin, Idi, 293n138, 317, 388n52, 486
Anglo-Canadians, 110, 154–55, 165n15
labour movement, 104–5
perceptions of, 118–19, 126, 135
Anglo-Saxons, 119, 156, 176, 181–84, 204, 302
Angola, 107, 203, 390n85
liberation struggle, 275, 317–20, 322, 325, 332, 339n97, 345, 506
Anishinaabeg people, 27–28, 31, 482
Annan, Kofi, 367–68
annexation, 110, 284
American, 39, 42, 105
Canadian, 59n22, 140
German, 147, 156, 176
A'nó:wara Tsi Kawè:note (Turtle Island), 508
anti-capitalist politics, 135–36, 239–40, 295, 324, 404, 506–9
anti-colonial politics, 3, 208–9, 242n9, 282, 288n23, 299
nationalism, 293n138, 305
solidarity in, 69, 275–77, 285, 295, 299, 506–9
struggles, 56, 88–89, 203–4, 227, 253–57, 303, 316, 445n128
as threatening, 135, 210, 238–41, 262–66, 315
anti-communism, 164n7, 165n15, 168n81, 375, 398
Asian, 200–1, 229, 232, 282–84
Canadian, 147–48, 204, 215–18, 225, 234–40
German Nazi, 158–59, 181, 197n65, 213, 247n131
government, 159–60, 192, 200–1, 305, 321, 371
media, *see* media, 145
propaganda, 135, 197n63, 323, 329
racism and, 135, 148, 153, 229, 323
work camps, 137, 150–51, 153, 215–16, 219

anti-fascism, 177, 197n63,65
Asian, 167n53, 213
Canadian, 151–54, 186
Spanish Civil War, 149–55
anti-Semitism, 102, 153, 416, 495n37
Canadian, 153, 165n15, 183, 419–21, 444n117, 457
Christie Pits Riot, 181–82
fascism versus, 179–82, 195n19
government, 157–61, 178, 183–85, 194n15
Nazism versus, 179–80
weaponizing accusations of, 419–21
see also Swastika Clubs
anti-war sentiment, 120–21, 146, 504
in Canada, 110, 124–25, 278
Apartheid, 332, 337n83
black people and, 54, 101, 299, 323
Canada's response to, 294, 312, 314–24, 504
Israel, 7, 54, 91, 202–9, 373, 414–21, 451
sanctions against, 258, 272–75, 294, 503
South Africa, 91, 178, 295–96, 303, 314–25
Apocalypse of Settler Colonialism (Horne), 68–69
Aquash, Anna Mae, 300, 334n16
Arabs, 257, 348
displacement of, 206–11
Israelis versus, 205–11, 304–7, 415–16
perceptions of, 106, 195n19, 346, 487, 501n160
violence against, 206–9, 396–98
see also Palestine
Arab Spring, 412–13
Arafat, Yasser, 296, 415
Arana Osorio, Carlos, 269
Arbenz, Jacobo, 233–34
Arbour, Louise, 368–69, 373, 380, 390n76, 413
Arcand, Adrien, 153, 180–81
Argentina, 134, 183, 234, 273, 479, 495n50
Aristide, Jean-Bertrand, 422, 424–29, 432, 445n131,144
aristocracy, 137, 148, 167n55, 178–80

Index

interests of, 17–18, 69
see also capitalist class
Armenia, 140–41, 166n29
Arone, Shidane, 353, 357
Asia, 383
    anti-colonial struggle, 253–55, 266, 333
    "Great Game," 115–16
    occupation of, 5, 138, 145–49, 175–77, 224–30
    perceptions of, 63, 118, 180, 200–3, 252–55
    Western powers in, 192, 217, 235–36, 255, 476
    see also South Asia
Asians,
    Canadian violence against, 84, 105, 211–12, 281
    immigrants, 103, 132–35
Assad, Bashar Al-, 412–14, 458, 475–76
Assembly of First Nations, 87
assimilation,
    immigrants, 135, 382, 408, 486
    Indigenous Peoples, 2, 43, 55, 78
Atlantic alliance, 177, 210, 240, 378, 384
Attawapiskat, 88
Australia, 53, 91, 183, 323
    as settler colonies, 75, 105, 131, 208, 320
Austria-Hungary, 116
autocracy, 133
Axis powers, 150, 173–74, 177, 185
Aztec society, 24

Ba'ath Party, 305–6, 335n30, 347–48, 412
Bagley, Fred, 51–52
Baker, I.G., 49, 69
Balkans, the
    immigrants from, 102, 136
    War, 352, 373–82, 392n123
band councils, Indigenous, 56–57
banking, 5, 178–79, 471
    international, 140–42, 271, 307, 325, 423–28
    profits from, 103, 272, 375, 379, 470, 475–76
    wartime expansion, 116–17, 140, 189
Bannerji, Himani, 381–82, 487

Basquia Cree, *see* Cree
Bata Shoes, 255, 268, 317
Batoche, resistance around, 45, 67–71, 80, 243n27
Battleford, SK, 49, 67, 71
beaver pelts, 45, 60n32
Belgium, 19, 106, 186, 350
    in the Congo, 254, 260, 262–65, 289n61
    in Rwanda, 360–61, 365, 368
Belize, 140, 142, 480
Bennett, R.B. 4, 143, 153
Beothuk people, 26, 32
Bercuson, David, 71, 193n4
Berlin Wall, 294, 326
Berthiaume, J.A., 264–65,
Bethune, Norman, 9, 150–51, 213, 504
Bezos, Jeff, 17
Bin Laden, Osama, 327, 396–99, 408
Black Panther Party, 298, 334n7
black people, 63, 109, 258, 279, 322, 354, 489
    enslavement of, 4, 93n20, 104
    labour conditions, 102–3, 289n49, 321, 325
    perceptions of, 100, 106, 111–12, 256, 261–63, 315, 360
    resistance movements, 297–98, 302, 323–24, 334n7, 423–24
    see also Black Panther Party; Black Power; racism; segregation
Black Power, 298–99
Blatchford, Christie, 400, 402
blockades, 395, 476–77
    Indigenous, 88–89, 300
Boers, the, 109–12, 122, 207, 315
Boer War, *see* South African War
Bolivarian Revolution, 458–67
Bolshevism, 122, 213
    Canada versus, 9, 117–18, 135–36, 172, 176, 507
    Hitler on, 158, 179–80
    Jewish, 178–83, 194n15, 195n19, 453, 456–57
    Russian, 117, 133, 340n127
    see also Russian Revolution
Bolsonaro, Jair, 472–74
Booh Booh, Jacques-Roger, 366–67
Borden, Robert, 117, 132, 140, 163n3,

513

212
Bosnia, 374, 377–78
Bothwell, Robert, 155, 218, 254
bourgeoisie, 169n91, 179, 362
    interests, 74, 119
    wealth of, 163
Boushie, Colten, 90–91
Brazil, 19, 183, 384
    Canadian companies in, 131, 141–43, 268, 273, 470
    far right in, 7, 142, 438, 466–67, 471–74
    Worker's Party (PT), 470–73
    see also Lula da Silva, Luis Ignacio; Rousseff, Dilma
Britain, 53–54, 72, 253, 423
    in Africa, 234–35, 256–59, 317, 325
    in Asia, 227, 230, 283
    Canadian support for, 5, 101–3, 112, 240, 409–10, 490–92
    colonialism, 19–23, 27–33, 44, 131, 138, 347–48, 397
    German versus, 109–17, 147–48, 161, 174–77, 183–84
    imperial favour, 39, 103–5, 113–14, 139
    War on Terror, 348
British Columbia, 33, 145, 484
    anti-Asian racism, 212, 214–15, 339n104
    Indigenous people of, 30–33, 71–74, 84
    settlers in, 30, 40, 103, 151, 480
    violence against women in, 84–85
British Empire, 4, 101–2, 490
    Canadian commitment to, 110, 121–25, 132–40, 155–57, 404
    control of, 105–11, 126n7, 128, 142, 190, 204–10
    expansion of, 40, 80, 109, 138, 251
British North America, 19, 23, 27–33, 43, 53, 107
British North America Act, 41–42
Brodeur, Victor, 143–44
Brown, Kyle, 357–58
Buchan, John, 111–12, 121, 124–25, 156, 279
buffalo, 200
    hunting, 41, 43, 45–46, 70–71, 74
    systematic slaughter, 48, 52, 65
Burkina Faso, 478–79
Burundi, 359–63, 365, 371
Bush, George H.W., 274, 314, 347, 372
Bush, George W., 396, 408, 425

Cáceres, Berta, 435–36
Cahokia, 25
Caledonia, 89, 507
Calgary, 74, 135, 468, 490
Canada,
    Dominion of, 41–42, 52–54, 72, 91, 144
    essence of, 78, 88, 135, 163, 229, 259
    as "middle power," 203–4, 303–4
    Nazi integration, 172, 189–91
    postwar, 124–26, 135, 172, 190, 210, 236–37
Canada 150, 37–39
Canadian Dimension, 419
Canadian International Development Agency (CIDA), 268, 441n43, 468, 479
Canadian Journal of Commerce, 141
Canadian Museum of Human Rights, 63–64
Canadian Pacific Railway (CPR), 44, 108, 117, 93n23
    construction of, 4, 52, 70, 103
capitalism, 28,
    advancement of, 7–9, 135–36, 138–44, 230–31, 437–38, 480–81
    Canada's commitment to, 4–7, 104–5, 190, 201–4, 226, 234, 311–16, 483
    colonial, 3, 20–24, 74, 100, 133, 228–39, 286, 505–8
    contradictions of, 20, 30, 125, 174, 382–83, 450
    crisis of, 138, 295, 438, 447n175
    definition, 16, 129n61, 320
    emergence of, 16–22, 78, 115, 509
    empire and, 114–19, 162–63, 173, 176, 404, 454, 505
    fascism and, 149, 163, 167n56, 173–77, 192–93, 211
    Indigenous Peoples, 1–2, 33, 74, 88–92, 203–4, 298–99, 432, 482
    industrial, 74, 105, 119, 138, 179

international, 6, 115, 138–44, 204, 305, 324–24, 362
liberal, 159, 173–75, 179, 238, 294–95, 329–30, 379
market, 202, 326, 375
revolutions, 17–18, 101, 147, 202, 332, 381, 459
rivalry in, 22, 27, 108–15, 138, 154, 164n6, 173–76, 190, 452
settler, *see* settler capitalism
violence with, 5–6, 120–21, 278, 282–86, 300, 477
war, 116–19, 172–75, 345–46, 384
see also anti-capitalist politics
capitalist class, the, 9, 267, 305, 332–33
in Canada, 4, 64, 137–38, 201, 249–50, 302, 418–20, 464–67
dictatorships and, 132, 319, 331, 345
international interests of, 4, 8–9, 101, 201, 240–41, 328, 473–77
profits of, 102–3, 109–10, 113, 296, 383–85
rise of, 16–22, 39, 78, 115, 208, 376, 482, 488
strategies of, 68–69, 93n23, 107–8, 149, 297, 427–28
threats to, 69, 101, 139, 295–97, 333n4, 381, 425–27
see also aristocracy; merchant class
Caribbean, the, 117, 141–42, 231, 465
Indigenous people in, 14, 266, 434
Carmichael, Stokely, 298
Carter, Jimmy, 269, 309, 416
Cartier, Jacques, 26–28, 31–33, 282
Castro, Fidel, 235, 274–75, 332, 339n97
Catholicism, 178, 182, 311, 426
cattle ranching, 48–49, 360, 362
CBC (Canadian Broadcasting Corporation), 266, 279, 281, 432, 473
International Service, 237
war, support for 172, 352, 376, 380, 394, 415, 487
Central America, 195n19, 234, 272, 295, 323, 436–37, 504, 507
Canadian corporations in, 141–42, 268, 312, 345
dictators in, 144–45, 232–33, 313
violence in, 303, 308–11, 314, 327, 336n58, 441n48, 485
Chamberlain, Neville, 152, 154–56, 162, 175, 193n3
Chávez, Hugo, 436, 445n140, 459–65, 468, 479
Chenoy, Anuradha M., 330–31
Cherry, Don, 123, 409, 488–89, 502n166
Chiang Kai-shek, 215, 241n3
child welfare system, 77–78; *see also* Millennium Scoop; Sixties Scoop
Chile, 6, 241n3, 286, 459, 466, 479, 503–5
violence in, 269–73
China, 17, 404, 504
anti-fascism, 151
communist, 151, 214–18, 223–25, 345
Japan versus, 200, 212–19
revolutionary movements, 134, 203–4, 241n3
Western powers and, 126n7, 214–15, 230, 297, 384, 452
Chinese people, 384
head tax, 103
perceptions of, 59n28, 119
railway construction, 4, 103, 112, 250–51
Chomiak, Michael, 247n137, 455–56
Chown, Alice, 9, 119–20, 130n81
Chrétien, Jean, 489
Christianity, 104, 107, 111, 119, 215, 221
anti-Semitism, 178–79
Indigenous conversion to, 73, 78–80
see also missionaries
Churchill, Winston, 107, 117, 180, 204, 208
fascism and, 147–49, 162, 167n53, 172
Clark, Gregory, 125–26
Clark, Joe, 311, 313, 324, 327, 347, 372
class, 84, 96n76, 210, 301–5, 504
conflict, 9, 114–15, 154, 202–3, 218, 283, 371
consciousness, 126, 131–33, 154
divisions along, 4–5, 101–2, 121–22, 163, 179, 330, 397
hierarchies, *see* hierarchy, belief in
professional, 102, 178, 394, 413
race and, 104, 119, 136, 182, 311, 360, 508

solidarity, 128n59, 145, 285, 466, 506–8
see also bourgeoisie; capitalist class; class struggle; middle class; ruling class; working class
class struggle, 138, 152, 179, 262, 276, 399
  emergence of, 17, 175–77, 322, 362, 507
  geopolitics and, 352, 374, 449, 467, 491
  postwar, 122, 133, 163, 202–3
Clearing the Plains (Daschuk), 49, 61n63
climate catastrophe, 7, 25, 438, 481–82, 508
Cockburn, Bruce, 313, 407, 441n48
Cold War, 5–6, 164n7, 397
  Canada in, 217–18, 252–54, 282, 294–96, 314, 345–46, 491
  capitalism in, 203–6, 210, 230–31, 239–41, 305–6, 400, 438
  ideology, 190, 223, 226–27, 230, 236, 278, 310
  post-, 240–41, 274, 349, 355, 366, 375–77, 388n51, 452
  rivalry in, 176, 202–4, 230, 241n3, 277, 354, 386n30
  Western powers in, 201–11, 223, 237–38, 303, 322–33, 382
Cold War Canada (Whitaker and Marcuse), 236–37
Colombia, 7–8, 340n119, 438, 466–71, 474; *see also* Fuerzas Armadas Revolucionarias de Colombia (FARC)
colonial imagination, Canada, 173, 240, 252–54, 346, 400, 408, 414, 490
  foreign policy, 24–26, 104, 122, 265, 356, 422, 431, 506–8
  Indigenous Peoples, 2–7, 51, 65, 68, 92, 140, 299
colonialism, 22, 27–29
  capitalism and, 18–26, 73–74, 91–92, 132–33, 201–9, 226–38, 286, 432, 506–8
  "civilizing" and, 19, 53–58, 110–12, 140–41, 251–63, 285, 352–60, 490–93
  effects of, 25, 37–41, 68–70, 86–90, 94n47, 303, 469, 475
  exoticization in, 53, 253–54, 351
  ideology of, 1–8, 24–30, 39–43, 52–53, 68–78, 91–92, 100–1, 111–12, 200–1, 282
  international, 100, 109–16, 131–34, 138–41, 201, 251, 352–60
  legacy of, 1–4, 15, 38, 51, 100–4, 225, 250–53, 400, 504
  military technologies, *see* military
  narratives of, 401–2
  neo-, 5–6, 239, 267, 285, 309, 317–19, 350, 360–66
  patriarchy, 51, 78–86, 118–21, 148–49, 344–50
  racism and, *see* racism
  resistance to, 3, 44, 87–91, 134, 201–10, 234–36, 252, 304, 376, 469; *see also* independence movements
  slavery and, 18–24, 33, 43, 69, 140, 186, 216, 251, 321, 423–24
  trickery, 8, 31–32, 45, 48–52, 73, 142, 405, 416
  types of, 19–20, 22–23
  violence, 19–23, 32, 37–45, 49–57, 94n47, 96n76, 185–87, 201, 358
  white supremacy and, *see* white supremacy
  see also anti-colonial politics; colonization; Indian Act; residential schools; settler colonialism; treaties
colonization, 55, 106
  competition in, 40–41, 109–10, 115–16, 138–41, 363
  death from, 19, 28–29, 48, 65, 70–91, 145, 256, 300, 396
  European, 18–19, 26–33, 108–10, 160, 208–10, 236–38, 255, 438
  geostrategic, 41, 174–75, 201–2, 277, 374, 400, 413
  logic of, 21, 57–58, 79–81, 104–6, 131, 180, 236–41, 350, 503–8
  Indigenous women and, 51–53, 79–86, 89, 282
  Japanese, 200, 212–13, 219, 225
  process of, 15–16, 72–81, 87, 140–41, 149, 380, 396, 505

violence of, 37, 44, 75–86, 94n47, 107, 137, 171, 185, 358–59
war and, 278–80, 286–87
see also colonialism
Columbus, Christopher, 14, 422
commodities, 81, 471
profit-making and, 16, 78, 129n61
Commonwealth countries, 155–56, 190, 203, 217, 253–54, 316, 373
communism, 292n101, 303, 509
alternative project, 509
anti-Semitism and, 178–82, 190, 215–18, 225
Asian, 213–30, 255, 277–85
fascism versus, 4–5, 138, 148–50, 176–77, 193n3, 375, 474
Indigenous people and, 4, 67, 143–44
perceptions of, 153–61, 201, 238–40
revolution, 133–34, 174, 216, 295–300, 310, 474
queer sexualities, 236–37, 299–301
worker organizing, 120–22, 143–47, 151–54, 177, 270, 283
see also anti-communism
communist bloc, 295, 297, 303, 315–16
Communist Party of Canada (CP), 135–36, 150–52, 165n20, 504
Communist Party of Germany (KPD), 158–59, 170n101
communists,
killing of, 6, 170n99
violence against, 158–59, 170n101, 208–10
Western governments versus, 153–60, 300–3, 310, 315–17, 329; *see also* anti-communism
companies, Canadian, *see* corporations, Canadian
concentration camps, 4, 256, 319
Nazi, 158–59, 229
South African, 111, 121, 124, 156, 279, 315
US, 7, 446n160, 485
Congo, the, 19, 371, 478
Canada in, 106–7, 124, 187, 259–66, 279, 282, 350, 359
independence of, 5–6, 252–63
Confederation, 139

Indigenous people during, 42–50, 101
legacy of, 3, 37–40, 86–88, 250
pre-, 23, 33, 75
racism and colonialism of, 23, 37–58, 104–5
conquest, 20, 81, 279, 490–92, 502–4
British, 22, 105–6, 208, 251
colonial Canada, 2–4, 49–53, 79, 90, 141
Indigenous people during, 25–31, 37–44, 50–57, 150, 157
international, 115, 146, 200, 211, 228–30, 265, 475
Conrad, Margaret, 31–32
conscription, 120–21, 125, 185
Contras, the, 303, 307–14, 335n41, 432, 486
Coodin, Freda, 9, 120
Cook, Ramsey, 26, 182
Co-operative Commonwealth Federation (CCF), 136, 165n20, 234, 236
Sixties Scoop and, 77
corporations, Canadian, 40, 103, 108, 301
aid projects, 256, 267–68, 284–86, 314, 403–11, 430, 483–84
monopolies, 4, 46, 115, 132, 141–43, 233, 267–68
international, 4, 132, 141–52, 255, 317–19, 418–19, 468–75
violence, 118, 132, 237, 322, 372, 385, 430
see also mining
corruption, 215, 391n100, 461
corporate, 118, 471–72, 476
state, 118, 143, 185, 422, 452, 462, 471–72
Côte d'Ivoire, 480
Coulthard, Glen Sean, 38, 56, 74, 92
coups d'etat, 386n30, 426–30, 483
Africa, 259, 317, 361, 451
Asia, 283
Latin American, 6, 143, 233–34, 268–73, 432–37, 460–66, 472–73
Crimea, 454–55
criminalization, 120, 149, 159, 233, 298–300
immigrants, 135
Indigenous people, 81–86, 90

structural factors of, 86
Cree, 47, 61n71, 68–69, 91, 122
   Basquia, 45
   Lubicon, 88
   Plains, 23–24, 57, 66–67
Croatia, 374, 376, 390n93, 391n99
Cuba, 131
   Canada and, 141, 234–35, 273–76, 328
   international solidarity, 285, 297–99, 319–24, 332, 345, 355, 507
   profit-making in, 4, 267
   Revolution, 203, 235, 241n3, 267, 310
   US invasion, 108, 116, 134, 274–75
Culhane, Claire, 9, 277–82
curriculum, Canadian, 353, 397, 510
   European settlement, 1, 63, 50, 107, 112
   Indigenous Peoples, 1, 25, 63–64, 75–76
Cypress Hills settlement, 49, 52, 66
Czechoslovakia, 176, 210, 326, 332

Daily Province (Vancouver), 103
Dakelh (Carrier) society, 79–80, 96n77
Dakota people, 52, 55
Dallaire, Roméo, 29, 359, 365–69, 388n66
Dark Threats and White Knights (Razack), 355
Daud, Muhammad, 397–98
decolonization,
   abroad, 6, 239–40, 283, 296, 320, 360
   movements for, 6, 208, 258, 265, 299–300, 503–10
   lack of support for, 77, 286, 314
   undermining, 201, 252–55, 316–18
Delaney, John, 66–67
democracy, 309, 330, 473, 490, 503
   in Africa, 255–59, 265–66, 317
   in Asia, 220–28, 277, 282
   fascism, 139, 148–50, 455–56
   Haiti, 422–32, 483
   Indigenous, 23–24
   in Latin America, 233–34, 268, 273, 307–10, 434–35, 459–68
   Middle East, 349, 405, 412
   radical, 133, 215, 310, 340n127, 462

   social-, 77, 136, 236, 272, 419
   Western, 115, 120, 146, 174, 201–7, 232, 252, 358, 448
de-Nazification, 189, 197n63, 237–38
Dene people, 56, 89
   pipelines and, 88, 92
   uranium mining, 192–93, 200
Denison, Flora MacDonald, 119, 504
Department of Indian Affairs (DIA), 56–57, 65–66, 71, 76
   structure of, 87
   see also Indian agents
Dewdney, Edger, 49, 56–57, 66, 70
Dextraze, Jacques A., 187, 260
Diaz, Porfirio, 141–42
Dick, Philip K., 173–74
dictatorships, 10, 108–10, 132, 147, 251, 264–76, 331, 354–55, 412
   Canada's support for, 6, 141–44, 231–34, 282–84, 314–21, 371–73, 436–37, 479–84
   fascist, 158, 174, 178, 187, 466–72
   US-backed, 134, 221–22, 229–30, 306–13, 348–49, 423–31
Diefenbaker, John, 217, 235, 261, 265–68, 289n61, 314–16, 321
Dien Bien Phu, 227–28, 276
disenfranchisement, 121, 131–32
Donnacona, Chief, 26–27, 32
Drinnon, Richard, 29–30
Dubois, W.E.B., 132, 258
Duck Lake attack, 70
Dumont, Gabriel, 9, 68, 70, 94n40
Duterte, Rodrigo, 474
Duvalier, Jean-Claude "Baby Doc," 424
Duvalier, François, 424
Dying from Improvement (Razack), 85–86

Eastern Europe, 237–39, 328–30, 375–76, 438, 451–52, 455–57
   immigrants from, 102, 118, 153, 165n15, 184
   Nazis in, 155–56, 190
   Soviet Union and, 241n3,5, 326–27, 345
East Indies, Dutch, 19, 282
East Timor, 282–86
economy, 48, 160, 219, 370, 462–66, 471
   capitalist, 24, 33, 105, 118, 163, 175,

362
political, *see* political economy
slave, 20–22
socialist, 226, 325–27, 330–31
US, 22, 138
world, 22, 115, 400
see also industrialization; nationalization; recession
Ecuador, 477, 479
Egypt, 18, 105–6, 131–34, 204–5, 209–11, 304–5, 351
elders, Indigenous, 73, 79–80
El Salvador, 308–11
    Canadian companies in, 143, 177, 267–68, 307, 340n119
    dictatorship, 143, 232, 312
    massacre in, 4, 132, 143–45, 187, 279
Empire Lite (Ignatieff), 489–90, 503
empires, 16, 19, 108, 134, 174, 194n15, 253
    American, 29, 141, 355, 373, 384, 399, 403–4, 449–52
    British, *see* British Empire
    capitalism and, 108, 114–19, 145, 173–76, 403–4, 454, 505
    colonial, 16, 19–20, 44, 114, 131, 210, 253, 350
    creation of, 16, 140–42, 204
    "Evil," 6, 328, 345
    First World War and, 101–3, 113–26, 132–33
    Japanese, 175, 211–12
    Ottoman, 166n29, 205–6
    rivalry between, 27, 101, 150, 162, 191, 383, 410
Empire's Ally (Klassen and Albo), 403
Endicott, James, 9, 28, 204, 215–16, 226, 236
enfranchisement, 57; *see also* disenfranchisement
England, 25, 101, 206
    colonial practices, 19, 29–32, 53, 75–78, 107–9
    colonies of, 19, 28, 42–45
    Enclosures, 17–18
    wartime, 123, 148, 157–61, 171, 176, 193n3
    see also Britain

Espinal, Edwin, 437
Ethiopia, 354–55
    Italian invasion, 139, 145, 169n86, 176
Euro-American powers, 180, 236, 354
    domination of, 115–16, 134, 138, 194n15, 200–4, 231
    Japan versus, 211–17
    resistance to, 5, 201, 206, 304, 376
    see also Western countries
Eurocentrism, 15, 17, 76
Euromaidan protests, 452, 455
Europeans, 114, 126, 166n29, 466
    capitalist logic, 1–2, 16–17, 24, 72, 175, 319–20
    Central, 118, 175
    feudalism, *see* feudalism
    hegemony of, 19, 63, 79–81, 101–7, 131–32, 210, 255, 297
    self-perceptions, 2–3, 17, 26, 106, 169, 180, 207–8, 254–55, 490–3
    settlers, *see* settlers
    wealth extraction, 20–22, 108–9, 129, 423
    see also colonialism; colonization; Eastern Europe
European Union, 454, 466
Export Development Corporation (EDC), 268, 271
extractive industries, 7, 438, 464, 473–76
    megaprojects, 88, 483
    see also natural resources

Facing West (Drinnon), 29
Falconbridge, 231–33, 255, 317, 321
famine, 14, 137, 266, 330
    state-involved, 49, 253, 453, 494n23
farming, 18, 67–69, 112, 103, 277, 309, 428
    death in, 4, 47–50, 102
    labour conditions, 16, 70–71, 136, 186, 220, 330, 407, 484, 500n150
far right, the, 4, 170n99, 181, 375, 452, 486–89
    ethnic nationalism, 237–38, 328, 376, 494n23
    government and, 163, 178, 195, 321
    movements, 126, 137–38, 146, 365, 391n99, 412, 417

support for, 408–9, 453–57, 466,
  474, 489–94, 510
 see also fascism
fascism, 145, 165n24, 317, 333
  anti-Semitism, 179–82, 195n19
  Canadian government and, 5, 7,
    151–55, 167, 185, 222, 449, 474
  elite interests and, 133, 142, 149,
    167n56, 173, 218, 273
  international rise, 4, 138, 151,
    159–62, 305–6, 420–21, 452–58,
    472–73, 509
  non-intervention, government,
    149–50, 155–57, 161–63, 187,
    191, 421
  Spanish Civil War, 139, 145–55,
    317–18
  support for, 111, 158, 167n55, 172,
    200–1, 211, 225, 233–34
  Western democracies, 161–62,
    172–78, 194n12, 375
federal government, 137, 274–76, 322,
  449
  corporate ties to, 113, 142–43
  dictatorships, 232–34, 259, 270–72,
    285–86, 317, 373, 463–65
  fascism, 150, 181–84, 190, 213, 217,
    256, 455
  Indigenous peoples, views on, 68,
    87–88, 102
  Indigenous resistance versus, 68–71,
    79–81, 469
  interracial solidarity versus, 68–70,
    256, 265, 407
Federici, Silvia, 78
feminism, 95n69, 458
  in Canada, 119–20, 300
feudalism, 349, 360–62, 397
  mismanagement in, 17–18, 212
Fifteen Days (Blatchford), 400
Figueres, José, 233
Findley, Timothy, 124
Finland, 135, 152, 165n15
First World War (the Great War), 113,
  156, 174
  Canada in, 101, 117–26, 128n52,
    135, 403, 503–4
  conditions during, 114–15, 163
  empire-building, 114–16, 132–33,
    174
  fascism, 111, 147–49, 162, 172
  left-wing rebellion, 115, 124, 135,
    158
  post-, 137–42, 205–6, 286
  responses to, 105, 121–26, 132,
    167n53,
  veterans, 124–25, 131, 150
  see also anti-war sentiment
fishing, Indigenous, 32, 54, 62n75, 434
Fontaine, Tina, 90–91, 96n76
food aid, Indigenous, 48–50, 57, 65, 137
foreign aid, 398, 425–27
  Canadian, 219, 229, 274, 284–86,
    317, 356, 411, 483
  colonialism and, 256, 430–31
  conditions of, 483, 267–68, 280, 283,
    313–14, 405–6
  to right-wing governments, 6, 232,
    259, 265, 270–71, 312, 370, 455
  workers, 277, 282, 313
  see also corporations, Canadian, aid
    projects
foreign policy, Canadian, 457–59
  assumptions of, 8–9, 105, 210
  framework of, 15, 38–40, 52–53,
    112, 404, 431
  Indigenous people and, 23–26, 46,
    65, 90–92
  interests, 139–41, 201, 268, 272, 396,
    483–84
  Middle East, 209, 405, 410, 414
foster care system, *see* welfare system
founding principles, Canada's, 320–23
  capitalism, 1–2, 4, 37–40, 201, 329
  European superiority, 2, 37–43, 68,
    89–90, 225, 241, 358
  multiculturalism, 249, 260, 381–82,
    485–88, 503
  patriarchy, 78–82
  peacekeeping, 5, 29, 201–4,
    340n126, 345, 350–52, 367
  perceptions of, 63–64, 102, 252, 369,
    491–92, 508
  territorial, 14, 37–40, 45, 90, 338n88
  war, 4, 123–24, 172–78, 186, 201,
    226
  see also Confederation; genocide,
    Indigenous Peoples; Heritage

Index

Minutes; Indian Act
France, 19, 101, 116, 123, 153, 206, 254, 298, 414
    Canadian support for, 139, 228, 257, 426–28, 451
    colonialism, 5, 26–30, 38, 54, 79–80, 131–34, 203, 209–10, 366
    feudalism, 17
    Germany versus, 108–9, 138, 146, 175–76, 185
    Indochina, control over, 227–28, 276–77
    slavery and, 22, 422–23
    see also New France
Franco, Francisco, 145–54, 317
Freeland, Chrystia, 247n137, 455–58, 473, 495n37; *see also* Chomiak, Michael
free market,
    effects of, 16–17, 438
    logic, 17, 53, 202
Frog Lake uprising, 66–67
Front de Libération du Québec (FLQ), 301–2
Fuerzas Armadas Revolucionarias de Colombia (FARC), 467, 469
Fukuyama, Francis, 294–95
fur trade, 27, 43, 45, 59n22, 74
    Hudson's Bay Company, 41, 46
    resistance to, 79–80

Gadhafi, Muammar, 411
Garífuna communities, 432, 434
Gaza, 209, 304, 351, 415–17, 420
gender dynamics, 5, 121, 301, 397
    colonial, 78–80
    Indigenous, 79–80
Generals Die in Red (Harrison), 124
genocide, Indigenous Peoples, 5, 358
    colonization, 19, 31–33, 119–20, 149, 297, 315
    Confederation and, 37–58, 101, 250
    cultural, 21, 55–56, 64, 71–78, 92
    process of, 64–66, 84, 193, 287n6, 308–13, 476, 480
    "Indian problem," 2, 23, 31, 43, 52–54, 77
    justification for, 2–3, 28–30
    portrayal of, 50–51, 63–64

    see also Holocaust, the; residential schools; Rwanda
George, Dudley, 88–89
Germany, 213, 298, 377, 456
    Britain versus, 109–10, 115–22, 138, 161, 175–76, 185
    Canada versus, 121–26, 155–61, 172–73, 186–89, 353
    expansion of, 132–39, 155, 162–63, 175–76, 185, 360
    France versus, 108–9, 138, 146, 175–76, 185
    immigrants from, 102, 121
    Nazi integration, 189–91
    resistance movements in, 146, 152, 158–59, 187–88
    Spanish Civil War, 146–54
    see also Hitler, Adolf; Nazis
Ghana, 59n28, 140, 239, 258–59, 262–64, 317, 478
Gildan Activewear, 426, 434, 437
Girouard, Percy, 107, 140, 338n91
glasnost, 325–26
globalization, 15–16, 299, 333, 404
    anti-, 392n130
Globe and Mail, 181, 253, 261, 264, 273, 306, 413, 477–78
god, *see* Christianity; Islam; Jewish people; Muslims; religion
Gold Coast, *see* Ghana
gold mining, 72, 109–10, 140, 231–33, 258, 414, 477
Gorbachev, Mikhail, 294, 325–28
Göring, Hermann, 157, 160
government, *see* federal government
Granatstein, J.L., 115, 155, 274
Grandin, Greg, 308
Grassy Narrows First Nation, 8, 449
Great Adventure: How the Mounties Conquered the West (Cruise and Griffiths), 50–51
Great Depression, 129n61, 136–39, 175, 260
Great Lakes region, Africa, 10, 359, 362
Great Lakes region, North America, 31–32, 52
Great Plains,
    genocide, Indigenous, 45–53, 86
    see also prairies

Great War, *see* First World War
Greece, 148–49
Grenada, 314
Guaído, Juan, 458, 466
Guatemala, 108, 145, 232–35, 284, 308–13
    Canadian mining in, 7, 234, 268–70, 476–78, 507
Guernica, 145–47, 157
Guevara, Ernesto "Che," 235, 267, 297, 303
Guggisberg, Gordon, 140
Gulf War, 346–49, 378, 492
Guyana, 140–41, 234

Habyarimana, Juvénal, 361–64, 368–71, 388n66, 389n74
Haida people, 24
Haiti, 424–25, 459, 486
    Canadians in, 7, 421–22, 426–32, 449, 451, 483
    sovereignty, 22, 423
Halifax, 30, 106, 183, 298
Harper, Stephen, 411, 419–20, 436, 448, 463–65, 468, 483, 498n98
Harris, Edgar, 9, 177
Harrison, Charles Yale, 124
Haudenosaunee Confederacy, 23–25, 31, 45, 132, 250
    Cartier versus, 26–28
Hawai'i, 116, 221, 243n28
health care, 310, 396, 411
    Indigenous, 71, 96n76
    universal, 150, 379, 460
Henderson, Nevile, 156–57, 162
Heritage Minutes, 201, 249–52, 259–66, 268
Hernández Martínez, Maximiliano, 143–45
hierarchy, belief in, 5, 18–19, 26, 78–81, 154, 286, 345, 360
    racial, 104, 179, 200, 208–13, 225, 255–57
    lack of, 24, 180, 300, 398
Hillier, Rick, 401, 411, 492
Hindus, 255, 474
Hirohito, Emperor, 216, 218
Hispaniola, 19
history,
    Canadian, 37–38, 42, 74–75, 86, 183, 345, 476; *see also* Heritage Minutes
    downplaying of, 15, 25–26, 71–75, 150, 155, 354–60, 448
    "end of," 294–95, 328–29
    fin de siècle, 74, 101–5
    focus of, 8, 81–84, 139–41, 172, 329–33, 508–10
    genocidal, 14–15, 189; 242n10, 494n23
    misrepresentation, 1, 42–44, 50–52, 109–12, 124–26, 223, 397–400
    right side of, 313, 324
    school curriculum, 1, 63–64, 148, 171, 238, 351–53, 397
Hitler, Adolf, 452
    admiration of Canada, 5, 54
    appeasement, myth of, 146, 161–63
    King, William Lyon Mackenzie, 155–62, 172, 183–85, 207, 231
    power of, 146–47, 171, 176, 179–83, 237, 421
    support for, 4, 145, 157–58, 177–85, 207, 464
    Western powers versus, 148–49, 172, 177–79, 185, 277
Hobsbawm, Eric, 116, 165n24
Hochelaga, 27
Ho Chi Minh, 132, 227–29, 277
Hockey Night in Canada, 408–9, 488–89
Holland, 17–19, 109, 134, 230, 282–84
Holodomor, 453, 494n23
Holocaust, the, 260, 320, 444n117
    Allied powers' complicity, 184, 188, 208, 211
    Jews fleeing, 145, 178, 184–88, 205–6, 251, 414, 457
    memorial, 159, 171, 421
    violence of, 171, 183–85, 205, 420
homelessness, 150, 188, 301, 450
    Indigenous, 84–85
Honduras, 232, 308, 336n43,58, 340n119, 432–38
    Canada in, 7–9, 16, 140–42, 426–38, 449–51, 463–66, 483–84
    golpistas, 433, 437–38
    Truth and Reconciliation Commission, 436

Index

Hong Kong, 185, 214
Horne, Gerald, 68–69
House of Commons, 37, 70, 153, 278, 457
Howe, C.D., 192
Hudson's Bay Company (HBC), 30, 39, 41, 44, 338n93
    Indigenous relations, 41–42, 46, 59n22
Hume Wrong, Humphrey, 232, 240
Hungary, 116, 134, 326, 474
hunting, 32, 41, 54, 60n28, 62n75, 265
    buffalo, 25, 43, 45–48, 71, 74, 157; *see also* buffalo
Hussein, Saddam, 306–7, 346–49, 385n8, 408, 412, 450
hydroelectricity, 4, 132, 142–45, 233, 378, 411–17, 428–29
    dams, 8, 88, 209, 318, 436, 469, 477–80, 481–83

Idle No More, 89
immigrants, 328, 455
    left-wing organizing and, 125, 135–36, 150–52, 165n15, 194n15, 238
    racism toward, 103–4, 118, 485
    sacrificing of, 4, 102–5 487; *see also* Chinese people, railway construction
immigration,
    attitudes towards, 9, 104, 118–19, 135, 382
    Canadian policies, 120–21, 190, 257, 337n 61, 485–88
    colonialism, 40, 43, 205–6
    discouraging, 103–4, 181–84, 208, 212
imperialism, 138–40, 200, 212–19, 235–37, 253–54, 396–99, 462, 483–89
    American, 267, 380–84, 404, 410, 423–26, 448, 451–55, 505
    British, 39, 59n28, 103, 109–10, 148, 283, 492
    Canadian, 105–6, 204, 211, 267, 359, 405, 429–32, 448–49, 464–67
    Great War and, 101–2, 113–25, 162–63
    rivalry, 109–12, 163, 174–76, 331–33, 366, 380–84, 438
independence movements, 31, 105, 134, 253, 328, 354, 423
    African, 6, 106–9, 209, 239, 254–63, 317–22, 397
    Asian, 5, 219–21, 227–30
    Canada's resistance to, 6, 230, 256–57
    Indigenous, 44
India, 5, 17–18, 474
    Canadians in, 105, 119, 253–54, 480
    colonialism in, 19–20, 137
    immigrants from, 103–4, 255, 339n104
    nationalist movements, 103–4, 253
Indian Act, 37, 53–58, 65, 78–80; *see also* Gradual Civilization Act
Indian agents, 49, 53–57, 66, 71, 87, 504
Indian Brotherhood organizations, 87–88, 241n3, 298–99
Indigeneity, definition of, 54, 57; *see also* status, Indian
Indigenous children,
    abuse of, 75–76
    kidnapping of, 72, 75, 77, 101
    residential schools, *see* residential schools
Indigenous Peoples, 122, 193
    capitalism, 1–2, 24, 33, 74, 88–92, 203–4, 298–99, 432, 482, 506–8
    civilizational destruction of, 14–15, 19–25, 30, 52–54, 73–78, 285, 387n44, 482, 490–93
    dehumanization, 14, 26–32, 51–52, 66–70, 82–84, 90, 106, 144, 252
    egalitarianism, 78–80
    elders, *see* elders, Indigenous
    governance structures, 2, 56, 68, 87, 132, 284, 405, 467, 482, 490
    genocide, *see* genocide, Indigenous Peoples
    homogenization of, 23–24
    inferiority, feelings of, 2, 14, 81
    Métis peoples, *see* Métis peoples
    militancy, 88–89, 255, 298–99, 334n16; *see also* anti-colonial politics; decolonization
    potlatch ceremonies, *see* potlatch ceremonies

slavery, 18–21, 43, 69
urbanization, 87–88, 97n85
White Paper (1969), 89
Indochina, 217–18, 274
    French control of, 227–28, 230, 276
Indonesia, 6, 134, 230, 282–86, 295
industrialization, 59n22, 74, 102–5, 115, 179, 194n12, 209, 219, 494n23
    Revolution, *see* revolution, industrial
    slower, 39, 118–19, 349, 378
Industrial Workers of the World (IWW), 121, 136
Innu people, 24, 27–28
Inouye, Kanao, 9, 214–15
Interahamwe, 361, 364, 368
International Control Commission (ICC), 228–29, 276, 280–82
International Criminal Tribunal for Rwanda (ICTR), 368–69, 390n76
International Monetary Fund (IMF), 271–72, 314, 322, 325
International Power (corporation), 132, 143, 168
internment camps, 212, 215
interwar years, 138–43, 145, 297–98
intifadas, Palestinian, 415–16, 419
investments, Canadian, 44–46, 284–86, 321, 324–28, 403, 483
    abroad, 5–6, 113, 202–3, 209, 255, 267–73, 312, 426–34
    capital, 141–42, 234, 418, 464–75, 479
inyenzi, 361, 387n49
Ipperwash Provincial Park, 88–89
Iran, 307, 385n8, 404, 412, 445n140, 449–52
    -Iraq War, 303–6, 340n119, 347–48, 505
Iraq, 113, 148, 305–7, 383–85, 449–50, 505–6
    invasion of, 7, 19, 346–49, 403–4, 408–14
    Iran versus, *see* Iran
    see also Hussein, Saddam; War on Terror
Ireland, 134, 182, 382
    British colonialism versus, 53, 167n51

Fenian rebels, 53
immigrants from, 102, 207
Islam, 19, 134, 307, 327
    right-wing, 327, 382, 398, 406, 408, 413
Islamic State (ISIS), 412–13, 450
Israel, 91, 304–7, 320
    Apartheid, 54, 373, 414–19, 451
    Canada's support for, 414–15, 417–18, 421
    creation of, 205–9
    fascism in, 7, 195n19, 348, 416–17, 420–21, 444n113
    settler capitalism, 185, 208–11, 315, 417–19
Israeli Defence Forces, 415, 417–18
Italy, 116, 134, 151–52, 298
    Ethiopia, invasion of, 139, 169n91, 176
    fascism in, 147–49, 154, 165n24, 167n55, 175
    immigrants from, 102
    Red Brigades, 298, 333n4

Jackson, William Henry, 68–69, 504
Jamaica, 43, 141
James, C.L.R., 258, 423
Japan, 18, 139, 211
    China versus, 169n91, 212–13, 219
    Communist Party in, 218
    expansion of, 145–46, 163, 175–76, 200–1, 212, 225–27
    fascism, 151, 167n53,56, 172–78, 214–18, 221, 255
    Germany and, 116, 172–73, 213–14
    immigrants from, 103, 132
    nuclear bombs, 191–93, 220–21
    Soviet invasion, 192
    stereotypes of, 191, 214–15
    war crimes, 216–18, 243n27
Jean, Michaëlle, 431
Jesuits, 78–79; *see also* missionaries
Jewish people, 157, 187, 211, 238, 242n9,16, 306, 419, 456–58
    anti-Semitism, *see* anti-Semitism
    Bolshevism, 178–83, 195n19
    perceptions of, 153, 179, 183–84, 194n15, 420–21
    persecution of, 131–32, 136, 153,

Index

184
refugees, 4, 145, 178, 183–5, 190, 205–8, 251, 414
women, 120
Jones, Burnley "Rocky," 9, 298

Kabila, Laurent, 371–72, 390n85
Kagame, Paul, 363–66, 369, 371–73, 388n54, 390n85
Karzai, Hamid, 399, 403, 405–6, 441n44
Kenya, 107, 239, 256–58, 288n23, 492
Kenyatta, Jomo, 256–57
Kergin, Michael, 436
Kim Il Sung, 222–23
King, William Lyon Mackenzie, 154, 171, 178–85, 212, 315
Hitler and, 5, 155–62, 175
King Jr., Martin Luther, 303, 314
Kipling, Rudyard, 105, 112, 204, 400–1
Kishi Nobosuke, 201, 216–17
Klassen, Jerome, 403–4, 410, 449
Komagata Maru, 103–4
Korean People's Republic (KPR), 220–22
Korean War,
Canada in, 187, 201, 205, 219–27, 282, 353
deaths, 223–24
Japan in, 175, 219, 230
left-wing struggles, 203, 210, 215, 218–20, 295
soldiers' disillusionment with, 224
United States in, 220–22, 228–30
violence in, 215–17, 223–26, 503–4
Kosovo, 377–78, 380, 413
Krehm, William, 150, 152
Ku Klux Klan (KKK), 136, 354, 358
Kumar, Rajan, 330–31
Kuwait, 340n119, 347, 349, 385n8, 451
Kwakwaka'wakw, 72

labour, 56, 219, 469, 475
conditions, 102–3, 135, 302, 312, 360, 379
division of, 79–80
exploitation, 2, 4, 102–3, 115, 212, 318, 372, 403, 482
Indigenous, 46–50, 65, 74, 78–80, 87, 97n85
migrant, *see* migrant workers
slave, 21–23, 33, 107, 140, 186, 216, 251, 321
wage, *see* wage labour
women's, 78–79, 460
labour movement, 234, 273
activism, 119–24, 136, 151, 165n15
Canadian, 103–5, 124, 135–36, 182
see also working class
land, 65, 220, 277, 435–36, 473, 481–82, 507
access to, 16–18, 47, 134, 179, 219, 283, 360–61, 479–80
claims to, colonial, 41–52, 382, 433;
see also land claims, Indigenous
dispossession, 27–33, 54, 90–92, 268, 438, 467–68
grants, 70–71
occupation of, 38, 45, 87, 209, 238, 360, 434, 444n113, 504
privatization, 2, 4, 16–19, 91–92
reform, 283, 310, 348, 397–98, 432
tenure, 44–47
theft, 1–3, 29–31, 69–74, 88–90, 100, 309, 421, 475
treaties, *see* treaties
Landa, Ishay, 179
land claims, Indigenous, 41–52, 382, 433
Laos, 227–28
Latin America, 84, 152, 195n19, 252, 507
Canadian companies in, 132, 140–41, 231–35, 267–68, 475–78
dictatorships, 108, 147, 232–34, 270–73, 468, 472–74
left wing in, 203, 235, 266–67, 270–72, 311, 438, 459–67
neocolonialism, 5, 138, 297, 312
Laurier, Wilfrid, 110, 144
Laxer, James, 22, 40
League of Nations, 132, 139, 212
left, the radical, 157, 165n15
government versus, 163, 218, 237, 334n7
opposition to, 122, 139, 149, 163, 296–301, 317
organizing, 133–36, 296–301, 322, 432
outlawing of, 158–59, 181, 415
violence against, 120, 163, 296–99, 301

525

left wing, the, 123, 126, 355, 420, 489
   governments versus, 4–6, 147, 158, 163, 273
   immigrants and, 165n15, 181, 238
   movements, 120–22, 136–39, 159, 211, 255, 298–300, 509
   political parties of, 220–21, 270, 347, 470–72
   right wing versus, 137, 158–63, 167n55, 191, 283, 398
   see also left, the radical
Le Jaune, Paul, 79
Leopold II, King, 106–7, 261–62, 265–66
Liberal Party of Canada, 413, 419, 489
Liebknecht, Karl, 121, 158
Lion, the Fox and the Eagle, The (Off), 369
Louis XIV, King, 22
L'Ouverture, Toussaint, 423
Lovelace, Sandra Nicholas, 300
Loyalists, 29–32, 135
Lubicon Cree, *see* Cree
Lula da Silva, Luis Ignacio, 470–72, 498n89
Lumumba, Patrice, 6, 258, 262–66, 289n61, 297, 303, 371
Luxemburg, Rosa, 158, 438, 508
Libya, 7, 410–14
literacy,
   programs, 310, 398, 425, 428
   universal, 330, 348

MacArthur, Douglas, 215, 218, 224
Macdonald, John A., 2, 40–44, 49, 68–73, 105, 250, 504
Mackenzie-Papineau Battalion (Mac-Paps), 150–55, 213, 507
MacLean, Ron, 409, 488–89
Maclean's, 215–16, 226, 280
Maduro, Nicolás, 461–62, 465–66
Malaysia, 167n53, 283
Malcolm X, 263, 303
Mali, 7, 414, 451
Maliseet people, 32, 300
Manchuria, 176, 211, 216–17, 225
Mandela, Nelson, 320, 323
Man in the High Castle (Dick), 173–74
Manitoba, 25, 44–47, 88, 91, 180, 480, 492
Manitoba Free Press, 125
Mantle, Craig Leslie, 113
Mao Zedong, 151, 215
Maracle, Lee, 9, 299
Marcuse, Gary, 236
Maritimes, the, 32–33
market, 54, 62n63, 268, 297, 331–33, 383, 483
   capital, 101, 107–8, 115, 129, 202, 326–28, 464
   free, 16–17, 53, 117, 310, 438
   labour, 119, 265, 375–78
Martin, Paul, 280, 284, 422
Marxism, 56, 122, 170n101, 270, 323
   overaccumulation, 108, 129n61, 383
masculinity, notions of, 119, 125, 208
Massachusetts, 28–32
Matchee, Clayton, 357–58
Mathieu, Carol, 127n28, 356–58
Mauritania, 478
Mayrand, Leon, 207, 241
McClung, Nellie, 119
McCrae, John, 112, 125, 128n52
McDougall, William, 42, 44
McFarlane, Peter, 141, 144–45
McKay, Ian, 106–7, 123–24, 236–37, 377, 492–93
McQuaig, Linda, 231
media, 111, 257, 266, 280–86, 306, 322, 401, 461–70, 477
   anti-communist, 135–36, 144–45, 158, 200, 216, 399
   anti-Semitic, 181
   foundational myths, 14, 50, 104, 349, 369, 380, 452, 491
   Indigenous people, portrayals of, 84, 86, 89–90, 253
   racism in, 8, 225–26, 253, 256, 260–65, 411–13
   social, *see* social media
merchant class, 17–18, 103, 423
Métis National Council, 87
Métis people,
   colonial government versus, 38, 43–47, 57–58, 70, 111, 122, 243n27
   gender dynamics, 80, 82–83
   Provisional Government, 43–44
   resistance, 54, 66–70, 94n40, 105,

205, 287n5
territory, defence of, 41, 43–47, 59n22/28, 68, 70
Mexican-American War, 39
Mexico, 31, 449
    Canadian companies in, 141–42, 478
    revolution, 134, 141–42, 234, 392n130
middle class, 17, 87, 119, 250, 279, 417, 452
    interests of, 40–42, 97n85, 182, 471
Middle East, the, 17, 205–10, 242n9, 295, 347, 382, 396
    Canada and, 303–7, 346, 413–14, 449–52, 505
"middle power," identification as, 5, 203–4, 303–4
Miéville, China, 332–33
migrant workers, 195n19, 349, 504
    conditions of, 16, 64, 484–87, 500n150
Mi'kmaq people, 24, 32, 54, 60n28, 85, 107, 300
militarism, 117, 128n52, 175, 345
    Canadian, 175, 408, 491–92
military, Canadian, 123, 137, 188, 250, 267–69, 317, 394, 405, 491–92
    college, 105
    Indigenous people versus, 44, 68–71
    -industrial complex, 185–86, 189, 418
    racism in, 8, 181–83, 215, 261, 357–58, 387n36, 401, 486–88
    restructuring of, 404–5
    technologies, 22, 113–14, 209, 223–25, 256–59, 351, 380–84, 417–18, 450–57
    violence, support of, 4, 50–52, 144–46, 181–87, 219, 232, 286, 346–55, 411–19, 436
    see also navy, Canadian; paramilitaries
Millennium Scoop, 77
Miller, Carman, 111, 113
Miller, J.R., 52, 67, 72–73
Mills of the Gods, The (documentary), 279
Milošević, Slobodan, 374, 376–80,

392n123, 464
mining, 88, 324, 427, 483
    coal, 135–36, 227
    corporations, Canadian, 5–8, 192–93, 372, 403, 427, 464–78, 479, 507
    diamond, 109, 116, 339n97, 480
    environmental destruction, 433–34, 478–80
    gold, *see* gold mining
    nickel, 234, 268–69, 312, 476
    resistance to, 135–36, 151, 269, 476–80
    uranium, 192–93, 200
    violence in, 142, 231–34, 269–70, 321, 403, 464–71, 475–78
    for weaponry, 192–93, 200, 213
missionaries, 3, 73, 107, 119, 213–15, 221, 225–27, 234, 407
    Indigenous people versus, 78–80, 251
Mississauga people, 32
Mobutu, Sese Seko, 264–65, 371
Modi, Narendra, 474
Mohawk people, 32, 88, 507, 510n3
monarchies, 194n15, 219, 305–6, 347–49, 360, 449–51
    feudal, 16–19
Monchalin, Lisa, 83–84
monopolies, Canadian companies, 46, 132, 267–68
    electricity, 4, 141–43, 233
Montreal, 27, 102, 132, 142–43, 151–53, 234, 265, 254–76, 409, 434
Montreal Gazette, 107, 321
Montreal Star, 135–36, 280
Morocco, 134, 257
Mortlach people, 25
Motkaluk, Jenny, 121–22
Mozambique, 285, 317–19, 325, 390n85
    FRELIMO, 285, 317–18
Mujahideen, 303, 327, 398–99, 406
Mulroney, Brian, 286, 311–14, 320–23, 328, 347, 371–72, 415
Murphy, Emily, 119
museums, 63–65, 73–74
Museveni, Yoweri, 362–63, 371, 388n52
Muslim Brotherhood, 209, 412
Muslims, 19, 195n19, 255, 346, 474,

485–87
Mussolini, Benito, 147–49, 165n24, 179, 231, 318
Myth of Ethnic War, The (Gagnon), 374

Namibia, 319, 321–25, 338n93
Nanjing massacre, 176, 200, 211–12, 215, 243n27
Nasser, Gamal Abdal, 205, 209, 211, 304–5
National Film Board (NFB) documentaries, 236, 340n 126, 350–53
National Inquiry into Missing and Murdered Indigenous Women and Girls, 84
nationalism, 38–40, 89, 206–9, 230, 283, 293n138, 305, 328, 374–76
  African, 254–55, 258, 265, 360–61, 365–66
  Canadian, 124, 128n52, 302, 311, 506–7
  fascism and, 134–37, 165n24, 175, 179–81, 215, 453–56, 494n23
  racism, 103–4, 149, 237, 424
nationalization, economic, 192, 209, 270, 283, 317, 323, 376, 464
National Post, 368, 406–7, 411, 414, 440n36, 490
Native Council of Canada, 87
NATO (North Atlantic Treaty Organization), 228, 239–41, 256, 322, 377–80, 412, 452
natural resources, extraction of, 19, 90, 97n82, 383, 403, 475
navy, Canadian, 144–45, 409
Nazis, the, 4, 149, 185, 208, 236, 457
  battle against, 146–48, 152, 171–73, 177, 241n5
  fascism, 149, 163, 167n56, 173–79, 191–93, 211, 454
  Freikorps, 158, 164n9, 169n87, 454
  neo-, 89, 171, 354, 358, 420–21, 454, 486–87
  support for, 153–59, 175–76, 181, 212, 451–56
  Western reintegration, 189–91, 197n65, 238, 328
  see also de-Nazification

Nehru, Jawaharlal, 254, 316
neocolonialism, 5–6, 239, 267, 309, 317–19, 350, 360, 366
neoliberalism, 325, 370–76, 400, 424, 432, 436, 459–60
  Canadian, 324, 411, 438, 449, 474, 484
  capitalism and, 313, 362, 379–82, 405, 428, 468
Newfoundland and Labrador, 26–27, 30, 261
New France, 23, 27–28, 30, 32, 79
New Zealand, 105, 131
Ngo Dinh Diem, 228–29
Nicaragua, 142, 145, 203, 307–14, 335n41, 458–59, 466
  Canadian mining in, 231–33
  see also Somoza dictatorship
Niemöller, Martin, 159
Nigeria, 107, 338n91
Nipissing people, 32
Nkrumah, Kwame, 258–59, 262, 296, 317
non-governmental organizations (NGOs), aid funding, 430–31, 483–84
  Canadian, 311, 323, 406–7, 432, 483–84
Norman, Herbert, 9, 217–18, 236
North Korea, 220, 222–24; *see also* Korean War
Northwest Mounted Police (NWMP), 48–51, 56, 70, 82, 103, 107, 112, 251
Nova Scotia, 27, 54, 107, 145, 300; *see also* Afro-Nova Scotians
nuclear bombs, 191, 202, 215, 221, 237
  Canada's role in, 192–93, 212, 332
Nyerere, Julius, 316–17

Obama, Barack, 462
Obote, Milton, 317, 362, 388n52
Odawa people, 31, 45
Off, Carol, 367, 369, 373
oil companies, 331, 385n8, 460, 462, 472
  Canadian, 410–11, 479–81
  colonial capitalism, 88, 116, 318, 466
Ojibwa people, 32, 88
Oka, 88–89, 300, 507
O'Kelly, Andrew, 153
oligarchy, 216–17, 331, 379, 453–54, 457,

Index

471
  Western interests and, 7, 142, 305, 314, 376, 434–35, 459–61
Ontario, 16, 39–40, 152, 157, 180, 301, 386n26, 485, 491
  Indigenous Peoples, 32–33, 44, 63, 70–73, 88, 92n3, 300
On-to-Ottawa trek, 150–52
Operation Paperclip, 189–90
Organization of American States (OAS), 463–64
Organization of Ukrainian Nationalists (OUN), 453, 459

Pacific Coast peoples, 72
Paivio, Jules, 150, 152
Pakistan, 253, 349, 398
Palestine, 91, 295, 304–5, 349
  British-fuelled tension, 205–6
  Liberation Organization (PLO), 306, 415
  partition of, 206, 208, 211, 416–19
  Zionism, 184–85, 207–10, 242n16, 243n19, 414
Panama, 314
Papua New Guinea, 5, 257, 284–85
paramilitaries, 206, 270, 303, 307–10, 318, 327, 454–57
  Canadian support, 9, 312–13, 427–28, 469, 474–77
Paris Commune, 180
Parrot, Jean Claude, 9
pass system, Indigenous people, 56–57, 52n75, 67, 71–72
patriarchy, 119, 148–49, 300, 344, 356, 398, 406, 432, 488
  colonialism and, 51, 78–84, 350
  see also violence
Paul, Frank, 85
peacekeeping, 386n29, 419, 451, 491–93
  Cold War, 201, 210–11
  failure at, 204–5, 219, 353, 367, 414, 445n144
  imperialism, 204, 211, 289n61, 304, 350–56, 371, 404
  mythology of Canadian, 5, 29, 201, 204–5, 350–52, 409
  portrayal of, 1, 9–10, 204, 252, 340n126, 344–50

racism, 204, 223–28, 260–66, 353, 357–58
  violence in, 261–66, 288n29, 350–55, 358, 377–80, 392n115, 401
Pearson, Lester, 176–77, 226, 230, 234–36, 249–59, 273, 277–80, 321
  Suez crisis, 204–6, 209–11, 304
peasants, 26, 143, 219–20, 268, 398, 453
  capitalism, transition to, 17–19, 40, 227, 258, 371, 467
  revolutionary movements, 126n7, 133–34, 194n12, 202, 270, 467
  violence against, 114, 144, 216, 278, 309–10, 360–65, 372, 474
  wage labour, *see* wage labour
People's Democratic Party of Afghanistan (PDPA), 397–99
Pequot people, 28–29, 34n26
Perry, Adele, 64
Persian Gulf, *see* Gulf War
Philippines, the, 140
  US military in, 19, 75, 116, 230
  violence in, 474, 314, 340n119, 474, 480
Pickton, Robert, 85
Piepot, Chief, 57, 66
pinkwashing, 301
Pinochet, Augusto, 6, 170n99, 270–72, 299, 486, 496n50
pipelines, 89, 97n89, 479, 489
  Mackenzie Valley, 88, 92, 480
  Trans Mountain, 449–50, 480
Plains Cree, *see* Cree
Podur, Justin, 418, 430–31
Poland, 102, 280, 326
  fascism in, 7, 147, 474
  Nazi invasion, 176, 184
policing, 62n75, 137, 189, 223, 301–2, 373, 435–37, 454–61, 488
  anti-communist, 181–82
  Indigenous people, 4, 50–53, 69–70, 76, 89, 96n77, 101, 299, 449, 504
  killing in, 70, 121–122, 167n55, 271, 284, 321, 334n7, 424
  training support, 401–10, 422
  violent, 58, 64, 151–53, 158, 298, 300, 428, 476–77, 485
  white supremacy, 82–86, 181–82,

529

251, 486
see also Northwest Mounted
  Police (NWMP); Royal Canadian
  Mounted Police (RCMP)
political economy, 387n47, 401
  of empire, 212, 417
  Indigenous, 1, 20, 25, 72, 482
  patterns of, 55, 178–79, 207, 243n19
popular movements, 6, 314, 319, 349
  neutralization of, 7, 211
Portugal, 4, 26, 107, 174–78, 254, 274,
  285, 317–21, 325
postwar era, 172, 175, 191–92, 207–20,
  270
  Canada in, 124, 190, 230, 236–37,
  240–41, 253
Potlatch ceremonies, 72–74
poverty, 180, 310, 354, 429, 446n160,
  454–55, 468
  capitalism and, 4, 102, 137, 175, 314,
  375, 422, 481–85
  colonialism, 84, 88, 144, 254, 257,
  371, 424
  endemic, 118, 270, 295, 301, 326–30,
  396, 411, 413–16, 459–61
  war against, 204, 250, 295–96, 330,
  366, 425, 465, 471–73
prairies, 104, 157, 200, 261
  colonization of, 41–46, 49, 67, 71,
  82, 141, 353
  resistance movements on, 68
private property, 31, 74
  in capitalism, 16, 58n8, 100
privatization, 314, 326, 331, 376–79, 428,
  432, 471, 477
  land, 2, 88–92
production, mode of, 56, 80, 460
  agricultural, 55, 102, 194n12, 219,
  268, 310, 362, 453
  capitalist, 16–17
propaganda, government, 195n19,
  243n28, 269, 431, 455–57, 488–91
  anti-communist, 135, 237, 329–30
  foundational myths, 14, 161
  resistance movements versus, 68,
  237, 363, 368
  wartime, 114–15, 156, 185–87, 190,
  219, 224–26
"Protestant ethic," 17, 28–31

Protestantism, 178
Puritanism, 28–32, 34n26, 35n50
Putin, Vladimir, 329–31, 413, 452–55

Québec, 26–27, 32–33, 39–40, 279, 427,
  481, 486
  anti-Semitism, 151, 180–81
  federal government versus, 110,
  301–2
  war, responses to, 110, 118, 121, 125
queer liberation struggles, 236, 300–1,
  432, 461
Quinn, Thomas, 66–67

racial science, 100–2, 118–19, 121
  hierarchy, 104, 179, 200, 212, 257
racism, 237, 473
  anti-African, 106, 169n93, 264–66,
  306, 387n44
  anti-Asian, 118, 167n53, 191,
  212–16, 223–27, 339n104
  anti-Indigenous, 42–43, 118
  anti-Semitic, 135–36, 153, 178, 420,
  453
  Canadian, 15, 86, 90, 104, 486–87,
  492
  colonialism, 3, 37, 45, 182, 320–21,
  370, 409
  institutional, 64, 104, 325, 354–56
  international, 5, 100–13, 314, 426
  nationalism and, 149, 250–51
  see also white supremacy
railroad, 40, 89, 141, 153, 298
  construction of, 4, 42, 67–70, 103,
  107–8, 112, 140, 250–51
  importance of, 41, 74, 102
  intercontinental, 45, 49, 72
  see also Canadian Pacific Railway
  (CPR)
Rainville, Michel, 356–58
rape, 95n69, 289n61, 407, 472, 476
  colonization, 19, 84, 288n29
  Indigenous women, 76, 82–86, 90,
  308, 478
  organized, 19, 243, 256, 308
  wartime, 186–87, 214, 225–26, 279,
  354, 378
Ray, Arthur J. 46
Razack, Sherene H., 85–86, 353, 355,

Index

357–58, 407–8
recession, 108, 113
   global, 68, 115, 135
Reagan, Ronald, 294, 309–14
Red Army, 117, 189, 296
red-baiting, 278, 291n101
Red Power movement, 88–89, 298–300, 323
Red River settlement, 41, 43–47, 50, 59n28, 60n30, 63, 68, 80
Red Scare, 135–37, 144–45, 181, 215, 234
Regina Riot, 137, 151
refugees, 29, 46, 194n15, 205–6, 272, 356–74, 378–79, 451, 485–86
   approach toward, 1, 151, 226, 237, 318–19, 336n61, 415, 425
   refusal of, 4, 145, 178, 183–84, 251, 312–13, 414, 504–7
Reid, Escott, 253–54
religion, 360, 426
   colonization and, 19, 24, 72, 420, 482
   divisions in, 5, 42, 178
   settler, 28–31
   zealotry, 17, 93n26, 398, 401, 406
Remembrance Day, 125, 150, 219
reparations, slavery, 22, 423–24
reserves, Indigenous Peoples on, 1, 32, 67, 75, 315, 323
   conditions on, 71, 86–88, 92n3
   confinement to, 37, 56–58, 62n75, 70–74, 101–2, 111, 135
   starvation on, 46–50, 54–55, 64–66, 504
residential schools,
   Canada's use of, 37, 75, 85, 91
   conditions in, 74–77, 95n47, 101
   Indian Act and, 76
   international use of, 75, 315
   survivors of, 76–78, 85; *see also* Truth and Reconciliation Commission
revolution, 4, 164n8, 208, 304–6, 423–24
   African, 258, 318–19, 322, 325, 354, 360–61, 387n47
   American, 30
   Chinese, 226–27
   counter-, 194n12, 259, 284, 303, 361, 399, 458, 467, 470

   Cuban, 235–36, 267, 273, 310, 313
   defeat of, 134–35, 158, 174, 283–84, 312–14
   Industrial, 40
   European, 17–18, 115, 163, 178, 326, 452
   Latin American, 141–44, 231–34, 267–69, 309–10, 345, 458–67
   left-wing, 4, 115, 149, 163, 169n87, 180–81, 269
   possibility of, 73, 121–22, 202–3, 241, 286, 298–99, 509
   Russian, *see* Russian Revolution
Rhee, Syngman, 221–23
Rhodes, Cecil, 109, 242n16
Riel, Louis, 43–44, 52, 70, 80, 250
Riel Rebellion, *see* War of 1885
Rousseff, Dilma, 470–73, 498n89
Roy, Arthur, 9, 118
Royal Canadian Mounted Police (RCMP), 50, 236, 256, 274–78, 301, 321, 409, 428
   Indigenous people versus, 83–85, 436, 449
   see also police
Rupert's Land, 30, 46–47
Russell, Ross, 150, 153
Russia, 116, 134, 174, 384, 397, 404, 412
   communism and, 147, 156, 181, 201–2, 241n5
   opposition to, 156, 186, 219, 326–28, 438, 456–58
   support for, 121, 453
   Tsarist, 133, 165n15, 194n12,15
   Ukraine crisis, *see* Ukraine
   see also Soviet Union
Russian Revolution, 4–5, 132–33, 147, 178, 194, 331–33, 340n127
   Canada versus, 117, 122, 135, 140, 144–47
   inspiration of, 134, 138, 330
Rutherford, Scott, 47
Rwanda, 387n44, 388n66
   Canada and, 10, 345, 350–52, 381–82, 413
   colonization and, 360–62
   genocide, 10, 29, 359–73
   nationalism, ethnic, 293n138, 360–61, 365–66

see also Dallaire, Roméo; Kagame, Paul
Rwandan Patriotic Front (RPF), 362–71, 388n54,66, 389n74, 390n76,85

Sahtugot'ine First Nation, 192–93
Sakimay reserve, 66
Salazar, António de Oliveira, 178, 317–18
Sale of the Century (Freeland), 456–57
sanctions, economic, 318, 321, 349, 444n113
    Western powers, 294, 322–23, 425, 462, 466
Sandinistas, 308–14
Sands, Charlie, 150, 152
Sankara, Thomas, 296–97, 479
Saulteaux people, 47
Saskatchewan, 25, 136, 450
    Indigenous-settler relations, 45, 70, 76, 82, 90–91
Saturday Night, 181, 253
Saudi Arabia, 307, 348, 385n8, 396–98
    Canada and, 7, 340n119, 449–51
scalping, 19, 32, 51, 90
Schabas, William, 369–70
scorched-earth policies, 111, 223–24
Scott, Duncan Campbell, 77
Second World War, 147, 169n91, 202, 225
    bombing during, 172–73, 187–88, 193n4; see also Second World War, nuclear bombs
    Canada in, 146, 174–78, 180–88, 190–93, 233, 251, 315
    deaths from, 171, 176–77, 185–88, 191, 200
    escalation to, 154, 161–64, 172–77, 205
    as "good war," 171–73, 177–78, 184–88, 191–93
    mythologization in, 4, 171–73, 236
    nuclear bombs, 191–93, 202, 215, 221, 237
    post-, 87, 142–44, 206, 230, 239, 255, 296, 375, 455
    profiteering, 185–86
    war crimes, 172, 190, 201, 216–17
Secwepemc people, 85
segregation, racial, 54, 90, 103–6, 131–32, 251, 261–62, 315–20, 325

Serbia, 374, 376–80, 390n93
settler capitalism, 25–26, 382, 480
    Canada and, 2, 24, 58, 68–69, 125, 173, 252, 506–8
    empire and, 101–2, 107–9, 113, 140
    expansion of, 39–40, 122, 208, 421, 475
    Indigenous communities versus, 39–40, 78, 88, 92
settlers, 62n75, 138, 208
    American, 30–31, 46, 105, 108, 208, 279
    anti-Indigenous, 8, 25–29, 37–50, 72–75, 81–89, 149, 167n53, 507
    attitudes of, 3, 23–28, 68–69, 102, 459
    British, 1, 19–23, 27–33, 42–44, 72, 105–6, 131, 251, 347–48, 397
    Canadian, 1, 3, 8, 40, 52, 65, 90, 102, 119, 204–5
    French, 1, 26–28, 42, 302
    Indigenous assistance and, 26–28, 43
    land, interest in, 19, 30–32, 40–55, 89–92, 102, 107–9, 304, 475
    rebellions, 39
    violence of, 8, 34n26, 84–85, 225, 318, 360–63, 416–19
    see also colonialism; colonization; Europeans; territorial expansion; settler capitalism
sex workers, 84–85, 91, 261
Shake Hands with the Devil (Dallaire), 359, 369
Shewell, Hugh, 87
Shoal Lake 40 First Nation, 64
"shock therapy," 326
Shola Jawid, 397, 406
Sikh community, 104, 336n61
Simpson, Leanne, 90
Singh, Mewa, 9, 104
Sioux people, 52–53, 71, 82
Sitting Bull, 52
Six Nations, 88–89, 92n3, 132
Sixties Scoop, 77
slavery, 43, 251
    abolition of, *see* abolitionism
    capitalism and, 18–24, 254, 265, 297, 422

colonialism and, 18–24, 33, 69, 107, 140, 186, 216, 251, 321, 423–24
justification for, 4, 22, 24, 102
resource extraction, 4, 19, 33, 107, 297, 321, 422
revolts, 22, 69, 107, 216, 423
trans-Atlantic, *see* trans-Atlantic slave trade
smallpox, 31, 41, 45–46
Smith, Goldwin, 182–83
Smuts, Jan Christian, 315
SNC-Lavalin, 403, 430, 450, 480
socialism, 5–6, 110, 330, 373, 503, 507
alternative project, 147, 165n15, 218, 326, 375–79, 391n100, 509
Canadian, 135, 151, 155, 299, 317
governments and, 6, 158, 174–75, 203, 221, 294–97, 305–13, 462–71
revolutionary, 134, 178, 235, 241n4, 322
socialists, 137, 226, 347, 361–62
bloc, 6, 316, 327
movements of, 110, 119, 166n49, 177, 325, 438
violence against, 158–59, 179–80, 271, 311–14, 335n31
social media, 89, 96n76, 472
Soekarno government, 282–84
Somalia, 8, 29, 345, 350–52, 367, 381–82
Affair, 353–59, 401, 403, 407
Somoza dictatorship, 145, 231, 309–12
Nazi affiliations, 232–33
Songhee people, 72
South Africa, 53, 208, 338n88, 339n104, 372
Apartheid, 54, 91, 243n19, 258, 272–75, 294–95, 314–20, 503
Canadians in, 124, 178, 251, 315–25, 475
concentration camps in, 4, 111, 121, 124–25, 156, 279
South African War, 53, 109–17, 125
South Asia, 281
Canadians in, 229, 253
immigrants from, 103–4, 293n138, 317
perceptions of, 5, 254
Southern Rhodesia, *see* Zimbabwe
South Korea,
Canadians in, 219, 225–26, 279
Japan in, 220–21
North Korea versus, 222–23
see also Korean War
sovereignty, Indigenous, 23–27, 31–33, 80
Soviet Union, the, 168n81, 291n101, 382, 452–57
Canada versus, 4, 150, 155, 165n20, 204, 238–41, 294–95, 312
defeat of, 294, 303, 325–29, 345, 349, 375, 399
as inspiration, 6, 121, 133–34, 203–4, 241n3, 316–23, 330–33
international assistance, 153, 210, 267, 274, 304–5, 310, 341n139, 397–98
portrayal of, 5, 194n12, 206, 222–23, 235–37, 297, 494n23
Second World War, 158, 164n6, 176–77, 185, 188–92, 197n63
United States versus, 174–75, 191–93, 202–3, 215, 220, 375, 381
see also Russia
Soweto uprising, 319, 321
Spain, 4, 168n81, 236, 317, 506
empire, 19, 423
fascism, 146–48, 151–54, 158, 162, 172–78, 213
left wing in, 134, 149–54, 159, 166n49, 177, 507
Spanish Civil War, 146–50
spies, 153, 224, 218
Canadian government, 70, 136, 235, 274–76, 280, 317
Nazi, 170n101, 233
Stadacona, 26–27
Stairs, William, 100, 105–7, 116, 140, 279
Stalin, Joseph, 157, 176, 197n63, 220, 240, 453, 494n23
left wing versus, 168n81, 170n101, 223, 241n3, 242n9
status, Indian, 57, 80, 300
Steele, Sam, 4, 112, 116, 251
St-Laurent, Louis, 223, 228–29, 238
St. Louis, SK, 82–83
Stonechild, Neil, 85–86
striking, 134–35, 258–59, 270, 278, 504
mobilization, 104, 120–22, 142–43,

533

151–52, 219–21, 298, 302
  rejection of, 118–19, 186, 218, 449
  see also Winnipeg, General Strike
structural-adjustment policies (SAPs), 313–14, 370
Sudan, 105, 124
Suez Crisis, 204–5, 209–11, 228, 304–5, 351
suffragists, 3, 119–20
Suharto dictatorship, 282–86
Sun Dances, 62n75, 73–74
superpowers, global rivalry, 202–4
Swastika Clubs, 180–82
Swift, Jamie, 106–7, 123–24, 236–37, 377, 492–93
Syria, 7, 304–5, 331, 450–51, 455, 505
  deaths in, 412–14
  refugee resettlement, 485–86

Taíno civilization, 19, 422
Taliban, 396, 399, 406–7
Tanzania, 255, 317, 325, 361–63, 475, 478
territorial expansion, 31, 133, 280
  colonial, 3, 14–15, 24, 29, 33, 41
  European, 107, 116, 138
  importance of, 39–40, 155, 160–61
  Japanese, 200, 211–13, 217
  myths of, 14, 102
  Nazi, 145–47, 157, 162–63, 175–77, 185
terrorism, 111, 135–36, 283, 319, 410–14
  attacks, 7, 345, 397–98
  Canada and, 274–75, 306–8, 313, 323–24, 394, 490
  fascist, 233
  see also War on Terror
The Pas, MB, 91–92, 97n99
Thomson, Susan, 360, 372
Tontons Macoutes, 424, 427
Toronto, 119, 135, 181–82, 204, 238, 274, 421, 458, 468, 476
  settlement in, 102, 488
Toronto Daily Star, 200
Toronto Mail, 70
Toronto Star, 50, 125, 261, 263–64, 279, 373, 469
trade, 39, 270, 321, 483
  agreements, 110, 327, 436, 465, 475
  international, 45, 107–10, 321, 258, 269, 274, 285, 473–74
  missions, 113, 117, 451
  unions, *see* unions
  within Canada, 27, 41, 45–46,
  see also fur trade
trans-Atlantic slave trade, 2
  economy of, 20–22
  rise of, 16, 482
  wealth from, 42–43
treaties, 89–90, 299
  deception in, 47–48, 55–57, 65, 92n3, 137
  forced signing of, 48–50, 52, 56
  international, 107, 138, 139, 156, 176, 315
  numbered, 46–47, 75
  terminology of, 48, 75, 93n20
  vagueness of, 31–33, 62n75, 72
Trigger, Bruce, 27
Trudeau, Justin, 8, 38, 235, 407, 420, 448–51, 455–58, 474, 485, 489
Trudeau, Pierre, 89, 268–76, 286, 301–2, 311, 314, 321–22, 328
Truman, Harry, 191–92
Trump, Donald, 445n140, 452, 462, 485, 489
Truth and Reconciliation Commission, 64
  report release, 37, 77
  survivor testimonies, 76–78
tuberculosis, 150
  Indigenous people and, 41, 46, 48, 71
Tudjman, Franjo, 376, 391n99
Tulchinsky, Gerald, 182
Turkey, 116, 139, 148, 166n29, 175, 480
Turtle Island, *see* A'nó:wara Tsi Kawè:note

Ubico, Jorge, 145, 232
Uganda, 250–51, 255, 293n138, 317, 359, 361–62, 366, 371
Ukraine, 328, 330, 491, 506
  Crisis, 452–58
  fascism in, 7, 421, 452–54, 457–58
  immigrants from, 102, 121, 237–38
unions, 159, 218, 272, 420, 471
  anti-war, 121, 311, 323
  breaking up of, 108, 119, 149, 182,

231–33, 236, 302
  formation of, 69, 114–15, 135–36, 236, 489
  Jewish women in, 120
  strikes by, 120, 167n51
Union of Soviet Socialist Republics (USSR), *see* Soviet Union
United Fruit Company, 108, 233
United Nations, the, 10, 249, 257, 296, 304, 359, 373, 466
  Canada in, 221–23, 230, 251, 300, 344–50, 378–81, 409, 451
  neocolonialism and, 239–40, 255, 263, 283–86, 296–97, 315–21, 337n83
  Palestine, 206–7, 306, 451
  peacekeeping, 210–11, 224, 260–66, 352, 366–68, 404, 414–19
  weapons and, 215–16, 275, 349, 429, 441n57, 450
United States, the, 221–25, 229, 279, 360, 397–99, 407, 417, 455
  Canada versus, 39–41, 140–41, 210, 231–40, 267–81, 382–84, 422, 464–66
  Central Intelligence Agency (CIA), 189–90, 221, 224, 235–36, 259, 270–75, 280, 347, 396–98, 425
  Civil War, 22
  Cold War, 6, 202–4, 240, 307–10, 345–47
  economic growth, 22, 138
  fascism and, 7, 146–49, 174, 195n19, 230, 377, 460
  imperialism, 29–31, 33, 42, 75, 91, 108, 116, 297, 313, 423–25, 452
  industrialization, 39
  Nazi integration, 189–91, 197n65, 238, 328
  in Second World War, 176, 183, 213–15
  slavery in, 22, 104
  Soviet Union versus, 174–75, 191–93, 202–3, 215, 220, 375, 381
  see also American Revolution
urbanization, 40, 97n85, 102, 179, 194n12, 310, 349, 362, 374
Uribe, Álvaro, 468
Usiskin, Roz, 120

Vallières, Pierre, 302
Valour and the Horror (documentary), 172–73, 193n4
Vancouver, 61n72, 103–4, 145, 372, 449, 501n160
  Downtown Eastside, 85
Vancouver Sun, 145, 212, 223
Van Horne, Cornelius, 4, 107–8, 127n31
VanKoughnet, Lawrence, 50
Varley, Frederick, 131–33
Venezuela, 7, 436–38, 445n140, 451, 458–73, 491, 496n50; *see also* Bolivarian Revolution
Versailles Treaty, 138–39, 156, 167n55, 169n87, 212
veterans, war, 124–25, 131, 150, 172–73, 222, 281
Victoria, BC, 72, 111, 118, 121, 507
Victorian era, 81–83
Viet Minh, 227–28
Vietnam, 203, 320
  Canadians in, 225, 228–29, 277–82
  Communist Party of, 227, 230
  freedom of, 132, 210, 227–28, 235, 296–97, 506
  North versus South, 229, 277–82, 292n104
  Viet Cong, 229, 277, 279
  violence in, 167n53, 278–81
  War, 227–31, 276–83
Vimyism, 122–26
Vimy Ridge, 112, 122–24, 128n52, 150
Vimy Trap, The (McKay and Swift), 124
von Neurath, Baron, 160–61

wage labour, 312, 330, 425, 432–33
  conditions of, 118, 135, 237
  Indigenous people and, 62n75, 74
  shift to, 16, 18
wages, low, 26, 142, 186, 268–70, 383, 427–28, 454–59, 475, 484
Walker, Barrington, 57
Walsh, Red, 9, 150–52
water, lack of clean, 251, 378, 411, 415–17, 428–34, 461, 478–80, 484, 500n150
  Indigenous communities and, 8, 64, 88, 92n3, 449, 482
war, *see* Afghanistan, war in; Balkans,

War; First World War; Second World War; War on Terror
War of 1885, 45, 51, 60n30, 66–73, 91, 93n26, 102, 111
War on Terror, the, 295, 328, 331, 373, 438, 505
    Canada in, 7, 345–46, 381–84, 395–415, 490–91, 506
wealth, 55, 120
    accumulation of, 2, 17, 20, 24, 72, 186, 310, 331, 383
    colonialism, 18–22, 43, 108–10, 422, 431
    gap, 17, 134, 137, 286, 333, 481
    redistribution, 72–73, 219, 277, 348, 398, 432
    transfer, 20–22, 263, 269, 371, 403, 464–69
weapons, export of, 307, 340n119, 400, 410
    atomic, *see* nuclear bombs
    biological, 226, 275, 332
    Canada's role, 7, 213–15, 255–56, 273, 312, 321–22, 413, 450–51, 505
    chemical, 145, 279, 281, 348
    to dictatorships, 228–31, 357, 366–68, 376
    imperialism and, 5, 304, 310, 318, 321, 354
    wartime, 114, 116, 121, 153–54, 167n56, 174, 277, 306–7
West Bank, 209, 304–5, 415–18
western Canada,
    conquest of, 3, 22, 41, 141
    Indigenous people in, 41, 71–74
Western countries, 173, 230, 277, 305, 412–14, 488
    capitalism and, 17, 116, 141, 149, 165, 202–3, 240, 319, 324–31, 452
    fascism within, 139, 149, 161–62, 172–77, 191, 194n12, 303, 479
    right-wing governments and, 7, 10, 146, 200, 218, 221–32, 285, 373–82, 449
    slavery and, 21–22
    wartime, 114–15, 172–77, 183–93, 206–15, 297, 409
Wet'suwet'en territory, 89, 449

white supremacy, 9, 103, 320–24
    Canada and, 5, 8, 14, 39, 181–83, 357, 486–88, 504
    colonialism, 39, 44, 59n28, 133
    logic of, 2–3, 51, 69, 100, 148, 508
    Confederation and, 38–39, 43
    hunting licences, 73–74
Whittaker, William, 180–81
Wilson, Woodrow, 117, 221
Winnipeg, 39, 97n85, 181, 253, 491
    General Strike, 121–22, 135, 504
    settlement in, 41, 44–45, 63–64, 102, 165n15
Wolfe, Patrick, 30
Wolseley, Garnet, 44, 59n28
women, 167n53, 182, 351, 385n8
    control of, 78–80, 95n69, 132, 300, 347–49
    imperialism, 110, 398–401
    Indigenous, *see* women, Indigenous
    mobilization of, 218, 300, 396, 434, 458–61, 470
    violence against, 80, 186, 214–16, 226, 279–85, 432, 478, 487
    working-class, 118–20
women, Indigenous,
    colonialism, 51–53, 78–84
    murder of, 3, 83–86
    police versus, 82–85
    traditional status of, 34n26, 78–80, 132
    violence against, 8, 66, 81–86, 89
    see also National Inquiry into Missing and Murdered Indigenous Women and Girls
working class, the, 40, 165n15, 279, 505
    capitalism and, 68, 119, 238, 327, 383
    far right and, 69, 102, 167n55, 175, 179
    mobilization of, 104–5, 115, 121–22, 126, 218
    revolutionary movements, 136, 180, 194n12, 202, 302–3, 348
    sacrificing of, 4, 117, 125, 131–33, 150, 185, 440n33
    violence against, 63–64, 182, 214
    women in, 118–20
World Bank, 325, 425, 428, 476

Index

World War I, *see* First World War
World War II, *see* Second World War
Wounded Knee occupation, 300
Wyandot people, 31

xenophobia, 487

Yeltsin, Boris, 326
Yemen, 450
Yugoslavia, 6–8, 152, 187, 345, 350–52, 373–81, 413

Zaire, 359, 371
Zelaya, Manuel, 433–37, 447n173
Zimbabwe (Southern Rhodesia), 318–21, 324–25, 337n83
Zionism, 205–7, 242n16, 243n19
    Canadian support for, 184, 304, 414–15, 419–21, 444n117
    colonialism and, 208, 242n9,10, 305–6
    settler capitalism, 208–11, 416, 420